Contents

RUSSIA AND THE REPUBLICS — PRACTICAL INFORMATION

RUSSIA AND THE REPUBLICS: THE COUNTRIES

The first part of each country chapter appears in the following order:

Climate — History — The People — Language — Getting There — Red
Tape — Money — Communications — Getting Around —
Accommodation — Eating and Drinking — Exploring — Entertainment —
Sport — Shopping — Health and Hygiene — Crime and Safety — Help and
Information.

Sections dealing with large cities are dealt with as follows:

City Layout — Arrival and Departure — City Transport — Accommodation —
Eating and Drinking — Exploring — Entertainment — Shopping — Crime and
Safety — Help and Information

Travellers
Survival
Kit

Russia &
The Republics

T**ravellers**
S**urvival**
K**it**

Russia &
The Republics

EMILY HATCHWELL &
SIMON CALDER

with additional research by
Carole Cadwalladr and Anna Sutton

Published by
VACATION WORK, 9 PARK END STREET, OXFORD

TRAVELLERS SURVIVAL KIT: RUSSIA & THE REPUBLICS

by Emily Hatchwell and Simon Calder
with Carole Cadwalladr and Anna Sutton

Copyright © Vacation Work 1995

ISBN 1 85458 132 5 (softback)

Publicity: Roger Musker

Cover Design
Mel Calman
Miller Craig Cocking Design Partnership

Illustrations by William Swan

Maps by Andrea Pullen

Imageset and Printed by Unwin Brothers Ltd, Old Woking, Surrey, England

MAPS

Acknowledgments

Many travellers and citizens of countries in the Commonwealth of Independent States have contributed to this book. In the order in which the material appears in the book, we would like to give special thanks to the following people:

A considerable amount of research on the **Russia** section was undertaken with the help of Jenny Lo, Lena Cook and Fiona Cushley, with valuable back-up from Angela Mitchell.

Moscow: Cathy Packe and Hannah Start.

St Petersburg: Mihai Cucos wrote the nightlife section. General thank-yous to Boris, Liana, Anna, Rico, Amy, Veronica, Katya, Janet, Evan and Carol.

The Baltics: Lester Wagman.

Belarus: Francine Danaher, Tim Gould and Toni.

Ukraine: Tim Gould.

Moldova: Dennis, Dean and Ian Birbek.

Central Asia: Boris, Sasha, Andrew Apostollon, Ildar, Adil, Graeme Loken, Paul Bergne, the Honorary Consul in Bishkek, Malika, Reza, Lexy, Jacksibek, Bradley Mayhew, Susie Grant, Tim Belk, Village and Issy, and Metin Göher for the sauna.

IMPORTANT NOTE: While every effort has been made to ensure that the information contained in this book was accurate at the time of going to press, some details are bound to change during the lifetime of this edition. If in the course of your travels you encounter errors or omissions, please write to Emily Hatchwell and Simon Calder at Vacation Work Publications, 9 Park End Street, Oxford OX1 1HJ, or e-mail to calder@cix.compulink.co.uk.

Those whose contributions are used will be sent a free copy of the next edition.

PREFACE

Congratulations: the fact that you are reading this makes you one of the relatively small number of people willing to consider a trip to the former USSR. By travelling to Russia, and the republics which were once satellites of Moscow, you have a unique opportunity to see a region in transition, and to overturn a host of preconceptions about a much-misunderstood part of the world.

Few predicted the timing and speed of the downfall of the Soviet Union. Now that the USSR has splintered into 15 separate republics (or more, depending upon whom you ask), independent travel has simultaneously become easier and more complex. Visitors have an unparalleled degree of freedom to decide where and how they travel.

The most intrepid traveller was no match for the USSR. Only a few parts of the Soviet Union were open to visitors, always under the watchful eye of the State Committee for Tourism — Intourist. Its bureaucrats kept tabs on every traveller. Intourist has survived the demise of the USSR, but is powerless to stop adventurous individuals from exploring the nooks, crannies and soul of the nations held in suspended animation for the last 75 years. An amorphous mass of land, riddled with regulations, has been transformed into fifteen distinct republics. With a smattering of Russian and a fistful of roubles you can go where you please, from the shiny new British Embassy in Vilnius to the Pacific shore at Vladivostok.

Visitors on pre-independence package tours could enjoy some of the delights of the old Soviet Union: Baroque palaces in the Baltics, glorious beaches on the Black Sea, Fabergé eggs and fabulous icons in the Kremlin, the deserts of Kazakhstan and the mosques of Samarkand. But the more remote archaeological sites and wildlife reserves were off-limits, as were most ordinary towns. Suddenly one-sixth of the world's land area has been opened up, stretching 6,000 miles and eleven time zones. You can ride with Cossacks on the Steppe, or take one of several headbangingly long train rides, without having to explain yourself to anyone.

The Party is over, the Union is dead — long live Russia and the republics.

Emily Hatchwell
Simon Calder
Oxford
May 1995

Of course we're glad 28 million of you chose to fly with us last year.
It must mean you like us.
Lufthansa
More than that, you trust us.

RUSSIA & THE REPUBLICS – PRACTICAL INFORMATION

When the Soviet Union collapsed, everyone thought the region would quickly lose its reputation as somewhere where travel is a battle with bureaucracy. For a few months after the CIS began, and you could travel freely all over the old USSR. Rapidly, however, the new frontiers between the constituent republics made travel a challenge once more. The good news, though, is that you can legally explore independently almost anywhere you wish. And gradually, the region is adapting to the needs of travellers who prefer to plan as they go along. But the long-established tourism infrastructure which provided heavily regimented tours is still mostly in place. So you can, if you wish, hand the burden of organisation to somebody else; suggestions of experienced companies are given in this section. It also contains options for getting to the region, what money to take, insurance recommendations, health advice, etc., and outlines what you can expect in terms of accommodation, public transport and so on.

AIR

The opening-up of Russia and its neighbours has spawned a whole new breed of air routes into the region. Besides Aeroflot and its offspring, the key players are Austrian Airlines, Lufthansa of Germany, SAS and Turkish Airlines. Eastern European carriers, such as Lot of Poland and the Czech carrier CSA, are getting in on the act too. Others are certain to follow as the economic and social potential of the former USSR is realised. Flights to the most popular destinations such as Moscow, St Petersburg, Kiev and the Baltic capitals are often cheaper than the equivalent train fare. Open-jaw flights (flying in to one city and returning from another) can offer good value, and increasingly many airlines are offering this facility. With Austrian Airlines, for example, you could fly into St Petersburg, cover the intervening territory by land and fly out of Odessa; SAS lets you fly into one of the Baltic capitals and out from either of the other two.

From Britain. Any travel agent should be able to book you a cheap flight to Moscow, but the best range of options and lowest fares are available through specialists. Furthermore, if you want to travel somewhere off-the-beaten-track, these agents will not just have heard of Almaty, Baku and Chisinau — they will also be able to sell you a ticket there, and help with visas. Most offer package deals in addition to flights.

Canterbury Travel (London) Ltd, 246 Streatfield Road, Kenton, Harrow,
    Middlesex HA3 9BY (tel 0181-206 0411, fax 0181-206 0427).
East-West Travel, 15 Kensington High St, London W8 5NP (tel 0171-938
    3211; fax 0171-938 1077)
Fregata Travel, 100 Dean Street, London W1V 6AQ (tel 0171-734 5101;
    fax 0171-734 5106).
Finlandia, 227 Regent St, London W1R 8PD (tel 0171-409 7334; fax 0171-
    409 7733).
Interchange, Interchange House, 27 Stafford Road, Croydon, Surrey CR0
    4NG (tel 0181-681 3612, fax 0181-760 0031).

Intourist Travel Ltd, Intourist House, 219 Marsh Wall, London E14 9FJ
    (0171-538 5965).
One Europe Travel, Research Travel, Fraser Rd, Perivale, Middlesex UB6
    7AQ (tel 0181-566 9424, fax 0181-566 8845).
Overseas Business Travel, 8 Minories, London EC3N 1BJ (tel 0171-702
    2468, fax 0171-488 1199).
Progressive Tours, 12 Porchester Place, Marble Arch, London W2 2BS (tel
    0171-262 1676, fax 0171-724 6941).
Regent Holidays, 15 John Street, Bristol BS1 1DE (tel 0117-921 1711, fax
    0117-925 4866).
The Russia House, 37 Kingly Court, Kingly St, London W1R 5LE (tel 0171-
    439 1271, fax 0171-434 0813); has 25 years experience arranging all

travel — flights, rail and cruises — plus invitations, visas and hotels throughout Russia and the Former Soviet Union (the Republics) — see inside front cover.

Time Travel, 7-11 Kensington High Street, London W8 5NP (tel 0171-376 1700; fax 0171-376 1722).

VIP Travel, 42 North Audley St, London W1Y 2DU (tel 0171-499 4221).

If you are under 26 or a full-time student, it is also worth calling agencies specialising in discount travel, such as STA Travel (86 Old Brompton Road, London SW7; 0171-937 9921) and Campus Travel (52 Grosvenor Gardens, London SW1; 0171-730 3402). Both these companies have networks of UK branches. Other agents advertise in the weekend newspapers or magazines such as *Time Out* or *TNT* in London.

From North America. While there is a growing number of links between North America and the former USSR (especially on the Delta network via Frankfurt), flying to London first is often your best option. Not only is it easy to get a cheap transatlantic ticket to the UK, onwards flights are normally excellent value too. Even with a day or two spent in an overpriced London hotel, you should still save money on the deal. Some specialist operators offer good deals, particularly to Russia and the Baltic Republics using SAS and Finnair flights via Scandinavia.

From Australasia. Similar advice applies to people from Australia and New Zealand who are visiting the western part of the region covered in this book: go via London to save money. If your destination is Siberia, the Russian Far East or Central Asia, however, it is probably worth travelling via Hong Kong or Delhi, both served by cheap flights from Australia. Red Bear Tours (320 Glenferrie Road, Malvern, Melbourne, Vic 3144; tel 03 824 7183) has a good range of travel and accommodation possibilities in the CIS, especially Russia. So too does Gateway Travel, 48 the Boulevarde, Strathfield NSW 2135; tel 02 745 3333.

From Southern Africa. The Balkan Bulgarian Airways link between Johannesburg and Sofia could provide a cut-price flight to the edge of the region. Similarly, Austrian Airlines' flights to Vienna, and Lufthansa's to Frankfurt, slot into a network of services to the CIS. Otherwise travel via London.

RAIL

Rail travel from Western Europe to the former Soviet Union is not necessarily cheap, though young people are eligible for significant discounts. The fastest route from London is on Eurostar trains through the Channel Tunnel to Brussels and onwards from there, but you may well save by travelling on the Harwich-Hook of Holland route. Once you reach the Baltic Republics, Belarus or Ukraine, train fares become much cheaper, but you won't benefit much from the price differential if you pay for your entire ticket at home. To save money, purchase a ticket just to the border (or to the first town across the frontier) and buy an onward ticket from there. (Note, however, that you should not try this in Belarus if you are heading from Poland to the Baltics — if you do not get a through-train, you become liable for an expensive Belarus visa.) For information in the UK, call the International Rail Centre at Victoria Station (0171-834 2345); many large rail stations should be able to help too. For more expert advice, you would do well to consult one of the agents listed under *Air*, above, or a company specialising in rail travel behind the former Iron Curtain: GW Travel, 6 Old Market Place, Altrincham, Cheshire WA14 4NP (tel 0161-928 9410, fax 0161-941 6101).

Useful sources for planning a travel by rail include *Thomas Cook's European Timetable* (covering the European parts of the former USSR), the *Overseas Timetable* (for Central Asia and the trans-Siberian routes, and the Far East) and the *Thomas Cook Rail Map of Europe*.

Rail Passes. Marketing transportation is a relatively new concept in the region, so rail passes have not really taken off. Only Baltic republics offer a rail pass (obtainable in the UK from Campus Travel, tel 0171-730 3402). Owing to the good value of rail travel in the region, this is rarely a worthwhile investment unless you plan to do a lot of travelling in a fairly short time.

BUS

The thought of spending a day or more in a bus may not appeal, but travelling by road is an excellent way to reach Belarus, the Baltics and Western Ukraine. For Brest, Kaliningrad, Minsk, Vilnius and beyond, it is well worth taking a bus to Warsaw and travelling from there by rail. Eurolines (52 Grosvenor Gardens, London SW1; 0171-730 0202) runs regular services to the Polish capital for around £100 return. It is also well worth checking the fares on the privately run companies such as Europol (0171-828 9008). The cheapest direct way from the UK to any of the destinations in this book is the London-Lviv bus, operated by Acton Holidays, 354 Uxbridge Road, London W3 9SL (0181-896 1642). This runs once a week (more frequently over Christmas/New Year), takes 45 hours and costs £134 return.

SEA

There are various ferry routes to the Baltic Republics from Germany, Sweden or Finland; from Turkey to Ukraine; and from Japan to the Russian Far East. Travelling by ship is not usually a cheap option, but can provide an unusual way to reach the former USSR. See the country chapters for further information.

 ## *Progressive Tours Ltd.*

12 Porchester Place, Marble Arch, London W2 2BS Tel: 0171-262 1676 Fax: 0171-724 6941 Telex: 25135

ABTA 50669

Russia,   **Ukraine,**   **Central Asia**

Political life has turned inside out, but the splendour of Moscow and St Petersburg shines brighter than ever: the great museums so well conserved by the state, the Danilov and St Sergius monasteries restored to glory by the Orthodox Church, the palaces and theatres of St Petersburg and the great country houses and parks around it, Smolny Cathedral and St. Isaacs; some perhaps, like the Mariinsky, changing name but changing nothing of the supreme achievement of the Kirov and Bolshoi companies.

There has never been a better price for visits to the great capitals (from £375 including the flights), or for venturing into the Volga country, the Urals or Siberia, with a new direct flight to Tashkent bringing fabulous Samarkand and Bokhara into easy reach.

Trans-Sib Train,   **Irkutsk,**   **Mongolia**

Take Eurostar (or fly to Moscow) for the world's longest and most exciting journey via Irkutsk and lake Baikal to Vladivostok, or turn south at Ulaan Ude for Mongolia and Beijing. This ride is one long special event, yet "everything went very smoothly, scenery and atmosphere excellent, Siberia and Baikal so beautiful, like a fairy tale" to quote one of our many happy travellers in 1995.

TOURS

The appeal of a package tour can be its low cost, or simply the fact that the logistics of a trip are taken out of your hands. The travel agents listed above run tours, together with a growing number of tour operators. Most of these cover straightforward city breaks to the Baltic capitals, Moscow or St Petersburg, but others specialise in activities. From the UK, Sherpa Expeditions (0181-577 2717) organises a wide range of tours in Russia and the other former republics of the USSR. In Russia, the company tackles Lake Baikal in Siberia and the Kamchatka Peninsula in the extreme east. It also runs treks to the Crimea, Tajikistan and the Altai Mountains of Kazakhstan. Durations and prices are around 15 days and £1,200, although Kamchatka costs £2,100. The company warns 'none of its treks is for the sedentary'.

Voyages Jules Verne (0171-723 5066) organises a series of tours by air, land and water within Russia and neighbouring republics. And Russian Nature Tours (01962 733051) organises natural history tours throughout the CIS.

DRIVING

If this book persuades you not to drive to or within the CIS, it will have performed at one very useful function. Despite some recent improvements, road conditions in the former Soviet Union are still way behind what most Western European drivers are used to. Some rural roads are positively Third World, and even main through routes have surfaces fit to break your axles. Motorways, as we know them in Western Europe, are scarce, although a lot of main roads are colloquially called 'motorways', earning the title mainly by the volume of traffic they are forced to carry. A few roads have benefitted from investment and are a joy to drive along, and the opening of modern service stations makes life for motorists a good deal more pleasant too. But the disadvantages of driving in the former Soviet Union should not be underestimated: everyone from underpaid traffic police to local criminal fraternities (often one and the same) is arrayed against the visiting motorist. Information about documentation and so on is given below, but for general hints and information about driving conditions see *Getting Around*.

Membership of a motoring organisation is a good investment: they offer information about the documents required and other advice. The main organisations in the UK and elsewhere are as follows:

AA, Fanum House, Basingstoke, Hampshire RG21 2EA (01256-20123).
RAC, PO Box 100, 7 Brighton Road, Croydon CR2 6XW (0181-686 0088).
AAA, 1000 AAA Drive, Heathrow, FL 32746, USA (407-444-7883/7000).
CAA, 60 Commerce Valley Drive East, Markham, Ontario L3T 7P9, Canada (416-771-3170).
AAA, 212 Northbourne Avenue, Canberra ACT 2601, Australia (062 477311).

Documents. An International Driving Permit (IDP) is not legally essential, but it will smooth your progress if you are stopped by the traffic police; unlike British licences, it shows your age and photograph, and has a Russian translation.

Insurance is mandatory: you need either a green card or frontier insurance. Not all motor insurers issue green cards for travel to the former USSR, even in such Western-looking republics as the Baltics. You are therefore compelled to purchase insurance at the border, where its cost and quality will be highly variable. See *Breakdowns*, below, for information on insurance policies available.

Maps. Good motoring maps are hard to find in the West. You could take advantage of the series of US Air Force Tactical Pilotage Charts, at a scale of 1:500,000. These are available from the Map Shop, 15 High Street, Upton-upon-Severn, Worcs WR8 0HJ (01684 593146).

Once you reach the former Soviet Union, there is a surprisingly good range of up-to-date maps, complete with new place names. Unfortunately those for Russia and Ukraine are in Cyrillic, which alone is a good reason for learning the alphabet.

Breakdowns. The best way to ensure against breakdowns is to make sure your car is in perfect working order before you set off. Have it thoroughly serviced and take a few spares, as they may be difficult to find abroad. The obvious ones are lights, fan belt, plugs, hoses, ignition coil, ignition key and fuses; also take your own pressure gauge. Reciprocal repair agreements with sister motoring organisations are of varying efficiency and usefulness in the former USSR.

If you have a breakdown or accident which is so bad that you abandon your vehicle, ensure that you obtain an official confirmation of this from the police or insurance authorities; border officials might otherwise assume that you have sold it illegally, and fine or detain you accordingly.

Fuel. Quality is a constant problem, and finding any fuel at all can sometimes be tricky. Furthermore, unleaded petrol is virtually unknown. Since the collapse of the USSR. the flow of petrol can be extremely erratic. It is a good rule to fill up whenever you can — also because petrol stations are few and far between in country areas. Be prepared to queue, as the supply rarely meets the demand of the region's new breed of private motorists.

MOTORCYCLING

The information and advice given above is relevant also for motorcyclists. Bear in mind too that uneven road surfaces can play havoc with your motorbike's suspension, and nuts and bolts have a nasty habit of falling off after a severe jolt. Clearly, good brakes and tyres are essential.

Note that filtering through columns of traffic is not always legal. Although most traffic officials turn a blind eye, don't disregard the rule too blatantly. In some instances, however, motorcyclists may be singled out for a hard time.

CYCLING

The vast majority of the territory covered in this book is relatively flat, and therefore theoretically ideal for most cyclists. Those who require a challenge could head for the Caucasus or Central Asia. Hire facilities are limited, and keen cyclists should take their own bicycle: when you need a rest, it is usually possible to load your bike onto a train (though not an express as a rule) or bus. You may be asked to pay an extra 10% of the normal fare.

The Cyclists' Touring Club provides members (£25 per annum) with general information sheets on cycling abroad, as well as trip reports. For further details contact the club at 69 Meadrow, Godalming, Surrey GU7 3HS (tel 01483-417217, fax 426994). If you'd like someone else to take over the logistics (and carry your bags), you might consider a cycling holiday organised by Bike Tours (PO Box 75, Bath BA1 1BX; tel 01225-480310). There may be as many as 100 people on one tour, but you travel at your own pace, covering an average of 60 miles a day.

What to Take. Owing to the dreadful state of roads, take a rugged bike with good chunky tyres, ideally a mountain bike; though anything which looks too flash is bound to attract unwanted attention.

Take your own supply of tools, and suggested spares include: brake pads; spokes (these can be taped to the frame of the bike and forgotten about); gear cable (long), which can double as brake cable if necessary; inner tubes; a small selection of nuts and bolts; and of course, a puncture repair kit.

Transporting your Bike. Always check with the airline, bus or train company about bicycle carriage before you buy a ticket: different companies have different policies. Most airlines allow you to take a bike free of charge. Some permit this in addition to your usual luggage limit, others say its weight must be deducted from the baggage allowance of 23kg per person). This should take in a touring bike plus two panniers (including one which you take on board as hand luggage).   When packing up the bike for transportation, tape cardboard around the whole thing or, failing that, just around the gear and brakes levers and the rear wheel gear assembly; remove the pedals and deflate the tyres to avoid explosions at high altitude, and turn the handlebars parallel to the frame: try this at home first.

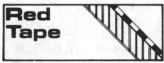

Passports. A full ten-year passport is required for travel to all the countries covered in this book. Most countries require your passport to be valid for at least six months beyond your projected date of arrival.

If your passport is lost or stolen while travelling, contact first the police and then your nearest Embassy. Obtaining replacement travel documents is easier if you have a record of the passport number and its date and place of issue, ideally a photocopy of the relevant pages. In most parts of the world the consular department of your Embassy can do the paperwork for you more or less immediately. In the former USSR, however, your wait could be several days. This is largely because the immigration officials of the country concerned need to supply you with an exit permit, and the bureaucracy involved can take a long time. If you lose your Russian visa along with your passport, it could prove an expensive exercise too.

Visas. If you were hoping the collapse of state communism would result in a reduction in red tape, you are out of luck. Previously one Soviet visa covered a whole trip. Now obtaining the proper permissions can be a tedious, time-consuming and expensive business.

Where possible, arrange any visas you require before you leave home, though this may depend on how long you plan to be away: most visas are valid for six months from the date of issue. The addresses of consulates in the UK and North America are given under *Red Tape* in each country section. You can also obtain a visa at the relevant consulate within the former Soviet Union or, usually, at the airport or at land borders, but you may face a longer-than-average wait and higher-than-average fee. Visas must almost always be paid for in hard currency.

Immigration. Assuming your visa is in order, entering the country is likely to be slow but sure. Customs officials tend to pay scant attention to most travellers, though crossing sensitive borders can still involve draconian searches complete with sniffer dogs. Elaborate electronic equipment, such as portable computers, can still arouse special interest wherever you are.

The fall of communism, and the adoption of free market policies, means that prices have risen substantially since 1991. This has affected local people far more than tourists, for whom the cost of living remains comparatively low. However, prices vary dramatically according to the levels of tourism and change. So while you'll encounter ludicrously high prices in parts of Moscow and Kiev, living becomes cheaper the further east you go.

Changing Money. Take your funds in cash and travellers cheques, with a credit card or two to fall back on. The US dollar has long held sway as the hard currency of choice, but its fall in value in 1995 *vis-à-vis* the Deutschmark has made the German currency increasingly popular. Rates for both these currencies are usually widely advertised and competitive; you are likely to get a much poorer deal exchanging other currencies, if indeed you can persuade anyone at all to accept them.

The former USSR is way behind the West in terms of personal finance. However, hole-in-the-wall cash dispensers are increasingly common and some city banks have automatic currency exchange machines. Normally, however, to change money out of banking hours, you'll have to rely either on bureaux de change or hotels, offering poor rates or outrageous commission charges. Changing currency at the border is usually a bad deal too. This is one reason to avoid having any surplus currency when you leave. If you want to change local money back into hard currency when leaving the country, you will usually be asked to show your original exchange receipts.

Travellers Cheques. The safest way to carry money is in travellers cheques, preferably as US dollars. In response to the number of stolen travellers cheques in circulation, some banks may ask to see the sales receipt: don't leave home without it.

American Express, Thomas Cook and Visa travellers cheques are equally acceptable in Eastern Europe, though you'll probably find it easier to obtain a refund for stolen cheques if you are an Amex customer: the company has numerous representatives in the former Soviet Union, and addresses are shown on the advertisement page 20.

Cash. Travellers to Russia and the republics should take a higher proportion of cash than they would on a trip in Western Europe. Travellers cheques are by no means universally accepted, even in banks. Many establishments are happy to accept either local or hard currency, whether you're buying souvenirs in a shop or paying for a private room. In Russia, however, you have to change hard currency into roubles first.

In some cases, certain goods and services must still be paid for in hard currency, including international train tickets. In these situations, only cash may be acceptable.

Credit and Charge Cards. American Express, Diners Club, Access/Master-Card and Visa are accepted by most airlines, leading hotels and smart restaurants and shops. Since some places occasionally run out of vouchers, it might be to your advantage to have a couple of credit cards. Note that most American Express offices will allow you to draw cash against your Amex card if you are in credit at home.

Withdrawing cash on a credit card is commonplace in Moscow and St Petersburg, but don't think that you could live off plastic in Ashkabad or Bishkek. Articles that are difficult to pay for with plastic wherever you are include train tickets and petrol- though, like everything else, this may change.

Emergency Cash. The local British Embassy will, with some reluctance, cash a cheque for up to £100 backed by a UK cheque guarantee card. This will not be enough to pay for a ticket out of the country, so if you're entirely destitute you'll have no option but to be repatriated and surrender your passport upon arrival back home; you won't get it back until you have paid the Foreign Office. Repatriation is unlikely, however, until all other avenues, such as finding someone at home to pay for your journey, have been tried.

You can ask your bank to wire money to a named bank abroad, but this is often an unreliable business which can soak up four or five days of your holiday. Alternatively, ask someone to send money through American Express, Thomas Cook or Western Union. You then pick up the cash at the local office (which could be some distance away).

Black Market. A little black market dabbling used to be part of the thrill for many visitors to the Soviet Union, but the potential gains have virtually disappeared in most countries. From Vilnius to Vladivostok you'll still find a few desperados trying to hatch deals with tourists, but all are unsavoury types, out to rip you off.

If you are tempted to trade, choose carefully with whom you deal. Rather than do business on the street, you may find it safer to deal with hotel or restaurant staff — though gone are the days when lift attendants stopped between floors for some covert trading. If you opt for the street, choose an individual and try to make sure he has no accomplices. Ideally there should be two of you. Firstly, agree how much you are going to exchange and the rate. The dealer should give your companion the money to count. He or she should check the notes, then move slightly away (out of grabbing range). Only when your companion has confirmed that the amount is correct, and has pocketed it, do you then hand over the dollars. Some rules should be observed to minimise the chances that you'll be conned.

1. Never try to change a huge amount of money; if you are going to be ripped off, better that it is just $10 or $20.
2. Keep the amount that you want to change in a separate pocket. It is foolish to reveal where all your funds are kept.
3. If, after agreeing to change money, you feel threatened, don't hesitate to pull out of the transaction.
4. Given the introduction of a range of new currencies in the former Soviet Union, check that you're not being fobbed off with either obsolete or foreign notes.

With all the care in the world, you cannot always avoid being cheated. Favourite tricks include excessive haste, to make you panic and pass over the dollars before you've checked the money, and the old chestnut of shouting 'police' and running off leaving you with insufficient notes or perhaps none at all.

Tipping. Illegal under communism, tipping has rapidly caught on. Ten per cent is the norm, and fancier restaurants often add this figure to the bill; a further tip is usually expected as well.

The best way to get to know the region properly is to live and work there. Do not expect to make money though, unless you work for a Western company. A local firm will pay a local salary, which will just about cover living costs but nothing else. The vast majority of jobs available for foreigners are as teachers of English. But as the barriers between East and West crumble through the 1990s, it is clear that opportunities for working travellers will increase.

TEACHING

English is now the first foreign language taught in schools. A knowledge of it is regarded as a crucial step towards economic regeneration, and there is a big demand for both qualified English teachers and native speakers. While it is harder now than a couple of years ago for someone without training and experience to get a job, anyone who looks for work on the spot still has a fair chance of being employed, particularly as many trained teachers simply aren't willing to accept the low salaries and working conditions offered in the former USSR. Anyone who is well qualified or experienced should be able to fix up a job without difficulty, whether you arrange it in advance or once in the region. Unqualified teachers will find it difficult to arrange a job from abroad.

Your chances of landing a job will be greatly enhanced if you head out of the big cities, particularly if you are unqualified. While simply being a native English-speaker will be enough for some places, most schools in the capital cities can afford to be more choosy.

Needless to say, experience and a teaching or TEFL qualification will get you the better-paid jobs. The RSA and Trinity Certificate Courses are the most sought after. Most schools express no preference for nationality, though Americans are probably in the ascendancy.

Jobs are available in state schools and universities as well as private language schools. Inexperienced teachers are used by state schools primarily for conversation classes. Teaching in state schools usually most rewarding — you see more a slice of life than in private schools. Working for the state also guarantees a salary, the possibility of accommodation, access to health insurance, and long-term contracts (which makes it easier to obtain a work permit). Jobs attached to universities usually offer stability and a light workload. At the university level you will normally require a degree. State schools and many other institutions have organized English lessons at the end of the working day, so anyone with initiative can create a job for him or herself with hours and a location to suit. Teachers in private schools must expect to teach everything from grammar to conversation. Private schools offer less financial and job security though they usually pay slightly better.

English language materials vary, and are not necessarily better in a private than a state school. Some have ancient texts, others the latest books and satellite TV. Pupils are generally keen and no problem to teach.Some pupils may find modern teaching methods strange as they are used to a more teacher-centred approach, and more creative techniques may take some getting used to.

Pay can vary enormously, but teachers can usually expect to earn $100-150 per month. It is essential to find out whether you pay is net or gross: in Russia, you could lose 38% of your earnings in tax. Some language projects are funded from the West, so pay better. A full-time salary should be just about adequate to live on by local standards but will not allow you to save anything for further travels, unless you take on lots of private teaching. The pay for private lessons can be $7 an hour, as high as $15 per hour for businesses. Some people manage to get free accommodation in exchange for giving conversation lessons. Given the choice, most employers will give priority to candidates who already have somewhere to stay, but most will try to help fix you up with a room. The advantage of working in the state system, particularly at a university, is that accommodation is likely to be provided.

When Russia and the republics first began rebuilding, teacher shortages were so dire that red tape for foreign teachers was kept to a minimum. But work permits are increasingly difficult to obtain. While those with qualifications and experience normally have nothing to worry about, people with only their native-speaker status may encounter problems. Short contracts make it more difficult to get a work permit, since the authorities are reluctant to undertake the paperwork for such short stints of work. Note too, that in some countries you may find it hard to change status if you were admitted on a tourist visa.

Finding a Job. Many of the native speaker teachers working in the former Soviet Union at present are under the auspices of a British or American agency, such as VSO and the Peace Corps. The Central Bureau for Educational Visits and Exchanges (Seymour Mews House, Seymour Mews, London W1H 9PE; 0171-486 5101) selects students and teachers to work at various UNESCO-sponsored holiday language camps. All you pay for is the flight. The organisations listed below, which recruit for more than one country in the region, will consider qualified teachers only.

Bell Educational Trust, Overseas Dept, The Lodge, Redcross Lane, Cambridge CB2 2QX.
British Council, 10 Spring Gardens, London SW1A 2BN (0171-389 4931).
East European Partnership, 15 Princeton Court, 53-55 Felsham Road, London SW15 1AZ (0181-780 2841).
International House, 106 Piccadilly, London W1 9FL (0171-491 2598).
Soros Professional English Teaching Program, 888 Seventh Avenue, Suite 1901, New York, NY 10106 (tel 212-757-2323, fax 974-0367).
Soros English Language Programme, 79 Lee Road, London SE3 9EN (tel 0181-852 5495, fax 0181-297 8788). The UK branch of the above.

If you opt to look for work once in the region, the local British Council can be a good place to start. Every office abroad keeps a list of English language teaching centres, and the main British Council offices have large English teachers' resource centres from which you may be able to benefit. Most have lists of language schools. At the very least, you would be able to read notices on the notice boards and meet teachers. Look in local English-language newspapers, if they exist, approach schools listed in the Yellow Pages.

Whether looking for work in advance or on the spot, *Teaching English Abroad* by Susan Griffith (Vacation Work, £9.95) is an excellent companion. It provides numerous addresses of state and private schools throughout the region as well as providing background information on red tape, pay, conditions of work and so on. Contacting private schools ahead of time is rarely productive (unless they recruit via a foreign agent), since most will want to interview you before making any commitment.

Teaching private lessons is the most lucrative but the most difficult to fix up. When looking for private teaching, a small notice placed on a prominent university notice board or in a daily newspaper would certainly produce results. Many executives need English for business, so you could even try approaching local companies.

VOLUNTARY WORK

While the decentralisation of power in the former communist bloc means that the old state-run voluntary organisations have either disintegrated or are losing their funding, there has been a dramatic increase in the number of contacts between voluntary groups in the East and West. The international workcamp organisations operating in Eastern Europe include the following:

International Voluntary Service, Old Hall, East Bergholt, Colchester, Essex CO7 6TQ.

Quaker International Social Projects, Friends House, Euston Road, London NW1 2BJ (0171-387 3601).

Christian Movement for Peace (CMP), 186 St Paul's Rd, Balsall Heath, Birmingham B12 8LZ.

United Nations Association (Wales), International Youth Service, Temple of Peace, Cathays Park, Cardiff, South Glamorgan (01222-223088).

British Trust for Conservation Volunteers (BTCV), 36 St Mary's Street, Wallingford, Oxfordshire OX10 0EU (01491-39766).

Some camps are agricultural since there is a severe shortage of labour in some rural areas. In many cases, the projects are a pretext for bringing together young people in an effort to dismantle prejudice on both sides. Often discussion sessions and excursions are a major part of the three-or four-week workcamps, with very little work expected. There is normally a registration fee of £25-£50; only travel expenses incurred once you have arrived at your destination will normally be paid for. Applications for workcamps should be sent through the partner organisation in the applicant's own country.

US and Canadian citizens should contact the CIEE (Council on International Educational Exchange at 205 East 42nd Street, New York NY 10017 (tel 212-661-1414), which runs study programmes and workcamps in the former USSR.

OTHER OPPORTUNITIES

The new democracies are all targeting tourism as a means of aiding their economies and are encouraging foreign tour operators to develop resorts; in time these may have large staff requirements. If you are looking for some casual work, ask discreetly around the universities or among expatriates teaching English. Your services as anything from a disc jockey to a freelance copy editor may be in demand. There are many niches which keen foreigners willing to stay for a while can fill.

People based in Russia and the republics are taking advantage of the new entrepreneurial spirit to take up more conventional forms of employment. The number of foreign firms in all the big capital cities is increasing rapidly.

Communications

Telephone. The Eastern bloc used to be cursed with some of the world's most inefficient telecommunications organisations. Foreign companies are busy upgrading the networks and have already made notable improvements, but progress is slow. Since the emphasis seems to have been laid on improving international connections, you'll often find it easier to call home than a neighbouring town: domestic telephone lines, when you eventually get through, vary between tolerable and inaudible. Some countries have wonderful new cardphones, but the older variety of public telephones are still a nightmare. Where new payphones don't yet exist, the easiest and cheapest way to make a call is to go to a public telephone station, which you'll find in every town of any size. The operators rarely speak English, but this is not usually a problem since all you need to do is to write down the number and wait. If you make a call from your hotel, expect to be charged at an exorbitant rate.

Phoning Ahead. You can dial direct to all the countries included in this book, though half the republics still use the old Soviet System routed via Moscow (prefixed 7 in the list below). Dial the international access code (00 from the UK, 16 from the Irish Republic, 011 from the USA or Canada, and 0011 from Australia or New Zealand), followed by the country code (listed in the order in which they appear in this book):

Russia 7	Armenia 7
Estonia 372	Azerbaijan 994
Latvia 371	Uzbekistan 7
Lithuania 370	Turkmenistan 7
Belarus 375	Kazakhstan 7
Ukraine 380	Kyrgyzstan 7
Moldova 373	Tajikistan 7
Georgia 7	

(You may see other codes listed for specific numbers, in particular 872. This is a satellite service, which has the great advantage of extra efficiency but the drawback of higher cost.) Next dial the area/city code, then the subscriber's number. Russia and the Republics are between two and 11 hours ahead of GMT.

Telegrams. These are a cheap and effective means of communication. Most post offices can handle them, and they are often more reliable and less stressful than the phone. Gradually, however, they are being replaced by fax communication.

Fax. Since fax transmissions use ordinary telephone lines, the service is not 100% reliable, but every enterprise from hotels to airlines seems to use them. The good thing from the traveller's point of view is that if you can produce a faxed confirmation of bookings. If you need to send one, post offices are usually cheaper than hotels.

Mail. Postal services are dismally slow. A letter posted abroad from Moscow or Kiev can take a fortnight, while those from off-the-beaten-track can take a month or more. The delivery of parcels is even more haphazard, wherever they are posted. If you want to post goods of any value, use a courier service such as DHL, which has opened up offices all over the place.

Poste Restante: in theory, poste restante should be available in any town, but in practice you would do best to rely on the central post office in the capital city (addresses are given under *Help and Information* in the relevant city sections). Check under both your first and last name, since letters are not always filed correctly.

The delivery of incoming mail is patchy whatever the address, but the chances of letters arriving are enhanced slightly if you use American Express. Any Amex customer can use their offices abroad for poste restante: addresses are given in the text, or call 0171-930 4411 for a worldwide directory.

KEEPING IN TOUCH

Newspapers. Keeping up on international events is increasingly easy given the blossoming of homegrown English-language newspapers and the expanding circulation of the foreign press in the CIS. There is already a choice of locally produced English-language dailies in Moscow, and *The Baltic Independent* circulates in Estonia, Latvia and Lithuania. The capital cities are where you're most likely to find foreign dailies, from the *Financial Times* and *Independent* to the ubiquitous (and dull) *Herald Tribune* and *USA Today*. The best places to find foreign newspapers are luxury hotels. In some of the more obscure capital cities, your embassy will be a good source of reading matter.

Broadcasting. While there is the odd broadcast in the English language by some radio stations, the BBC World Service provides the best source of news. Ring the Broadcast Coverage Department on 0171-257 2685 for information on World Service reception.

The influence of the West on the new democracies is perhaps most visible on television. Some new commercial TV channels have been set up with the aid of foreign money, but the most startling development has been the spread of satellite television. BBC Worldwide, CNN and ABC are beamed into thousands of hotel rooms, even the more modest establishments.

LANGUAGE

While English is the preferred foreign language in most of the capital cities, it is wrong to assume that everyone in the former USSR speaks English. Many Russians have only a shaky recollection of their English schooling, while easily the most common second language outside Russia is Russian (though many would rather not speak it for emotional/political reasons). In Moldova a little Italian will go a long way, while further east Turkish, Arabic or Persian could be useful. In Estonia, you're on your own. A basic vocabulary is included for most of the countries covered in this book. Learning a little more, however, will add considerably to your enjoyment.

Never underestimate the size of Russia and the republics of the former USSR when planning journeys in the region. If you choose to go from Vilnius to Vladivostok by train, you will be about ten days older when you get there. While sampling rail travel may be fun for a while, it is much slower than flying. Buses do not usually provide a third possibility; unlike in much of the world, buses are slow and peripheral to the main transport systems, except in the wilds of Central Asia.

AIR

It used to be easy: Aeroflot, the world's biggest airline, enjoyed a monopoly on services within the former USSR, setting services and fares at whatever levels it wished. Service was lousy, but given the range of difficulties the airline was up against — from technological obsolescence to appalling weather — it maintained technical standards and kept remarkably good time. Now the giant carrier has split into over 100 pieces, and many other airlines have started up. From one point of view, this is excellent news for the traveller: if there is a choice of three carriers between Moscow and Kiev, then service is likely to be better and fares keener than if there is just one. But safety standards are giving cause for concern, as a result of poor management, sloppy procedures and suspect maintenance on some airlines. In general, you are certainly going to be more comfortable and will probably feel safer on the Airbuses and Boeings of Ukraine International and Transaero than on ancient Antonovs, Ilyushins and Tupolevs handed down by Aeroflot to its successors.

Another effect of the diversification of air travel is that obtaining comprehensive information is difficult. Airports themselves are good venues, because all the competing airlines have offices where you can compare fares, schedules and aircraft.

You should assume that payment for tickets will need to be in local currency or cash US dollars; credit cards are rarely accepted.

TRAINS

The railways penetrate most corners of any country in the former Soviet Union. Thanks to the central power of Moscow, most places are linked to the Russian capital by express trains. If you're told the train is fully booked, this usually means that all tickets have been sold to touts, large quantities of whom you will find hanging around the entrance. For a premium they can get you a ticket to wherever you want to go. Finally, if all else fails, turn up at the train station and approach a *provodnik* or carriage attendant: for dollars they will almost certainly find you a seat on the train.

DRIVING

If you are persuaded that taking your own car into the CIS could be a mistake (see *Getting There*), you may consider the option of hiring a car once you have arrived. Given the relative low cost of public transport within the region, car rental is uneconomic. On the other hand, it may be the only realistic means by which you can reach the more isolated spots in the region.

Car Rental. International rental companies operate in many parts of the former Soviet Union. For a list of outlets, call the following UK numbers: Avis 0181-848 8733, Budget 0800 181181, EuroDollar 01895 233300 and Hertz 0345 555888. These multinationals are geared mainly for those planning ahead, with the price for prebooked rental often cheaper than on-the-spot deals.

Rates vary enormously, but $300-400 for a week is not unusual. You must generally be over 21, and you'll need to show your passport and leave a deposit- usually $100 or your full credit card details.

Rules and Regulations. All traffic travels on the right. In most countries it is an offence to drive even with a trace of alcohol in your blood. Lesser misdemeanours, such as breaking the speed limit, are punishable by on-the-spot fines, which are often negotiable. Enforcement is sporadic, though traffic police are not averse to picking on foreigners. Seat belts must be worn at all times.

Look out for local idiosyncracies, such as being able to turn right against a red light. Watch what local motorists are doing, though not to the extent where you imitate their reckless habits: few drivers have adapted to the fact that there is much more traffic on the roads than there was under communism. The sight of an oncoming vehicle overtaking on your own side of the road is distressingly common. Quick reactions are a huge asset and defensive driving is advisable at all times.

Accidents. If you're involved in an accident, the obvious rules apply: administer first aid or summon help for the injured; call the police; and take names and addresses of other drivers and any independent witnesses. If possible, don't move any of the vehicles, but if you have to because you're obstructing the traffic, mark their wheel positions in the road, and take some pictures if you have a camera.

The hassle following even a minor accident can be considerable. One easy way to enhance your chance of avoiding an accident is to drive only by day. Road markings and street lights are scarce, and there are still a lot of old cars about which do not have dipped headlights, or perhaps any headlights at all.

HITCHING

The increased number of private vehicles on the road means that hitching is easier than it used to be, at least in the west of the former Soviet Union. Hitch-hiking is an acceptable form of (free) transport in the Baltic Republics, but anywhere east from there hitch-hikers — particularly Western ones, perceived as being rich — are often expected to pay something towards the cost of the ride. Note that the practice of hailing private cars in cities, to act as informal taxis, always involves payment.

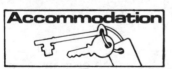

Most of the former Soviet Union has never really had much of a tourism industry, hence the current shortage of hotels. Historic buildings are being converted and new hotels are being constructed, but the demand still far outstrips supply. Furthermore, most of the attention is concentrated on business hotels, which means reasonably priced facilities for tourists are rare. Accommodation will almost certainly be you biggest single daily expense in the former USSR. You'll be hard pushed to find a hotel room for less than $40 for two, and may cost a good deal more than that. There is a general shortage of single hotel rooms.

Whether you stay in a smart or lowly establishment, you can usually rely on towels, soap and loo roll being provided. But take your own bathplug: there seems no good economic or cultural reason why the countries of the CIS should have a chronic shortage of bathplugs, but they do.

Private Accommodation. Staying in a private house will give you the chance to experience ordinary culture and lifestyles. Most families are extremely welcoming, though in cities you'll usually be given a key to your room and the flat and left to get on with your own thing. In rural areas, you'll feel much more at home, and will probably be asked to share family meals.

Special agencies have sprung up in some places, but elsewhere people will approach you direct, most commonly in transport terminals, or put signs up advertising vacancies. Given the competition for hotel rooms, going private is the most reliable way to find accommodation on the spot in the high season. It is also cheaper. Rooms cost an average of $10-15, though some cost double or half that.

If you wish to arrange private accommodation in advance, a good UK company to contact is Interchange, at Interchange House, 27 Stafford Road, Croydon CR0 4NG (tel 0181-681 3612, fax 0181-760 0031).

Hostels. The most welcome accommodation development in recent years has been the establishment of the first travellers' hostels in Moscow and St Petersburg. Membership of Hostelling International is not obligatory. As independent travel to the CIS increases, more hostels are likely to be created.

Camping. Like hostels, campsites can be good places to meet people, and are by far the cheapest form of accommodation: you will rarely pay more than a few dollars per person. In areas popular among hikers, the facilities and locations are often extremely good; elsewhere, however, you may find yourself under a flight path and with nothing but a couple of cold showers and evil-smelling lavatories. Freelance camping is not normally a problem if you ask permission to stay in a field first. Do not try this in Gorky Park.

Travel in the USSR used to be a relatively safe experience, but the collapse of health services and hygeine standards along with economies means that all kinds of previously rare diseases such as diphtheria are becoming prevalent. It is strongly advisable to contact a travel medicine specialist such as MASTA (0891 224100).

In general, however, few travellers fall ill, the most common complaint being a bout of diarrhoea or a bad hangover brought on by some lethal local liquor. But no one should take their good health for granted. While you are extremely unlikely to encounter any but one or two of the hazards listed here, by following the advice given below and taking sensible precautions, you can help prevent illness from spoiling your visit.

Stay Healthy Abroad by Rob Ryan (Health Education Authority, £6.99) is an most up-to-date and comprehensive guide for anyone concerned about their health.

NATURAL HAZARDS

Heat. You may not be in the tropics, but whether you're sightseeing in Samarkand or sunbathing by the Black Sea you should respect the sometimes intense summer heat. Wear a hat and drink plenty of non-alcoholic fluids even if you aren't thirsty. If you experience headaches or giddiness after a long day outside, you probably have a mild case of heat exhaustion; drink plenty of water and sit in the shade until the symptoms subside. Heatstroke brings on more severe headaches and delirium, and must be treated immediately; remove all your clothes and cover yourself with a wet sheet in order to stop the body temperature from rising further.

Sun. The most effective protection is to stay out of the sun between 10am and 3pm. The next best precaution is to expose yourself to the sun gradually and use a lotion with a high protection factor. Sea water, perfume and after-shave increase the rate of burning.

If, like most sun-starved travellers, you ignore this advice and get burnt, apply calamine lotion or cold cream liberally, or soak a towel in cold water and place it over the most tender areas. For severe burns use a mild antiseptic and keep the skin clean and dry.

Mosquitoes. While these hateful creatures are not (yet) carriers of malaria in the CIS, they can still be a darned nuisance: their bites itch a lot and can make summer nights a misery. At nightfall, cover your limbs and apply insect repellent to exposed parts. For the best protection, choose a repellent which contains the chemical called Deet, such as Jungle Formula. Eating copious amounts of garlic is also said to repel mosquitoes, as well as other people. Soap, calamine lotion or any of the sting relief creams on the market help to ease itching. Applying ice to the bites can also soothe irritation.

DISEASES AND OTHER HEALTH HAZARDS

The collapse of communism has led to an upsurge in the spread of infectious diseases. While most short-term visitors should not encounter problems, people intending to spend long periods in the former USSR are strongly advised to take specialist medical advice.

Diphtheria. Around 800 people died from this respiratory disease in Russia in 1994, and it is widespread in neighbouring republics. People who have not had a vaccination in the past ten years should consider having a booster.

Gastric Problems. Much of the food you will encounter is so bland that you may conclude that the risk of gastric trouble is low. Any food, however dull, can carry bacteria, though in practice cases of food poisoning are rare. Central Asia has the worst reputation for upset stomachs, but wherever the standards of hygiene are obviously low it is wise to avoid eating meat. Contaminated water (see below) is an equally common cause of gastric problems. Some travellers to Russia have returned home with giardiasis, which is caused by an intestinal parasite picked up from contaminated food or water.

Diarrhoea is likely to be the first clue that you have eaten something you shouldn't have. If left to its own devices it should clear up in a couple of days. Rather than take drugs, drink as much (bottled) water as possible and eat only dry bread, rice, pasta, etc. Lomotil, codeine and immodium alleviate the effects of the diarrhoea (and will block you up if you are going on a long bus journey), but do nothing about the cause. Antibiotics can have a detrimental effect, and they are best avoided unless fever or serious infection is suspected. In this case you should seek medical advice.

Water: a terrifying number of waterways in the CIS have been polluted by industry, and many people throughout the region choose to boil their tapwater.

Hepatitis. A viral infection of the liver, hepatitis comes in various forms. The one which is most likely to affect travellers is Hepatitis A. It is easy to catch from contaminated food and water and Romania will be the country you are most likely to pick it up.

Incubation takes two to six weeks and symptoms include loss of appetite, lethargy, fever, pains in the abdomen, followed by nausea and vomiting. The whites of the eyes and the skin turn yellow, urine turns deep orange and stools become white. If you suspect infection, rest and seek medical advice immediately. Do not smoke or drink alcohol, nor eat fat. Some people are only mildly affected, but hepatitis can sometimes take six months to clear up; therefore you are strongly advised to go straight home and recover in comfort.

The gamma globulin vaccine offers good protection against Hepatitis A. Since the effect of the vaccine wears off gradually after it is administered, have the injection shortly before departure. If you plan to be away for more than six months or are a frequent traveller, you should think about having the Havrix vaccine, which gives immunity for ten years: it is administered in three doses, two a month apart before a trip, followed by a further one about three months later.

Pollution and Smoking. It may not seem fair to lump pollution and smoking together, but both are so widespread that asthmatics could face serious problems. With the rapid increase in traffic, smog is becoming a serious problem in the big cities, while poisons are still churned into the atmosphere by industry.

An overwhelmingly large proportion of the male population smokes. Smokers from the West will be delighted at the lack of restrictions on the habit. Only the odd tourist-oriented restaurant has a non-smoking room; in bars and restaurants frequented mostly by local people, you can expect to sit in a smoky haze.

Other Diseases. The standard inoculations apart from those mentioned above are typhoid, tetanus and polio. Typhoid, like Hepatitis A, is caught by consuming contaminated food or water. The typhoid vaccination is administered in two doses, though travellers who have already had a course need only a booster injection. Polio and tetanus require a booster every ten years.

AIDS

The Acquired Immune Deficiency Syndrome (Aids) is caused by the Human Immunodeficiency Virus (HIV). This can damage the body's defence system so that it is unable to fight certain infections and other diseases. Statistics for the CIS are scarce, and it is difficult to discover the extent of the Aids and the virus which causes it. While there is a comparatively low incidence of intravenous drug abuse, prostitution is on the rise and hospitals strapped for cash cannot always maintain high levels of hygiene. Even so, for visitors who take sensible precautions against contracting the virus through unprotected sexual intercourse or intravenous drug abuse, risks are minimal.

You are strongly advised to avoid contact with male or female prostitutes and to take your own supply of condoms if there is a chance that you will have sex with somebody whose sexual history is unknown to you. In much of the former Soviet Union condoms are hard to find or of poor quality. Infection through contaminated blood transfusions is less easy to control. Although screening is now common, this is not always done effectively. In addition, hypodermic syringes may be reused and may not always be adequately sterilised. If you are in an accident and require a blood transfusion, try to get in touch with your nearest consulate or embassy; the staff there will know the nearest source of 'clean' blood. You should also consider taking an Aids Pack. A normal kit contains hypodermic needles, suture material (for stitches), intravenous drip needles and alcohol swabs. Your doctor should be able to make a kit up for you; ask him or her to supply a letter explaining that the kit is for medical use only- this will save you potential hassle at Customs among officials convinced you are a possible drug-user.

A growing trend (and one which is condemned internationally) among the countries of the former Soviet Union is to insist upon new arrivals producing a certificate showing them to be free of HIV. This is more likely to be applied against long-stay visitors such as students than short-term visitors, and may turn out to be a policy used only to exclude 'undesirables'.

Sources of Information. For up-to-date information on the extent of Aids, contact the Panos Institute at 9 White Lion Street, London N1 9PD (tel 0171-278 1111, fax 0171-278 0345). It publishes various books and a bi-monthly magazine called *WorldAIDS*. The Terrence Higgins Trust (52-54 Grays Inn Road, London WC1X 8SU; tel 0171-831 0330, fax 0171-242 0121) is the UK's leading Aids charity and offers good general information and advice on HIV and Aids. You can call its Advice Centre on 0171-242 1010. You can also talk to trained advisors by ringing the National Aids Helpline on 0800-567-123: calls are free and confidential.

MEDICAL TREATMENT

Most countries in Europe have a Reciprocal Health Agreement with the nations covered in this book, which entitles them to free medical treatment, though prescription charges must be paid for. Even so, you should still take out full medical insurance. Doctors throughout the region are generally well trained, but so short of money that the medicines and equipment at their disposal are severely limited. For the best treatment you should try to find a private (and expensive) clinic.

Medications. While medicines are much easier to buy in the former Soviet Union than they used to be, as a general rule you should bring with you all the medicines you are likely to need. Cures for indigestion and headaches can of course be purchased over the counter, but some pharmacies do not have a sufficient range of drugs to make up complicated prescriptions. Nevertheless, pharmacists can be very helpful, and can save you a trip to the doctor if all you have are minor and easily recognisable symptoms. Furthermore, if you can overcome language problems, medicines are very cheap.

OTHER HEALTH MATTERS

Women's Health. If you are planning to travel while pregnant, check carefully the effects of any vaccinations you might require. It is advisable not to be inoculated with a live vaccine such as polio, especially during the first three months of pregnancy.

While you can buy tampons and sanitary towels, prices tend to be high and supplies erratic in some areas. You are advised to bring all you need from home.

A book called *Bugs, Bites and Bowels* (Cadogan, £8.95) is particularly good on the subject of women's health.

Contraception. Take all the contraception you think you may require. Locally-produced condoms are best avoided, and sophistications such as spermicidal jelly or oral contraceptives are difficult or nigh impossible to obtain. Note that the effectiveness of the contraceptive pill is reduced if you have a stomach upset, or if you take certain types of antibiotics.

INSURANCE

While most people are scrupulously honest, there is a small contingent of thieves who are never happier than when robbing foreigners. So insurance is essential for your possessions as well as for your health. The cover provided by most policies is fairly standard: delay and cancellation insurance of up to £2,000; £2 million for medical expenses; the same amount for personal liability; £20,000 for permanent disability; and lost or stolen baggage up to about £1,000 (sometimes valuable single items are excluded). Most now also offer an emergency repatriation service.

Every airline, tour operator and travel agent is delighted to sell you insurance because of their high commission (sometimes over 60%). Shopping around can save you money or get better cover for the same premium. Endsleigh Insurance offers good rates for its worldwide insurance scheme. Information is available direct from the head office in Cheltenham (tel 0242-223300) or from any youth travel specialists. Annual travel insurance policies are well worth considering for longer trips or if you make more than a couple of international journeys each year.

If you're unfortunate enough to have to claim on your insurance, the golden rule is to amass as much documentation as possible to support your application. In particular, compensation is unlikely to be paid for lost baggage or cash unless your claim is accompanied by a police report of the loss.

Crime and Safety

During the oppressive regime under communism, most parts of the former Soviet Union had no tradition of lawbreaking. They are now making up for this with a vengeance. Economic crises of varying severity and the incursions of capitalism have resulted in an increase in crime at all levels across the former USSR. The incidence of murder and robbery has risen sharply, and gambling and prostitution are increasingly common. Organised crime is thriving, with activities ranging from small-time racketeering to high-level corruption. Mafias operate in all cities, often seeming immune from police action.

Most casual visitors will be completely unaffected by (and oblivious to) crime of this nature. Dodgy moneychangers can be a danger (see *Money: The Black Market*), but the main threat is from pickpockets and other petty thieves. As a Westerner, you could be carrying in cash what for the average former Soviet citizen represents several months' wages. Therefore theft of a wallet or purse presents understandable temptation; a worrying tendency is the use of violence in thefts.

How to Avoid Robbery. There is no need to feel paranoid about crime, but by taking a few precautions you can greatly reduce the chance that you will be robbed. Western visitors displaying ostentatious wealth in darkened backstreets are asking for trouble. It pays to try not to look too much like a tourist. Do not carry around shoulder bags that can be easily swiped. Cameras symbolise Western wealth and can be a major temptation too. Leave as much money as possible in your hotel and conceal what you take with you in a moneybelt beneath your clothes. Keep a small amount of change in your pocket, so you don't have to undress just to buy a coffee or a newspaper. (In some countries such as Ukraine, where inflation is high, means you may have to use a brick-sized wad of the local currency for even a small purchase.)

When in cities frequented by a large number of tourists, treat anyone you meet on the street with caution, initially at least. Avoid revealing where you are staying until you feel you trust your new friend. Be particularly wary of gypsy children. One may approach you alone after a few pennies but will then try to distract you while accomplices pick your pockets.

The Law. It used to the case that foreigners were automatically regarded with suspicion by the security forces. It was believed that a large proportion of visitors were there to subvert the state. These days, that view no longer prevails. In its place has arisen the idea that Westerners represent easy pickings for a woefully underpaid police force, and arbitrary fines for often-imagined offences are widely imposed. The good news is that the precise amounts of these fines is usually negotiable.

Drugs: potentially, the market for drugs in the former USSR is huge. The republics are becoming established on the narcotics trafficking network, and the level of lawlessness makes transportation and sale easy. Having said that, the authorities are anxious to keep their subjects off anything stronger than vodka. Penalties for possession always include a fine, plus a term in prison of up to five years. In reality, in the case of foreigners sentences tend to be shortened, followed by deportation. Sentences for selling and smuggling range from five to ten years.

Drunkenness: don't get overly drunk in public places. While over-indulgence is tolerated in the privacy of your own home, if you wander drunk around the streets you run the risk of being arrested and locked up until you sleep it off. Furthermore you greatly increase the risk of being a victim of crime. If you are robbed while drunk, expect little sympathy from the police.

Photography: formerly communist regimes may have a more relaxed approach towards security, but there are certain subjects which are still not considered suitable for photographs. As is the case in nations around the world, you should not take photographs of military or police installations or equipment, airports, power stations, border crossings, etc.

When it comes to taking pictures of local people, not everyone enjoys being photographed. It is good manners to always ask your subject for the go-ahead first. People in Central Asia can be particularly sensitive.

Help and Information *i*

Gay Travellers. Under communism, homosexuality was illegal, and the republics are liberalising this law at differing rates; in Lithuania, for example, anal sex is still forbidden. In practice the remaining laws are most unlikely to be enforced, but bear in mind that most former Soviet citizens share a conservative attitude towards gay people. There are still relatively few visible gay movements, with no real 'scene' as you'd find in Western Europe. Only a small number of bars cater overtly for the gay community, these being concentrated in the more developed capital cities like Moscow and Kiev.

The best source currently is the *Gay Guide: Eastern Europe*, published by Softpress in Poland but available from gay bookshops abroad, including Gay's The Word at 66 Marchmont Street, London WC1N 1AB (0171-278 7654). It is not much more than a booklet, but at £2.25 is better value than *Spartacus*, published in Germany by Bruno Gmunder, price £14.95. This country-by-country directory gives information about current laws on homosexuality, gay movements, etc., but it is not particularly accurate and is aimed primarily at gay men. In some towns, more research appears to have gone into locating cruising areas and public lavatories than in seeking out gay bars and clubs.

Women Travellers. Women outnumber men in the former Soviet Union, not that it has done them much good. Official equality between the sexes was declared in 1917, so complaints about discrimination, unequal pay and harrassment have traditionally had no public outlet. Independence has not done much to change the situation either. In the past, women have prospered in professional fields, becoming doctors, spacc scientists and tram-drivers. But you won't see the tram-driver behind the wheel of a private car, and the space scientist will still be expected to do all the shoppping and cleaning. The shortage of accommodation has meant that women often marry young in order to escape the parental home, and also have children young. Independence has brought all sorts of issues out into the open, but it has also made things harder economically. Whilst before, women were doing a full-time job as well as all the household chores, they are now frequently doing two jobs as well as all the household chores. The birth rate has dropped sharply. Widespread availability of contraception for the first time is one factor, but reluctance to start a family in such unstable times is undoubtedly another.

No amount of laws can dislodge male chauvinism, but harassment of women travellers is not common. The main aggravation may be the over-protective solicitude some local men display. The lobbies of smart city hotels are often gathering places for prostitutes, so female travellers would be wise to avoid sitting alone in such places.

In the Islamic republics in the south, religious fundamentalism is growing and women should dress modestly.

Young and Student Travellers. Anyone under the age of 26 should obtain an ISIC or FIYTO card, for students and other young people respectively. They are available from youth travel agencies or student unions and will entitle you to discounts on everything from museum admission fees to certain bus or train journeys. Student cards are widely available in the CIS, and enquiries as to your precise student status are unlikely to be extensive.

Travellers with Disabilities. The countries of the former USSR lag well behind in their provisions for people with disabilities, and financial constraints mean that this situation is unlikely to change in the near future. Those with wheelchairs will face constant impediments to mobility, and blind and partially sighted travellers will find it hard to get around. At present, the help of an able-bodied companion is, unfortunately, essential.

Anyone who is keen to travel around the former Soviet Union should try contacting the tour operators listed under *Getting There*, since these have some experience of circumventing the problems confronting the handicapped.

Useful source books include *Nothing Ventured: Disabled People Travel the World*, by Alison Walsh (Penguin, £7.99), available from bookshops, and *Holidays and Travel Abroad: A Guide for Disabled People* by John Stanford, available from the Royal Society for Disability and Rehabilitation (RADAR) at 25 Mortimer Street, London W1N 8AB (0171-637 5400), currently priced at £4.50 including postage. In the United States, you should contact the Society for the Advancement of Travel for the Handicapped at 345 Fifth Avenue, Suite 610, New York NY 10016 (tel 212-447-7284, fax 725-8253).

Electrical Items. Most sockets are standard Continental two-round-pin jobs, with an optional earth. Some hotels use twin flat prongs instead, like US sockets. A universal adaptor is advisable. The supply in all the countries in this book is nominally around 220v at 50Hz AC, roughly the same as in the UK. Voltage drops and frequency fluctuations are usual, however, so be prepared for equipment such as hair dryers and radios to function below normal, and think twice before connecting sensitive equipment such as portable computers.

Weights and Measures. The CIS uses the metric system. Distances are measured in millimetres (25.4mm = 1 inch), metres (0.3m = 1 foot) and kilometres (1.6km = 1 mile). Volume uses the millilitre (550ml = 1 Imperial pint) and the litre (4.5l = 1 Imperial gallon). Weights are given in grams (27g = 1 ounce) and kilograms (0.45kg = 1 lb).

SOURCES OF INFORMATION

Maps and Books. The best travel guides and maps are published in the West, but in the former Soviet Union new, independently-produced books are gradually replacing the turgid, authority-approved volumes of the past. In particular, the *Traveller's Yellow Pages* series is expanding, covering Moscow, St Petersburg, northwest Russia and the Baltics, with more to come. These books contain listings of services, but also valuable up-to-date advice on city life. In the UK, they are available from Zwemmer, 28 Denmark St, London WC2H 8NJ (tel 0171-379 6253; fax 379 6257); in the USA, from InfoServices International, 1 St Mark's Place, Cold Spring Harbor, NY 11724 (tel 516-549-0064; fax 516-549-2032).

City maps are easily available once you're in the former Soviet Union, but may be in an unfamiliar script and with out-of-date street names — check the publication date carefully. If you want to buy country maps before you leave home, the best ones are published by GeoCenter International, Freytag & Berndt, Kümmerley & Frey and Marco Polo. Some specialist shops stock maps imported from Eastern Europe, including the excellent Cartographia series from Budapest.

Periodicals covering the former Soviet Union are expanding, such as the monthly business magazine *New Markets*, available from Paper Mews Place, 290 High St, Dorking, Surrey RH4 1QT (tel 01306 877111, fax 01306 889191).

Bookshops: The following are travel specialists:

Daunt Books, 83 Marylebone High Street, London W1M 4DE (tel 0171-224 2295) — guides and travelogues as well as related literature, from biographies to cookery books.
Stanford's: 12-14 Long Acre, London WC2E 9LP (tel 0171-836 1321) —

has some of the more obscure guidebooks and is the best source of maps in London.

The Travel Bookshop: 13 Blenheim Crescent, London W11 2EE (tel 0171-221 5260) — also sells secondhand guidebooks and literature.

Travellers' Bookshop: 25 Cecil Court, London WC2N 4EZ (tel 0171-836 9132) — a good selection of new and secondhand guides, and a useful travellers' notice board.

Tourist Information. While tourist offices as we know them have begun to open up, most national tourist boards in the former Soviet Union are still unaccustomed to dealing with independent travellers. Their function is primarily to make bookings for accommodation, theatre seats, train tickets and so on, not to tell you which bus to catch to visit the local zoo. For this type of information, you'll do better at one of the private tourist organisations, which are already well-established in several capital cities and are gradually opening branches in smaller towns and cities. Failing that, of course, try asking any local person. Most people will try their best to help.

Embassies. If you get into difficulties, whether caused by theft, ill-health or involvement with crime, your first point of contact should be your Embassy (or the Embassy of the country which represents you). The staff have a thorough understanding of the way things work — or fail to work — in Eastern Europe. They can also cash cheques of up to £100, if it is backed with cheque card. In a real emergency, the staff will do their utmost to help you out; however, if your problem is that you've sprained your ankle while drunk, don't expect too much sympathy. Addresses of Embassies and Consulates are given in the text.

RUSSIA

The Russian Federative Republic, which includes Siberia and the Far East, covers 17 million square kilometres. Its domination of the former Soviet Union is easily explained: Russia occupied three-quarters of Soviet territory and was home to half of the population. The Ural mountains form the geographical boundary between Europe (Western Russia) and Asia (Siberia and the Far East).

The world's biggest country presents huge challenges to the traveller, but with patience, humour and dollars most of them can be overcome and the considerable rewards of visiting a nation in transition reaped. Life for the visitor to Russia is a kind of roulette, with much depending on chance. Will the hotel receptionist decide to help you out, or choose the safe option of 'no rooms'. Will the airline clerk sell you a ticket for roubles, or insist you go to a separate office? Will the waiter bring you a beer, or insist that only champagne is available today? People in Russia have been taught that 'no' is the best answer to many questions, and only gentle persuasion may change their hearts and minds.

You will often get frustrated by the heavy hand of bureaucracy, appalled at the ecological dereliction which is the legacy of a lifetime of state communism, and plain hungry, when your stomach's requirements are not matched by the offerings or the hours of the food-providing bureaucracy. At least, you must tell yourself several times each day, you are not obliged to live there. With time, the grace and generosity of most Russian people will become evident and the natural and man-made treasures of this great land revealed.

Distances are vast: from west to east Russia stretches for more than 10,000 kilometres. It spans eleven time zones and contains a huge variety of natural conditions. Extremes of climate range from a winter average of −60°C/−76°F in the tundra of the Central Siberian Plateau, through to average summer temperatures of over 30°C/86°F in the Caucasus. Perhaps the most important geographical fact about Russia is that it is both Asian and European, and the resulting diversity of natural habitats, peoples and cultures makes it arguably the world's most fascinating country.

THE PEOPLE

The population of Russia, around 160,000,000 makes it fourth in the world, behind China, India and the USA; Indonesia and Brazil are catching up fast. Russia's people are distributed very unevenly. The vast majority live in the European parts west of the Urals, but the rest of the country is, apart from the cities, almost empty. Most are Russians, but there are also significant numbers of Tatars and Bashkirs, whose designated homelands have about 6 millions and 1.5 millions respectively. Further north, the Buryats of eastern Siberia, the peoples of the far north and the Aleuts of the Far East are also significant.

Before the collapse of the Soviet Union, the term 'minor nationalities' was applied to ethnic groups such as the Chenchens and the Ossets of the Russian Caucasus, who — as with their neighbours to the south — are now experiencing the consequences of the lid being taken off festering political sores.

In addition, there are small communities of Germans, Jews and Koreans scattered across Russia.

Meeting the People. The first impression you gain of Russian people may be unfavourable: staff in shops and restaurants, etc. can be surly in the extreme, and it would be a mistake to expect any special treatment just because you're foreign. Furthermore visitors in the big cities are prime targets for petty criminals, and it is easy to form a poor opinion of a nation where everyone seems to be rude, or after your money, or both. Once you get out of the saturated tourist haunts of Moscow and St Petersburg, however, Russian people are extremely hospitable. Don't be surprised if they are rather conservative about appearance: even though fashion has escaped from the mauve-nylon-with-everything regime under communism, men with earrings, anyone with brightly coloured hair or a slightly racy hairstyle or outfit will be stared at. In winter, if you aren't wearing a hat, old ladies will come up to you and point at your head in a most concerned fashion.

A great virtue of Russian people is their respect for their friends and relatives, and in turn their friends' and relatives' friends and relatives. So even if you are just a distant acquaintance of someone they know, you will be welcomed into their house and treated as if you have known them all your life. Do not, therefore, be shy about ringing up people whose names and telephone numbers you have been given. It is usually well worth the effort.

Russians traditionally entertain at home rather than in restaurants, though this is changing as the number of places to eat out multiplies. As a guest, you are always expected to eat and drink copiously, whatever time of day. Do not imagine that if you turn up at 3 or 4 pm you can make the excuse that you have just had lunch; you will nonetheless be expected to eat. Teetotallers and vegetarians may have some difficulty as they are treated with great curiosity and even suspicion, these being such alien concepts to Russian mentality.

It is essential to take something with you when you visit, be it flowers, which Russians adore; rarely in summer will you board a bus or train without seeing people laden with flowers, chocolates or alcohol.

Women in Russia. Communism's aim of achieving complete equality between the sexes never did work out. Although many women work as doctors, scientists and lawyers, a large proportion of the remainder end up with the less prestigious, lower-paid work than men and are still expected to do all the cooking, domestic chores and shopping.In Russia, it is a woman's duty to give birth. Foreign couples are considered eccentric if they have no children; indeed it is often the first thing a Russian citizen will want to know about you (along with your salary). Tragically the most common form of birth control is abortion, which is legal and of which the average Russian woman has five or six. Most of these take place in European Russia, as in Russian Asia women have many more children. Contraceptive pills are almost impossible to find; they are generally only given to women who have a medical history of gynaecological problems, whilst condoms and diaphragms are primitive, to say the least. Methods of both abortion and childbirth are not very advanced. Neither the father of the child nor any other relation or friend is allowed to be present at the birth. Sometimes fathers do not see their new child until up to five days after he or she is born.

To date there is no official feminist movement in Russia, though there are a few women who are doing their utmost to create one. The term 'feminism' is severely frowned upon and leaders of feminist groups are often the objects of persecution. A worrying number of Russian women still believe that they achieved complete emancipation in 1917, but strong sex-stereotyping continues in behaviour and in the media.

Despite the prevailing sexism, Western women need not be as apprehensive about walking around Moscow, St Petersburg or Vladivistok by night as they would be in other European cities of that size. But given the growing incidence of attacks on both women and men for financial gain, it is sensible to choose more crowded and better lit streets.

Prostitution. Until 1986, paid sex did not officially exist in Russia; it was only then that it was made an offence. To the women who work the big hotels for Westerners, this is little deterrent. Single male visitors can expect unwelcome attention from prostitutes in their hotels. The bars are good hunting grounds, and there seems to be a degree of connivance between hotel managers and call girls. Some men are disturbed in their rooms in the middle of the night by phone calls from prostitutes, often calling them by name. It should not be necessary to point out the spectrum of sexually transmitted diseases which flourish in this world.

Gay People. Homosexual relations are now legal in Russia, but gay people are still largely ostracised. Only in Moscow and St Petersburg is there any significant gay scene.

Religion. Under Communism, Russia was officially an atheist state in line with Marxist doctrine. Despite frequent persecution of Christian, Jewish and Muslim leaders and the conversion of places of worship into secular buildings, religion endured the decades of state socialism. These days, the Russian Orthodox Church is the dominant religion but evangelical groups from abroad (mainly the USA) are moving in and establishing significant followings.

Orthodox services are moving, often in both the figurative and literal senses — there always seems to be a great deal of shuffling around.

The Muslim community is strongest in Tatarstan and the south. If you intend to visit an active mosque, note that women must cover their heads, everyone must remove their shoes and you should behave with the utmost decorum. Try to avoid the five daily prayer times, indicated by the calls to prayer broadcast over loudspeakers in every Muslim town.

LANGUAGE

Russian is spoken by almost everyone. It uses the Cyrillic alphabet, which you should endeavour to master; at the very least it will help you to decipher signposts. English is spoken by an increasing number of people, since these days it is widely regarded as the key to success in life, but this still represents only a small proportion of the total population.

A good starting point for learning the language is Michael Frewin's *Teach Yourself Russian* or the *Penguin Russian Course*; both books are moderately priced paperbacks. The BBC's *Get by in Russian* is good for short visits, and includes a cassette.

Useful Words and Phrases

hello — strastvitye
goodbye — do svidanya
excuse me — skazitye
yes — da
no — nyet
please — pazhalsta
Baris Yeltsin
how much — skalka
thank you — spasseeba
good — hurrasho
bad — plokha
left — nalyevo
right — napravo
today — sevodnya
tomorrow — zavtra
restaurant — restoran
hotel — gataneetsa
hot — gahryacho
cold — kholodna

water — voda
tea — chai
coffee — kofye
beer — peevo
vodka — vodka
cheers! — za vashev zdahrovye
toilet — tooalyet
(female) — zhenskee
(male) — moozhskoy
hospital — polycleenika
pharmacy — aptyeka
market — reenok
airport — aerovoksal
underground — metro
railway station — vokzal
taxi — taxi
bus — ahvtoboos
tram — tranvai
Boris Yeltsin — Baris Yeltsin

CLIMATE

It is impossible to generalize about the weather in a country as vast as Russia. The Arctic north has an almost constant winter whilst some of the southern republics enjoy a sub-tropical climate. The coldest part of the country, and indeed of the whole northern hemisphere, is the far northeastern corner of Siberia, where temperatures sometimes sink as low as −65°C. The mountains ranges to the south stop warm tropical air from reaching the Russian plains. As a result of this natural barrier, summers in Russia tend to be hot and dry — much less humid than in Central Europe. Spring and autumn are short seasons. Autumn tends to be wet, windy and foggy, although September can be pleasantly warm, rather like a good English autumn.

For most of the country, though, winter is the dominant season. Snow begins to fall at the beginning of November heralding freezing cold winters. Heavy snowfall is widespread. This is not just the case in remote areas like Siberia where few people ever go; St Petersburg is under snow for approximately 160 days a year. Fortunately, many visitors feel the extreme dryness of the air to be either invigorating or uncomfortable, particularly for those with sensitive skin. The dry air does mean that winter temperatures, which sink to −20°C/−4°F or below, do not feel as cold as you might fear. Furthermore, the snow highlights the beauty of the buildings and makes the dull countryside almost romantic. Skiing and skating are popular, not to mention drinking to stave off the cold.

In winter, tourists should take heavy clothing: warm overcoat, scarf, gloves, a hat that can cover the ears, snowproof shoes or boots and thermal underwear. It is best to dress in layers as hotels and public buildings tend to be very well heated. Do not forget that outdoor footwear and coats have to be left in the cloakrooms in many places and remember to sew a hook into your coat, as it makes life easier for the attendants; some will heckle you if they cannot find a hook.

The present visa restrictions mean that visiting Russia is far easier is you are travelling as part of an organised holiday. For this reason, tours are dealt with first.

TOURS

For those without substantial resources of initiative and cash, a package tour to Russia is a much easier proposition than trying to arrange an itinerary independently. For less than £300 (out of season), you can have a one week tour of Moscow and environs, while the same trip arranged individually would cost substantially more and involve much more bureaucracy. Only when you plan an adventure such as the Trans-Siberian railway do the sums change in favour of the independent traveller, and then the cash-consevong potential needs to be weighed against the bureaucratic hassle.

Plenty of tour operators organise inclusive tours to Russia, but if you want to get beyond the normal tourist trail — or combine a visit to Russia with neighbouring countries, then the companies listed on page 14 can help.

From North America. The leading operators of tours from North America to Russia are based in New York:

Intourist, 630 Fifth Avenue, Suite 868, New York, NY 10011 (tel: 212-757-3884/5).
Russian Travel Bureau, 225 East 44th Street, New York, NY 10017 (tel: 212-986-1500 or toll-free 1-800-847-1800).
The Russia House, 16 East 34th St, New York, NY 10016 (tel: 212-251-1375).

Tours are cheaper from London, and if you take advantage of low transatlantic fares you can save considerably. Some US and Canadian travel agents deal with British tour operators on your behalf, but even if you do it yourself the cost in international phone calls or faxes is small compared to the potential savings.

INDEPENDENT TRAVEL

Those determined to plan an individual itinerary should consult the relevant sections on *Red Tape* and *Getting Around* for advice on these aspects of travel in Russia. Business visitors requiring complex arrangements should contact a specialist company such as:

One Europe Travel, Research Travel, Fraser Rd, Perivale, Middlesex UB6 7AQ (tel 0181-566 9424, fax 0181-566 8845).
Overseas Business Travel, 8 Minories, London EC3N 1BJ (tel 0171-702 2468, fax 0171-488 1199).
The Russia House, 37 Kingly Court, Kingly St, London W1R 5LE (tel 0171-439 1271, fax 0171-434 0813); together with its partner organisation, The Russia Travel & Trade Company, has offices in Moscow and other capitals and can arrange personalised tours to suit individual travel requirements – see inside front cover.

From Britain. Scheduled flights between London Heathrow and Moscow and St Petersburg are operated by Aeroflot and British Airways. Discounted fares are easily available through the agencies on page 14, and you could expect to pay around £250 for a non-refundable ticket to either city. Transaero operates between Gatwick and Moscow via Riga, and sells Apex tickets for £229 through CIS Travel Services, 7 Buckingham Gate, London SW1E 6JP (0171-828 7613) and other agents. Other airlines have connecting flights to other parts of Russia, e.g. Lufthansa flying from London, Birmingham and Manchester via Frankfurt to Yekaterinburg and Novosibirsk.

From North America. Delta has flights from various US points via Frankfurt to Moscow and St Petersburg. Aeroflot flies non-stop from Moscow. The fastest connections are probably on Finnair or SAS via Helsinki or Stockholm. Approaching from the West, Alaska Airlines has a weekly flight from Seattle via Anchorage to Magadan, Khabarovsk and Vladivostok.

From the Far East. Vladivostok is served by flights from various points in Japan, and Seoul in Korea. Ferries operate between the Japanese ports of Niigata and Fushiki and Vladivostok. In summer 1995, services began between the Japanese island of Hokkaido and Korsakov on Sakhalin Island, which offers the prospect of a new — and inexpensive — way into Russia from Japan.

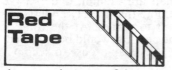

Red Tape

Despite the widespread changes occurring in Russia, getting into the country remains maddeningly bureaucratic. The traditional fear of foreign invasion is still a real part of the Russian psyche. Accordingly its borders remain some of the most tightly sealed in the world, and the information here is barely changed from before the collapse of communism.

Visas. All visitors to Russia from Western countries need a valid visa. If you are going to the Russia on a package tour, you will be sent a visa form through the post. Submit the completed form, with three photographs (bearing your name on the reverse) and a photocopy of the first six pages of your (old-style) passport or last two pages of your new one, at least three weeks before you intend to travel. If you are an individual traveller to Russia, you will have to organize your own visa. The above conditions apply, but you will also have to state your precise dates of arrival and departure, and your itinerary. These conditions would appear to adversely affect your flexibility, but note that you should apply for the maximum possible length that you might need to stay. This requires you to demonstrate that you have accommodation booked, but a fax from a hotel or hostel confirming a booking should suffice. As far as the itinerary is concerned, this should clearly bear some relation to your accommodation reservations. Fortunately, no-one seems to pay much attention if your visa says Moscow but you bowl up in Murmansk.

By far the simplest way to get a visa is to enlist the help of a specialist travel agency. Otherwise, you will have to take your chances at the visa section of a Russian Consulate: in the UK at 5 Kensington Palace Gardens, London W8 4QS (tel 0171-229 8027; fax 0171-229 3215); in the USA at 1125 16th St NW, Washington DC 20036 (tel 202-628-7551). The Consulate in London opens 10am-12.30pm on Monday, Tuesday, Thursday and Friday, but is closed on Russian and British public holidays. The officials who issue visas do not seem to be any more efficient than other branches of Russian officialdom, so allow plenty of time. Even if you apply three months in advance (the maximum allowed), you may still find that you have to go to the Consulate the day before you travel to pick up your visa.

The normal fee is £10, but at this price it will take at least two weeks to obtain. If you need one faster, then a sliding scale applies: £20 for a week, then doubling every day thereafter. Business travellers may be able to obtain an 'emergency' visa upon arrival, but only in exchange for a large number of dollar and then only if you can persuade the airline to let you on board.

Immigration. Formalities at Russian frontiers, ports and airports are fairly straightforward, if disconcerting. The passport control booths are equipped with bright spotlights and mirrors, an environment guaranteed to engender paranoia and perspiration. Most people believe that their passport photograph does not look like them, but to smooth your entry to Russia you should ideally resemble it as closely as possible. Under the steady gaze of the 18-year-old cadet checking your passport, you may get the distinct feeling of not being in control of your life. Bear in mind, however, that unlike, say, the USA or Australia, a visa is a guarantee of entry to Russia. So no matter how long it takes the official to compare the length of your eyebrows with those in the photo, you can be sure you'll be admitted eventually.

Medical Checks. As of 1 August 1995, foreigners planning to enter Russia for more than three months are obliged to 'prove' that they are not carrying the HIV virus, which can cause Aids. Diplomats are exempt. Others have to produce a certificate of HIV negativity, but note that merely undergoing a test may render life insurance cover difficult to obtain. At the time of writing, it was not not clear how assiduously the new law would be enforced; it seems possible that it will be used sparingly — ie as an excuse to keep out 'undesirables'.

Customs. As you arrive (or on the aircraft) you will be given a customs declaration form. On this document, unchanged since Soviet days, you say how many pieces of luggage you have and the amounts of cash in various denominations, plus any Soviet lottery tickets. Only the money part really matters, since strict exchange controls were re-introduced in 1995. Like the Aids test mentioned above, the rules may be only sketchily enforced, but the idea is that you can account for all the money you spend. Therefore keep currency exchange receipts, and receipts for any hard-currency transactions. You should then be able to leave the country safely.

As far as possessions are concerned, customs officials are much more concerned about Russians returning home than foreigners. Even so, you may suffer the indignity of having your underwear brought to public attention. Regulations are not too specific and customs officers have carte blanche to inspect your baggage and confiscate anything they think to be in excess of normal requirements (e.g. a dozen pairs of jeans).

Until the 1990s, the kopek was a small but effective part of the monetary system. That was before devaluation of 1,000,000 per cent (as measured in May 1995). The 15-kopek coin underwent a temporary reprieve because of its demand for use in telephones.

It used to be the case that anything you might want to do in Russia required endless bureaucracy and lots of pieces of paper. A supply of paper is still needed, but it has to be issued by the Federal Reserve and inscribed 'In God we trust'. In the country of the receding rouble, the US dollar is king. Inflation was once held to be an evil eradicated by socialism, but it is now generally accepted to be running at about 100% annually.

The simplest purchase, therefore, requires a wad of roubles. Although many things are priced in dollars, you may only pay in roubles at the prevailing rate (this is a vain attempt to maintain some sort of control over the money supply). Credit card payments are immune. But if plastic is unacceptable, then you have no choice but to pay a few million roubles or whatever.

Currency Exchange. Exchange bureaux have replaced the statues of Lenin in post-Soviet Moscow: there seems to be a kiosk or window on every street corner. All over Russia, booths have been set up, and the rates for dollars (and sometimes Deutschmarks) prominently displayed. For all financial transactions make sure you have your passport with you for identification. Keep your receipts to change money back, and to clear customs on the way out.

Credit and Charge Cards. Access/MasterCard, Visa, American Express and Diners Club are accepted in most hotels and fancy restaurants, but not necessarily by airlines.

Taxes. After decades without them, Russian bureaucrats are catching on quickly to the concept of taxes. It has even reached the stage where any enterprise with the word 'Russia' in its title must hand over 0.5% of its earnings to the state for the privilege. For travellers, the new 23% tax on 'luxuries' is a nuisance, since luxuries can include meals and drinks in hotels. Check if tax is going to be added before you order.

Communications

Telephone. Most hotels have international direct dial facilities. Although you may well pay over the odds for phone calls, the extra cost ($7 a minute to Britain compared with $3 or $4 at a telephone office) may be worth the convenience of dialling direct. Alternatively, go to the telephone section of a post offices (pochta) and hope for the best

Big post offices have special telephone booths with direct lines to all big Russian cities (i.e. you simply have to dial the required number without the area code) and also operator-controlled international lines. Queues tend to be long here, so unless you want to use the special interurban booths, you are probably better off at the smaller post offices.

Having ordered and pre-paid for your call at the desk (*pryom*), you then have to wait patiently and pay attention constantly as the city or country you are trying to ring will be announced over the loudspeaker followed by the number of the booth that the call is coming in on. It is advisable to try and convey to the people sitting next to you where you are ringing and they will then prod you when the call comes through and see that you go to the correct booth. The time you will have to wait depends upon how close you are to a major city such as Moscow, St Petersburg or Kiev. In, or close to, these cities, long-distance or international calls can be put through in a few minutes or less. In Siberia you may have to wait several hours. Local calls from most hotels are free, though some have started charging $0.50 — a complete rip-off.

In addition, you can ask at restaurants, shops, etc., if it is possible to use their telephone. The free local calls explain why Russian people spend so long on the phone.

Payphones are very common and located on most streets and in many public places, so you should have no problem at all finding one. Finding one working, and for which you have a token (*jeton*) is a much bigger problem. Only a few kiosks sell these tokens, and charge an arbitrary amount (usually $0.10-15)

Telegrams. Internal and international telegrams can be sent easily from any post office. Those within Russia are cheap to send and often prove an easier way of getting hold of someone than telephoning.

Telex. The telex is commonly used in Russia by all major organizations, and most telex machines are adapted for messages in Roman script. You should be able to send and receive telexes through your hotel reception.

Fax. Every booming business has a fax. You can send them from hotels and some post offices for about the same price as a telephone call.

Post. Post offices are usually open from 8am to 8pm, but the main post office in each city should be open 24 hours. Letters and postcards to Europe automatically go airmail and cost around $0.45 and $0.35 respectively. Letters to European destinations can take anything between five days and three weeks, sometimes more, and you should expect even longer delays for mail going into Russia from Europe.

MEDIA

Newspapers. English-language papers can be bought in some hotels. These are usually a couple of days old. In Moscow, competing companies produce excellent English-language papers, which are excellent and free. The main Russian newspapers, such as *Izvestiya* ('News') and *Trud* ('Labour') are survivors from communism. You will see these and other papers posted on billboards around the cities and towns. Important journals include the illustrated magazine *Ogonyok*, which carries news items, literature, features on current affairs and so on, the humorous *Krokodil* and the literary paper, *Literaturnaya Gazyeta*. These are all weeklies.

Television. Russian people watch a considerable amount of television, much of it terrible. More and more foreign programmes and films are broadcast in Russia, and advertising is also beginning to make its mark.

Radio. Big cities have dozens of stations, while other places have just one or two. Phil Collins could easily retire on the royalties he must be making on the hits played on various music stations.

Health and Hygiene

Water in Moscow should not do any harm to tourists, but that in St Petersburg should be avoided: it has the reputation of being the most impure water in Europe. Travellers should either drink mineral water — a problem in St Petersburg, as the local mineral water is extremely sulphurous and unsavoury — or use water purifying tablets, which should be obtained in advance of the trip. Do not drink the water on the trains, unless it has been boiled.

Standards of hygiene are not dreadful in public toilets, and no paper is provided outside hotels, so it is wise to pack some of that too. If you propose to be in Russia a long time — more than a month or so — you might consider taking vitamin tablets.

Smoking. Having realized that smoking is at least as bad for Soviet citizens as drinking, the authorities have cracked down on smoking in public places — not only obvious venues such as cinemas and post offices, but also outdoor targets such as Red Square in Moscow and the Black Sea beaches. Many places where smoking is forbidden, such as cafés and bars, do not display no-smoking signs since it is assumed that the locals know the rules. Therefore be careful not to light up unless others are smoking.

Aids. There have been reports of dirty needles being used in the treatment of foreigners, so to be safe you may wish to take a sterile pack containing syringes, available from doctors and medical suppliers in the West.

Medical Treatment. When called out by Westerners, medical staff respond quickly — especially the private health care enterprises. These cost a fortune, but if your insurance is paying they can be well worthhile.

Pharmacies. Chemists are open from 8am to 8pm and some are open all night. Do not rely on Russian chemists but take everything you envisage needing with you from home. Sanitary towels, deodorants, tissues, and contraceptives, for example, are not always of the same standard as in the West,

As far as independent travellers to Russia are concerned, the good news about the collapse of communism is that travel within Russia is no longer firmly in the hands of Intourist. You can book domestic flights or rail tickets anywhere in the Federation. The bad news is that it is often painfully difficult to do. Railway stations and airports sport an improbable number of ticket windows, and even when you (a) find the right one and (b) get to the front of the queue, there is no guarantee that you will be sold a ticket. Foreigners are expected to pay more than Russians for transportation, and since passports must be shown to buy any long-distance tickets this is an easy rule to enforce.

Frequently this discrimination is overlooked, and the authors of this book have travelled all over Russia on tickets which can best be described as dodgy. Rather than risk being turned away, or to alleviate the stress thus generated, you may prefer to book in advance through an agency. There is an increasing number of these, and they have the advantages of speaking English and providing the opportunity for some sort of comeback if things go horribly wrong. But mostly things do not go wrong, and you can achieve travel as free of hassles as is possible in Russia.

Potential motorists might now be appreciating the freedom to go where you choose in the comfort of your own vehicle. But the problems of driving are considerable, as described below.

Maps and Guides. Good maps of Russia are becoming commonplace. Atlases published in Russia itself have always been good, except for their propensity to omit areas sensitive for defence reasons, and the fact that they are in Cyrillic. Buy in advance if you can.

Place Names. All maps have been hard-pressed to keep pace with the changes towards 'traditional' names of towns and cities, rather than names imposed in honour of Soviet worthies (most of whom are now discredited). But the most substantial changes, such as St Petersburg for Leningrad and Yekaterinburg replacing Sverdlovsk have already happened. Street names are a much tougher proposition, since even when the local legislature has decided that Svetlana should replace Lenin (as in the case of the city of Vladivostok), it can be some time before the old signs are taken down.

AIR

The national airline, Aeroflot, has been divided into over 100 smaller carriers. Its aircraft are mostly poor copies of outmoded foreign planes, such as the French Caravelle (Tupolev 134) and the British VC-10 (Ilyushin 62). Cabin safety standards are dreadful: although smoking is officially prohibited on domestic flights, this is often not enforced and emergency drills are often omitted.

Fares are low — the 4,000 mile/6,400km stretch from Moscow to Vladivostok (the longest non-stop domestic route in the world, equal to a long transatlantic flight) costs around £230, partly because there is considerable competition on some routes. Transaero, using American-built planes leased from Ireland, has the best reputation, though check-in standards are woefully low.

TRAIN

Russia has the world's greatest train ride: see the Trans-Siberian Railway on page 158. Along with most of the 14 other republics it has an excellent network of rail services. The train is the primary mode of travel in Russia, and the national railways carry ten million passengers each day. There are two basic classes: soft and hard. The names sum up the difference. Soft seats are wide and comfortable, hard ones are usually narrow and plastic. At night, soft class passengers enjoy four-berth couchette compartments while hard class travellers may be consigned to bunks in noncompartment coaches, a miserable mobile dormitory. If you feel like splashing out, or are worried about security, pay extra for a *coupé*, a comfortable two-person compartment. Security is essential — a stout piece of wire should be used to secure the door from the inside.

Schedules operate according to Moscow time throughout Russia, which is disconcerting if you're in Khabarovsk and your 6am train leaves at what feels like lunchtime. Most station clocks show both Moscow and local time. Many stations (*vokzal*) are fine pieces of architecture. They are named after the original Vauxhall station in London, now called Victoria, which the first Russian railway engineers visited and from which they took the name for 'station'.

The trains themselves range from little local suburban services to crack expresses — ER200 — which hurtle between Moscow and St Petersburg at 125mph. For long-distance services, reservations must be made through stations or agencies. First of all you need to locate the right ticket office before you start queuing (the names of the destinations it serves are written above in Cyrillic), then you must wait. If you're told the train is fully booked, this usually means that all tickets have been sold to touts, large quantities of whom you will find hanging around the entrance. For a premium they can get you a ticket to wherever you want to go. Finally, if all else fails, turn up at the train station and approach a *provodnik* or carriage attendant: for dollars they will almost certainly find you a seat, a bunk or even a complete compartment on the train.

For suburban trains, you must buy your ticket in advance from an automatic machine. If you have any difficulties, keep repeating your destination and somebody will point you in the right direction.

BUS

Very much the poor relation of the train, buses operate infrequently and cost no less than hard-class trains. The advantages is that they go to a few places not served by train, and that the average city bus station is less chaotic and confusing than a rail terminus.

CAR

Road travel was always a poor relation to the railway in Russia, but cars have made something of a comeback now that almost everyone seems to own one. The basic rule of the road is simple: the hierarchy of the highway has pedestrians at the base, cyclists (a rare and probably dying breed) and motorcyclists as second-class citizens, and a hegemony of motorists which depends upon the power and size of your car.

Ladas were never as bad as the jokes cracked them up to be, coping with extremes of temperature and being sufficiently hardy to withstand road surfaces which would break the axles of most other vehicles. Larger models include the Volga, Chaika and Zil limousines, each of which looks like a 1960s car from the West; the Zil finally went out of production in 1995.

The highway network reflects the fact that until relatively recently traffic was light, and potholed roads were the norm. The accident rate is very high; ten times as many people die in motor accidents in Russia as in the UK. Defensive driving is called for at all times.

Fuel. The standard petrol is 72 octane, which keeps a Lada happy for years but which will not agree with most Western engines. In addition there are usually long queues at 72 octane pumps. The two-star equivalent is 95 octane, for which the queues are shorter. Ther are now plenty of modern, Western-style petrol stations, but the procedure at older ones is to pay for fuel at the *kassa*, and then wait your turn (you'll be barked at by overhead loudspeakers, and everyone will stare and point at you). Pumps are often faulty: they fail to start (or worse, fail to stop), and meters are not always set to zero which causes furious arguments.

Diesel is an altogether less predictable fuel. Often it is watered down, with disastrous consequences for the engine. Its availability is sporadic.

Breakdowns. All repair and towing costs must be paid for by the motorist. Although the terms of the cover issued by motoring organizations will allow you to recover the cost eventually, it is worth carrying plenty of spare cash just in case. Parts for foreign cars are hard to find outside of Moscow and St Petersburg: you should ensure your car is in peak condition and has a sensible selection of spares, or run the risk of a three-week wait in Smolensk while a new fan belt comes from Dagenham.

Rules and Regulations. The speed limit in towns is 60km/h, on the open road 90km/h. You are not permitted to drive with any alcohol in your bloodstream. Militia checks are frequent: the officer orders vehicles to stop by holding out his baton, and will want to see the Russian translation of your personal data. Many are after fines, and pick on foreigners as soft targets, citing often imaginary offences.

Fines for most offences are paid on the spot, with little investigation into claims of guilt or innocence. You can appeal against a fine in the local magistrate's court, but the onus is firmly on you to establish your innocence beyond doubt. So most people negotiate the 'fine' as low as possible and pay up.

Accidents involving physical injury could land you in jail (unless you can prove your innocence). There is widespread abuse of the law whereby all such damage or injury must be reported to the police: injured parties will exaggerate their injuries and offer to make an out-of-court settlement. If you refuse, and they can prove to the police that you were involved in an unreported accident (not difficult, as witnesses can always be offered a percentage), then you will find yourself on the wanted list when you try to leave the country.

Road Signs. Standard European warning signs are used. On major routes most destinations appear in both Cyrillic and Roman script. The placement of signs in Roman script, however, is haphazard, another good reason for mastering the Cyrillic alphabet.

Car Rental. Plenty of self-drive cars are available, but it is almost always cheaper and safer to rent a car and driver through an agency or other contact; you might get the use of both for $50 per day, less than the average rental charge.

CITY TRANSPORT

Taxis. These days almost any vehicle is a potential taxi. Private motorists pick up people who flag them down in the street, for a standard fare of perhaps $2 in Moscow and St Petersburg, $1 elsewhere, for an in-town journey. Second-class taxis (the battered looking ones) cost about the same, but luxury taxis — of the sort you order by telephone — cost a fortune. None have meters, or at least meters that work.

Public Transport. Moscow, St Petersburg and several other cities have an underground railway, known as the metro (*METPO*). The standard fare is around $0.10, which buys a plastic token. You drop the token into the gate at the entrance and walk through.

Most towns have a network of buses, trolleybuses and trams, again operating on a flat fare of around $0.10. Some larger cities have 'route taxis', minibuses which operate, like buses, on fixed routes, but which are faster and more frequent.

Until recently, Westerners had little option but to stay in top-class hotels, but now staying in private homes or youth hostels is feasible. At present, however, most people use hotels.

These fall into three main types: pre-revolutionary places with plenty of character; featureless modern Soviet monstrosities which have an unmistakeable air of catering for the masses, and brash new Western places. For independent travellers, prices are around $25, $50 and $150 for a single room in each of these types, $35, $65 and $200 for a double.

Whatever the standard, in most Russian hotel rooms you can expect a telephone (with a direct-dial-in facility), radio (if it is working, you are usually limited to a choice of four channels selected by push buttons — you cannot tune it), television and fridge. You can also expect the room to be ferociously overheated, and even when the outside temperature is below zero you may have to open a window to reduce the heat.

When you check in you have to hand over your passport and visa for registration, for which a fee of 10% of the minimum monthly wage is payable — currently $1. Your documents should be returned to you the next day, but you often have to keep reminding the desk-clerk, who might otherwise hold on to it for days. On checking in you will also receive a hotel pass (*propusk*) with your room key. The hotel doorman has the right to see your pass whenever you enter the hotel, and you will also need it to get into other hotels. In some hotels, residents are not actually issued with a room key but have to present their propusk to the floor attendant who looks after all the keys for the rooms on that particular floor. Guests from outside the hotel are allowed in your room until 11pm. The hotel management issues a pass for anyone who comes to visit you. For this purpose your guest should carry some form of identification. The pass will be carefully checked by the *dezhurnaya*, the formidable woman in charge of your floor. Noisy parties are frowned upon.

Youth Hostels. Moscow has one, and St Petersburg have several. Standards and prices are much the same as in the West, with a dorm bed costing around $15.

Staying in Private Homes. It is quite possible to stay with Russian people as a paying guest, and increasingly many people are offering *gastaneetsa v domou* ('hotel at home').

Camping and Cabins. In summer, this is a feasible prospect, though there are few sites and they tend to be well outside towns. Most campsites have restaurants or cafeterias and some have a bureau de change, post office, a petrol station and international telephones.

Eating in Russia is rarely a complete delight, but it is fascinating how many pre-Revolutionary dishes have survived. Even afternoon tea, cultivated by the upper classes in the last century, survives in many Russian homes. Some dishes have been absorbed as a result of contact with foreign invaders but most have come from within the former USSR, especially from Georgia and Uzbekistan, and have become part of the everyday diet.

Pies of various kinds are typically Russian: inside, you may find anything from cabbage to brains. *Pirozhki* (turnovers) are among the most common. More unusual and tastier varieties include *rastegai* and *kulebyaka* (types of fish pie) and *kurnik* (chicken pie). The most delicious Russian fish is the sterlet from the Volga; the trout caught around St Petersburg is also good. Beef and pork are the most common meats, and are often dismally cooked. Soups, popular all over the Soviet Union, are a staple in Western Russia. *Shchi* (cabbage soup) is the most traditional Russian soup, enjoying a similar status to *borshch* in the Ukraine. Those with a sweet tooth should look out for *tort-kolbasa* named after kolbasa (sausages), which are biscuits often served after a meal with tea and *bubliki* — tasty little rings of choux pastry. A drink that you are likely to see a lot of is *kvass*. This is the national Russian drink, made from fermented rye flour and sold in mugs from huge barrels in the street.

The great culinary advance of the past few years is the number of forign restaurants, from Italian to Mexican, which have set up. There is even an Australian restaurant in Vladivostok.

Breakfast. A proper Russian breakfast is a grand affair. Buckwheat, oats, rice or millet is made into a porridge-like dish and is served with milk and sugar or with fried egg and butter. In practice, however, you are unlikely to experience this treat. The typical offering is bread, butter and jam together with a hot dish such as fried eggs, sausages, etc. *Kefir* (a cross between yoghourt and buttermilk) is also popular at breakfast, or sometimes served with fruit as a dessert.

Appetizers (*zakuski*). Don't hold back on this course as this is usually the most impressive part of the meal. Caviar (*ikra*) is generally served with toast and butter, and if you're lucky a piece of lemon. The black variety, which is more sought after but not necessarily more flavoursome, comes from sturgeon, whilst the red comes from salmon. Like Scandinavians, Russians eat a vast quantity of cold fish-smoked salmon, sturgeon, fish in aspic, pickled herrings — all of which are highly recommended, especially with a glass of chilled vodka.

Russian will pickle almost anything — cucumbers, gherkins, beetroot, onions — and don't be surprised to see people eating whole heads of pickled garlic. *Salat* (Russian salad) also comes at this stage of the meal: huge mounds of egg, ham, chicken, carrot, peas, onion and cucumber all mixed together in a creamy mayonnaise dressmg.

Hot starters include chicken julienne, which is very thin strips of chicken served in a creamy, white sauce. Similar, and equally good are mushrooms in sour cream (*griby v smitane*) with black bread. Delicious, but often hard to get, are the famous *bliny* or pancakes with sour cream (*so smitanou*).

Soups. These are often served as the second of four courses at lunchtime; for some reason few restaurants serve soup after 4pm. Borshch varies from place to place, but essentially it is a hot beetroot and cabbage soup with pieces of often rather grisly boiled meat and a splodge of sour cream. It is often served with some form of pie or *pirozhok* (pasty). Other soups include *solyanka* (salty fish or meat soup with lots of salted cucumber), *shchi* (cabbage soup), *bulyon* (bouillon or broth), particularly good when made with *pelmeni* (a form of dumplings or ravioli) and *ukha* (fish soup). In summer cold borshch is very refreshing. For the more adventurous, *okroshka*, a chilled vegetable soup, has an interesting taste.

Main courses. Fish dishes, sadly, are rather limited. Even on the Black Sea you can sometimes only get very dreary fish from the Arctic. Restaurants often serve baked or steamed fish with creamy sauces or, occasionally, fish kebabs.

The choice of meat dishes is usually a little wider. The most common ones are probably *shashlik* (kebab) with tangy tomato sauce, which is actually a Caucasian dish but is served throughout Russia, *kotlyety* (cutlets), and meatballs. Beef Stroganov is braised beef in onions, mushrooms and sour cream. Traditionally, the pieces of beef are cut very thin. Legend has it that Count Stroganov, after whom the dish is named, was in Siberia, where it was so cold that the beef had frozen and could only be cut in wafer-thin strips before it was cooked.

Desserts. Soviet people have an extremely sweet tooth and many of the cakes and pastries served might be rather sickly for Western taste. They tend to be heavy and syrupy, and are often decorated with the most lurid icing. Excellent, however, is the ice cream (*marozhenoye*), which the Soviets take very seriously and will eat whatever the weather. There is not usually a choice of flavour at any one time, vanilla is the most common but creme brulée flavour is particularly delicious. Ice cream is served by weight: 100g is usually two scoops, 150g three scoops and so on. Also good but not that common is *kompot* or cold stewed fruit.

Restaurants. Eating out can be expensive by Western standards — a light lunch might be $15, while dinner could easily reach $30. Office canteens offer the best value.

Even if the restaurant is empty you must wait at the entrance until a member of staff assigns you a table. If you dare to sit down without asking, you will be roundly rebuked or ignored. You must also deposit your coats at the *garderob* before you go to your table, as it is not considered good manners to eat in your outer clothing. Dining out is a time-consuming process, as service tends to be very slow, so do not expect to be able to combine a trip to the theatre with a meal out-in any case some of the theatres have excellent buffets, serving open sandwiches with smoked fish or salami, fruit juices and cakes; no theatre outing is complete for a Russian without starting at the buffet.

Vegetarian Travellers. People who prefer not to eat meat will not have an easy time in Russia. They are regarded with the same degree of suspicion as teetotallers, and little effort is made to accommodate them. On an organized tour, let everyone-from the tour operator to individual waiters-know of your dietary requirements, but don't expect your wishes always to be respected. A common Russian view of vegetarians is that they dislike only solid pieces of flesh. Therefore you may be offered a soup from which the lumps of meat have been removed moments before. The best you can do is go to the fruit and vegetable markets (which is an interesting experience in itself), buy some of the often very good bread products from the bakeries, or bring supplies from home.

Fast Food. The Soviet equivalent of a hot-dog stand is a homely middle-aged woman with a wicker basket or steel barrel full of deep-fried pasties (pirozhki) made from yeast dough and filled with cabbage, carrot, minced meat or jam. She is being rendered obsolete by McDonald's, Pizza Hut and other international chains.

Buying Food from Shops. Almost anything is available from shops now, for a price. Specialist shops are as follows:

bakery (*bulochnaya*) — rye bread is probably the best. It is amusing to watch babushkas prodding the different varieties of bread to test for firmness and freshness. Special forks are even provided for this purpose. Bakeries also sell a limited variety of cakes; particularly delicious is *vatrushka*, which is a form of cheesecake made with curds. Some bakeries are combined with stand-up cafés.

charcuterie (*kulinariya*) — cold meats and sausages; some sell salads and cakes.

dairy (*moloko*) — milk, yoghourt and kefir.

greengrocery (*frukty* or *ovoshchi*) — rarely contain appetising fresh produce. The best fruit and vegetables can be bought at high prices in the markets.

DRINKING

Mikhail Gorbachev's crackdown on alcoholism had not the slightest impact on the average Russian's intake of alcohol. Vodka ('Russia's aspirin') should not be sipped but knocked back in one go (which explains why it is never drunk without food to accompany it). Often vodka is drunk throughout a meal. As well as straight vodka, there are numerous flavoured varieties including lemonnaya (lemon), pertsovka (chilli pepper), ryabinovka (ash-berry), zubrovka (bison grass) and vishnevka (cherry). Prices start at about $3 per bottle in kiosks. Don't expect your vodka to come with orange or tomato juice or a sweet and fizzy mixer. It is drunk neat. It is no joke that every glass must be drunk as a toast to someone or something, preferably a vague concept. The evening may begin with drinking to peace and inter-national friendshup, then deteriorate into drunken toasts to Moscow Dynamo football team and Bruce Springsteen. Drinkers in Russia can get spectacularly drunk, and usually become violent or subside into melancholy. Neither is a very pleasant sight.

Wine. Hard to find and overpriced, unless you get some digustingly sweet red Moldovan.

Beer. Russian beer (*pivo*) is almost universally terrible — flat, weak and watery. It costs about $0.60 for a bottle from kiosks, more in bars (if you can find any). Any self respecting beer-drinker quaffs foreign ale, the stronger the better. The best beers are from Kazan, or are imported.

Soft Drinks. Pepsi-Cola and Fanta (produced locally) are widely available. You might prefer an exotic juice (sok) such as berezovyi (birch tree), granatovyi (pomegranate) or aivovyi (quince). Russian mineral water (mineralnaya voda), which is always the carbonated variety, is often very sulphurous.

Tea. Chai is the most typical Soviet drink. The water is boiled in a samovar and the tea often served in tall glasses with metal holders. Milk is never added. At the end of a meal, the tea is sweetened with jam and flavoured with a slice of lemon.

Coffee. The coffee served in bars and cafes is usually Eastern style coffee (vostochny kofe), like Turkish coffee, which is quite widespread and very good. It may be too sweet, unless you order it without sugar (byez sakhara).

Museums and Galleries. Most are well laid out and cheap; the most expensive is the Hermitage in St Petersburg, costing around $10. Prices are invariably higher for foreigners. Labels are usually in Cyrillic only, but places on the tourist trail occasionally have signs bearing Roman transliterations or floor plans on the walls marked in English. Unlike in the West, the shop at the end of your tour is likely to be a disappointment; it may be closed, and if open will be poorly stocked.

Visual Art. After the persecution of artists (most notably by Stalin's henchmen, Andrei Zhdanov, and Mikhail Suslov in the Brezhnev years), Russian painters have a new-found freedom. Look out for post-Constructivist work by Edward Steinberg, and the avant-garde approach to Russian folk art tradition exemplified by Marina Tuchakova and Anna Birstein. But if you want Soviet era posters of smiling workers exhorting their comrades to work hard and join the heroic struggle, you will have a difficult search.

You should certainly make an effort to attend a concert or go to the theatre. To find out what's on, ask at your hotel, or your nearest *kassa*, kiosks dotted around every city. If a performance you really want to see is sold out, try standing outside the theatre itself just before the performance starts, as professional touts will help you. They invariably want payment in hard currency, and will ask anything from $10 upwards for a $5 ticket. Often the tickets they sell are poor ones with restricted views or even out-of-date, so check the details carefully (date and name of performance) before handing over any money.

Theatre. The new political climate has spawned some exciting new work, developing the tradition of the great 19th century Russian writers. In theatres, you must use the cloakroom (which is free). Opera glasses can be hired from the cloakroom attendant. Evening performances begin at 7 or 7.30pm and usually finish at 10 or 10.30pm. Matinees begin at noon. The buffets in the larger theatres are generally very good, selling open sandwiches with smoked fish or salami, juices and cakes.

Opera and Ballet. The most established ballet and opera companies in Russia are the Bolshoi in Moscow and the Mariinsky (formerly the Kirov) in St Petersburg. The ballet is recognized internationally as being of a very high standard, whilst the opera is good but not exceptional. Ballet in Russia has always been regarded as a particularly important art form, and has never been considered inferior to opera, as it was in the West in the 19th century. Both ballet and opera are sometimes criticized for being too conservative and classical in approach, but a tourist should nonetheless make an effort to see them. The strike of the Bolshoi in 1995 was not expected to last.

Traditional Dance. Performances of the traditional dances (*khorovods*) and songs (*chastoushki*) still take place to the accompaniment of concertinas. A traditional sport to look out for is *gorodki*, the object of which is to knock down an arrangement of wooden pins by throwing a metal-covered stick.

Music. Classical music is enjoyed throughout the USSR, and the big cities stage an impressive range of concerts. The local philharmonia is a feature of most Soviet towns. Many churches that are no longer functioning have been converted into concert halls.

For years rock was frowned upon as decadent, and performers forced underground. Now that it is out in the open, its true dreadfulness can be appreciated — heavy metal circa 1975 delivered with a complete lack of panache.

Cinema. The Soviet Union used to have half the world's cinemas, with 80 million paying customers each week. The spread of video means cinema attendances in Russia have dropped substantially. Most show films from 9am until midnight, in separate performances. All seats are numbered and reserved, wooden and uncomfortable. Programmes last around two hours (usually a short newsreel followed by the feature) and latecomers are not admitted. All foreign films are dubbed into Russian, usually badly, except in Westerners' cinemas in the largest cities.

Circus. Russian circus is the best in the world. Performances take place in purpose-built arenas rather than in tents, and artistes are of the highest calibre. Some Westerners find the use of performing animals upsetting, but increasingly only horses take part (and they look well cared for). The advice above for obtaining theatre tickets applies equally to circus seats, although prices tend to be lower. You might be able to get a good place for £5.

SPORT AND RECREATION

The Soviet system of sport was a major industry, producing champions as idolized as their counterparts in the West. Selection still begins at kinder-garten, and talent is nurtured throughout the formative years. The rewards for Russia take the shape of the hundreds of medals won at each Olympiad. This fervour rubs off onto the less talented, and a young Russian who is not interested in sport is a lonely one.

Spectator Sports. Soccer is easily the most popular game. Tickets for all spectator sports can be bought at the entrance to the stadium. Fans behave very well compared to their European counterparts, though they are catching on. There is always a heavy Militia presence at football matches for those that do step out of line. Other popular spectator sports are ice hockey, basketball, horseracing and motorsport. Saloon car races are the most popular form of motorsport. Rallying and karting are also well supported.

Gambling. One of the few legal ways to bet is at racecourses. All bets are lumped together under a totalisator system, with the state taking a large percentage of the stake money. (Needless to say a great deal of illegal betting takes place, but you are not advised to get involved.) Even for those proficient in Russian, studying the form is tricky: there is no Russian equivalent to *Sporting Life*. In general, the best horses are bred in the Pyatisgorsk region and subsequently trained in Moscow.

A day at the races is to be recommended. Most large cities have a course (*Hypodrom*) with regular races, particularly on Sundays. The horseracing lowlife breeds characters as fascinating as anywhere, and an awful lot of vodka is quaffed illicitly from concealed flasks despite the official ban on drinking at race meetings.

The most popular illegal game of chance is called 'thimble', and involves three thimbles and a pea. Like 'spot the lady', it is run by con-men who may let you win at first to build up your confidence before cleaning you out.

Beaches. Russian beaches, whether on rivers on the few stretches of sea, are usually crowded and polluted. They are organized in a rather regimented way: music often blares out of loudspeakers, but individuals are severely reproached if they bring their own. Queues for drinks and ice creams are long. Even in summer, beaches generally close in the evening. Nude bathing is strictly forbidden.

No-one comes to Russia to shop. Whether you look in the sad windows of a city kiosk, or at the goods on offer in Moscow markets, quality is shoddy. The system of payment for most shops is that a customer must decide what to buy, find out the price, pay at the central cash desk and then take the receipt back to first counter and pick up the goods. This often involves standing in three queues for one item, and shops are arranged such that the same procedure has to be carried out for each Item from a different section. Russians have therefore developed the art of keeping their place concurrently in several queues. You must also be quick at every stage, or you risk being shouted at by the sales assistant and everyone else waiting behind you in the queue.

Food shops (*produkti*) are open between 9am and 7pm daily except Sundays and public holidays. Some supermarkets (*Universam*) open daily. Department stores are open from 10am to 8pm. Locally produced records (on the Melodiya label) and CDs are excellent quality and value. Think very carefully before buying anything which could be construed as an antique. 'Works of art' may only be taken out with special permission, and customs officials will often decide arbitrarily to confiscate anything that looks remotely old.

Smoking. Western style cigarettes are known as *cigareti*. They have almost replaced the traditional Russian type (with half the volume taken up by an empty cardboard tube), known as *paperosi*. Belomor is the cheapest brand, while the more palatable Stewardess and Kosmos cost twice as much. Western cigarettes are available everywhere — the most common brands are Marlboro, Chesterfield and Dunhill (including menthol).

The most important thing is to take the normal precautions you would in any Western country and not pay too much attention to the horror stories people will insist on telling you before you go. Violence is rarely directed against tourists, and although the mafiosi do have a bad reputation they're much too busy trying to kill each other. Other forms of criminal activity are usually on a very minor scale such as pick-pocketing. Since travellers' cheques are difficult to exchange and you'll need to carry most of your money in cash, a money-belt when travelling is a good idea. Don't leave valuables lying around your hotel room, large hotels usually have safes.

On trains the safest place to stow your valuables is in the luggage hold beneath the lowest bunk. Compartment doors have locks, which a child can pick, but there's also a security latch on the left-hand side of the door. It's a piece of metal which when flipped out prevents the door from being opened any more than an inch. Women travelling alone can request a bunk in a compartment with other women when buying the ticket.

The other big threat is from armed conflict. The fringes of Russia are in some turmoil, and the events in the devastated region of Chechnya show the potential for conflict within Russia's borders. Check with the Foreign Office (0171-270 4129) before you go, and locally with the Embassy.

Tourist information in the sense understood in the West is an unknown concept in Russia. But like the Soviet Union itself, Intourist has been through some exciting changes, one of which is a travellers information hotline. It specialises on Moscow, St Petersburg and Kiev, but they'll try and answer your questions about anywhere else. The telephone number is 0891 516951 and they're obviously shaping up to capitalism quite nicely because your call is charged at 49 pence per minute (39p cheap rate). Unlike the old Intourist they are also exceptionally friendly.

The main Intourist hotel (which may well have been renamed) usually houses an Intourist Service Bureau. They can be useful for booking train or plane tickets though don't expect them to be of much other help. Begin by trying to find a local map; the shops in hotel foyers are worth trying, as are bookshops and kiosks.

For travellers heading to Moscow, St Petersburg or the far north, three invaluable publications are written by Michael R Dohan. The *Travellers' Yellow Pages* to each city are much more than lists of telephone numbers. Each one gives useful information such as a seating plan of the Mariinski and Bolshoi theatres to tips on Russian superstitions.: 'Don't sit on the corner of a table or you will end up single.' The books are available in Britain from Zwemmer, 28 Denmark St, London WC2H 8NJ (tel 0171-379 6253, fax 0171-379 6257). In the USA, they can be ordered by calling the publisher, InfoServices International, on 516-549-0064.

Moscow

St Basil's Cathedral

The biggest city of the world's largest country can easily overwhelm you. Everything seems to have been designed on a superhuman scale, from the agrophobic acres of Red Square to the alienating apartment blocks which hug the huge city. All other subway systems pale in comparison with Moscow's metro, while the Gotham-meets-Marx skyscrapers created by Stalin accentuate the vulnerability of mere mortals. Add the terror of the organised crime network that has filled the vacuum of state autonomy, and the trauma of the dispossessed forced to beg on the streets, and it seems a wonder that any would ever wish to go there. Yet it is a fine, exciting city, populated by generous and welcoming people. You might not always feel comfortable in Moscow, but these days you could never be bored.

From the air, the Russian capital looks like a muddy splodge on a huge featureless plain. Close up, it hardly improves. Summer evenings seem to last forever, but the dying sun only feebly penetrates the grimy pallor which hangs over the city. The spectrum of colour seems to extend from grey only as far as sepia. There are patches of what would be taken to be grass were it not for its complete denial of anything approaching the colour green. It is not all like that: the world's most stunning centre is the convocation of the Kremlin, Red Square, GUM, and, most glorious of all, St Basil's Cathedral. To miss Moscow is to miss Russia.

Moscow's official birth was in 1147. Yuri Dolgoruky (Yuri the long-armed), Prince of Suzdal, built a fortified settlement — a 'kremlin', or citadel — on the Borovitsky Hill, between the rivers Moskva and Neglinnaya. However, Slavs have inhabited this place since time immemorial. Moscow prospered as the city linked the rivers Volga and Oka and the river Moskva became one of the main trade arteries of medieval Russia.

59

In the 12th and 13th centuries Russia was a feudal state broken up into numerous principalities. Feuds between these principalities were bloody and destructive, and made them incapable of withstanding the devastating incursions of Tatars and Mongols. In 1238 Khan Baty of the Golden Horde invaded Moscow, sacked it and burnt the first wooden kremlin to ashes. He obliged all the princes of medieval Russia — of Kiev, Suzdal, Vladimir, Tver, Novgorod and Rostov — to pay homage to the Khan's tents thousands of miles to the east at Saray or even to the Great Khan at Karakorum in Mongolia. Furthermore, the rulers had to pay (in gold and men) for the right to rule. This domination lasted for more than 200 years, and left a permanent mark on the political, fiscal and military education of the Russian ruling princes.

The wily Ivan I (1325-41) known as Ivan Kalita (Money-Bags) married the Khan's sister and emerged as the most influential of all the princes. Subsequent Moscow princes aimed at strengthening the Moscow principality and uniting the Russian lands. In 1380 Prince Dmitri Donskoi won the important battle of Kulikovo on the River Don over Khan Mamai and the Horde, and the principality of Moscow became that of Vladimir and Moscow. It took another 100 years before the Moscow princes finally dared to default on paying the tribute to the East.

By the end of the 15th century Russia had become a centralized state when Ivan III (1462-1505), having married the overweight heiress Sophia, niece of the last Byzantine Emperor, adopted the Byzantine two-headed eagle for his coat of arms and took the title of 'Autocrat of all Russias'. The era of deceit, humiliation, treachery and corrupt collaboration with the ruling Khans was over, yet in the years to come Russia was to be invaded time and time again by Crimean Tatars, Poles, Cossacks, the French and finally the Germans. But the biggest enemy of Moscow was fire; between 1473 and 1493 alone there were ten great fires in the Kremlin, and the worst was still to come. Moscow was reduced to ashes by horrendous fires in 1547, 1571, 1595, 1612, 1701, 1712, 1737 and of course by Napoleon in 1812 in a blaze which gutted three out of every four buildings; but each time Moscow rose like a phoenix to be reborn with greater splendour.

The first Tsar of All the Russias, Ivan III, built the first two stone cathedrals in 1326 (those of the Assumption and of the Archangel Michael). The Kremlin's white stone walls, which twice resisted assaults by the Lithuanians, were replaced by new bricks and towers in 1485-1495. At the end of the 15th and early 16th centuries the Moscow Kremlin came to be regarded as one of the most sophisticated strongholds in Europe. The new fortress has nineteen towers, all different in size and shape, the space between them determined by the firing distance of the canon used in those days.

After the fire of 1547 Ivan the Terrible decreed that open spaces should be left between courtyards and households, and between the Kremlin and the surrounding settlements. People were encouraged to build with brick and stone, and the main settlement, the Kitaigorod (Chinese Town), east of the Kremlin was walled with massive stones. Tsar Alexis (1645-1676) built Moscow's first stone bridge in 1643.

In 1712, Peter the Great's new city of St Petersburg, founded in 1703, was declared capital, and Moscow went into decline. In 1714, Peter forbade the construction of brick and stone buildings outside his new city, in order to concentrate all the available raesources there, and this further halted the development of Moscow. It was also Peter the Great who, after the 1712 fire had destroyed a whole district of Moscow, ordered that all new streets be straight and symmetrical — something that was absolutely alien to medieval

Moscow. Moscow was proverbially known as the city which had 'forty times forty' churches. After each fire, where previously there had been one church, two would replace it. Almost every district had its fortified convent, monastery or major church; the Andronikov monastery (1359), the Simonov ('the sentinel of the city', 1405), the Rozhdestvensky (1501-5), the Novodevichy Convent (1524) and the Donskoy Monastery (1591) amongst others. The genius of Moscow's architects, masons and icon-painters fused the styles of Vladimir and Pskov with those of Byzantium or Renaissance Italy. As a result Moscow created its own version of Baroque and then Russian Gothic. The unique St Basil's Cathedral (1555-60) commissioned by Ivan the Terrible, continues to amaze people today; legend has it that Ivan had the architect blinded so that he would never again be able to build such a magnificent cathedral.

Sadly the construction of the Moscow Metro in the 1930s and 1950s caused much of medieval Moscow to disappear, including many famous towers and chapels and the grand Cathedral of the Redeemer, built after 1812 to thank God for delivering Moscow from the French. The Lenin Mausoleum replaced the chapel protecting the holy icon of the Ivernian Mother of God at the entrance to Red Square.

Despite the greatest blow to its pride in the early 18th century when Peter the Great moved his capital north, Moscow nevertheless remained Russia's unofficial second capital and the coronation of the new Tsars continued to take place in the Kremlin. The city's pride was resurrected by Napoleon occupying Russia's holiest city and then being forced to retreat in humiliating defeat. In the age of nationalism Napoleon had turned Moscow into the national capital of Russia.

Throughout the Tartar-Mongol domination, Moscow had lagged 300 years behind Europe. In the 1560s the first printers were accused of witchcraft and had to flee to Latvia to escape burning. A Kiev-inspired seminary teaching Greek and Latin was founded in Moscow only in 1680. The first Russian newspaper, *Vedomosti* (Records) did not appear until 1703. No proper survey of Moscow was made until 1739. The city's first bank was set up in 1753, but soon failed. Moscow university was founded in 1755-7, but on the initiative of a private individual — Count Ivan Shuvalov.

In the 19th century the contrast between Moscow and St Petersburg became increasingly pronounced and Russia's greatest writers, whose golden age was just beginning, were fascinated by it to the point of obsession. From Pushkin, Gogol, Lermontov and Herzen to Turgenev, Tolstoy and Dostoyevsky, all were enthralled by the rivalry between the two great cities.

After the October Revolution in 1917 Moscow emerged as a new force. In February 1918 Lenin personally initiated the move of the capital from Petrograd (the new name of St Petersburg until it became Leningrad) to Moscow. From then until New Year's Day 1991, the red banner, the state flag of the Republic of Soviets, flew above the Moscow Kremlin. In 1935 the double-headed eagles which were the emblem of the Tsars were taken from the Spasskaya, Nikolskaya, Troitskaya and Borovitskaya towers, and replaced with five-pointed stars. In 1937 they were replaced by new ones made from ruby-red glass and lit from inside. A fifth star was installed on the Vodovzvodnaya tower.

When the Soviet Union formally disintegrated in 1991, the Russian flag began to fly above the Kremlin. Later that year, attention switched to the White House, the Russian parliament, where Boris Yeltsin made his historic stand against the coup leaders. Within a few years, the face of Moscow had changed beyond recognition.

CLIMATE

The weather in Moscow is more or less predictable. In winter, though temperatures of −40°C have been recorded, the average temperature over recent years has been −8°C in December, −10.5°C in January, and −9.5°C in February. However this is cold enough for most Westerners and cold enough too for people wearing glasses to be severely inconvenienced as their breath freezes over the lenses reducing visibility to nil.

Summers in Moscow are fairly warm but sometimes the humidity can be oppressive. July is the hottest month, with an average of 18°C (though the temperature can reach 30°C or drop to 8°C). June and August are not so warm, with an average temperature of 16°C. Spring and autumn can be very pleasant but are comparatively short seasons with spring coming late and autumn early; frosts persist into April and the first snow can arrive as early as October. Although the last few years have seen some freak weather, it is normally possible to predict seasonal changes fairly accurately:

Around March 16	the snow begins to thaw
April 12	the ice breaks up in the river Moskva
May 2	first thunderstorms in Moscow
May 24	the apple and cherry trees blossom
August 26	leaves begin to fall
September 14	the first night frosts
October 28	the first snow
November 18	the river Moskva freezes
November 23	snow cover becomes general

THE PEOPLE

Moscow is a multinational city. Most of the Muscovites are Russian (more than six million) but the city is also inhabited by Ukranians, Byelorussians, Tatars, Armenians, Georgians, Letts and many other nationalities.   On the whole Muscovites are sociable, hospitable people, though many visitors have found them pretty surly in shops and on the street. However if you ask them for directions they'll mostly do their best to help. Most young people will probably understand English, but will be shy to reply in English; older people will speak only Russian. Muscovites provide the best form of entertainment in their homes. They are naturally hospitable and see themselves under an additional obligation to help foreigners gain a good impression of Moscow.

ARRIVAL AND DEPARTURE

Air. Moscow's main international airport is a disgrace. Sheremetyevo-2 (Sheremetyevo-1 is mainly for domestic flights) is surrounded by woodland, situated 20 miles/32km northwest of Moscow, and is complete chaos. Passport Control proceeds at a slow pace, and customs can be slower still. If you want a trolley you will need to change at least $2 into roubles. Then your problems start. Flights are met by phalanxes of touts, all trying to get you to ride in their taxi. Independent travellers should make for the bus stop and reject all offers. There is an Airport Express Bus which runs roughly every half an hour between Sheremetyevo and Rechnoy Voksal metro stop. Tickets cost between 1 and 2 dollars- sometimes you have to buy a ticket for your luggage too. Bus number 517 takes a little longer but runs to Planyornaya Metro station every 15 minutes. Both metro stations are in the north west of the city, about 40 minutes from Red Square.

Sheremetyevo-1 is older and further away, but less chaotic. It uses the same runway as terminal 2, but buses between the two take an age.

Domodedovo, the second largest airport in the Soviet Union, caters mainly for internal flights, and is about 30 miles southeast of Moscow. It serves Central Asia, Siberia and the Far East. Vnukovo serves Crimean and Caucasian resorts and the Baltic coast, and is the least catastrophic.

Air tickets from Moscow: the first 'bucket shops', offering air tickets afor much less than the regular fares, have begun to make an appearance in Moscow. Flights to Western Europe, particularly London, are much better value than official fares on Aeroflot and British Airways, while transatlantic tickets are positive bargains.

Time Travel, ul Pistovaya 12 (tel 257 9220).
Magellan, ul Khmeleva 21 (tel 208 4743, fax 975 2619)
Overseas Business Travel, Mayakovskaya Square, 2 Tverskaya Yamskaya no 6 (tel 250 2231, fax 250 2264)

In the spring of 1995, Moscow-London tickets on the Czech airline CSA (via Prague) were going for $325 one-way, $525 return. Moscow-New York round-trips were selling off-peak on SAS for $630, including a night in a Stockholm hotel at the airline's expense. In peak season, the lowest fare is on Aeroflot, for $655 return.

Rail. Moscow has nine main railway stations. Each one is a terminal which caters for a particular area of the country. Most of them are central with easy access by metro. Left luggage departments are available at each station, as are restaurants and buffets. The porters operate a cartel to keep their fees high, and some Westerners who have failed to negotiate a price in advance have been forced to pay $40 for five minutes' work. Always fix a fee in advance, with reference to the list of charges which should be attached to each trolley.

Byelorussian station (Byelorussky vokzal) is the most impressive. It stands in the big square of the same name at the top of Tverskaya. The station is over a hundred years old and boasts an architecturally interesting restaurant and very smelly lavatories. There are daily departures to Berlin and Warsaw which connect to London, Oslo and Stockholm. Information: 266-92-13.

Three stations — Kazan, Leningrad and Yaroslavl — are situated in Komsomolskaya Square, reached by metro to Komsomolskaya. The Kazan railway station caters for the former central Asian Republics and Siberia. For information dial 266-28-43.

Trains from Leningradski railway station go northwest to St Petersburg, Murmansk, Petrozavodsk, Tallinn and Helsinki; information: 266-91-11.

Yaroslavl railway station has the best amenities and is the starting point for the Trans-Siberian Express — see page 158. Information: 266-02-18.

The Kiev railway station serves the Ukraine and has trains to the capitals of Eastern Europe.

The Kursk railway station is, according to some Muscovites, the dirtiest and the liveliest of them all. It serves Georgia, Armenia, Azerbaijan, Crimea and the Caucasus. Be particularly careful of your belongings and wallet here, as there are usually lots of gypsy children about. Information: 227-20-03, 297-31-52.

The three others are Paveletsky Railway Station (metro Paveletskaya); the Riga Railway Station (metro Rizhskaya), with trains to resorts on the Gulf of Riga; and the Savelovsky Railway Station. For timetable information for all Moscow railway stations call 266-90-00.

River. With the construction of the Moskva Canal, Moscow is a major port linked with the Baltic, White, Caspian and Black Seas and passenger steamers go to destinations as far away as Astrakhan, Ufa and Rostov-on-Don. Departure is from the Northern River Terminal, 51 Leningrad Highway, (metro Rechnoy) tel 457-40-50, where timetable enquiries can be made.

CITY TRANSPORT

City Layout. Moscow stands on seven hills on either side of the river Moskva which is linked by the Moscow Canal to the great Russian river Volga. At the centre of Moscow is the Kremlin. The city is contained within five ring roads which mark the city's expanding boundaries over the years. Within the innermost ring, surrounding the Kremlin, there are squares and streets, some of which still preserve their old names like Nikitskiye Vorota (St Nikita's gate), Petrovskiye Vorota (Peter's gate), Zemlyanoi Val (Earthern Rampart), Valovaya Ulitsa (Rampart Street), Kitaisky Proyezd (Kitai Passage). These are all immediately outside the Kremlin. Nowadays this ring also includes Staraya Ploshchad (Old Square), Novaya Ploshchad (New Square), and Ulitsa Razina (Razin Street).

The second, incomplete, ring is known as Bulvarnoye Koltso (Boulevard Ring), and lies about a mile outside the inner ring. Its tree-lined central reservations and elegant 18th century mansions made it a perfect area for a stroll until traffic got too heavy. The third ring, the Sadovoye Koltso (Garden Ring), runs for nearly ten miles/16km around the city and is its most important road for heavy traffic. Most of the main tourist sights are contained within these three rings. The fourth ring used to be known as Kamer-Kolleshsky Rampart but now seems to be nameless while finally the fifth ring constitutes the Moscow Circular Road and marks the city's present boundaries.

From the centre and cutting across these rings run a series of long straight avenues. Prospekt Mira (Avenue of Peace) leads north to the former Exhibition of Economic Achievements and then becomes Yaroslavskoye Shosse (Yaroslavl Highway). Leningradsky Prospekt leads north-west to Sheremetyevo-2 airport. Running west is Novy Arbat, which becomes Kutuzovsky Prospekt and then Minskoye Shosse (Minsk Highway), while Leninsky Prospekt leads south-west towards Vnukovo airport. The two old streets Bolshaya Polyanka and Bolshaya Ordynka join to form the road south, and Volgogradsky Prospekt (Volgograd Avenue) and Shosse Entuziastov (Enthusiasts' Highway) lead to the east of the country.

Metro. Moscow has over 140 miles of underground railway and more than 130 stations, each of which is marked with an illuminated M sign outside. There are no tickets. To get to the platform you have to drop a token into a slot machine; if you do not a barrier appears from nowhere to block your path. If you have a monthly pass, show this to the attendant on the gate. Trains run daily from 6am to 1am (on national holidays they run until 2am) but do not expect to strike up cheerful conversations while you travel — no one seems to talk at all.

The underground system is safe, fast, spotlessly clean and most reliable. Furthermore a number of stations are works of art in themselves with marble arches and colonnades, mosaic floors and classical statues peering down at the hurrying commuters. Komsomolskaya depicts episodes from Russian history and has an entrance which resembles the helmet of a Russian warrior. Quite often stations will be linked in twos or threes so it is important to

MOSCOW

1 Air Terminal
2 Aerostar Hotel
3 Traveler's Guest House
4 Moscow Penta
5 Minsk Hotel
6 Revolution Museum
7 McDonald's I
8 Pizza Hut
9 Budapest Hotel
10 Post Office
11 Bolshaya Theatre
12 Intourist Hotel
13 GUM Department Store
14 St. Basil's Cathedral
15 Kremlin
16 Rossia Hotel
17 British Embassy
18 Pushkin Art Museum
19 Tretiakov Gallery
20 St. Nicholas' Church
21 Viewpoint

0   1 km

0   1/2 mile

know exactly which station you are heading for. Additionally some of the stations do not have the name well marked by the platforms so be prepared to count the stations and have the name of your destination written down in Cyrillic. Announcements are made at each station, but only in Russian.

Buses and trolleybuses on most routes run every few minutes from 6am to 1am. 'Microbuses' provide a shuttle service between the points which are difficult to reach by other means of transport. They run every 10 minutes and stop by request.

Trams start at 5.30am, mostly in the suburbs, and run until 1.30am. Most buses, trolleybuses and trams do not have conductors; you have to buy tickets (normally in sets of 10) from drivers during stops or in Metro stations. Upon boarding you must punch one ticket at one of the ticket punchers located throughout the bus and keep it until you get off.

Taxis. There are more than 11,000 official taxis in Moscow, roughly the same number as in New York City, and probably ten times as many unofficial ones. The standard fare in town is $2, except from the luxury cabs that you order by phone.

Moscow also has fixed-route taxis (*marshrutniye taxi*). They run every ten minutes between the main squares, railway stations, and other important points.

Riverboats provide an excellent way to see the city and cruise the river Moskva from May-June until September-October, depending on when the river is unfrozen. There are two routes, one lasting an hour and the other 80 minutes. The starting point is Kiev Terminal by the Kievskaya Metro station. The first route takes you via Krasnopresensky Park to Kuntsevo-Krylatskoye and also to Fili-Kuntsevo Park and the river beach. The second route takes you via the Lenin Hills — Gorky Park — Krymsky Bridge — Bolshoi Kamenny Bridge — Bolshoi Ustinsky Bridge — Krasnokholmsky Bridge — Novospassky Bridge, passing the Novodevichy Convent, the Lenin Stadium, Moscow University, the Moskva swimming pool, the Kremlin, the Rossiya Hotel, the Novospassky Monastery and other Moscow landmarks.

As elsewhere in Russia, Moscow hotels come in three types. Most of the old, pre-revolutionary ones (e.g. National, Berlin, Metropol) have been tarted up, and the newer post-revolutionary ones (e.g. Kosmos, Rossiya) have been joined by purpose-built Western-style places. The big hotels are as follows:

Aerostar, 37 Leningradsky Prospect, Korpus 9; tel 213 9000, fax 213 9001; for satellite links prefix these numbers with 7502.

Cosmos: 150 Mir Prospekt, built in 1979. One of the biggest hotels in the Soviet Union, nearly 2,000 rooms. Cosmos has a swimming pool, sauna and bowling alley. Four restaurants, late night bars.

Intourist: opposite Red Square. Opened in 1970. 540 rooms. Great location, dismal hotel.

Metropol: 1-4 Marx Prospekt. Built in 1900, 400 rooms, very ornate, conjuring up images of Tsarist Russia. Very opulent and very expensive.

Mezhdunarodnaya: World Trade Centre, smart and modern.

National: 1 Gorky St. Built in 1903 and expanded in 1960s, pleasant atmosphere. Excellent view from roof.

Radisson-Slavyanskaya: adjacent to Kiev Station. New, flashy, expensive and housing most of the Western media in Mosow, including the BBC.

Rossiya: 1 Moskvoretskaya Embankment, built in 1967. Claims to be the largest hotel in Europe with over 3,000 rooms. Certainly the ugliest in Europe. Cinemas, a large concert hall, several restaurants and cafes and a basement disco. Room service available. Overlooks the Kremlin.

Ukraine: 10/9 Kutuzovsky Prospekt. 1,500 rooms, lovely view of the Moskva River. Lifts are often out of order.

It is highly recommended that you ignore these in favour of the Budapest (central, comfortable and cheap, at Petrovskiye Linii 2/18, tel 921 1060) or the even cheaper Molodegny (some distance north at Dmitrovskoye Shosse 27). Better still, the Travellers Guest House at 50 Bolshaya Pereyaslavskaya ul, 10th floor (971 4059) will save you cash and plug you straight into the independent travel scene. To reach it, take the Metro to Prospekt Mira and head right (north) along Prospekt Mira itself until just before a 12-storey building at number 62. Turn right along Bannii Pereulok towards four grey chimneys. When you reach the end, turn left, find number 50 and take the lift to the 10th floor. The place is shabby but friendly.

Eating and Drinking

Fast Food. This section makes no excuses for beginning with fast food. It is often said by visitors to Moscow that McDonalds is the only place in the capital where you are guaranteed reasonably priced food and quick service- and it stays open until 10pm. You will find quite an array of people tucking into their Big Macs, from top western businessmen to former Soviet war heroes. Moscow now boasts three McDonalds: one on the Arbat (metro Smolensky- dark blue line) and two on Tverskaya. At weekends there may be queues, but these are usually fairly fast moving. Prices are currently the same as in the USA.

Kombis is a new American Sandwich Bar which offers an alternative to McDonalds. There are several branches in Moscow, the most central being on Tverskaya, opposite the Intourist Hotel. Expect to pay the rouble equivalent of $2-5 for a good-sized roll depending on the filling. If you are craving lettuce, Kombis even makes salads, and there is plenty of choice for vegetarians — a revolutionary idea.

Pizza Hut are old timers in Moscow now; the company has been trading for both roubles and hard currency since the early days of glasnost. You can buy a slice of take-away pizza (there is still only a choice of two) from their stand just before Pushinskaya Square on Tverskaya for the rouble equivalent of $2. Alternatively both the Tverskaya and Kutozovsky Prospect restaurants have take-away as well as eat-in sections.

Taco Bell, the American 'Mexican' fast-food chain has opened a stall at Park Kulturi metro station, selling cheesy burritos and New York hot dogs (each just under $1). You wil need a metro token to get into the stall. It seems to close around 7pm.

Steffi, a Danish hot dog firm, has recently set up several kiosks around Pushkin Square. Again expect to pay about $1 for a hot dog or burger.

Outside the Intourist Hotel there are a few kiosks selling Russian pizza, chips and so on. Sometimes the pizza is a little heavy on dough and light on topping, but they are often cheaper than their western counterparts. If you are vegetarian try asking for *bez massa* (without meat) — it may work.

If you are determined to try something really Russian, go for the shashliki or kebabs at the top of the Old Arbat near the Prague Restaurant, or the Papsi kiosk by the picture of Checkhov on Tverskaya. For over three years now this kiosk has been doing a good trade selling sausage, bread and pickled gherkin. Its popularity never seems to wane, and there is always a short queue. There is also a stall selling very tasty chicken on the top floor of GUM, near the toilets.

One local fast food dish does come highly recommended — machipuri. Originally from Georgia, it can only be described as a warm, doughy bread with a cheesy filling. Have a look for it in the kiosks in the park behind Kropotkinskaya metro station; if you can't find it here try the Georgia Cultural Centre, opposite the Pushkin House on the Old Arbat. Downstairs is a rather classy restaurant, but they do machipuri to take out for around $2). Apparently it is becoming fashionable in the United States, so make sure you can say you had the real thing in Moscow first.

Obviously fast-food outlets are relatively new to Moscow — a result of the spirit of free enterprise which has hit the country. But they are well beyond the means of many Russians, who are more likely to eat in the Stolovayas or self-service cafes. The food is certainly cheap, but it and the standards of hygiene are often poor. If you are interested in trying one of these cafes out, there is one behind the Bolshoi Theatre, at the corner of Petrovsky Street and Kuznetsky Most. For some reason, perhaps to protect the cook from angry diners, knives are very scarce in these places.

Cafés. Sadly, cafés seem to come and go very quickly. This may be because of the precarious economic climate, distribution problems, the mafia, or a combination of all three, but there seems to be little to encourage individual ventures.

U Tretyakov. Situated beside the Tretyakov Art Gallery, this café is a delight. Clean chairs and tables inside and out, waitress service. Tea, coffee, sandwiches and cake. Very reasonable prices: tea and cake will cost you around $0.50, Open till 7pm. Part of a German-Russian joint venture.

Margarita. Bright and cheerful café on the corner of Maly Kozikhinsky Pereulok (metro Pushkinskaya). Gets its name because it is close to Patriarch's Road, where the cat first appears in Bulgakov's novel *The Master and Margarita*. Delicious cakes. You may need to book.

Lux Café. Petrovsky Passage, Petrovska street (metro Kuznetsky Most). Right at the far end of this elegant glass-roofed shopping arcade. Cappuccino, expresso, traditional Russian cakes, sandwiches, and salads. The Lux is not cheap; prices are given in dollars and then converted to roubles. Bar on the second floor of the shopping arcade. Neither the café nor the bar have a toilet. Closes at 7pm.

Café Rosa, Old Arbat, halfway down on the left-hand side (metro Arbatskay/ Smolenskaya). A very Russian phenomenon. It advertises cappuccino but only sells expresso. Full of atmosphere, it is frequented by the young, trendy crowd, and is an excellent place to sit and watch them. Don't venture to the old Arbat at night, as it is poorly lit and becoming increasingly dangerous.

Café Cappuccino, 12 Suvorovsky Bulvar (metro Arbatskaya). Open 10am-11pm. A real artists' bistro, with walls lined with paintings by local artists. Sells cappuccino, expresso, ice-cream, pizza, soft drinks and some harder ones. Not cheap but very pleasant. Prices are given in dollars and converted to roubles. Expect to pay around $6-7 for a pizza. Very popular amongst Moscow's young foreign community.

Restaurants. Despite a long culinary tradition, Moscow certainly couldn't claim to be the food capital of the world, but the restaurant situation is improving all the time. Eating out in Moscow may be a little pricier than many other European cities, and it is always advisable to check the bill carefully. Unfortunately many establishments still see western tourists as walking dollar bills, and the price may be adjusted accordingly.

You may often find both the reception and food on offer in Russian restaurants to be decidedly cool. A full scale meal will usually include *zakuski* (appetizers) which consist of red (from salmon) or black (from beluga) *ikra* (caviar), smoked *osetrina* (sturgeon) or *semga* (salmon), or salads with *smetana* (sour cream) and *studen* (jellied meat). Zakuski are served with white or brown bread. Moscovsky, Borodinsky and Orlovsky bread are mixed grain with rye and are heavier than most British varieties.

Zakuski are normally followed by hot soups; such as *borshch* (beetroot soup), *shchi* (sauerkraut), *solyanka* (vegetable and meat or fish soup) and *rassolnik* (meat or fish soup with gherkins). Note that Russian soups tend to have a very high fat content which can leave an unpleasant taste in the mouth. As an alternative *okroshka* — cold vegetable soup — is popular in the summer. These soups are often served as a main course. By the time the soup arrives it is likely to be nearly cold — do not send it back to be re-heated, you will be unlikely to see it again. *Pelmeni* (similar to ravioli) and *bliny* (pancakes) with meat or cottage cheese fillings are also favourites among Muscovites as main courses. *Morozhennoe* (ice-cream), and *tort* (gateau) and *pryaniki* (gingerbread) served with Turkish-style coffee (if you are lucky) bring a lengthy and very filling meal to an end.

Some specific recommendations follow, beginning with a strictly Russian one:

Slaviansky Bazar, 25th October Street 13. One of Moscow's most famous and longest-established restaurants. Chekhov and Slaviansky were once among its clientele. It is said that this is where Chekhov agreed to put on *The Seagull* at the Moscow Arts Theatre. Russian cuisine is accompanied by an orchestra and cabaret. Very atmospheric. Not suitable for vegetarians.

Baku Restuaurant, Tverskaya 24 (metro Chekovskaya). Persian cuisine from Azerbaijan. Service may be rude unless you slip the waiter a tip at the beginning of the meal. Specialises in different kinds of pilav.

Pirosmani. Novodyevichi Proyezd 4 (metro Sportivnaya). A little way from the centre, but this elegant restaurant is well worth the trip. The food is Georgian, and is recommended by Georgians. A violinist plays at your table, and there are original paintings by Pirosmani on the walls. Very popular so it is advisable to book in advance. The prices are given in dollars converted to roubles.

La Cantina. Tverskaya, next to the Intourist hotel. Moscow's first Mexican restaurant. Casual, fairly reasonably priced, and with a lively atmosphere. La Cantina is very popular with Moscow's young foreign community, who have presumably either never tasted real Mexican food or are homesick for such transatlantic delicacies as Death by Chocolate.

Patio Pizza. Volkhonka St, opposite the Pushkin Museum of Fine Arts. One of Moscow's busiest restaurants, particularly at weekends. Help yourself salad bar- eat as much as you can for $6. Large variety of pizzas. Delghtful airy surroundings. Reservations advisable. Suitable for vegetarians.

Lily Wong Chinese, 3/5 Intourist Hotel, Tverskaya St Tel: 9568-301. Recently opened, this Chinese restaurant boasts traditional cooking made with authentic ingredients. Expensive — you could easily spend $60 per person on a meal and drinks.

There are also restaurants, coffee shops and bars in most Moscow hotels. Although they may be expensive ($5 for a cappuccino) those belonging to international chains are generally of a high standard. The Manhattan Express, an American-run restaurant in the Rossiya Hotel, was recently recommended in glowing terms by the *Moscow Times*: 'The food is great and the staff are so friendly and beautiful that they could have been imported from another planet'. Incidentally, the *Moscow Times* is a useful source of information about new or trendy restaurants, although some of its reviews should be taked with a pinch of Russian salt.

THE KREMLIN

Roughly triangular in shape and bordered on two sides by the Moskva River and Red Square, the Kremlin (Kreml = citadel) stands at the very heart of Moscow and is the oldest historical and architectural centre of the city. The building of the Kremlin began in 1156 when Prince Yuri Dolgoruky ordered a wooden fort to be built on Borovitsky Hill (now called Kremlin Hill) which became the residence of the ruling princes of Moscow. The fortress was burned to the ground in 1238 during the Tartar invasion but Moscow continued to live and grow. In 1382 the Tartar Khan Tokhtamysh and his hordes broke into the Kremlin, demolished the fortress, pillaged the churches, burnt the houses inside it, and slaughtered around half the population. Moscow had to start building all over again.

In 1485-95 the walls of white stone were replaced by new brick walls and towers, the originals of which, although much restored, are still standing. At the same time the area of the Kremlin was extended to its present size. The Kremlin suffered badly in 1812, when Napoleon's armies marched into Moscow which was abandoned by its people and the Russian army. The French soldiers were quartered in the Kremlin and when forced to retreat they tried, on Napoleon's orders, to blow it up. This they failed to do thanks to the courage of the Cossacks and native people who remained behind in the city but much damage was done.

You can view the Kremlin from many vantage points. You can walk right around it for 2,235 metres along the top of its walls. You can also get a very good view of the cathedrals, the Grand Kremlin Palace and the Kremlin walls and towers from the Moskvoretsky or Bolshoi Kamenny Bridges and also from the Morisa Toreza Embankment, which also houses the British Embassy in Moscow. You may also view it from Red Square or from the 50th Anniversary of the October Revolution Square (formally Manège Square), or from the National or Rossiya hotels.

The best way to visit the Kremlin is to take the Metro to Prospekt Marxa and go to the small kiosk in the park across the road where you can buy tickets for the various different palaces, cathedrals and museums inside the Kremlin. From here you may either enter through the Sobakina Tower at the Kremlin's northernmost point or walk south west through the beautiful Alexandrovsky Gardens, past the tomb of the unknown soldier to enter the Kremlin through the gate in the pyramid shaped Borovitskaya Tower. These are the only two pedestrian entrances, though there is an exit through the Spassky Gate into Red Square and also through the Troitskaya gate. All are open daily from 10am.

Passing through Alexandrovsky Gardens you come to the Troitskaya (Trinity) Tower, at 240 feet, the highest of all the Kremlin's 20 towers, which is guarded by the squat Kutafya Tower and linked to it by a white

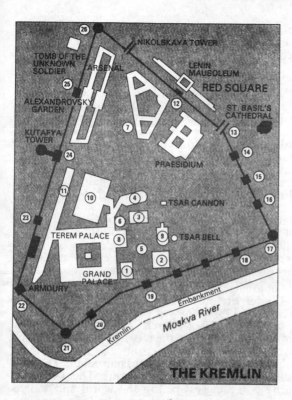

1 Cathedral of the Annunciation
2 Cathedral of the Archangel
3 Cathedral of the Assumption
4 Cathedral of the 12 Apostles
5 Cathedrals' Square
6 Church of the Deposition of the Robe
7 Council of Ministers Building
8 Granovitaya Palace
9 Ivan the Great Bell Tower
10 Kremlin Palace of Congress
11 Poteshny Palace
12 Senate Tower
13 Spassky Tower
14 Little Tsar Tower
15 Alarm Tower
16 Tower of Constantine and Helen
17 Beklemishevskaya Tower
18 Peter Tower
19 Tainitskaya Tower
20 Annunciation Tower
21 Vodovzvodanya Tower
22 Borovitiskaya Tower
23 Armoury Tower
24 Troitskaya Tower
25 Arsenal Tower
26 Sobakina Tower

stone bridge. Beyond Troitskaya Tower is the Palace of Congresses, a monumental structure of concrete and glass and the most modern building in the Kremlin. The Troitskaya Tower was erected in 1495 and it was through its gate that Napoleon's troops entered, and later fled from the Kremlin. Tsars and military leaders returning victorious from campaigns used to ride into the Kremlin either through the Troitskaya Gate or through the Spassky Gate. Lenin too entered the Kremlin through the Troitskaya Gate as head of the First Soviet Government in March 1918. To the left of Troitskaya Tower you can see a large two-storey building, the Arsenal. It was begun by Peter the Great in 1702 and was completed in 1736. Today it houses offices.

The Armoury. Not far from the Borovitzky entrance is the Armoury (Oruzhei-naya Palata) built in the 16th century. At the beginning of the 19th century the Armoury was rebuilt and converted into a museum. It is one of the oldest and most remarkable museums in the Soviet Union. Its collections include the famous golden Cap of Monomakh, the 11th century hero who defended the country against invaders from the east, which was to crown all Russian tsars up to Peter the Great, the first Russian Imperial crown of Catherine I made of silver-gilt, the dress of Catherine II (Catherine the Great) adorned with exquisite silver embroidery, and many other historic items. The museum also has a display of unique objets d'art in gold, silver, precious stones, ivory, and porcelain, and fabrics embroidered with pearls and adorned with precious stones. There is also an outstanding collection of ceremonial carriages, each one of which is a work of art in itself.

The Grand Palace (Bolshoi Kremlyovsky Dvorets) is a group of several buildings built in 1838-49. For centuries this was the home of the tsars. The present building was erected after the previous palace was badly damaged by Napoleon's troops.

There are several vast halls in the palace. The most famous and beautiful is the Georgievsky (St George) Hall. It is now used for state receptions and official ceremonies. Next to it, connected by mirrored doors, is the octagonal Vladimirsky (St Vladimir) Hall, founded in 1487. It contains one of the most ancient chambers, the Palace of Facets (Granovitaya Palata). Vladimirsky Hall is also connected with the Golden Tsarina Palace (Terem Palace) which dates from the seventeenth century and has a striking red and white tiled roof and where the Tsarina received her official visitors.

Opposite the Armoury stands a three-storey building, formally the *Senate*, and now the Council of Ministers. It was in this building that Lenin lived and worked.

Opposite the former Senate, to the right of the Palace of Congress is the small five-domed Church of the Twelve Apostles and The Patriarch's Palace built in 1635-56. It now houses the museum of 17th Century Life and Applied Art. There are over 700 exhibits of unique copper, tin and silver articles, fabrics and jewellery.

The Bell Tower. In the centre of the Kremlin rises one of the most remarkable structures of 16th century Russian architecture — the Ivan the Great Bell Tower. It is 263 feet (80m) high, and for many years was the tallest building in Moscow. In the past it served both as a church, and the main watchtower of the Kremlin providing a good view of the city and the surrounding area for up to 18 miles/30km around. The three-tier pillar construction was meant to symbolise the might of the centralized Russian state. The two towers together have 52 bells the largest weighing 70 tons. The Tsar Bell, standing on a pedestal nearby is the biggest bell in the world and weighs 200 tons. Nearby stands the Tsar Cannon cast in bronze in 1586 and with the world's greatest calibre of 35 inches.

The Cathedral Square. The massive bell tower unites all the Kremlin cathedrals into the magnificent Cathedral Square, the ancient main centre of the Kremlin, built in the early 14th century. On its northern side stands the five-domed Cathedral of the Assumption (Uspensky Sobor) which was built by the Italian Aristotle Fiorovanti in 1475 in the style of the Uspensky Cathedral at Vladimir. It became the main cathedral of old Russia and religious services are still held here. This was the place where the tsars were invested and the emperors crowned and the carved throne of Ivan the Terrible still stands here. It was also the Moscow burial place of the metropolitans and patriarchs of the Orthodox church.

Next to the Uspensky Cathedral is the smaller, single-domed Risopolozheniye (Church of the Deposition of the Robe) built in 1484-85. This graceful church became a private chapel in 1653 but is now a museum with exceptionally fine 17th century frescoes.

On the west side of the Cathedral Square but closer to the river stands The Blagoveshchensky Sobor (the Cathedral of the Annunciation) with nine gilt domes. This remarkable monument of Russian architecture links three centuries of art and religion. Although the foundations were laid in the 14th century it was built in 1484-89; after a fire in 1547 it was restored during the reign of Ivan the Terrible. Inside you will find icons by the great master Andrei Rublyev, paintings and a beautiful iconstasis and striking murals which depict themes from the apocalypse; the floor is of polished agate jasper given by the Shah of Persia. This cathedral used to be the Tsar's private chapel.

Opposite the Cathedral of Annunciation is another church, the Archangel Cathedral. It has five domes and is a splendid example of the combined style of early Russian Italian Renaissance architecture. Between 1540 and 1700 this was the burial place of the Moscow princes and tsars. In it there are 45 tombs which include those of Ivan the Terrible and his sons. During the architectural and archaeological work in the cathedral in 1962-65 several tombs were opened; from the remains of the skeleton and skull, the Soviet anthropologist and sculptor Mikhail Gersasimov was able to make the first documentary portrayal of Ivan the Terrible.

The Kremlin may be visited on an individual basis or excursions can be taken with one of the guides who hangs around in Red Square. Backpacks, carrier bags, parcels etc. are not permitted in the Kremlin. You may photograph any of the monuments from the outside, but not the interiors of the museums. You are expected to remove your headgear inside the museums and to refrain from smoking. You also have to wear felt slippers in some museums. There is an exit through the Spassky Tower gate to Red Square.

RED SQUARE (Krasnaya Ploshchad)

The history of Red Square goes back to the 1940s, when numerous buildings around the Kremlin walls were pulled down. Nearly all the roads to Moscow from all over Russia converged there and at first Red Square was known as Torg (Market) Square, then as Troitsky (Trinity) Square after the wooden church on its south side. But after St Basil's Cathedral was built in the 17th century people soon started to call it Krasnaya Square since the old Russian meaning of the word Krasnaya was beautiful, magnificent or stately. In the 16th century it became a place for ceremony as well as for state executions. Under the Soviet State the adjective 'Krasnaya' was identified with the colour of the revolutionary flag and Red Square became the venue for the annual military parades and civilian demonstrations.

The Cathedral of Intercession. St Basil's or Pokrovsky Cathedral (1555-61) was built on the order of Ivan the Terrible by the Russian architects Barma and Postnik (although documents uncovered in 1957 suggest that they were in fact one person — Postnik, nicknamed Barma). The old church of Trinity was pulled down to clear the site. St Basil's Cathedral has eight tower-like chapels with differently designed and coloured domes surrounding the principal chapel (107 feet high), all linked by an elevated gallery. In 1588 a small chapel was erected next to the Cathedral over the grave of the Blessed Vassily (Saint Basil) and since then the Cathedral of Intercession has been known as St Basil's Cathedral. The beauty and the splendour of the cathedral gave rise to a popular legend: asked by Ivan the Terrible if they could build anything finer or duplicate what they had already done, the architects Postnik and Barma answered that they could — Ivan was so outraged that he ordered them to be blinded so that there would never by anything more beautiful in the world than the Cathedral of Intercession.

In front of the cathedral stands Moscow's first secular monument to Minin (a butcher) and Pozharsky (a prince) who, in 1612, rallied the people to arms and liberated Moscow from the Polish invaders. Behind the cathedral, just beyond Red Square, is the huge *Rossiya Hotel* whose top floor restaurant gives a marvellous view of Red Square and the Kremlin.

The History Museum. (built in red brick, 1878-83) is at the opposite end of Red Square to St Basil's. At the time of writing this building was boarded up, and its future was uncertain.

The Lenin Mausoleum is a low red building sitting beside the wall of the Kremlin by the Spassky Tower. A guard of honour stands at the entrance and the goosestepping guards are changed every hour on the hour. Inside, dressed in a suit with a blue polka-dot tie, lies the embalmed body of Vladimir Ilyich Lenin, the founder of the Communist Party and of the Soviet State, who died in January 1924. The Lenin Mausoleum is open to visitors on Tuesdays, Wednesdays, Thursdays and Saturdays from 11am to 2pm and on Sundays from 11am to 4pm.

No one is allowed to dawdle when passing the crystal sarcophagus. No cameras are allowed inside nor are slouching or putting hands in pockets. Guards may check pockets which bulge unseemingly and turn away offenders.

Kazanski Sobor. The crisp new yellow building next to the history museum is a rebuilt version of an old cathedral, destroyed by Stalin. Compared with St Basil's it is very ordinary, but the startling iconostasis and gently crackling candles makes it seem more elderly than it actually is. It opens 8am-7pm daily.

Smoking is not permitted anywhere in Red Square. The nearest metro stations are Ploshchad Revolutsii and Prospekt Marksa.

TVERSKAYA STREET

Temporarily re-named after the writer Maxim Gorky in 1935, Gorky Street used to be known as Tverskaya Street. This was the road that led from the Kremlin to Tver (once Kalinin) and then on to St Petersburg. For centuries the street was narrow and twisting. Today it is a straight, broad (widened from 19 to 56 metres) modern boulevard, with considerable traffic and many museums, historic monuments, hotels, theatres, restaurants, cafés and shops. You can start your walk up Tverskaya from the corner of the National Hotel on the left side of the street and next door to the 22-storey Intourist Hotel (built in 1971). At the corner of the first major side street (Oganev Street) stands the Central Telegraph Office (open 24 hours a day). Here, if you look to your right across Tverskaya you will catch a glimpse of the Moscow Arts Theatre founded by the famous actor/director Stanislavsky in 1898 and where Chekhov and Gorky's plays were first produced. A bit further on is an equestrian statue (1959) of Prince Yuri Dolgoruky, the founder of Moscow. The city hall of Moscow or the Moscow Town Council (*Mossoviet*) stands opposite, originally built in 1782 as the residence of the governor general of Moscow, but since 1937 rebuilt and extended. It was even moved back 14 metres to widen the street.

Continuing on the right-hand side, you pass the Hotel Central (Tsentralnaya) whose restaurant specialises in Russian cuisine. In the same building is the best known old bakery in Moscow. Next to it is a jewellery shop and then you come to the very popular Yeliseyevsky's delicatessen. It was built in the early 19th century with big plate-glass windows, a high-ceilinged hall, huge chandeliers, and a sumptuous interior.

Next is Pushkin Square, where Tverskaya crosses the Boulevard Ring road. In the centre of the square is the bronze statue of the great Russian poet Alexander Pushkin. It was erected by public subscription in 1880.

There are always bouquets of flowers by the pedestal left by admirers of Pushkin.

On the right at the end of the square is the Rossiya Cinema (built 1961). The building is also used for the International and Soviet film festivals. Behind the Rossiya Cinema are the offices of the *Novosti* (APN) press agency. Also on Pushkin Square stands the new extension of the offices of *Izvestia* (News), on the other side of the square are the offices of *Moscow News*. In the same building is the All-Russia Theatrical Society and the Central Actors' Club, now renamed the Union of Theatrical Workers. It has a very good restaurant which accepts roubles only. Anyone, including foreigners, can get in.

Continuing along Tverskaya you will reach No 21. This old mansion with colonnades used to be the exclusive English Club of the aristocracy, and dates from 1787. It is now the Museum of the Revolution. The trolleybus outside was damaged in the attempted coup of 1991. A little further on in Sadovaya Lane is the Young Spectators' Theatre where plays for children are performed; opposite is another theatre, the Stanislavsky Drama Theatre. Sadly this is now chiefly notable for the shady characters who attend the nightclub here.

In Mayakovsky Square Tverskaya crosses the Sadovoye Ring Road, the grand boulevard of Moscow and a busy thoroughfare ten miles long. Mayakovsky Square is one of the centres of Moscow cultural life. On one corner stands the Tchaikovsky Concert Hall (built in 1940); nearby is the Mossoviet Theatre and on the west side of the square the Svremennik (Contemporary) Youth Theatre.

Tverskaya ends in the square of the Byelorussian railway station. In the small garden at the centre of the square is the monument to Maxim Gorky erected in 1957. The station itself is over 100 years old, built in the traditional Russian style.

THE ARBAT AND NEW ARBAT (Metro: Arbatskaya, Smolenskaya)

The Arbat lies at the centre of what was described as the St Germain of Moscow. During the 18th and 19th centuries this area was predominantly home to the court nobility. Indeed the Arbat, a cobbled, pedestrianised street stretching 1,000 yards is still one of Moscow's trendiest addresses.

In the 16th century the quarter was full of artisans, as demonstrated in the names of the small side streets, ul Serebrannaya (Silver Street), or ul Plotnikov (Carpentry Street). It was a century later that the Arbat first became one of Moscow's main shopping streets, and it remains so to this day. It has also become a total tourist trap. There is a whole host of souvenir shops, antique salons and small art galleries.

About halfway down the street is a relic of the cold war era, a Wall of Peace put together by children throughout the world for the Moscow Olympics of 1980. A little further along is a corner dedicated to graffiti; this was one of the first places of free expression in the early days of perestroika.

Keep your eyes open for Starokoninskeny Pereulok, a sidestreet on the right hand side where the Tsars' stablemen used to live. This green 'lace' house traveled to the World's Fair in Paris, where it was exhibited as a typical Moscow dwelling. Pushkin spent a brief period at no.53. His apartment is now a literary museum. Past Ivanov's house, on the same side of the street, is the Georgian Cultural Centre. Don't be afraid to walk in past the rather seedy-looking men who tend to hang around the door of this pale blue building. Once inside there is an exquisite cast-iron art nouveau staircase. Upstairs there are often exhibitions of Georgian paintings or applied art. Downstairs is a Georgian restaurant. There is a small entrance fee for the exhibitions.

As it draws to a close, the Arbat reaches one of the Stalinist Gothic Skyscrapers that mark a very different period in the city's history. This now houses the Ministry of the Interior. And then you reach McDonald's. To the right you should be able to catch a glimpse of the Bely Dom- the Russian White House, which was besieged by the supporters of Rutskoi and Khasbulatov during the troubles of October 1993. For a more striking view, take the no 34 trolleybus in the direction of Kutuzovsky Prospect, to the bridge.

As a well-known tourist area, the Arbat is a perfect haven for petty thieves. Watch you wallet, and be vigilant at all times. Be particularly careful of children asking for money; they are often only trying to distract you while one of their friends steals your purse. Stick to the main street, and don't be tempted to wander off down small, deserted side streets.

New Arbat. A more stark contrast to the Old Arbat is impossible to imagine. Formerly Kalinin Prospect, the Novy Arbat was allegedly the showcase of the Soviet capital. In the 1960s all the old buildings and the maze of streets and alleys were completely demolished to make way for this new thoroughfare. 26 government ministries were housed along the Prospect. Ironically the New Arbat is now one of the principal centres of western-style capitalist development. The Irish House Supermarket, the Vivaldi Centre (Moscow's first western shopping mall) and the Cherry Casino are replacing the soviet stores and government blocks.

In 1966 the Paris Centre of Architectural Research awarded the Grand Prix to the architects of Kalinin Prospect for their work renewing the existing buildings. However, unless you are fascinated by high-rise apartment buildings (there are nine in total) the buildings on the New Arbat are unremarkable. The exception to this is no.16, the House of Friendship. A 19th century Moscow merchant, Marizin, was fascinated by Spanish medieval architecture, and on returning from a visit to Spain he tried to recreate the style in his new home.

The underpass leading from Arbatskaya to the Old and New Arbats is a popular spot for Muscovites selling their unwanted pets. If you want a larger selection of kittens, snakes and other quasi-domestic wildlife, visit the Ptichy Rynok, Moscow's weekend market for pets and animal accessories. To get there, take any bus or trolleybus heading south from Taganskaya Metro Station, count 5 stops and get off. For more information phone 270-50-10.

OTHER PLACES TO VISIT

Tretyakov Gallery 10 Lavrushinski Pereulok (tel 231 1362). Open daily except Monday. This is one of the world's ten greatest art museums, and was sorely missed while it closed for ten years, reopening only in the summer of 1995.

Novodevichy (New Maiden) **Convent** lies in a tranquil spot in a loop of the Moscow River. The beautiful walled convent, for many years a place of retirement for noble women, was founded as early as 1524 to mark the defeat of the Lithuanians. Outside walls vary from 16 to 40 feet high and are up to 20 feet thick. It is here that in Mussorgsky's opera, Boris Godunov was invited by the Muscovites to be the Tsar of Russia. The huge, five-domed Smolensky Cathedral is famous for its frescoes and highly ornate multi-tiered iconostasis. The cemetery is full of notables including Chekhov, Gogol, Stalin's wife, Eisenstein and Kruschchev, the one Soviet leader not buried in the Kremlin Walls.

You can wander around the grounds for free and enter the Cathedral between 10am and 5.30pm every day except Tuesday and the first Monday of the month. The nearest metro station is Sportivnaya (do not take the exit marked Stadion). The convent is to the right, about five minutes from the station.

The **Park of Economic Achievement**, at the western end of Prospect Mira (metro VDKH- now Central Exhibition Centre) was once the showpiece of Soviet Russia. In the 533 acres of land every aspect of the Soviet economy was displayed; achievements in agriculture, nuclear energy and space. Nowadays the whole place is surreal, the mini-buses and trains no longer operate and the Cosmos Hall has become a night-club. Rather ironically the 80-odd pavilions are filled with traders selling a whole range of imported goods, from electronics to the usual snickers bars and German cakes.

A short walk from the park wavers the Ostankino television tower. Ostankino broadcasts all over Russia and was beseiged in October 1993 during the troubles. For fantastic views over Moscow take a trip up to the top — it is higher than the Eiffel Tower.

More central is **Gorky Central Park** Moscow's equivalent of Hyde Park. Attractions include boating, chess, ice-skating in winter and a big wheel. A good place to see the other life of Muscovites. At the weekend, there is a small entrance fee; buy your ticket from the kiosk (*kassa*) and go in through the main gates.

If you have had your fill of sightseeing and want to catch a glimpse of the life of an ordinary Muscovite, take the metro to one of the outlying districts of the capital. Journey time to Sokol in the northwest of the city or the Yugo-Zapadnaya in the southwestern tip is about 45 minutes from Teatralnaya. The rather bleak Yugo-Zapadnaya was built in 1980 as the Olympic Village for the Moscow Games. As a non-Russian speaking tourist it is unwise to venture to these parts after dark.

Entertainment

THE PERFORMING ARTS

Ballet and Theatre. Notwithstanding the exodus of some dancers to the West, nor the strike in spring 1995 against the management, the Bolshoi Ballet Theatre remains one of the greatest in the world.

The theatre is at Petrovka ul 1 (Metro to Teatralnaya); tel 292 3319 to find out what's on, 292 0050 to make bookings. The season lasts from September until June but the Bolshoi company (or some of its leading lights) is often abroad on tour. You can buy tickets at the theatre box office (open noon-3pm) or, in theory at least, from the *kassa* kiosks all over the city. In practice, the theatre is frequently sold out. You can either try to procure tickets through your hotel, or just turn up about an hour before the performance and buy from the touts who are invariably outside. In either case, expect to pay several times the face value of £5 to £15. Be warned that touts sometimes offload outdated tickets to hapless foreigners; check the date carefully.

Other theatres showing opera and ballet include the Stanislavsky and Nemirovich-Damchanko Musical Theatre at 17 Bolshaya Dmitrovka (tel

229 4250), and the Operetta Theatre along the street at number 6, which seats 2,000 and puts on classical and modern works.

For drama there is a wide selection of formal theatres showing works from Shakespeare to Gogol to Arthur Miller; among the more famous is the Maly theatre which has two houses, the major one close to the Bolshoi at Teatralnaya Ploshchad 1 (tel 924 4083) and its associated studio theatre at 60 Bolshaya Ordynka (tel 237 6420). To circumvent language problems the Obraztov Puppet Theatre, 3 Sadovo-Samotechnaya (tel 299 0904) has a world-famous troupe and puts on satirical shows as well as children's shows; the Moscow Puppet Theatre at 26 Spartakovskaya (261 2197) is mainly for children. There is also a Mime Theatre (Teatr Mimiki i Zhesta) at 41 Ismailovsky Blvd (tel 163 8150).

The Traveller's Yellow Pages to Moscow contains seating plans for the city's leading theatres, and comprehensive details about the others.

Cinemas. The weekly magazine *Kino Nedelya* ('Cinema Week') is on sale in every newspaper kiosk and lists all the current films that are showing. It also reviews new releases and gives information on how to get to the various cinemas (of which there are plenty). Kino Nedelya is in Russian, but the English-language press contains details of showings of Western movies. The two top venues for foreign films are the Americom House of Cinema in the Radisson Slavyanskaya Hotel (Metro to Kievskaya; tel 941 8386) and the Kinosentr na Krasnoy Presne at Druzhinnikovskaya 15 (Metro to Krasnopresnenskaya; tel 255 9237).

Circus. The Moscow State Circus is probably the best in the world, with 6,000 performers. The Old Circus is at 13 Tsvetnoi Boulevard (tel 200 6889) and the New Circus at 7 Vernadski Prospekt (tel 930 2815). In summer, a proper big top is set up in Ismailovski park.

NIGHTLIFE

Going clubbing in Moscow is not for beginners. Many of the city's clubs are run by and for the Mafia, and consequently prices are high and the clientele may not be the sort of people with whom you are inclined to mix.

The most prominent club is Night Flight at Tverskaya 17 (tel 299 4165), a Swedish-run establishment which has strict rules on dress (not casual) and age (men over 30, women over 21). Admission is around $30, with sky-high drink prices. Few of the women seem to pay for their drinks.

Further from the centre but cheaper is Lis's, in the Olympic Complex on Olympiski Prospekt (tel 288 4027). It occupies the gymnastics arena of the complex, and visiting the place is a bizarre experience — the club is surrounded by ten thousand empty chairs. The setting is rather like the National Exhibition Centre in Birmingham. Admission is $15, and you can expect a through search on the way in.

One of the few places where the occasional ordinary Muscovite turns up is the Bingo discoteque in one of the towers of the Ismailovo complex (tel 166 2001). Each Friday and Saturday is Latin night, when most of the city's Central and South American community (as well as a good number of Lebanese) turn up for beer, salsa and belly-dancing (as spectators).

SPORT AND RECREATION

As with belly-dancing, it is easier to be a sports spectator in Moscow than to participate, and there are 68 stadiums from which to make your choice.

The Lenin Stadium (Metro: Sportivnaya; tel 201 0955) accommodates over 100,000 spectators and is one of the largest sports centre in the world. You can watch football and athletics events in the summer, and ice hockey and figure skating in winter. But there are also facilities for every imaginable sport from fencing and boxing to badminton and tennis.

The second most prominent stadium is Dinamo, which stands in its own extensive grounds at 36 Leningradsky Prospekt (Metro: Dinamo; tel 212 7092). It stages football matches in the 55,000-capacity stadium, and has a large indoor swimming pool. The Olympic Sports Complex looks surprisingly shabby for a place which staged the Olympics less than 20 years ago. Its main stadium seats 45,000.

Swimming. A pool open to all is the Moscow City open-air pool at Prechistin-skaya 37 (Metro: Kropotkinskaya, tel 202 4725). This is a heated pool, open all year round, which opens early (6am) and closes at 10pm. You enter the pool indoors and then swim out through a tunnel into the open.

In summer you can swim in the Moskva river, at Serebryany Bor (Dinamo Beach, tel 199 4619) and Khimki reservoir. Boating is also available in these places as well as in Gorky Park. The Penta, Radisson Slavyanskaya, Rossiya and Kosmos hotels have heated indoor pools which are open to non-residents. Finally there is the Chaika pool, 1 Turchaninova pereulok (Metro: Park Kultury; tel 246 1354)

Horses. There is a riding school at the Bittsa Equestrian Complex, Balak-lavski Propckt 33 (Metro: Chertnovskaya; tel 318 0744).

The race course (*Hippodrom*) is at 22 Begovaya St (Metro: Begovaya, tel 945 4367 for information in English). Races begin at 6pm on Wednesdays and Fridays, and on Sundays at 1pm. At the Metelitsa Casino, you can bet on televised races from the UK.

Chess. The Central Chess Club is at 14 Gogolevsky Boulevard (Metro: Kropotkinskaya; tel 291 8595), but in summer you will see it played in parks everywhere.

Winter Sports. About 20 locations on the periphery of Moscow cater for cross-country skiers; consult the *Traveller's Yellow Pages* for full details. You will also see people skiing in Gorky Park in winter. Here the footpaths are flooded; they freeze overnight and turn into natural skating rinks.

Parks and Gardens. Moscow's parks and gardens play an integral part in the lives of Muscovites. In summer they are the scene of open-air theatres, concerts, carnivals and festivals while in winter they become a playground for skiers and skaters. Most are open from 10 am to 11 pm.

Gorky Central Park is the most central and the greatest. Forget the famous thriller by Martin Cruz-Smith; you are unlikely to be murdered in Gorky Park, but petty crime is not unknown. Gorky Park is the Russian equivalent to Hyde Park. In summer it hosts a huge fun-fair. Some rides are identical to those in the West, including a big wheel, carousels and a rifle range. There are concerts on most nights in summer with frequent pop concerts on Sunday nights.

Ismailovo Recreation Park (17 Narodny Prospekt, Metro: Ismailovsky Park) covers nearly 3,000 acres with large stretches of pine forest and was once the home of the Romanovs and a retreat of the Tzars. On most weekends a market is held around the old palace on the island with many little stalls selling paintings, prints, wooden carvings, jewellery, toys and puppets. Amusement park and open air theatre.

Sokolniki Park, ul Rusakovskaya 62 (Metro: Sokolniki). Sokolniki lives its name from Tsarist times when it was used for falcon hunting by the Tsars (the Russian name for falcon is *sokol*). In this park there are some well preserved churches and artifacts. The park is based around a Petrine estate, containing a reconstruction of Peter the Great's house is situated. If the weather is good you can swim in a nearby river. This is a very green and friendly park; horses and bicycles may be hired to explore its 1,500 acres.

Alexandrovsky Gardens (Metro: Prospekt Marksa). Laid out in 1820 on the bed of the Neglinnaya River running along the western wall of the Kremlin. The gardens were designed by the best gardeners in Russia and in December 1966 a monument was erected on the grave of an unknown soldier who fell defending Moscow against the Nazis in 1941. To the right of the grave are six urns holding soil from the six 'hero cities' of Odessa, Sevastopol, Volgograd, Kiev, Brest and Leningrad which so stubbornly resisted the German advance in the 'Great Patriotic War' of 1941-45.

To paraphrase an American marketing slogan, if you can't find it in Moscow you're better off without it. All the leading Western brands, from Benetton to Levi, have opened shops in the capital, while for more prosaic purchases there are thousands of kiosks selling anything from beer to pornography.

The four big department stores are: GUM, 3 Red Square; TsUM, 2 Petrovka Street (next to the Bolshoi Theatre); Detsky Mir (Children's World), 2 Prospekt Marksa; and Moskva Department Store, 54 Leninsky Prospekt. These are worth visiting for the spectacle of how the West has comprehensively taken over the Russian retail trade.

The main shopping street is Tverskaya, and its grandest shop is the Elyseevski (open 8am-9pm from Monday to Saturday and 8am-2pm on Sundays). The grandfather of the delicatessen, this Beaux Arts creation has been restored to its former Imperial glory.

Arbat Street is the main tourist haunt, but for standard souvenirs like Yeltsin dolls, head for Izmailovsky Park (metro station same name) on Sundays. The open-air market operates throughout the year, selling Red Army trinkets and rabbit-fur hats. Traditional hand-painted wood and ceramic souvenirs are usually not expensive, although often dismal quality.

For CDs and records, try Melodiya, at 24 New Arbat, while next-door-but-several is Dom Knigi (House of Books)

Around the Kuznetsky Most area there are many impromptu book markets where books can be swapped as well as bought. Contemporary Western books are highly valued. For a distinctive line in stationery try Shkolnik on Arbat, which sells a brand with pictures of the Kremlin on.

Markets. Since enterprise was liberated, these places have lost some of their attraction but are still worth seeing. Try Cheryomushkinsky Rynok, 1 Lomonosovsky Prospekt; Danilovsky Rynok, 78 Mytnaya St; Rizhsky Rynok, 94/96 Prospekt Mira; Tishinsky Rynok, 50 Bolshaya Gruzinskaya; Tsentralny (Central), 15 Tsvetnoy Blvd; and Yaroslavsky, 122 Prospekt Mira. Central market is the biggest and best known. Besides the farmers with their produce there will be people selling sweatshirts out of the back of lorries, lines of women looking for something to swap something else for, rabbit hats by the thousand and plenty of lads willing to lift your wallet.

Moscow is dangerous. The murder rate is around two per day. Although these are mostly underworld killings, the Foreign Office warns that 'incidents of mugging, theft and pickpocketing are increasing', and advises visitors to dress down.

The most dangerous areas are those heavily touristed — especially Arbat Street and the subways under New Arbat. Be particularly wary of gipsy children, who will often attack *en masse* in broad daylight.

The rapid expansion of Moscow in the last 50 years has seen the population double since 1945, with the result that many former historic villages and estates have now been submerged in modern suburbia. Some remain, and provide interesting oases of old Russia and a pleasant contrast to the overwhelmingly modern aspect of Moscow today.

Kolomenskoye Estate lies southeast of central Moscow, close to Kolomenskaya metro station. Its history goes back to the 14th century. It became the summer residence of the Moscow princes and later the tsars, including Ivan the Terrible and Peter the Great. Standing on the high bank of the river Moskva is the church of which Berlioz said 'Nothing has amazed me so much' — the beautiful Church of Ascension (1532) built in the old Russian tent style. Sct in a lovely park with 800-year-old oak trees is the famous museum of wooden architecture, including the log cabin in which Peter the Great lived in Arkhangelsk.

Kuskovo Estate and Ceramics Museum is about six miles/10km from Moscow but can easily be reached by train from Kursk Railway station or by metro to Ryazanskaya Prospekt and then bus number 208. The palace was built in the 18th century as a summer residence for the Prince Sheremetyev family, who at one time owned more than 200,000 serfs. It stands in magnificent grounds on the banks of a lake. The palace is often known as the Moscow Versailles, with its magnificent 18th-century buildings, orangery, grotto, etc. It is now a museum with an excellent collection of 18th century Russian paintings. The Ceramics Museum has a fine collection of glass, china and porcelain both Russian and from abroad.

Arkhangelskoye Estate is ten miles/16km west of Moscow on Volokolamsk Highway, along the road to Petrovo-Dalniye. The road to it passes through a beautiful forest of conifers, nut groves, and glades. The main complex was built in the 18th century by Prince Golitsyn; bought by the wealthy Yusupov it now houses his fabulous art collection and is surrounded by a splendid park, whose avenues are lined with statues and monuments.

Other trips worth considering would be to Zagorsk (75 miles/124km), the seat of the Russian Orthodox church and site of the 15th-century Trinity Cathedral, from Yaroslavsky Station; Peredelkino, about 15 minutes by train from Kievsky Station, a writers' village in typical Russian countryside and once the residence of Solzhenitsyn and Pasternak (who is buried there); Tver, 56 miles/89km out of Moscow on the St Petersburg highway, site of Tchaikovsky's house where he lived for nine years and an attractive old town; Borodino, 75 miles/124km from Moscow on the Minsk highway and the site of the famous battle of Borodino where Mikhail Kutuzov led the Russian army against Napoleon's troops; and finally Yasnaya Polyana Estate Museum, which lies south of Moscow along the Simferopolskoye Highway —

here Leo Tolstoy lived, worked and was eventually buried and his house has been kept just as it was during those 60 years.

 The closest you are likely to find to tourist information is the service desks at one of the more Western-oriented (i.e. expensive) Moscow hotels, or at the Travellers Guest House. There are free local telephones in these places, which at least means you can make your call in relative comfort without having to battle simultaneously with *jetons* and the Moscow climate.

EMBASSIES

UK: Sofiskaya Embankment (Nabreznaya) 14 (tel 230 6333 or 230 6555; fax 956 7420). Open Mon-Fri 9am-5pm, closed noon-12.30pm.
Canada: Starokonushenny Pereulok 23, tel 291-58-82, fax 291-44-00. Open Mon-Fri 9.30am-1pm, 2-6pm.
USA: Novinsky Blvd 19-23 (tel 252-24-51/59, fax: 956-42-61). Open 9am-1pm, 2-5pm.

EMERGENCY NUMBERS

Fire 01; Police 02; Ambulance 03; American Medical Centre, Shmitovsky Proyezd 3, tel: 256-82-12, 956-33-66

Medical and Dental Treatment: American Medical Center, 2nd Tverskoe-Yamskoi Pereulok 10, tel 956 3366 (Metro: Mayakovskaya). International Medical Clinic, 10th floor, Grokholsky Pereulok 31, tel 281 7138 or 280 8374 (Metro: Prospekt Mira).

24-hour Pharmacy: France Santé, ul Rudnevoy 4, tel 184 1663, 471 1442 (Metro: Babushkinskaya). Another is at Nikolskaya ul 19, tel 921-49-42.

Lost Property: in the metro: 222-20-85; in trams, trolleybuses or buses: 923-87-53

Lost Children: dial 401 9982, or the police on 02 if you are desperate.

Post. The most reliable place to post letters is at the Central Post Office on Tverskaya. If you want to guarantee delivery of anything (letters or parcels) in or out of the capital try DHL Worldwide, Chermshevskogog Pereulok 3 (tel 956-10-00) or RGW Express, Pogodinskaya ul 14/16 no.53 (tel: 245-52-45, 245-17-97)

St Petersburg

St Petersburg is the vision of one man, an emperor who decided to build a city on a bog at the edge of the Baltic Sea. In 1712, Peter the Great moved not only the entire imperial court but also the capital from the comfort of Moscow to this inhospitable northern outpost. St Petersburg now ranks among the world's most beautiful cities.

There has always been a lighthearted but none the less deep-felt rivalry between St Petersburg and Moscow. Petersburgers see themselves as more cultured, developed and European than 'backward' Muscovites; they refer to Moscow as 'the big village', which can bear no comparison with their own majestic city with its elegant palaces and wide boulevards.

St Petersburg is nearing the end of a turbulent 20th century, in which it has seen off Tsarism, Nazism and finally Marxism. On the surface, the city appears to be shrugging off its communist legacy, but behind the new Coca Cola sponsored road signs, you still find Lenin lurking, not least in the imagination of many of the inhabitants, for whom the city is still Leningrad. It is understandable if some of them feel confused: their city has been renamed three times so far this century: there are people alive today who were born in St Petersburg, educated in Petrograd, married in Leningrad and are now enjoying their twilight years once more in St Petersburg. In 1991, the local people voted overwhelmingly in favour of reverting to the original name.

The building of this city marked a fundamental change in Russian history. The traditional core of Russian settlement was to the south, around Moscow and Vladimir. With the economic development of western Europe, however, Russia's attention and trade turned increasingly westwards. The Baltic Sea became strategically vital to the Russian state, and Peter the Great founded the new capital in recognition of this new status. The city was constructed, mostly of stone, by serfs and Swedish prisoners-of-war labouring in appalling conditions and with horrific loss of life. The city was laid out in accordance with the latest theories on town planning, and strict regulations stipulated the height and architectural style of buildings. Once built, the city formed the Russian 'Window on Europe', and boosted trade through the Baltic. More than any other single event, the development of St Petersburg enabled Russia to become a major European power.

The new capital of the Russian Empire became associated with Western culture as well as trade. It became the cradle of Russian music, opera and ballet. Writers and poets such as Pushkin, Gogol, Turgenev and Dostoevsky lived and worked here. As Petrograd, the city was the major location for many of the events of the Russian Revolution, notably Lenin's return from Finland, and the firing of the gun on the cruiser *Aurora*, which marked the storming of the Winter Palace by the revolutionaries. Its position, however, made the city vulnerable to attack from the advancing counter-revolutionary armies. Accordingly, the capital was moved back to Moscow in 1918.

The Second World War was the darkest hour in the city's history. Leningrad was subjected to a 900-day siege by Nazi forces, in which around 650,000 civilians and soldiers died and much of the city was destroyed by enemy shelling. But the city was swiftly rebuilt, with priority given to restoring historical monuments. Fifty years on, St Petersburg is adapting to the changes which have swept across the whole of the former Soviet Union.

CLIMATE

St Petersburg's climate is notorious. Its location on a marshy bog just south of the Arctic Circle makes for bitterly cold winters and mosquito-infested summers, with year-round Baltic breezes to boot. Winter — when temperatures plummet to $-20°C/-4°F$ — is harsh, but the city looks absurdly beautiful covered in a thick layer of snow. Furthermore, the museums are virtually empty and tickets for the best ballet performances easily available. The early part of spring in March and April is miserable and damp as the snow thaws and turns to mud. Then, some time in mid-May, leaves appear overnight and everyone races to the nearest park to catch the first rays of summer. The city is at its most vibrant during the so-called 'White Nights' from mid-June to mid-July, when the sun never quite sets and the city is bathed in a delicate silvery twilight. Huge open-air concerts are staged on Yelagin Island during the annual festival which takes place in the last 10 days of June. Autumn is short and sweet. From September onwards, the days shrink rapidly until daylight is reduced to just six hours in December.

CITY LAYOUT

St Petersburg lies in the delta of the river Neva, occupying 44 islands and with over 60 rivers and canals crossed by 376 bridges. The easiest way to get your bearings is to think of the area south of the river as the mainland. This is where you'll find most of the city's famous landmarks as well as the modern commercial centre. The two best landmarks along this side of the river are the Admiralty, with its tall golden spire, and the gargantuan Winter Palace, overlooking Palace Square (Dvortsovaya ploshchad). The main drag, Nevsky Prospekt, runs from the Admiralty to the Alexander Nevsky monastery, 3 miles/5km southeast. All public transport and most people converge here, making it the crowded, dusty but lively hub of the city. The street is often referred to locally simply as 'Nevsky'.

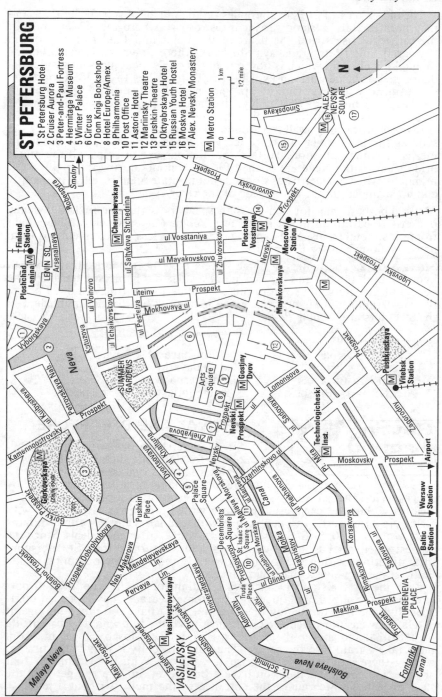

ST PETERSBURG

1 St Petersburg Hotel
2 Cruiser Aurora
3 Peter-and-Paul Fortress
4 Hermitage Museum
5 Winter Palace
6 Circus
7 Dom Knigi Bookshop
8 Hotel Europe/Amex
9 Philharmonia
10 Post Office
11 Astoria Hotel
12 Mariinsky Theatre
13 Pushkin Theatre
14 Oktyabrskaya Hotel
15 Russian Youth Hostel
16 Moskva Hotel
17 Alex. Nevsky Monastery

Ⓜ Metro Station

The oldest part of St Petersburg lies on the northern side of the river and incorporates Hare's Island (Zayachi Ostrov) — where the golden spire of the cathedral rises from the heart of the Peter and Paul fortress — and Petrograd Side (Petrogradskaya Storona), where Peter the Great intended to build his city and which is now one of the city's most pleasant residential districts. Vasilievsky Island (Vasilievsky Ostrov) lies to the west, opposite the Admiralty. Its easternmost tip, known as the Strelka or 'Spit', used to be the city's bustling port; today, the modern passenger sea terminal is located on its western flank, facing the Gulf of Finland.

A word of warning: walking around on summer nights can be tricky. As soon as the main river is free of ice, usually in early May, it is used as a means of communication. To facilitate the passage of ships, all the major bridges across the Neva are opened for a few hours during the night. After midnight, when the metro has stopped running, late night revellers frequently end up stranded on the wrong side of the river.

Maps. The best map for non-Russian speakers is the one included in the pocket-size edition of the St Petersburg *Yellow Pages*, which can be bought from most hotel shops. You can buy cheaper but less intelligible maps from hawkers along Nevsky Prospekt.

Street Names. The names of some streets have been changed. It is worth knowing both the old and the new names, since old habits die hard and the people of St Petersburg seem to prefer to stick to what they know. Four of the most important changes are given below, with a full list published in the St Petersburg *Yellow Pages*:

Old Name	New Name
ul Gertsena	ul Bolshaya Morskaya
ul Gogolya	ul Malaya Morskaya
ul Krasnaya	ul Galernaya
Kirovsky Prospekt	Kamennoostrovsky Prospekt

Getting Around

ARRIVAL AND DEPARTURE

Air. St Petersburg has two airports: Pulkovo 1 for domestic flights and Pulkovo 2 for international flights. Both lie about 12 miles/20km south of the city and are just a couple of miles apart, linked by a bus service. British Airways and Aeroflot each run a service from London Heathrow, but the cheapest flights are with Finnair via Helsinki or with Delta via Frankfurt. An open return with Finnair valid for three months costs around £250. SAS, Swissair and KLM also offer good deals. Since the domestic network has shrunk enormously, most journeys from St Petersburg to destinations within the former Soviet Union, with the exception of the Baltic states, involve a change in Moscow.

Both the Arrivals and Departures buildings of the international airport have been revamped, and queues for customs clearance have speeded up. If your flight arrives in the daytime and you don't have too much luggage, it is relatively easy to reach the city centre: take the bus which stops outside the terminal and goes to the nearest metro station, Moskovskaya, and from there take a train into the centre. The only difficulty is that at the time of writing there is no change office at the airport. Whilst it is unlikely that anyone will check whether you have a bus ticket, no one can get past the steel turnstiles which guard the entrance to the metro without a jeton —

which can only be bought for roubles. You can, however, get a taxi into town from Moskovskaya metro and pay in dollars; this should cost about $10. The other option (and the only option if your flight arrives late at night), is to take a taxi all the way, but this is likely to taint your first impression of Russia. However sharp your bargaining skills, the hard-nosed spivs who monopolise the airport run will still sting you for at least $30.

To reach the airport from the centre, you should get away with paying $15 or less if you go by taxi. Or take the bus from ulitsa Bolshaya Morskaya 18; this should run between 5.30am and 9pm, but check the timetable at the nearby Aeroflot offices. The addresses and telephone numbers of the main airline offices are as follows:

Aeroflot, Nevsky Prospekt 7 (104-3822).
Air France, Pulkovo-2 (104-3433).
British Airways, Nevsky Palace Hotel, Nevsky Prospekt 57 (119-6222).
Delta Airlines, Pulkovo-2, (104-3438).
Finnair, ul Malaya Morskaya 19 (315-9736).
KLM, Pulkovo-2 (104-3440).
Lot, Pulkovo-2 (104-3437).
Lufthansa, Voznesensky Prospekt 7 (314-4979).

You may find it easier to procure tickets through an agency such as Time Travel (tel 184 8282), which can also help with visas, accommodation and rail travel.

Rail. The main office for buying long-distance and international train tickets is at 24 Griboyedova Canal, on the left-hand side of Kazan Cathedral. It opens 8am-8pm Monday to Saturday, 8am-4pm on Sunday. Foreigners must go to the Intourist desks on the second floor. St Petersburg has five major rail termini. The name of each station is a good clue as to which destination it serves:

Moscow Station (Moscovsky Vokzal): for services to the Russian capital. The nearest metro is Mayakovskaya/Ploshchad Vosstanya. Trains to Moscow run several times a day, the journey taking 5 hours by day and 7-8 hours by night. The overnight Red Arrow service is popular among foreign travellers.
Baltic Station (Baltiysky Vokzal): for services to the southern outskirts and to Latvia, Lithuania and Estonia. The nearest metro is Baltiyskaya.
Warsaw Station (Varshavsky Vokzal): for services to Poland and northern Europe. The nearest metro is Baltiyskaya or Frunzenskaya.
Vitebsk Station (Vitebsky Vokzal): for services to the southwestern outskirts and to Belarus and Ukraine. The nearest metro is Pushkinskaya. The main hall is a beautiful example of the Style Moderne, and there is a model of the first Russian locomotive in a glass case by the platforms.
Finland Station (Finlandsky Vokzal): for services north of St Petersburg and to Helsinki in particular. The nearest metro is Ploshchad Lenina.

Bus. The two intercity bus terminals are located along the Obvodnovo Canal: one is just behind Warsaw Station, the other is further east, near Ligovsky Prospekt metro station.

Boat. Various Swedish companies operate regular services to and from Stockholm. Their ships moor at the main passenger terminal (Morskoy Vokzal), next to the floating Commodore Hotel on Sea Glory Square (Morskoy Slavy) on Vasilievsky Island. You can obtain further information and buy tickets for these crossings from an office on board the Commodore.

The River Port (Rechnoy Vokzal) is at Prospekt Obukhovskoi Oborony, near Lomonovskaya metro station. There are long-distance river services east to Lake Ladoga and south to Moscow and beyond. Most river cruises are expensive pre-booked packages, but if you want to join one once you are already in St Petersburg, contact Tatyana Tomnitskaya: her tour company, Russian Fair, has an office on the seventh floor of block Two of Hotel Pulkovskaya (tel 264-5870, fax 592-0245).

Road. The main approaches by road to St Petersburg are from Finland and Moscow. The road from the north runs into the centre along Primorsky and Kirovsky Prospekts, ending up at the Palace Embankment. The route from Moscow enters the city near Warsaw Station.

Car hire: you can rent cars from the Hotel Astoria (210-5858) and many of the other major hotels. The Hertz representative is Interavto, at Ipsolkom-skaya ul 9/11 (277-4032); Avis has an office at Konnogardeisky bulvar 4/34 (312-6318).

CITY TRANSPORT

St Petersburg's buses, trolleybuses, trams and metro are cheap to travel on but terrifyingly overcrowded. Whichever you use, stops are few and far between, so be prepared for lots of walking.

If you arrive at the very end or beginning of a month and intend to stay for a week or more, it is worth investing in a Yedni card, which is valid for all forms of city transport for one month and costs the rouble equivalent of $10 (1994). Otherwise, the standard ticket for a metro journey comes in the form of a metal jeton, which doubles as a phone token. Should you attempt to walk through the barriers without paying, you will face corporal punishment in the form of a painful prong delivered by a metal bar torpedoed at knee level. For other forms of transport, paper tickets can be bought from the driver; these come in strips of 10 called *talon* and need to be punched to be valid. Undercover agents of the Ministry of Transport cruise the buses and trams in search of law-infringing passengers. The humiliation apart, the fines are no longer negligible.

Metro. The metro is the easiest and most efficient way to travel around the city. Trains run from 5.30am to midnight and arrive on average every two minutes. Due to St Petersburg's marshy terrain, the metro had to be built extremely deep, so you're liable to spend more time travelling up and down the escalators than on the trains themselves. Monotone advertisements boom out of invisible speakers in 'Big Brother' style.

Travelling on the metro is easy since the network is made up of only four lines, but there is some scope for confusion. Where two lines intersect, for example, the stop will bear two names, one for the station on each line. At a link station, follow the *perekhod* signs to join the other line. Technologichesky Institut is an exception to the rule, since it is a link station with only one name, but this makes it twice as confusing. Here, you need to check the signs along the platforms and listen out for the announcements; be especially wary after 10pm, when for mysterious reasons a train which has so far been travelling on the blue line may decide to switch over to the red line. Your best bet will be to ask for advice from a fellow passenger.

All the stations on the green line have closed platforms with sliding doors which open only when the train pulls into the station. Note also that during the rush hour (4-5.30pm), the entrance to Nevsky Prospekt station is locked, so you have to go through Gostiny Dvor station to reach the blue line.

On the whole, St Petersburg's metro stations are not as impressive as Moscow's, but a few are worth a special detour. Vladimirskaya has a mosaic depicting strapping Soviet peasants celebrating a plentiful harvest and Ploshchad Lenina a huge mosaic of Lenin. Mayakovskaya station, named after the futurist painter Mayakovsky, is suitably loud and glaring: an oppressive vermillion red mosaic covers every inch of wall around the platform area.

Buses, trolleybuses and trams. In the city centre you are most likely to use trolleybuses, especially along Nevsky Prospekt. Useful trolleybuses include number 5, which goes from Smolny to St Isaacs' Square, and 1, 7 and 10, which run between Vasilievsky Island and Nevsky Prospekt.

Taxis. As in most cities of the former Soviet Union, taxis in St Petersburg come in two varieties. The real thing, usually a Volga with a sign on the roof, cruises around tourist areas and is likely to be a rip-off; the driver will usually quote a price in dollars. The other type of taxi, more often than not a Lada, is just a private car whose driver will probably (though not always) set a lower price than a regular taxi. If drivers just tell you to get in and sit down, give what you think is appropriate: $2 is fine for a short distance in the city centre during the day.

Water Transport. This is one of the most pleasant ways of travelling around the city, since the dust and dirt of street level are not visible from the canals. Boats run only for a short season, however, from the beginning of May to mid-September, as the waterways are frozen over for much of the year.

The cheapest way to cruise the waters is to join a tour on one of the long river boats: trips along the canals depart from Anichkov Bridge (where Nevsky Prospekt crosses the Fontanka); trips along the Neva depart from the pier at Decembrists' Square (Ploshchad Dekabristov) or from the pier opposite the Hermitage. The cost is about $1 per person. In both cases there is a non-stop commentary in Russian, which is tedious even if you understand it. For a more relaxing experience, hire your own boat and boatman for $20-50 per hour from the Anichkov Bridge or the Green Bridge (over the Moika Canal). Some boats take up to ten people, and you can devise your own itinerary.

Hotels. The hotel situation has improved slightly in the last few years, but for the most part you'll still have to pay way over the odds for mediocre service in a mediocre location. If money is no object, you may consider one of the three luxury hotels in the centre — the Astoria, the Nevsky Palace or the Europa — which charge $200-plus for a double room. Even those on a low budget become frequent visitors to these hotels, if only to take advantage of the exchange facilities and clean toilets.

The next category of hotels in order of price is that of the 'botel'. Baffling though it is, many tourists seem quite happy to pay in excess of $100 for a cabin on a geriatric ocean liner moored far from the city centre. You pay about the same to stay in one of the middle-range hotels housed in astoundingly ugly 70s high-rise blocks. At the bottom end of the scale, you can find a room for as little as $10 — albeit with shared bathroom and dodgy plumbing, but often in a more central location. There is also the recently opened Russian Youth Hostel.

Whichever hotel or price appeals, it is worth booking in advance, especially if you will be travelling between May and September.

Top range:

Astoria, ul Bolshaya Morskaya 39 (tel 210-5032, fax 315-9668). Fully renovated, the Astoria occupies the best location in town, right on St Isaacs'
Square. Doubles go for $210.
Europa, ul Mikhailovskaya 1/7 (tel 196-000, fax 119-6001). If you can make
it past the armed thugs at the door, this Swedish joint venture is very
luxurious and priced accordingly. Doubles start at $345 without breakfast.
Nevsky Palace Hotel, Nevsky Prospekt 57 (tel 275-2001, fax 850-1501). A
glitzy Austrian joint venture, with all the comforts you'd expect but no
charm. Its best feature is the Café Vienne on the ground floor. The
cheapest double costs $255.

Middle range:

Commodore, Morskoy Slavy on Vasilievsky Island (tel 119-6666, fax 119-
6667). With its tacky floorshow and American hamburgers, the Commodore boasts all the dubious delights of a former Carribean cruiser, though
the location is anything but tropical. It does, however, have a cinema,
which shows films in English every night at 7pm. Single rooms cost $110.
Hotelship Peterhof, moored by nab. Makarova on Vasilievsky Island (tel
213-6321, fax 213-3158). A Swiss botel with a double cabin for $190.
Moskva, 2 Ploshchad Alexandra Nevskovo (tel 274-2115, fax 274-2130).
Bad plumbing and cockroaches are an aggravation, but its location at the
end of Nevsky Prospekt is an advantage. Double rooms available for $87
upwards.
Olympia, moored at Morskoy Slavy (tel 119-6800, fax 119-6805). This is an
unattractive apartment complex perched on the hulk of a ferry. Pool
tables, Mexican food and a free shuttlebus to the centre provide some
consolation for the setting. A double will set you back $175.
Okhtinskaya, 4 Bolsheokhtinsky Prospekt (tel 227-3767, fax 227-2618). This
new French joint-venture hotel has good bathrooms, but the location
across the Neva from Smolny Convent is awkward for public transport.
Doubles cost from $95.
Pribaltiiskaya, ul Korablestroitely, Vasilievsky Island (tel 356-0263, fax 356-
0094). A huge Swedish-built hotel with good facilities, including saunas,
but the location on the Gulf of Finland is dismal as far as public transport
is concerned, and you'll end up spending a fortune on taxis. Doubles
cost $110.
St Petersburg Hotel, nab. Vyborgskaya 5/2 (tel 542-9411, fax 248-8002).
Some of the rooms have wonderful views over the river and the battleship
Aurora, but the location is not all that central. Doubles for $95.

Cheap range:

Oktyabrskaya, Ligovsky Prospekt 10 (277-6330). This hotel is rather shabby
but very well situated, just two minutes' walk from Moscow Railway
Station. It is an old-style establishment and foreigners are still eyed with
some suspicion, but the clean rooms are among the cheapest in town at
$30 for a double or a triple. Stay here while you can: rumours suggest
that it is to be turned into a Holiday Inn.
Nauka, ul Millionaya 27 (315-8696). Ulitsa Millionaya ('Millionaires'
Street'), which runs parallel to the embankment of the Neva, was the most
prestigious Petersburg address in tsarist times because of its vicinity to
the Winter Palace. Sadly, the building which houses the Nauka Hotel is
a dilapidated affair with hesitant supplies of hot water. But the rooms,

while basic, are excellent value at $10 for a double. It is best to reserve in advance.

Russian Youth Hostel, ul 3ya Sovietskaya 28 (tel 277-0569, fax 277-5102). Very central, close to metro Ploshchad Vosstanya, this hotel is a good option for short-term visitors. The rooms for two or three people are basic but bright and clean, and there is a kitchen too. The English-speaking staff are very friendly and can help with visas. The 1am curfew may put some people off. The hostel charges $15 per person.

St Petersburg Travel, 196 High Road, London N22 4HH (tel/fax 0171-249 7503) can arrange B&B with Russian families in advance.

Private Accommodation. Prices for staying in a rented flat or with a family vary a lot, depending on location and the length of stay, but this remains the cheapest option. In summer, travellers arriving by train — especially at Moscow Station — will see baboushkas and a few younger touts holding up notices offering a room. Bargaining usually opens at around $5 per person per night. There are also several agencies which can organise private accommodation for you. Try to book at least two weeks in advance and request the area you want.

Elpis, ul Kronverskaya 27 (tel 232-9838, fax 352-2688). Prices per person range from $10 basic to $25 for full board. The can also organise visas and transport from the airport.

Host Families Association, Flat 5, ul Tavricheskaya 5 (tel/fax 275-1992). Similar service to the above but more expensive: $25 per person for bed and breakfast, $40 for full board.

Campsites and Motels. The closest campsites are more than 10 miles/16km from the city, on the road to Finland, and are not very salubrious. The Olgino Campsite and Motel at Primorskoe Shosse 18km (tel 238-3552) charges from $7 per person. The Retur site at Primorskoe Shosse 29km (tel 237-7553, fax 273-9783) has two-room cottages on the Gulf of Finland.

Eating and Drinking

Whilst the choice has improved with the opening of new restaurants, it is becoming harder to find a reasonably-priced meal: the latest eateries tend to cater for the wallets of wealthy foreign businessmen and their even richer local counterparts. The only bargains are to be found in cafés, the best being those which serve Georgian or Central Asian food. The distinction between cafés and restaurants in the following listings is as follows: places listed under *Restaurants* are more expensive, more formal and stay open late; those listed under *Cafés* are cheaper and often close early.

For a city with a very high consumption of alcohol, St Petersburg has a surprising dearth of places to drink. It is only during the shortlived summer period, when outdoor cafés are set up on the pavements, that you'll catch ordinary Petersburgers having a beer with friends. Most of the bars which do exist, cater for the new rich, but there are also a handful of more down-to-earth places: these generally double up as music clubs, so see also the listings under *Entertainment: Live Music and Clubs.*

Ice cream (*marozhna*) is one of the joys of Russia, at any time of year. The creamy Russian variety available from street vendors all along Nevsky. But if you want a greater choice of flavours, you may be lured to Gino Ginelli's, an Italian ice cream parlour on Griboyeova Canal, or Baskin Robbins at Nevsky 79.

Restaurants. Reservations are not usually necessary unless you require a table for a large party. Unless it is stated otherwise, all restaurants listed below are within walking distance of Nevsky Prospekt metro station.

Bistrot, Nevsky Prospekt 40. Also known as Nevsky 40, the Bistrot serves filling — though not particularly inspired — international dishes such as lasagne. Main courses cost about $7.

Literary Café and Restaurant, Nevsky Prospekt 18. The café where Pushkin allegedly drank his last coffee before fighting his fatal duel is very elegant, with art nouveau light fittings and a string quartet. But it caters exclusively to tourists and prices are accordingly high: $15 minimum for lunch.

Sadkos, Hotel Europa ul. Mikhailovskaya. The cheapest of the Europa's many restaurants, with pub-style food priced at $5-10, Sadkos is good if you are craving pizza or feel hungry late at night (it stays open till 1am).

Senate Restaurant and Bar, ul Galernaya 1 (314-9253), accessible on trol-leybus 5 from Nevsky. The magnetic attraction of the Senate lies in its mouth-watering selection of main courses (which, given the portions, are reasonably priced at $15) and its choice of 60 different beers, mainly from Belgium. But it is an unashamedly slick place, with tacky empire-style décor and almost as many mobile phones as customers. The system for paying is also highly innovative: at the entrance you are issued with a card on which your bill is totted up, and then you pay as you leave. If however you lose your card, you are supposed to fork out $100 — so depending on your own and your companions' capacity for Belgian beer, a little loss could be profitable. Most credit cards are accepted.

Sirin Bar, 16 First Line, Vasilievsky Island (213-7282); metro Vasileostrov-skaya. A hearty Russian meal will set you back $5-10 in this tiny basement restaurant. The dark décor and telephones at every table make it the ideal venue to live out cold war spy fantasies.

Tandoor, on the corner of Admiralteysky and Voznesensky Prospekts (312-3886). Both the food and service at this authentic Indian restaurant are superb. If the prices (about $4 for a main course) remain as reasonable as they are now, it stands to become one of the most popular places in St Petersburg.

Cafés. With its illustrious literary ancestry, large student population and cold climate, St Petersburg should be home to a thriving café society, but sadly there isn't one. Most of the places listed here serve cheap tasty fare but are not sufficiently comfortable to make you linger for long.

Art Club, Griboyedova Canal 3; metro Nevsky Prospekt. By day this spacious club (see *Entertainment*) turns into a quiet café where you can read undisturbed for hours.

Baghdad, ul Furstadtskaya 35; metro Chernyshevskaya. Located in the heart of embassy land, this cosy basement is a good place to sample *plov* (an Uzbeky mutton dish) between obtaining visas or replacing a lost passport.

Cafè, ul Galernaya 3, just off Decembrists' Square. A small café with a warm, folksy interior. The hearty Russian fare is tasty and good value. Open 11am-8pm.

Cafè, on Moika Canal, around the corner from the Literary Café; if you walk past number 57, you'll know you've overshot it. When the bustle of Nevsky gets too much, this is a wonderful haven. It serves delicious ice cream in summer and shots of vodka to warm you in winter. Caviar is available any time.

Cafè 01, ul Caravannaya 1; metro Gostiny Dvor. A popular café serving typical Russian fare at reassuringly Russian prices.

Cafè Vienne, Nevsky 57, on the ground floor of the Nevsky Palace Hotel. Frothy hot chocolate, delectable cream cakes and a choice of foreign newspapers make the Vienne a thoroughly enjoyable, albeit expensive, place to shelter from the cold in winter.

Dom Uchonikh, Dvortsovaya nab 26. To get there, walk down the embankment from the Winter Palace and past the Hermitage theatre until you reach a large 19th-century building with a porch surmounted by a pair of griffins. Now the House of Scientists, this was once the residence of Grand Prince Vladimir and the scene of many a decadent party; the Prince's daughter, Elena, apparently once served herself up naked on a giant fish dish to a room full of Guards Officers. The scientists who now occupy the building are a rather more demure lot, and are often to be found chatting in their cosy café overlooking the Neva. This is not officially open to the public but no one seems to mind if you sit there enjoying the view.

Don Quixote, nab Reki Fontanki 23 (inside the House of Friendship); metro Gostiny Dvor. Despite the name and décor featuring Don and Sancho, there is nothing Spanish about this café apart from the accent of the Cuban waitress. The menu is uninspiring, but the wonderful views over the Fontanka and its central location make this an ideal spot to pause for coffee or read a newspaper between sightseeing. No smoking. Open 10am-10pm.

Falafel Bar, Griboyedova Canal: look out for a hole in the wall or a line of people just to the left of Kazan Cathedral. This place keeps erratic opening hours but is worth seeking out for the delicious and very cheap falafels.

Metekhi, ul Belinskovo 3; metro Gostiny Dvor. Tucked down a side street that links Liteiny to the Fontanka, Metekhi serves delicious Georgian specialities such as *satsivi* (chicken in a creamy garlic and walnut sauce) while barely making a dent in your pocket. Open 11am-7pm every day.

Russky Bliny, ul Furmanova 13; Chernyshevskaya is the nearest metro station, but is still not particularly close. Russky Bliny serves just that, Russian pancakes, in comfortable surroundings. A good place for brunch.

St Petersburg Cafè, Griboyedova Canal 7. It is often crowded in the evenings with the hungry overflow from the Art Club next door, but serves tasty food at reasonable prices. Open 3-11pm and noon-11pm at weekends.

Buying Food. If you're cooking for yourself, the best place to stock up on fresh produce is at one of the farmers' markets, where goods are flown in from the Caucasus and Central Asia ensuring an astounding year-round selection of delicious fruits and vegetables as well as cheeses, sausages and every herb imaginable — albeit at prices well beyond the reach of the average Russian. The largest of these markets is Kusnechny Rynok, right next to Vladimirskaya metro station. Vasileostrovsky Rynok on Bolshoi Prospekt (Vasilievsky Island) is another good one.

Searching for other foods can be a frustrating business, and you'll probably end up using the import shops, which are springing up around the city. Most of their wares come from Scandinavia and are ludicrously expensive. There are a few Western supermarkets on or just off Nevsky. The best of these are the one in the basement of the Passazh arcade (Gostiny Dvor metro) and a 24-hour supermarket on Ploshchad Vosstanya, convenient for last-minute supplies before boarding the Moscow train. Stockman, at Finlandsky Prospekt 1 (metro Ploshchad Lenina), is the largest Western supermarket but less convenient.

Being a tourist in St Petersburg can be daunting. All the main sights are concentrated in the historic centre, but this in itself is a vast area: go prepared for plenty of walking. In the first section below, the main sights have been grouped by area into five walking tours; a reasonable day's sightseeing would include just one or two of these. Sights which are out on a limb and other museums are dealt with individually afterwards.

WALK 1: Petrograd Side and Hare Island

Hare Island (Zayachi Ostrov), a tiny hexagon of land across the water from the Hermitage, and adjacent Petrograd Side (Petrogradskaya Storona) together comprise the oldest part of the city. This itinerary takes you from the most famous landmark of the October Revolution, the battleship *Aurora*, to the Peter and Paul fortress. The easiest way to reach the *Aurora* is to walk down to the river from Gorkovskaya metro and then follow the embankment for about 15 minutes. Alternatively, take tram 25 from Liteiny Prospekt.

Not all that big, and absurdly shiny for a 90-year old battleship, the **Aurora** looks more like an oversize toy than a powerful war machine. Launched on 11 May 1903, it was first used during the Russo-Japanese War of 1904-5. But its enduring fame dates from 25 October 1917 when, following Lenin's order, its cannon was fired as the signal for the storming of the Winter Palace. Until recent events marred its symbolic importance, this shrine was a compulsory stop on all Intourist tours and a rallying point for the young pioneers. Nowadays, Petersburgers cynically remark that it was the most powerful weapon in history: one blank shot leading to 74 years of communism. There is a small museum on board, which displays documents and relics from the ship's history.

Walking back along the embankment towards the Peter and Paul fortress, you will reach a tiny house dwarfed by the surrounding 20th-century sprawl. The brick walls are a protective shell for the earliest surviving wooden structure in the city, built in May 1703 as a home for Peter the Great while he supervised the construction of the neighbouring fortress. Though there is little to see inside, local inhabitants flock here to pay homage to their city's founder. From the embankment just below the cottage there are sweeping views of the city, stretching from the blue and white Smolny cathedral on the far left to the bulbous gold dome of St Isaac's over on the right.

A little further north you reach **Trinity Square** (Troitskaya ploshchad), which has reverted to its original name having been known for almost half a century as Revolution Square. This is the oldest square in the city, where public executions and festive occasions were held in the time of Peter the Great. It is a large, ungainly space and there would be little reason to linger were it not for the museum at ulitsa Kuibysheva 4 in the northeastern corner. The building, typical of the Style Moderne — St Petersburg's version of the Art Nouveau style — first belonged to the ballerina Mathilda Kschessinkaya, whose affair with Nicholas II caused much scandal at the beginning of the century. In 1917, the Bolsheviks turned the building into their headquarters for a few months and later deemed it a suitable venue for the Museum of the Great October Revolution. This museum has been replaced by the **Museum of Russian Political History**, which is a confusing hotch potch of semi-permanent exhibitions, each requiring a separate ticket. On the ground floor, the 'Democracy or Dictatorship' exhibition attempts to give an unbiassed appraisal of 20th-century Russian politics from Lenin onwards. Unfortunately, the labelling is in Russian only and English-speaking guides are thin on the ground.

If you are short of time, head straight to the excellent **Wax Museum**, which is at the back of the building and accessible via the basement. It was set up as a cooperative project by the artists who made the wax figures, and is simply excellent English-speaking guides are normally available at little or no extra cost and are essential for making the most of the displays. The theme is 'Terror or Democracy', with figures of terrorists and their victims set up in chronological order. Dim lighting and the guides' penchant for whispering in conspiratorial tones add to the atmosphere. All the early revolutionaries, such as Dostoevsky and Tolstoy, are dashing Byronic types with long hair and sincere expressions, but as the exhibition moves into the 20th century, romanticising gives way to the need to rewrite history. Lenin looks decidedly creepy and it's hard to know what to make of Stalin and Khrushchev: the former looks like a tin-pot dictator and the latter is portrayed as a benevolent old man, in a white suit and holding a panama hat. The final figure is of Boris Yeltsin, who points the way forward in a pose immediately reminiscent of that of Lenin.

Behind the museum, you can glimpse two minarets which belong to the St Petersburg mosque, built in 1914 in the style of Tamerlane's mausoleum in Samarkand. Cross Kamennoostrovsky Prospekt and you'll reach a small bridge at the southern tip of Lenin Park; this links Petrogradskaya to Hare Island.

The **Peter and Paul Fortress** (Petropavlovskaya Krepost), which covers almost the entire island, is as old as the city itself: St Petersburg was officially founded when work began here in May 1703. Built with the help of forced labour, it was intended to protect the land that Peter the Great had regained from the Swedes. But as the intruders never returned, the fortress was converted into a prison. The first inmate was Tsarevitch Alexei, imprisoned by his own father for not supporting his reforms; he subsequently died in mysterious circumstances, allegedly strangled by Peter himself. In the 19th century, many Decembrists and revolutionaries were imprisoned here, including Dostoevsky.

Since 1924 the fortress has been a museum. It is open at all times and you can wander freely within its walls, though you must pay to visit the cathedral, prison and mint. The main entrance, St Peter's Gate, is a beautifully ornamented arch bearing a large two-headed eagle — the emblem of Imperial Russia. At the heart of the fortress stands the **Cathedral**, built by Domenico Trezzini and consecrated in 1733. Its golden spire, which was wrapped in black canvas to protect it from enemy bombing during World War II, was the highest point in the city until the Television Tower was built in the 60s. The interior has recently been renovated, and the sugar pink and mint green paint seems rather gaudy in what is principally a mausoleum. All the tsars and tsarinas of Russia since Peter the Great — with the exception of Peter II, Ivan VI and Nicholas II — are buried here. The plain white marble tombs belong to nobility and those adorned with a double-headed eagle belong to members of the imperial family. Peter the Great lies to the right of the iconostasis. His tomb, easily recognisable with its array of military medals and surmounted by a bust of the man himself, is often strewn with fresh flowers. His wife Catherine and daughter Elizabeth are close by, while Catherine the Great is in the row behind. The only two coloured tombs, made of green jasper and pink rodena, belong to Alexander II and his wife, who were canonised by the Russian Orthodox church following the Tsar's assassination in 1881. Since Nicholas II and his family were unearthed in Ekaterinburg it has been decided to bury them here, but no date has yet been set.

Southwest of the cathedral is the Commandant's House, where revolutionaries were tried during the 19th century, and just beyond it the Mint (Monetny Dvor), which Peter the Great transferred from Moscow in 1724. From 1876 this was the only place where Russian coins were made. A cannon is fired every day at noon from the Naryashkin Bastion nearby. This old tradition used to signal the time for the tsar's lunch but was later appropriated by the communists, who claimed the daily explosion was a commemoration of the shot fired from the *Aurora*. Walking eastwards, you reach the popular Peter and Paul beach, to which Petersburgers flock at the first sign of sun: standing up with your back propped against the wall seems to be the favoured sunbathing position. In winter, members of a local swimming club, known as the Walruses, hack through the ice to take their daily dip. The views across the Neva from here are excellent, but for an even more sweeping perspective head to the roofs of the fortress, accessible via ladders — though this is not recommended in windy conditions.

The large horse-shoe shaped building north of Hare Island, across the Kronverk Ditch, is the **Artillery Museum** (Artilleriysky Muzey). This is great for teenage boys or anyone else with a passion for weaponry. Exhibits include Lenin's armoured car, which once graced the entrance to the now defunct Lenin museum. Next door is St Petersburg Zoo, a depressing place with wretched-looking animals living in cramped conditions. From here you can continue to Vasilievsky Island across Birshevoy Bridge or head back to Gorkovskaya metro through Lenin Park.

Opening times:

Battleship Aurora Museum, Petrogradskaya nab. Open 10.30am-4pm daily except Monday and Friday.

Peter the Great's Cottage (Domik Petra), Petrogradskaya nab. Open 10am-5pm daily except Tuesday and the last Monday of the month.

Museum of Political History, ul Kuibysheva 4. Open 10am-6pm daily except Thursday. The Wax Museum opens 10am-7pm every day.

Peter and Paul Cathedral. Open daily 10am-5.40pm, except on Tuesday when it closes at 4.40pm.
Museum of Artillery, Alexandrovsky Park 7. Open 11am-6pm daily except Monday, Tuesday and the last Thursday of the month.

WALK 2: Vasilievsky Island

Like Hare Island and Petrogradskaya, Vasilievsky Island (Vasilievsky Ostrov) was one of the earliest parts of the city to be settled. The following itinerary takes you from the Strelka, or Spit, to the Academy of Arts along the embankment of the Neva. If you're approaching from the Peter and Paul fortress, simply cross the Kronverk ditch and then the Birshevoy Bridge which leads straight to the Strelka. If you take a trolleybus from Nevsky (numbers 1, 7 or 10), alight at the first stop after you've crossed the Neva. The nearest metro station is Vasileostrovskaya.

Apart from its three main arteries, named literally Big Street, Middle Street and Little Street (Bolshoi Prospekt, Sredny Prospekt and Maly Prospekt respectively), virtually all of Vasilievsky's streets are referred to as numbered 'lines' or *liniyi* (*linia* singular). This strange system is the result of a grandiose urban plan that went wrong. When Peter decided to develop the island as the focus of his new capital, he ordered engineers to plan numerous canals so that all the houses would face water. The work was carried out in the emperor's absence, however, and the streets turned out too narrow to accommodate canals along the middle. But their names stuck, so each street has two numbers, one for either bank of the canal that was never dug.

The most interesting sights are concentrated along the embankment of the Neva and around the **Strelka**, a narrow promontory that juts out on the eastern side of the island, providing a fine vantage point for a panoramic view. This is a popular spot among newlyweds, who come to the Strelka to take photos, swig champagne and throw the empty bottles into the Neva for luck. The city's merchant seaport was located here until 1865. Its most important barometer was the Stock Exchange (Birzha), housed in the huge neoclassical building which was built 1804-10 and reigns over the whole area. Now that the merchant sailors have taken their trade elsewhere, the granite block has been given over to the Central Naval Museum, which documents the history of the Russian fleet. The two red Rostral Columns — which derive their name from the 'rostra' or prows imbedded in their flanks — have also been made redundant. In the good old days, the copper bowls on the top of the columns were filled with oil and burned as torches to direct ships into the port. Now, they can be seen in their full glory only on national holidays.

University Embankment (Universitetskaya Naberezhnaya), which runs west from the Strelka, has the greatest concentration of academic buildings in the city. The pretty blue and white baroque **Kunstkammer**, or Chamber of Arts, was built to house the Academy of Sciences and Russia's first museum. The scientists outgrew the premises and were relocated to the adjacent neoclassical building, which is considered the finest work of Italian architect, Giacomo Quarenghi. The Kunstkammer now houses the Museum of Anthropology and Ethnography, which includes Peter's private collection of oddities. Pots and pans, tools and totem poles and assorted bric a brac from every corner of the world fill glass cabinets on two floors. The main attraction, as proven by the hordes of schoolchildren who crowd into the circular observatory, is the display of deformed foetuses in jars which share shelf space with a stuffed two-headed calf. The original anatomical collection was much larger and visitors used to be given a shot of vodka as they entered the museum to prepare them for the horrors ahead.

On the other side of Mendeleevskaya linia, named after the chemist who invented the periodic table, the main façade of the **University** stretches out at right angles to the river. The building known as the Twelve Colleges was the administrative centre of the Russian Empire during the reign of Peter the Great. The story goes that in the original plans such an illustrious building was naturally designed to face the water, but that Alexander Menshikov (Peter's right-hand man) switched the drawings around in order to leave more room for his own palace. In 1819, it became the main building of St Petersburg University. Famous alumni include Pavlov, Mendeleev and Lenin himself. Today the university is considered one of the best in Russia and has over 20,000 students.

Around the corner, at Universitetskaya nab 15, is **Menshikov's Palace** (Dvorets Menshikova). The residence of the Governor General of St Petersburg, whose astounding career elevated him from humble beginnings to the position of second in command of the Russian Empire, was even more grandiose than Peter's own. The rooms, which have been restored to their 18th-century appearance, betray a strong Dutch influence, with blue and white tiled stoves and cosy wood panelling. Most sumptuous of all is the glittering gold ballroom overlooking the Neva.

One block west is the **Academy of Arts**, the world's largest art school. It was founded in 1757 and many famous Russian artists, including Repin, Klodt and Shishkin, studied here. Works by former students are exhibited in a small museum on the first floor. The rest of the building is divided into studios and lecture halls. If you're here at the beginning of May, you can see the students' annual show. The two sphinxes which sit in front of the Academy and were brought from Egypt in the 1830s are said to be over 3,000 years old.

From here you can hop on a trolleybus to return to the centre of town.

Opening times:

Kunstkammer (Museum of Anthropology and Ethnography), Tamozhenny pereulok 1. Open 11am-5pm daily except Friday and Saturday.
Menshikov Palace, Universitetskaya nab 15. Open 10.30am-4.30pm daily except Monday.
Academy of Arts Museum, Universitetskaya nab 17. Open 11am-7pm daily except Monday and Tuesday.

WALK 3: Nevsky Prospekt

Nevsky Prospekt is St Petersburg's main artery through which all the energy of the city is channelled. This is the place to come to shop, sightsee or have your pocket picked. The road runs for an exhausting 3 miles/4.5km, linking two points on the Neva across a huge loop in the river. This itinerary covers only the stretch from the Admiralty to the Fontanka, where the oldest and most interesting buildings are clustered.

Founded in 1704 as a shipyard, the **Admiralty** has undergone several facelifts before settling for its present appearance as designed by Andreyan Zakharov in 1823. The yellow and white edifice, which stretches from the far corner of Nevsky all the way to Decembrists' Square, is considered a masterpiece of Russian neoclassical architecture and has been included on

UNESCO's list of World Heritage sites. The needle sharp golden spire is crowned with a three-masted frigate which has become the emblem of the city — as featured on the new roadsigns sponsored by Coca Cola. The Admiralty now houses a Naval School whose pupils guard the entrance.

Across Nevsky from the Admiralty is **Palace Square** (Dvortsovaya ploshchad), the setting of many important events leading up to the Revolution. Most notable was Bloody Sunday in 1905: at least 1,000 people were killed when the Imperial Guard fired on protesters who had gathered to hand a petition to the Tsar. Today, official processions such as the Victory Parade on 9 May end up here, with much flag-waving and chanting. On ordinary days, the square is simply an immense empty space, where even 20 or so Intourist buses fail to have much impact.

The huge green and white building featured in so many travel brochures is the **Winter Palace** (Zimny Dvorets), designed by Bartolomeo Rastrelli in 1754. It was the chief residence of the tsars until 1917 and now houses the Hermitage Museum (see *Museums* below). The former General Staff Building opposite, designed by Carlo Rossi in 1919, provides a calm contrast to Rastrelli's baroque excesses. In the centre of the square stands the Alexander Column, built to commemorate the defeat of Napoleon in 1812 and named in honour of Alexander I, during whose reign the French Emperor was routed from the Russian Empire. At 156 ft/47.5m, it is the world's highest monolithic column and a remarkable feat of engineering: nothing holds it onto the pedestal except its own weight.

Leave the square through the splendid arch which links the two wings of the General Staff Building and is surmounted by a sculpture of Winged Glory in her chariot, also built to commemorate the victory over Napoleon. You will emerge on Nevsky Prospekt. Heading east across the Moyka Canal, the large green and white palace on the right was built by Rastrelli for the Stroganoff family — whose chef invented the famous beef stew and whose coat of arms can still be seen in the fine stucco work. A little further down on the left, statues of the saints Peter and Paul stand before the **Lutheran Church**, which is an example of the creative use made by the communists of confiscated sacred ground. Whilst the exterior was left untouched, the inside was turned into a diving pool. The church has been given back to the Lutherans, but insufficient funds have so far delayed restoration. The diving boards and stadium seating are still in place, and the now empty pool looks more incongruous than ever with a large cross hanging from the deep side.

Further down rises the mighty **Kazan Cathedral** (Kazansky Sobor), built by Vornikhin in 1801-1811. The crescent-shaped colonnade was modelled, albeit on a slightly smaller scale, on the Bernini colonnade in St Peter's Square in Rome. For many years, the cathedral housed a Museum of Atheism but this has been reorganised as a Museum of Religion, which displays various icons and ceremonial robes. The main entrance to the cathedral is on the right side, facing west as required by Orthodox tradition, but this is open only during Sunday services. On other days, when only the museum is open, you enter by a small basement door around to the left. Kazan Square has long been a popular setting for political demonstrations, which are still often initiated here. On a normal day, however, you are more likely to see a few hippy kids sitting around playing Bob Dylan songs in the garden opposite.

Opposite the cathedral is **Dom Knigi**, St Petersburg's biggest bookshop. The illuminated globe on the top of the building dates back to tsarist times, when the Singer sewing machine company was housed here.

Ulitsa Mikhailovskaya, the next street on the left (connecting Nevsky with

Arts Square, described in Walk 5) is exceptionally glamorous, with Mercedes limousines, armed thugs, high-class prostitutes and wealthy businessmen congregated around the entrance of the Europa, St Petersburg's flashest hotel. An underpass nearby provides safe passage across the road to the arcades of **Gostiny Dvor**, a vast trading house built in the 18th century and now the largest department store in the city (see *Shopping*). Beyond this frenetic bazaar and across Sadovaya ulitsa, you'll reach the huge State Public Library, where Lenin once worked. The main façade faces **Ostrovsky Square** (Ploshchad Ostrovskovo), a peaceful park dominated by a huge statue of Catherine the Great surrounded by courtiers. The impressive yellow building opposite is the Pushkin Theatre, designed by Carlo Rossi in 1823. The National Museum of Theatrical and Musical Arts at 6 Ostrovsky Square contains photographs and portraits of actors, as well as reconstructions of stage sets and old posters.

Walk behind the Pushkin Theatre and you reach **Ulitsa Rossi**, the most mathematically perfect street in St Petersburg. Named after its designer, the street is the same width as the height of the identical buildings on either side, and the length of the buildings is ten times their height. There are only three streets of this kind in the world, the other two being in Paris and Florence. On the east side is the Vaganova School of Choreography, where Rudolf Nureyev trained.

St Petersburg's most beautiful shop, Yeliseev's, occupies the ground floor of the Style Moderne building at Nevsky Prospekt 56, just across from Ploshchad Ostrovsky. During the communist years, it was known simply as Gastronom Number 1. The once barren shelves are now laden with pineapples, German yoghurts and other delicacies neatly stacked and illuminated by exquisite wrought-iron chandeliers. Just past Ostrovsky Square, overlooking the Fontanka river, is the **Anichkov Palace** (now a popular venue for share auctions), which was named after the engineer who built the city's first river bridge nearby: the Anichkov Bridge, with its lifesize bronze sculptures of rearing horses placed at each of its four corners, marks the southern boundary of the city centre and must once have provided a grand gateway to St Petersburg.

Opening times:

Museum of Religion, Kazan Cathedral. Open 11am-5pm daily except Wednesday.

National Museum of Theatrical and Musical Arts, Ploshchad Ostrovskovo 6, metro Gostiny Dvor. Open 11am-6pm daily except Tuesday and the last Friday of the month.

WALK 4: Southwest of Nevsky

This itinerary takes you from Decembrists' Square to St Nicholas Cathedral, one of the most beautiful churches in the city.

Decembrists' Square (Ploshchad Dekabristov) is named after the revolutionary noblemen who gathered here in December 1825 during an unsuccessful but none the less significant uprising against the newly-appointed Tsar Nicholas I. At its centre is the famous equestrian statue of Peter the Great, immortalised in Pushkin's poem *The Bronze Horseman*. Catherine the Great dedicated the statue to Peter I in 1782, as recorded in an inscription on the pedestal. Today, it is the second obligatory photo stop for newly-weds after the Strelka, and also a favourite spot with local kids, who enjoy sliding down the steep pedestal.

Just south of the square rises the imposing bulk of **St Isaac's Cathedral** (Isaakievsky Sobor). Built between 1818 and 1858 by another Frenchman, Auguste Montferrand, this is the largest church in the city. Mass is celebrated only at Christmas and Easter, attracting thousands of worshippers. The interior is extremely lavish, with malachite and lapis lazuli columns in front of the iconostasis, wall-to-wall marbling at the lower level and mosaic frescoes on every inch of remaining wall space. Another great attraction is the view from the dome: on a clear day it is the best in St Petersburg. The cathedral opens 10am-5pm daily except Wednesday.

The lower end of St Isaac's Square looks like one large strip of concrete, but it is in fact the widest bridge in St Petersburg, with a span of 328ft/100m. It leads over the Moyka Canal to the **Mariinsky Palace**, now part of the town hall but originally built as a residence for Maria, Nicholas I's daughter. Nicholas I himself is commemorated by an equestrian statue at the centre of the square.

Following naberezhnaya reki Moyki westwards you reach the **Yusupov Palace** at no. 94. This large neoclassical palace was the scene of one of Russia's most famous crimes: the murder of Grigory Rasputin. This man was a Siberian preacher who had become a protegé of the imperial family and was even rumoured to be the lover of the Russian Queen. In 1916, Prince Yusupov and others took it upon themselves to rid the nation of this dangerous mountebank. They lured him to Yusupov's palace, where they fed him cyanide-coated biscuits. When Rasputin showed no sign of expiring, however, they shot him. You can see the white marble staircase up which Rasputin allegedly escaped before being shot in the courtyard. To visit the rest of the palace, you must join a guided tour. Enquire at the ticket office in the basement since tours are not conducted very often, and you must book in advance for an English guide (tel 311-5353). Some tours are followed by a concert in the palace's private theatre.

After the Yusupov Palace, take the first left down ulitsa Glinka. This leads straight to Teatralnya ploshchad, home to the illustrious **Mariinsky Theatre**, where Pavlova, Nijinsky and Nureyev have all delighted audiences. The building is more familiar to contemporary ballet audiences as the Kirov Theatre, as it was known from 1935 to 1991. The auditorium, draped in blue and gold velvet, is infinitely more sumptuous than the austere exterior leads you to believe.

A short distance further down the street is the **St Nicholas Cathedral** (1753-62), one of the city's least publicised treasures. It is a delicate blue and white baroque structure, crowned with octagonal rather than the more usual smooth onion domes. The cathedral actually consists of two churches, one placed on top of the other. The lower one is darker and more spiritual, with incense burning and almost continuous services; the upper church has loftier ceilings and elegant gold and white décor, but is open only for important masses. Head towards the graceful free-standing belfry and you'll emerge on the edge of Kryukov Canal. The cobalt blue domes of the Trinity Cathedral further south loom over the top of the surrounding roofs.

From here it's about 30 minutes' walk back to Nevsky Prospekt along Griboyedova Canal, which is crossed by several picturesque wrought-iron bridges. The first part of the walk takes you through an area reminiscent of Amsterdam, with its shady embankment and scanty traffic. If it's raining, you can hop on the metro at the huge Sennaya ploshchad, notable for its crowds, dust and general air of disrepair.

WALK 5: Northeast of Nevsky Prospekt

This last itinerary takes you from Arts Square (Ploshchad Iskusstv) to Peter's

Summer Palace through the Mikhailovsky Park and the Summer Gardens, two havens of tranquillity in the heart of the city. Arts Square is about five minutes' walk from either Nevsky Prospekt or Gostiny Dvor metro stations.

Thus named because it is surrounded on all sides by museums and theatres, **Arts Square** is considered the finest neoclassical ensemble in the city and the masterpiece of Carlo Rossi. It is dominated by the **Mikhailovsky Palace** (1819-25), now the Russian Museum (see below). Other buildings in the square include the Maly Theatre, second only to the Mariinsky, and the **Museum of Ethnography**. If you're heading south, this excellent museum provides a wonderful insight into the carpets and fabrics you will find in Central Asia. To see the collection of priceless Scythian gold jewellery you need to join a guided tour: enquire at the excursion bureau on the ground floor.

At the centre of Arts Square is a small park where aspiring poets and other romantics come to pay homage to the monument to Pushkin. On the southern side of the square, on the corner of ulitsa Mikhailovskaya, stands the Bolshoi Philharmonic Hall, dedicated to Shostakovich. Many of his works were performed here for the first time, notably his seventh symphony in 1942, when the German blockade was still in force.

Just north of the square, on Griboyedova Canal, is a large neoclassical building which houses the Benois Wing (Korpus Benua) of the Russian Museum which, as well as housing the permanent collection of 20th-century Russian art, serves as a venue for temporary exhibitions. Nearby is the multicoloured **Church of the Saviour on Spilled Blood** (Khram Spasa na Krovi), so-called because it was built on the spot where Alexander II was assassinated in 1881. Topped by onion domes, the building is in marked contrast to the neoclassical and baroque architecture elsewhere in the city. These last two buildings back on to **Mikhailovsky Park**, once the private garden of the nearby palace and enclosed by a beautiful wrought-iron grille. At the other end of the park is the vermilion Mikhailovsky Castle, which houses another branch of the Russian Museum but was originally built by Paul I because he felt unsafe in the vast Winter Palace. Ironically, it was within these fortified walls that Paul was murdered in 1801. The building is also known as the Engineers' Castle, after the Military Engineers School that occupied the building for many years.

Two parks cover the area between the castle and the Neva, flanking Sadovaya ulitsa. On the west side is the Field of Mars (Marsovo Pole), a former parade ground. To the east is the **Summer Garden** (Letny Sad), the city's finest park. Surrounded by water on all sides, this garden is a favourite spot with the young and old alike: courting couples come to coo among the statues, young mothers promenade their offspring along the tree-lined avenues, and baboushkas congregate on the benches to exchange the latest gossip. When the gardens were originally laid out in 1704, Peter the Great used Versailles as his model, interspersing fountains and statues with geometric flowerbeds. Over the years, however, the fountains have been removed, many of the statues destroyed and the formal patterns replaced by a more naturalistic landscape. The gardens are beautiful all year round, but especially so in late May, when the new leaves have emerged in all their full glory. In winter, the statues are enclosed in wooden boxes to prevent them from cracking in the sub-zero temperatures. The Summer Palace, which overlooks the Neva at the end of the park, is one of the city's earliest stone buildings, designed by Trezzini in 1712 for Peter the Great. It is now a charming and cosy museum, with the smell of beeswax polish emanating from the oak furniture and fresh flowers placed in vases. The highlight is a huge barometer-cum-clock device which Peter the Great bought in Dresden.

From the Summer Garden, you can either head back to Nevsky along the Fontanka Canal, or you can follow the Neva embankment all the way back to the Winter Palace.

Opening times:

Museum of Ethnography, ulitsa Inzhenernaya, off Arts Square. Open 10am-6pm daily except Monday and the last Friday of the month.
Summer Palace, Summer Garden, nearest entrance on nab. Kutuzova. Tram 2, 34 or 53. Open 11am-6pm daily except Tuesday.

OTHER SIGHTS

Smolny. The area known as Smolny was once the hub of the city's ship-building industry. In 1748, however, Empress Elizabeth decided to put this strip of land overlooking the Neva to more elevated use and commissioned Rastrelli to build a a religious complex. The cathedral is a most beautifully proportioned building with its elegant domes, an exceptionally plain interior and excellent acoustics. It is now used as a concert hall.

To the right of the church and convent buildings stands the Smolny Institute. Built by Quarenghi in 1806 as an elite girls' school, it is more often associated with the Petrograd Soviet, which had its headquarters here in 1917. It was from Smolny that the October uprising was directed and the early decrees of the Soviet Government were issued. It is still used by local government and so can not be visited. The exterior remains a communist showpiece: the prototype statue of Lenin, erected in 1927, stands firm and the hammer and sickle medallion above the entrance remains equally unperturbed by late 20th-century history. In the nearby park, statues of Marx and Engels lurk among the shrubbery.

To reach Smolny, you can take the metro to Chernyshevskaya and from there walk east through the lovely Tauride Gardens. These were designed as the grounds of Tauride Palace, which was given by Catherine the Great to her lover Potyomkin as a reward for annexing the Crimea (known as Tauris in Greek). The building is now used for official receptions and international congresses.

Alexander Nevsky Monastery. Located at the far end of Nevsky Prospekt, St Petersburg's most famous monastery was founded in 1713 and dedicated to the Prince of Novgorod, acclaimed for his defeat of the Swedes on the banks of the Neva in the 13th century. It is one of only four lavras in the former Soviet Union, a title bestowed on the highest ranking monasteries in the Russian Orthodox Church. High protective walls enclose the monastic buildings, two churches and several cemeteries. The main attraction is the Tikhvin Cemetery (Tikhvinskoe Kladbishche), on the right as you enter the grounds. Also known as the Necropolis of the Masters of the Arts, this is where Dostoevsky, Tchaikovsky, Rimsky-Korsakov, Carlo Rossi and countless other famous people are interred. The tombs of the best-known figures are marked in both Russian and English, but if you have any trouble locating a particular grave just ask the baboushka at the entrance. Opposite the Tikhvin is the Lazarus Cemetery, the earliest burial site in the city. The baroque Church of the Annunciation beyond it is closed to visitors during restoration. The much larger Trinity Cathedral (Troitsky Sobor) is St Petersburg's most important working church. There are several services daily.

At all times visitors should dress respectfully, and it is usual for women to wear a headscarf. If you are lucky, you will hear the superb choir performing.

The monastic quarters are not officially open to the public, but it is not unheard of for visitors to be taken on an unofficial tour. Historical value apart, the grounds of the monastery are a peaceful place to while away an afternoon.

To reach the monastery, either take the metro to ploshchad Aleksandra Nevskovo or trolleybus 1 or 22 along Nevsky. The cemeteries are open 11am-6pm daily except Thursday. The Cathedral opens daily 8am-2pm and 5pm-7pm.

MUSEUMS

All museums charge two rates of entry, one which is minimal for Russians and another which is often absurdly high for foreigners. Anyone studying in Russia pays local prices, and if you are a student elsewhere you are entitled to a reduction. Most museums close at least one day a week, and in addition usually have one 'sanitary day' a month, when they close for cleaning. It is not unknown for some of the less popular museums to close at the whim of the curators if there is a dearth of visitors. In many museums, guided tours are still compulsory, a hangover from the Soviet era when the individual pursuit of culture was considered anarchical. These official tours are often conducted only in Russian and can be torture, particularly if you don't understand a word. In most museums, last admission is one hour before closing.

The list below does not include those mentioned in the walking tours, the Russian Museum being the one exception.

The Hermitage. This is one of the biggest and most impressive art museums in the world. Founded in 1764 to house Empress Catherine II's foreign paintings, in the course of the next 150 years, the collection grew rapidly. After 1917, the Hermitage was opened to the general public, and numerous private collections were added. The museum now houses more than two million exhibits in five separate buildings, the largest of which is the Winter Palace. The works of art on view constitute only 4% of the total treasures owned by the museum; the rest are kept in the vaults below. In order to see every gallery in the Hermitage, you would have to walk over 12 miles/20km, so it is worth being selective. You can buy a plan of the galleries in English, but if you get lost, there's an army of attendants to point you in the right direction. Paintings are labelled only in Russian, but the artists' names are at least transliterated into Roman script. Particular highlights include the collection of Rembrandts and the art of the Italian Renaissance (including works by Fra Angelico, Botticelli, Leonardo da Vinci and Titian) on the first floor, and the collection of works by 19th-and 20th-century French artists (including Monet, Van Gogh, Renoir, Cezanne, Rodin, Degas, Courbet, Bonnard, Matisse and Picasso) on the second floor. The Hermitage also has very rich Chinese and Classical collections.

Quite apart from the collection, the palace interiors form a spectacular backdrop. Of particular note are the Rastrelli Gallery by the main entrance, the Hall of Twenty Columns and the Malachite Hall, which are all in the Winter Palace itself; the Pavilion Hall, with its spectacular Peacock Clock, is on the first floor of the adjacent Small Hermitage. All the apartments on the north side of the buildings offer splendid views over the River Neva.

The main entrance to the Hermitage is on the north side of the Winter

Palace. The museum opens 10.30am-6pm, daily except Monday. The admission fee for foreigners is the rouble equivalent of $10 for adults, $5 for children, with heavy surcharges for cameras and videos. Touts and tour guides hang out around the entrance and may offer you cheaper tickets.

The Russian Museum. This museum contains one of the best collections of Russian art in the world, second only to Moscow's Tretyakov Gallery. The galleries are housed in the Mikhailovsky Palace overlooking Arts Square (see Walk 5) and the nearby Rossi and Benois wings. The permanent collection of 300,000 works covers Russian art from the 11th century up to the avant-garde of this century. If your time is limited, make sure you see the Russian icons on the first floor, including works attributed to Rublev. Also of great interest are the works of 19th-and early 20th-century painters such as Repin, Levitan, Ivanov, Malevich and Gonchorova. The rooms themselves are very attractive, particularly the White Hall.

The Mikhailovsky Palace is just a few minutes' walk from Nevsky Prospekt metro. It opens 10am-6pm daily except Tuesday, though on Monday it closes at 5pm. The entrance fee is approximately $5.

Museum of the Siege. At Solyanoi pereulok 9, metro Chernyshevskaya. Open 10am-5pm daily except Wednesday and the last Thursday of the month. This excellent museum set up a new exhibition in 1994, on the 50th anniversary of the end of German blockade of Leningrad. There is just one large hall with artwork from the period documenting daily life during the city's most difficult years. The staff, all survivors of the siege, are more than happy to explain the scenes depicted in the photographs and other pictures.

House Museums. A Russian speciality, these museums are the former homes of famous artists, writers, musicians and politicians which have been lovingly restored. In many cases, the original furnishings survive, making the houses interesting as period pieces and worth visiting on that basis alone.

Anna Akhmatova Museum: Liteiny Prospekt 53, metro Mayakovskaya or Gostiny Dvor; walk through the leafy courtyard and follow the signs round to your left. Open 10.30am-6.30am daily except Monday and the last Wednesday of the month. Anna Akhmatova (1889-1966) has been acclaimed as Russia's greatest woman poet. Along with intellectuals such as Boris Pasternak, she was part of the avant-garde which existed in St Petersburg in the early 20th century. Unlike many of her contemporaries, she remained in Russia after the Revolution.

The museum contains interesting old photographs of gatherings of glitterati at the turn of the century. In the bedroom there is a portrait of the poet by Modigliani, whom she met in Paris in 1922. There is a pleasant café on the ground floor of the building.

Dostoevsky Literary Memorial Museum: Kuznechny pereulok 5, metro Vladimirskaya or Dostoevskaya. Open 10.30m-6.30pm daily except Monday and the last Wednesday of the month. Dostoevsky lived in this flat for the last three years of his life (1878-1881), and it was here that he wrote *The Brothers Karamazov*. As well as a number of his personal belongings, the museum contains several beautiful pieces of 19th-century furniture and gives an accurate impression of a moderately wealthy St Petersburger's home at that time. Labelling is in English as well as Russian, and guided tours are available. Enthusiasts may like to go on the Dostoevsky walking tour, which can be booked from the ticket office. On Sundays at noon, the small cinema here shows films of Dostoevsky's novels.

Pushkin Memorial Museum: nab reki Moyki 12, Nevsky Prospekt metro.

Open 10.30am-6pm daily except Tuesday and the last Friday of the month. Alexander Pushkin's many years in exile have bequeathed a series of house museums throughout Russia, but none more evocative than this beautiful flat on Moyka Canal. This was where Russia's greatest poet spent the last year of his life and died. Pushkin challenged to a duel a young Frenchman who had persisted in making advances to the his wife, Natalia. The pair met on 27 January 1837. Pushkin received a fatal wound from which he died a few days later.

Rimsky-Korsakov Memorial Flat: Zagorodny Prospekt 28, metro Vladimirskaya. Open 11am-6pm Wednesday to Sunday. Rimsky-Korsakov began his career as a naval cadet but went on to become an extraordinarily prolific composer, writing 11 operas in just 15 years. More than any of the other houses described above, this feels more like a home than a museum. You need to ring a doorbell to be let in. Students from the Academy of Music are usually available to give informal tours in English. Concerts are held regularly in the small concert hall, with the most famous recital of all given every year on 18 March, the anniversary of the composer's death.

WAR MEMORIALS

The most painful chapter in the city's chequered history was the 900-day siege which lasted from September 1941 to January 1944. The exact number of dead has never been established, but estimates vary between 600,000 and a million — roughly a quarter of the population of Leningrad at the time. Some died engaged in active combat, but many more died from starvation and the cold. However, despite constant shelling, meagre food rations and no fuel for heating during the coldest winters this century, the people of Leningrad resisted the German blockade with astounding heroism. The dead are buried in Piskarovskoe Cemetery, and the Victory Monument pays tribute to all those who suffered to defend their city.

Victory Monument. Ploshchad Pobedy, 15 minutes' walk from metro Moskovskaya. If you arrive in St Petersburg by air, on your way into town from the airport you will pass Victory Square. A tall obelisk stands in the centre, surrounded by blackened statues of valiant soldiers and suffering women. Unveiled on 9 May 1975, the 30th anniversary of the victory against the Germans, this is a belated tribute to the survivors and victims of the siege.

The round shape of the memorial, with a gap torn through its southern side, is a symbolic representation of the end of the siege; it was on the southern front that the city first broke out of its imprisonment. To stand at the centre, with a skyline of 60s highrises beyond and listening to the strains of Shostakovich's seventh symphony (premiered during the siege), is both a disconcerting and moving experience. In the underground memorial museum, 900 giant red fairylights — one for every day of the siege — cast a dim light over a vast mausoleum-like hall. Here, Shostakovich is replaced by the ticking of a metronome, a sound that was constantly broadcast on local radio during the siege to symbolise the heartbeat of the city. In addition to a variety of exhibits, films with live footage are also shown.

Piskarovskoye Cemetery. This monumental World War II cemetery is built on the site of a village where the bodies of the victims of the siege were dumped. Mass graves are laid out on either side of a pathway which leads down to a giant statue of Mother Russia holding a laurel wreath. To add to the atmosphere of gloom, loud-speakers play an eerie funeral march. Approximately half a million people are buried here; civilian graves are marked with a hammer and sickle, military graves with a star. Flanking the entrance are two exhibition halls with photographic documentation of the siege.

Piskarovskoye cemetery (Piskarovskoye memorialnoye kladbishche) is at Prospekt Nepokorennykh 74; take the metro to Ploshchad Muzhestva and then bus 123 or 131. It is open daily 10am-6pm.

Opera, Ballet and Classical Music. Lovers of opera, ballet and music will find St Petersburg endlessly gratifying. On any given night there is an extensive choice of quality performances. Tickets, even for the best ballet, are reasonably easy to obtain and good value. Plays are not an obvious option for non-Russian speakers, but the fairytale plots of the Puppet Theatre do not present much of a problem. Most performances start at 7pm and dressing up is *de rigueur:* in winter this can lead to long queues at the *garderob* (cloakroom), as people fumble to remove their heavy boots and slip into evening shoes brought with them in a plastic bag.

Tickets can be obtained at the venues themselves or at a kassa. There are several of these booking offices along Nevsky Prospekt, advertising all of that month's performances and selling tickets to most of them. In summer, when seats are bought in bulk by tourist companies, tickets to the most popular performances may only be available from hotel desks at inflated prices. Throughout the year, but especially in winter, there's a good chance of obtaining a ticket by turning up at the theatre at the last minute and buying one off a tout for a price only slightly over the odds. As there are over 40 theatres and concert halls in the city, only the most famous are listed here.

Mariinsky Theatre, Teatralnya ploshchad (114-1211). Formerly known as the Kirov, the Mariinsky opera and ballet company is Russia's most famous. Winter is the best time to try and see a performance here, as the troupe is often on tour in the summer and tickets can be hard to come by in spring. The sumptuous building guarantees a glamorous night out.

Maly Theatre, Ploshchad Iskusstva (219-1978). This the city's second venue for ballet and opera. Standards are not nearly as high as at the Mariinsky, but the theatre itself is extremely attractive.

Hermitage Theatre, Dvortsovaya nab 34 (311-9025); a short walk from Palace Square. Catherine the Great's own private theatre is one of the most charming and intimate venues in the city. Modelled on a Roman theatre in Vicenza, the interior is almost entirely of marble, with the seating arranged in semicircular tiers. Ballets and plays are only occasionally staged here and not always very widely advertised. Enquire at the theatre ticket office inside the main entrance of the Hermitage Museum.

Bolshoi Philharmonic Hall, ul Mikhailovskaya 2 (311-7333). This, the Bolshoi, and the Glinka (also known as the Maly Philharmonic Hall, Nevsky Prospekt 30) together form the St Petersburg City Philharmonic. Both have a good varied programme with concerts every night of the week.

Kapella, nab Reki Moiki 20 (314-1058); metro Nevsky Prospekt. The Kapela specialises in choral concerts.

Drama and Comedy. The principal drama theatres include the Academic

Bolshoi Dramatic Theatre (nab Reki Fontanki 65; 310-9242) and the Pushkin Academic Drama Theatre in Ploshchad Ostrovskovo (312-1415), both near Gostiny Dvor metro station. For lighter performances, try the Theatre of Drama and Comedy (Liteiny Prospekt 51; 272-5335) or the Bolshoi Puppet Theatre (ul Nekrasova 10; 273-6672), both within walking distance of metro Chernyshevskaya.

Clubs and Live Music. St Petersburg has always been the centre of Russia's struggling pop music scene, and in the last few years music here has blossomed due to unprecedented access to Western trends. New venues have sprung up all over the city. The most interesting bands fall into the hardcore/alternative category. Look out for bands such as the Dolphins, Tequila Jazz, Bondzinsky and Spitfire, which head the so-called 'jazzcore' scene.

Check flyposters and the *St Petersburg Press* for details of concerts and festivals. Opportunities for clubbing in the city are limited, though raves are occasionally held in larger venues such as the circus. Music aside, the friendly atmosphere of Petersburg clubs makes them the obvious places to spend an evening.

Art Club, Griboyedova Canal 3; metro Nevsky Prospekt. A well-established café/bar with a large hall for concerts and a clientele made up predominantly of students. There is live music most evenings, plus all-nighters at weekends with a good variety of music. By day it is a good place to have a coffee.

Indie club, Troitsky Culture Centre, Obukhovsky Oborony Prospekt 223; metro Proletarskaya. Don't be deceived by the name of this club: its musical programme is far more wide-ranging than it indicates. There is a small seated auditorium for bands and a separate bar (cosy and cheap). Bands are interspersed with a disco, which is not unlike a sweaty student bop. Open 7pm-midnight.

Jazz Philharmonic Hall, Zagorodny Prospekt 27; metro Vladimirskaya. Perfect for a more sedate evening out. Tickets buy you a seat at one of several round tables, where you can settle down to listen to mainstream jazz. On Sunday evenings there is a 'jazz ball', when the audience is invited to dance to the tunes. Buy tickets from the box office at the same address during the day as seating is limited.

Kvadrat, ul Pravky 10; metro Vladimirskaya. A big jazz concert hall for performances mainly of modern jazz, often by foreign bands, and frequent jam sessions. Highly recommended and good value. Shows start after 8pm.

Tam Tam, Maly Prospekt 49; metro Vasileostrovskaya. This is the centre of St Petersburg's hardcore and punk scenes. The crowd consists of a mixture of Russsian punk and trendy students. Definitely worth a visit. Open 7pm to midnight.

Ten club, Dom Kultury Desyatiletiya Oktyabrya, nab Obvodnovo Canala 62; metro Pushkinskaya. A new, small and comfortable club, with bands and clientele similar to those of Tam Tam, but without the low life. The bar is good and cheap. Open 7pm-midnight.

Tunnel, on the corner of Lyubansky pereulok and ul Zverinskaya; metro Gorkovskaya. This dance club is open all night at weekends and offers the best techno music in the city. It is worth checking out not least because it is housed in an old nuclear bomb shelter. Open midnight-6am.

Wild Side, nab Bumazhnovo Canala 12; metro Narvskaya. A Western-style club frequented by ex-pats. Open all night Thursday to Saturday, with bands followed by a disco. Open 10pm-5.30am.

Circus. Though not in the same league as the one in Moscow, St Petersburg's circus can lay claim to being the oldest in Russia, founded in 1877. It always has a wide range of acts and has recently won an award for its performing hedgehogs. Definitely worth a visit if you enjoy that kind of thing. The permanent building of the St Petersburg Circus is at nab Reki Fontanki 3, near Mayakovskaya or Gostiny Dvor metro stations.

Cinema. The biggest concentration of cinemas is on Nevsky, but the calibre of films shown here is fairly dismal. The most popular genre in recent years has been bad action movies made even worse by appalling dubbing, though Znanie (Nevsky 72) shows documentary and art films. Stereokino at no. 88 specialises in 3-D films. Spartak (at ul Saltykova-Schedrina 8) shows old films, both domestic and foreign, but all in Russian.

For non Russian-speakers, films in English are shown every night at 7pm at the Commodore Hotel. There is a free shuttle bus which leaves from outside the National Library on Ploshchad Ostrovskovo, every hour on the half hour; admission to the cinema is free too. Check the *St Petersburg Press* to see what's on.

SPORT

Like elsewhere in Russia, soccer and ice-hockey are the most popular spectator sports. St Petersburg has a reasonable football team called Zenit, which plays in the spectacular Kirov stadium (capacity 100,000). It was built on land reclaimed from the sea and is located on Morskoi Prospekt, on Krestovsky Island in the northwest of the city. Ice hockey games are played at the Jubilee Palace of Sports (Yubileiny Stadion) at Dobrolyubov Prospekt 18, next to the Tuchkov bridge in Petrogradskaya. Tickets to these events can be obtained from the booking offices on Nevsky Prospekt or at the venues themselves.

Given the long winters and abundant snowfall, there are plenty of opportunities for cross-country skiing, though the equipment available for hire tends to be primitive. Even so, if you can lay your hands on a decent pair of skis, you can enjoy exploring one of the larger parks such as Park Pobedy (at the metro stop of the same name) or, better still, the vast grounds of Pavlovsk outside the city (see *Further Afield*).

Russian baths. The *banya* or Russian bath-house is not nearly as luxurious as its Turkish or Hungarian equivalent; it usually consists of just one small steam room, a pool of ice cold water and some showers. The only garment you're supposed to wear is a woollen hat to protect your hair, and when you've sweated copiously, the assistant or your bath companions will insist on beating you with birch twigs, allegedly to improve the circulation. If you're lucky, you may be offered a glass of vodka at the end of the ordeal. Every district of the city has its own banya, the most central being at ul Marata 5, near metro Mayakovskaya.

Parks. For boating in summer and skating in winter, head to one of the larger parks in the suburbs, such as Kirov Park on Yelagin Island (metro to Chernaya Rechka and then tram 2, 31 or 37) or Moskovsky Park Pobedy (metro Park Pobedy). The Botanical Gardens are at ul Professora Popova 2 (metro Petrogradskaya).

Nevsky Prospekt is St Petersburg's equivalent of London's Oxford Street, though since this is Russia, the choice of goods is not quite the same. International names, however, are gradually moving in: Reebok and Levis have already set up shop, and no doubt many more will follow, bringing the best and worst of Western consumerism.

The largest and most famous department store is Gostiny Dvor, which occupies a whole block above the metro station of the same name. Plans are afoot to turn it into a Western-style mall complete with fountains and piped music. For the moment, however, it is more like a giant bazaar with numerous different stalls. Most of the ground floor is taken up by import stalls selling Finnish chocolates and other luxuries; for genuine Russian merchandise, head to the first floor where you can still pick up cheap hats and clothes.

Directly opposite Gostiny Dvor is Passazh, another department store with a long gallery lined with shops, not unlike a section of Moscow's GUM. It too is moving upmarket as an increasing number of foreign import stores lease the premises. Shopping apart, Passazh is useful as a shortcut from Nevsky Prospekt to Arts Square.

A winter spent in St Petersburg is liable to convince all but the most diehard animal lovers that a fur hat is the only way to keep warm. Should you decide to throw your misgivings to the wind, one of the better value fur shops is at Zagorodny Prospekt 28 (metro Vladimirskaya). If you prefer to see live animals, head to Kondratevsky Ptichy Rynok, which calls itself a bird market but actually sells every kind of pet from puppies to piranha fish. The market is held at weekends on Polyustrovsky Prospekt. Take the metro to Ploshchad Lenina and then trolleybus 3, 38 or 43.

Books. Dom Knigi, the city's most famous bookshop at Nevsky 28, has a varied and varying range of books, mostly in Russian. Stalls all along Nevsky sell pocket dictionaries, coffee-table books on St Petersburg and maps of the city. For second-hand and antiquarian books, try Staraya Kniga, next to the Literary Café, at Nevsky Prospekt 18. There are many books in foreign languages, especially art and fiction, but prices are somewhat random. Prints are also on sale. The stretch of Liteiny Prospekt closest to Nevsky is also good for new and second-hand bookshops.

Foreign newspapers can be bought for about $5 at all the major hotels. They are cheapest at the Neva Star shop in the Hotel Moskva.

As with other major Russian cities, St Petersburg has seen a sharp rise in crime in the last few years. However, most of the crimes committed against foreigners involve extortion from wealthy businessmen and protection rackets, so the average tourist is not particularly at risk. Even so, take the usual precautions: avoid carrying around large sums of money and be vigilant against pickpockets, particularly along Nevsky and around the expensive hotels.

The main health hazard in St Petersburg is the water, which is infected with *giardia*, a nasty parasite which causes gastric problems. Only the most expensive hotels have water filters, so avoid drinking unboiled tap water. Mineral water is relatively easy to buy in hotel shops and foreign stores.

Medical Treatment. The standards at Policlinic 2, Moskovsky Prospekt 22 (292-6271, 292-6272), metro Technologichesky Institut, are much higher than average since this used to be the clinic for high-ranking Russian officials and diplomats. It is now independent and therefore fee-paying. The best general care in St Petersburg is provided by the AMC, the American Medical Centre, at nab reki Fontanki (119-6101), metro Gostiny Dvor. You have to pay a membership fee to avail yourself of all its services.

In an emergency, call one of the private ambulance services at either Policlinic 2 (110-1102) or Hospital 20 (108-4808). If major surgery is required, contact your consulate or the American Medical Centre to help organise evacuation.

The Damian pharmacy in Policlinic 2 has the widest selection of Western medicines.

Tourist Information: following the collapse of Intourist, it is not obvious to know where to obtain information. Most hotels still have service desks which can be either helpful way beyond the call of duty or utterly useless. The *St Petersburg Press*, a weekly paper in English, is good for listings; you can pick up a free copy from most hotels. For longer-term visitors, the St Petersburg *Yellow Pages* is a useful investment. Apart from the excellent map which comes with every copy, it provides up-to-date information on museum opening hours, restaurants and all sorts of other services.

Money: the American Express office is located on the ground floor of the Hotel Europa. Cash advances on Visa can be obtained from the exchange office by the mezzanine café in the same hotel, and also in the Nevsky Palace Hotel. Many of the tourist hotels now exchange travellers' cheques as well as cash, and there are numerous cash-only exchange offices (*obmen valut*) along Nevsky.

Communications: the central post office is at ul Pochtamtskaya 9 and the main telephone office at 3/5 ul Bolshaya Morskaya. But it is much easier to use the smaller combined branch opposite Gostiny Dvor on Nevsky Prospekt. The poste restante address is Nevsky Prospekt 6, 19044 St Petersburg, but don't count on anything ever reaching you. American Express cardholders can receive mail at its office inside the Europa Hotel. The service operates through Finland and the address is c/o American Express, PO Box 87, SF-53501, Lappeenranta. Finland. Non-cardholders can also use this service for outgoing mail, thereby bypassing the inefficient Russian postal service.

Embassies and Consulates

Estonia, ul Bolshaya Monetnaya 14 (233-5303, 333-5548).
Finland , ul Tchaikovskovo 71 (273-7321).
Germany, ul Furshtadskaya 39 (273-5598).
Latvia, ul Galernaya 69 (315-1774).
Lithuania, ul Dekabristov 54 (114-1210).
The Netherlands, Engels Prospekt 101 (554-4890).
Poland, 5-ya Sovetskaya ul 12/14 (274-4170).

UK, Ploshchad Proletarskoi Diktatury 5 (119-6036).
USA, ul Furshtadskaya 15 (274-8568).

Visa extension: the main visa registration office (*ovir*) is at ul Saltykova-Schedrina 4, metro Chernyshevskaya. To extend your visa, turn up early since queues can be long. Instant passport photos can be taken at a studio at ul Bolshaya Morskaya 32.

Further Afield 61

FIVE PALACES

Sometimes referred to as the 'ring of pearls', the five summer palaces outside St Petersburg are all within easy reach of the city and can be visited as day trips. Each has its own attractions. For the most lavish tsarist magnificence, head to Peterhof or the Catherine Palace at Tsarkoe Selo. The smaller Pavlovsk Palace is ideal for those with just one afternoon available. Oranienbaum and Gatchina are slightly further afield but still well worth a visit.

With the exception of Oranienbaum, all the palaces fell within the area occupied by the Germans during World War Two and were looted, mined and in some cases set on fire. Restoration work began as early as 1944 and is still ongoing. Hand-painted silks, delicate stuccowork and inlaid floors have all been faithfully reproduced from old drawings. The extent and quality of the restoration is in many ways more astounding than the fact that the tsars built such sumptuous abodes in the first place. It is ironic that the same communist regime which ousted the tsars and all they represented should have spared no expense to recreate the opulent surrundings in which they lived.

The easiest way to reach any of the palaces is by the suburban train service or *elektrichka*. It is best to go during the week to avoid the crowds; on Sunday evenings these trains are packed with St Petersburgers returning from their dachas. In summer, tour buses depart regularly from Gostiny Dvor and Kazan Cathedral, but you must endure a breathless commentary in Russian. For more details see the *Getting There* section for each individual palace.

PETERHOF (Petrodvorets)

Famed for its fountains and beautiful maritime location, Peterhof is the most popular palace with both Russians and foreign tourists. It is at its most beautiful in summer, when the golden fountains are switched on in the park that stretches from the palace down to the Gulf of Finland. (Be sure to put on plenty of repellent since the local mosquitos are large and numerous.)

Following a visit to Versailles, Peter the Great decided to build a palace and park ensemble that would rival, if not outshine, its French inspiration. He chose a site west of St Petersburg, where the palace could stand on a natural terrace and the formal gardens slope right down to the sea. Peter personally supervised the project, paying particular attention to the design of the fountains. These come in many guises, but the finest stands in the pool at the top of the Grand Canal. The colossal golden statue depicts Samson tearing the lion's mouth, an allegory of Russia's victory over Sweden at the battle of Poltava: it is a replica of the original, which was stolen and melted down by the Germans. At the time of writing, Samson is obscured by scaffolding set up while restoration work is carried out around the Grand

Cascade. Trick fountains which spurt up from the ground when you least expect it, musicians in period costume, and freelance pixies who will pose with you for a photographic memento, all contribute to the lively atmosphere at Peterhof.

The original palace was built in 1714-25 by the French architect, Alexandre Leblond, but the present structure owes more to Rastrelli, who worked here some 30 years later under the orders of Peter's daughter, the Empress Elizabeth. Most interiors date from the time of Catherine the Great, but a few formed part of the original palace. The set itinerary begins at the top of the grand baroque staircase and then leads you into the ceremonial halls, followed by the private apartments. All the rooms are sumptuous but the White Dining Room, bathed in light from the huge windows which overlook the park, stands out for its freshness and simplicity. The 366 portraits of young women in the Picture Gallery were all made by the same artist using just 8 models. To reach this room, you have to pass through two fine Chinese Studies adorned with lacquer panels; it's hard to enjoy the 18th-century chinoiserie, however, since baboushkas hurry you through, urging you to hold your breath to minimise damage from moisture.

The smaller exhibits, stuffed in cabinets in the private royal apartments, are at least as interesting as the rooms themselves. Curiosities, such as the flea boxes and delicate ivory back-scratcher modelled in the shape of a hand reveal the more mundane aspects of court life.

There are several other palaces in the grounds. Monplaisir, by the water's edge, is a brick pavilion where Peter loved to relax. Catherine the Great's favourite retreat was the Hermitage (closed for restoration at the time of writing), where she liked to dine undisturbed by tiresome staff; at the tinkle of a bell, part of the floor could be lowered so that the table would be cleared without any need for the servants to make an appearance.

Getting There. Also known as Petrodvorets (the name given to it by the Soviets), Peterhof lies 18 miles/29km west of St Petersburg. Trains run regularly from the Baltic station to Novy Petergof, the journey taking about 40 minutes. From the station, buses 350, 351 or 352 take you directly to the palace. From the end of May to mid-September, you can travel by hydrofoil, with departures every hour from the pier in front of the Hermitage Museum. The journey takes 40 minutes but queues for tickets can be long since this is a favourite route for tour groups.

The main palace is open 10.30am-6pm daily except Monday and the last Tuesday of the month. Monplaisir is open May to October only.

TSARSKOE SELO (Pushkin)

Tsarskoe Selo does not enjoy as stunning a location as Peterhof, but its sumptuous architecture more than makes up for the absence of a sea view. Located here are the Alexander Palace (where Nicholas II and his family were arrested in 1917), Pushkin's old school and the Catherine Palace — the most ornate of all the summer residences.

Painted bright cobalt blue and adorned with white pillars, golden caryatids and a myriad stucco frills, the 300-metre long façade of the Catherine Palace (Yekaterinensky Dvorets) is unrivalled for coquettish extravagance. It is mainly the creation of Bartolomeo Rastrelli, who was commissioned by the Empress Elizabeth to enlarge, improve and adorn the stone palace her mother had built some years earlier.

The interiors, a mixture of baroque and neoclassical modifications designed by the Scotsman, Charles Cameron, and Giacomo Quarenghi, are second only to the Winter Palace in richness. The ceremonial halls have been painstakingly restored since the damage inflicted during the war. Inlaid floors, elaborate chandeliers and tiled stoves feature throughout. Highlights include the Portrait Room, where every inch of wall is covered in canvases; the Green Dining Room, decorated with Wedgewood-style cameo medallions; and the Blue Dining Room, with exquisite floral silk upholstery and matching curtains. When restoration work is completed, the Amber Room will no doubt outshine all of these. Its original priceless amber panels, a gift to Peter the Great by Frederick I, King of Prussia, were looted by the Germans and have never been recovered. The work is progressing slowly due to the enormous cost of the amber required to return the room to its original appearance.

Formal French-style gardens are laid out in terraces in front of the palace, but the lower grounds are more interesting, with a large lake surrounded by follies. The tiny mosque-type building served as Turkish baths for the courtesans, and the red-brick admiralty (now a café) was a viewing platform from which to watch mock naval battles staged on the lake. Beyond are the ruins of a Chinese village, where Catherine the Great and her friends would play at being Chinese peasants.

Pushkin Lyceum, where a teenage Pushkin was taught by some of the best pedagogues in Russia, is now a museum, to the right of the palace. There is a small and peaceful park nearby with a statue of the poet and sweeping views over the wilder Alexander Park, which stretches out to the back of the Catherine Palace and over to the Alexander Palace itself. The latter served as a military barracks after the revolution. It is now undergoing restoration, but is unlikely to open to the public for a number of years. Outside the Catherine Palace grounds, on the way to the bus stop, you pass a crescent-shaped building which houses the Court Carriage Museum — well worth a visit if you haven't already seen the luxurious gilded carriages and troikas in the Armoury Museum in Moscow.

Getting There. Tsarskoe Selo has undergone more name changes than most other towns in Russia. After the revolution, the name Tsarskoe Selo ('Tsars' Village') was changed to Detskoe Selo, or 'Children's Village', due to the numerous sanatoria for children located here. In 1937 it was rechristened Pushkin, but has recently reverted back to its original name. You may have to try all three if your request for train tickets is met initially with blank stares.

Tsarskoe Selo is about 15 miles/24km south of St Petersburg. Trains leave regularly from Vitebsk station, journey time about 30 minutes. From Detskoe Selo (as the station is still known), it is a 20-minute walk to the palace through the town, or you can hop on buses 371 or 381.

The main palace opens 10am-6pm, daily except Tuesday and the last Monday of the month. In summer, you may have to buy a separate ticket for the parks as well. The Pushkin Lyceum is open 10.30am-4.30pm every day except Tuesday and the last Friday of the month. The Court Carriage Museum is open 11am-5pm Thursday to Monday.

PAVLOVSK

The Pavlovsk Palace, set in vast landscaped gardens, is a beautiful example of Russian neoclassical architecture. It was built in the late 18th century to the designs of Charles Cameron and Vincenzo Brenna. A modest abode by the standards of Russian tsars, Pavlovsk was the favourite summer residence of Paul I, whose statue stands in the main courtyard. The unpopular pug-nosed emperor inherited his father Peter III's obsession for military drills and all things Prussian. He lived in constant fear of a palace coup and spent as much time as possible away from the intrigues of the city — either here or at the even remoter palace in Gatchina. His paranoia eventually proved to be justified when he was poisoned by his courtiers in 1801.

The formal royal quarters occupy the first floor of the palace. The centrepiece is the domed Italian Hall, with a disturbing *trompe l'oeil* pattern. From here, the itinerary takes you through Paul I's own quarters, decorated with every military motif imaginable, to Brenna's Greek Hall, a large room lined with black Corinthian columns and white marble statues. The next suite of rooms belonged to Maria Fyodorvna, Paul I's wife, and are as ornate as her husband's were austere. The walls, furniture and windows are all draped with delicately embroidered silk fabrics, though the *pièce de resistance* is the 64-piece Sévres porcelain toilette set in the bedroom — a gift from Marie Antoinette.

The ground floor of the palace, where Paul and Maria actually lived, consists of smaller but still richly decorated rooms. Most beautiful of all is the lilac and yellow Corner Room, one of the earliest creations of the architect Carlo Rossi. An exhibition of photographs of the house at the end of World War Two reveals the extent of restoration work undertaken since.

If you haven't had your fill of interiors, you can visit the permanent exhibition of 19th-century Russian furniture on the second floor. Otherwise, head straight to the parks, which are at least as interesting as the palace itself. Many of the leading architects of the day including Cameron himself, Quarenghi and Brenna worked on the design of the 1,500-acre grounds. Instead of rigid geometric lines and formal parterres in the French style, the design follows the ground's natural slopes and curves. Rolling hills and wide open expanses attract cross-country skiers and sleighers in winter. In summer, the peaceful woodlands dotted with numerous classical temples and colonnades provide plenty of secluded spots for picnics.

Getting There. About 20 miles/32km south of St Petersburg, Pavlovsk is just one stop (and a couple of miles) beyond Tsarskoe Selo on the train. The entrance to the parks is through the large gate opposite the station: from here it's a 15-minute walk through the grounds to the palace, or you can catch bus 373, 370 or 493, which will take you straight to the palace. If you want to continue to Tsarskoe Selo afterwards, you can either go by train or on bus 282.

Pavlovsk Palace is open 10.30am-5.50pm, daily except Friday and the first Monday of the month.

ORANIENBAUM

This palace is exceptional in that it was not occupied or ravaged by the Germans during World War II. As a result it has been low on the list of priorities for restoration. The main palace has been closed for years and is not likely to reopen in the near future. However, the palace has an appealing air of melancholy, the parks are pleasant and a few buildings are open to the public.

At a time when Peter the Great had built only the relatively modest palace of Monplaisir at Peterhof, his flamboyant second-in-command, Prince Menshikov, was creating a colossal summer palace further west along the Gulf of Finland, on a site overlooking the island of Kronstadt. The name

Oranienbaum is a corruption of the German word for 'orange tree' — a reference to the orange trees which once covered the whole front lawn of the palace. Undeterred by unfavourable climatic conditions, the Russian aristocracy somehow succeeded where the best botanists would have thrown up their arms in despair.

Following Menshikov's death, the palace became another summer residence for the tsars. Catherine the Great was a regular here in the days before she usurped her husband's place on the throne. Frustrated ambitions and boredom encouraged a spate of construction in the parks that would have impressed even Marie Antoinette. The baby pavilion, which looks like a giant wedgewood sugar pot, was the starting point for a wooden rollercoaster. Unfortunately, the building is all that is left of what must have been a remarkable toy, but when the pavilion reopens after restoration you should be able to view a model of the the original. The finest structure artistically is the delicate Chinese pavilion a little further inland, its original interior being one of the best-preserved examples of rococo chinoiserie anywhere in the world. Closer to the entrance of the park, there is a miniature pink and white building — a gift from the Empress Elizabeth to her nephew, the Tsarevitch Peter III, who would supervise military parades from the balcony.

Getting There. Suburban trains run to Oranienbaum (renamed Lomonosov by the Soviets) about every half hour from the Baltic station; since it is on the same line as Peterhof, which lies just 6 miles/10km east, you could feasibly visit both palaces in a day. From Oranienbaum station, it is a 10-minute walk to the palace grounds: head for the church with its green onion domes and then ask. If you're hungry, there's a good pie shop on your left before you reach the church.

The Oranienbaum parks are open all year round. The Chinese pavilion opens only in summer (end of May to mid-September), from 11am-5pm daily except Tuesday and the last Monday of the month.

GATCHINA

This is the least ornate of the royal country residences, but it has a fine park where few tourists ever venture. The estate first belonged to Count Orlov, Catherine the Great's favourite lover, but many of its present features date from the period of Paul I. He added the moat (now empty) and stone bastions to the already austere building, lending it the appearance of a military stronghold.

Gatchina shared the fate of other palaces in the last war, sustaining extensive damage from mines and pillaging. Restoration work is ongoing and only a small section of the interior is open to visitors. On the ground floor there is a collection of weaponry, which includes pistols, bayonets and sabres inlaid wth ivory and encrusted with pearls, turquoise and coral. Paul I's state rooms can be visited on the first floor. Though more homely than those at the Peterhof or Catherine palaces, the spanking new floors and coat of fresh paint rather spoils the effect. It's worth venturing up to the top floor to see the numerous unflattering portraits of Paul, who was so ugly that he refused to have his portrait stamped on coins.

There is plenty of scope for walks and picnics in the parks, with their birch tree woods and silvery lakes. One of the most picturesque spots is by the Venus Pavilion, on a little promontory known as 'love island' which juts into the largest lake.

Getting There. Gatchina is a 70-minute train ride south of the city. Trains run fairly regularly from the Baltic station. The imposing bulk of the castle sits at the end of a tree-lined avenue behind the station. The palace opens 10am-5pm daily except Monday and the first Tuesday of the month.

KRONSTADT

Stranded in the Gulf of Finland on the tiny island of Kotlin and still officially a closed city, Kronstadt is caught in a strange time warp. In 1704, just one year after the founding of St Petersburg, Peter the Great established a fortress here to protect the approach to the city in case of Swedish attack. Kronstadt developed into an important naval base, most famous this century for the Kronstadt Rebellion in 1921, when Red Army troops crushed an uprising by sailors against the Bolsheviks, leaving 20,000 dead on both sides. Branded traitors by the communists, the sailors were only recently rehabilitated in a decree issued by Boris Yeltsin in 1994.

Kronstadt has remained a military base to this day, and for security reasons maintains a restrictive entrance policy. There is a checkpoint on the causeway that links Kronstadt to the mainland, and drivers are requested to show their documents before they can enter. Since 1992 foreigners have been allowed to visit, but like any other non-resident they are required to have a *propusk* or permit. Unless you happen to have friends in Kronstadt who can invite you over, the only legal way to visit is to join an official tour: see below.

With a population made up largely of sailors, who are confined to their ships in the harbour or to barracks, the town is eerily quiet. The streets, which have retained their Soviet names, with Lenin and Marx featuring prominently, are virtually devoid of traffic. Tourists are restricted to a handful of sights which are quirky rather than intrinsically interesting. They include a scaled-down version of the St Petersburg department store, Gostiny Dvor, several statues of brave Russian sailors and an enormous neo-byzantine cathedral that was built at the beginning of this century to glorify Russian naval achievements. The cupola still sports an anchor, but the interior is now shared by a cinema and a war museum. The battleships in the harbour can only be glimpsed from afar, but they look as though they haven't seen active service for a long time.

Getting There. As you officially require a permit to visit Kronstadt, the easiest and surest way to get there is to join a tour. Excursions in Russian can be booked from the Excursiu booths near Gostiny Dvor on ul Dumskava. These run once a week, usually on a Sunday, and deal with all the bureaucracy for you. Though joining a tour has the obvious benefit of guaranteeing that you will see the place, it can be frustrating since you are given little or no time to explore on your own. From the end of May to mid-September hydrofoils from Tuchkov Bridge on Vasilievsky Island run a regular service to Kronstadt. You don't need a permit to board, and with a bit of luck no one will ever check whether you have the right documentation at the other end. The other way to try and slip in unnoticed is to go by bus. There's a direct service which runs several times a day from near Chernaya Rechka metro station.

REPINO

The village of Repino lies 28 miles/45km northwest of St Petersburg on the Karelian Isthmus overlooking the Gulf of Finland. This whole coastline between the city and the Finnish border is very attractive, with pine forests extending right down to the sandy beaches. In summer the area is popular among Petersburgers, who come to swim and soak up the sun. In winter, when the sea freezes over, fishermen bore holes in the ice.

This area became part of Finland in 1917, but after the war with Finland in 1939-1940, it was annexed by the Soviet Union. Repino is named after the famous Russian realist painter Ilya Repin (1844-1930), who lived and worked here. His house, Penaty, was turned into a museum devoted to the life and work of the painter, but it is closed indefinitely for restoration.

Trains to Repino run from the Finland Station and take about an hour. To reach Penaty, head towards the sea from the station and after about 600m you come to a road named ulitsa Repina; turn left here. The house is at no. 63, some 500m from the turn.

Western Russia

Western Russia divides up into three main areas: Central Russia, the European North and the Volga region. The distances are vast but the terrain is not hugely varied. The rolling plains, broad valleys and dense woodland of Central Russia become lakes, turbulent rivers and granite hills in Karelia to the north; further south, undulating forest plain and meadows along the banks of the Volga.

Central Russia, whose heart is Moscow, is the most popular with visitors, the most publicized and the easiest to get around in. The cities in this heartland of Russia, including Vladimir, Suzdal and the other towns of the so-called Golden Ring, were the historical nucleus of the early Russian state.

The European North, of which St Petersburg is the kernel, takes up about a third of Western Russia. When the Russians talk of the 'north' they refer not so much to St Petersburg, but to Murmansk, the northernmost town in Russia, close to Norway. Its shores are lapped by the Arctic Ocean and embody the harsher aspect of the North. The green areas around Lake Onega and Kizhi Island further south provide much more humane conditions for those not accustomed to the extremities of the Russian climate.

The Volga area, with huge areas of unbroken monotonous steppe is an important industrial and agricultural area. The region is concentrated around the middle and lower reaches of the great Volga river. It has little of historical interest compared with the other areas of Russia, but the semi-autonomous republic of Tatarstan is one of the few success stories following the collapse of the Soviet Union.

The main centres of historical interest are northwest (Novgorod and Pskov) and northeast (the Golden Ring towns) of the capital, all treasure troves of national Russian architecture and art. Some have been sanitized by extensive restoration, but the overall effect of the white-stoned, gilt-domed churches and fortress-like monasteries has not been dulled. The beauty of the characteristic Byzantine-style churches is unsurpassed, and contrast sharply with the wooden peasant cottages that huddle around them.

All the cities of ancient Russia, such as Novgorod, Smolensk, Kursk, Suzdal and Yaroslavl, testify to a turbulent past. A distinguishing feature of many of these towns is the presence of massive fortifications built not only to protect the artisan and merchant communities but, ultimately, to defend Moscow itself. Successive invasions (notably by the Mongols), fires, feudal strife and Soviet excess are all to blame for the damage done to the treasures of these towns.

The area south of Moscow, towards Orel, is little visited, but it has a few literary connections which attract lovers of Russian literature. This section begins, however, with Europe's last remaining geo-political oddity: the splinter of former Prussia that is now part of Russia.

KALININGRAD

The size of Northern Ireland, Kaliningrad is a an anomaly, separated from the rest of the Russian Federation by the Baltic Republics and flanked on the west side by Poland — a pocket of the old Soviet Union marooned among changing Eastern European nations. From the 13th century until 1945, when Stalin annexed what was then part of East Prussia, Kaliningrad was a German province. But the expulsion of most Germans after the war and intense Russification means that little remains of its German past.

Home of the Baltic Fleet, Kaliningrad was always of too much strategic importance to be given over to any of the Soviet republics and was sealed off from the West completely for almost fifty years: foreigners have been allowed in only since 1991. It is still dominated by the military who, compared with a civilian population of about 800,000, number anything from 100,000 to 300,000 — as a result of the influx from former communist countries in Eastern Europe, no one really knows.

If the prospect of surrendering the splinter of Russia was to be seriously considered, the Kremlin could have a problem on its hands, given the restlessness of military commanders, the reluctance of thousands of troops to return home and the number of unused weapons which has spawned what is said to be one big arms market. A possible split between Lithuania and Poland has been discussed, though autonomy is also a possibility. For the moment, however, talk is mainly of a new free trade zone, and some optimists have already called Kaliningrad the 'Hong Kong on the Baltic'.

Not surprisingly, Kaliningrad does not have much of a tourist trade, though the number of German visitors is growing all the time. As one of the most curious places in Eastern Europe, Kaliningrad is a huge temptation just waiting to be explored.

Kaliningrad Town (Königsberg). British bombing and the Soviet assault wiped out most of Königsberg, the old capital of East Prussia, during the war. Now it is mostly new, with spiritless open spaces flanked by grim concrete blocks — ugliest of all the House of Soviets, begun in the 1960s but never finished and known locally as either 'the Monster' or, less imaginatively, the 'Uncompleted Project'; there is a Danish scheme to cover it with green glass and turn it into offices. The few remaining old buildings include the former stock exchange by the filthy river, and the ruined red-brick Gothic cathedral where Immanuel Kant is buried. The desire among some Kaliningraders to rediscover the German roots of the town has led to a few

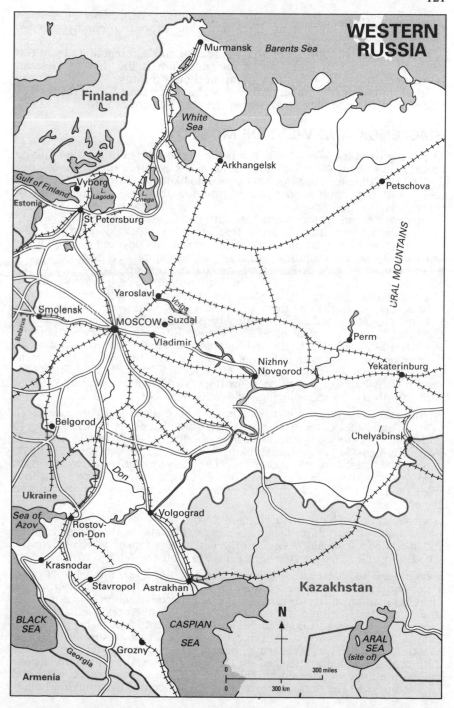

WESTERN RUSSIA

Barents Sea

Finland

Murmansk

White Sea

Arkhangelsk

Petschova

URAL MOUNTAINS

Gulf of Finland

Vyborg

L. Lagoda

L. Onega

Estonia

St Petersburg

Yaroslavl

Volga

Smolensk

MOSCOW • Suzdal

Belarus

Vladimir

Perm

Nizhny Novgorod

Yekaterinburg

Belgorod

Don

Chelyabinsk

Ukraine

Sea of Azov

Rostov-on-Don

Volgograd

Krasnodar

Stavropol

Astrakhan

Kazakhstan

BLACK SEA

Georgia

Grozny

CASPIAN SEA

N

ARAL SEA (site of)

Armenia

0   300 miles

0   300 km

restoration projects, but these are almost totally dependent on foreign (mainly German) investment. Even so, some pre-war monuments have already been resurrected.

There is a severe shortage of accommodation in Kaliningrad and you can count the number of hotels about on one hand. If the flow of German tourists continues, however, this situation should improve.

Street traders peddle amber. Kaliningrad has more than 80% of the world's amber, and you can pick up an amber necklace for under $10.

SMOLENSK AND WEST OF MOSCOW

Travelling from the West, Smolensk is the first big town in Russia that you reach. It lies about 40 miles/70km inside the Russian border with Belarus, 212 miles/340km west of Moscow. Few would liken it to Rome, but Smolensk and the Italian capital do share a common feature: the possession of seven hills.

Smolensk is one of the oldest Slav settlements in Russia, dating back to at least the sixth century. It grew steadily with the development of trade, the town's prosperity being largely dependent on its position on the Upper Dneiper. By the 12th century Smolensk was the capital of a principality and a large community of artisans and merchants grew up. At the end of the 16th century a huge stone wall was built to protect the city, symbolizing the important role Smolensk played in the defence of Russia and the town became known as the 'Western key to Moscow'. The walls, however, did not stop the Poles in the 17th century or Napoleon in 1812 from defeating the town. After the defeat of 1812 the town lost importance; by the time the Nazis attacked and devastated Smolensk it was just a provincial town. These days Smolensk is an industrial centre, but the Dneiper and the ancient city walls give it a certain character. The Kremlin, built in the 16th century on the right bank of the river, is an impressive sight as you arrive from Minsk, with its towers rising high above the Dneiper.

Arrival and Departure. Smolensk is on the rail route from Chop (Hungary), Warsaw and other cities to Moscow. There are also direct trains running to and from St Petersburg and the Baltic Republics. Approaching from the West, Smolensk is 200 miles/320km from the Belarusian capital Minsk, astride the Brest-Moscow motorway. The railway station is on the right bank; on the other side of the river lies the centre of town, enclosed within what remains of the old city walls. Tram 1 runs between the station and the centre.

Accommodation. The Rossiya Hotel at 25 ul Dzerzhinskovo is the epitome of a standard, dreary Intourlst hotel. You can also stay at the Phoenix Motel: it consists of a few chalets close to the Khvoiny campsite which lies in the woods ten miles/16km west of Smolensk, just off the road to Minsk.

Exploring. The oldest building in Smolensk is the Byzantine Church of SS Peter and Paul, which you reach by crossing the Dnieper Bridge on to the right bank and heading towards the station. Its construction began in 1146, and its greatest attribute is the majolica floor. On the opposite bank of the Dneiper, downstream along ul Malaya Krasnoflotskaya is the Svirskaya church, also 12th century and typical of the local architecture of the time. Walking up Bolshaya Sovietskaya, back across the river, you come to the 17th century cathedral, perched on the high bank. Of massive dimensions and with a huge wooden dome, the cathedral is a mixture of Baroque and Classical styles. The decoration inside is magnificent. The cathedral houses an icon of the Virgin Mary which is said to work miracles. Icon enthusiasts can go to the Art Museum at 7 ul Krupskaya which has a small but valuable collection. It includes some Western exhibits, such as work by Murillo.

Entertainment. The Philharmonia and the Puppet Theatre occupy the same building at 1 ul Soboleva, near the river.

Shopping. The Smolensk region is known for its 'northern silk' which is made from the local flax.

Further Afield. Ten miles/15km southeast of Smolensk along the Roslav Highway is the village of *Talashkino*. It contains the Teremok Museum, a branch of the Smolensk Museum of Local Lore, housed in a rather quaint, decorative wooden chalet built at the turn of the century. When newly built it was a popular centre among Russian artists. It now houses a large collection of folk art: the woodcarving, ceramics and embroidery are particularly beautiful.

Gnyozdovo is eight miles/13km from Smolensk along the Vitebsk road. You can also get there by train along the Koltso line or by bus number 2. This archaeological site includes thousands of graves and burial mounds, known as *kurgans*. A diverse collection of Arab, Russian and Scandinavian coins and jewellery has been found here.

SMOLENSK TO MOSCOW

Most of the towns east of Smolensk are not renowned for their charms, but some of them make convenient stops for motorists. Vyazma is 103 miles/165km east along the road to Moscow and was the site — like many of the towns in this area — of struggles with both Napoleon and the Nazis. It has an interesting 17th century cathedral on ul Nagomaya containing a miracle-working icon.

You can stop off at Gagarin (32 miles/54km east of Vyazma) for a bite to eat by the river in the centre of town; or carry on for a further 40miles/72km to Mozhaisk, just off the highway. The ruins of the Luzhetsky Monastery (16th-17th century) and the cathedral of St Nicholas (19th century) are both worth a detour. Seven miles/11km west of Mozhaisk, the Battle of Borodino took place in 1812 between Napoleon's and the Russian armies. You can wander among the battlefield which is littered with monuments: rather an eerie experience.

Continuing east, ten miles/16km north of the motorway from Kubinka and only 20 miles/32km from Moscow is Zvenigorod. The Moskva river cuts through the wooded hills forming dramatic ravines and creating a beautiful setting for the ancient town. The oldest part of Zvenigorod is Gordorok, an earthen rampart that stretches high above the Moskva river. The white-stone cathedral (Sobor na Gorodke), built in 1400, is a fine example of the early architecture of the Moscow school. Two kilometres upstream ls the Savvino-Storozhevsky Monastery with gold-domed cathedrals and churches, founded in the late 14th century and frequented by Ivan the Terrible. The gem of the complex is the Cathedral of the Nativity of the Virgin, built in 1404 and containing interesting frescoes.

NORTHWEST OF MOSCOW: KLIN AND TVER

Both these cities lie northwest of Moscow along Route 10, the St Petersburg Highway. Klin is 56 miles/90km from Moscow; Tver is 84 miles/145km from the capital and 340 miles/550km from St Petersburg. The two together can be visited in a day from Moscow, or you could break your journey between the capital and St Petersburg.

Klin. This ancient town lies beyond Lake Senezhskoye which is a popular weekend spot amongst walkers. Klin itself is famous for the Tchaikovsky Museum which lies just outside the town. Tchaikovsky lived here for two years shortly before his death in St Petersburg (in 1894). It was here that he composed the music for *The Nutcracker* and *Sleeping Beauty*. This small wooden house has been preserved as it was in his time, with his own books, piano and other personal effects. On 7 May and 6 November (the anniversaries of his birth and death) each year, eminent Russian pianists give recitals. Even for non-devotees it is a surprisingly moving museum.

Twenty-two miles (35km) north of Klin is the 'Moscow Sea' reservoir where the Sosa and Volga rivers meet. This is another popular picnic spot, much frequented by Muscovites.

Tver. This ancient trading port spreads out along the terraces on the banks of the Upper Volga. The town was founded as a military outpost but in the 14th and 15th centuries became an important cultural centre. The work of its stonemasons, jewellers and other artisans was renowned. The old buildings that managed to survive the feudal battles were almost totally destroyed by a great fire in 1763. Catherine the Great sent architects from Moscow to redesign the town and their layout has been largely preserved.

The heart of the city is ul Sovietskaya which runs parallel to the Volga for part of its course. Ul Utritsky traverses ul Sovietskaya at Lenin Square and leads down to the riverboat station.

Accommodation. The best rooms and services are in the fairly new Tver Motel which is off the Moscow-St Petersburg highway. As well as hotel rooms, there are also camping facilities here during the summer. The Chaikha restaurant near the riverboat station on the left bank, serves the best local food.

Exploring. The oldest monument is the White Trinity Church (Belaya Troitsa) dating from the 16th century. The jewel of Tver, however, is the perfectly proportioned Putyevoi Palace (Putyevoi Dvorets) between ul Sovietskaya and the Volga west of Lenin Square. It was built as a resting place for Catherine II when she travelled to St Petersburg from Moscow. Built in 1765 by Kazakov (the main exponent of Russian classicism), it is an imposing building with its graceful pavilions overlooking the vast square. The palace buildings now house the local museum and an art gallery: of these the best is the local museum (3/21 ul Nakhimova) which has displays of jewellery, textiles, ancient manuscripts and early printed books. For a glimpse of everyday life at Tver go to the Central Market on Ploshchad Kommuny; otherwise most of the good shops are along ul Sovietskaya and ul Utritsky. A trip to Tver in winter is especially exciting for sport fans, because speedway events and hockey matches are in full flow. Cross-country skiing tours are also arranged from the Tver Motel. From here you can go on skiing hikes and sled rides through the snow-covered forests and open country.

NOVGOROD

Novgorod translates simply to 'New Town', but it has little in common with Crawley or countless characterless Russian cities. It is one of the gems of Russia and full of interest for visitors. It stands on the banks of the broad

Volkhov river and beyond its boundaries fields stretch far into the distance. Novgorod is a majestic city, heavy with elegant buildings and the blue and gold domes of the churches and monasteries. Founded by Vikings, Novgorod is one of the oldest cities in Russia. It was first mentioned in the 9th century when it was part of the Kievan Rus, the first ancient Russian feudal state. Its position on the Volkhov — which links the Gulf of Finland via the Dnieper to the Black Sea — ensured its rapid development as a centre for trade, culture and crafts. Novgorod's chronicles are also the earliest records of Russian history and by this means influenced historical writing. Between the 12th and 15th centuries Novgorod was the capital of its own feudal state and as its power and territory increased, the city became known as 'Novgorod the Great'. The skill of both its soldiers and merchants was almost legendary.

It is easier today to appreciate the skill of its craftsmen who built and decorated the churches. The Novgorod school of artists was highly respected and was responsible for buildings all over Russia. In the 14th century Greek artists brought to Novgorod the innovations of the Byzantine renaissance, evidence of which can still be seen. In 1478 it became part of the Russian empire. Subsequently, with the building of St Petersburg in the 18th century, Novgorod lost its former importance. After the damage done by the Nazis during the Second World War, many of the buildings were restored. The result is a truly beautiful city.

Arrival and Departure. Novgorod is about 120 miles/190km southeast of St Petersburg and about 300 miles/500km northwest of Moscow, accessible by train from both cities. The journey from Moscow (via Chudovo) takes about 10 hours, from St Petersburg about three. By car you simply follow the St Petersburg Highway between St Petersburg and Moscow. From St Petersburg it is possible to take a tour of Novgorod in a day but to do the city justice you should stay longer.

City Layout. The Volkhov river cuts the city in two. The area on the left bank around the Kremlin is known as the Sophia Quarter (Sofiskaya Storona) and is the kernel of Novgorod. The zone on the other side of the river is called the Merchant Quarter (Torgovaya Storona). The main shopping street is ul Gorkova, which skirts the northern walls of the Kremlin.

Accommodation. The Intourist Hotel at 16 ul Dmitreivskaya (tel 7-5089) is smaller than most of its namesakes elsewhere in Russia and is relatively friendly. The Sadko at 16 Prospekt Gagarina (tel 9-5170) is just on the edge of the old city on the right bank. The Volkhov, behind the Kremlin at 24 ul Nekrasova (tel 92495) is smaller and of a slightly higher standard. Campers should seize the chance to stay on the Novgorodsky campsite in Savino, a delightful village six miles/10km from the centre of Novgorod (tel 7-2448).

Eating and Drinking. Outside the hotels the only real alternative is the Detinets Restaurant in the 14th century Pokrovsky Tower in the Kremlin. It serves a wide choice of national cuisine and there is a terrace open during the summer. Colin Thubron describes the place in *Among the Russians*: 'A maze of stairs and storeys twined church and tower indivisibly together. Embalmed in the monastic aura of rough-hewn benches and wrought-iron candelabra, the diners were slopping down borshch and solyanka where once the incense-blue spaces had thundered to the cherubikon or (if they were in the tower) to some less holy language.'

Exploring. The Kremlin — also known as the Detinets — was built in 1044 by Greek architects, but has been rebuilt many times since then. The origins of the present construction date from the 15th century and it is the oldest surviving Russian kremlin. Many of its buildings have been converted into museums but its striking character has not been lost. The St Sophia Cathedral with its six domes in the central square is the most notable monument. It is the oldest surviving stone building in Northern Russia, and for centuries was the centre of the political and religious life of Novgorod. The interior is rather austere save for the fragments of medieval murals. Do not miss the bronze Sigtuna door on the west side that was brought back from Sweden in the 12th century as war booty. West of St Sophia is the Vladichny Dvor or Archbishop's Palace. It was at this palace that Ivan the Terrible in 1570 had many of the nobles of Novgorod murdered as punishment for their refusal to toe the line. The most stunning feature of the Vladichny Dvor is the Hall of Facets (Granovitaya Palata), a huge Gothic hall on the second floor.

Leaving the Kremlin to the west you come out into the huge Victory Square. The Sophia Quarter on the left bank has numerous fascinating churches each of which is worth visiting. They form a semicircle around the Kremlin which is hemmed in by the river to the east. By walking upstream past Kremlin Park and St Blasius you come to Lake Myachino where the beautiful church of St Thomas is situated. From here you can begin a semicircular tour of the quarter by roughly following the old ramparts of the city from St Thomas right across to the Church of the Intercession (Pokrov) to the north. This route takes you past or near the major churches. One of the most interesting is the church of Peter and Paul on Blue Tit Hill (Petrai-Pavla-na-Sinicei-Gorye) which stands to the west of the lake. It has survived almost intact from the 12th century.

From the left bank there is a bridge across to the Merchant Quarter, just downstream from the Kremlin, where the Moscow-St Petersburg road crosses the Volkhov. The Yaroslav Court (Yaroslavov Dvor) was the heart of the quarter and an important meeting place and commercial centre. It is partially enclosed, and there is an arcaded Market Hall (Gostinov Dvor) by the river which provides a great view of the Kremlin on the opposite bank. The hall and its octagonal tower dates from the 17th century. There is a remarkably compact group of seven churches in the immediate area. The rather severe St Nicholas Cathedral (Nikolo-Dvorishchensky Sobor) dominates the Court. It has in fact replaced St Sophia as Novgorod's main cathedral.

To see the other churches in the quarter you could follow a semi-circular route almost parallel to the one recommended for the Sophia churches. Don't miss any out if possible but there are two of particular interest. Beyond ul Ilyinskaya is the Spas-na-Ilyine Church. Built in 1374, it is one of the most magnificent churches in Novgorod. Some of the decoration is a little over the top but the murals, painted by the Greek artist Theophanes in 1378, are spectacular and went beyond the the strict canons laid down by Byzantine religious painting. North of here on ul Moskovskaya (the Moscow-St Petersburg Highway) is the Feodor Stratilates Church (Fiodora Stratilata na Routchiou). It dates from the 14th century and became a model for the architects of Novgorod. The Byzantine influence evident in the lovely 14th century frescoes has prompted speculation that they were by Theophanes himself, but this is thought to be unlikely.

Entertainment. Evening entertainment centres around the Kremlin where you will find both the Philharmonia and the Drama Theatre. Between 25 December and 5 January every year, the Russian Winter Festival takes place within the Vitoslavlitsy Museum of Folk Architecture (see below). There is folk dancing and people play games, drink old Russian mead and eat hot pancakes.

Around Novgorod. As within the city, most of the sights around Novgorod are churches. The majority lie on or near the Volldlov River or Lake Ilmen, which is four miles/7km south of the city. Visiting them by riverboat is the pleasantest way to see them. Three miles/5km south of Novgorod is the village of Yuriev where you can visit the open air Vitoslavlitsy Museum of Folk Architecture. For something a little more unusual, go to the nearby St George's Church and Monastery which is not far from Lake Ilmen. Built in the 12th century, it has distinctive blue domes. Further east down the river is where you can visit the village of Seltso and the Church of the Redeemer (Spasa na Gorie Nereditse), dating from the 12th century. It is a small, elegant church but unfortunately only fragments of the once magnificent frescoes now remain due to damage done during the war. The church is only open in the summer, and accessible only by boat.

PSKOV

Pskov lies on the Novgorod-Riga highway near the border of Estonia and Latvia at the confluence of the Velikaya and Pskov rivers, on the south bank of Lake Pskov. Throughout its history Pskov has had to defend its western borders against attack from Teutonic Knights, Lithuanians, Poles and Swedes. The town was under the power of Novgorod for many years but also had a period of independence before it was swallowed up by Moscow in the 15th century. Perhaps Pskov's greatest fame came in 1917 when Nicholas II, the last Russian tsar, signed his abdication here.

Like other towns in western Russia, Pskov suffered severely during the Second World War but a large number of monuments — dating from the 12th century onwards — survived and have been restored. Pskov deserves greater attention than it generally receives at present.

Arrival and Departure. Trains run to Pskov from Novgorod, a distance of 150 miles/240km. From Moscow (430 miles/690km) the journey takes about 12 hours. Pskov lies 140 miles/226km southwest of St Petersburg (four hours by train). The train and bus station is in Privokzalnaya Square at the end of Oktyabrsky Prospekt, the town's main street.

Accommodation. The Rizhskaya is at 2-6 Rizhskoye Shosse (tcl 2-4301/3-3243). For meals out try the Pskov Restaurant at 5a ul Jana Fabritsius or the Gera down the road at number 2/117.

Exploring. There is a wealth of sights in Pskov warranting a stay of at least two or three days if possible. A map is essential, and one can be obtained from the tourist office at 4 ul Krasnoznamenskaya.

The Kremlin, one of Pskov's oldest monuments, is the highlight of the town and perches high on the cliff at the confluence of the rivers. Its largest monument is the elegant Trinity Cathedral which was built in 1699 and became the focal point of Pskov. An arcade beneath the cathedral leads to the castle walls from where you reach the Dovmontov Gorod, south of the Krernlin. During the Middle Ages there were 19 churches in this district and some of their foundations have been restored to show what the medieval town was like. There are some interesting buildings here, such as the Prikaznaya Palace. From Dovmontov Gorod there is a fine view of Sredny Gorod (Central Quarter), formerly known as Lenin Square. Walking down ul Sovietskaya towards October Square, next to the Central Post Office is the Church of St Michael the Archangel. This was the first stone church in Pskov, built in the 14th century. At number 50 ul Sovietskaya is the Menshikov Mansion which is a former merchant home dating from the 17th century. From here you can climb up to the Church of St Basil on the Hill (Vasily-na-Gorke), built in the mid-15th century. It is a beautifully elegant church and the simple decoration is typical of the Pskov school of the time. From ul Sovietskaya take ul Sverdlov to the river where there are various churches worth exploring.

Wandering down ul Marksa in Stary Torg (Old Market quarter), notice the interesting merchant house at number 10. You reach the old Okolny quarter which is a particularly beautiful part of town. Go down some of the streets near the river and around ul Krasnykh Partizan and you will see some of the best examples of Pskov's mercantile heritage, such as the 17th century Solodezhnya (Malt House) at number 42 ul Gogolevskaya, near the river. Southwest from here is the Polish Quarter where there are a couple of interesting 16th and 17th century churches. At 3 ul Nekrasova is the Pogankin Mansion which belonged to a merchant family and is one of Pskov's most famous 17th century buildings. It was once a fortress and contained warehouses, a shop and living quarters. It now houses the Museum of History, Architecture and Art with a collection of icons, ancient manuscripts and books.

One of the gems of Pskov is the 11th century Mirozhsky Monastery on the left bank of the Velikaya. In its grounds is the Cathedral of Our Saviour, one of Pskov's earliest stone buildings. The Byzantine influence is seen most in the frescoes. Crossing the river at Sovietskaya Square takes you into the Zapskovye district on the right bank of the river. Both the churches and the secular buildings are concentrated in the vicinity of ul Leon Pozemsky. A couple to notice are the Kozma and Demian (churches close to the river, dating from the 15th century), and Trubinksy House on ul Leon Pozemsky which is probably the finest secular building in Pskov.

Entertainment. The main concert hall is in the Musical College at 2 ul Libknekhta. There is also a puppet theatre at 3 ul Konnaya. For outdoor entertainment, the Pushkin Summer Gardens in Ploshchad Zhertv Revolutsii is the best place to go. For horse racing fans there is a racecourse on ul Ippodromnaya.

Excursions from Pskov

The Pechory Monastery: the town of Pechory is 31 miles/52km west of Pskov, close to the Estonian border. The monastery was founded in the 15th century when monks sought refuge within the caves here. In the 16th century walls were built around the monastery complex which became an important defensive outpost up to the 18th century. There are caves above the steep banks of a stream which are still used as a graveyard.

The Alexander Pushkin Museum: this museum actually comprises the villages of Mikhailovskoye, Trigorskoye, Petrovskoye and Svakina Gorka and the Svyatogorsk Monastery, all of which are associated with Pushkin. It is worth touring even if you aren't an ardent Pushkin fan since you cover picturesque forested country. Perhaps the loveliest spot is the monastery which stands on the Pushkin Hills above a sea of woods. Pushkin, shot during a duel in 1837, is buried here. Every year on the first Sunday of June admirers, poets and writers gather together for the traditional Poetry Festival to celebrate his birth.

KIZHI ISLAND

The local Karelians call Kizhi the eighth wonder of the world. A trip to

Kizhi Island is a superb excursion that gives you the chance to explore the charm of the Karelian region with its dense forests, turbulent rivers, the huge Lake Onega and enjoy the tranquillity which is the hallmark of Northern Russia. Petrozavodsk is the capital of Karelia and lies on the shores of Lake Onega of which Kizhi is one of the numerous islands. The lake forms part of the canal (Belomorkanal) linking the White Sea and the Baltic. Kizhi actually lies some 250 miles/400km northeast of St Petersburg and can be an easy extension on to a tour of northern Russia. Kizhi Island is only open between May and October.

You can go by train (9 hours from St Petersburg and 15 hours from Moscow) to Petrozavodsk, from where the Kometa hydrofoil takes people to the island. You can also catch a boat from the river port in St Petersburg (195 Prospekt Obukovskoi), though this service is somewhat erratic. This trip can be done individually or in tour groups and is best done over a weekend. The best time to visit is in May and June when you should get a breathtaking view of the Northern Lights. Petrozavodsk itself is of little interest, but visitors to Kizhi are likely to be based at the Intourist Hotel here. If you are staying overnight eat at the Petrovsky Restaurant in ul Marksa: it has 18th century-style decor and is quite fun.

Kizhi Island is one of the oldest settlements in Russia. Its name comes from *Kizhasuari* which means 'Island of Games'. At one time, as well as being the site for games, Kizhi was an important stop on the trade route to the White Sea. It is now an open-air museum consisting of secular and religious buildings which have been brought from various parts of northern Russia, mostly from Karelia and other islands of Omega. They are all built of wood and date from the 18th century. Wandering around the island you come across villages (most of the islanders live in the north of the island), windmills, huts and chapels. The only churches actually to be built on the island are easily the most impressive: the Church of the Transfiguration (Preobrazhenskaya Tserkov) has 22 domes and was built without the help of one nail. The Church of the Intercession (Pokrovskaya Tserkov) is simpler but no less beautiful with its crown of domes around the central cupola and the sumptuous iconostasis.

Kivach National Park is 53 miles/85km northwest of Petrozavodsk. The journey there by train takes about 90 minutes. The area is covered in pine and fir forest where bears and lynxes roam, and is full of waterfalls. Of these the most beautiful — the 'mother of waterfalls' — is the Kivach Waterfall.

MURMANSK

'Murman' in the local Saami language means 'the edge of the world'. The northernmost city in the world, Murmansk lies on the Kola Peninsula in the northwest corner of Russia, 125 miles/200km above the Arctic Circle. Thanks to the Gulf Stream, winters are fairly mild and the sea never actually freezes. The average temperature in July is 8°C and in January −5°C. Between November and January the sun disppears beyond the horizon bringing on the long polar nights, which last for more than 50 days. The long Arctic nights end on the last Sunday of January. Between May and July the sun never sets.

You can get to Murmansk from Moscow in two hours by air or 32 hours by train. All trains go via St Petersburg.

There isn't much to do in Murmansk apart from soak in the air and appreciate the novelty of being within the Arctic Circle. There is the ubiquitous local museum (in ul Lenina), but summer visitors would do best to go on an excursion along the River Tuloma to see the migration of salmon to their spawning grounds, which takes place from June to September. There are also hydrofoil trips across Kola Bay to permit a casual exploration of the Arctic coast. April is a good time to visit, when the Festival of the Peoples of the North takes place. There are various competitions such as, harnessed dog and reindeer races, hammer throwing contests, lassoing and crosscountry ski races.

THE GOLDEN RING

This area northeast of Moscow is a fascinating part of Russia: it is the home of a group of old towns known as the Golden Ring. These towns, which possess great architectural treasures, are Zagorsk, Pereslavl-Zalessky, Rostov-Veliky, Yaroslavl, Vladimir and Suzdal. Winter or summer are both good times to go since both the snow and sunlight highlight the beauty of the gilt domes and ivory-coloured buildings.

FROM ZAGORSK TO YAROSLAVL

This area is ideally covered by car, but there are also trains to Rostov and Yaroslavl, leaving Moscow from the Yaroslavl station. By car you must follow the M9 Moscow-Yaroslavl highway. Yaroslavl is 155 miles/248km from Moscow so the distances to cover are not great.

Zagorsk. The road to Zagorsk crosses lovely countryside and pretty villages with old churches. About 40 miles/70km from Moscow the domes of Zagorsk's churches and the huge Trinity and St Sergius monastery appear on the left.

The Trinity Monastery of St Sergius (Troitse-Sergiyeva Lavra) is the biggest monastery in Russia. It was founded in 1340 by Sergius, who came from the Rostov area on an evangelizing crusade. Sergievo, as the town was then known, became an important religious centre and the monastery itself was also important culturally and politically in this northeastern area. Its popularity amongst pilgrims grew when Sergius' body was removed intact after the wooden church where it lay had been burnt down by Tatars in 1408. Such was the affection and reverence felt by the Russians for the monastery that the Bolsheviks refrained from sacking it, and turned it into a museum after the Revolution. Now most of the churches are once more open for worship and pilgrims continue to flock to Zagorsk. The seminary and monastery still function and are very lively.

The monastery is a breathtaking sight as it emerges from behind the rather intimidating white walls with its beautiful gold and blue domes lavishly decorated with stars. The distinctive Baroque bell-tower was built in the 18th century by Rastrelli, the architect of the Winter Palace in St Petersburg. The churches and monastery contain staggering collections of icons (some of which are the work of major Russian icon painters), sculpture and folk craft. The buildings themselves do not date from one period. The Church of the Trinity (Troitsky Sobor) dates from the 15th century and although rather severe looking, is the highlight of the monastery with its single dome. The iconostasis inside was painted by Rublyev, one of Russia's best known icon-painters. Unfortunately what you see today are just copies, the originals having been transferred to the Tretyakov Gallery in Moscow. The atmosphere created by the uplifting sound of chanting, the pleasantly intoxicating smell of incense and the sight of pilgrims lighting candles, is quite moving.

There is often a queue of people waiting to kiss the ornate sarcophagus where Sergius lies. The distinctive domes in the monastery belong to the Cathedral (Uspensky Sobor) built in 1554. Next to a tiny chapel nearby is the tomb of Boris Godunov, former Tsar of Russia.

Pereslavl-Zalessky. Pereslavl lies 42 miles/67km north of Zagorsk (87 miles/ 140km from Moscow, 80 miles/130km from Yaroslavl). The town lies on the shores of Lake Plescheyevo where it joins River Trubezh, hence its name 'city of waters'. Throughout its life it has been subject to foreign invaders including Turks and Poles, and its architecture is visibly defensive in style. It was here, on Lake Pleshcheyevo that Peter the Great's fleet was born at the end of the 17th century.

Pereslavl is one of the most interesting Russian towns and is full of beautiful churches. The white, single-domed Cathedral of the Tranfflguration of Our Lord is the finest monument; it is in Red Square (Krasnaya Plosh-chad), the historical centre of Pereslavl. It was built in 1152 — the year of Pereslavl's foundation — on the spot where, according to local legend, Alcxander Nevsky, the great Russian military leader, was born. It is an extremely elegant building and an early example of the prestigious Vladimir-Suzdal school of architecture. The Church of St Peter the Metropolitan nearby, with an extraordinary tent-roof, dates from the 16th century.

It is the monasteries just outside Pereslavl, however, which are the most distinctive feature of the town. To the north is the Nikitsky Monastery (largely 16th century) with its fortified walls and towers; its complex includes a cathedral, church and a rather gloomy refectory. To the south, high on a hill, is the 17th century Goritsky Monastery. It houses a collection of wooden sculpture and icons, but the most fascinating things here are the beautifully carved Holy Gates. The monastery is closed on Tuesdays. You can walk around the northern shore to Mount Alexander (Alexandrova Gora) from where there is a fine view of Pereslavl.

Rostov-Veliky. This town, more commonly abbreviated to Rostov, lies on the banks of Lake Nero. It is 40 miles/65km north of Pereslavl and 35 miles/ 57km southwest of Yaroslavl. A contemporary of Novgorod, Rostov has been an important centre throughout its history. Founded in 852, by the 10th century it was the capital of the Rostov-Suzdal principality and then in 1207 of the powerful Rostov principality. A period of decline followed Rostov's annexation to Muscovy in the 15th century. The 17th century was Rostov's zenith when the Metropolitan, Iona Sysoyevitch, was behind the building of many of Rostov's present monuments, including the Kremlin. People flocked here in their thousands during the 18th and 19th centuries, from as far away as Greece, for its famous annual trade fair. In 989 Lake Nero was the scene of a mass baptism: Vladimir I, a fierce ruler turned saint, ordered the conversion to Chrishanity of the whole population. Priests from Constantinople rowed around the lake baptizing all the inhabitants.

Begin at the Kremlin which encloses within imposing walls a complex of buildings with silvery roofs and gilded domes. The Metropolitan Palace — also known as the White Palace (Belaya Palata) — is the main attraction of the Kremlin. It is a large hall that was used for official ceremonies and was built as the Metropolitan's residence in the 1670s. From here you can walk on to the Kremlin walls which give access to the main courtyard and the churches over the entrance gates. Outside the Kremlin is the Cathedral (Uspenksy Sobor) dating from the 16th century and a bell-tower boasting 13 bells: seeing a performance of Rostov bell-ringers is a real treat. From Cathedral Square all the main roads fan out in a radial plan. There are two monasteries, east and west of the Kremlin, on the banks of the lake. Both are worth seeing. The best view of the town is to be had from a boat: these boats are on hire from the park by the lake. On your wanderings keep an eye open for the finiftware (copperware decorated with enamel) for which Rostov was famous in the 18th century and which it still produces.

YAROSLAVL

Yaroslavl lies on the Upper Volga 40 miles/57km northeast of Rostov. The history books say that in 1010 Yaroslavl the Wise, Prince of Rostov, conquered the Slavic settlement here and built a fortress. Being on the Volga the town developed fast and by the 13th century was the centre of its own principality which was incorporated into Muscovy in 1463. Yaroslavl developed a widespread reputation for its art and architecture, especially in the 17th century — this was Yaroslavl's golden age — when the town had a great cultural influence on the rest of Central Russia. Having become a major centre for trade it lost importance in the 18th century when the port of St Petersburg was built. Today Yaroslavl is a major industrial centre with 600,000 inhabitants. It is still rich in ancient monuments, however, the majority dating from the 17th century; Yaroslavl avoided the devastation of World War II suffered by so many Russian cities. Thankfully most of the industrial buildings have been built in the suburbs; as you wander amongst the churches and fine classical mansions built by rich merchants and nobles it is easy to forget the smoking factories on the outskirts.

City Layout. The oldest part of the town is on the high right bank of the Volga which is called Nagorny Bereg (Hill Bank) by the locals; the low left bank where there are orchards and colourful wooden houses is called the Pugovoy Bereg (Meadow Bank).

Arrival and Departure. Yaroslavl has two railway stations, Glavny (main) and Moscovsky. Travellers from Moscow and other big cities will arrive, surprisingly, in Glavny. The number 1 trolleybus takes you directly to the centre of town. Moscovsky is a smaller station for mainly local trains; passengers from other Golden Ring towns may arrive at Moscovsky.

Accommodation. The Intourist Hotel on the banks of the Kotorosol River is rather seedy and rundown. Try the Volga on ul Kirova or Druzhba on ul Pushkina instead.

Eating and Drinking. By Russian standards Yaroslavl has a few pleasant cafes. Try the Lira on Volskaya Nabreznaya, not far from the harbour or Yartek off ul Kieva. For some bizarre reason the Reebok shop on ul Ustinsky sells trainers, coffee and delicious chocolate eclairs.

The choice of restaurants is rather limited. The Hungaria, past the Children's Theatre (Ploshad Unost) on Ul. Cvobodi is highly recommended but quite pricey. Expect to pay up to $10 for a main course. If you are on a limited budget, the Raduga on Prospect Tolbrukina sells cheap, solid pizzas. Vegetarians should ask for one *s lukom* (with onion). Hop on the number 2 or 3 tram for 3 stops. The large road to the right is Prospect Tolbukina. Cafe Argo on ul Pervomaiskaya is also quite reasonably priced but service is slow. It is best to avoid the Chinese restaurants on Ploschad Karla Marksa; a meal will set you back about $30 and it tends to be a hang out for the local mafiosi.

Exploring. The principal sights are concentrated in an area called the Strelka. It grew up in the 17th century on the right bank of the Volga. Soviet Square is a good starting place for a tour of the town. The church of Elijah the Prophet with elegant open porches, brightly painted portals and interesting icons, dominates the Square. Notice the fresco above the door, like other 17th century churches in Yaroslavl it is particularly vivid. From here head straight towards the white walled Spassky Monastery. As you wander past the painted merchants houses, the Bell Tower and Cathedral of Transfiguration should be visible in the distance. The monastery in Epiphany Square (formerly Podbelsky) has long been a dominant feature of Yaroslavl's architectural heritage. It was founded in the 13th century. but the building now dates from 1640, when a new fortress was constructed. It is unfortunately no longer a working monastery, but houses the local history and craft museums.

Next to the monastery is the church of the Epiphany. Dating from 1684, this church, with green shutters and domes, is remarkable for its enamel work. The nearly Rostov Beliky was the centre in the 17th century for brightly coloured enamel work. Outside the monastery and Church of the Epiphany you will notice the yellow collonaded building. This is Gostinny Dvor, the old trading centre. Beyond it, the golden dome on the white tower marks the old entrance to Yaroslavl. The tower was built in 1659 to replace one burnt down the preceding year.

Yaroslavl, once renowned for its array of over 80 glittering domes, has only one permanent working church. St Fyoder's is situated a little out of the centre but it is worth the trek for both the atmosphere and the magnificent frescoes. Take the no. 2 tram over the bridge. St Fyoder's is five minutes walk from the stop — services are held daily at 11am and 6pm.

When you've had your fill of churches, an attractive 19th century merchant's house on the banks off the Volga. now houses a collection of local paintings. The museum is open daily, from 10-6 except on Fridays. Music lovers might be interested in a new private museum further along the river bank call Music and Time. It includes a collection of traditional Russian instruments and clocks. In the summer you can go on a boat ride along the Volga, in the winter you can walk across it.

Entertainment. Concerts are often held at the Philharmonic Hall at Komitetskaya ul 13. The cinema programme is billboarded at the beginning of Svobodi ul. There is no need to understand Russian as the dubbing is so appalling that the English is perfectly clear.

VLADIMIR AND SUZDAL

A trip to these two beautiful towns is one of the highlights of any trip to Russla, such is the concentration of magnificent monuments spanning seven centuries. An exciting time to go is during the annual Russian Winter Festival between December 25 and January 5. There are great festivities in both towns, including sideshows, troika rides and so on, or you could spend a day or two skiing cross-country.

Arrival and Departure. Trains run frequently from Kursk station in Moscow. Motorists should follow M8, the Vladimir Highway, which is also the main road for Gorky and Kazan. This road was once notorious as the Vladimirka Road along which convicts were taken in droves to exile in Siberia. Vladimir is 120 miles/190km east of Moscow and Suzdal, off the main road, is 25 miles/40km northeast of Vladimir. The best route is via the village of Bogolyubovo, six miles/10km east of Vladimir. A good place for lunch is the Russkaya Skazka Restaurant along this road

VLADIMIR

Vladimir is one of the greatest cities of art in central Russia, thanks to its beautiful 12th and 13th century monuments. The splendid white stone and gold-domed churches and other monuments dominate the steep right bank of the river Klyazma, a tributary of the Volga. Vladimir Monomakh, Prince of Kiev, built a fortress at Vladimir in 1108 and by 1157 this young town was already the capital of the large Vladimir-Suzdal principality. It was during this period that the town became an important artistic centre and that the Vladimir-Suzdal style of painting and architecture was developed. Political decline, however, began with the Mongol invasion of 1238. In the 15th century Vladimir was absorbed into Russia.

The part Vladimir played in the emergence of the Russian people and the Russian state is often underestimated: much of this Republic's cultural heritage was created or collected here. In the 18th century stone houses, arcades of shops and other buildings appeared and these have survived alongside earlier monuments and modern industrial buildings. The city centre lies between the rivers Klyazma and Lybed. The main square is Freedom Square, in the old town, across which runs the main thoroughfare, ul Tretyevo Internatsionala (Third International Street).

Eating and Drinking. Make the most of the restaurants here as they are the best you'll find in the area. The Traktir Restaurant at 2 ul Stolyarova is in the form of a rather stylized Russian peasant cottage but they serve good national cuisine. The Golden Gates Restaurant at 17 ul Tretyevo Internatsionala has a novel interior too, the walls being laden with the coats of arms of local towns. The Russkaya Derevnya gives you good old-fashioned food and high-quality vodka (mostly Swedish).

Exploring. As you approach Vladimir from the west the Golden Gates (Zolotye vorota) appear before you. These are the first of several 12th century monuments characteristic of the Vladimir-Suzdal school. They are modelled on the gates of Kiev and were at one time a vital part of the town's fortifications. They are made of white stone and are crowned by a domed chapel. Heading up ul Tretyevo Internatsionala, which climbs up the hill from behind the gates, you pass the indoor market on the left. High up on the right of Freedom Square is the Cathedral of the Assumption (Uspensky Sobor), with its five domes. Built in 1158 by Andrei Bogolyubsky — who was responsible for making Vladimir capital of the principality — it later served as a model for the Moscow cathedrals. Long after power had shifted to Moscow this cathedral was the most important cathedral in Russia, a position it still seems to relish as it perches on the edge of a plateau, overlooking the forest and meadows below. The decoration is lavish and some of the old murals have survived, but the majority are those restored by Rublyev (whose icons you can see in Zagorsk) and Daniil Cherny in 1408. Observing a service in the cathedral, which is very active, can be a most moving experience.

The austere Cathedral of St Demetrius (Dimitrievsky sobor), built by Bogolyubsky's successor, Vsevolod, in 1193-7, lies nearby to the east. Some consider it the finest building in Vladimir and it is one of the most beautiful cathedrals you are likely to see in the country. It is perfectly proportioned with its single dome. There are some superb reliefs on the facade, depicting rampaging demons alongside rows of serene apostles. It is no longer in use but you can go inside and admire the fragments of frescoes inside.

The other monuments in Vladimir are meagre in comparison, but Pushkin Park, off the main street, gives you an excellent view of the Klyazma River.

Bolgoiyubovo. Six miles/10km east of Vladimir on the Gorky road, where the river Nerl flows into the Klyazma, this is a village whose main site is a mile outside, and accessible by foot. This is one of the pearls of Russian architecture: the Church of the Intercession on the Nerl (Pokrovskaya tserkov na Nerli). It was built in 1165 by Andrei Bogolyubovo in typical Vladimir-Suzdal style, as part of a monastery which has since disaPpcarcd. The solitary, white stone structure is elegant and well-nigh perfect in its design. Andrei Bolgolyubovo, a notorious tyrant (with remarkable taste) met with an untlmely death in 1174 when he was murdered by nobles in collaboration with his wife. In true Russian style the despot was canonized and is buried in his great cathedral in Vladimir.

SUZDAL

Russia is not renowned for its overpoweringly beautiful towns, but Suzdal is a notable exception to the rule that every conurbation must be surrounded by dreary industry. It also has some of the most beautiful monuments in Russia. The road from Vladimir takes you through attractive villages which are a suitable build-up to sumptuously picturesque Suzdal. Relics of the town's heritage, spanning the 12th to 19th centuries, have survived both time and catastrophe and now provide a unique gamut of the Old Russian architectural styles. More than 50 monuments are gathered together on the steep left bank and the flat right bank of the winding river Kamenka. In the oldest districts the distinctive wooden cottages have also survived.

Suzdal was founded in 1024 and, like Vladimir, became a popular desti-nation among traders coming from far and wide. It also came under the power of Prince Monomakh of the Kievan Rus in the 11th century and in th*f* 12th century Yuri Dolgoruky made Suzdal the capital of the RostovSuzdal principality. Suzdal's brief supremacy over Kiev as Russia's foremost city ended when Vladimir was made capital. It remained an important political, cultural and artistic centre, however, as well as retaining its religious import-ance. Suzdal's artistic golden age — in the 12th and 13th centuries — was brought to an abrupt halt: in 1238 the Tatars caused extensive damage and there were further invasions by Poles and Crimean Tatars. Suzdal survived, however, and the 16th century saw another architectural peak when a lot of restoration work was done. Suzdal is now an important tourist centre with hotels and restaurants, most of which are concentrated in the western part of the city.

Accommodation. The only hotel in the centre is the modern Intourist Hotel on ul Lenina looking on to the central Soviet Square. Just north of Suzdal, on the banks of the Kamenka, is the State Tourist Centre. This austere name conceals the modern Suzdal Hotel and Motel on Ivanovskaya Zastava (tel 2-1137) and the delights of the Pokrovskaya Hotel (tel 2-0131). Set within the former Monastery of the Intercession, the latter hotel consists of stylized wooden cottages and one of Russia's best restaurants, located in the old chapel.

From the Centre you can go swimming and hire boats. In winter, cross-country skiing and other activities are on offer; skiing along the frozen river is both exhilarating and unstressful.

Eating and Drinking. Several Russian specialities are best tried at Suzdal. These include shchi (cabbage soup), mushrooms baked in sour cream and horse-radish salad. The medovukha (mead) is an acquired taste but palatable none the less. If you can persuade the staff at the Pokrovskaya Hotel to serve you in addition to their quota of Romanians, you will enjoy some delicious and beautifully presented dishes. Most of the other restaurants are down ul Kremlyovskaya and the majority close on Mondays. The most atmospheric restaurant is Trapeznaya, in the Kremlin itself. The Pogrebok on the same street serves better food but is only open from 11am to 7pm.

Exploring. Near the southern entrance to the town on the left bank is the Kremlin, surrounded on three sides by the tortuous Kamenka. Having been the residence of both princes and bishops it contains an intriguing mixture of lay and ecclesiastical buildings. The oldest parts are the ramparts (12th century) and the Cathedral of the Nativity of the Virgin (Rozhdestvo Bogoroditsi), built in 1222-25 and later restored. Its blue domes decorated with gold stars rise above the rest of the Kremlin buildings and it is not unlike the Trinity and St Sergius monastery in Zagorsk. The Golden Gates surrounded by decorative portals are stunning. Next to it are the white Archbishop's Chambers which include some beautifully preserved 15th-18th century buildings with attractive galleries, staircases and carved window frames. They house a collection of jewellery, manuscripts and other treasures. In the western area of the Kremlin is the Church of St Nicholas an unusual wooden building dating from 1766. The other Church of St Nicholas is a fine example of the Moscow style with its elegant bell-tower and distinctive window frames. Most of the churches in Suzdal were built in pairs made up of a 'summer' and a 'winter' church. The former tends to be richly decorated and the latter is usually distinguishable by the bell-tower.

Across the river from the Kremlin is the museum of wooden architecture whose exhibits include some 18th century windmills. Outside the Kremlin by heading northeast you come to the Torg (Market), the old trading quarter and the home of artisans and the centre of Suzdal. The heart of the Torg is Soviet Square which is dominated by the Church of the Resurrection with its high steeple. Between the church and the river is the old 19th century shopping centre (Gostinny Dvor), with its unusual double row of columns. There are various 17th and 18th century churches in this area as well as in the rest of the town.

Of greater importance, however, are the monasteries which were designed as defensive strongholds at the approaches to the Kremlin and were later incorporated into the city itself. The Monastery of the Deposition of the Virgin's Robe (Monastyr Rizpolozhenia), north of Soviet Square, was founded in 1207 and is the oldest in Suzdal. It contains various churches and you can get a marvellous view from the top of the bell-tower. The unusual red and white Holy Gates are on the southern side. Further north, continuing along ul Lenina, is the Spaso-Evfimiyevsky Monastery, which stands on the cliffs above the river, dominating the left bank. It was founded in the 14th century and the fortress-like wall with its imposing towers demonstrates its role as a stronghold. For centuries it served as a prison for political opponents, disgraced nobles and other traitors. The centre of the complex is the five-domed Cathedral of the Transfiguration (Spaso-Preobrazheniye) built in 1594, with beautiful murals. It contains an interesting collection of rare printed books.

Walking along the river south from here, on the opposite bank, you see the white-walled Monastery of the Intercession (Pokrovsky monastyr), overlooking the calm waters of the Kamenka. Founded in 1364 it contains various early 16th century buildings as well as modern (but tasteful) chalets. The convent became a prison for noble women and rejected tsarinas, among them Solomoniya, the wife of Vassily III (Ivan the Terrible's father). The theory is that Solomoniya (exiled because she was barren) gave birth to a son and the rightful heir to Russia. It appears that she hid her son and staged his funeral, for during excavations in 1934 the small sarcophagus, which lay next to Solomoniya's, was found to contain a dummy wrapped in a shirt and nothing else. All the buildings are of interest but the most remarkable is the triple-domed Cathedral of the Intercession (1518).

You can also make a short excursion, three miles/5km east of Suzdal, to the Church of St Boris and St Gleb in the village of Kideksha, where Prince Yuri Dolgoruky built a Palace on the banks of the Nerl. Built in 1152 its white walls and simple design laid down the rules for the new Vladimir-Suzdal architectural style.

SOUTHERN RUSSIA

SOUTH OF MOSCOW

This area does not really hold much interest for travellers. There are a number of places, largely with literary connections, that are worth a visit if you happen to be driving south to Ukraine. The places described below are all along the Moscow-Simferopol Highway which goes right down to the Crimea, passing through forested land typical of Central Russia. The two main towns before you get to the Ukraine are Orel (or Oryol) and Kursk. Trains run from the Kursk station in Moscow (or from Kharkiv if you are approaching from Ukraine).

Podolsk and Chekhov. Podolsk, 25 miles/40km south of Moscow, earned its fame by the fact that Lenin lived here at the turn of the century. His house on ul Moskovskaya has been turned into a museum. Chekhov, 22 miles/35km further south, is named after the writer who worked as a doctor in the village of Melikhovo eight miles/13km to the east. Anton Chekhov wrote *The Seagull* and *Uncle Vanya* among other works while he was here from 1892-98. A museum has been set up with various personal possessions on display.

Tula. About 115 miles/180km further south you come to Tula, which for centuries was a defensive post against the Crirnean Tatars and the site of the first Russian arms factory, founded here in 1712 by Peter the Great. You can still see the 17th century Kremlin. Tula is more famous, however, for its connection with Tolstoy who lived in Yasnaya Polyana, 14km south of the town (tum right by a bust of Tolstoy). The author lived here for more than 50 years and it was here that he wrote *War and Peace* and *Anna Karenina*. The vast estate has been kept exactly as it was in Tolstoy's time. His grave — unadorned as was Tolstoy's wish — is in a corner of the grounds, surrounded by oak trees. The simple 19th-century house contains portraits, his library and other possessions. The unorthodox school which Tolstoy ran for peasant children has also been tumed into a museum. The estate is closed on Wednesdays. The Polyana restaurant, near the ticket office at the main gate, serves quite decent food.

Continuing south for about 80 miles/130km (until you are six miles/10km from Mtsensk) there is a turning to the left marked by a bust of Turgenev. This leads to the village of Spasskoye-Lutovinovo where Ivan Turgenev spent his childhood and later wrote *Fathers and Sons* and *A Nest of Gentlefolk*.

Orel. This big industrial town was founded in 1566 under Ivan the Terrible. It is 30 miles/50km south of Mtsensk and 215 miles/340km south of Moscow, nine hours by train from Moscow. The best place to stay is the Motel Shipka (Intourist) at 169 Moskovskoye shosse (tel 3-0704/3-0682) which is four miles/7km north of the centre. There are also camping facilities. The best restaurant is the Orlik at 228 ul Komsomolskaya.

The main interest in Orel is the Turgenev Museum at 11 ul Turgeneva. Turgenev lived in and often visited the town, and many of his works are linked with Orel and the surrounding area. The museum contains, among other things, first editions and correspondence. Orel is also known for its theatre: the Turgenev in Theatre Square. It is one of the oldest permanent theatres in Russia and was opened in 1815 as a theatre of serf actors. Guides are likely to treat you to stories about the cruelty of a certain Count Kamensky who was responsible for vile treatment of the serfs. For lighter entertainment try the puppet theatre in the 18th century Epiphany Church, at 1/3 ul Moskovskaya.

Kursk. This ancient town, a former outpost of Kievan Rus, is surrounded by one of the largest iron ore fields in the world. The greenery and a few 17th-19th century monuments give the modern industrial town some charm. The memory of the devastating World War II battle here, however, persists in the minds of the people. If you have to stay here there is the Solovinaya Roshcha Motel at 142a ul Engelsa, where your car at least is cosy in its heated garage. Campers can try the Sosnovy Bor Campsite (150 ul Engelsa) which is in the south of the city, in the Solyanka Park by the river.

Most of the interesting sights are along the main streets which meet at Red Square (Krasnaya Ploshchad). The most interesting of these is the St Sergius Cathedral on ul Gorkovo. It was designed by Rastrelli, the architect of the Winter Palace in St Petersburg, in the 18th century. The only museum worth visiting is the Alexander Deineka Picture Gallery at 3 ul Sovietskaya (closed on Mondays). A must for aficionados of 19th century art, it includes works by Repin, Deineka, and Levitan.

THE VOLGA

The southwestern area of Russia is best visited by boat down the Volga, although the main towns are, of course, perfectly accessible by other means of transport. The Volga, affectionately known as Matushka ('dear little mother') is the longest river in Europe. It winds its way for 2,300 miles/ 3,700km from northern Russia down to the Caspian Sea, linking five seas by means of its canals: the White, Baltic, Caspian, Black and Azov seas. The Volga towns are not comparable to the historical towns north of Moscow, as far as cultural interest is concerned. For this reason a trip by boat adds novelty to what could otherwise be a dull part of the country: the southern reaches of the Volga are particularly impressive. As you float along, you might want to read *Volga, Volga: a Voyage Down the Great River* by Lesley Chamberlain (Picador, £15.99).

Volga cruises usually begin from Kazan, east of Moscow, and finish up at Rostov-on-Don by following the Volga-Don Canal. The route can also be done in the opposite direction. Cruises last for about ten days and operate only between June and September (and even then spasmodically) while regular steamers run all year (but hard to get a place on). Check with Intourist for details. The best time to do the trip is between May and October: the highest summer temperatures range from 18°C to 29°C.

KAZAN

Kazan is one of the oldest towns on the Volga but it is now a big industrial city. It is the capital of Tatarstan, a semi-autonomous republic, incorporated into the Russian state during the reign of Ivan the Terrible in the 16th century.

Life in Kazan centres around ul Bauman, the main street. The Intourist hotel is the Kazan at 9/15 ul Bauman, which is preferable to the monolithic Tatarstan. The most intriguing place to eat is the Dom Chai (tea house), and the best drink is Jubilee-beer brewed at the Krasnaya Vostok ('beautiful east') brewery.

The 16th century Kremlin is the main sight in Kazan, and you should try to wheedle your way in past the guard on the door. Walking down ul Lenina you pass the university from which Lenin was expelled for his political activities. Maxim Gorky also spent time in Kazan in the 1880s, a period reflected in his autobiographical *My Universities*. Islamic resurgence is evident on the streets, particularly at the elegant Nurullah mosque which re-opened in 1995.

ULYANOVSK

Surrounded by forest and black earth steppe, Ulyanovsk is some 11 hours down the Volga from Kazan. It is the home town of Lenin and still a popular place of pilgrimage, especially from April 15-24 when Lenin's birthday is celebrated. The major part of the town is on the high right bank of the Volga which is broad and tranquil just here. The centre of old Simbirsk (as the town was called before it was renamed after Lenin's family name) has retained many of its low wooden houses and narrow streets.

The main Lenin museum is housed in the small wooden house at 58 ul Lenina where Lenin lived with his family until he left for Kazan. It has changed little and actually manages to retain some atmosphere despite the hordes which traiPse through here every year. Virtually every building where Lenin set foot has been turned into a museum or place of pilgrimage, including the library and the school he frequented on ul Kommunisticheskaya. To avoid Lenin overdose go for a relaxing walk down Bulvar Novy Venets which runs along the hilly banks of the Volga.

VOLGOGRAD

Beyond Togliatti (eight hours south of Ulyanovsk) the scenery is particularly beautiful, as the Volga curves through forested hills past the Zhiguli and Hawk Mountains. Volgograd, 36 hours further south (and formerly known as Stalingrad) is the largest port on the Volga. Its economic and strategic importance made it a natural target for the Nazis during World War II. The famous Battle of Stalingrad in 1942-3 is frequently regarded as a turning point of that war, making the defeat of the Germans feasible. But Stalingrad was obliterated by the battle and all that you see today was created by Russian town planners.

From the harbour Alleya Geroyev leads to the Square of the Fallen Soldiers (Ploshchad Pavshkikh Borktsov), the heart of the city. Prospekt Lenina, which runs parallel to the Volga, is the main street of the city: most shops are along here and Alleya Geroyev. The Beriozka is at 2 Alleya Geroyev. There is little difference between the two main hotels, the Volgograd at 12 ul Mira and the Intourist at 14 ul Mira. Outside the hotels the Leto Restaurant in the municipal park is very lively in the summer. The Molodyozhnoye Cafe (10 Prospekt Lenina) is also an entertaining place for a coffee and cake.

Most of what there is to see in Volgograd relates to its victory in 1943 and those who died in the struggle. The most dramatic memorials are on the hill called Mamayev-Kurgan. It is the highest point of Volgograd and from here there is a magnificent view of the city and river. The hill is crowned by the awe-inspiring statue of the Motherland: a woman brandishing a sword, standing 85 metres high. You can catch a bus from Prospekt Lenina to the base of the hill. At 21 Prospekt Lenina there is one of the best art museums in the country outside Moscow and St Petersburg. It has exhibitions of works from the Hermitage, the Tretyakov Gallery and other important galleries in the country. The collection includes the works of Rembrandt, Repin and Rodin. It is closed on Wednesdays. The Philharmonia is at 1 Naberezhnaya Shestdesyat Vtoroi Armii, overlooking the river.

ROSTOV-ON-DON

From Volgograd many of the cruises carry on down to Rostov-on-Don, by means of the Volga-Don Canal which begins 18 miles/29km south of Volgograd. The port of Rostov, surrounded by trees and wheatfields, lies on the hugh banks of the river Don, immortalized in the novels of Mikhail Sholokhov. It is a big city with one million inhabitants and is an important junction for all types of traffic, especially those travelling to and from the Caucasus. Unfortunately its Cossack heritage is not very evident these days. Ul Engelsa is the main street with shops, the train station and so on.

The city is well stocked with hotels. The two main Intourist hotels are the Moskovskaya at 62 ul Engelsa and the Intourist at 115 ul Engelsa (tel 65-9065/9066). There is also a campsite on the Oktyabrskoye shosse, seven miles/12km from Rostov, along the Kharkov road.

Strolling down ul Pushkinskaya is perhaps the most interesting pastime in Rostov but there are a couple of museums worth visiting too. The Fine Arts Museum, at 115 ul Pushkinskaya, has a good collection of 19th century Russian painting (including Repin and Levitan). Of more interest, however, is the Museum of Local Lore at 79 ul Engelsa, which traces the history of the Cossacks in Rostov. Three kilometres along the river from Rostov is the Petrovsky Quay Complex, a favourite spot for the locals. You can hire boats, go swimming, horse-riding and even have a Russian steam bath. Another entertaining place to go and watch the local people is at the market on ul Oborony.

A worthwhile excursion is to the Don Cossack History Museum at Novocherkassk, 25 miles/40km from Rostov. It is the only one of its kind in the country. 'Cossack' is a Turkic word meaning 'fugitive'. It refers to the serfs who fled from the feudal lords of Central Russia during the 14th-17th centuries. The Don Cossacks, descendants of these serfs, won fame as warriors, especially during the war against Napoleon. The museum has exhibits illustrating the Cossack way of life.

THE RUSSIAN CAUCASUS

This geographical area clips the northern half of the Caucasus mountains and stretches up through the industrial Krasnodar, Stavropol and Rostov territories. Travellers should bypass these dull industrial zones and head south to the mountains or to the Black Sea coast. The Northern Caucasus is not very well-known among foreign visitors but Sochi, on the coast, has more visitors than Yalta in the Crimea, and the mountains here include Mount Elbrus, the highest peak in Europe.

SOCHI

Having become a health spa only last century, Sochi is now the most popular famous resort on the Caucasian Black Sea and is easily accessible by air from Moscow. Greater Sochi is the name given to the resorts along the coast which cover some 90 miles/145km and which are visited (locals might say 'invaded') by millions of sunseekers every year. The climate, mineral water, warm sea and mountains are the great attractions. The Caucasian mountains protect the coast from northern winds, and the climate is mild all year round. Between May and October the weather is hot and reliable, with little rain. Autumn is probably the best time to go as the humidity is lower.

The sulphur springs which produce the mineral water known as Matsesta ('fire water') attracted people to Sochi last century, but it was only after the Revolution that rest homes were built by the dozen: the seafront and slopes are now thick with sanatoria. Kurortny Prospekt is the main street and crosses the entire city. Terraces run along the seafront and decorative staircases go down to the beach.

Arrival and Departure. Flights arrive at Adler, 19 miles/28km from Sochi. Local trains cover the distance frequently, taking about an hour. From Moscow the flight takes a little over two hours. Sochi is also accessible by rail, the journey taking 40 hours from Moscow. This is for the direct services, which go via Kharkiv in Ukraine. In order to avoid potential problems with Ukrainian frontier officials (a transit visa may or may not be granted; it may or may not be highly expensive), you may prefer to take the longer route via Voronezh or Volgograd, which skirts around Ukrainian territory. There are connections at Volgograd for elsewhere in Russia (notably Kazan).

Access by sea is possible although limited. Sochi is featured on some cruise routes to the Black Sea (e.g. Swan Hellenic operates a mammoth cruise from Europe calling at Sochi) and boats also run from Yalta and Odessa. The Caucasian resorts are linked by hydrofoil.

Accommodation. The Zhemchuzhina (3 ul Chernomorskaya) is the most luxurious of the old Intourist hotels and has a swimming pool, sauna and sports facilities. The Kamelia (91 Kurortny Prospekt) boasts a billiard room but also has other facilities more typical of a sea-resort. Alternatively, you could probably negotiate a good rate at one of the sanatoria in Sochi.

Eating and Drinking. Most of Sochi's restaurants are on Kurortny Prospekt, but the ones further afield are better, such as the Akhun Restaurant on Bolshoi Akhun Mountain (12 miles/20km from Sochi, see below) or the Kavkazki Aul Restaurant, in a forest clearing in the River Agura Valley (five miles/8km south of Sochi, on the slopes above the Matsesta springs). Finally, there is the Staraya Melnitsa retaurant on Bytkha Hill (four miles/6km from town) which serves Ukrainian dishes.

Exploring. Sochi's greatest asset is perhaps the Dendrarium Arboretum, off Kurortny Prospekt, which is among the best botanical gardens in the former Soviet Union. There is also a local museum at 29 ul Orzhonihdze which will fill you in on the historical and natural features of the area. Evening concerts are held in the Philharmonia at 2 ul Teatralnaya.

AROUND SOCHI

The beaches of Greater Sochi are as crowded as those found anywhere else along the Black Sea coast, and there is little to characterize or distinguish them. The principal beach resorts are Khosta (12 miles/20km) and Adler (22 miles/35km) to the south and Dagomys (12 miles/20km) to the north. The Georgian border is three miles/5km south of Adler. Unless you want to laze on sun-kissed beaches you would do best to avoid the coast and head out into the mountains. One of the most spectacular is Mount Aibga, where there is a Caucasian tavern serving good kebabs. It is also worth going down the Akhchu Gorge or — if and when the border zone is safe — making excursions across into Georgia, for example to Lake Ritsa.

Matsesta. Five miles/8km southeast (inland) of Sochi is Matsesta, famous for its caves and springs. Of greater natural interest, however, is Mount Bolshoi Akhun, about 12 miles/20km from Sochi. This is one of the most picturesque spots in the Russian Caucasus. From the top there is a fine view of the mountains and the coast. A winding path leads to the double waterfall on the Agura river.

Dagomys. Twenty kilometres north of Sochi, Dagomys — once the property of the Tsars — lies among wooded hills and subtropical vegetation. The capital of Russian tea, Dagomys is the home of a tea farm where you can sit at the confluence of two mountain rivers to drink tea and eat the local Kuban cakes. There are restaurants, cafes and bars and all kinds of sports facilities, including a mini-golf course, windsurfers, waterskis and motor-boats.

THE MINERALNIYE VODI

Literally 'Mineral Waters', this is the name given to the four Caucasian spa towns of Pyatigorsk, Kislovodsk, Essentuki and Zheleznovodsk. They first became popular in the 18th and 19th centuries when the wealthy arrived to take the waters. The resorts are also renowned for their mild (almost rain-free) climate. Temperatures are never extreme and if you can wait until October (when the crowds begin to disperse) the air is still warm. Essentuki and Zheleznovodsk offer accommodatlon only in sanatoria, but Pyatigorsk and Kislovodsk have hotels which means you can explore the countryside rather than undergo treatment.

Mineralniye Vodi is actually a small town which is the transport centre linking traffic with the four resorts. Flights and trains from elsewhere in Russia, notably Moscow, arrive here. The resorts themselves are connected by electric train. Pyatigorsk, the biggest, is the only one served by trains from elsewhere: from Moscow the journey takes about 29 hours. It is 1,060 miles/1,700km to Mineralniye Vodi from Moscow, 303 miles/485km from Rostov-on-Don to Pyatigorsk.

Pyatigorsk. This is the oldest spa and lies on the slopes of Mount Mashuk. The town retains some of its 19th century grace but it is largely modern and full of robust-looking people. Many of the sights in and around the town are linked with one of the most loved Russian poets, Mikhail Lermontov, who was exiled here for writing *On the Death of the Poet* (about Pushkin) and later killed in a duel in 1841. The best excursions in the area can most easily be done from Pyatigorsk. These include Mount Elbrus, about 105 miles/170km to the south (see below), the Churchkhur waterfalls and various other gorges.

There are walks nearer home too, such as to the top of Mount Mashuk, from where there is a magnificent view of the surrounding area.

The Mashuk Hotel (tel 53431) is the place where foreigners tend to stay, though the Volna Motel and Campsite is cheaper. The restaurant in the Mashuk Hotel is good, but for more atmosphere try the Lesnaya Polyana which is in the spot where Lermontov died.

Essentuki. The least attractive of the four, Essentuki is 12 miles/20km from Pyatigorsk on the road to Kislovodsk. It has some unique mud baths, but has little else going for it apart from an attractive valley with waterfalls, called Dolina Ocharovaniya, to the south.

Kislovodsk. This resort is situated on a high plateau in the valley of the Olkhovka and Berezovka rivers. It has more sun than any of the other spas especially in winter. From the town you can visit the waterfalls in the Olkhovka and Alikonovka valleys and the Zamok (Castle) Rock, an unusual rock formation southeast of Kislovodsk. Trips to Mount Elbrus can also be done from here.

Zheleznovodsk. This is the smallest and most picturesque spa of the group and lies in the thickly wooded foothills of Mount Zheleznaya. It is 12 miles/20km north of Pyatigorsk, about six miles/10km off the Rostov road. The most interesting site in the town is the former palace of the Emir of Bukhara. You can also climb Mount Zheleznaya from where there is a fine view.

KABARDIN-BALKAR

This region of snow-covered mountains and sunbaked steppe is undoubtedly most famous for Mount Elbrus, the highest peak in Europe at 18,478ft/5,642m. This mountain and the surrounding area, Prielbrusye, are the highlights of the Northern Caucasus. Some excursions can be made from Pyatigorsk or Ordzhohikidze (125 miles/200km to the south, see below), but a pleasant and less touristy base is the capital, Nalchik. It lies on the Tbilisi road 100km south of Pyatigorsk, and is accessible by air from Moscow.

Mount Elbrus. Whether approaching from Nalchik to the south or Pyatigorsk to the north, the road to Mount Elbrus branches off the Tbilisi road at Baksan and follows the Baksan Valley, one of the most attractive in the Caucasus. Once at Elbrus itself, there are cable cars which take you up to an altitude of 11,500ft/3,500m, from where the views are magnificent. The hiking season lasts from June 1 to October 20. There are beautiful walks in these mountains, e.g. in the Adir-Su Valley and up the Adir-Su-Bashi and Cheget-Tau-Chan mountains, both about 11,500/3,500m. The Adil-Su Valley is one of the most beautiful and leads to Shkhelda Peak. Autumn is the best time for hiking when the weather is stable and all the routes are open.

Skiing. The ski resorts are so high that summer skiing is a possibility, although the most reliable season is spring. Dombai, west of Elbrus, is the main resort. Teberda and Terksol are also important Caucasian resorts, but accommodation is scarce. From Terskol you can go by foot or cable car up Mount Cheget.

Chegem and Cherek Gorge. Chegem Gorge is 26 miles/42km from Nalchik: the road passes beautiful waterfalls and the gorge, at its narrowest point, is just 66 feet/20m wide. It contains archaeological relics including burial mounds and fortifications. The Cherek Gorge is 33 miles/56km from Nalchik, via the Balkar valley. From here you can visit beautiful gorges, mountain streams, waterfalls, glaciers and the Blue Lakes, the finest of which is the Cherek-Koel Tarn, surrounded by snow-topped mountains.

ORDZHONIKIDZE

About midway along the road between Pyatigorsk and Tbilisi, in the foothills of the Greater Caucasus, is Ordzhonikidze. On the banks of the River Terek, it is the capital of North Ossetia, a region of mountaill and plain whose inhabitants have both Persian and Caucasian roots. From Ordzhonikidze you can go up Mount Lysaya which is on the Tbilisi road, three miles/5km from town. There is a funicular which goes to the summit, from where you get a panoramic view of the Caucasus mountains. The most popular excursion, however, is to the grisly 'city of the dead' at Dargavs, 37 miles/60km from Ordzhonikidze. The village is the site of a necropolis, built between the 13th and 18th centuries, where you can see mummified bodies which the dry climate has helped to preserve. A little further on is the Kurtatin Gorge where there are some unusual gravestones, known as *tsyrty*.

Ordzhonikidze is 1,184 miles/1,897km from Moscow, 435 miles/700km from Rostov-on-Don and 125 miles/200km from Tbilisi. It is also accessible by train, the journey from Moscow taking 35 hours. Flights go to Mineralniye Vodi, from where the distance to Ordzhonikidze is 150 miles/240km.

CHECHNYA

The ruins of the Chechen capital, Grozny, lie 120 miles/192km due east of Nalchik. Even before the attack by Russian forces on the self-styled independent republic of Chechnya, there was little of interest for travellers in the region. At the time of writing the area was quiet, President Yeltsin's forces had succeeded in quelling the rebellion (at considerable political cost in Moscow). But given the amount of military supplies remaining in Chechnya, a low-level guerrilla war seems likely. Visitors should therefore avoid the area.

Siberia

Siberia is an immense and much misunderstood territory. The Greek historian Herodotus claimed it was inhabited by one-eyed monsters, and in the Western popular imagination it consists mainly of snow and salt mines. The magnitude of Siberia is fantastic: it stretches 2,200 miles/3,500km from the Arctic Ocean to Mongolia and 4,350 miles/7,000km from the Urals to the Pacific. Larger than either China or the USA, Siberia occupies well over half of Russia and a quarter of Asia. Yet this vast area has a population of only 30 million, most living in a handful of cities close to the Trans-Siberian Railway.

Although sparsely populated, Siberia is a land rich in natural resources. The name, of Tartar origin and meaning 'the sleeping land', is remarkably appropriate; man's influence on the land is still restricted to comparatively small areas. A Russian legend says that Siberia was the last place on Earth that God created. He poured out what was left in his sack of minerals, but finding there were too many he buried them under the ice and marshes to make them hard to get at.

Siberia is crossed by some mighty rivers including the Ob, Yenisei, Amur and Lena. It is divided up into three geographical and economical regions: Western Siberia, Eastern Siberia and the Russian Far East. The Urals lie to the extreme west and form the boundary between Europe and Asia. Western Siberia stretches from this low range of mountains to the great Yenisei river. East Siberia extends from the Yenisei to the mountain ranges east of the Lena River, and the Russian Far East occupies the land south of the Bering Sea down to the region north of the Amur in the south above China.

Topographically the land is extremely varied. West Siberia includes the vast plain which runs from the Urals for 750 miles/1,200km east to the Krasnoyarsk region north of the Altai mountains. The plain, traversed by the huge Ob and Irtysh rivers, is often marshy and unsalubrious and vast expanses are covered in taiga (Siberian pine-forest). Close to towns and the railway the forest has been cleared to some extent but in other areas it is as dense as it ever was. Towards the south and China the forest becomes steppe. In the north and Arctic regions the land is desolate and much of it is a permafrost zone: the soil is frozen to a depth of hundreds of metres in places, the earth only thawing at the very top. The Far North is frozen tundra.

History. The first settlements — by Stone Age nomads — in Siberia have been traced to the area around Lake Baikal and further north towards the Arctic Circle. The Mongols played a large part in the early history of Siberia. Mongol tribes had begun venturing from the south long before the Huns arrived in the 3rd century BC. The Huns continued westwards but their descendants, the Buryats, still live around Lake Baikal. Much later, Central Asian tribes moved up to dominate southern and central Siberia: among these were the Kyrghyzs who had already established a vast empire for themselves stretching as far as China. In the 13th century, Genghis Khan induced the Kyrghyzs and others to join his Mongol hordes; by the time he died in 1227 he had created an empire which occupied the area between the China Sea and the Dnieper.

One effect of the Mongol Empire was to open up the roads between Europe and Asia. The Mongols and Kublai Khan, elected Great Khan in 1259, fell increasingly under the influence of Chinese and Tibetan culture. The Mongols originally practised Animism and Shamanism (a religion centred around the Shaman, a kind of medium who communicated with the spirits). Their acceptance of pacifying Buddhism, together with the bureaucratic nightmare of administering such a vast empire, led to the gradual collapse of the Mongolian Empire.

There had been several expeditions eastwards to the Ob from Novgorod between the 11th and 15th centuries but it was Ivan the Terrible who began the real penetration of Siberia. Having conquered the Kazan Tatars east of Moscow, Asia was at his fingertips. The first move involved a man called Yediger. He was Khan of Sibir, a small kingdom east of Urals. In the face of the powerful Tsar he offered to become Ivan's vassal and promised him a fur tribute. After Yediger's death his son, Kuchum, refused to continue giving this tribute. Ivan enlisted the help of the Stroganovs, a family of merchant-adventurers. On the Tsar's promise of land and permission to extend their commercial activities beyond the Urals, the Stroganovs successfully conquered the Tartar kingdom of Sibir in 1581.

The army, made up largely of Don Cossacks, was led by Yermak, a former pirate. He is known as 'The Conqueror of Siberia'. After his death the Russians continued to push and a few *ostrogi* (military outposts, which later grew into towns) were founded. Some of Siberia's most important towns date from this period e.g. Tomsk, Krasnoyarsk, Irkutsk and Yakutsk. The indigenous tribes either accepted the newcomers as being less ruthless than the Tatars or else were too scattered to provide any real opposition. The terrain did not present many difficulties to the invaders either. In 1584 Ivan added 'King of Sibir' to his list of titles, and in the space of about 50 years much of Siberia was colonized. As the Russians progressed eastwards they cleared a ribbon of land which eventually went from Perm to Irkutsk: this was the great Siberian Trakt, later known as the Siberian Post Road. By 1639 the Russians had gone beyond the Lena to the Sea of Okhotsk by the east coast.

Fur, especially sable, was a great attraction to Russians. The new region was rich in this valuable commodity, which triggered an inflow of adventurous traders. In 1649 a rich fur merchant called Khabarov, supported by the Tsar, explored the region around the Amur in the east and reached as far as Manchuria. He and his men were barbaric in their treatment of the natives. The indigenous tribes of the Amur region appealed to the Manchus, who beat the Tsar's men back. In 1689 a treaty fixed the Sino-Russian frontier about 200km north of the Amur.

Only in the 18th century were the first real attempts were made by the Russian Tsars to exploit Siberia's mineral resources. Peter the Great backed a series of scientific expeditions stretching right across Siberia. The region's population was still largely indigenous, and in the 19th century Moscow encouraged voluntary emigration to Siberia: both to reinforce the Russian presence, and to free overpopulated areas in Western Russia for cultivation. Migration was accelerated by the building of the Trans-Siberian Railway (1893-1904) and by incentives, such as a free plot of land, offered to settlers by the government. Even these stimuli failed to attract volunteers to the mines and forests north of Irkutsk, so slave labour was employed widely (see *Exiles*, below).

The 20th century saw much industrialization and increasing exploitation of Siberia's considerable mineral resources: coal, diamonds, metals, oil and natural gas, gold and silver. Factories have sprung up to use the power provided by massive hydro-electric stations, and — in some of the most inhospitable regions on earth — entire new towns such as Bratsk have been developed.

Exile. From the 17th century onwards, men were marched along the Siberian Trakt on the way to a life of exile or hard labour. At first Siberia was merely a dumping ground for those who had already been punished or mutilated and were of no further use to society. When the region's resources began to be harnessed, prisoners were put to work in the gold and silver mines and in the forests. In 1753 capital punishment was abolished in Russia, in favour of perpetual exile in Siberia. As the need for labour increased, so the list of offences punishable by exile grew and even included 'begging with pretence to being in distress'. Many died during the long march there. Only in the 19th century were overnight camps built along the route; these were the so-called *etapes*, some of which still survive.

Prisoners were divided into four categories: hard-labour convicts, penal colonists, non-criminal exiles (mostly vagrants) and voluntary exiles, usually wives and children accompanying exiled husbands. Political exiles, such as the Decembrists, were treated well in comparison to the criminals and sometimes had their own homes. For most people, the camps were horrific: overcrowding and disease were the two main problems.

The exile system was abolished in 1900 but under Stalin concentration camps sprang up. Prisoners, both political and otherwise, were reduced to the status of slaves and used to promote large-scale development east of the Urals in the 1930s and 40s. It is thought that ten million were exiled. Those who survived were forced to settle there after they had served their full term. After Stalin, the Kremlin relied upon recruiting young settlers by offering high wages and special bonuses.

The People. Siberia has long been considered an inhospitable land used only for exile but, despite the jokes that you'll have to put up with before you go, travellers do generally return home — if they can bear to, that is. The people of Siberia are earthy, friendly and welcoming, with a good sense of humour. One reason for this may be the relatively small number of travellers who visit the region; those who do are paid more attention to than elsewhere.

The term 'Siberian' is a loose term with which to describe the inhabitants of Siberia. A Siberian is, in fact, a Russian who has gone to live in Siberia or a descendant of same. Various indigenous tribes lived in Siberia long before its annexation to Russia, but were unable to offer much resistance to the onslaught from the west. They were originally nomadic groups, and most followed a form of either Shamanism or Buddhism. These natives make up less than one-fifth of the present population and are concentrated in the interior. Some have settled in the cities now and have adopted the Russian way of life, but many continue to herd reindeer and other animals. Traditional dances and songs also survive.

Of these ethnic minority groups the Buryats are the most numerous, followed by the Yakuts and Evenks. The Buryats are descended from the Mongols and lived a nomadic life herding animals between Lake Baikal and Mongolia, although some lived off fishing or timber work. Of all the indigenous groups they were the most uncooperative when the Russians first arrived but were quick to see the advantages of getting involved in the fur trade. Like Central Asian nomads, they lived in yurts. There present homeland is Buryatia, a semi-autonomous republic south of Lake Baikal.

The Yakuts used to herd and hunt along the banks of the Lena River, where they now have their own homeland too: the capital is Yakutsk. These people are similar in many ways to Eskimos and Laplanders. The Evenks belong to the Tungu group of people (of northern Chinese origin) and were originally nomadic herders and hunters. They live in the northern regions. Although most now live on collective farms, some continue their old traditions.

Religion is strong in Siberia, visible above all at Easter. The blue and green (seen in the paintwork of the wooden cottages) are symbolic colours of the Russian Orthodox Church.

Climate. Siberia is known for its extremes of temperature. Hot summers alternate with rigorous and seemingly interminable winters, lasting up to six months in the south and eight months in the north. It is an unforgettable sight when the sun shines to see the air sparkling as the moisture freezes. You may well find that you use a credit card more in Siberia than anywhere else in Russia: it is very useful for scraping the ice off bus windows so that you can see outside.

Summer temperatures of 35°C/95°F and winter temperatures of −30°C/ −32°F are not unusual, and can be even more extreme. In the warmer Western areas the snow begins to melt from March onwards but in Eastern Siberia the rivers are frozen over until April or May. In the east, however, the air is so dry, the sun so bright and the sky so cloudless that it creates an illusion of mild weather. In summer, take plenty of mosquito repellant.

The climate in the Far East, owing to its proximity to the sea, is milder.

Getting Around. Travellers can hope to see only a tiny fraction of this vast land. Although travel is no longer heavily restriced, the sheer impracticality of getting around tends to keep visitors to the larger settlements and their environs. Yet wherever you go, Siberia is guaranteed to make a lasting impression — whether you aim for Novosibirsk, the 'heart of Russia', Irkutsk with its architectural treasures and lively atmosphere, or for Lake Baikal, surrounded by wild taiga forest and quiet villages. Some modern towns, such as Bratsk, like their counterparts in Western Russia, lack individuality. They are of little interest except to fans of hydro-electric power or modern industrial architecture.

The distances, of course, are huge. Air and rail are the only sensible

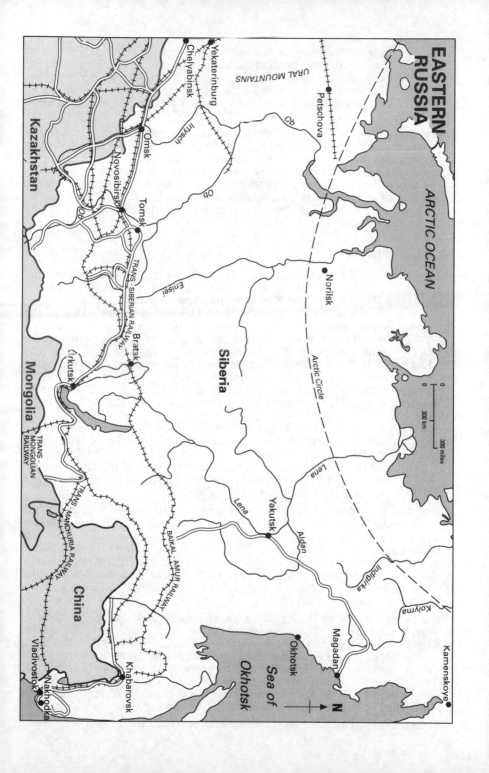

methods of travel. Novosibirsk, Irkutsk, Bratsk and Khabarovsk are access-ible by air. Excursions can be made from each of these, but if you wanted an overall view of Siberia and the Far East, you should consider going on the Trans-Siberian Railway. (For details of this journey see the following chapter.) Alternatively, you could take a summer river cruise along the Lena or Amur river.

Eating and Drinking. Siberian cuisine has little to be proud of. Availability of produce is extremely spasmodic, and fresh fruit and vegetables do not figure large on menus: when they do the quality is usually poor. At the worst you will get lots of pickles, gristly meat and rice. If you are planning to spend much time in Siberia it is wise to take vitamin tablets. The food in hotels and good restaurants is reasonable, however. The best known Siberian food is *pelmeni*, meat-filled dumplings served in soup or on their own. The other staple is alcohol.

NOVOSIBIRSK

Often called the 'Chicago of Siberia', Novosibirsk is the largest city in the region with a population of one and a half million. It lies on the river Ob, which flows through Western Siberia to the Arctic Ocean.

The village of Gusevka was founded in 1893 with the building of the bridge across the river Ob for the Trans-Siberian Railway. It developed rapidly as the railway was vital for the transportation of coal mined in the Kuznetsk Basin, east of the city. It also became a transit point for settlers heading south to the Altai mountains or further into Siberia. The renaming of the town in 1925 as Novosibirsk, meaning 'New Siberian Town', heralded the greatest period of growth with the building of the Turksib, the Turkestan-Siberian Railway. This was used to transport grain and timber to Central Asia.

Apart from a few wooden houses built before 1914, Novosibirsk is devoid of old monuments and is characterized more by the forests of cranes and huge ships on the river.Ice reduces the port to impotence for half the year, but in summer the river becomes the recreational artery of the city. Because the nearest sea is (a) 1,000 miles away and (b) the Arctic Ocean, the banks of the river are pressed into service as beaches.

Arrival and Departure. Most Westerners arrive on the direct Lufthansa flight from Frankfurt, though fares are high. There are flights from Moscow on Transaero, and from Irkutsk, Vladivostok and other Russian cities on Aeroflot and its derivatives. The flight time from Moscow is about four hours, from Frankfurt 11 including a stop in Yekaterinburg. By rail Moscow is 2,074 miles/3,336km and 48 hours away. There is a three-hour time difference, i.e. noon in Novosibirsk is 9am in Moscow. The airport is 12 miles/20km outside the city.

City Layout. The heart of the city is on the right bank of the Ob. Krasny Prospekt, a typical tree-lined boulevard, is the main street. It is 10km long and leads north from the Ob, crossing the central Lenin Square. Vokzalnaya Magistral leads from Lenin Square to the train station and the Novosibirsk Hotel. A metro system has been built recently and is still being extended. In 1995, however, the money ran out and a charity was formed to pay for future building. The Metro Development Fund placed collection boxes at stations, and obtained the equivalent of $2,500 in the first week alone.

Accommodation. The Sibir Hotel, at the end of Vokzalnaya Magistral, is the usual second-rate hulk. The excellent pelmeni in the hotel restaurant is the only saving grace. There is another, older hotel, the Novosibirsk, at 3 ul Lenina (tel 220313).

Exploring. A stay of a couple of days is ample; some would say a couple of hours is enough.

Walking around Novosibirsk, you would be forgiven for thinking that communism has made a comeback, all forgiven. The people look like extras from Dr Zhivago as they shuffle diligently along Lenin Street, past Revolution and Soviet Streets to Lenin Square. On your right is the modest redbrick building where, a sign boasts, 'Soviet power was established on 14 December 1917'. Across the road is the man responsible. Several granite tons of V I Lenin stand scowling a little as he urges communism forward. Newly-weds still pose for pictures near his left boot, with the uncompromising pillars and dome of the opera house providing a suitably stirring backdrop.

To the right of the founder of the Soviet Union, three stone riflemen look unthreatening beneath the afternoon's gentle dusting of snow, despite their weapons. To his left, a peasant and a worker complete the Leninist collective trinity.

It says much about railway engineering, and the general level of architecture in Novosibirsk, that by far the most attractive building is that of the station. This green and white palace of the railway, presiding over the east bank of the Ob, is better still in real life. The best thing about any Russian station is the departure board, and since the city functions (like Chicago) as the nation's Clapham Junction, it consequently has the best of the lot. Omsk to Tomsk, Almaty to Moscow, St Petersburg to Tashkent — all lines lead to Novosibirsk.

You enter through a fairly triumphal arch into a cavernous hall decorated with the icons of communist achievement. A statue of Lenin dominates the centre, striding off purposely towards the ticket office. A pair of cherubic Young Pioneers gaze skyward in the general direction of a mural of soldier-peasant-worker synergy at its most potent.

A short way south, past some attractive old wooden cottages, is Locomotive 3000, a 2-10-2 steam engine called Felix Dzerzhinsky, a henchman of Stalin.

If you prefer wandering around the shops, these are mostly down ul Lenina and Vokzalnaya Magistral. The local market — north of Lenin Square, off Krasny Prospekt — sells fruit, woolly hats etc. and is quite entertaining. The main bookshop is at 29 Krasny Prospekt.

Entertainment. The silver-domed Opera House — the largest in the Russian Union — on Lenin Square is the city's pride and joy. It gives Novosibirsk the chance to call itself the cultural centre of Siberia, not a difficult title to claim.

For musical entertainment there are regular concerts (given by the Philharmonic and Chamber Orchestras) at the Art Gallery at 13 ul Sverdlova. The city opera and ballet company also has a good reputation.

IRKUTSK

In The Incredible Mile (1970), Harold Elvin described Irkutsk thus: 'Dreary, soulless. Not a nice café or shop in town. No architecture at all since the revolution: only buildings, monuments to melancholy. Not one item in one shop meriting one glance. Even the bookshops: full of paper and print signifying deadness . . . The guide-books acclaimed Irkutsk as one of the most beautiful cities in Siberia. Blimey!'

Yet it could easily prove the highlight of any visit to Siberia as well as an excellent base from which to see Lake Baikal and typical Siberian villages and taiga forest. Irkutsk is particularly entertaining during the Winter Festival between 25 December and 5 January when there are great festivities: you can go for troika and sleigh rides, and every night there are performances of opera, ballet and folk dancing. All through the winter you can see the men fishlng on the frozen river, children skiing in the parks and snow clearers constantly at work.

Irkutsk is officially the capital of a region the size of France and the UK put together, but is often regarded as the capital of the whole of Eastern Siberia. It has a population of over 500,000. A modern, busy city, it is still relaxed and friendly in comparison to its Western Russian counterparts. Lying on the broad Angara River, Irkutsk has been admired by many (except Harold Elvin) and was described by Anton Chekhov in 1890 as the best town in Siberia. This still holds true today. Despite a devastating fire in 1879 and the construction of modern blocks, some of the old-style wooden houses — with carved eaves, window frames and shutters — have survived. Some are even being refurbished. Plans are being made to turn the old areas in the centre into a pedestrian zone.

Irkutsk began as a camp for the Cossacks who were sent here in 1652 to encourage the uncooperative native Buryats to pay their fur tribute to the Tsar. It later grew into a large trading centre and by the beginning of the 19th century was also the administrative centre of Siberia. Caravans came through the Gobi Desert from China, loaded with silk and tea, and returned home with fur and the occasional mammoth tusk from the Arctic. (Tusks from these prehistoric creatures were greatly prized). From Irkutsk, goods were sent further west and the town soon became known as the 'Paris of Siberia': Russian and foreign merchants flocked to its trade fairs which were the biggest in Siberia.

It was from Irkutsk that the first Russian merchants ventured into China, further into Siberia, along the Lena north to the Arctic and across the Bering Straits to Alaska. The discovery in the mid-19th century of gold to the north and east of Irkutsk brought a period of affluence: gambling, drinking and general decadence became as rife as in any gold rush city.

Many political prisoners were exiled here in the 19th century. Among them were the Decembrists, banished in 1825 after a failed *coup d'état* in St Petersburg. They were mainly educated aristocrats, and were the forerunners of a faction of revolutionaries which in the 20th century included Stalin. Many of the Decembrists, after a stint of hard labour, were joined by their wives and were allowed to take up residence in Irkutsk and other towns. Even after they were pardoned in 1855, many stayed on and made an impression on the cultural and political development of the town and its people.

You will notice a marked variety of faces in Irkutsk: Russian descendants of exiles and early settlers, and the Eastem faces of Mongolian, Buryat and other tribal groups.

Irkutsk developed fast after first Trans-Siberian train reached the town in 1898. Previously, journeys along the Siberian Post Road in wooden carriages had proved extremely arduous, with the added risk of attacks by escaped criminals. The criminals these days are less desperate but better armed.

Arrival and Departure. The flight from Moscow takes seven hours. Irkutsk is also linked by air to Khabarovsk, Novosibirsk and Omsk, and some international flights operate to Almaty and Tashkent. The airport is 15 minutes from the centre of town along ul Baikalskaya. On the Trans-Siberian

Railway, Irkutsk is about 87 hours from Moscow. Irkutsk is five hours ahead of Moscow time.

City Layout. The main city is on the right bank of the Angara, although the train station is on the left bank. Ul K Marksa is the main shopping street. Ul Lenina and ul Sukhe-Bator lead off ul K Marksa and cross the large Kirov Square which extends to the banks of the Angara. The Post and Telegraph Office is on ul K Marksa.

Accommodation. The only hotel used by foreign tourists is the Intourist at 44 Bulvar Gagarina (tel 91-353/4). It overlooks the Angara and is in a quiet part of town. The service desks are helpful and the restaurants serve good Siberian food. The Angara Hotel restaurant is not so good or friendly but tends to be cheaper. As in the Intourist, you can eat *omul*, the delicious fish native to Lake Baikal. Your next best choice is the Almaz Restaurant at 46 ul Lenina which also senes local food. Of the cafés on Lenin Square, the Café Bilnia specializes in selling heavy-looking but palatable dumplings and horrendously sweet hot chocolate: a popular mid-morning snack for the locals. On ul Uritskova is a video café popular with the younger Irkutskians.

Exploring. Irkutsk is a compact city. and it is quite possible to see its sights on foot, if time and temperatures permit. A day's visit, however, would never do the town justice. Of the churches in Irkutsk the most attractive is the white, gold-domed Church of Our Saviour at the end of ul Sukhe-Bator by the river. It is now an excellent folklore museum and includes exhibits relating to Buryat, Yakut and other tribes as well as beautiful tribal costumes.

Across the road is the Cathedral of the Epiphany which now houses a small collection of icons. Nearby is the Gothic style Catholic Church, built by exiled Poles. The small Museum of Regional History at 2 ul K Marksa, by the river, is one of the friendliest museums in Russia. It illustrates the customs and culture of the local indigenous tribes and the exploration of Eastern Siberia and the Far East. Notice the outstanding political-style stained glass window half way up the stairs. Opposite is the Classical 'White House', the former palace of the Governor of Irkutsk. The Art Gallery at 8 ul Lenina has the best collection of Siberian art in the country, as well as original works by Poussin and Landseer. Another place of interest is the Decembrists' Museum, housed in an elegant wooden house at 64 ul Dzerzhinskova. Those without Russian can admire the fine array of bearded men in the photographs.

In the outskirts is the Znamensky Convent and the small Church of the Holy Saviour. Services are still held here and you often find old women in black busy polishing candlesticks, or offering you mass-produced icons. Photography is forbidden. In the cemetery is the grave of Gregory Shelekhov, the Siberian fur-trader who founded Russia's first permanent colony in Alaska in 1784. Several Decembrists are also buried here.

Those interested in the fur industry can go on an organized tour to the Fur Distribution Centre where you can see pelts of all kinds, from Barguzin sable (the most prized) to water rat — popular with the locals, and of which 200 skins are needed to make a coat. In the summer you can go on boat trips down the Angara: boats leave from opposite the White House at 9am every morning.

Entertainment. Concerts and organ recitals are held in the Cathedral of the Epiphany and Catholic Church on ul Sukhe-Bator: posters outside advertise these and tickets cost about R1.50. There is an Opera House on ul K Marksa, just north of the White House, and the Philharmonia is at 2 ul Dzerzhinskova, opposite the Palace of Sport.

Shopping. Irkutsk is a lively shopping town. Most activity is concentrated along ul K Marksa and ul Uritskova, the pedestrian street which leads from ul K Marksa to the department store on ul Dzerzhinskova. (Buses 20 and 21 run along ul Sukhe-Bator and ul K Marksa.) Along the pedestrian precinct there are cafés, plus street stalls selling clothes, cassettes and piping hot pasties. The central market, where you can get an insight into the variety of nationalities here, is just to the left of here. It is full of pushy flower sellers, butchers wielding heavy meat cleavers chopping up fatty cuts of meat and, in winter, people selling milk in frozen blocks.

LAKE BAIKAL

One of the most amazing sights in the world, Lake Baikal enchants most visitors. As you approach from Irkutsk (65km south) you pass picturesque villages and vast expanses of taiga forest before crossing the Primorsky mountains that skirt the southern end of the lake. Once at the shore, Lake Baikal is an awesome sight. The Russian writer, Valentin Rasputin, calls it 'a great cathedral of nature.'

Intourist guides used to have a field day with statistics when bringing tour groups to here. Lake Baikal is 395 miles/636km long and is the deepest (some say the oldest) lake in the world: it contains one-sixth of the world's fresh water. The water is beautifully clear partly thanks to a crustacean, native to Baikal, which has a voracious appetite for bacteria. Two-thirds of the fauna and flora found in the lake — totalling more than a thousand species — are unique to Baikal: the high oxygen content of the water has meant that species extinct elsewhere have survived here. Fresh water seals, called nerpas, are found nowhere else in the world. Neither is the omul (a type of salmon that turns up on many local restaurant menus), nor the golomanka, a fish that produces live young as opposed to eggs. It lives at a great depth and when brought to the surface explodes or melts like ice leaving a pool of oil, rich in Vitamin A. Sturgeon can grow up to six feet/two metres in length and when they reach maturity at 20 years, can produce 20lb/9kg of caviar. The lake certainly deserves its name Bai-kul, meaning 'rich lake', given to it by the Buryat tribe indigenous to the area.

Being such a rich natural repository, Lake Baikal is the subject of fears for its ecological well-being. Since 1967 a pulp factory has been the source of pollution, and periodically other threats — in the form of industrial plans or schemes to divert the rivers which feed it — have appeared.

The climate at Lake Baikal is different from that of the Irkutsk region due to the mountains that surround the lake. In winter, the temperature by Lake Baikal is noticeably warmer than in Irkutsk. The lake doesn't freeze over until January and stays frozen until May. The ice can be a metre thick in places but gases coming up from the depths warm the water and can make the ice unsafe for skating. In winter, before the water freezes, these gases make the water appear to smoke.

The Angara, which is the only river to flow out of the lake (while over 300 flow in), freezes much later than most Siberian rivers due to its strong current. In summer the sun is extremely hot and the mosquitoes can be a real pest so bring lots of repellant. Lake Baikal is also affected by extremely strong winds which can create large waves and could turn a boat trip into quite an experience. To add to the natural thrills, earth tremors are not infrequent.

Arrival and Departure. Buses for Listvyanka, the village on the shore of Lake

Baikal, leave from Irkutsk bus station (on ul Revolutsii, not far from the Decembrists' Museum) frequently through the day. Hydrofoils run from Irkutsk in summer. A third alternative is by taxi: $30-$50 should secure a driver and car for the day.

Accommodation. The Baikal Hotel is a standard Intourist hotel but its position is perfect. It is a few minutes' walk from the village of Listvyanka and overlooks the lake. The restaurant serves good food, including fish caught fresh from the lake, pickled mushrooms and cowberries. The water here is delicious and is said to make you a year younger. In winter you can hire sledges, skis and boots from the hotel.

Exploring. The main village of Listvyanka is a few minutes' walk from the hotel. This has unfortunately become something of a show town for tourists. With its smouldering chimneys and wooden cottages it is, nonetheless, extremely picturesque and tranquil. The pink church of St Nicholas, dating from the 1850s, nestles among the houses. It can be quite unnerving to walk up the small frozen river in winter but the hollow sound of footsteps is deceptive as the ice here is good and thick.

Across the mouth of the Angara from the hotel is Port Baikal, once a hive of activity. Before the railway was built around the southern tip of the lake in 1904, passengers on Trans-Siberian trains had to cross Lake Baikal by ferry. Two ferries — the *Baikal* and the *Angara*, both sent over in pieces from Newcastle-upon-Tyne and assembled locally — made the journey from Port Baikal to Mysovaya. Sadly, this port has now fallen into disuse.

Close by you can see the so-called Shaman Rock, whose tip just breaks the surface of the water. Legend has it that Baikal had 337 daughters, one of which, Angara, was particularly stubborn. She fell in love with Yenisei and when Baikal forbade their marriage the two eloped; as they fled Baikal threw the great Shaman Rock after them: this rock now stands where the river Angara leaves the lake on its way to be united with Yenisei. The fate of alleged criminals was decided by chaining them to the rock: if they drowned it meant they were innocent and would reach Paradise but if they reached the shore they were guilty and must have their throats cut. Opposite here is the entrance to the Limnological Institute and Museum. The museum is small and contains many specimens of fauna and flora found in and around Lake Baikal. There are also models showing the structure of the whole lake. It is an interesting museum but do not venture in if you don't like seeing rather bedraggled stuffed animals or baby seals in jars. The exhibits are labelled in Latin which is useful for zoology scholars but little help for laymen. Some find the visitors' book more entertaining; as one American put it: 'I like the fish, what about the chips?'

One of the best things to do in Listvyanka is to walk. By walking up a clear path to the left of Baikal Hotel you reach the hilltop from where there is a magnificent view of the lake on a clear day: it takes about an hour there and back. At the top is a tree to which people traditionally tie ribbons for good luck.

On the road to Listvyanka, 29 miles/47km from Irkutsk, is a reconstructed 18th-century village. It is definitely worth a visit if you have the time. This museum is only open in the summer but it is possible to wander around the grounds in autumn and spring.

BRATSK

On its course to the Arctic Ocean, the River Angara flows through Bratsk,

400 miles/650km north of Irkutsk. It was founded as a Cossack fort in the 17th century, and remained a quiet village in the taiga until the 1960s when a huge hydroelectric plant was built. It is the second largest plant in the former USSR, after the one at Krasnoyarsk. Bratsk is often featured on Siberian package tours since the authorities are always proud to show off their electric power stations. This is perhaps a legacy of Lenin who, in 1920, said: 'Communism is Soviet power plus the electrification of the whole country.' Some tours honour Bratsk with a two-day visit but this really is excessive unless you go on out-of-town excursions. You can go to the open-air Ethnographical Museum with, among other things, the 'Evenk Village' showing the lifestyle of this indigenous nomadic tribe. Other excursions include trips into the taiga forest (lethal in the summer when the mosquitoes are at their most voracious) or crosscountry skiing expeditions in winter. Summer boat trips up the Angara from Irkutsk to Bratsk may be possible.

KHABAROVSK

The Trans-Siberian crosses the Amur at the confluence with the Ussuri, a river almost as big as the Amur. On the right bank stands Khabarovsk, with a population of 600,000, just 22km from the border with China. The Amur — 'Little Father Amur' to the Russians — can be rough and even smashes ships during storms and sweeps away villages when it floods. The Chinese call it the 'Black Dragon'.

Khabarovsk was founded in 1858 by Count Muravyev-Amurski, the Governor of East Siberia, as a military outpost guarding access to Manchuria. It was named after Erofey Khabarov, the Russian explorer who made several expeditions to the Amur in the mid-17th century, and actually reached this point in 1649. In 1884 the Far Eastern Territories were separated from Eastern Siberia and Khabarovsk became the administrative centre. Centuries ago it was believed that this part of Siberia rested on the backs of three great whales. Modern developments have made these hard to discern but the city does in fact stand on three long hills — known locally as sopka — which lie side by side. At one time it was a trading centre for sable pelts. The opening of the railway connection with Vladivostock in 1897 added greatly to the industrial development of the town. Until this stretch of the railway was completed, passengers sailed up and down the Amur and Ussuri rivers between Khabarovsk and Vladivostock. Considerable damage was done during the Revolution and subsequent unrest, so much of the building is new.

Khabarovsk is a pleasant town, worth exploring. Laurens van der Post in *Journey into Russia* writes: 'Like a true frontier outpost Khabarovsk's people were generous, informal and hospitable to the extreme'. Few old wooden houses have survived but there are still some stone buildings. The surrounding area is rich in minerals but is basically swampy forest. The average temperature is −26°C in January, 18°C in July. Sometimes there is snow on the ground for half the year, and there are areas where the permafrost penetrates to 1000 metres. Khabarovsk has on average 256 cloudless days a year. In an attempt to make the city self-sufficient in vegetables, gardeners take advantage of the sunny skies to cultivate produce under glass.

Arrival and Departure. Khabarovsk is an important transit area for tourist routes from Europe and Central Asia to countries of the Pacific, especially Japan. There are flights to Moscow (eight hours), Irkutsk and other Russian cities, and services to Niigata in Japan and Seattle in the USA. Bus 3 and trolley-bus 1 go to the airport from ul K Marksa. The airport has a decent restaurant if you are delayed. Khabarovsk lies at the 8,531km mark of the Trans-Siberian Railway, some 143 hours from Moscow (almost 6 days). The train station on ul Leningradskaya is accessible from Komsomol Square on bus 1. Khabarovsk is seven hours ahead of Moscow.

City Layout. The city is laid out in a grid pattern. The main street-with cafes, theatres, shops — is ul K Marksa, which starts at Komsomol Square on the banks of the Amur and runs east across the central Lenin Square towards the airport. A wide flight of steps leads from Lenin Square down to the Amur embankment and the beach. Amursky Bulvar runs parallel to ul K Marksa and leads from the river to the train station.

Accommodation. The Intourist Hotel is at 2 Amursky Bulvar (tel 34-4347), close to the river. It is nine miles/15km from the airport and a couple of miles from the station.

Eating and Drinking. The hotels are probably as good as anywhere but try also the Ussuri Restaurant at 34 ul K Marksa which serves local as well as standard fare. There is a pleasant café in the tower on Amursky Cliff (see below) where you can eat good ice cream.

Exploring. Behind Komsomol Square is a park and Amursky Cliff, the river embankment which is a favourite spot for the locals. There is a magnificent view over the Amur and across the steppe to China in the distance. You can go on two-hour boat trips (not long enough to reach the People's Republic) from the jetty. The river is frozen for five months of the year; in winter people fish through the ice for carp, pike and 'Jaws', the super sturgeon. In summer people swim from the sandy shores of the Amur. Wandering along ul K Marksa you see a few red-brick houses and some public buildings built in the 1930s Constructivist style. Down side streets there is the odd wooden house. In Komsomol Square are the offices of the Amur Steamship Company — a fine building of the Belle Epoque.

The Local History Museum, by the park at 21 ul Shevchenko, has a collection of ethnography, fauna and flora of the Far East and the taiga. Explorers' and hunters' donations have made interesting additions: these include two Amur tigers, and a sea-otter whose fur is the most sought after in the world. In the garden is the skelcton of a whale caught in 1891. There are also exhibits relating to the customs and lifestyle of tribes who lived on the land around the Ussuri and Amur. The Art Museum has the usual collection of icons and 18th-20th century Russian art. In addition, you can see the works of Rubens and Rembrandt as well as Japanese and Chinese applied arts. Perhaps the most interesting are the arts and crafts of the Amur and Ussuri tribes, such as the Olchis and Goldis. Both museums are closed on Mondays.

The Arboretum claims to possess specimens of all the trees and shrubs (1,300) to be found in the Russian Far East.

Entertainment. The best entertainment in Khabarovsk is to be had in the circus at 20 ul Tolstovo. The clowns are hilarious. The Philharmonia is at 7 ul Shevchenko and the Musical Comedy Theatre at 64 ul K Marksa.

The Trans-Siberian Railway

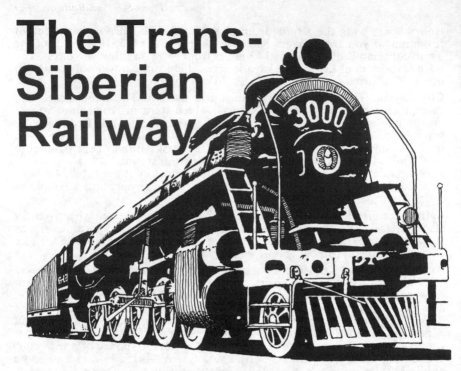

'There is no railway journey of comparable length anywhere in the world . . .
The Trans-Siberian is the big train ride. All the rest are peanuts.'

Eric Newby, *The Big Red Train Ride*

The greatest railway on earth runs for nearly 6,000 miles between Moscow
and Vladivostok. It passes through eight hundred stations (all of which look
very much the same, many of them still adorned with Soviet propaganda),
seven time zones, two massive mountain ranges and crosses four mighty
rivers. And, if you are not suited to long-distance rail travel, it can be
stultifyingly dull.

Tsar Alexander III authorized the building of a railway in 1886 to help
the development of the country beyond the Urals and to transport troops
to the Amur region, at the time under dispute with the Chinese. It was built
in separate stages: only in 1916 did the Trans-Siberian reach from Europe
to the Pacific. The West Siberian stretch (from Moscow as far as present-
day Novosibirsk) was finished in 1895 and the Mid Siberian section to
Irkutsk in 1898. The Transbaikal track was laid down by 1900: this linked
Mysovaya on Lake Baikal to Sretensk, on the Shilka River. Passengers had
to cross the lake by ferry and then go by steamer down the Shilka and Amur
rivers to Khabarovsk; from there they went on the Ussuri line — built
in 1897 — down to Vladivostok. The East Chinese Railway, connecting
Transbaikal to Vladivostok via Manchuria, was completed in 1901. With
the building of the Circumbaikal Line in 1904, Irkutsk was linked by rail to
Mysovaya. The Amur Railway linking Sretensk to Khabarovsk was finished
in 1916, thus completing the Trans-Siberian route.

In the 1920s a plan was hatched to build a northern branch of the
TransSiberian. This would begin at Tayshet, east of Krasnoyarsk, and run

north of the existing line to Sovetskaya Gavan on the Pacific. Construction began at Tayshet but was abandoned at the beginning of World War II. In 1976 Leonid Brezhnev announced that building would be resumed, but it proved a mammoth task due to the severe conditions. Now that the Baikal-Amur-Magistral (BAM) railway is fully operational, its true irrelevance to most travellers has become clear. It has, however, provided a new freight service between Europe and the Far East, giving it important international status and removing some of the burden from the original Trans-Siberian line.

The multiplicity of choices and bureaucracy involved in planning a trip on the Trans-Siberian — and its offshoots, the Trans-Mongolian and Trans Manchurian to China — is as mind-wrenching as the statistics of the railway itself. You must choose when and where to go, and decide between the easier option of booking on an organized tour, or the more complex (and cheaper) business of travelling independently. If you are using the Trans-Siberian as a cheap option to travel overland from Europe to Asia or vice-versa it may not matter to you that there are no overnight stops during the journey. But if your purpose is to explore Siberia — beyond the views through dirty windows and in the stations — it may be worth planning a stopover or two.

Choosing a Route. Now that Vladivostok has become an 'open' city, Western travellers bound for Japan can follow the TransSiberian for its entire length. Foreigners were previously obliged to change trains at Khabarovsk for Nakhodka and the ferry for Yokohama. Now you can take the boat at Vladivostok for Niigata and Fushiki. These ships operate only between June and early October; in winter you have to fly, which can add greatly to the cost. If China is your destination, take either the Trans-Mongolian or Trans-Manchurian to Beijing. The Mongolian route uses a Chinese train which serves better food and the journey takes only six days. The Manchurian train takes a week.

When to Go. Those hesitant about braving a Siberian winter can be assured that the heating on the trains is (too) efficient. If you wish to make the journey in summer, it may be necessary to book five or six months in advance. Between October and April trains are much less crowded and so late bookings are feasible, except for Christmas when tourism picks up slightly. Scenically, most seasoned travellers prefer late spring or early autumn.

Red Tape. Only after all your travel and hotel reservations have been confirmed will your Russian visa be issued. Furthermore you must have a visa for your country of destination beyond Russia, whether it is China, Belarus, etc. (Western travellers do not need a visa for Japan). This means getting your visas in reverse order i.e. if you're going from Beijing to Belarus you must get your Belarusian visa first and then your Russian one. Those going east to China via Mongolia need visas for both these countries before applying for a Russian visa. If applying through the embassy, rather than through Intourist or another agency, you must take confirmation of your ticket with you. A Russian transit visa is usually valid for a maximum of 10 days, quite sufficient if you don't plan to stop over at all during the journey across. Those staying for longer should apply for a tourist visa.

LONDON-VLADIVOSTOK   *TRANS-SIBERIAN*

<u>22nd May - 24th June 1996</u> - A 34 day trip from London, travelling 16,000 km to Berlin, Moscow and Vladivostok. Includes return air flights, off train tours and side trips to Mongolia etc.

<u>23rd June - 14th July 1996</u> - A 22 day trip from Vladivostok to Moscow. Includes flights to Vladivostok and same side trips as above.

Tours feature new first class sleeping cars, saloons, restaurant and bar cars. The train will be hauled by fully restored Russian Trans-Siberian steam locomotives.

GW Travel also organise rail tours to the Caucasus and Crimea. For further details contact the tour operators.

 **GW Travel Limited**
Continental Rail Tour Operators

GW Travel Limited, 6 Old Market Place, Altrincham, Cheshire WA14 4NP
Tel: 0161 928 9410 Fax: 0161 941 6101

Buying a Ticket. You can just bowl up in Moscow and buy a ticket there, but enlisting the help of a specialist agent, such as the following, can speed your progress greatly. If you book everything in the UK, then obtaining visas becomes infinitely easier.

China Travel Service, 7 Upper St Martin's Lane, London WC2H 9DL (0171-836 3688).
GW Travel, 6 Old Market Place, Altrincham, Cheshire WA14 4NP (tel 0161-928 9410, fax 0161-941 6101).
St Petersburg Travel, 196 High Road, London N22 4HH (tel/fax 0171-249 7503).
One Europe Travel, Research House, Fraser Rd, Perivale, Middlesex UB6 7AQ (tel 0181-566 9424, fax 0181-566 8845).
Intourist, 219 Marsh Wall, London E14 9FJ (tel 0171-538 3202).

These agents can spell out the various options, including the potentially wise one of missing out many of the most boring bits. For example, you could go Moscow to Irkutsk by rail, Irkutsk to Khabarovsk by air, Khabarovsk to Vladivostok by rail and by boat to Niigata, for around £500.

Westbound from China. Within the People's Republic, the China International Travel Service (CITS) is the Chinese version of Intourist. You can book Trans-Mongolian tickets through CITS — at lower prices than outside China — but at least one month's notice is required. If you are planning to travel around China, book your ticket as soon as you get there. During the low season, the minimum time required to arrange a ticket on the Trans-Manchurian is a week (excluding the time needed to get a Russian visa) although this depends on which train you wish to go on. Bookings for the Chinese train open one month ahead and the service is often fully booked by the afternoon of the first day. The Russian train is less popular due to the inferior dining car and it has been known for people to buy a ticket on the day of departure (try this only if your Russian visa is in order, which will be something of an achievement if you have no ticket).

CITS has a special Foreign Independent Travel (FIT) department in the Chongwenmen Hotel in Beijing. Tickets are available from the International Ticket Office on the third floor. You can buy tickets to several European capitals besides Moscow. Getting a visa for Russia in Beijing poses few difficulties as the Russian Embassy (4 Dongzhirnenwei, Beizhongjie; tel 521-267) is highly efficient. Transit visas cost 25 FEC and take about a week to process. If you pay 45 FEC it can even be issued the following working day. Note that the embassy is only open on Monday, Wednesday and Friday mornings. It is, in theory, necessary to show proof of travel out of Russia but not many people are actually asked to show any reservation details.

The Mongolian Embassy is at 2 Xiushui Beijie, Jianguomenwei (tel 521-203). Visas can be collected the next working day, for a fee of US$30 paid in cash. Some travellers have omitted to obtain a Mongolian visa yet succeeded in having their passport stamped at the border free of charge, but do not rely upon this; it's a long way back from the frontier to Beijing.

Westbound from Hong Kong. It is cheaper to buy in Beijing than in Hong Kong, but you may feel that the reduction in hassle justifies the extra expense. There are three main agencies in Hong Kong through which you can buy Trans-Siberian tickets: China Travel Service, 78-83 Connaught Road, Central; Hong Kong Student Travel, 305 Entertainment Building, 30 Queen's Road, Central or 833-835 Star House, 3 Salisbury Road, Kowloon; Wallem Travel, 46th Floor, Hopewell Centre, 183 Queen's Road East.

If you wish to make your own way to Beijing, you can cross into China by bus, train, ferry or plane. One route you could take would be to catch the express train to Canton and then the train to Beijing, which takes about 34 hours. Air China runs daily flights to Beijing from Hong Kong.

ON THE TRAIN

The time spent at a station varies from two to twenty minutes (much longer at border posts). If you're not sure check on the timetable in the corridor or ask the *provodnik* (carriage attendant). There is little warning (and no whistle) of departure, so make sure you are back on board in time. If you cross the tracks to get to a shop, check that another train isn't going to block your path: freight trains pass frequently. It is wise not to wander too far from the train.

The train and stations both keep Moscow time right the way across. You are advised to change your watches to local time as you go along to help you adjust to 'train lag' (a gentler version of jet lag). Drivers have even been known to make unscheduled stops in spring and summer so that passengers can pick flowers, which grow in abundance on the Siberian steppe.

Kilometre posts are on the southern side of the track. The train averages 70 km/h; promised acceleration from newer engines have never materialised. The trains between Moscow and Irkutsk are electric, but beyond here electrification is not yet complete and diesel engines are used.

Customs Formalities. Stops at border stations usually take between one and two hours. Customs officials board the train and check passports, visas and currency declaration forms. Luggage inspections also take place; the thoroughness of these varies; the Mongolian officials have a reputation for being extremely conscientious. On the whole customs officials are most interested in illegal migrants.

Money. Those travelling straight through should allow $100 in order to eat and drink well en route. In Russia, these will need to be in roubles, since no (official) change facilities are available on the train. For the Trans-Mongolian you will need some US dollars, since only these are acceptable in the restaurant car while passing through Mongolia. Those crossing into China should note that station banks have erratic opening hours and the border exchange rate for Yuan is usually unfavourable. Bartering seems to be most successful in Mongolia, where cassettes of Western music go down particularly well.

Provodniks. Each carriage has an attendant known as the *provodnik* in Russian (*fuwuren* in Chinese). They vacuum the carpets, keep the samovar full for hot drinks, look after the heating and are usually willing to answer any questions you have about the length of station stops, etc. They may well expect a tip at the end.

Compartments. The compartments are basic but clean and perfectly adequate. Windows are kept locked in winter and usually opened in May when they often don't shut properly and are prone to let in dirt, especially when passing through industrial zones. The solid-fuel boilers in each carriage are very effective but also give off rather a lot of coal dust. In summer natural dust replaces that produced by the boilers. You will need to clean your window regularly if you want to take photographs from the train. Smoking is not allowed in the compartments. You can only smoke between the doors at the end of the carriages: this can be a freezing experience in winter but it is always a good way to make friends. There are also fold-down seats in the corridor which make a pleasant change from your bunk.

There are 'soft' and 'hard' class compartments. 'Soft' class compartments come in two categories: de luxe first class and first class: the former have two berths and a washbasin, the latter four berths. All four berths are used in the Hard or second class compartment but otherwise the quality is much the same, the bunks being equally well-padded etc. Travelling first class tends to be quieter and not such fun. The second class compartments on the Chinese trains are, in fact, the equivalent of first class on ordinary trains in China.

Bedding is provided and changed once during the journey. Compartments are mixed. Women sharing with Russian men often find that they will offer you the upper (and more discreet) bunk, will get you cups of tea and are generally very kind; rarely might they become a nuisance.

Washing. If you are planning to go the distance, have a thorough scrub before you get on the train since there are no showers on board, although these may come in the future. The carriages have a washroom at each end, the one nearest the provodnik invariably being the cleanest. The washroom consists of a basin and lavatory and is tiny. There is hot water but this can take some time to warm up or simply not appear at all. It is a good idea to bring a strong bottle or thermos flask which you can fill with hot water at the samovar and then use for washing or for a rudimentary shower. There is a plug in the floor which can be lifted out to allow water to drain. There is no plug in the sink but there is a 220v socket for those with electric shavers. Loo paper is not always on offer or runs out along the way, so take your own.

Eating and Drinking. Do not deceive yourself into thinking that a trip on the Trans-Siberian is going to be a culinary delight. Dining cars have erratic opening hours and seem to follow neither Moscow nor local time (although officially you should sit down to eat at about the same time as President Yeltsin). The provodnik will usually know but it is best to check for yourself as often as possible. As it is more than likely that you will miss the odd meal, a limited supply of provisions is advisable: biscuits, black bread, tinned food, dried fruit, nuts and similar snacks are recommended. Russian travellers often take their own food and don't use the dining car at all. Unless you have special dietary requirements or are travelling in winter it is probably unnecessary, however, to take a large food stock.

The restaurant tends to be most reliable at the beginning of your journey. Remember too that there are kiosks at the stations where you can buy food, and hawkers who descend on the arriving train to sell snacks, although there is seldom much to excite your appetite. Now and again the treats on offer include: pirozkhi (pasties), blini (pancakes), kebabs, cakes, ice-cream and milk. Your are also more likely to find fresh vegetables — usually bundles of radishes or spring onions-at the stations than on the train. In addition, sometimes trolleys with meagre offerings of food are pushed up and down the corridors.

The Russian dining car sports a vast menu — in Russian, Chinese, English, German and French — but by no means all of what is printed on it is actually available: the dishes on offer are the ones with the price pencilled in. The variety of food seems to depend on the time of year, the choice diminishing during the winter. The kitchen is stocked along the way. So, for example, fish is suddenly included on the menu after the stop by Lake Baikal. Constants on the menu are beef Stroganov or goulash, chicken soup or borshch, fried or hard-boiled eggs and black bread. Occasionally caviar (the cheaper red salmon variety), sturgeon, chicken or even moose steaks are available. Meals are relatively cheap: an average meal consisting of soup, bread, beef Stroganov and Potatoes and tea costs not much more than $5.

The mineral water is rather metallic tasting and the over-sweet juices only make you thirstier so buy water in advance. Beer and (sometimes) vodka are sold by the provodnik. You can order hot drinks throughout the day from the provodnik. If you're fussy about coffee take your own: you can use the water from the samovar to make your own drinks. Cigarettes, sweets and chocolate are on sale in the dining car.

The dining cars change nationality as you cross the borders. The Mongolian one (which accepts only US dollars) is as unexciting as that in Russia but the Chinese dining car generally meets with praise largely because of the change of menu and higher-quality food. There are drawbacks, however: there is no menu, portions can be small and the food more expensive. Expect to pay about $5 for breakfast and $8 for lunch or supper.

Entertaiment. This may sound like a contradiction in terms, but it is unlikely that you will get bored during the journey. The compartments and corridors are a constant hive of activity and there are often parties in the evening. What with taking in the scenery, trying to take photographs, studying people in the dining car, avoiding crooks and jumping out at stations for food or exercise, there is plenty to keep you occupied. It makes sense, however, to take a few diversions along with you: a thick novel (or three), a diary, playing cards, chess or draughts, Scrabble, a sketchbook. Writing letters is a good timefiller: take paper and postcards with you in case you cannot get any along the way. A Walkman is also useful if you have a garrulous companion in your compartment or if the piped music gets a little too much.

Advice. For general information on what to take and how to behave in Russia see the Introduction; there are, however, certain things which apply specifically to the Trans-Siberian. Remember you are not travelling on the 8.03 from Woking to Waterloo, but on the world's longest train ride. An expanding number of books are devoted to the train ride, the most recently published is *The Trans-Siberian Rail Guide* (Compass Star, £11.99).

Photography is no longer taboo, though the odd official may take exception to it. Use fast camera film (at least ASA 400) for taking pictures on the move.

Although there is ample storage space in the compartments, travel as light as possible (soft bags rather than hard suitcases are recommended). One Trans-Siberian traveller took just an executive case containing his book, toothbrush and one change of thermals. Washing clothes is difficult, however; there is not much room in your compartment for dripping underwear so take plenty with you. Thin clothes and a light pair of shoes are as vital as your winter woollies. The Russians often wander around in pyjamas and you are best off wearing sweatshirts or a tracksuit. Other useful things to take on the train include a torch, plate, mug, penknife, tin-opener, insect repellent (for summer) — and strong wire to secure the door of your compartment.

THE TRANS-SIBERIAN ROUTE (showing distances from Moscow)

Yaroslavl station, Moscow — departure at 2pm.

Zagorsk (45 miles/73km). For details of the history of this town see page 130. From the train you should get a glimpse of the stunning blue and gold cupolas of the Cathedral of the Assumption and the bell-tower, within the St Sergius monastery complex.

Yaroslavl (175 miles/282km). Tolstoy lovers might remember that it was at Yaroslavl station that Count Vronski met Anna Karenina. If it is summer, and therefore a light evening on the eastbound journey, the best view of Yaroslavl's ancient cathedrals (described on page 133) is to be had as you leave the town, as the train crosses the huge bridge that spans the Volga. After Yaroslavl you begin to see the vast coniferous forests, which soon become tediously typical of Northern Russia.

Kirov (621 miles/957km). This modern city lies on the Vyatka River. It was named Kirov in 1934 after the Communist leader, Sergei Kirov, who was murdered in the same year, and has hung on to the name against the tide of de-communisation. The death of Kirov precipitated the Great Terror of Stalin during which some say 12 million were executed, exiled or imprisoned. Many suspect that Stalin himself authorized Kirov's murder and used this as a pretext for his purges.

As you pull out of Kirov, try not to remind yourself that you are only one-tenth of the way to Vladivostok.

Perm (893 miles/1437km). The train runs by the Vyatka and Chepta rivers before reachin Perm, some nine hours beyond Kirov (the train stops for about ten minutes, at lunchtime Moscow time). This city lies on the huge Kama river which flows into the Volga. A member of the Stroganov merchant family established a village here; being on the Kama, the Siberian Post Road and later the railway, it was perfectly situated for trade. Beyond here the train enters the Urals, which resemble rocky hills more than mountains and are dotted with open-cast mines.

Approaching the 1,777km point, 1104 miles from Moscow, crowds gather in the corridor to catch a gllmpse of the puny white obelisk which marks the continental divide, the border between Europe and Asia. Eastbound, this tcnds to happen only in May to August, when the late evening is light enough to see it.

Yekaterinburg (1130 miles/1818km). With a population today of over a million, Yekaterinburg was founded in 1721 during the reign of Catherine the Great. It was known as Sverdlovsk from 1924 until 1991, when a local lad, Boris Yeltsin, ensured the name was changed to the historically resonant original.

On 16 July 1918 Tsar Nicholas II, his wife, son and daughters met violent deaths here. Details of the murders are scanty; some still believe that a few membcrs of the royal family survived.

Yekaterinburg is an important railway junction; the train makes a 15-minute stop before continuing down the Urals to the rather dreary Great Siberian Plain, much of which is covered in taiga. This is one of the flattest areas in the world: it stretches from the Arctic Ocean to the Caspian and covers about 930 miles/1,500km east to west. This is the time to get your book(s) out.

At the 2078km post (1291 miles from Moscow) Siberia officially begins, at the point where the Yekaterinburg and Tyumen regions meet.

Tyumen (1322 miles/2144km). This is the oldest town in Siberia. It was founded in 1586, on the site of a Tatar settlement said to date from the 14th century. Many exiles and convicts passed through here on their way east.

Omsk (1688 miles/2716km). Beyond the Tobol and Ishim rivers is Omsk. It was originally an *ostrog* (military outpost) founded in 1719 where the river Om joins the Irtysh (which has its source in China). It was an important military headquarters and later many exiles ended up here. They included Feodor Dostoycvsky (1849-53), who describes the experiencc in *Buried Alive in Siberia*. It is now the second-largest city in Siberia. There is a stop of 15 minutes which even then is too long. Eric Newby records: 'Very few people have had a good word to say for Omsk . . . windy, cold, dusty (according to the seasons) and always dirty.' Beyond Omsk the railway is busier than at any other time, with trains passing about every two minutes. The scenery is also dreary as the train crosses 375 miles/600km of the Baraba steppe which is scattered with mosquito-infested lakes. Some of these get into the train, so wear repellent in summer.

Novosibirsk (2078 miles/3343km). There is a stop of 15 minutes here. See page 150 for details about the Siberian capital, the official heart of Russia.

Taiga (2219 miles/3571km). Here a line branches off through the dense taiga forest to Tomsk, 56 miles/90km to the north. Tomsk was founded in 1604 and was visited by many merchants, travellers and exiles when it lay on the Siberian Post Road. It declined after the railway was built to the south but it is still one of the main Siberian towns.

At the 3820km point (2374 miles from Moscow) you pass from Western into Eastern Siberia, where the vast administratlve region of Krasnoyarsk begins.

Kranoyarsk (2550 miles/4104km). This city, founded in 1628, lies on the

Yenisei River, which means 'wide water' in the language of the local (originally nomadic) Evenk tribe. It almost cuts Siberia in two as it flows north into the Arctic Ocean. Lenin was exiled here at the end of last century.

Krasnoyarsk means both 'red' and 'beautiful', neither of which is true, the town being surrounded by hydro-electric plants. There is a 15-minute stop here. Beyond Krasnoyarsk the scenery gradually becomes more hilly and less monotonous.

Tayshet (2810 miles/4522km). Tayshet is the junction of the Baikal-Amur-Magistral Railway (BAM). It has indeed opened up a vast new area of Eastern Siberia, but most people (Russians included) are inclined to ask 'So what?'. The only point of real interest is Severobaikalsk, at the northern tip of Lake Baikal. Rail buffs and masochists should note that to cover the whole stretch to Sovietskaya Gavan requires changes at Tynda and Konsomolsk na Amure.

Some 60 miles/100km further on the train hits the foothills of the Sayan mountains, on the other side of which lies Mongolia. The forests become less dense after this stretch and the land flattens out again.

There is a 20-minute stop at **Irkutsk** (3226 miles/5148km); see page 151 for further information on this city. Leaving Irkutsk the train passes through a tunnel for the first time since Moscow. The line penetrates the Primorsky Mountains and the excitement grows as you approach Lake Baikal. Although Moscow time is in the small hours, the six-hour time difference with local time means it should be light.

The track follows the southern shore of the lake, affording some splendid views. Now you are in Transbaikal, which some would call real Siberia. With thick forest at every glance, the scenery begins to improve.

Ulan-Ude (3510 miles/5647km). This is the capital of the Buryat homeland, which lies around the southern part of Lake Baikal. Traditionally a nomadic people, known as 'the people of the forest' among their neighbouring Mongols, most of the Buryats have adapted to a modern way of life as farmers.

Ulan-Ude was an important trading post on the caravan route from China. After a stop the train continues through countryside which is a combination of forest, mountains and wide valleys. Eight kilometres east of Ulan-Ude is Zaudinsky which is the beginning of the Trans-Mongolian line (see below). Beyond Khilok (3687 miles/5932km) the train climbs into the Yablonovy (Apple Tree) Range which runs northwards between the Amur and Lena rivers and has peaks of up to 9,075ft/2,750 metres and severe temperatures in winter.

Chita (3559 miles/6204km). Built by the Cossacks in the 17th century, Chita was also an important stop on trade routes from the East. A large group of Decembrists were exiled here in 1827 — many remained and their descendants live here still. There is a stop of 15 minutes.

Karimskaya (3915 miles/6300km). This is the junction for the Trans-Manchurian route (see below). If you are sticking to the Vladivostok line, the countryside becomes drier as you skirt the Gobi Desert and later picturesque — almost Tyrolean — as the train follows the magnificent Shilka river, a tributary of the Amur. Unfortunately this takes place in early morning local time, going east, so you miss much in winter or through sleep. This area consists of high plateaux, interspersed with almost inaccessible valleys.

At the 7075km post (4397 miles from Moscow) the train crosses from Siberia into the Russian Far East, and the Amurskaya region. Over 625 miles/ 1,000km to the north is the Yakut homeland, a huge area much of which is in a permafrost zone. Its capital is Yakutsk, which lies on the Lena river and was one of the earliest fortresses in Siberia. Here the soil is frozen to a depth of 330 feet/100m, and some of the buildings are elevated on concrete pillars. The Yakut people comprise the largest ethnic group in the Russian Far East.

The stretch along the Amur — hidden by hills and the heavily guarded Chinese border — is particularly beautiful as you cross the river Zeya. The area beyond, along the Bureya river, is a wildlife sanctuary, rich in fauna and flora.

Birobidzhan (5195 miles/8358km). This is the capital of a swampy Jewish autonomous region, created in 1934 for Jewish people wishing to emigrate from Western Russia. Not many Jews wished to make the journey and many who did left disenchanted. Less than 10% of the present population is Jewish. Station names remain, however, in both Russian and Yiddish.

At 5289 miles/8511km you cross the magnificent Amur river.

Khabarovsk (5302 miles/8531km): see page 156. From here the train runs along the Ussuri river, extremely close to the Chinese border — at times you can look across into the People's Republic. A new route due south from here to Beijing may become possible. The cold currents coming off the Sea of Japan make the summers long and the climate humid, hence the lush vegetation. The train used to branch off and head through oriental scenery towards Nakhodka, bypassing Vladivostok; it was felt that passengers might otherwise be tempted to spy on the Russian Pacific Fleet.

Ussurisk (5708 miles/9185km). Shortly before reaching Vladivostok, the line splits with one branch continuing south to Khasan and the border with North Korea; travellers heading in this direction need to apply for a visa well in advance.

The splendid thing about the final approach is that the last few miles cling to the coast of the Vladivostok peninsula, your first sight of sea for goodness knows how long.

Vladivostok (5778 miles/9297km) The end of the line. See page 169.

If you are continuing by air or sea to Japan, the contrast with the USSR will seem almost unreal. After your battles with Russian bureaucracy, you may be relieved to learn that Western visitors do not need a visa to enter Japan for stays of up to 90 days, and that most frontier officials are all smiles.

THE TRANS-MONGOLIAN ROUTE

This section of railway, linking Moscow with Beijing, has been open since 1956. It follows the trade route frequented in the past by caravans of camels that came across the Gobi Desert from the Chinese capital. This route takes you through Mongolia, a republic that is more than twice the size of France yet with only two million people. The eastern part through which you travel is mostly grassy plain — actually part of the Gobi Desert — dotted with yurts (traditional nomadic tents), yaks and other animals and the odd horseman. Genghis and Kublai Khan brought their Mongol hordes from this area to terrorize 13th century Europe.

Mongolia is predominantly Buddhist and became independent from China in 1911. It has had a communist govermnent since 1921 and is proving more recalcitrant than most state socialist countries to shake off its past.

Naushki (3668 miles/5902km). From the main Trans-Siberian route at Zaudinsky, the train heads south across the Buryat region for 155 miles/ 250km to this town, which lies on the Russian border with Mongolia. Across the frontier at Sukhe Bator (3682 miles/5925km), Mongolian officials — sometimes unduly harsh and with a penchant for making petty confis- cations — search luggage and compartments. Camera film has sometimes been confiscated from those who insist on photographing the border. Be careful about taking pictures anywhere in Mongolia as it can provoke a violent reaction.

Ulan-Bator (3918 miles/6304km). The capital of Mongolia lies some 250 miles/400km south of the border and the train stops for 30 minutes. You may wish to bore fellow travellers with the information that Ulan Bator is the most distant from the ocean, and the coldest, capital in the world. It is also one of the few places where a statue of Stalin has survived. Some people get off as it is possible to stay here, but this must be arranged in advance. Vegetarians should note that Mongolia is so extremely carnivorous that some locals refuse to eat vegetables on religious grounds (to do with the soul of the earth).

The journey to the Chinese border town of Dzanun Ude (4359 miles/ 7013km) takes about ten hours. There can sometimes be a ten-hour delay while the bogeys are changed. The loos on the train are also locked during this time.

Erlyan (4365 miles/7023km). This time it is the Chinese customs officials' turn. The atmosphere is much less daunting than at previous border posts. It is sadly unlikely these days that an old steam locomotive will haul this part of the route.

You cross the Great Wall before reaching Datong (4874 miles/7483km) and finally, at the 7865km mark (4888 miles from Moscow), the Chinese capital.

THE TRANS-MANCHURIAN ROUTE

At Tarskaya the train leaves the Trans-Siberian line and joins the East Chinese Railway (completed in 1901), crossing the Chinese border and on to Harbin before heading south to Beijing. On the Russian side the border formalities are performed on the train at Zabaikalsk (4143 miles/6666km). At Manzhouli (4150 miles/6678km), the Chinese border town, you can go to the bank, stock up on food and even take photographs. Compared to the rigours of life on a Russian train the atmosphere seems incredibly relaxed. You travel south through the Inner Mongolian steppe and aaoss the foothills of the Great Khingan Range.

Harbin (4732 miles/7613km). This town was built by White Russian exiles and the Russian influence is clearly visible in the strangely incongruous domes and spires that survive in what otherwise is an ordinary Chinese town. The other stops between here and the capital include Changchun (4882 miles/7855km), Shenyang (5071 miles/8160km), Shanhaiguan (5336 miles/8586km) — the eastern end of the Great Wall — and Tianjin (5511 miles/8868km).

Beijing (5594 miles/9001km). You can have your first (or last) wash for a week.

The Far East

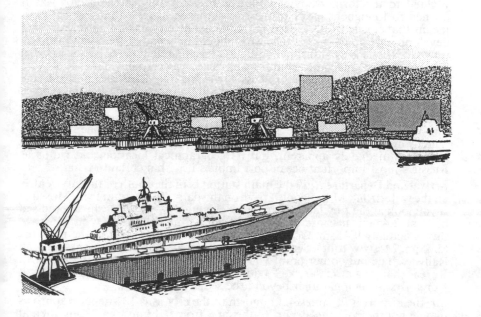

Vladivostok

Decades of communism failed to obscure the fact that this region of Russia has little in common with the European part of the Federation. The Far East is, well, far east — on the other side of the world, a nine-hour flight from Moscow or a week by train, and much closer to a dozen or more capitals than to the heart of Russian power. The physical and mental distance from Moscow means that life in the Far East has always difficult for central government to control. Since the collapse of the Soviet Union, the region's inclination to go its own way has become increasingly marked. But it will be some time before the nation's 'window on Asia' shakes off the detritus of state communism.

Vladivostok is the heart of the Wild East, a bewildering city where Chinese entrepreneurs meet Californian investors under the watchful eyes of the city's Mafiosi. Elsewhere, life continues less frenetically, and the traditions of the peoples of the north are as unaffected by capitalism as they were by communism.

VLADIVOSTOK

In a 1930s guide book called *Brazilian Adventure*, Peter Fleming imaginatively described Sao Paulo as 'like Reading, only further away'. But it doesn't take much imagination to see Vladivostok as 'like Minsk, only further away'. Japan is just a boat ride away, while North Korea is a short hop and China an even shorter one. Yet architecturally Vladivostok has nothing in common with the East. Despite the potential of its setting, a terrace of hills running down to the Pacific, it is not the great port city you might expect.

One reason why 'the Lord of the East', as the name translates, is so wedded to the former Soviet Union is because only in the 1990s was it opened to foreigners. Prior to that, its status as home of the Pacific Fleet meant that it was firmly closed to visitors. The city has a kind of retarded development, which means that what should be some of the wealthiest real estate in Russia is a confusion of dilapidated concrete monstrosities, wooden cabins hardly changed in a century, and bleak wasteground. The people who call it the 'San Francisco of Russia' are risking legal action from the California city. All it has in common are hills, a bay, Pacific fog and crooks.

Gradually, though, it is taking on the airs of an important trading point. The population of 750,000 is expanding. The fact that it is the end of the line from Moscow, and the jumping-off point for Japan, means that an increasing number of tourists are passing through the city. Its charms may not be immediately apparent, but its geographical location and status as Russia's most important ocean port imbues it with a certain raciness.

Arrival and Departure *Rail:* the main station is in the south of the city centre, on the waterfront. Most people arrive on the daily *Rossia* train from Moscow. If you look at the timetable, it appears scheduled to pull in at the uncivilised hour of 2.45am; because of the seven-hour time difference with Moscow, this is actually 9.45am. Going west, it leaves at five to one in the morning (5.55pm Moscow time). See page 158 for more details of the Trans-Siberian Railway. The only other point you can arrive from is Pyongyang in North Korea, changing at Ussurisk. To do this, however, you need to get to North Korea first, which is rather beyond the scope of this book.

Air: the airport is 28 miles/45km north of the city. Bus 101 departs approximately hourly from the airport to the city, from 7.13am to 6.33pm, then at 9.28pm. Ignore the sign just outside the airport promising 32km to the city; the actual distance is nearly half as much again.

Vladivostok is the eastern end of the longest non-stop air route in Russia. There are frequent flights from Moscow on Transaero, Orient Avia and the Aeroflot splinter airline Domodedovo Air. The fare is around $350 one-way, and the journey time is around 10 hours; rather than overfly China, a roundabout route is taken, flying over Kharbarovsk. For bookings in Vladivostok, the central sales agency is at ul Pasietskaya 17. Transaero's airport number is 26 08 80.

From the USA, Alaskan Airlines has a weekly flight from Seattle and Anchorage, for which the non-discountable price is $737. Orient Avia is talking about launching services linking Vladivostok with Honolulu and San Francisco, as well as Singapore, Bangkok, Saigon and Shanghai. Flights from Japan and Seoul (South Korea) operate on a seasonal basis.

Sea: the Far Eastern Shipping Co, which seems to have fingers in many pies in Vladivostok, operates a ferry approximately weekly between June and September to Fushiki and Niigata in Japan. This is your chance to sail with a company awarded the Orders of Lenin and the October Revolution.

City Layout. Vladivostok occupies a spit of land which protrudes like an arm between the Amur and Ussuri Gulfs. To continue the analogy, the main part of the city is around the palm, with the commercial centre on the knuckle from which a finger of land extends. The railway station is on this finger, which protects shipping in the dog-leg shaped harbour — the Golden Horn bay, and Vladivostok's *raison d'etre*. It is a deep bay, rarely frozen and therefore ideal for ocean-going shipping.

The main landmark is the disgracefully ugly Supreme Soviet, which was destined to be a hotel until the local apparatchiks got their hands on it.

Getting Around. The trams in Vladivostok look like battered garden sheds, but comprise a better form of public transport than the poisonously foul buses. Because of the implausibly large number of private vehicles (many left-hand drive, procured in Hong Kong or Japan), it is easy to find a freelance taxi. Traffic congestion can be appallingly bad.

Accommodation. The plushest hotel in town is the Versailles, fairly central at ul Svetlanskaya 10 (tel 26 51 24, e-mail /pn = vers/o = vladivostok/admd = sovmail/c = sufsprint.com). It has been newly refurbished after a fire, and costs $180 single/$240 double.

The Vladivostok hotel, on a hill above the modest beach, is a standard Soviet-issue concrete monolith. A single room costs $50 a night, but if you can find a friend a double costs only two dollars more.

The good news is that the second-floor flat at 7/11 ul Semyonovskaya is a *gostanitsa na domu* (bed and breakfast), charging around $15 per person per night. The bad news is that it's immediately above the Korea House restuarant (see below), and suitable only for guests who don't mind high-volume karaoke until the early hours from the bar downstairs.

The Golden Horn hotel, on the corner of Svetlanaskaya, is the most central, overlooking the city's main crossroads. This attractive early 20th-century building was being refurbished in the summer of 1995, and if the Versailles is anything to go by then it will charge very high rates when it re-opens.

If you want to retreat to the comfort of the Canadian Prairie, then the Vlad Motor Inn is the place for you. It is halfway between the airport and the city, and has everything from butter to bed linen imported from Canada.

Eating and Drinking. Vladivostok's unique culinary claim is for a range of restaurants from the Pacific rim, notably its closest neighbours — Japan and Korea. For Japanese food, the restaurant at the Versailles (third floor, past the casino) is good but expensive — $12 for a bowl of miso soup and a modest amount of tempura (seafood and vegetables fried in batter). The lunch specials at the Versailles, priced at around $8 for four courses, are much better value. On the ground floor of the Vladivostok hotel, the Sakura restaurant is also good, and offers the possibility of adjourning next door to the Fujiyama karaoke bar.

East along ul Svetlanskaya, the Russki offers more salubrious surroundings than the average Russian restaurant.

For Korean food, try the Korea House at 7/11 ul Semyonovskaya, near the Dinamo stadium. Kim chi, the pickled cabbage beloved by Koreans, is an acquired taste. The most improbable eating establishment in Vladivostok (actually in the northern suburbs, 12 miles/20km from the city centre) is Captain Cook's, an Australian restaurant. The menu includes crocodile and kangaroo. The address is ul Devyata 14, in the Sanatornaya suburb (tel 21 53 41).

Exploring. If you have only 24 hours in Vladivostok between train and ferry to Japan, you need not fret unduly about missing some of the sights. A city built in the last 140 years is likely to be short of historical interest, and Vladivostok certainly is. The museum on ul Svetlanskaya has an eclectic collection covering the short history of the city and beyond, ranging from an antique Japanese motorcycle to a crown coin commemorating a visit to New Zealand by the British Royal Family.

Shopping. Assuming you do not wish to buy anything from the Sniper Gun Shop at ul Aleutskaya 26, there is not much to get excited about on the retail front in Vladivostok. Some old Soviet memorabilia is still available, with a huge red hammer-and-sickle flag fetching about $15.

Crime and Safety. The murder rate in Vladivostok is high — around two killings a day. The vast majority of these, however, are underworld operations, and the visitor need not be too fretful.

Because of the general air of lawlessness, driving seems to be even worse in Vladivostok than in the rest of Russia

Help and Information. The dialling code for Vladivostok is 4232. The local Intourist office is in room 1022 on the first floor of the Vladivostok hotel (tel 22 50 22).

Further Afield. About 125 miles/200km from Vladivostok, Nakhodka lies in a sheltered bay of the Sea of Japan. It was founded last century and is a major fishing port. Its importance grew in 1958 when Vladivostok was deemed to be of too much military importance for foreign ships to continue docking there. It went into decline in 1991 when that decision was reversed, opening up Vladivostok to foreigners. It is now a free economic zone, and has little to offer the visitor.

Estonia

Tallinn

Population: 1.6 million   **Capital:** Tallinn (population 500,000)

Just 50 miles from Helsinki, three hours by ferry from the Finnish capital, Estonia is the northernmost of the Baltic states. It lies on Russia's western border and extricated itself only relatively recently from the drab homogeneity of the former Soviet Union. Yet even as part of the USSR, Estonia's proximity to Scandinavia made it more Westernised than any of the Soviet republics. Most Estonians still seem to consider themselves the *crème de la crème* of the Baltic states (of which it is the smallest), and they are confidently ahead in terms of opening up to Western economics and tourism.

Estonia is an ancient country with a colourful history. The influences of its people's language and culture combine uneasily with its recent Soviet past and longstanding Scandinavian heritage. Notwithstanding, Estonia is a forward-thinking and progressive state with a problematic but burgeoning eceonomy: Estonia is probably the most successful of the former Soviet republics. Even so, it is not an expensive place in which to travel.

Despite the ravages of state communism and weekend visits by Finns in search of cheap alcohol, Tallinn retains great charm, with some superb architecture dating from its days as an old Hanseatic port. The other trading centres, such as Narva, have survived less well. The Estonian countryside is flat and consists mostly of forest and marshy plains dotted with lakes, with few particularly attractive towns. If you really want to explore, try visiting some of the country's 1,500 coastal islands. The largest, Saaremaa, is easily accessible and offers rural scenes that have more appeal than most sights in the country.

For those using Estonia as an entry or exit point to or from Russia, the

173

contrast will be staggering. But Estonia has much to offer in terms of history, culture, beer, food and interesting people.

CLIMATE

Winter can be very cold with frequent heavy snowfalls. It lasts from November to mid-March: you sometimes see trees in blossom as late as June. In summer, the average temperature is 17°C/62°F. July and August are the hottest months, with temperatures often in the region of 26°C/79°F. Thunderstorms are not uncommon during this same period. Try to visit in June, when the days extend well into the night — the so-called *White Nights*.

HISTORY

Estonia was referred to by the Roman historian Tacitus as 'Aesti', which is still the name the people use to describe their country- except that they now spell it 'Eesti'. Tacitus also described to Estonia as a Germanic country, probably referring to the Danes' peaceable occupation of its northern shore, on which they built a fortified port called Taani Linn (Danish Town), the modern day capital. This prevailed until early medieval times when the expansionist German Teutonic Knights bought Tallinn from the Danes for the equivalent of 450kg of silver and named it Reval. By the 15th century, the city had become a wealthy and influential member of the Hanseatic League. The crusading knights had introduced a fiercely feudal system, however, which aroused much resentment locally. When Sweden succeeded in occupying the country in the 16th century (having helped to expel the Russian invader, Ivan the Terrible), was not unwelcome. Following a crippling affliction with the black death, Tallinn surrendered to tsar Peter the Great.

In 1721 the country was annexed by Russia. Only then did Estonia really begin to develop as a nation. In 1905 a revolution was brutally repressed, but Estonian nationalism grew and in 1918 freedom-fighters declared independence. Two years later in the Tartu Peace Treaty, the Russians renounced territorial claims on Estonia 'for all time'. Perperuity turned out to be 20 years. Estonia was independent until 1940 when it was annexed by the USSR following the Molotov-Ribbentrop Pact — the deal under which Germany and the Soviet Union carved up Eastern Europe. A puppet government was set up and Tallinn was made capital of the Estonian Soviet Socialist Republic.

Having borne the damage wrought by the German invasion during the Second World War, the Estonian people went on to suffer even more at the hands of Stalin. The Soviet leader was responsible for the deportation and execution of more than 60,000 Estonians from 1945 to 1949. After such harrowing events, Estonia did well to recover and become one of the richest republics in the Union.

Independence. Estonia was the first of the Baltic states to set up a People's Front, which began calling for autonomy and democracy in October 1988. A broad unity was established between the reformist majority of the Estonian Communist Party leadership and the popular movements. While supposedly in support of Gorbachev's *perestroika*, the reformists gradually eroded the powers of the Russians and their Soviet institutions and independence was eventually declared on 20 August 1991, shortly after the failed coup against Gorbachev.

Elections in 1992 landed the country with an unstable coalition government led by President Lennart Meri, head of the right-wing Fatherland Party. Progress towards political and economic has been rapid, due to three factors: the proximity to the West (especially the wealthy economies of Finland and Sweden); a small population (Estonia was the least populous republic in the USSR); and the fact that Estonia has started from a far more advanced position than most of the former Soviet Union.

Like other former Soviet republics struggling to make a go of independence, the country still faces severe economic difficulties, including high unemployment and growing debts. The sinking of the ferry MS *Estonia*, en route to Stockholm in 1994, killed nearly 1,000 passengers and crew. The disaster also cast a shadow over Estonia's progress towards the West. And although Tallinn has the aura of a boom town which has swept aside its Soviet past, as long as Estonia depends on Russia for energy supplies, the country will continue to feel vulnerable.

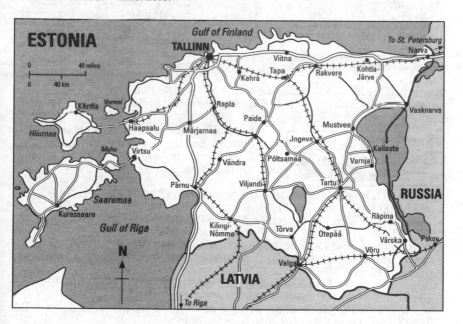

THE PEOPLE

Estonians make up 61% of the population. They often look typically Scandinavian, and some feel that they are part of a 'lost' Scandinavian nation. Finns regard them similarly as their first cousins. This serves to alienate Russians, who number a substantial 30%; they are in the majority in several towns and cities, including Tallinn itself. With Estonian nationalist feelings aggravated by the number of Russian immigrants, some people have demanded a stop to immigration and even the repatriation of Russians. In 1993, only intense political and economic pressure from Russia forced the Estonian parliament to revise a controversial law to limit the rights of Russian citizens.

Language. Estonian replaced Russian as the national language in 1989. It is totally different from Latvian and Lithuanian, which are Indo-European languages. With its large number of vowel sounds, Estonian is close to Finnish and Hungarian. Here are a few basic rules about the pronunciation of consonants:

č — ch	g — more like a k
š — sh	j — y as in yes
ž — s as in measure	r — usually rolled

Estonians speak more English than their Baltic neighbours, but the most common second language is still Russian — though given the racial tension, it is best to avoid using it in conversations with an Estonian. Sometimes a little German is helpful to communicate. Bookshops sell English-Estonian phrasebooks, and a short list of useful words and phrases follows.

yes — *jah*	train station — *raudteejaam*
no — *ei*	bus station — *autobussijamm*
hello — *tere*	street — *tänav (tn.), tee*
goodbye — *head aega*	avenue — *puiestee (pst.)*
thank you — *tänan, aitäh*	highway — *maantee (mnt.)*
please — *palun*	square — *väljak*
where? — kus?	hospital — *haigla*
how much? is it? — *kui palju see maksab?*	market — *turg*
Do you speak English? — Kas teie räägite inglise keelt?	

Several agencies have particular experience in dealing with travel to the Baltics from Western Europe. Most can arrange tours as well as book flights. They include:

Canterbury Travel, 248 Streatfield Road, Harrow, Middlesex HA3 9BY (tel 0181-206 0411, fax 206 0427).
Finlandia, 227 Regent St, London W1R 8PD (tel 0171-409 7334; fax 0171-409 7733).
Fregata Travel, 100 Deal St, London W1V 6AQ (0171-734 5101).
Gunnel Travel Service Ltd, Hayling Cottage, Stratford St Mary, Colchester, Essex CO7 6JW (01206-322352).
Instone Travel, 83 Whitechapel High Street, London E1 7QX (0171-377 1859).
One Europe Travel, Research Travel, Fraser Rd, Perivale, Middlesex UB6 7AQ (tel 0181-566 9424, fax 0181-566 8845).
Progressive Tours, 12 Porchester Place, London W2 (0171-262 1676).
Regent Holidays, 15 John St, Bristol BS1 2HR (0117-921 1711).

AIR

You can reach Tallinn from Britain or North America on SAS via Stockholm or Copenhagen daily. Other airlines serving Tallinn include Finnair (with daily flights from Helsinki) and Lufthansa from Frankfurt. The national carrier, Estonian Air, has a limited network only, with flights from Frankfurt, several cities in Scandinavia (including daily runs from Helsinki) and the CIS. Flights to and from London are due to start in the winter of 1995/96, operating three days a week.

An alternative from the UK is to fly to Vilnius on Lithuanian Airlines and travel overland from there: for further information see *Lithuania: Getting There*. Helsinki is also an easy jumping-off point for Estonia, but Finland is not cheap to reach, and hideously expensive once you're there. Finlandia Travel has flights to Helsinki for around £250, with the short extra hop to Tallinn costing an additional £50 or so return. An advantage of Finnair and SAS flights is that you can fly into Tallinn and back from Riga or Vilnius for little or no extra cost. You could even fly one way into St Petersburg and return from Vilnius, thus seeing four countries for little more than the price of one.

TRAIN

Trains from Minsk in Belarus run daily to Tallinn (17 hours) via Vilnius, Riga and Tartu, with another more comfortable service starting from Riga. There is also a daily service from Warsaw (30 hours). From Russia, trains serve Estonia from Pskov, southeast of Tartu, and St Petersburg. There are two trains daily to and from the Baltic Station in the latter, travel overnight in both directions. There is also a twice-daily direct service from Moscow.

BUS

Services run daily to Tallinn from both Riga (six hours) and from Vilnius (12 hours). Buses also run every day from St Petersburg (8 hours) and Pskov (3 hours), and once a week from Warsaw (22 hours).

BOAT

From Stockholm. Estline car and passenger ferries sail on alternate days (all year round) between Stockholm and Tallinn. The journey takes 15 hours and costs $70 one-way: the cost of taking a car is about the same again. For the latest timetable and fares call Estline in Stockholm (46 8 667 0001) or E Line Ltd in Tallinn (372 6 31 36 36).

From Helsinki. The advantage of travelling via Finland is the short crossing time and the frequency of services, currently running at about ten a day in summer. Ferries take four hours, hydrofoils two, catamarans 100 minutes. If you fly to Helsinki, your agent should be able to book a ticket for you. Try to travel during the week, since fares increase at weekends.

Ferries are run by Tallink, with six sailings a day. The *Georg Ots* (which once hosted a Reagan–Gorbachev Superpower Summit) is passenger only ($15-20 one-way), while the *Tallink* and *Vana Tallinn* take cars ($20-40 one-way, plus about $40 per car). Tallink also runs four hydrofoils a day in summer. The central booking agency in Helsinki is Saimaa Lines, with offices at Fabianinkatu 14 (65 87 33) and at the western harbour (Länsisatama) for ferries and Makasiiniterminaali for hydrofoils.

Viking Line (358 28 26011) operates two catamarans on the Helsinki-Tallinn route, one of them (*Viking Express I*) taking cars. Estonian New Line (ENL) operates twice-daily catamarans, while Eestin Linjat has a daily ferry.

DRIVING

The M12 between Riga and Tallinn is a reasonable road, following a picturesque route along the coast as far as Pärnu. In contrast with this fairly pleasant drive, the highway from St Petersburg is in a poor state (though it improves markedly west of Narva) and is flanked by a pipeline carried on concrete pillars. Tallinn lies 224 miles/358km west of St Petersburg, a comfortable day's drive with time for stops en route.

Red Tape

Many nationalities, including British, American and Australian citizens, can now enter Estonia without a visa. On arrival, you will normally be granted a stay of 30 days. Note that Irish passport holders require visas. If you need one, it will be issued on the spot if you go in person to an Estonian consulate, or by return post if you apply in writing. You can also obtain a visa on arrival at Tallinn airport, but it is easier to do all the paperwork in advance. Note that a visa for Estonia is also valid for the other Baltic Republics.

The addresses of Estonian missions abroad are as follows:

UK: 16 Hyde Park Gate, London W11 2RB (0171-589 3428).
USA: 630 5th Avenue, Suite 2415, New York, NY 10111 (tel 212 262 7634, fax 212 262 0893).
Canada: Suite 202, 958 Broadview Avenue, Toronto, Ontario M4K 2R6 (tel 416 461 0764, fax 416 461 0448).
Australia: 29 Wentworth Street, Point Piper, NSW 2027, Sydney (02-773 8069).
Finland: Kasarmikatu 28 A 1, Helsinki (90 17 97 19).
Russia: Sobinovsky pereulok 5, 103009 Moscow (290 5013).
Sweden: Storgatan 38, 1tr, Stockholm (tel 08 661-5810, fax 662-9980).

Money

1 kroon (kr) = 100 sents
1995: £1 = 17kr   US$1 = 11kr

Estonia introduced its own currency in 1992. This has made life easier for visitors in that it has reduced the ramifications of the two-tier price structure, in which Estonians paid less (in roubles) than tourists (in hard currency). The kroon is pegged to the Deutschmark at DM1 to 8kr.

Currency. Notes are issued in denominations of 1, 2, 5, 10, 25, 100 and 500 kroon, and coins in denominations of 1, 2, 5, 20 and 50 sents and 1 kroon and 5 kroon.

Changing Money. Dollars or Deutschmarks in cash are the most acceptable currencies, though you shouldn't have problems changing other currencies, be they French francs or Dutch guilders. You can also buy other Baltic currencies and roubles.

Travellers cheques are accepted in a growing number of places. For the best deals rely on the banks (*panki*) — Tartu Kommertspank usually offers the most competitive rate. Other exchange bureaux (*valuuta-vahetuskontor*) have appeared in Tallinn. These sometimes offer a poor deal (as do the hotels) so shop around.

Credit cards can be used at many hotels and in some restaurants.

Telephone. You can make local calls free from public phones, but it is hard to find one in working order. If calling long-distance within Estonia or abroad, you may do better at a telephone office (usually attached to the post office). There are many new magnetic phonecard telephones in Tallinn: for example in the central telephone office, the large hotels and in the central rail station. To call abroad direct dial 8 + 10 followed by the country code. When phoning from a hotel, you may have to book the call with the operator (dial 007).

Estonia is two hours ahead of GMT, three hours ahead from March to September. The country code for Estonia is 372.

Useful numbers: Directory Inquiries: 065, Fire Brigade 01, Police 02, Ambulance 03.

Mail. To send a postcard within Europe costs about $0.25 and takes 10-14 days. Poste restante is available at Tallinn's central post office (*postkontor*) at Narva maantee 1, but the delivery of inbound mail cannot be relied upon.

Maps. The Cartographia map of the Baltic Republics (£5.95) is commonly available in Western Europe and features street plans of all three capitals. Within Estonia, look out for the *Eesti Maanteed,* a reasonably up-to-date road atlas. You can find street plans to most sizeable towns, though some of these are still in Cyrillic, with the (now inaccurate) street names in Cyrillic.

Bus. Buses are cheaper, faster and more frequent than trains. The fast (*kiir*) buses are slightly slower than the express (*expres*) services, but you'll not notice a huge difference in the journey time. Try to book your ticket a day in advance.

Train. The often-crowded trains are most useful if you want to save a bit of money or if you simply prefer rail travel. Book two days in advance whenever possible, particularly when heading abroad, though hops to Riga are normally possible without reservation on the daytime services.

Taxi. Cabs charge such low fares that it isn't outrageous to use them for long-distance journeys if you are part of a group or in a mad rush. You would pay $20-25 for the 120-mile ride between Tallinn and Tartu, for example. It's not unusual for people to travel between the Baltic capitals by taxi.

Driving. Road accidents are common in Estonia, mostly due to drink-driving and the poor condition of minor roads. The police are clamping down heavily on drink-driving, however, and they have now been equipped with breathalysers. Do not drink even a drop of alcohol.

The police are tightening up in other areas too. The speed limit on most roads is 55mph/90kmh in rural areas (30mph/50km in urban zones). If you are caught doing more than 110kmh, you can be fined 50kr on the spot. Anyone caught driving over 110km/h will have their licence confiscated and will have to pay 100-300kr to recover it.

The wearing of seatbelts is compulsory.

Local police advise drivers never to leave valuables inside their cars.

Fuel: unleaded and four-star petrol are increasingly widely available outside the capital.

Car hire: several international car rental agencies are represented in Tallinn, including Hertz (Baltlink Ltd, Tartu maantee 13; tel 42 10 03), Avis (Hotel Olimpia, Linalaia 33; tel 631 59 30) and Europcar (REFIT Ltd, Merepuiestee 6; tel 44 16 37). A few local firms have started up operations.

Hotels tend to be either expensive Soviet-style blocks with no character or scruffy Soviet-style blocks with no hot water, an interesting repertoire of insect life and few home comforts — though some of these are being refurbished. A new breed of joint ventures in Tallinn has smartened up establishments at the top end of the market. For a comfortable room expect to pay at least $50. A cheap room costs anything from $5 to $25. The fledgling Estonian Tourist Board publishes a booklet giving the addresses of over 100 hotels.

Homes and Hostels. The main alternatives to hotels are private rooms or hostels. The number of families renting out rooms or whole flats is fast increasing. Several agencies can arrange this, including the Family Hotel Service in Tallinn (Mere Pst. 6; tel/fax 44 11 87). The FHS grades its accommodation from A to C. You can rent a perfectly comfortable grade C one-bedroom apartment for under $20; the fact that it may be in a grim concrete housing estate adds to the whole experience. The Bed and Breakfast agency (Sadama 11, Tallinn; 60 20 91) offers accommodation for around $15 per night. Both these agencies can arrange rooms in the other Baltic states.

The Estonian Youth Hostel Association (Lembita 4; tel 45 49 00) runs most of the country's hostels. These are generally open in the summer only and are in country areas. You'll pay around $5 (no Hostelling International membership card is necessary). Try to book ahead in mid-summer.

Estonia has a few campsites (*kämpingud*), mostly near Tallinn and in the resort of Pärnu. Some have chalets as well as space for pitching tents.

Old habits die hard, and restaurants rarely offer everything listed on the menu, though some of the new places in Tallinn do a better job of offering only what they've actually got. Fish is widely available, particularly trout and herring (try *rossolye*, herring served with vinaigrette). Veal is popular: *sult* or jellied veal is the most typical. As a rule, however, meals start well and then tail off, so pigging out on the hors d'oeuvres is often a good move.

Make the most of the restaurants in Tallinn because those in the provinces are extremely poor by comparison. You'll find it difficult to eat after 10pm outside the capital.

Here are a few terms to help you interpret a menu:

hors d'oeuvres — *külmad road*
main course — *teised road*
meat dish — *liharoad*
fish — *kala*
trout — *forrell*
vegetables — *köögiviljad*
fruit — *puuviljad*

snack bar — *einelaud*
drink — *joogid*
ice cream — *jäätis*
water — *vesi*
tea — *tea*
coffee — *kohv*

For those in self catering accommodation, there are good Western-style supermarkets in Tallinn (with prices to match). In the surrounding housing estates there are usually more basic self-service shops and the occasional outdoor market.

Drinking. The most common drink is beer (*õlu*), which is imported in cans and bottles. Saku, available in both bottles and draft, is a palatable local lager. For variation, try mulled wine (*hoogvein*), available in a few bars. Avoid Vana Tallinn, a dark, ruby firewater made locally, unless you want to end up like a Finn.

Tea and coffee are both easily availble, the café scene being a long-established part of life in the capital.

The biggest tourist office in Estonia is the Tallinn City Tourist Office (Tallinna Turismiamet) at 18 Raekoja Plats (tel 66 69 59, fax 44 12 21). Several books, all published since the revolution, are available. *Tallinn — A Practical Guide* contains general information about Estonia and the main provincial towns as well as the capital. So too does *Tallinn — This Week* which, curiously, is only published every couple of months. *The Baltic States: A Reference Book* (last edition published in 1991), with remarkably thorough listings, maps, useful words and phrases and even a Who's Who section, is available in some travel bookshops abroad.

The *Baltic Independent* and *Baltic Observer* are both English-language weeklies. *Tallinn City Paper* is published four times a year.

Eesti Radio (103.5MHz FM in Tallinn) or 50.6m (5.935kHz) short-wave broadcasts news in English at 6.20pm Monday to Friday, and programmes in English on Monday and Thursday from 11.30pm to midnight.

TALLINN

The Estonian capital, on the shores of the Gulf of Finland, started out as a small fortified town at the crossroads of trade routes. With the development of commerce, it grew into a large community of merchants and artisans and by the fourteenth and fifteenth centuries was a major Hanseatic port — some of the city's finest architecture is Gothic, dating from this period. Plague and war brought decline, but with annexation to Russia in the 18th century there was further expansion. Tallinn is still a big trade and fishing port, with a population approaching half a million.

The quiet cobbled streets, gently decaying palaces and elegant spires in the centre of Tallinn are a world away from the busy port and grim concrete blocks built to house Russian workers, but the different atmospheres combine to generate a relaxed and cosmopolitan capital. A twinning link with Venice may raise too many hopes, but Tallinn is well worth seeing: go now before foreign investors and tourists take over completely.

CITY LAYOUT

The centre of Tallinn is compact and easy to get around on foot. The oldest part of the city, known as Upper Town, centres on Toompea Hill, topped by a castle; down below is the walled Lower Town, with Raekoja plats as its focus. Both districts make up the Old Town or Vanalinn, where you'll probably spend most of your time. Lai is one of the main streets through

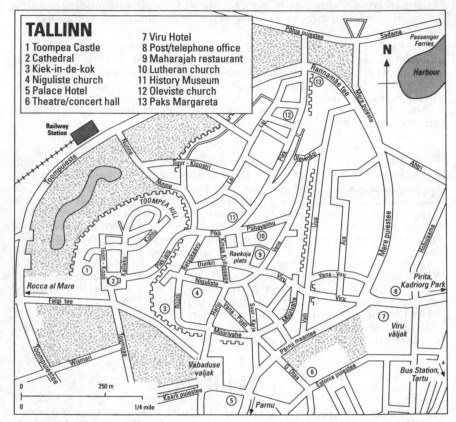

TALLINN

1 Toompea Castle
2 Cathedral
3 Kiek-in-de-kok
4 Niguliste church
5 Palace Hotel
6 Theatre/concert hall
7 Viru Hotel
8 Post/telephone office
9 Maharajah restaurant
10 Lutheran church
11 History Museum
12 Oleviste church
13 Paks Margareta

the centre, running from the foot of Toompea Hill north to Oleviste church, whose tall Gothic spire is a useful landmark. The New Town developed outside the city walls: with the old fortifications so well preserved, it is easy to keep track of which part of the city you are in. The focus of the more modern district is Vabaduse väljak, just south of the old town. From here Estonia puiestee runs east to Viru väljak, overlooked by the high-rise Viru Hotel (appallingly ugly, but another useful reference point).

Maps. Several city plans are available, including a tourist map with information in English as well as Estonian and Russian. The best, however, is the *Jana Seta* 1:25 000 city map, which shows all the bus, tram, trolleybus and route taxi (see *City Transport*) routes, has a useful street index and marks places of interest.

ARRIVAL AND DEPARTURE

Air. The airport (*lennujaam*) is the easiest in Eastern Europe for links with the city. It lies just a couple of miles southeast of the centre along the Tartu road. Buses 22 and 24 runs every 20-30 minutes between the airport and the railway station, also calling at the bus terminal and Viru väljak. A taxi to the centre will cost about 70kr. For general flight information call 21 10 92. Otherwise call the airlines direct:

Estonian Air: 44 02 95, 44 43 84, 44 63 82 (10 Vabaduse väljak).
Lufthansa: 21 52 59/44 40 37.
Finnair: 31 14 55.
SAS: 31 22 40/41, 21 25 53.

Train. The railway station or *Balti jaam* is on Toompuiestee (44 67 56), northwest of Toompea Hill and about ten minutes' walk from the centre.

Bus. The international and inter-city bus station or Maaliinide Autobussi-jaam (42 25 49) lies about a mile southeast of the centre at Lastekodu 46, off Tartu Maantee and a 20-minute walk or a short tram ride (number 2 or 4) from downtown. For information and tickets, it is easier to go to the office at Pärnu maantee 24. Local buses leave from the station next to the rail terminal and from the bus terminus on A. Laikmaa (adjacent to Viru Väljak).

Boat. Passenger ferries arrive at the dock, Tallinn Reisisadam (44 94 27) at the end of Sadama, northeast of the old town. Follow the locals to the nearby bus and tram stop, from where several services (including trams 1 and 2 and bus 65) head into the centre. You can buy tickets for the *George Ots* from the port and for the *Tallinn* from the Tallink office by Hotel Palace on Vabaduse Väljak. Hydrofoil tickets are sold both at the port and in the Viru Hotel. Information about ferries to Stockholm is available from the Estline office at Sadama 29 near the port (31 36 36).

Driving. Central Tallinn is heavily congested. Parking is not free. There is an entrance fee to drive in to the old city.

City Transport. Buses and tram fares are low: the flat fare is 10kr (half that for students). Buy a ticket (*pileteid*) in advance from a kiosk, then punch it when you board.

There are also route taxis (small minibuses) which leave from the bus station, outside Hotel Viru, and follow predetermined routes; these are shown on city maps. Stops are not always marked, but a small (or large) clump of people should indicate when you are in the right place.

Taxi fares are low if you avoid the ranks outside the smart hotels. Yellow state taxis are the most reliable, and usually turn on their meter without any prompting. If they don't or won't, be sure to agree the price in advance, or better still get out and seek another taxi. They really do want your custom, so this move will usually achieve results. Expect to pay 40-50kr for a trip from the city centre to the suburbs, for example.

Accommodation

There is an acknowledged shortage of hotels in Tallinn, particularly at the lower end of the market. The Family Hotel Association (Vanu Viru; tel/fax 44 11 87) in the old town can arrange private accom-modation. The nearest camping facilities are at the Kloostrimetsa campsite (23 86 86) near the cemetery in Pirita, 7 miles/11km around the bay northeast of the city and accessible on bus 34 from Viru väljak.

The following hotels are listed in ascending order of cost.

Agnes Youth Hostel, Narva maantee 7 (43 88 70). About $13 per person, open April to September. Reservations recommended.
Barn Youth Hostel, Viru 1 (31 38 53) in the old town is very central. Basic but clean dormitory accommodation available for around $15 per night. It has a snack bar on the premises which is open until midnight.

Kungla, Kreutzwaldi 23 (42 14 60). A Soviet relic with resident mice helping to control the cockroach population, and double rooms for around $40. A last resort.

Viru, Viru väljak (30 13 81/90). A former Intourist monolith billed as 'unpretentious', this place is better known as Hotel Virus. All the drunken Finns wash up here, as do the city's prostitutes. Still, it's comfortable if you can get a room; even though the standard rate is $115 for two, the place is usually full of Finns on package tours. Besides several bars and restaurants (the view from the one on the 22nd floor is better than the food), it has a sauna and useful information desks.

Palace, Vabaduse väljak 3 (44 47 61). A 19th-century gem restored with Scandinavian money and now the best of Tallinn's hotels. If you can't afford the $200-a-night rooms, splash out in the restaurant, which is dazzlingly good; it used to be the very best in the Soviet Union. Hard currency or a robust credit card essential.

Olümpia, Liivalaia 33. A 25-storey refurbished ex-communist hotel, with solarium. Price range falls between the Viru and the Palace.

Peo Les Hotel/Motel, Parnu Mantee 555 (2-77 16 01). Twin rooms with en suite bathrooms.

EATING AND DRINKING

If there's one thing to thank the Finnish tourists for, it's that their custom has helped make Tallinn the best place to eat in the Baltics. In addition to spectacular cuisine — in terms of taste and price — at the Palace, there are plenty of atmospheric places in the old town, and an increasing number of new places.

Vana Toomas, 8 Raekoja Plats (44 58 18). In a tastefully decorated cellar oozing with atmosphere and delicious food. A good place to try local specialities. Friendly waiters and jazz at weekends.

Maharajah, Raekoja plats 13. An English-Indian restaurant serving superb Asian food — the best between Pakistan and the East End of London. Moderately expensive but probably the best in town.

Eeslitall, Dunkri 4, off Kullassepa. A small, friendly and buzzing restaurant with better-than-average Estonian food; the cellar bar below is open late.

Reeder Restoran, Vene 33. Decent, meat-oriented menu. Reasonable prices, novel décor, less grasping waiters than elsewhere. You can also order meals from the main menu from the less formal bar downstairs.

Bistro, Narva maantee 6. A partly Swiss-managed fast food bar, serving a mix of salads, pasta and other simple meals. Good value, closes early.

Sanjay's, Rataskaevu 3/5. An oriental mixed bag, serving Indian and Chinese food. The food is good if not entirely authentic, and the prices are certainly more reasonable than at the Maharajah.

Nord, Rataskaevu 3/5. A good Estonian restaurant on the ground floor of the same building as Sanjay's, with a fair choice of dishes, reasonable prices and courteous staff. Seafood is the main speciality.

Ai Sha Ni Ya, Mere Pst. 6. This restaurant serves superb but expensive Chinese cuisine. There is a courtyard and seating both inside and outside.

Bars and Cafés. Old Tallinn is full of cosy cellar bars, where you can while away a pleasant evening; some double up as restaurants. Particuarly recommended are Karikabaar, at the corner of Kuninga and Suur-Karja (with dancing later on) and Bar Viarosse at Lai 23, in a gorgeous 15th-century building. Western-style bars tend to be pricey: one such is the Mundi

(Mundi 3), which attracts a young and trendy crowd and is very busy at weekends. The Rebaseurg is a cosy cellar bar beneath the Nord Restaurant at Rataskaevu 3/5. There are also the ubiquitous Irish pubs, including George Brownes at Harju 6. Toovo Pub at Suur-kaja 18 is a lively new pub, which serves soups and other hot food (at moderate but not cheap prices) and occasionally has live music.

Tallinn is famous for its cafés (*kohvik*); indeed its first one opened in 1702, before even Paris had one. There are a couple of good examples on Pikk and another at Harju 48, which has a garden; try also the Moskva in Vabaduse väljak. The Khovik Mary, at Vene 1, has classic 20s decor and serves delicious home-made cakes, salads and sandwiches. A great place to eat and drink and enjoy city views is in Fat Margaret at Pikk 70. There is an open-air American sandwich bar in the courtyard of the maritime museum (see *Exploring*). Harju Café at Suur-kaja 4 serves reasonable food at reasonable prices.

EXPLORING

Tallinn's old town is a superb example of medieval urban architecture, with a mixture of styles reflecting German, Russian and Scandinavian influences. Many of the buildings have been converted into museums, offices, cafés and souvenir shops, but the squiggly cobbled streets still exude atmosphere.

Lai and Pikk are particularly rewarding streets to explore. Along Lai, the houses at numbers 23 and 29 are characteristic of the burgher residences of the 15th century and still have the pulleys used to raise goods to store rooms. Pikk, which runs parallel, has many interesting medieval buildings too, notably numbers 17, 24 and 16. The first is a gem of the Northern Gothic style: visit the History Museum inside just to get a closer look at the marvellous interior. Beyond the Oleviste church, a 16th-century bastion called Paks Margareta (Fat Margaret) commands the northern end of Pikk near the seafront; it was used as a jail for political prisoners at one time. It now houses an interesting maritime museum (with limited labelling in English) and a great bar with an observation tower. Near the bottom of Pikk on Pühavaimu, Tallinn's most notable Lutheran church (Pühavaimu Kirik or the Holy Trinity Church) has a superb altar, painted by Bernt Nothe in the 15th century.

Raekoja plats, the main square in the old town, is dominated by the Town Hall (Raekoda), completed in 1404 and one of the greatest Gothic buildings of its kind in Northern Europe. Its weathervane (the 16th-century original of which is in the City Museum) represents a soldier, Vana Toomas, who guards the city and is the symbol of Tallinn. There is also an apothecary's shop in the square, in operation for more than 500 years and said to have been used by Peter the Great.

For some of the best views of Tallinn, climb the Kiek-in-de-Kok (Peek-into-the-Kitchen) Tower, part of the old city wall at the southern edge of the centre. The museum inside traces the history of the capital from the 13th century onwards, with a few good models of the old town. It also houses occasional exhibitions of crafts, art and photography.

Also well worth a look are the Dominican monks' cloisters (Dominiklaste Klooster) at Vene 14. Founded in 1246, these are set around a secluded garden courtyard, and there are displays of ancient stonework and other archaeological finds. Concerts of medieval music are staged here every night in summer (9pm). Leave via the cosy café/bar at Kloostri Ait (Vene 14).

Toompea Hill. At the southern end of Pikk, Pikk Yalg and Luhike Yalg ('long leg' and 'short leg') connect the lower town to Toompea Hill. Climbing through the medieval townscape to the summit is like walking through a Gothic fairytale. Pastel-washed houses merge with jocular twirls of iron, and ornate gutters droop from steep red roofs.

Toompea itself is on a limestone plateau which, according to legend, is the grave mound of the folk hero Kalev, made by his mother whose tears formed the lake beyond. Toompea Castle presides over the hill and the republic — it is the seat of the Estonian parliament. The ornate and newly renovated Alexander Nevsky Cathedral, at the top of Pikk jalg, is a rather more incongruous sight: the 19th-century Russian Orthodox church comes complete with onion domes. Walk up Kohtu east from the cathedral to a platform, which provides yet more panoramic views of Tallinn's roofs and spires.

Kadriorg Park. About a mile east of the centre along Narva maantee, Kadriorg Park is an excellent place to watch the locals relaxing. You can also visit the Kadriorg Palace (Kadrioru Loss), a delicious but much neglected 18th-century Baroque mansion, built at the request of Peter the Great in honour of his wife Catherine. It is now an art gallery, open daily except Tuesdays. Traditional and popular song festivals take place periodically in the park, including a folk festival every year towards the end of July. Tram 1 or 3 from Pärnu maantee runs along Narva maantee, within spitting distance of the park.

Ethnography Museum. At Rocca al Mare, 4 miles/6km west of the city, the Ethnography Museum has exhibitions of rural wooden architecture, mostly dating from the 18th and 19th centuries. It opens daily from May to October; folk and dance concerts are staged on weekend mornings. Take bus 45 from Vabaduse väljak.

Pirita. To most locals, Pirita (north of Kadriorg Park) means beaches. If you consider the sea too dirty or too rough for bathing (most people do), you can hire boats at the Yachting Centre built for the 1980 Olympic regatta, or stroll in the nearby pine forest. Take buses 1, 8 or 34 from Tallinn. For information on boat hire call 2-23 70 55.

ENTERTAINMENT

Tallinn has its own accomplished opera company which performs at the Opera and Ballet Theatre on Estonia puiestee. The Estonia Concert Hall, next door, has a fairly full programme, and smaller concerts are held in the old Town Hall in Raekoja plats and the nearby St Nicholas (Niguliste) church. A free handout called *What? Where? When? In Tallinn* provides a fairly comprehensive list of cultural events.

Several of Tallinn's beer cellars metamorphose into discos late at night, or have a club attached: one such is the Eeslitall Baari, perhaps the liveliest place in town and with a mixed clientele (including sailors). It is open into the early hours. Lucky Luke's at Mere Pst. 20 has a disco Mondays to Wednesdays and live music on Friday and Saturday. The Piraat night club at Regati 1, Block 5 of the Pirita Yachting Centre, is popular with young Finns. A bus service back to town is laid on for punters.

Paan-Casino at Mere Pst. 5 is an expensive Western-style casino and bar, open 6pm to 6am. You can play on the gaming machines from midday though. There is also a casino in the Palace Hotel.

For more sedate entertainment, the Helios cinema on Viru and Soprus cinema on Vana-Posti show films in English.

SHOPPING

Cultural freedom is not completely new to the Estonian capital, and the shops were always far better stocked than in rest of the old Soviet Union. Even so, shopping in Tallinn is still a good deal more rewarding than it used to be, with a growing number of places selling things you might actually consider giving to friends. Most arts and crafts shops are in the old town, with several along Pikk including numbers 9, 18 and 27; amber can be a good buy and is not too expensive. Look out for women in the streets of the old town peddling high-quality handmade knitwear, including socks for the equivalent of about $5and exquisite sweaters for around $30.

One of the city's best bookshops is Homeros at Mundi 3, which has English-language titles and guide books. You can buy traditional Estonian music at the record shop in Raekoja plats.

There are several Western-style department stores, such as the expensive Stockmann at Viru Väljak 4. Also try the Tallinna Kaubmaja store and food hall at Gonsiori 2. Western brands of alcohol and cigarettes can be particularly good buys, if that is what you're after. There is a daily market on the north side of Balti Jamm, which sells food, novelties and household items.

HELP AND INFORMATION

Tourist Information: Tourist Office (Tallinna Turismiamet) at 18 Raekoja Plats (tel 66 69 59, fax 44 12 21). Or try Estonian Holidays, a travel agency at Viru väljak 4. *Tallinn This Week* is a good source of general information, with listings, etc.

Communications: the main post and telephone office is at Narva maantee 1, on Viru väljak. The post office opens 8am-8pm Monday to Saturday, but you can make calls daily 7am-10pm.

Money: good rates at Tartu Kommertspank at Dunkri 9, open 9am-5pm and Hansa bank at Viru 20, Sadama 25 (in the port) and at Gonsiori 2 (inside Tallinna Kaubmaja department store). American Express is represented by Estonia Tours at Roosikrantsi 4B (44 20 34). there is a good currency exchange desk in the main railway station.

Central Hospital: Ravi 18, south of downtown.

Embassies and Consulates

UK: Kentmanni 20 (tel 31 33 53, fax 31 33 54).
USA: Kentmanni 20 (31 20 21/22).
Canada: Tolli 3 (44 90 56).
Belarus: Kuramaa 15-111 (32 70 62).
Finland: Liivalaia 12 (31 14 44).
Latvia: Tõnismägi 10 (31 13 66).
Lithuania: Vabaduse väljak 10 (44 89 17).
Poland: Pärnu mantee 8 (44 06 09).
Russia: Pikk 19 (44 30 14).
Sweden: Endla 4a (45 03 50).
Ukraine: Sakala 3 (31 15 55).

Further Afield 61

NARVA

Some 125 miles/200km east of Tallinn on the Russian border, Narva was once a moderately important trading town. Devastation in the Second World War means little of its medieval architecture has survived, though some restoration work has been done. Industry is Narva's main *raison d'être* these days. There's not a lot to detain you, but the town makes a useful stopping-off point if you are heading into Russia. Indeed Narva may as well be in Russia, the homeland of the majority of the town's inhabitants. In 1993 a controversial referendum in the town voted for autonomy from Tallinn.

The main attraction is Narva Castle, by the river, which dates from the 13th century and contains a modest museum. Art festivals are held in the castle grounds, and painters display their work in the open air. There is a pleasant café in the roofed gallery of the Western Citadel.

Narva lies on the main road and rail route to St Petersburg (90 miles/144km east) and is therefore easy to get to by bus or train. There is little to choose between the town's two hotels, the Narva (Pushkini 6) and the Vanalinn (Koidula 6), both a short walk from the castle.

TARTU

Situated 110 miles/176km southeast of Tallinn, Tartu is the oldest — and undoubtedly the most interesting — of Estonia's provincial towns. The large and lively student population is a great asset to the city's atmosphere too. Despite having been razed to the ground more than 50 times, Tartu retains some fine architecture, much of it classical in style.

The centre of the city occupies the west bank of the river Emajogi, with Raekoja plats the focus of the old town. Splendid classical buildings flank the square and include the 18th-century Town Hall. Just to the north is the heart of Tartu's ancient university, founded in 1632 and housed in another magnificent classical building on Ullkooli. There is an art museum inside.

Toomemägy Hill, to the west, marks the site of the first settlement and is topped by the 13th-century Vyshgorod Cathedral, a partial ruin containing a museum which traces the history of the university. You can enjoy good views over the town below.

Arrival and Departure. Four trains a day serve Tartu from Tallinn, taking three or four hours, but buses are much more frequent and slightly faster. The bus station is also more central — on Turu, four blocks southeast of Raekoja plats. The train station lies southwest of Toomemägi Hill on Vaksali, just under a mile from the main square.

Accommodation and Food. Hotel Park (Vallikraavi 23; 234-336 63), at the southwest foot of Toomemägi Hill, is the best place to stay. It has a modicum of character and rooms are comparatively cheap at around $30. Hotel Tartu, at Soola 3 (234-320 91), is just around the corner from the bus station and also cheaper.

For a relaxed evening, you can't do better than go to the Püssirohukelder at Lossi 28 (234-342 24), a wonderful cellar bar on Toomemägi Hill. The food is unexceptional but the décor and atmosphere provide ample compensation. Groups performing traditional song and dance entertain punters at weekends.

SAAREMAA ISLAND

To leave the beaten track, head for Saaremaa, Estonia's largest coastal island and once the favourite haunt of Soviet party officials. It is an attractive blend of pine woods and grasslands, with comparatively little modern development. The main town of Kuressaare feels thoroughly rural but has some interesting architecture, including a 14th-century castle.

To get to Saaremaa, take the ferry (which runs several times a day) from Virstu, 80 miles/130km southwest of Tallinn, to the island of Muhu, from where a three-mile causeway leads to Saaremaa. You can travel to Kuressaare direct by bus from Tallinn, which takes about five hours. There are buses also from Pärnu (3 hours) and Tartu (5 hours).

The tourist office in Kuressaare's main square can help with everything from accommodation to currency exchange (though you would do well to have changed money before your arrival). The best small hotels include Hotel Lossi (Lossi 27; 544 43) and Hotel Panga (Tallina 27; 577 02), a clean place close to the bus station. Don't leave town without visiting Café Veski at Pärna 19, in an old windmill just east of the main square.

PARNU

This town of 55,000 lies 80 miles/130km southwest of Tallinn, where the Pärnu river flows into the Gulf of Riga. Archaeological finds in the local museum show that Pärnu was inhabited in the Stone Age, although the 'modern' town dates from 1251. It retains a few interesting medieval features from its days as a Hanseatic port, but most Estonians are attracted more by the beach and the local health-giving mud than the architecture.

The resort area is deserted and rather forlorn out of season, but perks up when rich Scandinavian tourists arrive. Many people are still reluctant to swim through fear of pollution. The liveliest area is the promenade along the beach, where there are some pleasant bars and cafés and a few small parks.

Arrival and Departure. Pärnu is served by frequent buses from Tallinn, which take about two hours. There are daily buses also to Tartu, Riga and Vilnius. The bus station is slightly east of the centre on Ringi. Riga is four to five hours away by rail, with departures from the train station east of the bus terminal.

Accommodation. Given that Pärnu is a resort, it's no surprise that budget accommodation is limited. Hotel Pärnu at Rüütli 44 (244-421 45) is a characterless but convenient Soviet affair, located close to the bus station. Further east, Hotel Emmi (Laine 2; 244-220 43) is friendly and has hot water, though you'll find cheaper rooms at the Kajakas (Seedri 2; 244-430 98), just north of Rannapark and the beach.

Calendar of Events

January 1	**New Year's Day**
February 24	**Independence Day**
March/April	**Good Friday, Easter Monday**
May 1	**May Day**
May	Cultural Days, Tartu
June 23	**Victory Day (Anniversary of the Battle of Vonnu)**
Late June	**Midsummer Day**
June	Estonian Song Festival, attracting 30,000 performers and staged in both Tallinn and Tartu; held every five years, with the next in 1999
July	Summer Music Festival, Estonian dance festival at Kalev Central Stadium, Rock Summer Festival, all in Tallinn; Music Festival, Pärnu
September	Flower Fair, Tallinn
October	'Tartu Autumn' Rock Festival, Tartu
November	International Music Festival, Tallinn
December 25	**Christmas Day**
December 26	**Boxing Day**

Public Holidays are shown in **bold.**

Latvia

Riga

Population: 2.7 million **Capital:** Riga (population 917,000)

Latvia, about the size of Scotland, will never win any prizes for scenery: pine and birch forest covers well over a third of the land, punctuated by over 4,000 lakes and a staggering 12,000 rivers. The rest is often dull wide open space, given over to agriculture or industry. Under Soviet rule, Latvia produced some of the finest consumer goods in the USSR and earned itself the title 'workshop of the Baltic'.

Latvia has found it harder than the other Baltic Republics to shake off its Marxist past. This is due to both economic mismanagement — exacerbating the huge drops in salaries and industrial output and rising unemployment — and political considerations: given that almost half of the population is Russian, there is a large body of people that is not entirely keen on a total divorce from all that the old Soviet Union stood for.

Most of Latvia has changed little since independence. The biggest advances have been made in Riga, visible in both the reconstruction work and the rise in organised crime, which has won the capital a reputation as a Wild West city. For most visitors, however, Riga is one of the loveliest cities in Europe; before the war it was known as the 'Paris of the Baltic', not altogether unreasonably. There are other historical towns worth exploring too, and the wooded gorge of the Gauja National Park is one of the most scenic spots in the whole region.

CLIMATE

Latvian weather is invigorating, changeable and wet. The best time to visit

191

is in August or September, when the wind drops and the sea is warm. June and July tend to be rainy: go prepared as you would for a capricious English summer. Winters are harsh and long, with thermals essential.

HISTORY

The people of Latvia have shared with the Estonians the burden of occupation by foreigners. In the 11th and 12th centuries they were dominated by crusading Teutonic Knights, who left an indelible mark on the country in the form of solid merchant houses and the Lutheran faith. Half the population was German even in the early 20th century, and German agricultural practices persist in the orderly farms that stretch across the country.

Like its Baltic neighbours, Latvia was ruled by Sweden in the 17th century and annexed by Russia in the 18th, but then refused to associate with the Bolsheviks in 1919. The country was devastated in the First World War, losing about a fifth of its population. Ever-resilient, however, Latvia was one of the most prosperous countries in Eastern Europe by the 1930s. 'Sovietisation' after 1940 set the country back initially, but the construction of factories gradually brought comparative prosperity, as well as shocking pollution and a huge influx of Russian immigrants.

Independence. Latvia's Communist Party was always more loyal to Moscow than others in the region. Even so, Party officials made up about a third of the members of the Popular Front which was formed in July 1988 and led Latvia into independence. Following victory for the Popular Front in elections in March 1990, an alliance of communists and the military began a propaganda campaign against the government. Events came to a head with an attempted coup in January 1991, when Soviet troops began seizing key buildings in the capital and barricades were set up outside the Communist Party headquarters. The coup failed and Latvia declared independence in August of that year.

Independence did not bring political stability to Latvia and the first elections were held only in June 1993. Latvian Way, a coalition of moderate nationalists won a surprisingly comfortable victory — surprising because it was led by Antolys Gorbunovs, once a secretary of the Communist Party. The more radical National Independence Movement coming a poor second. Support for the Popular Front totally collapsed — as elsewhere in the region, it had been a broad coalition useful for ousting but not holding onto power.

THE PEOPLE

Letts, the native people of Latvia, make up 54% of the population, Russian-speaking minorities around 45% and other Slavs (mostly Poles) a mere one in a hundred.

With such a large number of Russian inhabitants (they are the majority in the country's six biggest cities), the issue of race has kept a high profile in Latvian politics. One in three Russians voted for independence (the idea of returning home certainly doesn't hold much appeal), and many have made an effort to learn the official language — this is the only way they are likely to be successful in business or government. But they continue to campaign for increased rights: in the 1993 elections only about 40% of non-Latvians had the vote. Concord, the single multi-ethnic political grouping in Latvia, came third.

Language. Latvian has been the official language since 1988, but far more

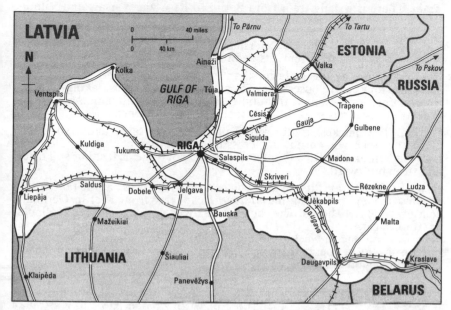

people speak Russian than the native tongue. This is due both to the number of Russians in the country and the fact that most native Latvians speak good Russian (though they may not like to admit it). The correct pronunciation of consonants should enable you to deal adequately with most Latvian words:

c — as ts   č — ch
j — as y   š — sh
ĝ — j   ž — s as in measure
ņ — ny

Useful words and phrases include:

yes — *jā*
no — *nē*
hello — *sveicināti*
goodbye — *uz redzēšanos*
please — *lūdzu*
thank you — *paldies*
how much? — *cik?*

do you speak English? — *vai jūs runājat angliski?*
airport — *lidostu*
train station — *dzelzcela staciju*
market — *tirgus*
hospital — *slimnīca*

Getting There

Air. Although flights from London City airport to Riga ceased in 1994, there are plenty of good links between the UK and Latvia. Baltic International Airlines has flights from both London Gatwick and Manchester for around £250 return, with slightly higher fares from other UK airports via Gatwick or Amsterdam. SAS flies to Riga from the UK and North America via either Copenhagen or Stockholm, and allows open-jaw tickets (into one Baltic capital, out from another). Connections from Birmingham, Heathrow and Manchester via Germany are good on Lufthansa. The specialist agents listed on page 176 also cover Latvia.

Train. There is a daily train from Berlin to Riga via Warsaw and Vilnius, with several additional trains from the Lithuanian capital. Direct trains also run from Kaliningrad and Kiev. There are three or four trains a day from Moscow (13 hours) and St Petersburg (11 hours). If you are heading to Russia, check visa requirements before you travel.

Bus. Travelling by bus is faster than by train, and usually less crowded. There are four or five buses a day from Tallinn and Vilnius, taking six hours from both cities, as well as from other Estonian and Lithuanian towns. The Warsaw-Tallinn bus stops in Riga too, but runs just once a week.

Driving. The quickest route from Tallinn to Riga takes about six hours, along the M12 via Pärnu and crossing the border at Ainazi. The M12 between Vilnius and Riga (via Panevėžys) is not quite as fast but still direct and straightforward.

Boat. If you are travelling by car, you can save long waits at the border (but not any money) by taking the *Mercuri-I* car ferry from Kiel in Germany. Journey time is 40 hours. The cheapest one-way passenger fare is $160, plus $140 for a car.

Ferries run once a week from Stockholm, taking 18 hours. The cheapest fare on the *Ilich*, operated by Baltic Express Line, is $140, but most fares are in the region of $200.

Red Tape

UK citizens do not need a visa, but at the time of writing, Irish, US and Australian nationals do. Note that a Latvian visa is also valid for Estonia and Lithuania.

The usual cost of a visa is £7 (£10 for postal applications), though Americans pay no fee. You may apply for one on arrival at the airport, but are advised to obtain one in advance from a Latvian mission abroad:

UK: 72 Queensborough Terrace, London W2 3SP (tel 0171-727 1698; fax 0171-221 9740), open 11am-3pm Monday to Friday.
USA: 4325 17th Street NW, Washington DC 20011 (tel 202-726-8213, fax 202-726-6785).
Canada: 230 Clemow Avenue, Ottawa K1S 2B6 (613-238-6868).
Russia: ul. Chaplygina 3, Moscow 103062.

Upon arrival, most travellers are granted a stay of three months.

Money

£1 = LS0.90 $1 = LS0.60
LS1 = £1.11   LS1 = $1.66

The lats (LS) has been in circulation since May 1993, but you'll still find a few Latvian roubles (an interim currency) and possibly even older Russian roubles knocking about. If you have dealings with a black marketeer, you can guarantee to be given out-of-date notes.

Life for visitors remains fairly cheap, despite the fact that prices previously in roubles have shot up and that there are still hotels and other establishments which insist on charging a 'foreigners' price' of two or three times the locals' rate.

Changing Money. US dollars or Deutschmarks in low-denomination notes are the things to take. Travellers cheques are an even bigger problem in

Latvia than in Estonia, and you can rely on a credit card only in a few top hotels and restaurants — certainly not for withdrawing cash at a bank.

Try to change money in Riga, where branches of the Bank of the Republic of Latvia tend to offer the best rates. Bureaux de change have opened up in hotels, stations and so on, but watch out for high commission charges.

An organisation in Latvia is enthusiastic to recruit English-speaking volunteers for its summer programme. The International Exchange Center (2 Republic Square, 1010 Riga; fax 83 02 57) needs over 100 volunteers for at least a month to work as leaders and sports instructors on children's camps on the Baltic. No special qualifications are required and a tourist visa will suffice. It is possible to apply direct to the IEC (registration fee US$50). IEC also arranges au pair placements and places on workcamps.

Qualified EFL teachers can become Volunteers for Latvia through the Latvian National Council in Great Britain (53 Gotthard Way, West Wickham, Kent BR4 OER). Two American organisations send volunteer teachers to the Baltic states on short contracts: American Latvian Association (400 Hurley Ave, Rockville, MD 20850) and Places at workcamps can be arranged through the Latvian Student Centre, Elisabetes 45/47, Room 514, 1010 Riga.

Telephone. Latvia may be independent, but most international telephone calls are still connected via Moscow. The least stressful way to phone, either within or from Latvia, is to do it through your hotel. Going to the nearest public telephone office is likely to involve a wait of several hours, even if you are phoning within Latvia. In Riga, if you are willing to pay slightly over the odds, there is a new telecommunications office which can connect your call almost immediately.

Some payphones can be used for long-distance calls, but until the telecommunications network is given an overhaul (foreign companies are competing for the privilege), using them is likely to lead only to frustration. Most take tokens known as *žetoni*, available at the post office, though you still find some demanding 15-kopeck coins.

Useful numbers: fire brigade 01, police 02, ambulance 03.

Mail. Sending an airmail letter or postcard abroad from Latvia doesn't cost more than about $0.10, but delivery can take 10-14 days. The Latvian for post office is *pasts*, usually with a *telegrafs* office attached for the sending of telegrams.

The rail network serves most main towns, but — as in the other Baltic states — buses are the best way to explore the country, being more frequent and faster than the trains. For short journeys covered by few buses, you could consider taking a taxi.

Driving. Petrol shortages have become a feature of everyday life since independence, so fill up whenever you can and be prepared to queue. You'll have no trouble finding four-star or diesel, but unleaded petrol is uncommon outside Riga. The speed limit is 80km/h (50mph) in the country and 50km/h (32mph) in built-up areas.

Rented cars are in big demand, and you should try to arrange this in advance. In Riga, the main car rental desk is in the Hotel Latvija (21 25 05), although Avis has an agent at the airport (20 73 53). Car theft is a problem in the capital, so consider picking up a vehicle at the airport and heading straight out of town.

The hotel (*viesnīcu*) scene in Latvia is similar to that in Estonia, with wide-ranging and unpredictable prices, whether you're staying in high-class or simple places. While many hotels in Riga have been spruced up with the aid of foreign cash, in provincial towns you'll still often find charming hotels and pensions which have been around since before independence.

The Latvian University Tourist Club (LUTK), at Raiņa bulvāris 19 (tel 22 31 14; fax 22 50 39), offers information about youth hostels open in summer, but the network is still small. Campsites are also scarce (and basic), though in rural villages you should be able to pitch your tent in a field.

LUTK, as well as the tourist board, can arrange private accommodation in Riga and elsewhere, and the number of homes renting out rooms is growing.

Eating is not a delight in Latvia. Hard rye bread, tinned sprats and unappetising cucumbers are depressingly common. Even so, you should get the chance to have at least one feast. Traditionally, Latvians prefer fish to meat, one of the best local dishes being *Riga Tel'noe*, deep-fried fish fillets stuffed with a mushroom and anchovy mixture. Smoked salmon (*lasis*) can be good too. Fish aside, pork and chicken dominate restaurant menus, though hare and rabbit are also popular: a traditional way of cooking them is with mushrooms, cheese, wine and herbs. Sausages (*desa*) tend to be of uncertain provenance and gristly. If none of the above sound tempting, try the soups (*zupa*), which are often a meal in themselves, or fill up on cakes such as *biezpienmaize*, bread with curd, or Alexander Torte, a wonderful raspberry-filled pastry.

café — *kafejnīca*	cheese — *siers*
snack bar — *bufete*	fruit — *augli*
menu — *ēdienkarte*	ice cream — *saldējums*
starters — *uzkoda*	drinks — *dzērieni*
meat/main dishes — *gaļas ēdieni*	tea — *tēja*
fish — *zivis*	coffee — *kafija*
vegetables — *saknes*	(fruit) juice — *sulas*
bread — *maize*	water — *ūdens*

Drinking. Latvia, particularly the Aldaris brewery in Riga, produces the only good beer (*alus*) in the Baltics. Mērnieku Laiku is delicious though quite bitter. Bauskas Tumsais, also brewed locally, is a dark beer.

Kvas, fermented ryebread water with a taste of honey sounds and looks unappealing, but is ideal for quenching summer thirst (despite being slightly alcoholic). Riga's Black Balsam, on the other hand, is dark, thick and very potent, flavoured with ginger, oak bark and cognac among other things. Most people also consume vodka in large quantities.

You're advised not to drink the tapwater. See the general introduction for information on water purification.

RIGA

As you first approach, the Latvian capital resembles a typical Soviet city, with hulking great apartment blocks, muddy grey and dismal, scattered as far as the horizon. Hideous housing is punctuated by towers belching poisons and linked by an artless network of cracked concrete highways. Not only does the city look Russian architecturally: more Rigans are of Russian descent than Latvian. Ten miles/16km inland from the Baltic Sea, on the banks of the broad Daugava river, Riga was an important military and shipping centre in the former USSR. With a population of over 900,000, it is bigger than Stockholm and Helsinki and almost twice the size of the other Baltic capitals.

Now that the main street is named after Freedom rather than Lenin, a certain colour has returned to the cheeks of Riga. Its heart has never been less than handsome, with the austere good looks of Lutheran architecture. Many streets are pedestrianised and now dotted with smart shops, new cafés and restaurants. You can walk off the coffee and cakes by exploring bulky churches clad in silvery grey tiles and the Baroque mansions of Hanseatic merchants.

Despite restoration and reconstruction, there is an appealing shabbiness about old Riga, though this also acts as a timely reminder that the new prosperity has benefited only a minority of Rigans and has been achieved at a cost. Appalling poverty persists and the capital boasts some of the most notorious gangsters in Eastern Europe. But don't let this put you off. Riga offers a fine combination of old architecture, well-kept parks, culture and fun, which is enjoyed by surprisingly few tourists. Furthermore, some of the best things in Latvia can be visited as day trips from Riga.

CITY LAYOUT

Riga straddles the Daugava river, but its heart occupies the east bank. The main October Bridge (Oktobra Tilts) leads from Pardaugava, the industrial quarter on the left bank, into Kalu iela, which bisects the old city (Vecriga). This is a compact area — you can walk from one side to the other in quarter of an hour — bound on the eastern side by a tree-lined canal (Pilsētas kanāls) which was once the old castle moat. Doma laukums, overlooked by the cathedral, is the heart of the old town. Beyond the canal are predictable modern boulevards, principally Brivibas bulvāris which continues into Brivibas iela.

Maps. *Riga City Map*, a post-independence street plan showing transport routes, is available from kiosks and some bookshops: try Centrālā Grāmatnica at Aspazijas bulvārus 24.

ARRIVAL AND DEPARTURE

Air. Spilva airport lies 5 miles/8km southwest of downtown. It is poorly equipped, though there is at least a currency exchange desk. Bus 22 runs into the centre every half hour.

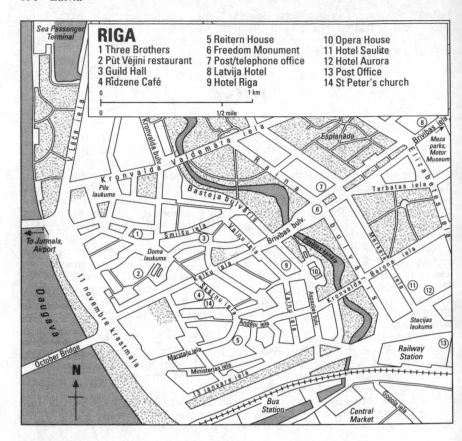

RIGA
1 Three Brothers
2 Pūt Vējini restaurant
3 Guild Hall
4 Rīdzene Café
5 Reitern House
6 Freedom Monument
7 Post/telephone office
8 Latvija Hotel
9 Hotel Riga
10 Opera House
11 Hotel Saulīte
12 Hotel Aurora
13 Post Office
14 St Peter's church

Train. The main train station or *centrālā stacija* (23 21 34) is at the southern end of Raiņa bulvāris, on the edge of the new city. Information is also available from the travel desk in the Latvija Hotel.

Bus. The bus terminal (*autoosta*) is on Prāgas, a short walk southwest of the train station. Call 21 36 11 for information.

Boat. The boat landing stage in Riga is at Eksporta iela 1 (32 98 82), about a mile north of October Bridge.

CITY TRANSPORT

Buses and trams are decrepit but just manage to hold together a reasonable service; buy tickets from kiosks before boarding. There is also a waterbus service, most active in summer — the Daugava freezes over in winter. The most useful boats go to Mežaparks (see below), though it's worth taking any boat just for the fun of the ride. Boats leave from Piestantne (Pier) 1 by October Bridge.

Taxis fares are moderately high due to fuel shortages. Some drivers seem to take tourists only if they wave dollars or Marlboro cigarettes around.

ACCOMMODATION

Riga has a fairly good range of hotels, though some of the cheaper places have been spruced up. In summer, try to book in advance.

Latvija, Elizabetes iela 55 (tel 21 26 45, 21 25 03; fax 28 35 95), by Brīvības iela. A former Intourist hotel and an ugly 27-storey hulk of glass and plastic. Double rooms go for around $120.
Riga, Aspazijas bulvāris 22 (21 60 00, 21 67 00). A stately 19th-century building in the old town, but noisy, decaying and poor value (around $120 for two). It also has a miserable restaurant.
Tūrists, Slokas iela 1 (61 54 55). Big Soviet-style place in Agenskalus on the west bank, about 1km from October bridge. Clean and well-priced double rooms for about $25.
Saulīte, Merķela 12 (22 45 46), near the train station. Drab but clean rooms for $25 for two.
Aurora, Marijas 5 (22 44 79), opposite the train station. Most central of the cheap options, but definitely no frills.
Victorija, A. Caka 55 (27 23 05). Just over a mile northeast of the old town, bus 23 from the train station. Basic but cheap and better than the Aurora.

Hostels and Private Rooms. The Youth Hostel Interpoint (33 21 31), run by the YMCA at Kalnciema iela 10-12, is open in summer only. It is on the west bank and accessible on bus 22 (same as for the airport). Facilities are simple but cost less than $10 per person. The BATS hostel at Greciniēku iela 28 charges a similar rate.

The LUTK, the Latvian University Club (Raiņa bulvāris 19) has information about student residences open as hostels in the summer. It also arranges accommodation in a family home, as does Koop Viesis at Merkela iela 12 (22 28 02).

EATING AND DRINKING

Riga's selection of restaurants and cafés improves almost daily. The pick of the city's best restaurants follows:

Pūt Vējini, Jauniela 18 (22 88 41), just south of Doma laukums. A small cosy place offering quality cooking and good service. It's popular so book to be sure of a table.
Rostock, Tērbatas 13. Pleasant atmosphere, reasonably tasty Latvian dishes, mostly meat.
Astorija, 16 Audeju iela, on top of a department store. Specialises in local dishes.
Forum, Kalku 24. A café-cum-restaurant, with predominantly young clientele, live music and passable food at good prices. Hard currency only at present (as is the casino upstairs).
Latvija, the restaurant on the 25th floor of the hotel isn't bad and there is a good view of the city.

Cafés. There are a few old-fashioned cafes in the old city, particularly near the cathedral square. The Doma, at the top of Smilšu iela, serves great pastries and other snacks. The Ridzene at Skārnu 9, on the other side of the cathedral, has conspiratorial booths where lovers sip and simper. The Peter Gailis (Skārnu 21) is a pleasant enough place for a coffee break but the Balta Roze, at the southern end of Meistaru iela is much better: the coffee and cakes generate queues, so allow plenty of time.

EXPLORING

Unless you have a penchant for Latvian architecture of this and the last century, you should spend most of your time in the old part of town, where architectural styles from Romanesque and Gothic to Renaissance and Baroque rub shoulders. Narrow alleys link spacious squares, some of them so narrow that they can only just take two people.

Overlooking Doma laukums, a pleasant cobbled square with stalls and buskers, the Dome Cathedral is a magnificent building that was begun in the 13th century but took over 500 years to complete. The result is a conglomeration of styles which yet remains remarkably simple. The interior, with a towering Romanesque nave, is decorated with beautiful woodcarvings and portraits of Lutheran worthies. The cathedral also houses the fourth largest organ in the world, with a total of 6,768 pipes. You'll find a museum about the history of Riga in the cloisters.

A short walk northwest is Pils laukums and Riga Castle, built in the 13th century but added to since. It contains the Latvian History Museum, the Foreign Art Museum and the Rainis Literary Museum (the latter dedicated to Latvia's most famous poet, Jānis Rainis). But you'll have more fun strolling the streets. East along the nearby Maza Pils iela, a trio of houses (numbers 17, 19 and 21) known as the 'Tris Brali' or Three Brothers have lavishly decorated facades and are typical of Rigan medieval architecture.

On the other side of Kalku iela, Skārnu has a fine collection of churches, the gem being the Church of St Peter, a large Gothic building constructed mostly in the 15th century: it was the tallest building in the old city until Intourist built the Latvija Hotel. There is a viewing platform 72 metres above ground which gives a wonderful panorama over the rooftops of Vecriga. The Museum of Applied Arts in the church opposite contains an excellent collection of Latvian arts and crafts. Following Skārnu around towards the river, you turn into Mārstalu iela, with two fine 17th-century houses: the mansion of Reitern at no. 2, named after a wealthy merchant and a Baroque mansion at no. 21, built by a burgher called Dannenstern. In nearby streets, Sarkanas Gvardes iela and Veepilsetas iela, several 17th-century warehouses still have their original hoisting equipment.

The compulsory sight in the new town is the Freedom Monument (Brivibas Pieminkelis) near the southern end of Brivibas iela. Erected during independence in 1935, the monument has been a focus for political activity since the late 80s and is the nearest thing Riga has to 'Speaker's Corner'. Outside the former Communist Party headquarters, there is a fragment of the Berlin Wall alongside pieces of the barricades which were set up in January 1991 in defiance of Soviet troops. While in the new town, it's also worth strolling along Elizabetes and Alberta streets, where there are several fine Art Nouveau houses.

Mežaparks. The city's largest park is set among pine forests on the shore of Lake Kišezers, 4 miles/7km north of the centre. There is an amusement park, several boathouses and sandy beaches, but strolling or sitting about usually provides ample entertainment, particularly when the park is busy at weekends. You can reach Mežaparks by waterbus along the Daugava or or tram 11 from Kr. Valdemāra iela.

Ethnography Museum. Situated by Lake Jugla and dedicated to rural Latvian architecture, this is the best open-air ethnographic museum in the Baltics. The buildings (of which there are more than 100) and artefacts date mostly from the 17th to 19th centuries. To get there catch bus 1, 18 or 19 from the bus terminal and get off at the Balozi stop. Lake Jugla is also connected to Lake Kišezers by a canal which is plied by boats in summer. The museum is open between May and October.

Motor Museum. Located at S. Eizenšteina iela 6, 5 miles/8km east of downtown, the Motor Museum (Motor muzejas) is the wackiest thing in Latvia, containing cars that once belonged to some of the most hated men in the world. In one corner, seated at the wheel of a damaged Rolls Royce, is a wax effigy of a panic-stricken Brezhnev: he crashed the car in 1980 and for years it was kept hidden in a garage at the Kremlin. In another, Stalin sits in the back of a Zil limousine which weighs seven tons and has windows 8cm thick. The museum opens 10am-8pm Tuesday to Sunday. To get there take the special bus which leaves from outside the Orthodox church on Brīvības bulvāris, most frequently at weekends.

ENTERTAINMENT

The Opera and Ballet Theatre on Aspazijas bulvāris (22 88 34) is Riga's greatest venue. Wagner was resident conductor at the opera house until he had to flee his creditors, and Schumann gave concerts here — though he wrote home once saying that Rigans knew nothing about music. Whatever the truth, there is plenty of choice as far as music is concerned. Regular and well-attended concerts and organ recitals are staged in the Dome Cathedral. The German choral traditions are still very much alive here and any concert in the cathedral could be one of the highlights of a stay in Riga. High calibre recitals are also staged at the Wagner Concert Hall (R. Vāgnera 4) and in the old Guild Hall (Amatu iela 6), home of the Latvian Philharmonic Orchestra where concerts are held in the splendid Gothic banqueting hall.

Several restaurants in Riga double as dance halls, where you can usually choose between enjoying a spot of live music, usually jazz and rock, or bopping to songs that your parents probably danced to. All kinds of music, from classical to traditional folk, are performed in the open air during the summer, including in Komunāru Park near the Latvija Hotel, at the Ethnography Museum and in Mežaparks.

SHOPPING

You can spend a surprising amount of time in Riga shopping, or at least window-shopping. Souvenir shops usually have a good line in cheap woollen socks and gloves as well as very cheap amber jewellery. Most of the best crafts shops are along Kalku iela, Brīvības iela and Aspazijas bulvāris, though you can also buy crafts at the Ethnography Museum, particularly when special fairs are laid on. There is a fabulous daily market held in and spilling out of old zeppelin hangars behind the bus station; most stalls sell fresh produce and other food.

CRIME AND SAFETY

Riga is much troubled by organised crime — there are said to be at least five drug-dealing mafia groups, and bomb attacks are not unheard of. The ill-lit city-centre streets are unsafe after dark and few people venture out. Assuming you manage to elude organised crime, petty theft seems no worse than in any other Eastern European capital.

HELP AND INFORMATION

Tourist Information: the tourist office is at Brīvības bulvāris 36 (tel 22 99 45, fax 28 45 72). *Riga This Week* (published every three months) and the *Riga Success Guide* both have listings and other information.

Central Post Office: Brīvibus bulvāris 21, open 24 hours. You can also phone or fax abroad and send telegrams from here. There is another office at Stacijas laukums 1 by the train station.

American Express: represented by Latvia Tours, Grecineku Str. 22/24 (21 36 52, 22 00 47).

Hospital: Maskavas iela 122 (24 17 70).

Embassies and Consulates

UK: Elizabetes iela 2, 3rd floor (tel 883 01 13, 32 07 37; fax 883 01 12).
USA: Raiņa bulvāris 7 (22 70 45, 22 05 02).
Canada: Elizabetes iela 45 (33 33 55).
Poland: Elizabetes iela 2 (32 22 33).
Lithuania: Elizabetes iela 2 (32 15 19, 32 17 44).

AROUND RIGA

Jūrmala. Just half an hour by suburban train from Riga, the thought of a Baltic Riviera sounds appealing. The sandy beaches, backed by dunes and pine trees, are very pleasant. Sadly, being so close to the polluted Daugava river, swimming is not recommended. Still, it's a nice day out, with plenty of scope for strolls along the beach or through the woods.

Jūrmala consists of a string of resorts, the best of which is Majori, with lively shops and cafés along the main street. In summer, take the one-hour hydrofoil journey from Riga, which adds to the fun of the trip.

Jelgava. This is a sizeable town, with a population of 75,000, 25 miles/40km southwest of Riga. The only reason to visit is to see the fabulous Rundale Palace, one of the finest buildings in the Baltics and once the residence of the Dukes of Courland (an order of Teutonic knights). It was built in the 18th century according to a design by Bartolomeo Rastrelli, the architect of the Winter Palace in St Petersburg. It sustained damaged in both the world wars, but has been rebuilt. There are more than ten buses a day to Jelgava, taking about an hour. Allow a day if you can since there are extensive grounds to explore.

Salaspils. Ten miles/16km southeast of Riga, Salaspils was the site of one of Hitler's death camps. Virtually all Riga's 45,000 Jews died here, as well as perhaps another 40,000 brought from other countries. A moving monument has been erected amid pine forest, the large stone figures the epitome of Soviet sculpture at its most potent. To get there, take the train to Dārziņi from where you can walk to the monument.

SIGULDA AND GAUJA NATIONAL PARK

Sigulda lies 30 miles/48km northeast of Riga in the gorgeous Gauja valley. A large area running northeast from Sigulda to beyond Cēsis has been designated as the Gauja National Park, taking in woods, caves and lakes as well as several old castles. For a dramatic view of the gorge, take the cable car from Sigulda across to the north bank of the river. Nearby are the ruins of Krimulda Castle and, at the bottom of the gorge, the Gūtmaṇa Cave, with graffiti dating back to the 17th century. You can carry on east up the hill to Turaida Castle (past stables where you can rent horses), founded in the thirteenth century but heavily restored: not great to look at but the views from the main tower are magnificent.

Served by regular buses and trains from Riga, Sigulda can easily be visited as a day trip; but since the surrounding scenery is — by Baltic standards — more than just pleasant, you should consider staying overnight. The Sigulda Hotel at Televizijas iela 19 (97 31 21) offers cheap bed and breakfast.

Cēsis. If you want to explore further up the valley, take the bus to Cēsis, 25 miles/40km northeast of Sigulda. Parts of this old walled city, once a member of the Hanseatic League, have survived a turbulent history, and the castle houses a museum. Hotel Tērvete at Vienibas laukums (223 92) offers simple accommodation.

WEST OF RIGA

Kuldīga. This town, 100 miles/160km west of Riga, was briefly capital of the German Dukes of Courland. There are many well-preserved buildings in the centre, dating mostly from the 16th to 18th centuries. Hotel Kursa at Pilsetas laukums 6 (33-224 30) has adequate rooms and an attached restaurant.

Liepāja. As Latvia's second port (with a population of over 110,000), Liepāja would not seem to have a lot going for it. But it is surprisingly provincial, has a few interesting old buildings and is a good place to stop off if you want to follow an alternative route to Lithuania. Buses run every couple of hours from Riga and take about four hours. You can stay at the Hotel Liva on Liela, with doubles for $20.

Calendar of Events

January 1	New Year's Day
March/April	Good Friday
May 1	Labour Day
June 23-24	St John's Day (Jāni). The summer solstice is Latvia's most important festival. Beer is brewed specially and people don flowers and greenery and sit around bonfires all night singing traditional songs.
July 2-4	Latvian Song and Dance Festival, Riga
November 18	**National Day**
December 25-26	**Christmas**
December 31	**New Year's Eve**

Public holidays are given in **bold**.

Lithuania

Population: 3.7 million **Capital:** Vilnius (population 595,000)

The largest Baltic republic once commanded a huge slab of Eastern Europe, stretching as far south as the Black Sea. Now, however, Lithuania's frontiers have shrunk to enclose a slice of territory the size of Ireland. The countryside, consisting mostly of plains and forest cut through by innumerable rivers, is about as dull as that of its neighbours, though inland from the dunes and pine woods, gentle hills bring some added interest. Trakai and Kaunas are both pleasant historical towns and the beaches around Klaipėda are better than in both Latvia and Estonia. But Lithuania's saving grace is Vilnius. More relaxed and friendly than Tallinn and Riga, the capital is set apart from its Baltic neighbours also by the strong Catholic bias of both the city's architecture and its people. The religious allegiance of most Lithuanians recalls the country's long-standing political and cultural links with Poland which, along with Kaliningrad — a curious, lost corner of Russia — flanks Lithuania's western border.

CLIMATE

The coastal climate is milder than that inland, but Arctic currents can bring frost as late as June. The hottest period runs from June to August, July being the warmest month. While August is the wettest inland, on the coast the heaviest rain falls in October. For the most pleasant conditions, travel in the spring or autumn.

HISTORY

The first known state of Lithuania was recorded in 1293, when a number of tribes joined together to resist the threat of invasion by the Teutonic knights. In the 14th century, under Grand Duke Gediminas (now recognised as the founder of Lithuania), the state's borders were gradually extended until they reached as far as the Black Sea. In 1410 a joint Lithuanian, Russian and Polish force defeated the Teutonic order, but it was the Poles who gradually established control. Following the Union of Lublin in 1569, a Polish-Lithuanian feudal state was formed, known as the *Rzeczpospolita*. This did not provide for long-term peace or tranquillity, however, and spates of plague and war brought decline. In 1795 the state was split up among its neighbours, with Lithuania being handed to the Russians, who held onto it until 1915, when the Germans drove them out. Lithuania was independent between the wars, then occupied by the USSR following the 1939 Nazi-Soviet Pact. Under Moscow's control, there was the inevitable process of industrialisation and colonisation, though not on a scale seen in the other Baltic states.

Independence. Sajūdis, Lithuania's main nationalist group formed in June 1988, led the country into independence with a haste which both outpaced the more tentative approach favoured by Estonia and Latvia and also greatly disturbed the Kremlin. There is an argument, indeed, that Sajūdis was the force which began to drive in the wedge which eventually split the Soviet Union. Economic sanctions imposed by the USSR forced the suspension of independence for a time, but in January 1991 Vytautas Landsbergis, the leader of Sajūdis and effectively Lithuania's president, redeclared independence. A bitter battle with Moscow ensued, with an attempt by Soviet troops to take over key buildings in Vilnius, including parliament. But the coup against Gorbachev brought the Kremlin's resistance to Lithuania's independence to an end.

Landsbergis made a series of blunders after independence which resulted in divisions within his right-of-centre party and the loss of the parliamentary majority in 1992 to Agirdas Brazauskas and his Democratic Labour Party. The economic crisis had exacerbated the already shaky position of Landsbergis, but Brazauskas — former leader of the Latvian Communist Party — also won respect for his toughness over the handing back of land taken into collectivisation. In elections held in Februry 1993, in which Lithuanians chose the first president of an independent nation, Brazauskas won a sweeping victory. But while Lithuania now enjoys surprisingly good relations with Russia, the republic remains the poorest of the three Baltic states. Inflation, an unstable currency and an industry still trapped in a timewarp are pressing problems for the government.

PEOPLE

About 80% of the population is Lithuanian, 10% Russian and 7% Poles. Many Poles live in the southern Vilnius region, where they are actually in the majority, with their own schools and newspapers. While Lithuania has faced its own problems with its Russian and Polish minorities, anti-immigrant feeling has never matched that in neighbouring Baltic states. In 1992, Lithuania settled a long-standing border dispute with Poland and also gave a commitment to safeguard the rights of the Polish minority. The presence of Kalinigrad, a splinter of Russia at its western frontier, remains a potential source of conflict.

Language. Lithuanian is an Indo — European language like Latvian, with similar pronunciation but very different vocabulary. In Vilnius, a surprising number of people know English. A few useful words and phrases are as follows:

yes — *taip*
no — *ne*
please — *prašom*
thank you — *ačiū*
hello — *sveiki, labas*
goodbye — *viso gero*
how much? — *kiek?*

where? — *kur?*
do you speak English? — *ar kalbate angliškai?*
airport — *aerouostą*
train station — *geležinkelio stoti*
hotel — *viešbuti*
hospital — *ligonine*
street — *gatvė (abbr g.)*

Air. LAL or Lithuanian Airlines (Lietuvos Avialinijos) flies to Vilnius four times a week from London Gatwick. A so-called Instant Purchase fare, which is non-refundable, currently costs about £275 return for a seven-day advance purchase ticket through the airline direct (01293 551737), but lower fares may be available through the agents mentioned on page 176. LAL also flies from other European cities, including Berlin, Frankfurt, Copenhagen and Budapest. SAS flies daily from Copenhagen, Lufthansa three times a week from Frankfurt.

Rail. Vilnius is the rail hub of the Baltic region, with direct several times daily from Riga (6-8 hours) as well as St Petersburg (14 hours), Moscow (13 hours) and Warsaw (12 hours). A sleeper train runs every day from Berlin (22 hours) via Warsaw, with services daily also from Prague (36 hours) and Tallinn (14 hours on the 'Chayka' bound for Minsk) and twice-daily from Kaliningrad (6 hours).

Note that most trains from Warsaw go via Grodno in Belarus; passengers on trains which travel straight through the rail corridor do not require a Belarus transit visa, but local services do; check before departure.

The towns of Kaunas and Klaipėda are easily reached by rail, either direct or via Vilnius.

Bus. There are daily international services from Tallinn (12 hours) and Riga (6 hours), Warsaw (9 hours), Berlin (17 hours), Kaliningrad (5 hours) and Minsk (4 hours). Book as far in advance as possible, particularly if you're travelling from Poland. Some buses from Warsaw go via Belarus, so (as with trains) check visa requirements.

Driving. The main border crossing from Poland is via Ogrodniki/Lazdijai, but delays are notorious. You may find it quicker to travel via Belarus or to take a ferry from Germany.

Boat. Ferries operate from the German port Mukran, (near Sassnitz on the island of Rügen), to Klaipėda, taking about 20 hours. Book at least a month ahead, preferably more in high season. For further information, contact Deutsche Seereederei Touristik in Rostock (tel 381-458 4672). Another ferry connects Kiel, also in Germany, with Klaipėda five days a week, taking 24-30 hours. Contact Lisco (the Lithuanian Shipping Co) in Klaipėda, on 61-56116 or fax 61-18479.

British passport holders do not require a visa, but most other foreign nationals (including the Irish) do. Transit visas are issued free of charge, but a normal tourist visa costs £14 (with an additional £7 for same-day service, and £3 extra for postal applications). In summer 1995 it seemed likely that the option of obtaining one at the border might disappear, so try to obtain one from a Lithuanian consulate abroad — or use one from one of the other Baltic states, since each recognises the others' visas.

You can extend your stay at the Emigracijos Tarnyba, Verkių 3 in Vilnius (75 64 53). Lithuanian consulates abroad are as follows:

UK: 17 Essex Villas, London W8 7BP (tel 0171-938 2481, fax 0171-938 3329).
USA: 2622 16th St NW, Washington DC, 20009 (tel 202-234-5860, fax 202-328-0466).
Canada: 235 Yorkland Blvd, Willowdale, Ont. M2J 4Y6 (416-494 4099).
Australia: 26 Jalanga Crescent, Aranda, ACT 1614 (06-253 2062).
Poland: aleje Ujazdowskie 13-23, Warsaw (62-3194).
Russia: ul. Pisemskogo 10, Moscow 121069 (291 2643).

lita = 100 centu
£1 = 6 lita   US$1 = 4 lita
The Lithuanian currency, the lita, was introduced in 1993. The two-tier system of prices in the local currency for Lithuanians and in hard currency for visitors has not completely disappeared, but the system has certainly been simplified.

Changing Money. While US dollars in cash are easily the most useful, Deutschmarks are the accepted currency in the resorts around Klaipėda. Changing travellers cheques is not as difficult in Lithuania as it is elsewhere in the Baltics. Big tourist hotels and several banks handle cheques, both in Vilnius and in large towns such as Kaunas. The main drawback is the commission, which can be as much as 5% in some banks.

Work. Opportunities for earning cash are limited in Lithuania, but are likely to expand as the economy becomes more westward-looking. At present, your labour is in demand as a volunteer. Minta (Perkuno al. 4, 3000 Kaunas Lithuania; 3707-202560/fax 208321) places up to 50 foreigners as group leaders and conversation assistants at summer language camps on the Baltic coast. Volunteers can be of any nationality but must be over the age of 20; the placement fee is $65. Minta also arranges au pair placements. An American organisation sends volunteer teachers to Lithuania on short contracts: American Professional Partnership for Lithuanian Education (PO Box 1370, West Hartford, CT 06119).

Telephone. Telephone calls are easier (though more expensive) in Lithuania than in the other Baltic states. In Vilnius, you should be able to dial direct abroad from your hotel. You'll probably have to wait for at least an hour in a public telephone office. If you have an urgent message and don't have the time to waste, send a telegram from the nearest post office (*paštas*).

While the majority of payphones are worse than useless, cardphones are great — particularly for international calls. When making a long-distance internal call from the capital, dial 8 and wait for the dialling tone.

Emergency numbers: fire brigade 01, police 02, ambulance 03.

Mail. Try to post all letters in Vilnius, from where they should reach European destinations in a week or ten days; within Lithuania the postal service is poor.

Buses are generally the best way to get about. Nevertheless, there is a well-developed rail network, the *greit* or fast services being the best for long journeys. For overnight trips, the four-person *coupe* compartments are recommended. Timetables in stations are minimalist, giving the starting-point and destination but rarely stops in between.

Driving. Roads are quiet since there are still comparatively few private cars and petrol is prohibitively expensive for those on local salaries. Unleaded petrol is available only in the main cities, but even then you'll have to hunt for it. The speed limit is 80km/h (50mph) on the open road and 50km/h (31mph) in built-up areas.

Car Rental: Balticar has offices in Vilnius (tel 46 09 98; fax 75 89 24) and Kaunas (75 92 45), and rents out both Western and Eastern European models. International agents are opening up.

Book ahead in summer if you want to be sure of a room. Hostel and private accommodation is only in its infancy. While this means you'll be restricted to hotels in most places, the situation can only improve (and the range of hotels is already reasonably good).

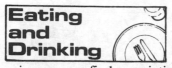

Eating and Drinking

Cuisine is rarely limited by political boundaries and Lithuanian cooking shares dishes with both Poland and Western Russia. *Zrazy* — roulades of beef or veal — are found all over the Baltics, but in Lithuania you may find a variation which is made with chopped meat, shaped like a burger and spread with a filling of, for example, grated horseradish root and sour cream. In winter the most common things on a menu are pork, sausages and pickled salads.

As in the other Baltic Republics, the cabbage is ubiquitous but cooked with great versatility e.g. with bacon, apples and lots of black pepper. A favourite dish is *golubtsy* (stuffed cabbage leaves), which dates back to the 14th century and was probably brought in by the Tatars. Potatoes also abound in many different forms, such as *bulvinai blynai* (potato pancakes) or *vedarai* (potato sausage), and even as a pudding (*kugelis*). A particular favourite is the *zeppelin*, a type of potato cake stuffed with meat and shaped like an airship (and usually saturated in grease). *Virtinukai*, similar to ravioli, are popular too, usually stuffed with meat but sometimes mushrooms (*grybai*) and cheese. Lithuania is not a bad place for vegetarians, though ostensibly meatless dishes are often fried in pork fat.

café — *kavinė*
menu — *valgiaraštis*
soup — *sriuba*
meat/main dish — *mėsos patiekalai*
fish — *uvis*
vegetables — *daržovės*
fruit — *vaisiai*

bread — *duona*
ice cream — *ledai*
drinks — *gėrimai*
beer — *alus*
tea — *arbata*
coffee — *kava*
(mineral) water — *(mineralinis) vanduo*

Help and Information

Lithuanian embassies abroad can send limited tourist information. This actually comprises photocopied pages from *Vilnius in Your Pocket*, an excellent guidebook published every two months, which you can pick up once you're there. It concentrates on the capital, but has some information on the rest of the country too.

VILNIUS

The capital of Lithuania, draped over terraces in the broad, wooded valley of the river Neris, was founded as a fortress by Grand Duke Gedinimas in 1323. By the 16th century, Vilnius was one of the biggest and most important cities in Eastern Europe. Now the old and new town are closely merged, with towers and churches mingling with residential blocks and newly-planted trees.

Vilnius differs from Tallinn and Riga in that the architecture has been shaped by Catholic rather than Germanic tastes — more specifically, by the Italian branches of the Gothic, Renaissance and Baroque styles. Along the labyrinthine cobbled streets of the old town, imposing churches and palaces rub shoulders with more humble cottages painted in pastel shades. Impressive restoration work has succeeded (on the whole) in preserving the

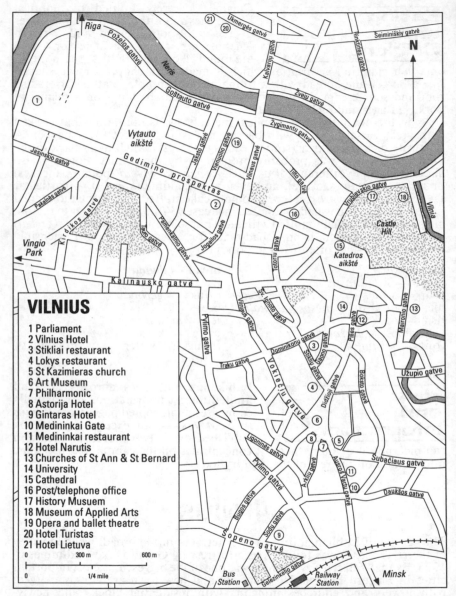

VILNIUS

1 Parliament
2 Vilnius Hotel
3 Stikliai restaurant
4 Lokys restaurant
5 St Kazimieras church
6 Art Museum
7 Philharmonic
8 Astorija Hotel
9 Gintaras Hotel
10 Medininkai Gate
11 Medininkai restaurant
12 Hotel Narutis
13 Churches of St Ann & St Bernard
14 University
15 Cathedral
16 Post/telephone office
17 History Musuem
18 Museum of Applied Arts
19 Opera and ballet theatre
20 Hotel Turistas
21 Hotel Lietuva

integrity of the exteriors while converting the interiors into shops, galleries and cafés.

The gap between the rich and poor is as wide as in the other ex-communist capitals, but the city centre lacks the *nouveau riche* atmosphere that afflicts some of its counterparts. Vilnius is lively and relaxed, and the local people seem to enjoy living here. There is a romantic air about the city and it is easy to get attached to the place.

CITY LAYOUT

The ancient and modern centre of Vilnius occupies the south bank of the Neris (all the less attractive workings of the city have been shunted across the river) and this is where you'll spend the vast majority of your time. The river Vilnia joins the Neris at the northeastern edge of the centre: Castle Hill (Piles Kalnas), which rises above the confluence, is a useful reference point. At the base of the hill, Katedros aikštė marks the heart of the old town, which spreads south from the square. Gedimino prospektas strikes west from Katedros aikštė as the principal road through the modern town.

Maps. There are maps in *Vilnius In Your Pocket*, available from news stands and decent bookshops (of which there are several on Pilies gatvė).

ARRIVAL AND DEPARTURE

Air. The airport (63 02 01) is 5 miles/8km south of the centre, linked to the train station downtown by bus. Facilities have improved greatly with the recent renovation; there is an exchange desk and duty-free shop. Lithuanian Airlines has an office at Ukmergės 12 (tel 75 25 88, fax 35 48 52).

Train. The railway station (63 00 86/88) is on Geležinkelio, due south of the old city. Trolleybus 2 runs to Katedros aikštė. You can book international tickets at Sopeno 3 (62 30 44), near the station, or in the Lietuva Hotel on Ukmergės, north of the river.

Bus. The main bus terminal (Autobusų Stotis) is at Sodų 22, next door to the train station. The timetables are pleasantly comprehensible. You can call for information on 66 04 81, but may find it a lot easier to wander in and look at the schedules.

CITY TRANSPORT

You can easily walk around the city centre, but there is a good system of buses and trolleybuses, with a few battered yellow trams. Buy tickets before boarding at kiosks marked *spaudos*.

State taxis (with a green sign) are most easily hired from the official ranks, which are dotted all over the centre. Cabs hailed in the street are likely to be private (with a chequered signs), since these are more accustomed to looking for business. Don't be persuaded to pay in hard currency, often the habit of private cabs.

ACCOMMODATION

Hotels in Vilnius have been slow to shed their Soviet atmosphere, but there are a few new joint ventures, catering to the top end of the market. A few cheap hotels charge around $20 a night, though the easiest way to pay less than this is to arrange bed and breakfast privately or through an agency.

Astorija, Didžioji 35 (tel 62 99 14, fax 22 00 97). A good, partly Scandinavian-owned hotel in the old town, with rooms from $40 to $100.

Turistas, Ukmergės 14 (tel 73 31 06, fax 35 31 61). On the north bank (a 15-minute walk from the old town or take trolleybus 2 from the train station), next to the 23-storey ex-Intourist Lietuva Hotel. Large and ugly but comfortable, and not bad value with rooms for $70.

Vilnius, Gedimino pr. 20 (62 41 57, 62 36 65). In the old town, with annex down the road. The rooms are best in the main building, $30-60 for two.

Narutis, Pilies 24 (62 28 82). Characterful place in good location in old town, but restoration has increased room rates to over $30.
Gintaras, Sodų 14 (63 44 96). Gloomy, but convenient for the train station. Room prices range from $10 to $35.
BATS Backpackers' Hostel, Geležinio Vilko gatvė 27 (66 16 92), west of downtown. Usually open only in summer, $14 per person.
Litinterp, Vokiečių 10 (tel 61 20 40, fax 22 29 82). Can arrange bed and breakfast accommodation ($15 per person), plus flats to rent.
Norwegian Information Office, Didžioji 14 (22 41 40). Arranges rooms for $15-20 a night.

EATING AND DRINKING

There is a reasonable choice of cafés all over the town, particularly along Gedimino prospektas, but most cellar bars (*alaus baras*) are in the old town. One of the best is the Rudininkai, at Rūdininkų 14 south of the main square. The city's best restaurants are also concentrated in the historic quarter:

Medininkai, Aušros Vartų gatvė (61 40 19). In a restored 16th-century building with cellar. Reasonable food and café attached.
Lokys, Stiklių gatvė 8 (62 90 46). Also in the old town, with interesting interior. Specialises in game, including moose and wild boar.
Stikliai, Stikilių gatvė 7 (62 79 71). The best place in town, with a long-standing reputation dating from pre-independence days. Mitterrand is among the rich and famous to have dined here. It closes at 10pm and a reservation is essential.
Viola, Kalvarijų 3, on the north bank (just across the main bridge). Wonderful Armenian restaurant serving delights such as kebabs and meat salads.

EXPLORING

In Katedros aikštė, the most natural starting-point for a tour of Vilnius, the most striking sight is the squat and rather cumbersome Catholic cathedral (Arkikatedra Bazilika), dating mainly from the 18th century and with a facade lifted straight from the Parthenon. Until 1988 it was an art gallery and concert hall, but now it is once again a place of worship. Inside, the highlight is the Chapel of St Kazimieras, a Baroque confection of marble, stucco and granite.
   A path leads from the square up Castle Hill. All that remains of the castle is the Gothic tower, from which you can survey the mosaic of steeples and roofs. It houses a branch of the History and Ethnography Museum, whose main building is at 1 Vrublevskio gatvė, at the bottom of the hill just north of the cathedral. The latter's collection covers Lithuanian history from the Stone Age up to the 20th century. Following the road east around the foot of the hill, you'll come to the Museum of Applied Arts (Taikomosios Dailės Muziejus) at Arsenalo gatvė 2, with a superb collection of Lithuanian decorative arts including furniture, jewellery and ceramics. About five minutes' walk further east, in the new town, the graceful Peter and Paul church sits marooned above a particularly arcane road layout by the junction of Kosciuškos and Olandų. Probably the finest example of late baroque architecture in Lithuania, its simple white exterior contrasts with the interior, which is like a wedding cake turned inside out and iced with stucco — a riot of frescoes, reliefs and life-size sculptures.
   The key streets of the old city are Pilies and Didžioji, which run one after

the other south of Katedros aikšte. Near the top of Pilies gatvė, a narrow little street leads east to St Ann's church, a stunning example of 16th-century Gothic architecture. The church of St Bernard next to it is much more austere but has some beautiful frescoes. Occupying the block on the other side of Pilies is Vilnius university, dating back 400 years and retaining its charming courtyards and arcades. There is also an extraordinary Astronomical Observatory, built in the 17th-century and with a facade decorated with signs of the zodiac. Didžioji, which contains many interesting 16th-century buildings, finishes up at the former town hall — now the home of the Lithuanian Art Museum (Lietuvos Dailės Muziejus), dedicated to 20th-century works; the legacy of state-approved art still lingers. The Jesuit church of St Kazimieras, a huge Baroque creation, marks the beginning of Aušros Vartu, which is an attractive street running southeast to the Medininkai Gate (Aušros Vartai), the only city gate to have survived intact. On top perches a white madonna, dirtied by pollution.

All the strects around Katedros aikštė are worth exploring. The area southwest of the square once formed the heart of Vilnius' Jewish quarter. One synagogue (at Pylimo 39) and a Jewish museum (Pamenkalnio 12) recall the city's Jewish population — half that of the entire city before World War II.

Gedimino prospektas runs west from Katedros aikštė right to the river. You can still see evidence of the 1991 independence struggles, though the barricades erected to defend the Parliament Building (at the western end) have been pulled down and the anti-tank ditches filled in. South along the river, Vingio parkas is the city's main park — a very pleasant place to stroll and with a huge open-air theatre where festivals are held.

One of the few things to tempt you north of the river is the Lithuanian State Museum (Lietuvos Valstybės Muziejus), near the western end of Ukmergės gatvė. The collection includes folk costumes and crafts as well as superbly carved crosses and other religious artefacts. Other displays relate to 20th-century events, from the deportations of the Stalinist era to the 1991 nationalist uprising. Further west from the museum you can see the TV tower where 15 Lithuanians were killed by Soviet troops in 1991; crosses commemorate those who died.

ENTERTAINMENT

If the opportunity arises, don't miss a performance by the Lithuanian State Dance and Song Company, the Lithuanian Chamber Orchestra or the Galve Village Choir; they are all renowned throughout the region. The main concert hall is the Philarmonic at Didžioji gatvė 45. The Opera and Ballet Theatre is a modern building at Vienuolio gatvė 1, northwest of the main square, and there is a puppet (Lele) theatre at Arkliu 5, south off Didžioji.

For a more energetic night out, try one of the local nightclubs such as the Erfurtas (Architektų 19) and the Dainava (Vienuolio 4); both sometimes put on variety shows which can be good for a laugh.

SHOPPING

Amber, or fossil tree resin, is found throughout the world. However, the largest deposits are found along the Baltic coast, in sands which are 40-60 million years old. Lithuania has for centuries been the main source, and in ancient times was known as the 'Land of Amber'. You can buy amber jewellery in many shops in Vilnius, but try not to be palmed off with amberoid, which is small pieces of amber fused together. You also see imitation amber knocking about, but it is not a patch on the real thing and rarely fools anyone.

For this and other souvenirs, try the shop in the Art Exhibition Centre, at Vokiečių 2 near the Lithuanian Art Museum, or Dailė (Gedimino prospektas 1). Folk craft festivals are staged periodically in Vingio parkas too.

HELP AND INFORMATION

Tourist information: several offices dispense information to visitors. Of longest standing is the Lithuania Travel Company at Ukmergės 20 (tel 35 65 26, fax 35 62 70), attached to the Lietuva Hotel. The *Norwegian Information Office*, at Didžioji 14 (22 41 40), is rather more convenient and does not deal solely with travellers from Norway. *Vilnius In Your Pocket* includes information on everything imaginable, from train timetables to the location of petrol stations.

Post Office: the central post office is at Gedimino prospektas 7 (61 66 14), with facilities for telephoning too, though the newer office at Vilniaus 33 (61 99 50/60) is generally more efficient and open 24 hours for telephone calls and telegrams. A fax service is available at the Foreign Tourists Service Bureau in the Hotel Lietuva (35 60 74).

Money: several banks on Gedimino prospektas will change money, including the Bank of Lithuania at no. 6 (open in morning only). Good rates also from Vilniaus Bankas: the branch in the main post office is the best one to use. American Express is represented by Lithuanian Tours at Vilniaus gatvė 2/30 (61 59 75).

Hospital: Siltnamių 29 (26 90 69).

Embassies and Consulates

UK: Antakalnio gatvė 2 (tel 22 20 70/71, fax 35 75 79).
USA: Akmenų gatvė 6 (tel 22 27 24, 22 30 31; fax 22 27 79).
Estonia: Turniškių gatvė 20 (tel/fax 76 98 48).
Latvia: Tumo-Vaižganto gatvė 2 (22 05 58).
Poland: Aušros Vartų gatvė 7 (22 44 44).
Czech Republic: Gedimino prospektas 54b-2 (62 97 13).
Russia: Juozapavičiaus 11 (26 16 37).
Romania: Turniškių 25 (77 98 40).

TRAKAI

In the days when the Grand Duchy stretched from the Baltic to the Black Sea, Trakai was capital of Lithuania and one of the most important cities in Europe. Located on a peninsula between two lakes, 15 miles/24km west of Vilnius, Trakai is now a tranquil town with just echoes of its former life — including two castles north of the main square: one in ruins near Lake Luka, the other on an island in Lake Galvès. The latter is a magnificent red-brick Gothic complex dating from the late 14th century. It has been restored and contains an historical museum, with portraits of the Grand Dukes (the last pagan rulers of Europe) and a curious assembly of other objects. On summer Sundays, folk groups perform in the courtyard. You can also hire rowing boats, and other sports facilities for riding, etc. are being developed.

Look out for hot meat-filled pasties called *kibinai*, a local speciality: the surest place to find them is at the Kibininė restaurant. Although almost certainly Central Asian in origin, the pastie recipe was reputedly brought from the Crimea by a number of tradesmen employed as servants and bodyguards by the dukes. About 200 of their descendants, known as the Karaimes or Karaites, still live in Trakai. One of their few remaining prayer houses is at Karaimų 30, north of the main square.

Buses and trains serve Trakai frequently from Vilnius, journey time around half an hour.

KAUNAS

Sixty miles/96km west of Vilnius, Kaunas is Lithuania's second largest city, with a population of 440,000. Founded in the 11th century and at one time a major trading centre, Kaunas was the country's capital for most of the inter-war period. There are plenty of interesting buildings and several museums, and a pleasantly relaxed atmosphere. In addition, some of the best musical events in Lithuania are held in Kaunas.

The centre of the city lies in the triangle of land formed by the confluence of the Nemunas and Neris rivers, the historic quarter situated near the western point. The main street through the new town is Laisvės alėja.

Arrival and Departure. Buses run every 30 minutes or so from Vilnius (journey time two hours), with services also from Klaipėda and other main towns. The bus station is at Vytauto 26 (22 79 42), southeast of the centre. The train station (22 10 93) lies a couple of blocks further out, with frequent services to Vilnius.

Accommodation and Food. Hotel Baltija at Vytauto 71 (22 36 39), near the transport terminals, is comfortable and good value at under $30. There are several smarter places on Laisvės alėja, including the Nemunas at no. 88 (22 31 02). This street also has some of the town's best restaurants, or try Medžiotoju Užeiga on the old town square.

Exploring. The focus of the old town is Rotušes aikštė, lined with some beautifully restored German merchants' houses dating from the city's peak trading days in the 15th and 16th centuries. The most important buildings in the square are Baroque, including the old city hall and the cathedral (though the latter was originally Gothic). Kaunas castle, a short distance north, is in ruins, the 11th-century tower one of the few bits to have survived.

The city's best museums are on Putvinskio, north of Laisvės alėja. The Ciurlionis Art Gallery (closed on Mondays) at no. 55 contains works by Lithuania's most famous artist, M. K. Ciurlionis (1875-1911), who some say influenced Kandinsky and therefore indirectly had a hand in the development of abstract art. Opposite, at no. 64, is the Museum of Devil's Sculptures (officially the A. Zmuidzinavičiaus muziejus), which has a compelling collection of Lucifers from around the world, though most are wooden figures carved in Lithuania.

The former Russian Orthodox cathedral, at the eastern end of Laisvės alėja in Nepriklausomybės aikštė, is in a fairly poor state inside despite its handsome exterior. It functions as a concert hall and also houses a Gallery of Sculpture and Stained Glass. Further east still is Vytauto Park and, adjacent, Europe's largest and oldest city forest, Ažuolynas. The presence of the latter has been good for the town since there are heavy restrictions on construction and air pollution in an effort to preserve the centuries-old trees.

KLAIPEDA AND PALANGA

From Kaunas, the A228 follows the wide Nemunas valley 140 miles/224km west to Klaipėda. This is a big port with around 200,000 inhabitants, and also a popular destination for holidaymakers, particularly from Germany. While swimming in the murk of the Baltic Sea may not sound appealing, the nearby beaches are some of the region's cleanest. Klaipėda was badly damaged by the Red Army in the war and little old architecture has survived (what remains is mostly south of the Danės river), but it is a cosmopolitan place and has about the liveliest nightlife in the country.

Buses serve Klaipėda from Vilnius, Kaunas and also Kaliningrad and the Latvian town of Liepāja. Trains run twice daily from Kaunas and the capital. Boats from Germany also dock here: see *Getting There*.

Hotel Klaipėda at Naujo Sodo 1 (199 60) is central and has good facilities including a fine restaurant. Rooms ($40 upwards) are often booked up in season. Less central but good value is the Vėtrungė at Taikos prospektas 28 (548 01).

Palanga. Fifteen miles/24km north of Klaipėda, this is the supposed gem of the Baltic coast, with its broad sandy beach, dunes and shallow sea. Locals gather on the long wooden pier in the evening to watch the sunset. Most accommodation is in the form of sanatoria, so you'll do best to visit on a day trip. There is an amber museum in the botanical gardens in the main town, north of the Ronze river.

Neringa. Klaipėda faces the Neringa peninsula, a narrow spit of land which extends 30 miles/48km and separates the Kuršių lagoon from the Baltic Sea; only the northern half belongs to Lithuania, the rest being part of Kaliningrad (see page 120). Most of the peninsula, made up mainly of dunes and pine trees, is protected and the entry fee seems efficient in keeping a lot of Lithuanians away.

A road stretches the length of Neringa, giving access to fishing villages along the lagoon side and deserted beaches on the Baltic side. At the southern end is Nida, where the home of Thomas Mann, who lived here in the 30s, has been turned into a museum. The best way to reach Nida from the mainland in summer is to take a motorboat from Kaunas, a fun four-hour ride along the Nemunas river.

Boats take foot passengers and cars from Klaipėda across to the peninsula.

Calendar of Events

January 1	**New Year's Day**
February 16	**Restoration of Lithuanian State (1918)**
March/April	**Easter Monday**
March	International jazz festival in Birštonas in even-numbered years
May 2	**Labour Day**
May (1st Sunday)	**Mothers' Day**
June 14	Day of Mourning and Hope
July 6	**Day of Statehood (Anniversary of Coronation of Grand Duke Mindaugas in 13th century)**
Mid-July	Baltika international folklore festival, held in each republic in turn. Next in Lithuania in 1996. Well worth seeing, with many people wearing traditional costume.
November 1	**All Saints' Day**
December 25-26	**Christmas**

Public holidays are listed in **bold**.

Belarus

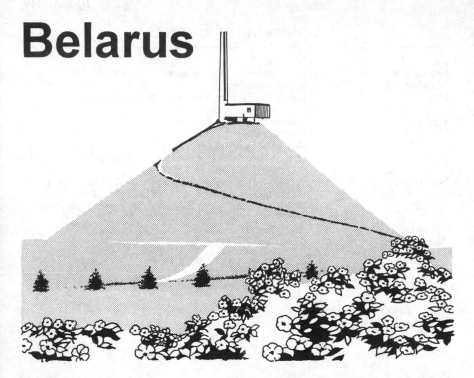

Population: 10.2 million   **Capital:** Minsk (population 1.6 million)

At every point throughout its history, Belarus has lain in the path of western armies heading east and eastern armies heading west. Caught in the crossfire of national rivalries, the country has had to fight every step of the way to maintain its identity, and even its very existence. It was nearly wiped out during World War Two: a quarter of the population was killed, and in the capital city barely a single building was left standing. But the survivors rebuilt the country almost from scratch, and their stoicism in the face of disaster holds them in good stead for the difficult times of today.

For many people Belarus is a blank space on the map of Europe. About the same size as Great Britain, the country is no great beauty, consisting largely of rolling plains. Belarus is a waterlogged land: there are more than 4,000 lakes, and marshy wetlands spread across most of the southern region. This is not a country to cross Europe for, but its proximity to the West make it an easily accessible place in which to sample what life is like in a former Soviet republic.

CLIMATE

Belarus has a continental climate. Although the average winter temperature is −6°C/20°F, this disguises lows of up to −25°C/−13°F in January. The best time to visit is perhaps spring, when the countryside is at its most verdant. The average summer temperature is 18°C/65°F, though temperatures rise to around 30-35°C/86-95°F for a couple of weeks in July. In late summer and autumn it rains heavily.

HISTORY

The history of Belarus has been dictated largely by the different forces around it. At one time or another it has been ruled by Poles, Lithuanians, Russians and Germans. In the ninth century, the area became part of the great Kievan Rus, one of the most powerful trading and cultural entities in Europe. The union disintegrated in 1240 and Belarus was gradually absorbed into the Grand Duchy of Lithuania, within which it enjoyed a relatively high degree of autonomy. This later diminished when Lithuania entered into political union with Poland in 1569. Polish influence succeeded in bringing the Belarusian Orthodox Church under the authority of the Vatican with the creation of the Uniate Church.

In the late 18th century, the Polish-Lithuanian Commonwealth collapsed and Belarus fell into the hands of the Russian tsars. There followed a massive crackdown on the Uniate Church, but the cultural and religious attachment with Poland lived on, particularly among the aristocracy. Despite the tsars' policy of Russification, by the end of the 19th century the idea of a distinct Belarusian identity had crystallised among intellectuals.

A revolutionary movement in the early part of the 20th century culminated in the proclamation of the Belarusian Democratic Republic in 1918, but a brief period of independence was crushed by a Polish invasion in the following year. With the end of the Russo-Polish War in 1921 came the peace settlement, which placed about 3.5 million Belarusians under Polish sovereignty. A brutal process of Polonisation followed. In contrast, the Belarusians living in the eastern half of the country, which was incorporated into the new Soviet Republic, enjoyed a renaissance of their own culture through most of the 1920s. This revival came to an abrupt end with the rise of Stalin. The Belarusian Soviet Socialist Republic was particularly badly hit by the purges, when first intellectuals and then hundreds of thousands of ordinary people disappeared overnight.

The Molotov-Ribbentrop pact between Stalin and Hitler in 1939 led to the reunification of Belarus under Soviet control, but in 1941 the German armies swept eastwards and gained control of the new republic. The campaign was fierce and by the time it was liberated, the country had been devastated: most Belarusian cities had been razed to the ground.

The country's wartime experiences were pivotal in the country's development over the next 40 years. After 1945, Soviet leaders set out to construct a model society in Belarus out of the ashes left by the war. The city of Minsk is still a prime example of Stalin-era architectural planning and social engineering. A traditionally agricultural nation, Belarus underwent rapid urbanisation and 'proletarianisation'. These processes went hand in hand with linguistic and cultural Russification. Belarus seems to have enjoyed the best standard of living in the former Soviet Union.

Following the entry of Mikhail Gorabachev into the political arena, several events turned vague nationalist sentiments into something more concrete. The first was the discovery of a mass grave of an estimated 100,000 victims of Stalin. The authorities' inept handling of the protest led to what is now referred to as 'Black Sunday', when tear gas was used against demonstrators at the mass grave. The Chernobyl accident in 1986 catalysed the movement still further: Chernobyl lies just eight miles/12km south of the Belarusian border and prevailing winds carried the heaviest radioactive releases into the republic. Calculated misinformation spread by the government was exposed by the Popular Front, a political organistion formed in 1988. Multi-party elections took place in spring 1990, and the Popular Front managed to gain 16% of the votes in the Supreme Soviet.

Belarus declared its state sovereignty on 27 July 1990, becoming the third Soviet Republic to do so after Russia and Ukraine, and in the following year declared its political and economic independence from the USSR. Belarus participated in the talks which led to the creation of the CIS. The selection of Minsk as the union's coordinating centre was a touch bizarre, given its location at the western extreme of the CIS, but solved the problem that neither Russia nor Ukraine would countenance the centre in the other's country. The Belarusian authorities are firm advocates of a reintegration of the former Soviet republics.

THE PEOPLE

It wasn't until 1979 that Belarus recovered from the devastation wreaked by the Nazis and regained its pre-war population level. According to a 1989 survey, ethnic Belarusians make up 78% of the population, Russians 13%, Poles 4%, Ukrainians 3% and Jews 1%, while more than two million Belarusians live in other former Soviet republics, primarily Russia.

Belarus has a tradition of tolerance and its Declaration of Sovereignty stressed that 'citizens of all nationalities constitute the Belarusian people'. Minority languages are positively encouraged, and the nationalism found in other republics finds little support here.

LANGUAGE

About 90% of Belarusians are fluent in their own language, with 80% also fluent in Russian. Belarusian is a Slavic language with strong similarities to Polish and Ukrainian, but an even stronger similarity to Russian. It uses the Cyrillic alphabet but has one extra letter, 'i'. The spelling of Belarusian is more phonetic than Russian, with the Russian 'o' becoming an 'a' in Belarusian.

Air. Belarus has its own international airline, Belavia, but its flight network cannot be decribed as extensive. Until recently, the only service was from Minsk to New York, though in 1995 twice-weekly flights between London Gatwick and Minsk began. The number of connections with western Europe on other airlines is increasing more rapidly. International airlines operating to Minsk include Lufthansa from Munich, Austrian Airlines from Vienna, Lot Polish Airlines from Warsaw and Transaero from Moscow. The agents listed on page 14 should be able to offer good fares.

Rail. The Berlin-Moscow express runs through Poland, crossing into Belarus at Brest, and then continues east via Minsk, Borisov and Smolensk. There are also links to the Baltic states and Ukraine. British Rail International (0171-834 2345) sells tickets for a direct train from the Hook of Holland to Minsk (part of the London-Moscow service), but the return fare is more expensive than the cheapest return flight.

Bus. Cheap bus services from the UK to various points in Poland make this a good option for reaching Belarus. Bus services continue from Warsaw (and arrive from Moscow and the Baltic states), but the trains are as cheap and infinitely more comfortable as a means of making the final approach to Minsk.

Car. Belarus lies at an important crossroads in eastern Europe. The country is crossed by three major roads: the M1, connecting Brest on the Polish border to Moscow; the M20, which runs north-south linking Riga, Vitebsk and Kiev; and the M13, which runs along the southern border from Brest eastwards into Russia. In addition, the M12 links Minsk to Vilnius and other Lithuanian cities. If you are travelling by car be prepared for a preposterously long wait at the border. Small-time traders driving cars stuffed with cheap cigarettes, alchohol and produce create huge tailbacks at the border crossings

See the general introduction for a list of the documents you should carry with you.

Visas. All foreign nationals entering Belarus require a visa. The London consulate charges £20 for both transit and tourist visas, and can issue them within three working days. The difficult part is obtaining the required letter of invitation. If you don't have friends inside the republic, there are two ways to obtain one. The first is to pay a visa shop such as Action Visas (0171-388 4498) in London; the second is to use Intourist (0171-538 8600) which, for a £20 service charge plus the price of the visa, will organise everything for you. You are supposed to pre-book accommodation with them, but this rule is not always enforced.

It is possible to buy a transit visa at the border, though it is likely to be expensive — $50 was being demanded from people arriving from Poland or Russia in 1995. The concession that anyone with a Russian visa is entitled to enter the country and stay for 48 hours appears to have been permanently withdrawn. Note that it is possible to cross Belarusian territory from Lithuania into Poland without a visa, so long as you travel on a direct international train.

You can extend your visa at the Ministry of Foreign Affairs in Minsk (ul Lenina; 27-29-47).

The addresses of Belarusian embassies and consulates abroad are as follows:

Germany: 56/61 Unterden Linden 10117 Berlin (229-95-94).
Lithuania: 8 Klima, Vilnius (66-88-99).
Poland: 67 Atenska, Warsaw (17-39-54).
Russia: 17 Maroseika, Moscow (324-70-31).
Ukraine: 8 Kutusov, Kiev (294-80-06).
UK: 1 St Stephen's Crescent, London W2 5QT (0171-221 3941).
USA: 1619 New Hampshire Avenue, NW Washington DC 20009 (986-16-04).

In 1992 Belarus introduced its own currency, the Belarusian Rouble. It is usually known by its unofficial name, the zaichik, or 'rabbit', in reference to the engraving on the one rouble note — or perhaps because of its renowned reproductive ability. Regardless of talk that the Russian rouble may be reintroduced, the most sought-after currency is still the dollar, followed closely by the Deutschmark.

Cash can be exchanged either in banks or at unofficial change points (the latter usually in the form of kiosks). It is possible to cash travellers' cheques in Minsk, but don't count on it anywhere else.

There is a thriving black market in Belarus, though it is more grey than the colour of pitch. The authorities seem to turn a blind eye to the unofficial exchange kiosks, which offer better rates of exchange than the banks. If the Russian rouble is reintroduced, however, there will almost certainly be a clampdown. Travelling to or from Poland, beware of crooks passing off old zloties — the Polish currency was revalued by a factor of 4,000 in 1995.

Telephone. Communications in and out of Belarus are notoriously unreliable. Calls within cities from public phones are free simply because there are no coins. To make an inter-city or international call, you must go to a telegraph office. Belarus is in the same time zone as Moscow, three hours ahead of GMT.

Media. The Belarusian government maintains a complete monopoly of national broadcasting and controls 80% of total press distribution. The authorities deny that censorship exists, but since late 1992 there have been no independent television or radio channels in Belarus. The main national newspapers are *Zvyozda* (in Belarusian) and *Sovyetskaya Belorussiya* (Soviet Byelorussia). Russia Federation newpapers such as *Izvestia* are widely available and popular.

Getting Around

Air. Although each of the six regions (or *oblasts*) has its own airport, a shortage of fuel means that domestic flights are both expensive and services erratic. The time spent trying to buy a ticket would probably be better spent travelling by train. You are also likely to be safer.

Rail. Trains offer much the best possibility for getting around the country. The rail network is extensive and the trains are not only comfortable but also highly sociable. On intercity trains there are three classes of accommodation. The most expensive is a two-berth compartment referred to as 'Lux', half the price and equally comfortable is a four-berth compartment referred to as 'coupe'. If you ask simply for a *bilyet* (ticket), it will be assumed that you want a bunk in hard class — open-plan carriages with harder and narrower bunks.

Buying tickets: foreigners are no longer required to buy their tickets through Intourist. This means that although fares are now much cheaper for tourists, obtaining a ticket is more difficult. First of all you need to locate the right ticket office before you start queuing (the names of the destinations it serves are written above in Cyrillic), then you must wait. If you're told the train is fully booked, this usually means that all tickets have been sold to touts, large quantities of whom you will find hanging around the entrance. For a premium they can get you a ticket to wherever you want to go. Finally, if all else fails, turn up at the train station and approach a *provodnik* or carriage attendant: for dollars they will almost certainly find you a seat on the train.

Bus. Buses are not nearly as comfortable as trains and only really worth taking if you fail to find a train ticket or if your destination is not on the rail network.

Car. The surfaces along the main roads are generally good: the Minsk-Brest dual carriageway is one of the best roads in the former Soviet Union. Signs on highways are given in Cyrillic and Roman script.

Belarus is still receiving cheap fuel from Russia, so the availability of petrol is not generally a problem — though supplies are more reliable at petrol stations accepting hard currency. Quality is not always good since as yet there are no Western service stations in Belarus.

International car hire companies now have outlets in Minsk, where you can hire a Western car for Western prices. If you have a credit card, this could be your one chance to use it. See *Minsk* for addresses.

Accommodation

You won't find a great array of cheap accommodation in Belarus. Tourism has yet to make much of an impact on the country and most hotels are busy chasing the businessmen who have begun to arrive with company chargecards. As in other republics in the CIS, private accommodation is best from every point of view — price and comfort not the least of them.

Eating and Drinking

Food is a serious business in Belarus, and if you are invited into somebody's home you are likely to be entertained in some style. Sadly, the same can not be said of most restaurants.

The cuisine, like the country, is a complex mix of influences: Russian, Lithuanian, Ukrainian and Jewish traditions have all left their mark. Meat and particularly pork is the central element in most dishes, and predominant flavourings include garlic and caraway. Some local dishes include *mokanka* (a mixture of curd cheese, sour cream and buttermilk, onions and herbs, served with tomatoes and cucumbers as a first course) and *galushki* or *kletski* (dumplings). Belarusian apples, known as *antonovka*, are a favourite, especially when cooked. So too are mushrooms. Mushroom hunting is a very popular autumn activity, and traditional Belarusian cooking has always featured them prominently. It is therefore a particularly poignant legacy of the Chernobyl accident that mushrooms must now be avoided.

Drinking. Beer is usually available for hard currency and is mostly imported. Vodka on the other hand can often be bought with roubles, and is the more traditional accompaniment to meals. A local alternative to vodka is the famous Belovezhskaya Bitter, an infusion said to be made of over a hundred herbs.

MINSK

The knowledge that only one building was left standing after World War II may well make you approach Minsk with a degree of trepidation. The predominance of post-war Soviet architecture, while not a great selling point, is at least a source of historical interest. Minsk was conceived by Stalin as a showpiece designed to illustrate to the world how socialism could build a city from the ashes of Fascist destruction. Along with the high-rise tower blocks and factory chimneys, there are also wide treelined boulevards and well-planned public parks.

CITY LAYOUT

It is not just the streets of Minsk which look uniform, but also the very fabric of the city, which extends 10 miles/16km from both north to south and from east to west. The winding River Svisloch slices the city into two halves. Linking the two sides is Prospekt Skoriny, which forms part of the Brest-Moscow motorway and is very broad, very long and very straight. This is the busiest street in Minsk, full of shops, cinemas and cafés. It begins at Ploshchad Nezalejhnosty (Independence Square) in the southwest and runs northeastwards, crossing Central Square (Ploshchad Tsentralnaya) and Victory Square (Ploshchad Pobedy).

ARRIVAL AND DEPARTURE

Air. The city has two airports — Minsk 1 and Minsk 2. The first is right in the centre of town at the end of ulitsa Chkalova, a couple of miles south of Ploshchad Nezalejhnosty. This mostly serves the closer destinations within the CIS, and any domestic routes which may be operating. Minsk 2 opened in 1989 and is some 25 miles/40km east of the centre, off the Moscow-Brest motorway. You are well advised to try to catch one of the hourly buses into Minsk since taxi drivers charge anything from $50 to $100.

The addresses of the principal airline offices are as follows:

Belavia, Prospekt Masherova 19 (Hotel Yubileyna) and at Minsk 1 airport (25-02-31).

Lot, Prospekt Masherova 7 (26-66-28).
Lufthansa, Minsk-2 Airport (97-37-45).
Swissair/Austrian Airlines, Propekt Masherova 19 (76-89-70, 76-89-71).
Transaero, Prospekt Masherova 19 (26-92-33), Hotel Yubileyna.

Rail. The train station is in the town centre on Privoksalnaya ploshchad, just five minutes' walk south of Ploshchad Nezalejhnosty. There are two daily trains to and from Berlin (19 hours), ten a day to Moscow (10 hours), and about five a day to Warsaw (9-11 hours). There are also daily connections with Kiev (11 hours), St Petersburg (16 hours), Vilnius (4 hours), Riga (10 hours) and Tallinn (18 hours). You can book tickets at ul Chkalova 9 or Prospekt Skoriny 18 (both offices open 9am-6pm, closed Sundays), or else from the Intourist office at Prospekt Masherova 19 — where you won't have to wait so long but will have to pay in dollars.

Bus. There are two bus stations in Minsk. The Central Station or Tsentralny Autovokzal (ul Babruskaya 12; 27-37-25) serves most destinations within the former USSR, including Vilnius, Riga and Kaliningrad. The Eastern Station or Vostochny Autovokzal at ul Vanyeva 34 (48-58-21) serves mainly destinations to the west, including Warsaw.

Car. You can hire a car from Avis, which has one outlet at Minsk 2 Airport (97-34-86) and another at the Belarus Hotel (ul Starazouskaya 15; 39-16-13). Europcar has a branch at Prospekt Masherova 11 (23-87-16). Petrol is available for hard currency at ul Karastrayanova 10 and ul Samakhvalovichi 26.

CITY TRANSPORT

Minsk has a two-line metro system which is efficient and easy to use. It runs from 6am to 12.30am daily. Tokens are available from the cash desks at each entrance. Above ground, buses, trolleybuses and trams run from 5.30am to 1am. You can buy tickets from newpaper kiosks and these must be punched on board. Be prepared for a crush as all forms of transport are desperately overcrowded.

You can order a taxi by dialling 061; otherwise, stand in the street, stick out your arm and see who stops first. State taxis, yellow or grey Volgas, are the least likely to overcharge you.

ACCOMMODATION

Three of Minsk's biggest hotels face each other across the river. Hotel Belarus (ul Starazouskaya 15; 39-17-05) is an enormous place on the east bank. All rooms have a bath or shower and TV and cost $30 (single) or $35 (double). On the opposite bank at Prospekt Masherova 19 is the Yubileyna Hotel (26-90-24) — not a pretty sight but the best place in town. Every room has satellite TV, and there is a sauna, hard currency bar and a pleasant terrace overlooking the river. Room rates are $53 (single), $63 (double) and $95 (luxury) both here and at the nearby Plancta (Prospekt Masherova 31; 22-85-87). This last hotel offers the same facilities, but is generally a gloomy place.

Set apart from the others is Hotel Minsk, Prospekt Skoriny 11 (20-01-32), near metro Ploshchad Nezalejhnosty. The central location is the best thing about this huge but very ordinary hotel. Single $30, double $35.

The Hotel and Excursion Bureau (Prospekt Skoriny 93; 96-54-69), near metro Park Chaluskintsev, can book the best-value rooms in town. Rates begin at around $10.

Camping. Minsk Motel and Campsite is 11 miles/18km southwest of Minsk on the Brest road (96-51-40), set in the middle of thick forest on the banks of the Ptich river. It is a complete holiday complex with a restaurant, bar, communal kitchen, post office and other services. Cottages can be rented for $3 per person, summer houses for $2 per person and tents for $1. The motel can organise skiing and sled rides during the winter.

EATING AND DRINKING

One of the most popular restaurants in Minsk is the Warsteiner Embassy at Nemiga 8 (near metro Nemiga). The food, consisting of a wide selection of traditional Belarusian dishes, is exellent but pricey, and you have to dress up: the no-jeans rule is strictly enforced. You'll also need to book to be sure of a table. Hard currency and credit cards only. From metro Nemiga, you can also explore the Trinity district (Troitskoe Predmestye), which is the best place in Minsk for bars, cafés and restaurants. At the Italian Restaurant off ulitsa Maksima Bogdanovicha, real Italian food is cooked by a real Italian chef.

Other places to try are the Steakhouse at Prospekt Masherova 13, which serves great steaks, and Uzbekistan (ul Kirova 25), which serves authentic Uzbeki food in a lively atmosphere and is popular with students and foreigners. Dinamo, at ul Daumana 23, is housed inside the enormous Dinamo stadium and is a great place to try good home-style Belarusian cooking. The food is cheap and tasty, and space is rarely a problem. Note that it closes at 9pm.

EXPLORING

Independence Square is a soulless place. It is dominated by the Belarusian parliament, housed in the largest building in Minsk, with the State University opposite. Heading northeast up Prospekt Skoriny (formerly Lenina), when you reach the GUM department store, turn left on to ulitsa Lenina and take the next right and then the first left. You will end up at Ploshchad Svobody, which is the centre of what is known as the old town. The medieval market place is now a concrete flyover, but there are a handful of pre-war churches and buildings left. Although they have been reconstructed, this is a pleasant area in which to stroll around. The twin towers belong to the Orthodox Cathedral, which is usually packed at evening mass. For a taste of how the city might once have looked, you'll find some attractive reconstructed wooden buildings from the 17th century across the river just west of Maksima Bogdanovicha, in the Trinity district.

Back on Prospekt Skoriny, just beyond GUM, the boulevard opens out into Tsentralnaya. If this square is not the heart of the city it is at least the hub. The northern side is dominated by the grand neoclassical façade of the Trade Union Culture Palace, behind which is the Museum of the Great Patriotic War (open 11am-7pm, closed Monday). The sheer size of the museum can be daunting (there are 25 rooms), but there are some fascinating exhibits, such as partisan leaflets printed on bark; and in the 'Black Hall' you can see a scaled-down reconstruction of the third largest concentration camp in Europe, which was located just outside of Minsk.

Prospekt Skoriny then crosses the river and leads down to Gorky Children's

Park, where local people come to relax. The street then opens out into Ploshchad Pobedy, dominated by a massive granite obelisk and an eternal flame, both dedicated to the heroes of World War II. A couple of miles further up is Park Cheluskintsev, accessible on the metro. The fun fair provides the best view of the city: from the top of the big wheel you can see for miles. You can also take a ride on the Children's Railway, which is run entirely by local youngsters. The nearby Botanical Gardens have about 90,000 different types of plants. The hot-houses are a good escape in the middle of winter with bananas, magnolia and orchids.

ENTERTAINMENT

The performing arts thrive in Minsk. Tickets for all performances can be bought from the central ticket office at Prospekt Skoriny 13, which is open 9am-7pm. The annual arts festival, the 'Belarusian Musical Autumn', is held in the last ten days of November.

The National Academic Opera and Ballet Theatre (ul Paskevic 23; 34-07-21) puts on all the usual favourites from *Giselle* to *The Nutcracker Suite*. Also look out for performances by the Capella Belarusian Choir and the Belarusian Folk Choir. Other theatres suitable for those without knowledge of Belarusian include the Theatre of Musical Comedy (ul Myasnikova 44) and the Puppet Theatre (ul Engelsa 20). At the State Circus (Prospekt Skoriny 32) you can see all the traditional tricks, not the least of which is Isabela Hentonova and her performing pink poodles.

Nightclubs. Most evening entertainment revolves around large amounts of vodka drunk at home. The most famous club in Minsk is Xantia, Krasnoarmeyskaya 3, Dom Offitserov (21-06-02), which leads a strange double life: by day it's a car showroom, by night it is allegedly the best disco between Warsaw and Moscow. Admission is free for women, $15 for men. For a more low-key evening, go to the Rendezvous at ulitsa Mayakovskaya 115. This is a restaurant-cum-bar, but with the added enticement of a cabaret. Admission $5.

Sport. Dinamo Minsk is a Premier League soccer team and you can catch a game in season at the stadium on ul. Kirova. The soccer competition during the 1980 Moscow Olympics was held here.

SHOPPING

Prospekt Skoriny is the best street for both window and actual shopping. Tsentralny, at no. 23, has recently been renovated by Italian investors and is now a Western-style supermarket. A hard currency shop inside stocks Italian delicacies, alcohol, toiletries and household items. Another good shop for browsing and stocking up on food and other essentials is Yubileynaya at ul Zaslavskaya 23, which opens 24 hours. The Nemiga store at Nemiga 8 sells Western goods for dollars and has a photo-processing department.

Prospekt Skoriny is also the best place to buy souvenirs. Local artists and craftsman display their work in the street and several shops, including the Mastatski Salon at no. 12 stock paintings and handicrafts. Lyanok, at no. 48, specialises in traditional Belarusian linen, such as patterned flax towels and table cloths, made by women in rural Belarus. Anyone in search of icons and communist memorabilia, should head to Soyuzdruk at ul Lenina 15.

At weekends Dinamo Stadium is taken over by a huge fleamarket where it is possible to buy just about anything from a bicycle to a video camera.

HELP AND INFORMATION

Tourist Information: Belintourist, next to Hotel Yubileyna (26-98-40), caters mainly for groups but organises numerous excursions which individual travellers should be able to join. There is an excursion bureau at Prospekt Skoriny 43 another information office opposite the train station on Privokzalnaya ploshchad.

Communications: the Central Post Office is at Prospekt Skoriny 10, open 8am-8pm. There is a telegraph office inside (open 7.30am-11pm) for calls within the CIS. To make an international call, go to the telegraph office at ul Surganova 24 (metro Akademia Nauk), open 10am-9.30pm. Local calls are free from any telephone box. The code for Minsk is 0172.

Embassies and consulates

Germany: ul Zakharova 26 (33-27-14).
Poland: ul Rumyantsava 6 (33-11-14).
UK: ul Zakharova 26 (33-07-52).
Ukraine: ul Kirova 17 (27-23-54).
USA: ul Staravilenskaya 48 (34-79-61).

KHATYN MEMORIAL COMPLEX

The Khatyn Memorial Complex, 35 miles/56km north of Minsk, was built in 1968 as a memorial to 185 villages destroyed by the Nazis during World War II. It stands on the site of a village which was burnt to the ground with all its 149 inhabitants in 1943. The complex is a place much visited by Belarusians. Day and night an eerie tolling of bells breaks the silence, and emotional music emanates from loudspeakers. At the centre of the site is a plateau with an eternal flame and three birch trees with an empty space where the fourth should be — a graphic representation of the one in four Belarusians who did not survive the war. Some say that the construction of the Khatyn memorial was ordered by Moscow to distract attention from Katyn in Russia, the site of a massacre of thousands of Polish officers in 1941.

There is no scheduled public transport to Khatyn, so unless you drive you must opt for an organised excursion.

BREST

Anyone travelling to or from Poland will have to make a special effort to avoid Brest. The city of 230,000 lies just a few miles from the border. It was here that in 1941 Operation Barbarossa got under way, during which German troops attacked the town and signalled the entrance of the Soviet Union into the war. Nowadays, Brest is under siege by small-time traders and smugglers. Shops are extraordinarily well-stocked and every weekend, the largest fleamarket in Belarus takes place on the outskirts of the town.

Brest has existed for over a millenium, but its attractiveness to invaders means that there are few reminders of its long past. The city's main sight is the 19th-century fortress situated in the outskirts and accessible on bus no. 12. Two Soviet regiments endured six weeks of bombardment by the Germans here in 1941, and you can still see pockmarks in the walls from the bullets and shelling. The fortress holds a memorial complex and a museum covering Brest's history since the mid-1800s. You can visit the fortress at any time; the museum opens 10am-6pm daily except Mondays.

Arrival and departure. Brest is the main border crossing for trains travelling to or from the CIS. There are frequent trains between Brest and Warsaw (4-6 hours) and Minsk (6-8 hours), with less frequent but regular ones to Moscow (13 hours), Kiev (12 hours) and Berlin (about 14 hours). If you're not on a through train and need to purchase an onward ticket, allow plenty of time: the queues can be enormous, and determined shoppers won't hesitate to elbow past you. After buying your ticket, you must pass through customs and immigration to get to the platform on the other side of the station. This can be even more time-consuming and crowded, as huge bales of goods and people are squeezed through a building which was not constructed with such a crowd in mind.

If travelling by car, you also need to allow plenty of time to cross the border.

Accommodation. If you have to stay overnight, choose either the Intourist Hotel (ul Moskovskaya 17; 5-10373), which charges $30 (single) and $50 (double) and has a passable restaurant; or Hotel Belarus at Shevchenko Bulvar 150, which is somewhat cheaper, charging $14 (single) and $26 (double).

Ukraine

Population: 52 million   **Capital:** Kiev (population 2.6 million)

Ukraine means 'borderlands' or 'edge', a rather accurate description of the marginal position it occupies in the European consciousness — a strange place for the biggest country in the continent. Known for well over a century as 'Little Russians', Ukrainians are struggling not only to assert an identity which is distinct from their Big Brother to the east, but also simply to survive.

According to a Russian proverb, while Moscow is the heart of Russia, and St Petersburg the head, Kiev is the Mother. But the Russians aren't mourning the loss of a parent; they are irked at having been left out of the will. From the old empire, Ukraine has inherited some of the prime pieces of real estate: the finest slice of the Black Sea Coast including Yalta, every Soviet's favourite beach resort, the Crimean and Carpathian mountain ranges and the cosmopolitan port of Odessa.

Change has been painful for Ukraine. The average monthly wage is one of the lowest in Europe, while the rate of inflation is among the highest. The fact that people are not starving is a tribute to their ingenuity rather than the government's performance. But as the first line of the national anthem points out, 'Ukraine is not dead yet'. Furthermore, it is one of the most fascinating destinations for travellers to the former Soviet Union, with a fine combination of natural beauty and culture.

GEOGRAPHY

Lying between Russia and the rest of Europe, Ukraine has always been of major strategic importance. It shares borders with an impressive list of countries: Russia, Poland, Hungary, the Slovak Republic, Romania, Moldova and Belarus, with the Black Sea lapping a a long stretch of its southern coast.

230

The black earth steppe in the central and eastern areas is highly fertile and Ukraine used to produce much of the former Soviet Union's grain. Heavy industry and coal reserves are concentrated in the east of the country in the Donbass region around Donetsk. There are two mountain ranges, the Carpathians in the west and the Crimean in the south.

CLIMATE

According to the official literature, Ukraine has a moderate continental climate with four distinct seasons. The icy winds and lows of –10°C/14°F which hit Kiev each February are anything but moderate. From November to March the temperature hovers around freezing, but can plunge much lower. From May to September the weather is warm, the average temperature in July being 20°C/68°F. The Black Sea coast has a sub-tropical climate with frost-free winters and sunshine most of the year.

HISTORY

Modern Ukraine was invented out of the geo-political chaos that followed World War I, a largely artificial creation that did not follow ethnic or religious divisions. For centuries the different regions that make up the country were incorporated into neighbouring empires obscuring any sense of a united Ukrainian identity. However, most Ukrainians view the principality of Kievan Rus that flourished between the ninth and thirteenth centuries as their true historical forebear.

Kievan Rus was an alliance of principalities which had grown rich from the trade moving up and down the rivers from the Baltic to the Black Sea. After the year 988 and the adoption of Christianity by Prince Vladimir, the region developed close relations with both the Byzantine Empire and Western Europe, becoming one of the most important trading and cultural entities in Europe. Kiev, its capital, is considered the cradle of both eastern Slavic and Russian civilisations, which goes some way towards explaining Russia's continuing attachment to Ukrainian soil.

In 1240, a wave of Tatar invaders from the East devastated Kievan Rus, leaving a power vacuum that was swiftly filled by the Poles and Lithuanians. Four centuries later, however, the Ukrainian Cossack armies drove the invaders from eastern and central Ukraine. Their leader, Bogdan Khmelnitsky, then succeeded in carving out a somewhat ambiguous niche in Ukrainian history by turning to the Russian tsar for help. The Treaty of Pereyaslav in 1654 pronounced the union of Ukraine with Russia and led to a long period of domination by the Russian Empire. It was not until the collapse of the empire in 1917 that there were attempts to form an independent Ukrainian state. This was overtaken by the revolutionary wave, however, and in 1922 Ukraine was incorporated into the USSR.

This is the story of just one part of the country. The western region of Ukraine enjoyed greater independence. In 1772, western Ukraine became part of the Habsburg Empire and after World War I was divided between Czechoslovakia and Poland. Home to the majority of ethnic Ukrainians and the powerhouse of the movement for Ukrainian autonomy, western Ukraine joined the Soviet republic only in 1939.

Ukraine was subjected to an aggressive campaign of 'Sovietisation'. Opposition to the forced collectivisation of agriculture in the 1930s was brutally quashed, by an artificially caused famine, the detail of which have come to light only in recent years. Estimates of the numbers of deaths vary from two to seven million. During World War II, the Ukrainians suffered further horrific losses. Post-war Ukraine was kept on a tight leash by Moscow, even after Stalin's death. A major change came in April 1986, when the explosion at Chernobyl made many ordinary people question the way that Soviet power was treating their country. With the demise of the USSR came massive popular support for an independent Ukraine, supported by around 90% of the population in a referendum in 1991.

Known as 'The Bread Basket of Europe', newly independent Ukraine confidently expected to achieve economic prosperity within a few years. Instead, Ukrainians have had to endure a severe economic crisis, with a currency that was almost worthless and average monthly incomes falling to just $10. More recently, however, it seems that the economic freefall may have slowed significantly, if not come to a halt. Given the country's fertile soil and huge industrial capacity, Ukraine should have a good chance of achieving stability in the future.

Chernobyl. While the world knows the name Chernobyl, it is Ukraine and Belarus which have to live with the consequences of the worst nuclear accident in history. On 26 April 1986, Reactor Number 4 exploded, releasing massive amounts of radiation into the atmosphere. Chernobyl lies only 50 miles/80km north of Kiev, but the capital was saved by the prevailing winds which were blowing north towards Belarus. The result was nonetheless catastrophic. Furthermore, government misinformation and an official policy which brought too little, too late, catalysed many people's desire for an independent Ukrainian state.

The workers inside the plant were placed under martial law and forbidden to leave. The mopping-up operation took months, as staff worked around the clock sacrificing their health and in many cases their lives to encase the core in a concrete blanket. A 20-mile/32-km exclusion zone has been established and a Ministry of Chernobyl set up, whose sole task has been to deal with the after-effects, spending an estimated 12-18% of total GDP. No consensus on the health consequences for the average Ukrainian exists, but there has been a substantial increase in the incidence of thyroid cancer and leukemia in children.

Despite international concerns for safety, reactors one and three are still in operation. With a severe energy crisis on its hands the government claims that it cannot afford to shut the complex down completely.

THE PEOPLE

Ukrainians account for 72% of the population and Russians 22%. There are also sizeable minorities of Jews, Belarusians, Moldovans, Bulgarians, Poles, Hungarians, Romanians, Tatars, Greeks and Armenians. Western Ukraine, home to the highest percentage of ethnic Ukrainians, was the region which most vehemently supported the idea of autonomy from Moscow. To some extent this has alienated people in other regions, who are wary of such nationalism — particularly in eastern areas, where most Russians live. In western Ukraine, the names of streets and squares have been quite systematically changed, while in central and eastern parts you will find that few changes have been made.

Despite the hard times, Ukrainians are an incredibly generous people and what little they have they will insist on sharing with you. Rather than risk offending someone by turning down their hospitality, bring a selection of presents with which you can show your appreciation. Ukrainians tel jokes about themselves and are generally more open than Russians, especially in the south where an abundance of sunshine, fresh fruit and good wines lends a Mediterranean warmth.

LANGUAGE

Ukrainian is a Slavic language with similarities to Russian, Polish and Czech. Like Russian, it uses the Cyrillic alphabet. Ukrainian has been the official language since independence, to the embarrassment of many politicians who are still struggling with its finer points. Street and shop signs in Kiev and the western region are mostly in Ukrainian, but Russian is still widely spoken. In eastern Ukraine and Crimea, Russian is the first language. The Ukrainian words listed below are written phonetically.

Useful Words and Phrases

Yes — *tak*

No — *nee*

Thank you — *dyakuyo*

Pardon — *probachteh*

I don't understand — *yah ne rozumeyou*

Do you speak English? — *chi veh rozmovliayeteh anhliskoyou movoyou?*

Hello — *dobry den*

Goodbye — *do pobachenya*

When? — *koly?*

Where? — *deh?*

How much? — *skilky?*

AIR

From London, there are daily flights to Kiev with SAS, Lufthansa and Austrian Airlines, and regular services on KLM and Finnair. Ukraine International operates several flights a week from Britain, three from Gatwick to Kiev and and one from Manchester to Lviv. The agents listed on page 14 should be able to offer good fares. At the time of writing the cheapest fare, with SAS, costs about £280 and allows an open-dated return. There are also direct flights from to Kiev from many central and eastern European cities, including Prague and Warsaw. Odessa is served by Austrian Airlines from Vienna.

TRAIN

Taking the train from countries within the former Eastern bloc is undoubtedly the best way to enter Ukraine, combining cheapness, comfort and conviviality. Trains from Prague, Vienna, Budapest and Bratislava all enter the country at Chop, 15 miles/24km south of Uzhgorod. You could be delayed here several hours while your train has its undercarriage changed (with the passengers still on board), to change from European to Soviet gauge. Trains from Bulgaria and Istanbul enter Ukraine at the Romanian border point of Vadul Siret. If you're coming from Berlin or Warsaw, bear in mind that as you now cross Belarus territory you are required to buy a Belarusian transit visa (See *Belarus: Red Tape*).

There are good direct links between Ukrainian cities and other places within the former USSR, including Moscow, St Petersburg, Minsk, Tashkent and Almaty.

BUS

There are international bus services to several destinations inside Ukraine from most neighbouring countries, but generally the trains are as cheap and infinitely more comfortable. The exceptions are buses from Istanbul, which are modern, fast and air-conditioned. There is also a direct service from London to Lviv in western Ukraine which represents the cheapest method if you're coming straight from England: see page 264.

BOAT

Unless you have chartered your own yacht or booked a cruise on the Black Sea, you are unlikely to approach Ukraine by boat. However, it is not impossible. Throughout the summer, the state-run Blasco company runs regular services between Odessa and Istanbul, Piraeus (for Athens), Port Said (Egypt) and Limassol in Cyprus (see *Odessa: Getting There*). Ships make chartered voyages even in winter — usually taking shoppers to Istanbul — and it is quite possible to hitch a ride. In Istanbul, the Odessa Restaurant in the port at Karakoy will broker some sort of deal for you.

CAR

See the general introduction for tips on how to prepare yourself and your car for a driving trip. Above all, make sure that your visa states that you will be travelling by car. Also be prepared for long queues at the border points as traders, legal and illegal, now clog every available exit. From Slovakia you enter the country along the E58, which runs from Košice via the border town of Vyšne Německé to Uzhgorod, the first Ukrainian town. From Hungary the border crossing is near the Hungarian town of Zakhon, a mile or so from the Ukrainian border town of Chop. Coming from the Romanian border town of Siret, you enter Ukraine at Porubnoye, 23 miles/ 37km south of Chernovtsy.

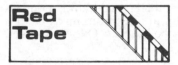

Red Tape

Visas. All foreigners travelling to Ukraine require a visa. Unless you are wealthy and/ or badly organised, get one in advance from a Ukrainian consulate abroad. To obtain a tourist visa, you are theoretically required to present an official invitation or a voucher, fax or receipt proving that you have pre-booked accommodation in Ukraine. However, in practice some consuls will issue a 30-day tourist visa with no questions asked provided you hand over the right number of dollar bills. The official price varies from $30-80, at the discretion of the individual consul; in summer 1995, the London consulate was charging £40, and £20 or £40 more if you wanted it more quickly than a week. Nobody is too sure of the rules anymore, and consuls can manipulate the rules according to whim.

Previously, you needed to list every town you intended to visit on your visa application form, and every hotel you stayed in would then register your presence with the local police station. The form has not changed, but in practice you will have no problems staying in a hotel in Odessa, for example, even if your visa is officially only for Kiev.

Intourist Travel (219 Marsh Wall, London E14 9FS; 0171-538 8600) can obtain Ukrainian visas without you having to prebook any accommodation. Acton Holidays (354 Uxbridge Road, London W3 9SL; 0181-896 1642), which runs a bus service from London to Lviv, can arrange an invitation for you for £15, and will process your visa application for a further £20 on top of the Ukrainians' fee.

If you arrive at the border (or airport) without a visa, it is unlikely you will be turned away, but you will have to pay an exorbitant fee to enter the country. Travellers arriving without a visa can pay a fee of $150, possibly the highest sum demanded anywhere in the world. Emergency visas, which have replaced transit visas, are usually valid for 24 hours and are in principle available at any border.

The addresses of Ukrainian embassies and consulates abroad are as follows:

Canada: 331 Metcalfe Sreet, Ottawa, Ontario (613-230-2961).
Germany: Wald Strasse 42, 53177 Bonn (31-21-39).
Poland: Ul-Szucha 7, 00-580 Warsaw (625-01-27).
Romania: Sector 1, Strada Rabat 1, Bucharest (312-4547).
Russia: ul Stanislavskoho 18, 103009 Moscow (229-1079).
UK: 78 Kensington Park Road, London W11 2PL (0171-727 6312); recorded
   visa information on 0891 515919, a premium-rate number.
USA: 3350 M Street, NW Washington DC 20036 (202-333-0606).

Visa extensions: if you decide to lengthen your stay, head to the nearest visa registration office (Ovir), and expect several hours if not several days of queueing before parting with an arbitrary sum in dollars and receiving yet another stamp in your passport. If you don't extend your visa, you may leave Ukraine unscathed, particularly if you exit via a former Soviet state. But the rules are getting tougher, and you could face a fine of up to $100.

Given the dismal state of the economy, foreign workers cannot expect to prosper in Ukraine. The shortfall of English teachers matches the shortages elsewhere in the country; one of the teaching placement organisations issues a list of suggested gifts to pack, and the first item is a stainless steel potato peeler. Several emigré organisations in the US recruit volunteer teachers; they warn that teachers do not live particularly well in Ukraine.

Ukrainian National Association, Inc, PO Box 17a, 30 Montgomery St, Jersey
   City, NJ 07303 (201-451-2200/fax 451-2093). This organisation sponsors
   an English-teaching programme for volunteers who stay for at least four
   weeks between May and August. Applicants from the US, Canada and
   Europe must pay a non-refundable application fee of $25.
Ukrainian-American Educational Exchange Association Inc, PO Box 116,
   Castle Creek, NY 13744 (tel/fax 607-648-2224). Volunteers receive a local
   teacher's salary, equivalent to about $5 a month, plus free accommodation
   and meals if staying with a host family. The program fee is $530.

An organisation based in the Ukraine which does the same thing for native English speakers of all nationalities is Mir-V-Mig, PO Box 1085, 310168 Kharkov (fax 572-22-76-14).

Ukraine's national currency, the coupon, is of scant more use than Monopoly money, costing more to print than it is actually worth: in late 1994, there were about 52,000 coupons to the dollar. Introduced in 1992, the coupon was intended to be only a temporary currency, to be replaced by something more solid when the economy stabilised. At one stage it seemed that this would never happen, but given the gradually improving financial situation, a new currency may indeed emerge. A measure of the coupon's present weakness, however, is that in Ukraine the Russian rouble is considered to be a hard currency.

Changing money. Ukraine is very much a cash economy. Travellers' cheques are accepted in only a few places, and you will simply have to carry large amounts of cash — i.e. dollars — around with you. The deutschmark is also popular, unlike pound sterling, which is much more difficult to change.

Do not change too much money at any one time, and check the number of zeros carefully as all the notes look very similar.

Credit cards. A few major hotels and hard currency stores accept credit cards, but on the whole they are of little use.

Black Market. Ukraine has a flourishing black economy, which is the only thing which saves many people from starvation. When changing money, you will inevitably find yourself using Ukraine's shadow economy. Banks are inconvenient and time-consuming, while kiosks, vans and booths of a semi-legal nature are everywhere: look out for signs saying *Obmen Valut*. Outside any public building, such as a railway station or department store, individuals hang around offering to change money. They either carry a piece of cardboard with a dollar sign, or will be fingering wads of ready cash. They are usually reliable, but make sure that you have the coupons in your hand before handing over the dollars.

Telephone. As the government can no longer afford to mint coins, local calls made from public payphones are free. To use inter-city (*mezhdygorod*) payphones, you need to buy jetons from the nearest post office (*pochta*). Phoning abroad is best done from a post or telegraph office, or from your hotel room. In both cases, you need to book the call in advance and then wait for the connection, which may take several hours or not arrive at all. If you have access to a private telephone, you can call direct to almost anywhere in the world — but be prepared to try, try and try again.

If you're calling Ukraine from the UK, the codes have remained unchanged since the break-up of the Soviet Union: dial 010 followed by 7 and then the city code, e.g. 044 for Kiev, 0322 for Lviv and 0482 for Odessa.

Time: with independence, Ukraine decided to mark its difference from Moscow by entering a different time zone, moving its clocks forward an hour. It is now GMT +2 hours. Crimea, however, decided to play the same game and voted to return to Moscow time, making it GMT +3 hours.

Mail. Post office opening hours are usually 9am-6pm every day of the week. Stamps even for international letters are absurdly cheap, which is just as well as there is a strong chance they will never reach their destination.

THE MEDIA

Newspapers. The failed coup in Moscow finally succeeded in breaking the stranglehold upon the press, but even before this hundreds of anti-communist papers had begun to appear. The first mass circulation newspaper was *Za Vilnu Ukrainu* (For a Free Ukraine). Many communist newspapers disappeared, changed their names and came back on the scene, including *Radyanska Ukraina* (Soviet Ukraine), which has returned rather unconvincingly as *Demokratychna Ukraina* (Democratic Ukraine). Although the political control has gone, rising printing costs and paper shortages have forced many new independents out of the market.

Kiev is the only city where foreign newspapers are easily available. The *International Guardian* is on sale at about 6pm on the day of publication in the Nika Bar (see page 246).

Television. Depending on where you are in Ukraine, you can receive up to seven TV stations. Channel 7 broadcasts CNN news in English twice a day. Several channels specialise in broadcasting pirated American videos (dubbed).

Air. Air Ukraine operates services from Kiev to Kharkiv, Lviv, Odessa and Simferopol. The cost of these flights for foreigners is about $90 one way, regardless of destination. The planes most often used on domestic routes are the propeller-driven Russian Antonovs.

Rail. One of the most best legacies of the Soviet era is the extensive rail network, which connects most cities in Ukraine. For just a few dollars you can buy a ticket which will not only get you to your destination but will give you a bed for the night, clean sheets, hot water in the samovar to make tea, and, as often as not, companions who will invite you to share their picnic, life story and bottle of vodka. Even if you're not hungry, it's worth taking provisions with you to be able to reciprocate hospitality.

On local trains only one class of travel exists: wooden benches. For longer train journeys, there are three classes: lux, a two-berth compartment; coupe, a four-berth compartment; and hard class (*platskarta*), open carriages where seated accommodation turns into narrow, multi-storied bunk-beds at night. Lux is available only on some trains. The best option for comfort combined with sociability is coupé. You'll need about a $0.50 in coupons to pay for bedding once you're on board the train.

Buying tickets: the old rules no longer apply when it comes to buying train tickets. It is not only the prices that are now the same for both Ukrainians and foreigners — also the availability and the queues. Buying a ticket can be a frustrating process, as lines are long, move slowly and the cashier will inevitably slam down the shutters when it is your turn next. Check the writing above the booth to establish not only which destinations it serves, but also at what time the next break is scheduled. An alternative is to use a tout: in some situations it is unavoidable since they are perfectly capable of buying up all the seats on the train. Don't worry about finding them, they'll find you.

Bus. Buses cover most of the country but the distances involved in getting around usually make the trains a much better bet.

Cycling. The condition of the roads together with the bad behaviour of motorists in Ukraine can be off-putting for cyclists. Probably the best place to cycle is the Crimea, where the national cycling team trains. The roads are some of the best in the country, and as long as you avoid the main highways, this is an excellent means of exploring the region.

DRIVING

You are free to drive where you please in Ukraine, although the erratic supply of petrol outside Kiev may restrict your mobility. Petrol stations tend to be few and far between, so fill your tank when you find one. High octane fuel is now widely available.

On main highways, signs are in both the Cyrillic and Roman script. If you're heading off the beaten track, it is worthwhile mastering enough Cyrillic to know where you're going.

Rules and regulations. In cities, the speed limit is 60km/h (37mph) and 90km/h (56mph) on highways. The percentage of alcohol to blood allowed is a non-negotiable 0%. Seat belts should be worn at all times. Traffic coming from the right has the right of way, as do trams coming from any direction.

Ukrainians drive in much the same way as their Russian neighbours. The faster your car the faster you drive — which, with the increasing numbers of BMWs on the road, can be very fast indeed. Police checks are frequent but designed not so much to enforce safety regulations as to augment the meagre salaries of police officers. You can try disputing the alleged offence, but since everyone knows that this is not the real issue, you would do better to try to simply drive the price down. All fines (*shtraf*) are payable on the spot.

Ukrainian women don't seem to drive at all, so if you're female expect attention from boy-racers and traffic cops alike.

Parking. Many parking places within cities are regulated by heavily-armed security men, and if you're driving a private car it can be in your own interests to pay out for protection. In remoter places, little boys have learnt the same trick and have taken to demanding money to 'protect' your car from the possibility of them vandalising it.

Car hire. In Kiev, cars can be hired from the major hotels and from a handful of agencies. In other cities, you may get your hands on an antiquated Lada if someone at the hotel service bureau happens to own one. In some places you won't be able to hire a car without a driver. If this is the case, you may find it cheaper to negoatiate an hourly price with a taxi driver.

CITY TRANSPORT

Most cities are served by a combination of trams, buses and trolley-buses. The standard single fare is so low that it's not possible to convert it into Western currency. Paper tickets come in strips of ten and can be bought from the driver or at a kiosk close to the stop. You need to punch one when you board for every trip you take. Kiev and Kharkiv both have spotless metro systems, for which you buy jetons at the station entrance.

Taxis. Ukraine is a nation either of hitch-hikers or of taxi-drivers, depending upon your point of view. To catch a cab, stick out your hand and wait for a car, any car, to stop. Tell them your destination, which they may or may not agree to, and fix a price. A few people may try and overcharge you because you're a foreigner, but the system generally works very well. There are also state taxis, usually Volgas, which have an official meter. This calculates a price in roubles, however, and bears no relation whatsoever to the price you'll be charged. You shouldn't pay more than one or two dollars for most journeys. Be wary of the taxis at any of the airports, where drivers are used to fleecing foreigners.

Hotels. Hotel accommodation in Ukraine ranges from the uninspiring to the unappealing, and neither is cheap. The situation has improved little since independence and finding a room is likely to be the biggest blow to any budget. You can try your luck with the cheaper hotels which used to cater solely for Soviet citizens, but many are still staffed by the old guard who tend to view foreigners at best with suspicion and at worst with hostility.

Private accommodation. There are no longer restrictions against people lodging foreigners in their flats, and this definitely provides the most comfortable and interesting option. Finding a host is not a problem in places commonly visited by tourists, such as the Black Sea coast, but elsewhere you may have to hunt around. The average nightly price is about $5, and you can usually negotiate a price for meals if you want to try some home cooking.

Camping. Most cities have a campsite a few miles from the city centre, but the quality and range of facilities vary enormously. Most, however, do have some sort of chalets or sited tents which you can rent for the night if you don't have your own gear. Travellers have reported pitching a tent outside official sites without any hassle.

Ukrainian specialities. Ukrainian cooking has close ties with the cuisine of its neighbours, and Polish, Slovak and Russian influences have all left their mark. It is hearty peasant fare, designed to fill you up and keep you warm rather than set your tastebuds on fire. Gastronomically, summer is the best season, when fresh fruit and vegetables are abundant. In winter, vegetables are prohibitively expensive and you'll come across a lot of pickles.

Ukraine is the original home of *borshch*, the thick soup popular both here and in Russia. The only two staple ingredients are beetroot and soured cream, and the variations are numerous. Beetroot is also used in a casserole known as *vereshchaka*, in which the other main ingredient is pork. The Ukrainian form of the dumpling is the *vareniki*, which can be filled with meat, potato or, most frequently, with sweetened curd cheese. *Galushki* and *pampushki* are less popular variations on the dumpling. *Cotlet po Kievsky* is chicken with garlic, and bears no relation to what we in the West call Chicken Kiev. *Drachena* is similar to an omelette and usually fairly tasty. Sweets to look out for include *bubliki*, small rings of choux pastry; *kvorost*, a deep-fried doughnut plait; and *medivynk*, a spicy honey cake. The most popular type of bread is made from a mixture of rye and wheat and is chewy and flavoursome.

Restaurants. Despite food shortages, there is no lack of good restaurants in Ukraine, and Lviv has arguably the best restaurant in the whole of the former Soviet Union. Many restaurants accept payment in either dollars or coupons. If the menu is priced in coupons count the zeroes carefully, as the five portions of caviar you have just eaten could easily turn out to be priced at $10 each rather than $1.

Menus can be in Ukrainian or Russian and may not be as extensive as they first seem. The standard procedure is for the chef to list every thing he would like to make in a perfect world. The waiter or waitress will tell you what exactly is available on the day. The most important part of the meal, and the course with the most extensive choice, is the starter or *zakuski*. It's usual to order two or even three. Several salads are frequently on offer as are selections of cold cuts, cheese and caviar. *Griby s smetanoi*, mushrooms in a thick creamy sauce, is a Ukrainian speciality. The main courses offer less variety — often just *myaso* or meat, which will probably be beef or pork.

Restaurants tend to close early, and in many places you'll be pushed to find any food at all after 10pm. In the newer swankier places, you are expected to dress up a bit. It is also standard for restaurants to have some sort of entertainment, from an electric organ to an energetic floorshow. After a few vodkas people will not only get up and dance, they may well ask you to dance too.

Vegetarians. Not eating meat is a concept that is almost unheard of in Ukraine, but menus usually include several meatless starters including cheese, salads and often mushroom soup. *Vareniki* dumplings filled with cheese are bland but ubiquitous, and a good standby. In summer, it is possible to eat well by shopping in markets, where you will find an excellent supply of fresh fruit and vegetables — much of which is organically grown.

DRINKING

As in Russia, drinking in Ukraine is both an essential part of hospitality and a national sport. Vodka is still the most popular tipple and is usually drunk neat. Pepper vodka is a Ukrainian speciality and an acquired taste. Sickly imported liqueurs are also gaining in popularity, especially Polish cherry liqueur and Amaretto. In bars and restaurants, vodka is served in 100-gram shots; you can buy bottles from state grocery shops (*gastronoms*) and slightly more expensively in kiosks. Be warned, however, that much of what is sold is reputed to be *falsificatsia* — lethal home-produced moonshine. A litre costs about $2.

Most beer available from kiosks and restaurants is imported. Ukrainian-produced beer is sold from tin trucks by the side of the road, poured directly into paper cups.

Wine. Crimean wines are considered to be some of the best in the former Soviet Union, though sadly the most-praised Massandran wines are rarely available. Both reds and whites tend to be very sweet. Crimean champagne is almost unbearably sweet, though the Novy Svet label is better than most. Champagne labelled simply 'Ukrainian' or 'Sovietsky' is slightly dryer but still sickly. If imported wines are sold in a restaurant, they will be suitably expensive.

Hiking. With the Crimean and Carpathian mountains, Ukraine has two wild open spaces that are ideal for hiking. There are no longer any restrictions on where you go, but you'll need to bring your own equipment, and stock up on food in a city. Maps could be your biggest problem and you're probably better off trying to find one before you leave home. A book giving extensive coverage of routes in Crimea is *Trekking in Russia and Central Asia*, by Frith Maier and published by Cordee Press; do not be put off by the misleading title.

Beaches. Ukraine has been decidedly lucky in inheriting the best beaches in the former Soviet Union. The Black Sea is in fact a deep blue colour and is moderately clean, though not everywhere. By June the water heats up to a comfortable 20°C/68°F, although it is at its warmest in October, when it reaches about 25°C/77°F. Beaches in Crimea tend to be narrow, shingle and crowded, while Odessa has some fine sandy stretches. Nudity is probably no longer illegal but few women go topless.

Most entertaining takes place in other peoples houses, where you'll find that despite hyper-inflation and economic collapse, Ukrainians will still pull out all the stops when they have a guest. You'll be expected to eat and drink and quite possibly even sing or dance. If you want to take a present, flowers and alcohol go down well. Outside the home, high culture is very good and very cheap, and low culture very bad and very expensive.

The largest cities have their own opera and ballet companies. Standards are generally high and the seats cheap. Puppet shows draw big crowds and are often very good, as are the circuses: both bypass the language barrier.

Unless your Russian or Ukrainian is very good you won't get much joy from going to the cinema. Films tend to be extrememly badly dubbed, often with one voice taking all the parts.

SPORT

Football is a national obsession, although the country has yet to make much of an impact on the international scene. Nonetheless, most major towns have a huge stadium and the turn-out is usually high.

The Soviet Olympic machine produced some fine gymnasts and Ukraine participates at the highest level. The World Championships produced a winner in 1994, although it took the organisers a good 20 minutes to locate the Ukrainian national anthem for the medal ceremony.

The most popular sport of recent times is gambling. Casinos have appeared everywhere and are the favourite hang-out of the new business elite. Most places take dollars only, although they may also have a coupon table where it is quite possible to win a million. The smart accessory is a personal bodyguard.

People don't go to Ukraine to shop but there is some scope for buying souvenirs. Caviar is still a bargain, at about $5 a tin, although you'll have problems finding it outside Kiev and Odessa. Check the sell-by date and try to keep it in a cool place. Outdoor vendors sell hand-made tablecloths, folkloric shirts and ceramics. Champagne and vodka are possible gifts and they're easy to find in state gastronoms and kiosks. Matrioshka dolls are also widely available, although most of them are made in Russia, not Ukraine.

Most major towns and cities have huge fleamarkets where imported (usually illegally) goods are on sale. Much of it comes from Turkey — most noticeably clothes and chocolate — but you'll also find Italian shoes, German electronics and Polish medicines.

Tobacco. If you're trying to give up smoking, Ukraine is not the place to go. Not only does everybody smoke, but Ukraine is also home to the cheapest cigarettes in Europe. A pack of 200 Marlboro costs about $3 in Odessa.

Health and Hygiene

If you're worried by Chernobyl, the good news is that unless you decide to pitch a tent in the northern section of the Zhytomir Oblast, the area worst affected by the nuclear disaster, the risks are minimal. The US Embassy in Kiev reports that background levels of radiation are now normal in the capital, although it also recommends avoiding water, fish and mushrooms. The latter are especially susceptible to radioactivity, but they are also a staple ingredient of Ukrainian cooking and are eaten regardless.

Crime and Safety

Crime is on the rise in Ukraine but it has not yet reached the level of that in Russia. Take sensible precautions, and call the Foreign Office Advice Line (0171-270 4129) or check the latest State Department travel advisory on CompuServe.

Help and Information

Tourist Information. The Intourist Travel information hotline in the UK (0891-516951) is a reasonable source of information on Kiev, but not for other Ukrainian destinations on the whole. In the country itself, the main Intourist hotels (which may well soon be renamed) usually house an Intourist Service Bureau. This can be useful for booking train or plane tickets, but do not expect the staff to be of much other help.

KIEV

It is unfair that Kiev is best known for a chicken dish which wasn't even invented here. The city which gave birth to the Eastern Orthodox church is a surprisingly handsome capital given its history. The Nazis destroyed about 80% of the houses during World War II, but the scars are not obvious. The golden domes of numerous churches pepper the skyline. Ancient monuments have been lovingly restored, and although the standard Soviet eyesores exist, they have largely been confined to the suburbs. Compared with the tawdriness of Moscow and the cool austerity of St Petersburg, Kiev possesses a quiet dignity.

Kiev was founded in the fifth century. In the ninth it became the capital of Kievan-Rus and, following the official conversion of the state to Christianity, grew quickly: by the 11th century it had 400 churches and 100,000 inhabitants. Sacked by the Tatars and controlled at various points by Poles, Russians and Lithuanians, the city's path back to fame came in 1934, when it replaced Kharkiv as the state capital.

As capital of an independent Ukraine, Kiev has been given a new lease of life. Local entrepreneurs flaunt their winnings in fancy foreign cars and designer suits; new ventures have sprung up to cater to the tastes and the wallets of the new class of foreign diplomats; and Western consumer goods fill the markets. Meanwhile, the vast majority are barely managing to eke out an existence on their devalued wages. Although much has changed, much has also stayed the same. Kiev still bears the hallmarks of a Soviet rather than a Ukrainian city: Lenin sits undisturbed in the centre of town, and fewer streets than in many other ex-Soviet cities have been renamed.

CITY LAYOUT

The vast River Dnepr flows through the centre of the city, dividing Kiev into two easy pieces. All the places of historic interest are on the right bank, the left bank consisting largely of post-war tower blocks. The city's main artery, running from Bessarabsky Market (Bessarabsky Rynok) to the Dinamo football stadium near the river, is vulitsa Kreshchatik, a broad boulevard that is home to a fair proportion of Kiev's shops, hotels and restaurants. Vulitsa Volodmirska, which runs parallel to the west, is the main street through Old Kiev (Stary Kiev).

The only up-to-date map of Kiev currently available is in Hungarian and hard to find.

ARRIVAL AND DEPARTURE

Air. Boryspil airport, 25 miles/40km east of the city, caters for both international and domestic flights. There are direct flights from most cities in Western Europe and the former Soviet Union, including three services weekly from London Gatwick on Ukraine International.

Buses run to the Air Ukraine office on Ploshcha Peremohy, at the western end of bulvar Shevchenka. Since services are irregular, however, you may be forced to take a taxi, which will set you back at least $20.

Jhulianny Airport, 7 miles/11km west of the city, serves domestic destinations only. Trolleybus 9 will take you to and from Ploshcha Peremohy, or a taxi should cost no more than $5.

Airline offices:

Air Ukraine, Karla Marxa 4 and Dmytrivska 1 (224-05-01).
Air Ukraine International, Prospekt Peremohy 14 (216-67-30) and Hospitalna 12 (224-29-50).
Transaero, Pushkinska 14; Prospekt Peremohy 4; and inside the Kievska Hotel at Hospitalna 12 (292-75-13).
KLM, Horkovo 102 (268-90-23 or, at the airport, 296-78-64).
Lufthansa, Hotel Kreshchatik, Kreshchatik 14 (229-69-97).
SAS, Chernoarmyiska 9/2 (224-35-40 to 42).

Rail. The main station is at the end of vulitsa Kominterna (Metro Vokzalnaya), just south of bulvar Shevchenka. Unlike other cities in the former Soviet Union, like Moscow and St Petersburg, Kiev has only a single main terminus. It is therefore the biggest and busiest station in the whole of the old USSR, and initially overwhelming.

There are daily trains to all cities in Ukraine including Lviv (18 hours), Simferopol (18 hours), Kharkiv (10 hours) and Odessa (11 hours). There is a fast daily train to Moscow (13 hours), a sluggish one to St Petersburg (33 hours), and other services to European destinations including Prague (34 hours), Berlin (25 hours) and Minsk (12 hours). Tickets can be bought at the central office at Shevchenka 38, but the queues can be long. However, there are always people trying to sell spare tickets and touts who can get you a ticket to anywhere for a price.

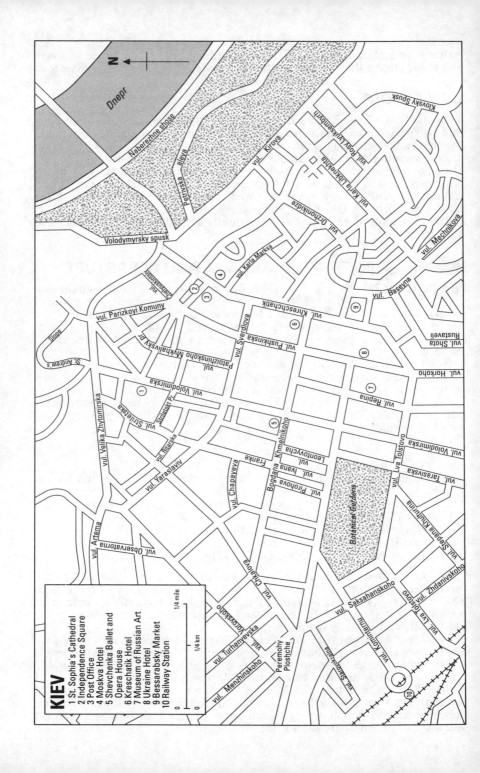

KIEV

1 St Sophia's Cathedral
2 Independence Square
3 Post Office
4 Moskva Hotel
5 Shevchenka Ballet and
  Opera House
6 Kreschatik Hotel
7 Museum of Russian Art
8 Ukraine Hotel
9 Bessarabsky Market
10 Railway Station

0   1/4 km
0   1/4 mile

Dnepr

Naberezhne shose

Petrivska aleya

Volodymyrsky spusk

vul. Kirova

vul. Rosy Luksemburh

Klovsky Spusk

vul. Karla Libknehta

vul. Ordzhonikidze

vul. Mechnikova

vul. Parizkoyi Komuny

vul. Chekistskiy

vul. Katla Marksa

vul. Khreschchatik

vul. Baseyna

Slope

St Andrew's

vul. Patolzinskoho Mykhalivsky Pl.

vul. Sverdlova

vul. Pushkinska

vul. Shota Rustaveli

vul. Velika Zhytomirska

vul. Volodimirska

Striletski Pr.

vul. Reptna

vul. Horkoho

vul. Striletska

vul. Rilska

vul. Leontovicha

vul. Lva Tolstovo

vul. Volodimirska

vul. Yaraslaviv

Bogdana Khmelnikoho

vul. Ivana Franke

vul. Pirohova

vul. Tarasivska

Botanical Gardens

vul. Artema

vul. Observatorna

vul. Chapayeva

vul. Chkalova

vul. Stepana Khmurinna

vul. Saksahanskoho

vul. Lva Tolstovo

vul. Zhdanivskoho

vul. Turhenyevska

vul. Volovskoho

vul. Menzhinskoho

Peremohy
Ploshche

vul. Kommutana

vul. Starovokzaina

Bus. Inter-city buses leave from the central bus station on Moskovska ploshcha (265-04-30), a couple of miles south of the city centre. Buses to Belarus depart from Polissia terminal on Ploshcha Tarasa Shevchenka (430-35-54) and Pivdenna terminal at Akademika Hlushkova 3. Tickets to all destinations can be bought from the ticket office at bulvar Lesi Ukrainki 14 (225-50-15).

Car. Finding petrol can be a problem, with both state and private filling stations equally likely to be out of stock. Try the following stations: Saratovska 63; Frunze 58; Kudriavsky Uzviz 10; and D Korotchenka 61. There is a Fist Aid station for cars at Prospekt Vozyednannya 7B (559-79-55).

Boat. The river terminal is on the right bank of the Dnepr river at Postova ploshcha 3 (416-7372), accessible by metro. You can go on short trips during the summer season, when hydrofoils serve local towns and villages. There are also long-distance passenger services between major cities and the Black Sea. UkrRichFlot, the Ukrainian River Fleet Company, operates cruises to Odessa and Crimea. Boats are modern and well-equipped: all cabins have showers and hot water and there is also a hairdresser, disco and sauna on board.

CITY TRANSPORT

Kiev is an easy city in which to get around. In addition to the buses, trolleybuses, and trams there is also an efficient metro system. Tickets called *talons*, which you validate upon entry, are needed for the overland services. For the metro you have to buy *jetons*, sold by the station entrance: at 150 coupons per ride (currently worth 0.0025 pence), this is probably the biggest travel bargain in the world. If you have mastered Cyrillic, the system is easy to use since it consists of just three lines.

Any car is a potential taxi, just stick out your hand and hail a ride; $1 is the average price for anywhere in the centre, rising to $2 for somewhere a little further out. Alternatively, you can order ahead by dialing 058.

 **Accommodation**

Hotels. No new hotels have opened since independence, so the choice is limited to a handful of bland, over-priced Soviet-era establishments. Choose from one of the following:

Druzhba, bulvar Druzhba Narodiv (268-3406). Not central, but the Lybidska metro stop is nearby. A room costs about $15-20 per person.

Kreschatik, vul Kreschatik 14 (tel 229-7193/7339; fax 229-8544). Single $100, double $120. Not as luxurious as the prices imply, but the comfortable rooms have a telephone, kettle and microwave, together with satin bedcovers.

Myr, Prospekt Sorokorichcha Zhovtnya 70 (263-33-81); metro Libydska and then trolleybus 4, or $2 by taxi from the centre. A double with breakfast costs about $23. The Myr, used by Sputnik, is a considerable hike from the centre of town, with little to recommend it beyond the price. In the evening the adjoining nightclub and casino is a favourite mafia haunt.

Moskva, Ploshcha Maidan Nezalezhnosty 4 (228-2804); metro Kreshchatik. In a good location, right in the centre, and with reasonable rates: single $55, double $77.

Ukraina, bulvar Shevchenka 5 (229-2807), close to the Bessarabsky Market.

A turn-of-the-century hotel with a handsome staircase and rooms for $70-90.

Private Accommodation. The best alternative in town to an overpriced hotel room is an overpriced apartment. The Private 'Hotel Service', Staronovodnitska 8a, Apt 3 (tel/fax 296-8583) has flats near the centre ranging in price from $30-50 for one room to $50-80 for two. The flats are cleaned daily and they will even meet you at the airport if you ask nicely. Kievantour at Volodomirska 47 (229-3115) also organises private rooms and a variety of other services, including interpreters or a car with driver for $25-30 a day.

Camping. There are two main sites. Campsite Kiev (31, Richcha Zhotvnia 60; tel 544-1802) is a cheap place on the left bank of the city, with a motel, café and bar attached. Campsite Prolisok (Prospekt Peremohy 139; tel 444293), set amid pine forest, is classier than most city campgrounds.

Eating and Drinking

New restaurants are opening all the time but as the choice increases so do the prices. At the time of writing, the cheapest meal costs about $10, and at the upper end of the scale you can pay as much as $100. Foreign restaurants tend to accept payment in dollars only. Other restaurants accept coupons or dollars, but the rate for dollars is likely to be unfavourable. The list below begins with restaurants serving Ukrainian food.

Hostynniny Dvir, Kontractova ploshcha 4 (416-68-76). A good place to go once for that authentic all-singing, all-dancing, all-Ukrainian experience, though a hearty meal plus drinks will set you back at least $30.

Lesnitsa, Borisa Hrinchenko 7 (229-86-29). Very good Ukrainian food served in a romantic vaulted room with live music and occasional dancing.

Slavyanski, Horkoho 125a (269-66-95). Splendidly kitsch surroundings with a pink leatherette settee in the foyer and lush fuchsia curtains throughout. Good Ukrainian fare.

Vavilon, Saksahanskoho 6 (227-45-13). This restaurant is in Dom Kino, the National Cinematographers' Association, and attracts a young crowd. There is a grand piano for impromptu entertainment. Reservations are essential.

Nika, a Swiss-Ukrainian joint venture at the foot of bulvar Shevchenka. Serves good pizzas for dollars.

Apollo, on Passazh, just off Kreshchatik (229-04-37). The upmarket end of the Nika empire, providing expensive but good European cuisine.

Italia, Prorisna 8 (224-20-54). This restaurant's crispy pizzas are the closest you'll find to Italian cuisine in Kiev. Medium prices for dollars or coupons.

Kavkaz, Kreschatik 6. The choice of dishes is not extensive at this Georgian restaurant but the food is delicious and good value.

Montana, Volodimirska 10. A Lebanese restaurant highly recommended for both value and quality.

Cafés and bars. Passazh, a short and narrow street running east off Kreshchatik, is the best place to go for coffee or a light lunch. The whole street is lined with cafés and restaurants. The best are Caffe Bonbon, which seves good coffee and cream cakes, and spills out into the street in summer, and Kreshchatik Café, where you can eat cheap, hot dishes in snug surroundings. Kiev's best bars include:

Karamboul, Zankovetskoy, at the top of Passazh. The eight pool tables and Guinness on tap attract both the expat community and mafia moguls.

Eskimo Bar, Chervonoarmiyska 64, just south of vul Pushkinska. Open 24 hours every day of the week. The prefab exterior disguises a cosy café which serves the best cappuccino in town, as well as a wide selection of cocktails and ice cream sundaes.

Four Seasons, Sichneveho Povstannya, next to the Salyut Hotel. A café by day and a bar by night. Attractions include the best pin-ball machine in Kiev.

Kreshchatik, the broad boulevard created in the 1950s and lined with apartment buildings built in a Stalinist Gothic style, is more attractive than you might suspect. Heading west from the river, you come to Independence Square (Maidan Nezalezhnosti), full of fountains and lined with monumental skyscrapers. It is the centre of the city and the traditional location for demonstrations, parades and celebrations. Formerly known as the Square of the Great October Revolution, it is one of the few concessions made in Kiev to deposing the names of the old order. Further along is Passazh, with its ornamental archway and cafés, and beyond Bessarabsky Market. Built at the turn of the century, the immense wrought-iron hall has been decidedly under-used in the past but is now the best place in Kiev for fresh fruit and vegetables. Sumptuous displays of fresh produce are piled up beneath the glass roof, and even in the height of winter goods are flown in from the Caucasus and Central Asia. Perched high on a pedestal opposite the market, a statue of Lenin shows no signs of moving.

Bulvar Shevchenka is an august street running northwest from the market. It is named after the city's favourite son, Taras Shevchenko, a 19th-century poet, painter, nationalist and all-round Ukrainian hero. The boulevard leads up past vul Repina (the Russian Art Museum at number 9 has one of the best collections outside Moscow and St Petersburg) and the University to the Church of St Vladimir. Built in 1882 in an opulent neo-Byzantine style, the interior is covered in Art Nouveau murals. You'll eventually reach Ploshcha Pobedy (Victory Square), dominated by a granite obelisk topped by a red star commemorating the city's role in World War II. It is also home to Ukraina, one of the biggest department stores in Kiev. Buried among the plastic light fittings on the ground floor, you'll find busts of Lenin and Stalin for sale, aimed not at tourists but the old faithful. At night the square fills with expensive German cars and personal bodyguards. Playoffs Casino and Nightclub, inside the Hotel Lybid, is the premier hangout of the city's New Rich.

St Sophia's Cathedral and St Andrew's Slope. A short walk north from Independence Square, through old streets lined with attractive Ukrainian Baroque buildings, brings you to Sofiyivska Ploshcha (formerly Bogdan Khmenelitsky Square). An 18th-century belltower, painted sky blue with white stucco and a gold cupola, stands alongside St Sophia Cathedral (Sofiysky Sobor), one of the oldest centres of Christianity in the Slavic lands. Named after and modelled on the Haghia Sofia in Constantinople, St Sophia's dates from 1037 and has changed little over the millenium. A couple of galleries have been added, and the 19th-century restorers made a ham-fisted job of patching up some of the frescoes, but inside the fabric of the church has remained virtually intact.

The exceedingly plain exterior in no way prepares you for the Byzantine brilliance of the inside. The walls are decorated with murals and rich geometric patterns of blues, reds and golds, covering over 3,000 square metres and mostly the 11th-century originals. Opposite the entrance, above the spot where the altar would have stood, is an unusually masculine-looking Virgin Mary, in a blue coat set against a glittering gold mosaic background. On the left of the altar, a marble coffin contains the remains of Yaroslav the Wise, who commissioned the building. Turned into a museum by the communists and a stables by the Nazis, St Sophia was offered to the Orthodox Church in the late 1980s, but for the time being it has been left in the hands of the state as sadly the church does not have the money to pay for its upkeep. It is closed on Thursdays.

If you turn left when you leave the quiet tree-lined courtyard, and head past the Bogdan Khmenelitsky monument and along Volodimirska, you eventually come to Andreuvsky Uzviz, or St Andrew's Slope. This narrow, cobbled pedestrian street, lined with pastel-coloured houses, twists and turns half a mile down the hill to Podoli or 'Lower District'. On Sundays and public holidays, this is where the public comes to promenade and it is full of hawkers, vendors and bad portrait artists. Even on other days, it is the place where you are most likely to pick up a matrioshka doll, Ukrainian tablecloth or Hard Rock Café Kiev t-shirt. At the top of the street stands the 18th-century excess of St Andrew's Church, painted blue and heavy with gold and green decoration. Inspired by Bartolomeo Rastrelli, the architect of the Winter Palace in St Petersburg, its interior — currently closed — is allegedly even more garish. At number 13 is the house where Mikail Bulgakov, author of *The Master and Margarita* and other novels, once lived and which is now a museum dedicated to his life (open 10am-5pm daily except Wednesday). At the bottom of the hill, you reach the Square of Contracts (Kontraktova Ploshcha), the heart of the old merchant district. There is a funicular railway in nearby Postova Square, which will take you back to the top. Boat cruises up the river leave from just opposite.

The Lavra and Motherland Statue. The Lavra, a vast monastic complex dating from the 11th century, and the Motherland Statue, Kiev's most impressive landmark from the Soviet era, are perched together high on the banks of the River Dnepr a few miles southeast of the city centre. You can take trolleybus 20 to the end of the line, or the metro to Arsenalnya and walk from there; or alternatively walk all the way, which should take about 40 minutes. The route takes you from the northern end of Kreshchatik (where a large metal rainbow built to celebrate Russian and Ukrainian unity is probably living on borrowed time) and then south along vulitsa Kirova. Right at the top, at no. 6, you pass the Ukrainian Art Museum (open 10am-5pm, closed Friday), which contains a fine collection, with some folk art. Further on is the Ukrainian Parliament, topped by an enormous hammer and sickle, and the Mariisnky Palace, near the top end of Central Park. The latter was built in the 18th century as a local residence for the tsar and is now the presidential residence. About two miles further down you reach the main entrance to the monastery, the Trinity Gate.

The Pecherskaya Lavra or Monastery of the Caves (open daily 9.30am-5pm) comprises about 80 buildings and is one of the outstanding monuments of Ukrainian history and architecture, as well as a major centre for Orthodox pilgrims. It was founded in 1051, when the first monks settled in caves dug into the steep bank of the Dnepr. Buildings were added over the centuries and the result is an intriguing mixture of Italian Baroque, Russian and typically Ukrainian motifs. The upper monastery is home to a number of museums which were established here at different times after 1922, when the whole Lavra was confiscated from the Church and declared state property. The lower Lavra is the working part of the monastery, where hordes of bearded monks gliding around in long black robes and terrorising the tourists are proof that since 1988 the Church has re-established its authority in these parts.

The most impressive buildings in the Upper Lavra include the 315ft/96m high belltower, which offers splendid views over Kiev, and the 19th-century refectory hall, adorned with highly decorative frescoes. The building site to the right of the refectory marks the early phase of the reconstruction of the Dormitian Cathedral, the most sumptuous church in the monastic complex until it was razed to the ground during World War II. The best museum is the Museum of Historical Treasures (open daily 10am-5pm), which has a priceless collection of Scythian gold. To see this glittering display of necklaces, coins and breastplates you must join a guided tour. A guard dressed in military fatigues and brandishing a machine gun follows the group just in case.

The highlight of a visit to the Lavra is undoubtedly an excursion through the caves which link the upper and lower monasteries. Visitors are required to join a tour which is conducted by one of the monks. The maze of narrow underground corridors which once formed the original monastery were turned into catacombs in the following centuries. Freeze-dried by an ungodly draught, the bodies of the monks are kept in glass coffins. Most are covered up but you can catch sight from time to time of a withered hand or toe.

Next door to the Lavra and dominating the skyline of the southern part of the city, stands the monument symbolising the Soviet Motherland. She is represented as a strapping 190ft/65m high Amazonian and is usually referred to simply as the 'Zheleznaya Baba' (steel wench) or simply 'Baba'. Conceived as a memorial to the city's role in what is still known as the Great Patriotic War, it took an entire year's supply of the Soviet Union's titanium stocks to build. Although from a distance it is ostensibly a massive piece of communist kitsch, the complex is still a moving memorial to the 200,000 Kievites who died defending the city. Facing towards Moscow with a huge hammer and sickle emblazoned on her shield, Baba is a testament to the difficulty of revisionist history in a country as confusing as Ukraine.

To reach the entrance, you walk through a concrete tunnel lined with massive bronze reliefs of young men toting machine guns. Old men come to sit and listen to the great patriotic songs which emanate from hidden speakers. The tunnel delivers you onto a huge concourse decorated with the names of other 'Hero Cities'. There is a museum on the war in the plinth of the statue, but most rooms are currently closed for restoration. On the second floor, a circular belt of windows gives you a view of post-war Soviet Kiev, stretching across the river to the tower blocks and factories on the other side. Next door to Baba is a military museum with a comprehensive selection of anti-personnel devices and a surprisingly enlightened exhibition on the USSR's involvement in Afghanistan

Parks and Gardens. Hidropark (metro Hidropark), which occupies several islands in the middle of the Dnepr, is the most popular spot in town for sunbathing, swimming and jogging. In summer, the sandy shores of the river are as crowded as the Italian riviera. Undeterred by reports that the waters of the Dnepr are some of the most polluted in Europe, and quite possibly radioactive, Kievans swim here in their thousands. An even more foolhardy minority, usually male pensioners, take a daily dip every day of the year — even if this means hacking through the ice.

The Botanical Gardens, which overlook the ruins of the 11th-century Vydubetsky Monastery, are one of the most beautiful spots in the city, particularly from May to June when the city's famous chestnut trees are blossoming. Trolleybus 14 from Bessarabsky Market takes you there, though you can walk there easily if you're already at the Lavra.

The principal and most beautiful theatre in Kiev is the Taras Shevchenko Ballet and Opera House at Volodomirska 50 (224-71-65). It is one of the loveliest small opera houses in Europe, where the best classical ballet in town is performed. Dramatic productions are staged at the Ivan Franko Ukrainian Theatre at Ploshcha Ivan Franko 3 (229-59-91); the Youth Theatre, at vul Lypska 15 in Pechersk district, specialises in foreign plays in translation. There is a Puppet Theatre at Shota Rustaveli 13 (220-90-65).

Classical music is performed at the House of Organ and Chamber Music at Chervonoarmiyska 77, at the Conservatory (Karla Marxa 1) and at the Philharmonia at Volodymirsky Uzviz 2.

Tickets to all performances can be bought from the Central Booking Office and its branches at Chervonoarmiyska 16, Volodomirska 51 and Priorzna 9.

Live Music and Clubs. Although you couldn't claim that Kiev's nightlife is thriving, it does at least have one. Nightclubs are glitzy and expensive, the floorshows generally appalling, but you will have the chance to rub shoulders with the local nouveaux riches and mafiosi. Included in this category are the Flamingo, in Hotel Myr (Sorokorichcha Zhovtnya 70) and Playoffs, in Hotel Lybid. Possibly more exciting are the discos organised by students, but they are impossible to track down without local friends.

The big department stores are the Central Department Store at Khmelnitskoho 2 (with an entrance on Kreshchatik) and Ukraina Department Store on Ploshcha Peremohy — though it's doubtful that you'll find anything you could possibly want to buy. Shops for souvenir-hunters include Keramika (Kostianynivska 71), which sells traditional Ukrainian ceramics and porcelains and Ukrainsky Souvenir (Chernovoarmiyska 23), a state-owned shop selling hand painted wooden eggs, inlaid boxes and so on.

Tourist Information: Intourist has a service desk inside Hotel Kievskaya Rus at Gospitalnaya 12, but provides neither maps nor organises excursions. Keep your eyes open for an English language publication called *Kiev in your Pocket,* which appears every couple of months and has good up-to-date information.

Communications: the central post office is at Kreshchatik 22. International telephone calls can be made from UTEL cardphones, found at various hard currency enclaves around the city, including the Hotel National (Lypska 3), Hotel Dnipro (Kreshchatik 1), and the Nika Bar (bulvar Shevchenko 2). They have the advantage of using satellite connections and will always get through. For the English operator dial 8-192. The code for Kiev is 044.

Money: streets are littered with vans serving as informal exchange offices. The Interbank at Yaroslav Val 36 gives cash advances against a Visa or Amex card, and Hotel Kievskaya Rus will normally cash travellers cheques.

Medical treatment: Emergency Ambulance Service: call 03.
Regional Clinical Hospital, Budyonoho 1 (211-89-2).
Central Clinical Hospital, Kotsubinskoho 9 (216-69-48).
Hard Currency Pharmacy: Prorizna 3 (228-28-71).

Consulates and Embassies

Australia, Malopidvalna 8 (228-74-26).
Belarus, Kutuzova 8 (294-82-12).
Moldova, Hotel National, Lypska 3 (291-87-44).
Romania, M Kotsubinskoho 8 (224-52-61).
Russia, Kutuzova 8 (294-79-36, 294-63-89).
UK, Desyatynna 9 (229-12-87, 228-05-04, fax 228-39-72).
USA, M Kotsubinskoho 10 (244-73-44, fax 244-73-50).

THE BLACK SEA COAST

ODESSA

With its balconied apartment buildings, leafy boulevards and seaside location, Odessa doesn't have the look or feel of a Ukrainian city, and in many ways it is not. If the Black Sea coast is the former Soviet Union's best approximation to California, then Odessa is its Los Angeles. It may not have great surfing, but neither does it have earthquakes and infernal traffic. It has always been one of the most cosmopolitan towns in the Soviet Union, with large communities of Greeks, Armenians, Bulgarians, Italians and Jews, who have arrived from across the Black Sea. A sunny climate helps give Odessa an easy-going charm. Off-duty sailors wander along the promenades, as do the city's population, well-dressed and disarmingly friendly.

The 19th century left a legacy of bourgeois monuments and elegant terraces, which although shabby are in no sense drab, with graceful tree-lined avenues and flowers that bloom from early spring to late autumn. If all this isn't enough, Odessa has sandy beaches just a short bus or boat ride away. The warm weather begins around May, and you can swim comfortably from June to October; September is usually the sunniest month.

Given its proximity to the markets of Turkey, Odessa has always had a thriving black market. This early start at entrepreneurial activity has held Odessa in good stead for life since independence.

Being relatively compact and laid out on a grid pattern, Odessa is an easy place to get around on foot. A good up-to-date map of the city is available from kiosks or the accommodation agency at the railway station. Note that Russian names of streets have been employed in this chapter since they are still widely used in Odessa.

History. As a port town, Odessa first came to prominence during the 1500s, when it was ruled by the Ottoman Turks. The Russians marched into the city in 1789 and five years later Catherine II founded the new city of Odessa, shipping down some of her finest architects from St Petersburg to help build it. Located close to the mouth of the Dnepr, Bug, Dniester and Danube rivers, Odessa's importance grew rapidly, though it was in the 19th century that the city really thrived. Governed by the Duc de Richlieu (who had sought refuge in Russia following the French Revolution), Odessa became an august and dignified city.

The city's greatest claim to fame came in 1905. Just a few days before the uprising in St Petersburg, workers in Odessa revolted and sailors (who had been sent by Nicholas II to quell disturbances) mutinied aboard the battleship Potemkin. The incident has been immortalised in a film by Russia's great director, Eisenstein. According to his film, *Battleship Potemkin*, following the 1905 mutiny civilians were massacred by tsarist soldiers on the steps leading down to the port; this, howeverm is the director's own invention.

Arrival and Departure. *Air:* Transaero, Air Ukraine and Aeroflot operate flights to and from Kiev and Moscow. You can buy tickets from the Intourist Service bureau in the Hotel Krasnaya, and there is an Aeroflot office at Karla Marxa 17. The only Western airline flying to Odessa in summer 1995 was Austrian Airlines from Vienna.

The airport is 8 miles/12km southwest of the city centre. Bus number 156 links the airport with the railway station.

Rail: trains run daily between Odessa and Moscow (23 hours), Simferopol (15 hours), Kiev (11 hours) and Chernovtsy (16 hours). There are several trains a day to Chişinau in Moldova, but they are all slow local services, taking four hours on a good day (of which there are few). The magnificent rail station is on Privokzalnaya ploshchad, south of the centre. Trolleybuses run along Pushkinskaya to the port.

Bus: the inter-city bus station is at ul Dzerzhinskogo.

Boat: Blasco, the shipping agency which has replaced Morflot, operates sailings between Odessa and Haifa, Istanbul, Piraeus, Port Said and Limassol. Boats run at all times of year, from the Sea Passenger Terminal (Morskaya Vokzal) at the bottom of the Potemkin steps, being most frequent during the summer season. There are also cruises along the river from Kiev (about $60 one way). Tickets and information are available from the office on Potemkinsev ploshcha (25 35 39, 22 91 43). See also *Ukraine: Getting There*.

Accommodation. Private accommodation in a flat or with a family is the cheapest option, and in Odessa it is remarkably easy to organise. There is an excellent agency at the train station, run by two enterprising women who meet most of the long-distance trains. If you don't see them on the platform, go direct to the kiosk: head out of the station, turn right and it is a short walk down the side of the station building. They have an extensive choice of rooms and flats for about $5 per person — less if you intend to stay for a week or more. You can call them on 24 61 18.

The best of the hotels is the Londynska (Primorsky bulvar 11; 22 50 19), a fully-restored 19th-century pile with the best location in town and rooms which have balconies overlooking the sea. Doubles cost $148. A notch or two down, Hotel Krasnaya (ul Pushkinskaya 15; tel 22 72 20, fax 25 52 09) is a grand old hotel with huge rooms and original turn-of-the-century fittings. Double rooms cost $90-125. Hotel Spartak (Deribasovskaya 25; 26 06 51) is a crumbling building in the centre of town, but is not without charm; doubles cost $50. You can book rooms here for hotels Passazh, Tsentralny and Bolshaya Moskovskaya, each with similar facilities. Tram 5 from the station threads through the suburbs down to Arkadia, a seaside enclave where various hotels, including the Victoria, may be prepared to offer a good deal.

You can camp at the Delfin campsite at Kotovskogo 299 in Luzanovka, about 6 miles/10km northeast of town, and accessible on a ferry from Odessa. There are small shacks for rent and a private beach.

Eating and Drinking. The two most popular places to gather, particularly in the evening, are at the top of the Potemkin steps and along the main pedestrian street, Deribasovskaya. There are many open-air cafés, and in summer several places serve delicious shashliks cooked over a barbecue. Kafé Vuldai (Ploshchad Potemkintsev 3) is in a prime location near the top of the Potemkin Steps. It serves shashliks (all year) and imported beer.

Restaurant Blisnitsi (Pushkinskaya 6) is pricey, coming complete with white-gloved waiters, but serves the best blinis in Odessa. The restaurant in Hotel Londynska on Primorsky bulvar is set in a beautiful inner courtyard, where peppermint green walls and an electric band complement fine food and wine. Expect to pay $5 for a starter, $15 for the main course.

Down in the beach suburb of Arkadia is the Palmira restaurant, who steps are lapped by the Black Sea An ordinary exterior conceals a remarkable interior, as though the great hall of a grand imperial palace had been translated to a beach in Odessa. Pastel pink walls are embellished with white stucco and draped with satin curtains. The culinary highlight is blini stuffed with wild mushrooms, braised in butter and garlic.

Exploring. The most popular place for a stroll, and the best place to catch the spirit of the city, is Primorsky bulvar, a Spanish-style promenade overlooking the sea and sheltered from the sun and sea breezes by rows of lime trees. At its eastern end stands the former Soviet — a neoclassical building supported by Corinthian columns and topped by two languorous women representing Night and Day. Heading westwards you reach the famous Potemkin Steps, built in 1837-41. There is a magnificent view of the bay from the top, with ten flights of steps and ten landings descending to the Morsokye Voksal or boat station. An escalator, installed in 1970, means that you need not climb the 192 steps back up (assuming it is working). The bronze statue at the top is of the Duc de Richclicu.

Continuing west along Primorsky bulvar, past the neoclassical Vorontsov Palace, built in the 1820s, you reach a pedestrian suspension bridge, with a fine view of the sprawling port below. Beyond lies one of the oldest parts of the city. Here, open-air cafés cluster around an old well, and a picturesque arched wooden bridge provides the favoured backdrop for newly-weds.

Just south from the Potemkin steps is Ploshchad Potemkinsev, an attractive square lined with ivy-clad 19th-century buildings. The huge bronze sculpture in the centre shows the mutineers engaged in revolutionary struggle. Continuing south along Karla Marxa and taking the first left on to Lastoch-kina, you come to the Opera House. Decorated with flying sculptures and a multitude of cherubs, this is an inspired piece of 19th-century pomposity. The surrounding square is very pleasant, leafy and full of cafés and cooling fountains. Beyond, around the junction of ulitsa Pushkinskaya, are several museums. The Maritime Museum (open 10am-4pm Saturday to Thursday) is a good place to get acquainted with Odessa's sea-faring heritage, though the rooms covered with frescoes are generally more exciting than the exhibits. The Archeological Museum (open 10am-5pm daily except Monday), housed in another neoclassical gem, has an excellent collection of Egyptian sarco-phogi and a good selection of Greek urns. The highlight is the Gold Room in the basement, which has Scythian jewellery and coins dramatically lit against a darkened background. The Literature Museum (open 10am-6pm, closed Mondays) is worth a visit if only to enjoy the café in the quiet courtyard garden.

Ulitsa Pushkinskaya runs south from the eastern end of Primorsky bulvar. You can visit the house where Pushkin lived for several years in exile at no. 13, though the nearby Museum of Western and Eastern Art (open 10am-5pm, closed Wednesdays) is more interesting. Housed in a fine baroque building adorned in blue and white stucco, it has a wide range of art including works by Caravaggio, Brueghel and Rubens. The truly extravagant building near the corner of Karla Liebknekhta — designed in the Moorish style and inlaid with coloured terracotta tiles and twisted columns of marble — used to be the Stock Exchange, and is now home to the Odessa Philharmonia.

The main pedestrian street, ulitsa Deribasovskaya, runs west off the northern end of Pushkinskaya. Benetton, Reebok and others have appeared along here, giving central Odessa an air of positive affluence. This will no doubt be reinforced with the opening of Passazh — an elegant neo-baroque arcade — which will connect the street with ulitsa Sovietskiye Armii at the western end.

Every weekend there is a huge flea market just south of Ovidiopolsaya Doroga, at the western edge of the city, with enormous amounts of consumer goods shipped in from Istanbul.

Entertainment. The main entertainment in the evening is to promenade up and down Primorsky bulvar or Deribasovskaya in your best clothes. The cafés stay open relatively late, and when they close there is an open-air disco down by the Potemkin steps. At all times of year there are performances of opera, ballet and classical music, and in summer there are frequent visits by foreign companies. You shouldn't miss the chance to see the Opera House in action: tickets are on sale from the *kassa* inside. The Philharmonia is also well worth a visit.

Help and Information. The Intourist service bureau is located on the ground floor of the Hotel Krasnaya at Pushkinskaya 15.

The telephone code for Odessa is 0482. If you want to phone from the city, go to the telegraph office at ulitsa Sadovaya 3, though it may well be easier to ask nicely in the reception of the Hotel Krasnaya. They will usually let you use the telephone for inter-city and possibly international calls too.

AROUND ODESSA

During the siege of World War II, Odessa held out for 72 days with no water and no food, defended by Odessites and Slovaks. Partisans set up their headquarters inside an extensive network of underground tunnels covering hundreds of miles outside the city boundaries. These were originally limestone quarries, from which most of the city's building material was taken, but later became a hiding place for smugglers. A part of the tunnels has been turned into the Museum of Partisan Glory (Muzey Partizanskaya Slava), with reconstructions showing how the fighters lived in the inhospitable conditions. It constitutes a fascinating contrast to the elegant facades of Odessa itself. Beneath the museum, which shows the methods and heroism of the resistance, you descend the spiral staircase to explore the caves themselves. The gloomy and oppressive sandstone walls are decorated with the graffiti of freedom fighters.

Guided tours are in Russian. To get there take bus number 84 along the Kiev road, and ask the driver for 'katakombi'. Since visitors are relatively few, you may need to search around for the attendant to let you in. The museum is open 9am-7.30pm.

Beaches. Some miracle of bureaucracy has ensured that the grassy banks running down to the sand on the shores around Odessa are occupied by trees and shrubs, not hotels. Behind the wooded fringe you can find lavish 19th-century villas in elaborate gardens dotted with sculptures. They have withstood three-quarters of a century of state communism by adapting to it. Most became sanatoria, primitive health farms for improving the chances of achieving production norms back in the smelly northern factories.

Beaches stretch both ways, but the most attractive are south of Odessa, and particularly Arkadia Beach. Trolleybus 5 or tram 5 (from the station) will take you there, or you can catch a boat from the Morsky Voksal. The sand is fine and golden, the sea looks clean and there is enough space for it not to get too crowded. Behind the beach is a pleasant park with vendors selling kebabs and ice-creams, and there are several cafés serving cold beer.

THE CRIMEA

A sub-tropical peninsula jutting out into the Black Sea and fringed with jagged mountains and swaying palm trees, the Crimea is the best place in the former Soviet Union to go in search of the last remaining vestiges of the workers' paradise. Geographical advantages undoubtedly make the usual Soviet unsubtleties more palatable than usual, and it was in the Crimea that the USSR came the closest to achieving the communist dream: a land of plenty for ordinary people as well as the party élite — with a warm sea, fresh food and good wines. Until 1991, it was a place of escape, so much so that it was here that Gorbachev was caught off guard during the failed coup which effectively destroyed the Soviet Union. And now even the Crimea has been unable to evade the political reality of the collapse of communism. The trouble is that everyone wants it. However, the Crimea decided in 1994 that it would rather be left alone.

While Western tourists have always been able to come here, they used to be confined to a few overpriced hotels. Now they are free to wander as they please and stay where they like. There has been a sharp fall in the number of visitors, so it is easy to find a room and a place to lay your beachmat. It is also one of the few places in the former Soviet Union to have a thriving restaurant culture aimed at the ordinary people.

History. Separated from the rest of Ukraine and exposed on all sides to external attack, the Crimea has changed hands a number of times over the centuries. The first people to inhabit the Crimea were nomadic Scythians and Cimmerians, but they were driven out by enthusiastic Greek colonists in the eighth century. The peninsula's early development was entirely distinct from that of Ukraine, but the same Tatar hordes which destroyed the Kievan Rus also took over the Crimea. In 1475, the Ottoman Turks finally gained control and settled along the coast, while the Tatars stayed up in the hills. Despite constant threats from the North, the Tatar population and their Ottoman rulers co-existed happily for 300 years. They eventually succumbed to the imperial army sent in by Catherine the Great, and the Crimea was annexed to Russia in 1783.

Throughout the 19th century, the Western powers became increasingly fearful of Russian expansionism southwards and believed the tsars to have designs upon the ailing Ottoman Empire. Matters came to head with the outbreak of the Crimean War in 1853: Turkey, Britain and France aligned themselves against the Russian army and within three years had driven them into the ground. Defeat came as a severe psychological and military blow to Russia. Even so, the Crimean War is not well-known in Britain as a victorious conflict; rather it is best remembered for the misconceived and ill-fated Charge of the Light Brigade, and for the work of the nurse Florence Nightingale in looking after casualties.

Today, the Crimea has the status of an autonomous republic within Ukraine. In 1994, the much-coveted region declared its independence from Ukraine, but this was a move which neither Russia nor Ukraine accepted. The issue is complicated by arguments over control of the Black Sea Fleet, based on Ukrainian territory but largely run by Russians. Adding their voice to the debate are returning Crimean Tatars, a Turkic people with a strong historical claim to the territory.

Geography and Climate. The Crimea is practically an island, surrounded on all sides by the Black Sea and with only a few threads of land connecting it to the rest of Ukraine. Simferopol, the capital, is the dividing point between two distinct regions: the large, flat plateau to the north and the mountainous coastal region to the south. The southern region is by far the more interesting and beautiful part of the Crimea. There is an extensive network of trekking routes in the mountains and plateaux just inland from Yalta.

The sea resorts enjoy a sub-tropical climate, with the mountains shielding the area from northern winds. The average July temperature is 24°C/75°F, with sea breezes preventing the heat from becoming too unbearable. Even in October, a temperature of 15°C/59F° is perfectly normal. There are few frosts in winter and spring comes early, with almond trees blossoming in February. In the mountains, the climate is considerably harsher: thick mists can bring the temperature down to a chilly 5°C/41°F in summer and in winter skiing is possible.

SIMFEROPOL

You cannot avoid passing through Simferopol, the capital of the Crimea, on your way to the south coast, but there is little to hang around for. Even so, it is not an unpleasant place, with some nice enough streets in the centre and several parks. If you need to stay the night, try the Moskva (Kievskaya 1), the Ukraina (ul Rosi Luxemburg 9) or the Simferopol (ul Kirova 22).

Moscow is 24 hours away by train, Kiev is 19 hours. Daily trains to Odessa take about 14 hours. There are also flights to Simferopol from many points within the CIS. The cheapest flight from Kiev is about $75 one way. The railway terminates at Simferopol, but the bus station is conveniently located next to the train terminal, so it is easy to continue your journey.

YALTA

Yalta is twinned with Margate in Kent, but while the towns may be joined in the spirit of international understanding, Margate simply wasn't born with the same natural advantages. Yalta is built around a perfect bay, backed by the rugged Ai-Petri mountains and with lush vegetation and vineyards all around. It also enjoys more sunny days a year than Nice (and a lot more than Margate). Despite the growing number of harsh concrete buildings, Yalta still has a certain old-fashioned charm, and the Black Sea is every bit as blue as it has always been.

Yalta developed around the turn of the century, when doctors declared the mild climate of southern Crimea beneficial to the health, and Nicholas II abandoned the Gulf of Finland in favour of sunny holidays by the Black Sea. He built the beautiful palace of Livadia nearby, while lesser aristocrats and sycophants colonised Yalta, creating a fashionable resort. It was to be expected, then that one of Lenin's first decrees was 'On the use of the Crimea for Rest and Treatment of Working People'. Ever since, Yalta has been a place for the common people, who came for cheap holidays in subsidised sanatoria — although you also see the private dachas of the party élite scattered among the hills. Yalta still has all the essentials for a traditional seaside holiday, based around the simple pleasures of sun and sea with the old-time attractions of fairground rides and ice-cream.

Arrival and departure. From Simferopol, 55 miles/88km north, you have the choice of a trolley-bus (the longest such ride in the world) or an ordinary bus for the two-hour journey to Yalta. Take the regular bus if you can, since it is more comfortable and slightly quicker. Tickets cost less than a dollar. A taxi ride will cost you $20-25, and touts offer places in shared taxis (*marshrutnoe*) for about $5. There are also direct buses from Simferopol airport. If you are driving, the road to Yalta is clearly signposted and winds through the picturesque Salgir River valley before veering west along the coast beyond Alushta.

There used to be regular boat, ferry, and hovercraft services along the Black Sea coast to Odessa and to coastal towns in Georgia, but at the time of writing these were no longer operating.

If leaving Yalta in high season, it is worth buying a train ticket in advance. The rail ticket sales office (Zheleznodorozhny Kacci) is just off Ploshchad Radina on ulitsa Sverdlova, open 8am-7pm. Even the bus services from Yalta to Simferopol can get over-booked.

Accommodation. There are more hotels around Yalta than in any other part of the former Soviet Union: see the list below. If you are looking for a room in a private house or apartment, be warned that there are no agencies. However, dozens of touts hang around the bus station waiting to mob all arriving passengers. Fix a price and check curfew rules before you set off with your new-found host. Expect to pay about $5 per person.

Until recently, few foreigners ever stayed outside Yalta, but now there is nothing to stop you rolling up in any of the other resorts along the coast. If you're looking for unspoilt beaches or picturesque villages, however, you are likely to be disappointed as the entire area has been heavily developed. To escape from it all, you will have to venture beyond Greater Yalta, either westwards as far as Foros (where Gorbachev used to have his dacha) or eastwards as far as Sudak, or better still up into the mountains. In these small towns and rural areas, private accommodation or camping are the best and often the only options. The Polyana Skazok Campsite lies in the hills about 2 miles/3km north of Yalta, with bungalows and a restaurant, and there is a motel nearby. The pick of the hotels in Yalta are as follows:

Gostinitsa Otdich, ul Drazhinskovo 14 (35 30 79). This is a very friendly guest house newly opened up to foreigners. Rooms are about $35 for a double, less if you stay for more than a week. All rooms have a view of the sea, a clean bathroom, fridge and television.

Oreanda, nab Lenina 35/3 (32 82 86). Centrally located on the main promenade, the Oreanda is the most attractive tourist hotel in town, with balconies overlooking the sea and its own private beach. About $100 for a double with breakfast.

Yalta, ul Drazhinskovo 50 (tel 35 01 50, fax 35 30 93). A huge monolithic Soviet structure perched on the cliffs at the eastern end of the resort, accessible on buses 16, 23 and 24. Room rates are $40 (single) and $60 (double). Facilities include a sea-water swimming pool, windsurfers, tennis courts and a high-speed lift which transports you down to the private beach. The Intourist service bureau is on the ground floor and you can buy airline tickets on the second floor.

Eating and Drinking. Crimean specialities include charcoal-grilled lamb and pork shashliks; *chibule*, an onion and meat-filled pie not unlike a Cornish pastie; and 'Crimean chicken', which is cooked in spices and served with a tangy tomato sauce. The Crimea produces some of the best wines in the former Soviet Union but all are sweet and probably best drunk as dessert wines. Bar Marino, on the main promenade, has about the best choice of wines in Yalta. The main market for fruit and vegetables is at the bottom of ulitsa Rudanskovo.

If you have your own transport, there are a couple of good restaurants up in the mountains: the Uchan-Su, at the waterfalls of the same name, five miles/8km west of Yalta on the Bakhchisarai road; and the Lesnoi, by nearby Lake Karagol and specialising in game dishes. Cafés and restaurants in Yalta itself are as follows:

Crimskiye Blyuda: an open-air café on the road leading up to the Hotel Yalta. Shashliks are cooked on the barbecue and sold along with imported beer and Crimean champagne. Lively and good value.

Gurman restaurant: a leafy outdoor terrace on the upper tier of the promenade, not far from the cable car station, serving among the best food in Yalta. Always reserve a table.

Rycha Restaurant: on Pushkinskaya, at the edge of the park opposite the Exhibition Hall. Good food, young crowd, loud music.

Vostok Restaurant: on nab Lenina, midway between the Lenin statue and the Oreanda hotel. Reasonably priced traditional Ukrainian and Russian fare in a prime location for watching the world go by.

Exploring. The split-level Lenin Embankment (Naberezhnaya Lenina), which runs along the edge of the bay, is Yalta's main street and promenade — the place to shop, eat and be seen. The evening stroll is as much a ritual here as it is in Italy. If you tire of walking up and down, there are plenty of benches and walls to slump on and watch street entertainment provided by anything from concert violinists to singing dogs. Most of the bars, cafés and restaurants along here stay open late. Opposite Hotel Oreanda, at the western end, sits a fake Spanish galleon, left over from a film shoot and now marooned high above the sea in the concrete harbour wall. This is where the evening crowds tend to congregate to get their definitive portrait painted or to buy souvenirs. For the best views of the city, take a ride up the mountain in the cable car which departs from the upper tier of the embankment, near ulitsa Kirova.

Opposite the harbour, at the eastern end of the embankment, is Ploshchad Lenina, with a handsome statue of the man himself casting his gaze out to sea. The post office, also on the square, is worth visiting for the highly imaginative socialist realist décor. Among the ceramic decorations is a picture of Hermes handing a letter to a cosmonaut — which goes some way to explaining why your mail may never reach its destination. Walk eastwards from here and you'll pass through the oldest parts of town, where the crumbling balconied buildings and spreading vines give the area a distinctly Mediterranean air. The best beaches are also in this area. Beachboys patrol the shore collecting money for the sunbeds and enforcing the local laws which forbid eating, smoking and dangerous games.

Yalta's most famous museum is the one dedicated to Anton Chekhov at ulitsa Kirova 112 (open 10am-5pm, Wednesday to Sunday). Chekhov came to Yalta as an ailing consumptive in 1899. The villa where he lived until his death in 1904 has been preserved as a museum. You can see the desk where he worked on *The Cherry Orchard* and the rooms where he entertained Rachmaninov and Gorky.

Another sight worth seeing is the Armenian church (ulitsa Zagorodnaya 3), which was built in 1914 as a replica of St Ripsime near Yerevan, the widely acknowledged masterpiece of medieval Armenian architecture. It now houses the Museum of History and Archeaology.

Help and Information. The Intourist desk in Hotel Yalta (35 01 32) opens 8am-8pm daily and is very helpful. It organises excursions, including to Sevastopol, which is still the only way to visit this closed port.

AROUND YALTA

There are many possible day trips from Yalta to cater for all tastes. Most of the sights in the immediate vicinity can be reached by boat. Cutters or *keteri* depart regularly from the Lenin embankment and are by far the most pleasant way to travel around, though there are also regular bus services to all nearby destinations. If you prefer to be more independent, you can hire a clapped-out Lada for about $55 per day. The major roads around Yalta are good, but once you head up into the mountains, surfaces deteriorate, signposts are few and far between, and the cloud which looks so picturesque from the beach descends in seconds — reducing the visibility dramatically on the mountain roads which consist entirely of hairpin bends.

West of Yalta. Just a mile or so west of Yalta is the Livadia Palace, built at the beginning of this century as a summer residence for Tsar Nicholas II. It is more famous, however, as the site of the Yalta Conference in which Stalin, Roosevelt and Churchill carved up Europe in 1945. The neo-Renaissance palace is now a museum with two permanent exhibitions: the first relates to the conference, with photographs of the 'Big Three' and a reproduction of the round table where they sat; the second, set up recently, relates to the Romanov years at Livadia, which Nicholas II always considered his favourite home. The beautifully tended park surrounding the palace offers good views of Oreanda bay, where some of the most luxurious sanatoria are located — including the place where the KGB came to unwind, and Brezhnev's old holiday home. Livadia Palace opens 9am-6pm daily except Wednesday. To reach it, go on foot or take bus 5 from the Spartak cinema at the top of ulitsa Pushkinskaya in Yalta.

If you are travelling by boat, a short distance west of Livadia you will pass Swallow's Nest (Lastochkino Gnezdo), a miniature pseudo-Bavarian castle perched on the clifftop and star of a thousand postcards, as well as the illustration at the start of this chapter. It was built for a homesick German baron at the beginning of this century and now houses a restaurant.

The Vorontsov Palace, which dominates the resort of Alupka, is the most interesting sight west of Yalta. The imposing grey mansion was built by Count Vorontsov in a strange mixture of neo-Gothic and Moorish styles in the 1830s. He apparently acquired his fondness for austere baronial architecture in England, where he spent much of his youth. Fragrant gardens with rosemary hedges and an abundance of rose beds are laid out in terraces right down to the sea. The palace is open 10am-5pm daily except Monday and Friday.

Foros: according to the locals, Foros, 30 miles/48km west of Yalta, has the cleanest waters along the whole Crimean coast. Gorbachev was obviously in agreement as he built a dacha on the cliffs just outside the village. It was here that he was held during the attempted coup in 1991. Foros can be reached by bus from both Yalta and Sevastopol, but you will need some impressive credentials to get past the armed guard who protects the entrance.

East of Yalta. Close to the highway above Yalta (accessible only by car, taxi or on an excursion) stands Alexander III's Palace. Built in the style of a French chateau, the palace was considered sufficiently opulent to be turned into Stalin's private dacha. In 1992 it was reopened as a museum of 19th-century art (open 9am-6pm Saturday to Wednesday).

Four miles/6km east of Yalta and accessible by *keteri* are the Nikita Botanical Gardens (Nikitsky Boatanichesky Sad), established in the early 19th century. These extensive gardens are at their most colourful in spring, when the air is filled with the scent of jasmine and lilac. About six miles/10km further on is Gurzuf, where you can visit the ruins of a Byzantine fortress and wander through the narrow streets of Pushkin's most beloved resort.

Sudak: sixty miles/96km east of Yalta, Sudak is one of the most historically interesting sights along the Crimean coast, with its quiet streets making a refreshing change from the crowds of Yalta. Sudak was colonised by the Venetians as early as the 12th century, when enterprising individuals sought to establish a lucrative trading route between Europe and Asia. In 1260, Niccolo and Maffeo Polo, father and uncle of Marco, landed here and stepped straight into the prologue of one of the world's classics. It was from Sudak that they set out on their expedition overland to the court of Kublai Khan, where they lived for several years. The Genoese superseded the Venetians and established a fort to protect their trading interests, of which there are extensive ruins left today.

From the top of the ramparts there is a fine view of the coast, and you can see tiny houses tucked in beneath the outer walls. Sudak can be reached by bus from both Yalta and Simferopol. You should be able to find private accommodation here if you decide to stay overnight.

BAKHCHISARAI

The town of Bakhchisarai lies 60 miles/96km inland from Yalta, on the other side of the Ai-Petri mountain range. The Crimean hinterland has a quite different feel from the crowded coastal areas. Beyond the mountains extends a vast plateau where you'll find the most interesting evidence of the region's past. Bakhchisarai is the site both of an ancient Byzantine settlement and the former capital of the Tatar Khans. The Tatars invaded in the 13th century and held sway over the plains of Crimea until Russia annexed the region in the 1700s. The most important surviving monument to their period of rule is the 16th-century palace of Khan Abdul Sahal Girey in Bakhchisarai. With the return of the Crimean Tatars in the last few years, the palace's status has shifted from being merely a tourist attraction to a sacred site, the burial place of the Tatars' forefathers.

The palace is built around a large and tranquil inner courtyard, which is filled with flowers, fountains and chestnut trees and surrounded by frescoed walls, wooden balconies and ornately carved minarets. To see the inside you must join a guided tour, but many of the rooms are currently closed for renovation. You can peek through a few doors, though, and have a look around the cemetery with its carved sarcophagi and strangely-shaped head-stones. The palace opens 9am-5pm, daily except Tuesday.

The vast limestone plateau near Bakhchisarai is pockmarked with cave dwellings gathered into small 'cities' which are reminiscent of parts of

Cappadocia in central Turkey. The most extensive cave cities are at least 6 miles/10km south of Bakhchisarai and difficult to get to without your own vehicle, but there are a couple within walking distance of the Khan's palace. Turn right out of the palace and walk for about a mile, past a mosque, and you will see the Uspensky Monastery carved into the rockface high up on the right. A small community of monks has recently moved back and is toiling painstakingly to transform it once again into a working monastery; some have already moved back into the ancient stone cells.

Continuing for less than a mile beyond the monastery, you will see fortified walls at the top of the high plateau on the left. This is Chufut Kaleh, first settled by Byzantine Greeks before being redeveloped by Tatars in the 13th century, and most recently inhabited by a Jewish sect in the 19th century. The earliest remains are the chambers carved out of the rock at the edge of the cliff. The later Tatar additions, including an Islamic mausoleum and several intact fortifcations and arches, are further up on the desolate plateau. The fortress is now the site of an annual Tatar festival.

The surrounding countryside offers some of the best hiking possibilities in Ukraine, and an eight-day trek will take you past the main cave cities and many other minor ones, and back to Yalta. The trails are well marked. The best map to explore the region is the one found in *Cave Cities of the Crimea*, a small Russian publication which you can pick up in Yalta or Simferopol.

Arrival and Departure. There is no direct bus from Yalta to Bakchisarai. You must go to Simferopol and catch a local bus from there. If you are travelling by car, the most direct route from Yalta is through the mountains: the road winds its way up to a height of 3,300ft/1,000m and then down again. The views are spectacular on a clear day, but the drive is not for the faint-hearted, particularly if the weather changes unexpectedly. The alternative is to drive to Simferopol and then cut west from there along the Sevastopol road.

SEVASTOPOL

The port of Sevastopol lies on the southwestern coast of the Crimea, 60 miles/96km from Yalta. As home to the Black Sea fleet, Sevastopol was the most important naval base in the former USSR. Though no one is quite sure of its status these days — at present Ukraine is officially in command of the town and Russia of the fleet — it remains a military stronghold and a closed port.

Sevastopol is officially out-of-bounds to foreigners, but you can join a guided tour. Not surprisingly, most of the sights relate to the town's nautical heritage. A vast circular tableau known as the Panorama depicts the Defence of Sevastopol in the Crimean War. There is also a memorial to Russian and Soviet sailors at the restored fortifications on Malakhov Hill.

Guided tours of Sevastopol can be booked in Yalta, at the Hotel Yalta or from the excursion office next to the *keteri* piers on the Lenin embankment.

BALAKLAVA

The Crimean War brought Balaklava fame on two counts. The town lends its name to an unattractive but effective piece of headgear which was invented during the war and is now a household name worldwide. Balaklava was also the site of the ill-fated Charge of the Light Brigade, led by Lord

Cardigan (only distantly related to the inventor of another woollen garment). Ruined fortifications recall the devastating battle. Located on a lagoon 10 miles/16km south of Sevastopol, Balaklava dates back to the 2nd century, when the Scythians settled here. Some believe it to be the port of Lostrigones, mentioned in the *Odyssey* as one of the places where Ulysses landed.

Balaklava can be reached by bus from Sevastopol.

EASTERN UKRAINE

Eastern Ukraine is the industrial powerhouse of the country and as such is low in tourist attractions. The workers here used to be among the best paid in the Soviet Union, but decline set in during the early 1980s and the majority Russian population supported Ukrainian independence in the hope that it would bring about the economic revival of the region. But since things have got even worse, many people now favour union with Russia. Kharkiv and Donetsk are not great destinations, but they at least make convenient overnight stops.

KHARKIV (formerly Kharkov)

With a population of 1.5 million, Kharkiv is the Birmingham of Ukraine. Its size and status as an important industrial base does not make it immediately appealing. Perched on the edge of the Ukrainian steppe 25 miles/40km south of the Russian border, and with a largely Russian speaking population, Kharkiv nonetheless has its surprises — including some interesting Modernist architecture, and a flourishing cultural life.

Arrival and Departure. Transaero runs daily flights to and from Kiev and Moscow, and Kharkiv is also an important rail junction. There are trains daily to Kiev (10 hours), Odessa (20 hours), Simferopol (10 hours) and Moscow (12 hours). The main railway station is Yuzhny Vokzal on Privokzalnaya Square, a mile west of the centre. Yuzhny Vokzal metro is adjacent, or you can catch tram 14 into the centre.

The main bus station, Tsentralnaya Avtovokzal, is at Prospekt Gagarina near the metro of the same name.

Kharkiv lies at the crossroads of two main routes — from Moscow to Yalta, and Kiev to Rostov-on-Don. The traffic can be heavy on the road from Moscow and the speed limit on some sections is only 50km/h (30 mph). The Kiev-Kharkiv highway, on the other hand, is a fast road. A good place to break your journey along this last route is Poltava, where there are a few reasonable hotels.

Accommodation and Food. There is little to choose between Kharkiv's main hotels. The main difference is that Hotel Mir (Prospekt Lenina 27a; 30 55 43) is slightly out of the centre and Hotel Kharkiv is more conveniently located at Ploshcha Dzerzhinskovo 8. There is campsite in Vysoky village, several miles out of town (22 52 00).

For food, try the restaurants in the hotels or else head to ulitsa Sumskaya. This has a variety of eateries, including the Vareniki Café at no 14, which specialises in the Ukrainian staple — the dumpling. The Teatralnaya at no. 2 has the reputation for being the best restaurant in Kharkiv, and is certainly very good.

Exploring. The Lopan river cuts a swathe through the city from north to south. On its east bank is Dzerzhinsky Square (Ploshcha Dzerzhinskovo), the heart of the city and a major traffic concourse. It is a massive space surrounded by equally massive buildings; these were revolutionary at the time they were built and remain some of the finest pieces of Constructivist architecture in the former Soviet Union. Constructivism, which grew out of the avant-garde movements of the 1920s, enjoyed only a brief period of popularity before Stalin stamped upon it, but its principles were copied and bastardised in a million post-war tower blocks. The Palace of State Industry, built in 1926-28 using glass and concrete, was the first skyscraper in the Soviet Union. The Gorky University building on the south side of the square and the Hotel Kharkiv on the north were designed to complement it in the 1930s, though the ceramic decoration was added after the war.

To reach the historic core of the town, walk down ulitsa Sumskaya to Ploshcha Rosi Luxembourg, close to the banks of the river. On the square's north side stands Pokrovsky Cathedral, which was built in 1689 in the style of traditional Ukrainian wooden churches — though stone was used instead of wood. Kharkiv's most famous landmark, however, is the nearby Uspensky Cathedral, whose golden domes and prominent bell-tower can be seen from most points in the city. The main part of the church dates from 1777, but the bell-tower was added in the 19th century to celebrate the victory over Napoleon's armies in 1812. You will hear its famous carillon chiming out on the hour.

The Fine Arts Museum at ulitsa Sovnarkomovskaya 11 (reached on trams 5, 10, 11 or trolleybuses 1 or 2) has a huge collection of pre-revolutionary art including some fine 16th-century icons.

DONETSK

Another large city, with over one million inhabitants, Donetsk lies at the heart of the Donbass coal field. Until 1924 it was called Hughesovka, an unlikely name for a Russian city and the result of an even unlikelier story. In 1880, a Welshman called John Hughes from Merthyr Tydfil took it upon himself to ship furnace equipment through the Mediterranean, Black Sea and the Aral Sea and then lug it by bullock cart overland to build blast furnaces in Ukraine. This is where he ended up. Unlike in South Wales, there are about 50 mines still working, although it is uncertain for how much longer. Apart from the quirky Welsh connection, there is little to delay you in Donetsk. Should you need to stay overnight, try the Hotel Druzhba at Universitetskaya prospekt 48 (91-19-68).

WESTERN UKRAINE

LVIV (formerly Lvov)

With its Gothic towers, dark medieval alleyways and faded but flamboyant Baroque churches, Lviv is a quintessential Central European city. Vienna and Prague may be bigger and grander, but Lviv is in some ways just as beautiful. Isolation from the rest of Europe and decades of neglect have kept Lviv in a time-warp. The fabric of the city remains untouched by the 20th century, and it is almost entirely unknown to Western eyes. Lviv was incorporated into the Soviet Union only in 1939, and centuries of Polish and Habsburg rule have left a much stronger imprint on the city than Moscow ever managed to do. Lviv must not be missed.

History. Lviv has always been a pawn in the hands of empire-builders, and even in this century a person who had never left the city would have lived in five different countries. The city was founded in the 13th century by Prince Danilo Galitsky and named after his son Lev or Leo. The name translates as 'Lion', which is a symbol that you see used all over the city. Throughout most of the Middle Ages, Lviv was in Polish hands. The aristocracy adopted the Polish language and culture, but the ordinary people remained largely unimpressed by the new rulers and kept the Orthodox faith until a bizarre religious compromise was agreed in 1596, with the foundation of the Uniate Church. The liturgy remained Orthodox but the Pope was adopted as head of the Church. In 1772, Lviv fell into the sphere of influence of the Catholic Habsburgs, whose ideology and religious convictions can be seen in the proliferation of extravagant baroque churches.

The collapse of the Habsburg empire at the close of World War I gave the city a brief taste of what independence might be like, before it fell once again to the Poles. The Red Army marched into town in 1939, but the Russians were in turn superseded by the Germans in 1941. More than 500,000 people are believed to have perished in the vicinity of Lviv during World War II, though the town itself was barely touched. With perestroika came the re-emergence of the Uniate Church, which spearheaded a burgeoning nationalist movement that spread outwards from Lviv to the rest of the country and culminated in the split from Moscow in 1991.

City Layout. Lviv is a big place, with a population of 750,000, but its old town is compact. This focusses on Market Square (Ploshcha Rynok) and is hemmed in by Castle Hill to the east and Ivana Franka Park to the west. The main street, Prospekt Svobody (formerly Prospekt Lenina) consists of two streets running either side of a thin park — from the Opera house at the northern end to Ploshcha Mistkevicha.

Most kiosks and bookshops sell an excellent street map of Lviv, which is one of the few up-to-date maps in Ukraine, complete with the new street names in Ukrainian. Alternatively, you can pick up a simple but clear plan of the centre from the reception at the Grand Hotel.

Arrival and departure. *Air:* getting to Lviv direct from the UK is feasible on Air Ukraine International from Manchester. There are also regular flights from Kiev and Moscow. The airport is 4 miles/7km west of the centre and is connected to town by trolleybus 9.

Train: Lviv has good rail connections to both the east and the west. There are several trains a day to Kiev (10 hours) and Moscow (21 hours). Trains also run direct to Prague (21 hours), Sofia (29 hours), Vilnius (13 hours) and Budapest (12 hours). The attractive turn-of-the-century railway station lies a couple of miles west of the centre on Privokzalnaya ploshcha and is accessible on tram 2 from Ploshcha Mitskevicha. Tickets are available either here or at the Intourist Service Bureau in Hotel Dzhorzh.

Bus: the bus station is a few miles south of the centre and can be reached on trolleybus 5. As well as long-distance buses within Ukraine, there is also a direct service to and from London. This runs once a week (more frequently over Christmas), takes 45 hours and costs £134 return. Contact Acton Holidays, 354 Uxbridge Road, London W3 9SL (0181-896 1642).

Car: driving from Kiev, start early since it's a long haul. Those coming from Slovakia or Poland should start even earlier as the border crossings at Shegini and Medyka have seen a huge increase in traffic with little corresponding relaxation of bureaucracy.

Accommodation. Recent restoration has done wonders to the Grand Hotel at Prospekt Svobody 13 (tel 76 90 60, 72 40 42; fax 72 76 65). Every room has satellite television and a luxury bathroom, the staff are extremely helpful and the restaurant is the best this side of the Carpathians. A single room costs $70-120, a double $110 upwards.

Hotel Dzhorzh on Ploshcha Mitskevicha (72 59 53, 79 90 11) is down several notches, with the cheapest double going for as little as $18. Housed in an opulent but crumbling turn-of-the-century building, the Dzorzh is the perfect place to come for a dose of faded grandeur. The rooms are ordinary and the water supply is erratic, but the surroundings provide ample compensation. If you're prepared to pay a little extra, you can get a room with a wrought-iron balcony overlooking the square.

Hotel Lviv (7 vul 700 Richyalvova; 79 22 71) is a standard Intourist hotel and only worth considering if you fail to get a room at the Dzhorzh. The sleazy basement bar — where sociability is guaranteed by long tables and a young, friendly crowd — is worth a visit though.

Eating and Drinking. Do not fail to treat yourself to a meal at the Grand Hotel, where traditional Ukrainian recipes have been unearthed and given the gourmet treatment. For $10 you get five enormous courses, mineral water and coffee. The other tolerable places in Lviv are notable more for the surroundings than the food:

Restaurant Pod Levom, Ploshcha Rynok. A fine mixture of the naff and magnificent, where pop music throbs beneath a peeling frescoed ceiling and locals get lively on Ukrainian champagne.
Restaurant Stary Royal, Stavropiriskaya 4. Elegant restaurant with wood panelled walls and a grand piano.
Ararat, Birmenska 31. Pleasant café in a vaulted room off Ploshcha Rynok.
History Museum, Ploshcha Rynok 6. This branch of the history museum is closed for restoration, but you can walk through the building to the stunning inner courtyard, where Renaissance galleries line the walls and coffee is served under the arcades.

Exploring. Unlike in most of Ukraine's cities, it is possible to trace Lviv's history through its architecture, from the Polish influences of the Middle Ages to the dignified civic monuments built during the national revival at the end of the 19th century. The best time to see Lviv is at dawn or dusk, when the churches are full and the streets empty.

The historic core of Lviv centres on Ploshcha Rynok, the old medieval market place. Surrounded by fine Renaissance patrician houses, the style of the square has been somewhat cramped by the 19th-century town hall in the centre, which bristles with the blue and yellow flags of an independent Ukraine. There are a number of museums around the square, including several branches of the Lviv History Museum and, on the corner of Ploshcha Rynok and vulitsya Drukarska, the Pharmacy Museum (open 9am-7pm weekdays, 10am-5pm weekends). This is a working pharmacy first and a museum second. The old wooden shelves in the shop display medicines stored in multi-coloured flasks. If you want to see the exhibition of alchemical instruments in the back room, you'll have to catch the pharmacist-curator when she's not busy.

The narrow streets leading off Ploshcha Rynok are home to many of Lviv's finest churches and are perfect for idle wandering. Following vulitsa Teatralnaya west of Ploshcha Rynok, you come to the Roman Catholic Cathedral. The large Gothic tower and high single nave were built in the

14th century, but the rest of the building has accrued over the ages, creating a striking juxtaposition of styles. Darkened chapels surround the airy nave elaborately decorated with a floral motif and recently restored frescoes. The church is open to visitors 10am-noon, and services are held in Polish every evening at 7pm. Nearby, partially incorporated into a neighbouring apartment building, is the Boim Chapel, the mausoleum of one of the richest men in 17th-century Lviv. The exterior is highly ornate, with unusual stone carvings of artisans and peasants.

It is worth checking if the Armenian Cathedral, on a narrow lane between Birmenska and Lesi Ukrainky has been re-opened. Built by Armenian artisans between the 14th and 16th centuries, the church was closed by the communists and is now in a ruinous state. However, a huge stash of priceless icons, uncovered recently, have somehow managed to survive the damp and cold. There are plans to exhibit them as soon as restoration work is complete.

Heading east off Ploscha Rynok towards vulitsa Pidvalna, you pass a dense conglomeration of churches. The most immediately striking is the former Dominican Church on Ivana Federova. This beautiful example of late baroque, with a large dome and a curvaceous façade, was built in the mid-18th century. Under the communists it was a museum of atheism, but a quick reorganisation of the labels has produced a Museum of Historical Religion (open 10am-6pm daily). From here, if you turn left and go through the courtyard opposite, you reach the Church of the Assumption. Only recently re-opened, its spanking new iconostasis blends with the equally garish original baroque gold altars. Further east, set amid parkland, stands the twin-towered Carmelite Church. Below it is a simple stone building dating from 1554, with a doorway guarded by two of Lviv's loveliest stone lions.

Head down vulitsa Pidvalna, which runs along the line of the old city walls, and you'll eventually reach Vozzednannya Ploshcha and the old Bernardine Monastery Church, now known as St Andrew's. Built in the early 17th century, this is perhaps the most atmospheric church in the city, with the relative simplicity of the single nave structure being completely offset by the flamboyance of its baroque decoration. Heavy gold altars swarming with cherubs line the sides and the ceiling is heavily frescoed. A vegetable market in the square outside is a great sight in autumn, when stalls are piled high with unusual mushrooms.

While Ploshcha Rynok is the centre of old Lviv, the focus of the new town is Prospekt Svobody. Formerly Prospekt Lenina, this is the most popular place in town to throw a nationalist rally. It was built on an ambitious scale in the 19th century, and is now lined with increasingly westernised shops. The climax of the avenue is the grandiose Opera and Ballet Theatre. Further south stands the elegant Grand Hotel Lviv, the most luxurious in Ukraine. The large green domes visible just east of here in the old town belong to the 18th-century Church of the Transfiguration. The main entrance is on vulitsa Krakivska: on the way you pass a small arts market where you can buy the usual Soviet memorabilia as well as embroidered Ukrainian folk shirts.

Southeast of Prospekt Svobody, through Ivana Franka Park, stands St George's Cathedral (Sobor Yura), a fine baroque building which was recently returned to its rightful owner, the Uniate Church. It now attracts hundreds of worshippers every Sunday. En route it is worth taking a diversion along Stefanika, which runs along the northern edge of Ivana Franka park. A picture gallery at no. 8 has a fine collection of paintings which includes works by Goya, Titian, Tintoretto and Rubens.

To stretch your legs and strain your eyes, head to Castle Hill (Park Visoki Zamok), 15 minutes' walk northeast of the centre. It is a steep climb to the top, but the sweeping views over the city and the surrounding countryside are well worth the effort.

Shopping. There are several fruit and vegetable markets, the most central of which is on Galitska Ploshcha, just east of Ploshcha Mitskevicha. Northeast of the city centre on vulitsa Shpitalna, is a large weekend market which sells everything from fishing rods to fur coats. For old-fashioned handmade hats, try the excellent shop at Ploshcha Rynok 13. Druzhba, on the corner of Ploshcha Mitskevicha and Teatralna, has a good selection of books on the city as well as maps.

Help and Information. Hotel Dzhorzh has a travel bureau on the ground floor, where you can book train tickets but not much else. The Itar Tourist Agency (79 90 11, 72 91 68) on the 4th floor is altogether friendlier. The owner speaks fluent English and is very helpful.

The main Post Office is on Slovatskoho, at the bottom of Ivana Franka Park. The central telegraph office is just around the corner at Petra Dorozhenka 39. The telephone code for Lviv is 0322.

TRANSCARPATHIA

South of Lviv and bordering on Slovakia, Romania, Hungary and Poland, Transcarpathia is the wildest part of Ukraine. It is an area of forested valleys, ravines, lakes and waterfalls dominated by the Carpathian mountains. In winter it's possible to come skiing here, and hiking is popular in summer. You'll pass through impossibly isolated villages, where both the houses and churches are made from wood with shiny tin roofs, and the inhabitants eke out a peasant subsistence from the soil. The people of this region have been governed from Vienna, Budapest, Prague, Moscow and now Kiev, but being so far from the centres of power their way of life has changed little over the last century. The locals are ethnically mixed, but generally consider themselves Ruthenians — a geographical identity that takes no account of existing national boundaries and has more in common with people over the borders in Slovakia and Hungary than in Kiev. Ruthenia as an entity has enjoyed independence for only a single day this century, in the immediate aftermath of World War I. The biggest change came during World War II when, as part of Slovakia, the area was ruled by a Nazi-appointed puppet government and its large Jewish population was wiped out.

The road from Uzhgorod to Lviv is stunning. It takes you through typical Transcarpathian countryside with wooded mountain passes and ravines. Some of the best views are from Veretsky Pass, 2,790ft/850m above sea level.

Uzhgorod. With a population of around 115,000, Uzhgorod is the largest town in Transcarpathia and its regional capital. It lies in the valley of the River Uzh, surrounded by vineyards which cover the foothills of the Carpathian mountains, and is the best base for exploring the area.

The main attraction and the town's most distinctive landmark is the walled castle. It dates from the ninth century and for most of the Middle Ages was inhabited by a displaced Italian aristocratic family. It is now a Museum of Local Lore. At the foot of the hill is the excellent open-air Museum of Folk Architecture, which contains traditional old wooden buildings taken from the surrounding area, carefully re-built and authentically furnished. Both museums close on Mondays.

The town's two central squares, Teatralna and Vozzednannya, are separated by the river but linked by a wooden pedestrian bridge. Teatralna ploshcha is home to the Opera and Drama Theatre and frequently hosts performances by the Transcarpathia Folk Choir.

A good day trip into the mountains from Uzhgorod is to Nevitskoe, 8 miles/12km north, which has a 13th-century castle and is the starting-point for the hike up Atalovetskaya Polyana. This extinct volcano is 3,185ft/971m high and can be climbed in about four hours.

Arrival and Departure: there are domestic flights to Uzhgorod, but the city is easily accessible by train. It lies only 15 miles/24km north of Chop, on the Hungarian border, and is the first Ukrainian stop for many trains coming from Budapest, Prague, Vienna, and Sofia. The train station is on vul Stantsionnaya 9, south of the centre, with the long-distance bus terminal is opposite. Rail tickets can be bought at the station or from the office at Ploshcha Vozzednannya 46.

Accommodation and Food: there is not a great choice of hotels or restaurants. Hotel Kiev (vul Koryatovicha 1; tel 35890) is the best hotel in Uzhgorod, with a good restaurant and an open-air terrace in summer. Hotel Zakarpatye, less than a mile south of the city centre (ploshcha 50-letia SSSR 5; tel 97140) is the largest hotel in town, with over 300 rooms. Hotel Uzhgorod on Ploshcha Bogdana Khmnelitskogo (tel 35065) is the Sputnik hotel and consequently the cheapest.

The best restaurants are in the Hotels Kiev and Zakarpatye. Otherwise try the Varalya café on vul Zhovtneva.

Public Holidays

New Years Eve	December 31
Christmas	January 7
International Women's Day	March 8
Easter	March/April
Labour Day	May 1
Victory Day, Mother's Day	May 9
Kiev Days	End of May
Independence Day	August 24
Anniversary of the Russian Revolution	November 7

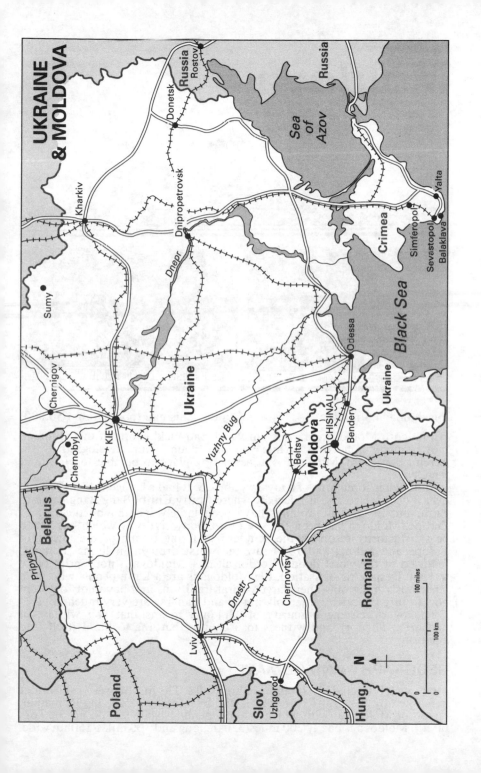

Moldova

Population: 4.3 million   **Capital:** Chişinau (population 650,000)

'To be born Moldovan is to be born with bad luck' is one of the country's most popular aphorisms. While you may count your blessings that you weren't born here, Moldova is a fascinating place to be able to visit (and then leave).

Moldova is something of a mystery abroad. It had a cameo role in *Dynasty* over a decade ago and is allegedly where Chitty Chitty Bang Bang came to earth, but its present troubles have been largely ignored by the rest of Europe. Moldova has been the site of a bloody civil war which has yet to be satisfactorily resolved; the standard of living is one of the lowest in Europe and falling; and 1994 saw the worst drought in living memory, followed by the worst floods. Yet for all this, Moldova is not a grim place to visit. Despite Sovietisation, the Moldovans are a Latin people who have tenaciously hung onto their largely rural traditions and have not forgotten how to throw a celebration: folk music and dancing are very much alive.

The overwhelming obscurity of Moldova means that you will be in uncharted territory and witness to a country battling to build itself into a nation.

GEOGRAPHY AND CLIMATE

Moldova is bordered by Ukraine on three sides. The fourth (western) frontier is marked by the Prut River, which divides Moldova from the Romanian region of Moldavia (with which the independent state should not be confused). Moldova is barely 200 miles/320km long and 100 miles/160km wide.

Most of it consists of flat plain, with the hilliest parts in the area northwest of the capital, Chișinau. The Dniestr River separates a long narrow strip of land in the far eastern part of the country from the rest of Moldova. This industrialised area, known as Transdniestr, declared its independence from the rest of Moldova in 1992.

Between droughts and floods, Moldova has a temperate climate with a relatively high average temperature of 10°C/50°F, moderate winters and reasonable rainfall.

HISTORY

Lodged between powerful empires for the best part of a millenium, Moldova has long been a political football, occupied, re-occupied, fought over and plundered continually. As a result, its history is so convoluted as to be almost incomprehensible, and its borders are still fiercely contested. Most of the territory encompassed by present-day Moldova was part of an independent principality of Moldavia, which existed from 1359 to 1523 and which to most Moldovans was their Golden Age — and their only taste, prior to 1991, of independence. The Turks put paid to that first period of sovereignty, and for the next 300 years the area remained at the heart of territorial disputes between the Turkish Ottomans, Hungarians and Russians. In 1812, the Russians gained the upper hand and incorporated it into their empire.

Over the next 150 years the ownership of Bessarabia (the largest region of modern Moldova) became a burning issue for both the Kremlin and Romania. The latter triumphed, and in 1924 the Moldovan Autonomous Soviet Republic was formed without Bessarabia. In 1939, however, it was returned to the USSR and after the war Romania renounced all claims upon the region. Sovietisation was then swift and systematic: the Cyrillic script was imposed on the Romanian language, and Russians and Ukrainians were shipped in to dilute the population.

During the 1980s, a number of opposition groups campaigned for independence, and in August 1989 Moldova became the first Soviet republic to proclaim its local language the official language. Full independence was achieved in the aftermath of the failed coup in Moscow: Moldova is a brand new country in the sense that it has never existed as an independent state within its present borders.

THE PEOPLE

Moldovans account for 64.5% of the population, with the bulk of the rest split into the following: Ukrainians 13.8%, Russians 13%, the Gagauz (a Turkish Christian group) 3.5% and Bulgarians 2%. The country's ethnic diversity has been the main cause of the political unrest which has plagued Moldova since independence. Non-Moldovans were justifiably concerned that the ultimate aim of independence from the USSR was to rejoin Romania. This was most acutely felt in Transdniestr, a region which had never been part of Romania and where ethnic Ukrainians accounted for 28% of the population and ethnic Russians 25%. The outcome was a violent and bloody conflict which erupted in 1990 and intensified in the spring of 1992, when Transdniestr separatists declared the region's independence from Moldova. A ceasefire was orchestrated in July 1992 and Russian troops were sent in, allowing Russia to bring pressure to bear upon the Moldovan government. It is largely as a result of the Transdniestr situation that the reunification of Romania and Moldova has been taken off the political agenda. Direct aid from Russia including fuel and food continues to pour into the region, but talks between the rebels and the government have still not reached a resolution.

LANGUAGE

The official language is referred to as Moldavian, Moldovan or Romanian, according to whom you're talking to. Moldovan is basically Romanian spoken with a regional accent. If you speak a Latin language (and Italian in particular), you may be pleasantly surprised by how much you can understand, especially now that Moldova has replaced Cyrillic with the Latin alphabet. However, while Moldovan is the first language of a large percentage of ethnic Moldovans, Russian is still the most widely used language in the country. In Chişinau, street signs are in both Moldovan and Russian.

Moldovan words are pronounced more or less as they look, with the following variations:

ă is pronounced as the vowel sound in 'hurt' or 'merge'.
ce or ci is pronounced ch: *ceai* (tea) becomes 'chai'.
ch before e or i is pronounced k: Chişinau is pronounced Kishinow.
e at the start of a word is pronounced ye: Elena becomes Yelana.
g is hard (as in 'go'), except before e or i when it is soft (as in 'gin').
î is similar to the French pronunciation of 'u', lying between the vowel sounds of the English words reed and rude.
ş is pronounced sh: Stefan is pronounced Shtefan.
ţ is pronounced ts: *tigan* becomes 'tsigan'.

Useful words and phrases

yes — *da*	1 — *unu*
no — *nu*	2 — *doi*
hello — *norok*	3 — *trei*
goodbye — *la revedere*	4 — *patru*
my name is — *mă numesc*	5 — *cinci*
please — *poftim*	6 — *şase*
thank you — *multumesc*	7 — *şapte*
how much — *cit costă?*	8 — *opt*
toilet — *toaleta*	9 — *nouă*
good — *bene*	10 — *zece*
water — *apă*	station — *gară*

GETTING THERE

You can fly to Chişinau from cities within the former Soviet Union as well as from Bucharest and, interestingly, Tel Aviv. Moldovan Airlines and Aeroflot and several other carriers fly from Bucharest, so if you wish to fly the whole way from western Europe, this is one of the easiest routes.

Train is probably the easiest way into Moldova. There are daily trains to Chişinau from Simferopol (16 hours), Odessa (6 hours), Moscow via Lviv (30 hours), Bucharest (12 hours) and Kiev (15 hours). The cheapest way to get to Chişinau from Britain is by taking the direct bus from London to Lviv (see page 264) in Ukraine and then catching the train from there, each part of the journey taking 45 hours. There are regular bus services between Bucharest and the Moldovan capital, and modern air-conditioned coaches also run from Istanbul via Bulgaria and Romania.

If you are driving, the M14 road links Odessa (110 miles/177km south) and Chernovtsy (205 miles/330km north) to Chişinau. From Romania, you enter Moldova via Leusheny (30 miles/48km from Chişinau).

RED TAPE

Officially, all foreigners require visas to enter Moldova. Unofficially, you can get in without one depending upon your point of entry and exit. If you enter from Ukraine on a local train, there is no border checkpoint at all, though this is likely to change. If you enter from Romania, however, you will be obliged to pay $50 for a tourist visa or $20 for a transit visa. Matters are complicated further should you enter via the Transdneistr: see below.

MONEY

In 1993 Moldova introduced the lei (pronounced 'lay') as its national currency. It is a comparatively stable currency compared with that of neighbouring Ukraine: in late 1994, you could get 4 leis for one dollar. At the time of writing, it is not possible to exchange travellers' cheques or use credit cards anywhere in Moldova, so bring dollars in cash. You should also change as much money as you think you might need in the capital, either in the main hotels or at a kiosk: most exchange facilities are operated by enterprising individuals who set up kiosks in obvious locations such as train stations, and operate without being troubled by the authorities.

WORK

Given the small size of the country and the severely limited funds for paying foreigners, opportunities in Moldova are poor. One possibility is to contact the Didactic Centre at apartment 4, 18 Bdul Moscow, Chişinau 277045 (tel 232458/fax 321817). This organisation manages English courses in various educational institutions throughout the country, ranging from kindergartens to science universities. English-speaking people are needed to assist, but payment takes the form of board and lodging with a local family.

GETTING AROUND

Trains link the major towns and cities, but otherwise you will have to rely on buses. All internal trains have hard seats, but since the longest journey you can make within the country is about four hours, the scope for prolonged discomfort is limited. Ukrainian or Romanian trains cover international services and are more comfortable. When travelling by bus be prepared for long journeys, even if the distance you intend to cover is short, since the road conditions are poor and the buses antiquated.

Driving regulations and conditions are the same as in neighbouring Ukraine, the main local quirk being that the traffic police wear cowboy hats. You can hire cars at the Moldova Tur office in the Hotel National in Chişinau, which charges about $5 an hour.

ACCOMMODATION

Moldova has never had a thriving tourist industry and still sees few visitors, so the number of hotels is limited. Those which exist are, for the most part, overpriced and under-equipped Intourist affairs. Staying in private accommodation or camping are always an option.

EATING AND DRINKING

Moldova's cuisine reflects its historical turmoil, with influences left behind by its many invaders. You will probably recognise many dishes from the Balkans, including an aubergine paté similar to baba ganoush, stuffed cabbage or vine leaves, goulash-type dishes made with lots of peppers, and cheeses similar to Greek feta. *Chorba* is a spicy soup, often served with *mamalyga*, a type of maize cake which is as much of a staple as bread. Sadly, restaurants are few and far between, and your best chance of eating a good Moldovan meal is in someone's home. Otherwise, try the markets, where peasant women often sell home-made specialities.

Moldovan wines were considered the best in the former Soviet Union, and most meals are washed down with quantities of red and white wines. The brandies are also good, the most famous being Yubileiny, Doina and Syurprizny.

CHIȘINAU (Kishinev)

Some cities are born great, while others have greatness thrust upon them. Chișinau is still reeling from the shock of finding itself at the helm of an independent country. One of the first moves was to change its name from Kishinev to Chișinau. There is little to disguise the fact that the Moldovan capital is still basically a sleepy, provincial town: there can't be many cities in Europe where a ten-minute walk from the main square will take you to open fields. The absence of streetlights and traffic means that you can stand in the middle of town at night and listen to the cicadas. Chișinau is not beautiful or stuffed with historic monuments and won't divert you for long. But it is green, pleasant and decidedly quirky.

CITY LAYOUT

The centre of Chișinau lies on the west bank of the diminutive Bîc river. The layout follows a grid pattern, and you should have no trouble finding your way around. The main street, which stretches several miles, is called Bulvardul Ștefan cel Mare. The only map of the city currently available is a little box on a poster-size map of Moldova, sold at a few kiosks and at Moldova Tur in the Hotel National. Finding buildings can be tricky as the usual formalities such as numbers are often eschewed.

Trolleybuses are the only form of city transport (for which you buy tickets from the driver), but you are unlikely to need to use even these in this small place.

ARRIVAL AND DEPARTURE

Air. International and domestic flights arrive at the airport 5 miles/8km south of town. There is an erratic bus service into the centre, but you may have to take a taxi. The Moldovan Airlines office is located on the 4th floor of the Hotel National (266021).

Train. The railway station is on Bdul Gagarin, a short distance southeast of the city centre. The Intourist Bureau on the first floor is the best place to buy tickets.

Bus. The main bus station is at Stradă Mitropolit Varlaam 58. Information on bus services is available from Oz Gulen Turizm (tel 263748), opposite the train station.

ACCOMMODATION

There are few hotels in Chişinau, but finding a room should not be a problem since there are correspondingly few visitors. Choose from among the following:

Codru, 31 August Stradă 127 (225506). A modern hotel overlooking Pushkin Park in the centre of the city, with doubles for $60.

Seabaco Moldova, M Chibotaru Stradă 37 (277012). The smartest of Chişinau's hotels, charging $180 for a double and catering almost exclusively to visiting business travellers. Facilities include an indoor swimming pool and casino.

National, Bdul Ştefan cel Mare 4 (266083). The former Intourist Hotel, with exceptionally helpful staff. A double room costs $30.

Cosmos, Bdul Negrutsi (223041), within spitting distance of the train station. A shabbier version of the National, with doubles for $30.

For private accommodation, look out for old ladies with signs at the station, or try calling Madame Eugenia on 262096 or 266514.

EATING AND DRINKING

Café Centrul, on Stradă Pushkina near Victory Square, serves the best and cheapest food in Chişinau, although the only element of choice is whether you want a pizza with meat or without meat. It is a bustling place with a young clientele. Restaurant Seabeco Moldova (M Chibotaru 37), in the hotel of the same name, is one of the few places to serve traditional food, but the prices are aimed towards the businessman's budget, at $10-15 per head. The menu includes delicacies such as 'grease and garlic' and 'hot Moldovans'.

The Ig Iorc, at the junction of Mateevici and Hincesti and accessible on trolleybus 10, 7 or 2 (from Bdul Ştefan cel Mare) is a pleasant outdoor café serving drinks and snacks and popular with everyone. There are several good wine shops on Ştefan cel Mare if you want to try the local stuff in the privacy of your hotel.

EXPLORING

Little in Chişinau dates back more than a century. The main street, Bulevardul Ştefan cel Mare, was rebuilt after World War II on a massive scale to accommodate May Day parades, but now it is sadly underused: a handful of trolleybuses are more or less the only traffic to rattle up and down it. The hub of downtown Chişinau is halfway along the street at Ploshchad Pobedy (Victory Square), a communist attempt to inject some Soviet-style glamour into the city. It is a vast space, flanked on one side by the monumental former Soviet, now the parliament, which dwarfs the rest of the town. Opposite, a commemorative arch erected by the Russians in the 19th century to celebrate victory over the Turks leads to a park overlooked by Chişinau's Cathedral, a dilapidated neoclassical structure topped by a shiny copper dome. It has recently been reconsecrated, and despite the scaffolding and the noise of ongoing repairs, the faithful gather here for Sunday services.

On the other side of the square is Pushkin Park, which was recently filled with statues and busts of Moldovan heroes. Outside the entrance stands the figure of Ştefan cel Mare (Stephen the Great), who was the head of an independent Moldova in the 15th century. The park is especially pleasant at weekends, when there is an impromptu speakers' corner near Stephen the Great's statue and old ladies come to practise folk songs and lay flowers at the feet of the country's national heroes.

Heading a few blocks southwest of Pushkin Park, you reach Parcul Valea Morilor (formerly Leninska Komsomola). This contains a lake (with rowing boats for hire) and the Park of Moldovan Economic Achievments. Abbreviated to EREN in Moldovan or VDNKh in Russian, this museum has a collection of agricultural machinery and mass-produced furniture, plus statues of deposed socialists.

The streets northeast of Ştefan cel Mare contain some pleasant 19th-century houses and are worth exploring, but you will soon reach mud tracks and rolling fields. Of the city's museums, the most worthwhile is the Museum of Ethnography and National History, at Stradă M Kogalniceanu 82 (open 10am-6pm, Tuesday to Saturday). It is housed in an exceptional Moorish-style building, built in 1905 and decorated with turquoise, red and yellow tiles. There is a sweeping diorama of Moldovan history in the basement. Among the most enjoyable displays (for the non-Russian/Moldovan speaker) in the National Museum, at August Stradă 31, are the photographs of old Chişinau.

ENTERTAINMENT

Several of Chişinau's theatres and other cultural centres are closed for restoration, but the main venues are the Opera and Ballet Theatre at Bdul Ştefan cel Mare 12; the Pushkin Music and Drama Theatre at Bdul Ştefan cel Mare 79: and the Philharmonia, at the corner of Stradă Metropolit Varlaam and Stradă Mihail Eminescu.

If you want to dance, try the Magic Club off Stradă Albisoara (any taxi driver will know the way). Housed in the Palace of Youth, this club attracts a young crowd which dances to suprisingly good music.

HELP AND INFORMATION

Moldova Tur, Intourist's replacement, has a service bureau on the second floor of the Hotel National. The staff are exceptionally helpful. Sputnik, the old youth travel organisation, is located in the Dvorets Maladoyzhe, or Palace of Youth off Stradă Albisoara (263637, 260720). The central post and telegraph office is at Bdul Ştefan cel Mare 134.

The Ukrainian consulate is in Hotel Codru (see above). There is no British embassy at present in Moldova. In an emergency contact the American Embassy located on Stradă A Mateevici (233698).

FURTHER AFIELD

Moldova is not large, so it is easy to explore beyond the capital. All the places below are accessible by public transport. Tiraspol and Bendery can be reached by train, with other destinations served by bus.

CRICOVA

Located just six miles/10km north of Chişinau, Cricova is a huge underground city where five million bottles of wine are produced a year. More than 850 women are employed to look after the wine, and they scuttle along the maze of tunnels and cellars. The collection includes a bottle of 1902 Jerusalem red which is allegedly worth over $1 billion. Unfortunately, unless you have friends in high places it is not easy to arrange a visit. Enquire at the Moldava Tur office in the Hotel National or consider showing up and seeing if you can tag on to a private guided tour.

CAPRIANA

There are several old monasteries in Moldova which have been given back to the Orthodox Church in recent years. Of these, the most easily accessible is Capriana, about 12 miles/20km north of Chişinau. This 15th-century monastic complex is associated with the early history of Moldova: Stephen the Great may or may not have founded it, but Alexander the Kind (less famous, but he was nice to small animals and children) was definitely born here. Forty monks now live at Capriana, and they have started the monumental task of restoring the six churches on the premises. Though a quantity of fine icons have survived, many more were plundered when the monastery was closed.

The countryside around Capriana is ideal for some gentle hiking, with lots of scenic spots for a picnic. If you've failed to stock up on food and drink in Chişinau, you'll have to rely on the kindness of monks: the one local shop closes just before the first bus arrives and only re-opens once the last bus is on its way back to the capital.

SOROCA

The town of Soroca, 115 miles/185km north of Chişinau and close to the Ukrainian border, is a good stopping-off point if you're driving north. A fort built in the 15th century by Ştefan Cel Mare overlooks the Dniestr river, with views across to Ukraine on the other side. There are also caves in the area which you can explore, but Soroca is above all a good place for relaxation and gentle trekking. Camp Luna, 45 minutes' walk from the bus station (over the bridge and left down a little track), provides accommodation in little huts for less than $1 per person. The river is clean but the strong current will deter all but very strong swimmers from taking the plunge.

You can also visit Vadul Lui Voda, a nature reserve 10 miles/16km southeast of Chişinau, on the edge of the Dniestr river. If you have your own tent it's possible to camp in the forest.

TRANSDNEISTR

The Transdneistr region, which lies sandwiched between the Dneistr river and the Ukrainian border, is heavily industrialised and strategically and economically crucial for Moldova's survival as an independent state. It is at present site of a bloody and largely unreported civil war (page XXX). The UK Foreign Office currently advises travellers not to go there.

Although not recognised by the rest of the world, Transdneistr has declared itself an independent republic. It is possible that a visa payment will be demanded if you enter the country from the Ukrainian side. The region also has its own version of the rouble: Russian bills have been overstamped with the Transdneistr symbol.

Tiraspol. An ancient Greek colony called Tiras once existed here, but you won't find much evidence of it among the high-rise tower blocks. The modern city of Tiraspol, the capital of Transdneistr, was founded in 1792 by the Russians in order to protect their interests against the Turks. With a population of 200,000, only Chişinau is bigger. Russia is very much the first language in Tiraspol and you may well see Russian soldiers, members of the 14th Army, wandering the streets.

Bendery (Tighina). Moldovans have renamed this town Tighina, but its name remains something of a political issue: the majority Russian population prefer the old name of Bendery. Another large industrial town, Tighina is also one of the oldest sites in Moldova, with some Roman remains dating from the time the area was part of Ancient Dacia. The most interesting building is the pentagonal fort above the river. It dates from Roman times, although it was largely reconstructed by the Genoese to protect the important river trade and was later extended by the Turks. It is now an army barracks.

The Caucasus

The Caucasus is the end of the Slavic world, the crossroads between Russia, Turkey and Iran. In the past, the Caucasus mountains, stretching from the Black Sea to the Caspian Sea, created an impassable barrier separating Europe and Asia, and marking the southern extent of Christianity. Christian tradition still holds in Georgia and Armenia, while Azerbaijan is firmly — almost Central Asian in character.

As with the Russian Caucasus to the north, this beautiful part of the world often appears to be tearing itself apart. The ethnic tensions between Armenia and Azerbaijan began at the time when the Soviet Union began to collapse, and show little sign of ending. Georgia has proved to be one of the most explosive regions in the former Soviet Union. For this reason, the region is firmly off-limits to most visitors. It is to be hoped that the cults of violence which are presently holding sway soon end, and that travellers can once again visit one of the most fascinating parts of the former Soviet Union.

The Caucasus defies simple description. Visitors find a mixture of minarets, churches, oil derricks, seaside resorts, spa towns, mountain lakes and tea plantations. They also encounter evidence of violent struggles. The overenthusiastic description of the region as 'the Garden of Eden' looks especially ridiculous against a background of political, religious and racial strife. But Transcaucasia is beguiling: Georgia with its castles and delicious wine, Armenia with its monasteries and cognac and Azerbaijan with its mosques and subtropical plantations.

The area itself has a complex history. The Transcaucasian republics were on the ancient trade route from the East known as the Silk Road. This partly explains the mix of Western and Eastern influences, although the string of invasions to which the Caucasus was subjected is also responsible. The Scythians and Huns were among the early invaders; the Greeks and Romans came on the scene in the early centuries AD and later Byzantium and Persia joined in. Nothing could stand in the way of Genghis Khan and Tamerlane in the 13th and 14th centuries, whose Mongolian hordes arrived from the east. After the fall of Constantinopole to the Turks in 1453, Transcaucasia was split between Persia and the Ottoman Empire. In the light of history, the diversity of the Caucasian cultures is understandable.

Russia's conquest of the Caucasus was a long and difficult process. It started at the beginning of the 18th century, at the instigation of Peter the Great, and continued until 1864. Not only was this in direct conflict with the ambitions of Persia and Turkey but the mountain people also put up fierce resistance. Shamil was the most famous figure of the resistance and is regarded as a hero, fighting against Tsarist imperialism. The Russian occupation was followed by another invasion, this time a peaceful one by the aristocracy attracted by the Caucasian mineral spas. The Caucasus even became a place of exile, but those deported from the north were enchanted by it. Tolstoy immortalized the place in his *Prisoner of the Caucasus*. The journals of 19th-century travellers such as Alexandre Dumas also show fascination in the ethnic diversity here.

After the Revolution in 1917, the three revolutionary parties of Georgia, Armenia and Azerbaiian formed a provisional government that was anti-Bolshevik. In 1918 Transcaucasia declared itself an independent federal state. It offered little effective resistance to Moscow and by 1921 all three republics were part of the USSR. The discontent caused by territorial decisions made in the 1920s has surfaced violently since the collapse of communism. Inter-ethnic relations were the main cause of the troubles which began in 1988 between Armenia and Azerbaijan over Nagorno-Karabakh, an ethnically Armenian territory within the borders of Azerbaijan over which both republics want control. Stress remains between and within these two republics, while when the Soviet Union fell apart, Georgia became the battleground for a long and twisted war between all sorts of maverick elements — notably radical nationalists and residual communists. Its two main breakaway republics are Abkhazia in the northwest and Abzhar in the southwest, on the Turkish frontier.

The Arabs used to call the Caucasus the 'Mountain of Languages'. The three ethno-linguistic groups are the Caucasian group (mainly Georgians), the Turkic group (the Turks of Azerbaijan being the most important) and the Indo-European group (represented by the Armenians, and further north by the Ossets, Slavs and Russians). Religion is also inextricably linked with the region: Armenia was the first nation in the world to adopt Christianity as its offcial religion. This was in the 3rd century, and Georgia followed suit a few decades rater. The church has always been a symbol of national identity and resistance against all forms of invasion; it remains strong in Armenia and Georgia to this day. Islam was introduced by the Arabs in the 8th century and spread among the Turks and the mountain peoples of Azerbaijan. As a faith it reveals itself mostly in the community spirit but the laws of tribal revenge and dominance of the male still linger.

Climate. The Caucasus mountains protect Transcaucasia from the cold north winds, and (at lower altitudes, at least), the region is about the warmest place in the former USSR in winter: temperatures seldom drop below zero.

Eating and Drinking. The food is varied but there are certain constants which show Middle Eastern and Mediterranean influences. Mutton is the favourite meat of the Caucasians. Try *harsho* (a spicy mutton soup, heavily flavoured with garlic). Beans, tomatoes and aubergines are the commonest

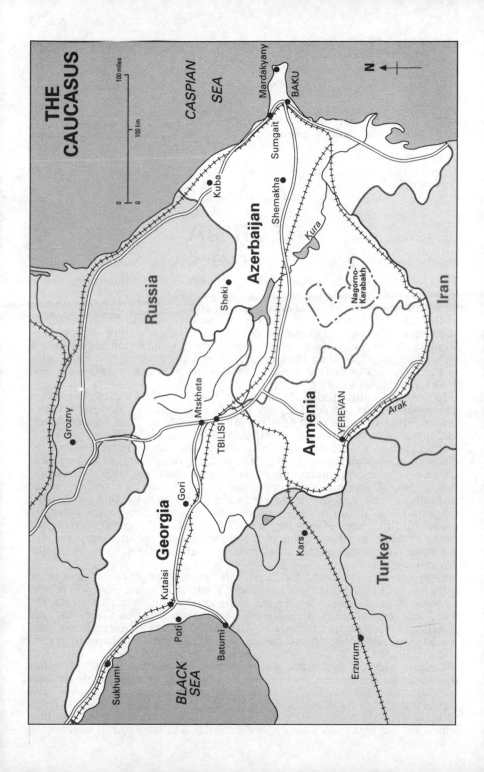

vegetables. Herbs and vegetables are often put on to the table and eaten raw e.g. coriander (*kinza*), which the locals claim will make you live to a hundred; extreme longevity is a trait of the Caucasians. Caucasian pies called *chebureki* (similar to pirozhki found in Russia) are made of unleavened dough and have a filling of spiced mutton; these are most often found in Armenian and Georgian restaurants and in shops called *cheburechnaya*. Cheeses and other dairy products are common. *Kefir* is the Caucasian equivalent of *kumiss* (from Central Asia), the buttermilk which is served in restaurants all over the former Soviet Union. Cakes are also Middle Eastern in nature; halva and cakes made with honey and nuts (such as *baklava*) are particularly popular.

GEORGIA

Population: 5.4 million   **Capital:** Tbilisi (population 1 million)

The Georgian republic is one of the most colourful and interesting in the former Soviet Union. Lying south of Russia beyond the Caucasus Mountains, Georgia is enclosed by the Turkish border to the southeast, the Black Sea to the east, and the republics of Armenia and Azerbaijan to the west and southwest. Although small in terms of area (Georgia accounts for only one-300th of the territory of the former Soviet Union), the republic embraces a wide range of physical conditions: from the high snow-capped mountains of the Caucasus to the agricultural lands of the Kura river valley and the Mediterranean-like coastal strip.

In terms of cultural identity, however, the Georgians regard themselves as a mountainous people. They are also fiercely nationalistic, and retain a certain pride in their most famous son, Josef Stalin. The former Soviet leader was born in Gori and educated for a time in the capital, Tbilisi.

If you arrive in Tbilisi from Russia, the republic immediately seems very different. The population is ethnically distinct from the Slavs. Georgians have a much darker complexion, most of the men sporting large moustaches. A southern, Mediterranean feel predominates. It would be wrong, however, to think of the Georgians as an ethnically homogenous people: whilst the majority (3.4 million) belongs to the so-called Kartvelian group, there are profound differences of language and culture between those occupying the western plains, and those living in the mountainous regions. Georgia is also the home for many immigrants from the various Slavic peoples of the Soviet Union.

Georgians are renowned for their keen business sense, one that in some cases has spilt over into organized crime. That Stalin was a Georgian is held by some Russians as explaining the intrigues that surrounded his rule. On a cultural level there is considerable antagonism between Georgians and Russians. Georgians are regarded by Russians, often condescendingly, as a hot-blooded and hot-tempered people, whilst Georgians see Russians as cold and uncultured.

Despite Moscow's decades of domination of Georgia, the republic has maintained a distinctive culture, thanks largely to its own highly distinct language. Georgia has had its own alphabet since at least 450 AD. The republic is at the crossroads of Asian and European culture, a fact that helps to make Georgia a fascinating destination, and also explains the conflicts which are continuing to flare up in the capital, Tbilisi, and elsewhere.

Money. The Georgian 'coupon' is virtually worthless. The real currencies are (in descending order of acceptability), the US dollar, the Deutschmark and the Russian rouble.

Getting There. *Air.* Georgian Air does not at present operate to the UK, so the best route (or, in the words of one British travel agent, 'the least unsafe route') is probably via Baku in Azerbaijan. You can get to Baku on British Airways' twice-weekly flight from London Gatwick, with connections from the USA. As of summer 1995, however, no discounted flights were offered on this service. A better deal, therefore, is on Azerbaijan Airlines — around £550 from London, including the Baku-Tbilisi sector.

Rail. At the time of writing, services from Russia were suspended because of hostilities. Links remain from Armenia (three expresses daily from Yerevan, around 11 hours) and Azerbaijan (twice daily, one fast and one slow, taking 12 and 18 hours respectively).

Eating and Drinking. The Georgians are an extremly hospitable and sociable people. Should you be invited back to a Georgian household (and it would be unlucky not to be), you will experience this at first hand. The food supply in Georgia is usually excellent, with fresh fruit and vegetables of all sorts being relatively easy to find. Dishes to look out for include *khachapuri* (not dissimiliar to a cheese pizza), *tzatzivi* (cold chicken pieces in a walnut sauce), *sulguni* (a smoked cheese), *nodun* (cream cheese with mint), *adjika* (hot red pepper and coriander paste), and many different fruits and vegetables.

Georgian meals tend to last an age, and are washed down with vast quantities of Georgian wine. The toastmaster (*Tamada*) is a vital part of any celebratory meal in Georgia. He (Georgia is still a strongly patriarchal society) is chosen for his wit, eloquence and — especially — drinking abilities. Toasts will last for 10-15 minutes, and having finished the toast the Tamada will often drink from a Georgian drinking horn, completing the toast by turning the horn upside-down-to prove that it is empty.

Safety. Georgians as a whole tend to be nationalistic, but since the collapse of communism the republic has splintered into several equally nationalistic blocs. South Ossetia, Abkhazia and Adjaria are all in various states of independence from, and conflict with, the government in Tbilisi. Therefore you should check local conditions both before visiting Georgia and, once you arrive, before exploring too deeply.

TBILISI

The capital (formerly known as Tiflis) is a charming city astride the River Kura in a natural bowl, surrounded by mountains on all sides. Its name is derived from the Georgian word *tbili* meaning warm, and is due to the fact that there are many hot springs in the city. Water emerges from the earth at a temperature of 30°C/86°F. Visitors wishing to experience the 'Turkish' baths can find a working sulphur bath along Gorgassali Street. Nevertheless, it was not merely the springs that gave rise to Tbilisi's importance. It was an important trading centre between Georgia's rich agricultural land and the Northem Caucasus and Persia. Archeologists have dated the remains of the huge Narikala fortress standing on the high bluff above the Kura to the early 4th century.

Arrival and Departure. The airport is about 25 minutes from the centre, served by plenty of buses and taxis.

Accommodation. The premier hotel in Tbilisi, and hence the whole of

Georgia, is the Metechi Palace Hotel, run by the Marco Polo group. This functions both as an upmarket hotel and *de facto* 'business' centre for the city. A sign at the door informs visitors that handguns are allowed into guest rooms, but semi-automatic weapons must be checked in at reception. Other hotels include the Iveria, the venerable Tbilisi, and the Adzhariya, which is a little further from the centre. Whilst there is a Metro, and plenty of buses, virtually all the sights are located within an easy walking distance of the hotels.

Exploring. When peace reigns, Tbilisi is still a pleasure to walk around. Its centre is still dominated by its original layout, a network of narrow cobbled streets and alleys often beginning or ending in stairways. The traditional houses, with their intricately carved wooden railings bannisters and cornices, provide a striking contrast to the typically over-pianned Soviet city with wide boulevards and huge squares. The main street in Tbilisi is Rustaveli Avenue, named in honour of the famous 19th century Georgian poet Shota Rustaveli. It is lined with trees which makes it a very pleasant walk in the hot summer months.

The Georgian Museum and Museum of Georgian Art are good places to get a good grounding in the nation's culture. Famous pieces include the Trialeti gold goblet, which is over 4,000 years old. The works by more recent Georgian artists, such as Niko Pirosmani, are also superb. Tbilisi today is the home of a thriving artistic scene, being particularly strong in the graphical and cinematic arts.

The city's churches, mosques and synagogues are spectacular. The distinctive architectural style and floor plan of Georgian churches owes a great deal to Byzantium. One of the finest examples is the 13th century Metekha Cathedral, perhaps the most impressive symbol of the Georgian nation. The equestrian statue is a representation of the supposed founder of Tbilisi, Vakhtang Gorgasali, King of Karthli. Just beside the church is a terrace of shops and houses in traditional Georgian style. Upstream from the Metekha Cathedral, the River Kura is enchsed by high cliffs. At the top are some very pretty, typically Georgian houses. Another church worth seeing is the Sioni Cathedral, the Residence of the Catholikos (Head of the Georgian Orthodox Church). The present structure dates from the sixth century.

Outside the immediate centre of the city there are several points of interest. A cable railway will take you up to Stalin Park, home to the monstrous TV mast that dominates the skyline of Tbilisi. A more pleasing sight is the open-air Museum of Georgian Folk Architecture and Everyday Llfe. The best way to reach this Museum is to take the cable car at the station on Chavchavadze Street, and go up to Cherepashye (Tortoise) Lake. The Museum is halfway up to the Lake. It features traditional Georgian peasant dwellings and demonstrations of craftsmanship.

Further Afield. Several interesting excursions can be made as day trips from Tbilisi: a trip up into the high Caucasus along the Georgian Military Road and the Aragvi River Valley; a visit to Gori, Stalin's birthplace, passing along the Kura river valley; and to Mtskheta, the ancient capital of Georgia.

Mtskheta. There has been a settlement at Mtskheta, ten miles/16km north of the capital, for four millenia. It is situated at the confluence of the two great Georgian rivers, the Kura and the Aragvi. Its greatest period was as capital of the Kingdom of Kartli from the 4th century BC to the 5th century AD, and it has played a pivotal role in the evolution of Georgian culture. The origins of the Georgian written language and the establishment of Christianity in the region are intimately linked with the city. The Sveti

Tskhoveli Cathedral is the largest Georgian church and dates from the 11th century. It is said that the builder of the cathedral, Arsukisdze, had a hand chopped off by his tutor because he had surpassed his teacher's ability. Other sights include the Armaz Acropolis, and the beautiful Byzantine Dzhvari Church standing on a bluff high above the city. This church was built between 585 AD and 604 AD, and its name means 'cross' in Georgian.

The Georgian Military Road. From Mtskheta the road follows the valley of the River Aragvi, which climbs up into spectacular scenery. For centuries this road was the main artery of communication between Georgia and Russia, but lost sigrlificance upon the completion of the railway from present-day Ordzhonihdze to Baku and Tbilisi in 1883. Its military importance is graphically illustrated in the form of the medieval castle at Ananuri, which once dominated the whole Aragvi valley. Inside the walls are two beautiful churches. From Ananuri, the road climbs through a series of spectacular gorges to the village of Pasanauri — over 3,300ft/1,000m high. From here, the road winds its way through a spectacular series of hairpin bends up to the Krestovy Pass at 7,850ft/2,380m, and thence down into Russia.

Gori. The centre of a rich agricultural region, Gori lies on the River Kura. It is the birthplace of Josef Dzhugashvili, more commonly known as Stalin. There is a museum in the house where he was born. The skyline is dominated by the Goristsikhe Fortress, the present structure of which dates from the 13th century. Six miles/10km along the Kura valley lies the fascinating Uplistsikhe Fortress dating from the sixth century AD. As can be seen from its dominant position, this fortress controlled the Kura Valley. Only in the thirteenth century was it stormed and taken by Khulagu, son of Ghengis Khan.

The Black Sea Coast. Most of the Georgian part of the Black Sea coastline is a spectacular riviera: high mountains which come right down to the coast in the north, and long sandy beaches in the south. It is also largely off-limits due to conflict with separatists. Before venturing there, seek advice in Tbilisi.

The southern Black Sea coast is dominated by the city of Batumi, capital of the former Adzharia Autonomous Republic, which borders Turkey to the south. Even if the simmering conflict with Adzhari separatists settles, Batumi is chiefly a large commercial port, with little of interest to visitors. In contrast, the ancient settlements of Sukhumi and Kutaisi — on the northern part of the coast — are excellent bases.

Sukhumi. Greek traders founded the port of Dioscurius, which in antiquity was one of the main points of communication between Greece and the Caucasus. The remains of Dioscurius now lie under the Black Sea, and indeed Sukhumi itself is slowly sinking. The Romans built a new city, and Sukhumi subsequently passed into Byzantine, then Turkish hands. It was only in 1810 that control passed to the Russian Empire. It is now capital of the breakaway republic of Abkhazia, and at present out-of-bounds.

Some of the most spectacular coastal views can be had from the small coastal towns of Gagra and Pitsunda. From the coast there are excursions into the mountainous interior and to Lake Ritsa, a spectacularly beautiful spot.

Kutaisi. Georgia's second city, Kutaisi was the capital of the ancient Kingdom of Colchis. Today it is modern and bustling. There is a great deal of evidence of the past glories of Kutaisi, the most spectacular being the 11th century Church of King Bagrat.

ARMENIA

Population: 3.29 million   **Capital:** Yerevan (population 750,000)

According to one of Armenia's many legends, when God created the world He sieved the soil and threw the softest part to one side and the stones to the other, exactly where Armenia now stands. The terrain is exceedingly rocky: Mount Aragats is the highest peak at 4,090m/13,400ft. Mount Ararat, where Noah's Ark is said to have settled after the flood, is higher still; although visible from the republic's capital, Yerevan, the mountain now lies in Turkish territory. This is a constant cause of anguish among the Armenians, whose empire once stretched as far west as the Mediterranean. They see Ararat as their symbol; it decorates their flag, and church roofs in Yerevan seem to echo its shape.

The republic lies in the southern part of Transcaucasia, with Turkey and Iran to the west and south. The Armenians are one of the oldest peoples in the world, but throughout their history they have been the prey of such neighbours as Turkey and Persia who were covetous of Armenia's position on important trade routes. Many Armenians have emigrated over the years, and their communities can be found in places as diverse as Germany and New York City. The exodus reached a peak in 1915 when they were virtually annihilated by the Turks. But despite this and the later atrocities committed by Stalin, they have preserved their own distinctive culture as well as a deep-rooted attachment to their homeland.

In 1988 Armenia hit the world's headlines on two counts. First, there was the unprecedented (in Soviet terms) unrest over the treatment of ethnic Armenians in the neighbouring Islamic republic of Azerbaijan. Thousands of people demonstrated in Yerevan, demanding the return of the region of Nagorno-Karabakh, which was incorporated into neighbouring Azerbaijan in 1923. More than 80% of the population in the disputed area is Armenian. The conflict is exacerbated by the fact that Armenians are Christian and traditionally at odds with the Muslim Azerbaijanis, whom they call 'Soviet Turks'. Calls for the return of the disputed region to Armenia were marked by mass demonstrations, handled brutally by the authorities. The dissent was quickly overshadowed by the Soviet Union's worst natural disaster, when an earthquake devastated western Armenia. The town of Spitak was totally destroyed and serious damage was done to Leninakan. About 26,000 people died and some were 500,000 left homeless.

With 70% of the land being mountainous, Armenia is one of the most beautiful areas in the Caucasus. It is unfortunate, therefore, that travel to the region is likely to continue to be hazardous over the next few years.

Climate. Armenia's geographical position and its average altitude of 3,300ft/ 1,000m make the weather variable. While grapes are ripening in the plains, it is still summer in the foothills, poppies are in flower further up the slopes and higher still the peaks are permanently snowcapped. During the summer, subtropical areas can rise above 40°C/104°F while in winter temperatures at high altitudes drop to −30°C/−22°F. These temperatures are extremes, however, and basically it is pleasantly warm in spring and hot in summer with winters being cold but short. The climate must largely be thanked for the fact that around 10% of the population is over 80. This, together with the high birth rate, makes it fortunate that the young traditionally hold great respect for the elderly. Older males tend to rule the roost. Few women pursue a career, since the family is of prime importance in Armenian culture.

Eating and Drinking. Armenian food alone justifies a visit to the republic. Bulgar wheat, chick peas and nuts are common ingredients as in Middle Eastern countries. Herbs and spices (especially cayenne and allspice) are also used liberally. Milk products are popular too, with *matzun* (similar to yoghurt) being used in many dishes and *tvorog* (a type of curd cheese) being a popular starter when served with fresh vegetables. Traditional starters are generally pungent and bitter and without seasoning or sauce of any kind.

Armenians are masters at cooking lamb: try *bozbash* (lamb stew with sour fruit), *kharput kiouftas* (meatballs made of lamb cooked in a chicken casserole) and *yarpakh dolmassy* (vine leaves stuffed with lamb and rice and served with a cinnamon-flavoured yoghurt sauce). The hot and cold soups are particularly tasty, but if you're feeling homesick try an Armenian omelette (*skrob*) made with *brynza* (feta cheese), vegetables and lots of cayenne. *Lavash* is the local bread which is traditionally made in the country in craters hollowed in the ground. Look out for the cakes, too, especially nut and honey *baklava* — sticky but delicious.

The local wine is recuperating from the vine-clearing excesses of Mikhail Gorbachev, but the brandy is excellent. Cognac is made in various parts of Armenia but the best, Erevanskii razliv, is made in Yerevan (you can visit the local distillery).

YEREVAN

The Armenian capital is 175 miles/280km by road from Tbilisi. Beyond Idzhevan and Dilizhan you come to the shores of Lake Sevan, and 44 miles/ 70km further on, dropping through the hills, is Yerevan. Colin Thubron in *Among the Russians* gives an interesting account of this drive, being stopped at 11 police posts and being forbidden to turn off the road. These days there are few restrictions: try not to be too perturbed by the crashed cars displayed at the side of the road as a warning to motorists — the Armenians certainly don't take any notice.

On the banks of the Razdan river and surrounded by vineyards that cascade down the mountain slopes, the Armenian capital nestles in the Ararat Valley; if the haze and pollution permit there is a fine view of the famous mountain. The city is full of hustle and bustle with dusty streets and noisy cars existing alongside ample greenery and fountains. Perhaps the most lasting impression of Yerevan is the colour and inventiveness of its architecture. The colours of the luxuriant decoration and the pink of the local *tufa* (limestone) seem to change according to the time of day. Yerevan is colourful in more than just the literal sense: go prepared for a city teeming with students and black marketeers.

Arrival and Departure. In 1994 and 1995, provisional plans were made to begin flights from London to Yerevan (including some services via Riga in Latvia), but at the time of writing nothing had come to fruition. The best existing service is on Turkish Airlines via Istanbul, costing around £500 from London or Manchester. The flight time from Moscow is about three hours.

The airport lies southwest of the city along ul Echmiadzin. There are rail connectlons from the Russian main line at Rostov-on-Don via Tbilisi to Yerevan; from Moscow the journey takes about 55 hours. Tbilisi is 14 hours away by train (three daily), while the daily 200-mile/320km journey from Mindzhevan in Azerbaijan to Yerevan takes 12 hours — if it is running. You can also travel by train from Erzurum in Turkey via Leninakan, a distance of 184 miles/294km.

Accommodation. There are three main hotels: the Armenia at 1 ul Amiryana (tel 52 53 03) is one up on the others with a wine cellar, as well as the usual facilities such as a dismal danceband. Near the river, northwest of the Armenia, is the Dvin at 40 ul Proshyana (tel 52 63 84) where you can experience the joys of their cabaret. Down from the opera house is the Ani Hotel at 19 Sayat-Nova Prospekt, which has a cinema and concert hall.

Exploring. Few of the old adobe houses have survived but the spaciousness and the monumental architecture make the city both a fun and interesting place to wander around. Both the History Museum (with national costume, carpets, etc.) and the National Picture Gallery (whose collection includes the works of Tintoretto and Rubens) are on the main square. The Market Hall is impressive both for its architecture and for the colourful atmosphere. Nearby is the remarkably Museum of Modern Art, which was the most non-conformist gallery in the Soviet Union and has a throving collection of local art.

Heading north, behind the park and the Opera House you can turn into ul Barekamu, one of Yerevan's prettiest streets, or carry on up to the Matenadaran, a splendid museum which is the pride of the city. It contains a fine collection of Armenian manuscripts, some with magnificent illuminations and some of great international importance since they are translations of old manuscripts of which the originals have been lost.

If you prefer to stroll around there are pleasant promenades along the river which forms a deep ravine near the city. Abovyan Park, on the right bank of the river west of the centre, is a popular spot with a special railway that goes to a nearby swimming pool. From Abovyan Square in the north, ul Kanakeri leads to Kanaker Plateau from where there is a fine view of Yerevan. Also from Abovyan Square, ul Norki joins a forest path which leads southeast to Komsomol Park. South of here is Arin-Berd ('bleeding fortress'), the ruined palace of King Argistis of Urartu, the founder of Yerevan and monarch of one of the oldest kingdoms in the world. The frescoes and friezes are beautiful. There is another Urartu fortress on Kamir-Blur hill in the southwestern suburbs, whose ruins indude some 150 buildings. There is always a good atmosphere up here on a Sunday; on any day, the view of the city and entire valley is worth the trip.

Entertainment. As well as the Opera and Ballet Theatre, already mentioned, the Tumanyan Puppet Theeatre at 4 Prospekt Sayat-Nova also has a good reputation. Music is the most respected art form in Armenia and there is a music school in virtually every village. People without a love of music are considered uneducated. It touches many fields of activity, both religious and secular.

Shopping. Armenian trading abilities are at their most visible on the streets of Yerevan. Armenian carpets are about the best buy in the whole of the Caucasus if you can afford them. Embroidery work is worth looking out for too, although you are likely to get a better deal outside the capital. The designs of Armenian silver jewellery can also be surprisingly modern. Be warned that customs officials can be awkward about taking antiques and even brand-new carpets out of the country.

Further Afield. Armenia is the smallest of the former Soviet republics, and distances seem short compared with the other countries in this book. Armenia has plenty to sustain you for a visit of at least a week, whether you prefer beautiful countryside or magnificent architecture. There are thousands of churches, monasteries and *khatchkars* (stone crosses erected for symbolic or commemorative purposes), many of which are in remote mountain areas and completely inaccessible. Some, however, are accessible enough to give some idea of how influential Armenia was in the history of architecture, having an important role in the development of the dome and the circular church. Armenians were also instrumental in the transmission to the West of the cruciform (cross-shaped) church. Leonardo da Vinci himself visited Armenia in the 15th century.

Zvartnots and Echmiadzhin. Ul Echmiadzin leads across the river from Yerevan into the heart of the Ararat Valley. Passing St Ripsime, a gem of a church dating from the 7th century, at the 15km mark, carry on for two miles/3km to Zvartnots cathedral, set among vineyards and orchards. Erected in the seventh century, it was then the largest circular church in the world. Unfortunately Arab sackings and earthquakes have left it in ruins, but there is a moving atmosphere about the place, especially at twilight.

Echmiadzin, an ancient capital of Armenia but now a busy market town, is two miles/3km further on. Since the 14th century it has been the seat of the Patriarch of the Armenian Church and is visited by many pilgrims. The cathedral, built in 303 AD but rebuilt in the fifth century, is the highlight of the tour. The Persian latticework is stunning, and if you go on a Sunday the excellent choir provides a concert-worthy performance. If you happen to be around on a feast day you could witness the Patriarch and his hooded monks processing to the cathedral. Devotees also offer lambs up for sacrifice, which are then cooked in huge pots and eaten by families amongst the tombstones. Vegetarians should keep away: if you refuse the meat offered to you, the wish made before the sacrifice will not be granted.

The trip can be extended another ten miles/16km by going to Lake Aygerlich where otters breed in the reeds and the setting is idyllic. You can visit the above churches by bus or car, and bicycles can be hired in Yerevan.

Garni and Gegard. Travelling 20 miles/32km east of Yerevan along the ridge of the Gegami range and descending through a pass you reach Garni. The Temple of the Sun perches high on a cliff above a deep valley. Dating from the first century and skilfully restored, it rises in the centre of a fortress built in the 3rd century BC as a summer residence for the Armenian kings. Notice the marvellous friezes and mosaics depicting sea monsters and other mythical creatures. Four miles/7km further east is the Gegard Monastery, set in a beautiful gorge and carved out of solid rock. People say that the holy lance which pierced the body of Christ was once kept here. As well as priests dozing inthe shade you may see people tying coloured ribbons to trees; the local belief is that so doing makes wishes come true.

Ashtarak. The town of Ashtarak, nestled on the slopes of Mount Aragats and 12 miles/20km northwest of Yerevan, is of little interest in itself but the surrounding area rewards exploration. The countryside is thick with picturesque villages, ancient burial grounds, dolmen and other megalithic monuments. Parbi and Oshakan warrant a visit but Ovanavank, three miles/5km from Ashtarak, deserves the greatest attention: here there are various ecclesiastical buildings and *khatchkars* (stone crosses) in a beautiful spot at the edge of a deep gorge. From Byurakan, six miles/10km west of Ashtarak, you can walk through forest and valleys to where the Arkhansen and Amberd rivers converge. High above are the ruins of the 10th century Amberd fortress.

Lake Sevan. You could choose to make Lake Sevan a base and explore the rest of Armenia from here; and sleeping in lakeside lodgings could be a pleasant change from faceless hotels. Lake Sevan, with the somewhat eerie atmosphere that hangs over it, is one of the largest mountain lakes in the world. The distance around its shores measures about 125 miles/200km. Maxim Gorky described it as a piece of sky that had fallen amongst the mountains, and it is easy to understand how legends have grown up around it. On the northwest shore stands a statue of Tamara, a medieval princess kept prisoner in a convent by the lake. Every night her lover rowed across to visit her by following the light of a fire that she lit for him, until one night a storm put the fire out causing the young man's death. Unfortunately the legend originated from Turkey and there never was an Armenian princess called Tamara. But this does not deter visitors and many come here to picnic. The air is fresh, the sun shines just about all year round and the water is beautifully clear, but so cold that only the brave dare swim.

The area is rich in monuments to explore. These include the ninth century monastery perched on the rocky slopes of the Sevan Peninsula near the town, and prehistoric cave dwellings near the village of Lohasen. Otherwise you could go on a hydrofoil trip round the lake or go boating, (but avoid the middle of the day, as the winds tend to pick up and sometimes develop into storms).

Accommodation. You can stay in the Motel Sevan, on the northwest shore near Sevan town, 62 miles/100km from Yerevan airport, 46 miles/70km from the capital itself. It is a lively place although it looks somewhat run down; you should be particularly aware of security (there have been several reports of theft). The restaurant serves national food including the famous *ishkhan*, the trout native to the lake. You would actually do better to go to the Ishkhan Restaurant near the Sevan monastery which specializes in serving fresh ishkhan: brushed with oil, cayenne and basil and grilled. The Hotel Akhtamar also has a good restaurant and is in a lovely position high above the lake.

Dilizhan and Tsakhkadzor. North from Lake Sevan the road climbs and then descends through beautiful gorges to Dilizhan, 20 miles/32km away. Surrounded by dense woods and mountain springs, it is one of the most picturesque resorts in the Caucasus. It was the most important cultural centre of medieval Armenia. If you are heading for Georgia you could stop here on the way. Tsakhkadzor is another country retreat about 35 miles/57km north of Yerevan, set in the so-called 'Valley of Flowers'. By following a forest path you can climb Mount Tegenis from where there is a magnificent view. This is a popular skiing place in winter. If you want to go on a day trip, trains run from Yerevan to Razdan (just west of Sevan) from where you can get a bus.

AZERBAIJAN

Population: 7.22 million   **Capital:** Baku (population 1.8 million)

Azerbaijan, with a population of 6.8 million, spreads south from the wooded slopes of the Caucasus. These mountains cover half the republic and at the Caspian Sea plunge downwards forming the Apsheron Peninsula where Baku, the capital, lies. Azerbaijan is a country of great variety: the people in tbe north and west belong to the mountain world of the Caucasus with their own lively traditions, while the southeastern areas of arid and almost deserted steppe are linked geographically and culturally to Iran, which has its own region called Azerbaijan.

Like Armenia, Azerbaijan was traversed by historic trading routes and as such attracted many conquerors, especially from Turkey and Persia. Caravans of Eastern traders travelled along this part of the route when it was known as Bab-ul-Abvad, the 'Gate of the East'; in this capacity Azerbaijan was also of strategic interest to Peter the Great, keen to expand his 18th-century empire. Islam, the climate and the language (Turk Azeri is the official language but you may hear Iranian and Arabic spoken, as well as some Russian) in many ways bring Azerbaijan close to Central Asia. As in Iran, most of the people are Shi'ite Muslims.

Although banners of the Iranian Ayatollahs have appeared on the streets, the Azeri, on the whole, are unfanatical about religion. Some Azeris, however, are not averse to the idea of reunion with Iranian Azerbaijan. The Azeri interpretation of the faith creates a great sense of community but they follow a fairly enlightened view of Islam. Women have greater freedom than in many Muslim countries, and were the first in a Muslim nation to receive the vote. All these elements, with the combination of sun, sea and mountains make it a fascinating republic to visit and is also a sharp cultural contrast to Christian Armenia. The disputed region of Nagorno-Karabakh — an Armenian enclave within Azerbaijan — is still the location for upsurges of violence, and in 1995 the Foreign Office was warning British visitors against travelling to the republic. The ethnic unrest in Azerbaijan has tended to be more violent than in Armenia. Demonstrators have also brandished Turkish flags in remembrance of the help the Turks gave Azerbaijan in an effort to save their independence after the Russian Revolution.

Recently the focus of conflict has switched from ethnic differences to a broader struggle for political control. In March 1995, violence flared up when the military police force, Opon, mutinied against the poltical leaders.

If and when it is safe to visit, there is plenty to keep you occupied in the rest of the republic, with its curious mixture of mosques, orchards and oil derricks. Since the 19th century Azerbaijan's fate has been closely linked to oil although Atropatena, 'the land of eternal flames', has been seeping oil for centuries and drew the attention of explorers such as Marco Polo.

Climate. You can test no less than nine of the world's thirteen climatic zones in Azerbaijan, an extraordinary figure given the realtively small size of the country. The climatic contrasts match the cultural and ethnic diversity. While the mountains in the north are perpetually freezing, further south you find subtropical valleys where exotic fruit grows abundantly. In the lower altitudes the temperatures are fairly mild. The winter average in Baku is just above freezing, while in summer the temperature in the valleys and coastal areas averages 30°C/86°F.

Red Tape. The good news is that visas are free if you apply in advance through the Azeri Embassy, Room 208, London House, 19 Old Court Place, London W8 4PL (0171-938 2222) *and* you have an invitation from a state department or company in Azerbaijan. If you elect to get a visa upon arrival, you pay $40 at the airport and wave goodbye to your passport for 24 hours, while it goes off to the Foreign Ministry for processing.

Money. The unit of currency is the Manat. It is like the Russian rouble in two ways: it maintains a similar value against the US dollar, ie around 5,000 to 1 in May 1995; and it devalues frequently due to high inflation.

BAKU

The Azeri capital lies on the Caspian Sea and has a population of around 1,800,000. The name derives from *Bad-Kube* a Turk Azeri word meaning 'city of winds' due to the powerful north wind that can rage there. The city forms an amphitheatre overlooking the bay and the offshore oilfields. A popular but curious local saying goes: 'If oil is the queen of Azerbaijan, Baku is her crown,' but it is hard to romanticize about the fact that the city can be hell at times: exceedingly hot, unhygienic and polluted. The city parks, however, go some way to mitigate the sultry heat and Baku is still a welcoming, cosmopolitan city. It was built on a second-century settlement and grew, as Azerbaijan did as a whole during the Middle Ages. The plentiful oil reserves created considerable attention, the oil being used mainly for military and medicinal purposes. Between the 12th and 15th centuries Baku was the capital of the powerful state of the Shirvan Shahs. Interesting features of the city date from this period although subsequent invasions, by Persians among others, and modernization have taken their toll.

Arrival and Departure. Flights link Baku with London and other Western European cities. Azerbaijan Airlines flies weekly from Gatwick, and fares of around £420 are available from agents such as those on page 14. This non-stop flight takes around six hours, while British Airways' twice weekly service stops at Bucharest and takes two hours longer. Furthermore, BA is (as of summer 1995) not discounting fares below the official excursion rate of over £900. Flights from Moscow take about three hours, while Yerevan is an hour away and Tbilisi 90 minutes.

Most international trains from the north go via Rostov-on-Don before proceeding to Baku via Tbilisi; this route is subject to interruption as a result of fighting. When it is running, the journey from Moscow take about 42 hours.

There have been reports of a ferry link to Baku from Bandar-e-Anzali (Iran) over the Caspian Sea, but with the political situation being rather unstable only the more intrepid may want to try this. The ferry to across the Caspian to Krasnovodsk (Turkmenistan) is more reliable.

City Layout. Old Baku (*Icheri Shekher*), enclosed within walls with tortuous streets and flat-roofed houses huddled together, is the heart of the city. Shemakha Gate takes you into Nizami Square in the outer city (*Bayir Skekher*), from where ul Kommunististicheskaya leads to Primorski Bulvar, which runs alongside the sea. Parallel to Primorski Bulvar is the main street, Prospekt Neftyanikov. There is a metro system which connects the northeastern district to the centre.

Be careful when you are crossing roads as drIvers tend to be temperamental and are not keen to relinquish rights of way to pedestrians.

Accommodation. A *caravanserai* (old traders' inn) in Icheri Shekher has recently been converted into the Karavan Sarai Hotel, which is certainly the most atmospheric option. The old Hotel Intourist by the sea at 63 Prospekt Neftyanikov (tel: 92-1265/1251) is the most likely bet. The restaurant serves tolerable food, and the waiters are more helpful than usual. Hotel Azerbaijan at 1 Prospekt Lenina (tel: 92-9842/9843) is a characterless, standard-issue tourist hotel.

Eating and Drinking. While you're in Baku take advantage of the proximity of the Caspian which is brimming with delicious fish. Azerbaijan is paradise for those with a weakness for caviar, called *ikra*, the best of which is found in Baku (and most of which goes straight for export or onto the black market). Other fish caught in the Caspian include *vobla*, a kind of roach served fresh or dried and sturgeon. *Shashlyks*, shish kebabs eaten most in Central Asia but also popular in the Caucasus, and Azerbaijan's many varieties of *pilaf* are popular dishes. The Azerbaijanis share with Armenia a penchant for lamb: try *dyushpara* (like ravioli, filled with lamb, garlic and lots of herbs). Other interesting meat dishes include *dovta* (a meat casserole with sour milk) and *nur kurma* (roasted meat garnished with pomegranates). *Narsharab* is a pomegranate sauce for meat and fish and an essential feature of Azerbaijani cooking. Milk foods are plentiful and a popular starter is yoghurt or buttermilk served with raw vegetables such as spring onions, followed by fresh fruit, ideally damsons and peaches, sauteed in butter: absolutely delicious.

The restaurants in the old town are the best: the Bukhara, set in a 16th century caravanserai, serves exotic local dishes including the delicious nut cakes called *shekerbur*. The Multani is housed in a 14th century caravanserai and upstairs there is a tea-room serving various traditional oriental sweets. If you want a different atmosphere, try the restaurants along the seaside boulevard where there are kebab stalls. This is also the place to come if you are more interested in drinking: there are various *chaikhanas* (teahouses) and open-air cafés. The chaikhanas are similar to those in Central Asia in that they are a popular meeting place but differ in that you cannot buy hot meals; in Azerbaijan you can only buy tea, in the traditional pear-shaped glasses called *armuds*. You can drink *kumiss* — fermented mare's milk common in Central Asia and an acquired taste — or try the local cognac or wine. Azeri wines are poor, and the strange pseudo-European names like *portwein* are probably the most amusing thing about them.

Exploring. From Prospekt Neftyanikov it is just a few minutes' walk to Shemakha Gate; if it is oppressively hot, catch trolleybus 3 to Dom Pechati or take the metro to Baky Soveti station. This is the best place to begin exploring the old city which, with its gates and towers, has largely retained its original structure. Simply wandering around is good entertainment in itself, but there are several features to look out for. The Maiden's Tower (Kyz Galasy) dates from the 12th century; climbing up to the top gives you a good panorama of the city. The maiden of the tower is the subject of many legends and poems but none solve the mystery as to who she actually was. Nearby are caravanserais (traders' inns) and baths, and the oldest building in Baku: the Sinik-Kala minaret with beautifully simple decoration. Up the hill past some 19th-century mansions, some now back in private hands, is the Palace of the Shirvan Shahs with rich decoration and stunning tilework. It houses the Historical and Architectural Museum, but of more interest is the Carpet and Folk Art Museum in the Djuma Mosque at 49 ul Asafa Zeinally. It claims to be the first of its kind in the world, and contains ancient carpets, fabric and jewellery.

The new quarter will be of interest to followers of Constructivist architecture, which had an important role in the transformation of the city in the 1920s. The best examples are the Press Palace (Dom Pechati) in Nizami Square and the old Hotel Intourist, a cut above its namesakes elsewhere in the former Soviet Union. Otherwise, strolling down the shady promenade is perhaps the best thing to do in the outer city. Primorski Bulvar is one of the busiest spots in town and is positively teeming on feast days. There is an area along here known as 'Baku's Venice', an unconvincing system of canals where you can go boating. You can also go for 45-minute trips around the bay, but your negotiation skills may be needed; gone are the days of the 45-kopeck ride. Ul Djaparidze, near the Maiden's Tower, is closed to traffic and is another favourite promenade place in Baku. From the end of Prospekt Neftyanikov you can go by funicular up to the park, from where there are splendid views of the city, especially at sunset. Stairs lead back down to the seafront.

Entertainment. The Opera House is on ul Nizami but the parks and promenades are the most likely source of evening entertainment. The park at the top of the funicular has an open-air theatre, and along Primorski Bulvar there is an open air cinema and a stage where concerts are held in summer. The main concert hall adjoins Nizami Square, but if possible go and see a performance of *mugam*, traditional Azerbaijani music. Mugam contains Iranian elements, with its fiery dance rhythms and lyrically emotionally songs, and is the most oriental music you'll find in Transcaucasia.

There are various sports facilities along the boulevard. The sea around Baku is not clean enough for bathing but there is a swimming pool at 39 Prospekt Narimanova. The traditional sports of *gyulesh* (wrestling) and *chavgan*, in which two teams chase a rag ball with sticks (along the lines of hockey), are most likely to be seen in the country.

Shopping. Of the local crafts you are more likely to find *djourabki* (thick woollen socks decorated with traditional colours and designs) and embroidered shawls than carpets. Around the Maiden's Tower, there are hundreds of local artists and craftspeople, and not a few spivs. There is an entertaining Eastern style bazaar — Sharg Bazary — behind the Sabunchinsky Railway Station; troUeybus 10 takes you there.

Help and Information. The British Ambassador, like many others, resides at the Old Intourist Hotel (tel 92 89 56). When a permanent residence is found, the hotel should know where to contact the embassy.

Further Afield. Although longer trips from Baku are more rewarding there are things to do in the immediate environs. Mardakyany, Ramana and Nardaran on the Apsheron Peninsula, each within 22 miles/35km of Baku, are all accessible by bus and have interesting 13th and 14th century castles. Between May and September you can go swimming at Zagulba, 25 miles/40km south of the city.

Kobustan. Heading south towards the areas with lush vegetation and tea and rice plantations, after 44 miles/70km you come to Kobustan where there is a fascinating collection of rock drawings that date back to the Stone Age, and also some cave dwellings.

Ateshgyakh Temple. The Fire Worshippers' Temple can be visited at Surakhany, about 12 miles/20km northeast of Baku. The temple was built close to the site of natural vents of flaming gas coming straight from the earth creating the 'everlasting fires' often mentioned by past travellers such as Alexandre Dumas. Fire worshippers believed that the fire had hypnotic powers. The place is surrounded by legend, but it is believed that the temple and monastery as they stand today were built in the 18th century by a group from Hindustan. These Hindustani fire worshippers are thought to have been members of an Indian colony that settled in Baku in the early 18th century. The low, dark cells for monks and pilgrims now house a museum tracing the history of the temple. There is still a mysterious feel to the place.

Kuba. There is little of interest along the coast immediately north of the capital. Sumgait, 25 miles/40km away, is an industrial town and not worth a special visit. Further north the road leads past fairly barren country, the Dzherainbatan Reservoir and limestone cliffs. It then begins to climb and takes you through the attractive villages of Gizib Gurum and Divichi, on the old caravan route. A few kilometres further on is Kuba (125 miles/ 200km from Baku) one of Azerbaijan's most beautiful towns, set in the foothills of the Greater Caucasus. It is full of apple orchards and in spring is a mass of blossom. Kuba is famous for its carpets and its 16th century fortress and 19th century mosques. If you're lucky or go high enough you might see wild boar or Daghestan mountain goats which are hunted between July and September.

Shemakha, Sheki and Zakataly. A round trip northwest of Baku to these three towns covers about 440 miles/700km but is most worthwhile if it can be accomplished safely. It gives you a good idea of how the terrain varies, taking you through mountains, orchards, foresi and plains. If you haven't time to do the whole tour just do parts of it, but don't miss Sheki.

Uzbekistan and Turkmenistan

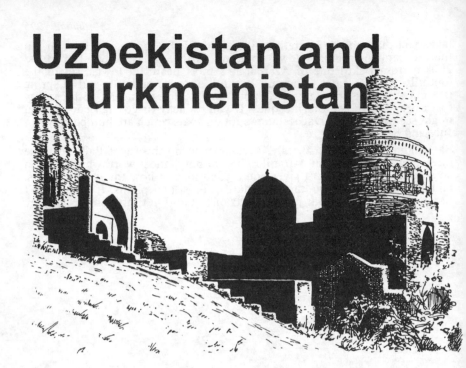

UZBEKISTAN

Population: 21.2 million   **Capital:** Tashkent (2.1 million)

In the jigsaw of nations that make up Central Asia, Uzbekistan is the most important piece. This is where you will find the essence of Central Asia, the heart of the mysterious region that has confounded and inspired explorers and writers in equal measure from Marco Polo onwards.

When the Russians arrived in the 19th century they found a land suspended in time, locked within walled citadels, ruled by khans of unimaginable cruelty, impervious to the world beyond the desert. This was the land that had seen the full fury of Genghis Khan, nurtured the ambitions of Tamerlane, and for over a thousand years been criss-crossed by camel caravans following a dense skein of paths which became known as the Silk Road. In 1924 the country was given a new name and the Soviet planners set about creating a modern industrial nation. But they only partially succeeded. The monuments of Samarkand remain undiminished, in spite of the new town that has sprung up around them; in Khiva you still find an isolated desert oasis; and perhaps best of all is Bukhara, where you can stroll among a daunting array of treasures and wash beneath the domes of a 16th-century bath house. Although Uzbekistan's bazaars may now be covered by concrete roofs, the taste for trade on which the country's fame and wealth was originally built, is as strong as ever.

On the other hand, Uzbekistan is still a one-party state, where the press is censored, the opposition is banned and the red-tape involved in obtaining a visa is a positive ordeal. Tourists find themselves checked up on by the police and snooped on by ex-KGB personnel. However, this becomes part of the challenge involved in going to one of the most secretive and mysterious countries that the East has to offer.

GEOGRAPHY

Uzbekistan covers an area approximately the size of Sweden, and shares frontiers with all the other Central Asian republics and also Afghanistan.

The Amu Darya river flows 1,500 miles/2,410km across the country, from the heights of the Pamirs north to the lifeless Aral Sea. Split between Kazakhstan and Uzbekistan, this inland sea is slowly being swallowed up by the rolling expanses of the Kyzyl-Kum desert. The far east of the country, a spit of land almost enclosed by Kyrgyzstan, is the fertile, populous and heavily industrialised Fergana Valley. To the south, hugging the borders with Tajikistan, are ranges of snow-peaked mountains.

CLIMATE

Uzbekistan's climate follows the classic continental pattern with long hot summers and cool winters. In the west of the country the desert conditions further exaggerate these extremes. In July and August temperatures can reach 40°C/ °F or more, while by the end of November they drop well below zero. The best time to visit is either in spring, when the desert comes to life, or between September and early November, when the summer heat has subsided but the skies are still blue and clear. Most rain falls during the autumn. In the south of the country winter barely lasts two months. Termez, on the Afghanistan border, is the warmest place in the ex-Soviet Union, where even in December it can be t-shirt weather.

HISTORY

Uzbekistan was born in 1924, a socialist republic being invented from the remains of three 19th-century khanates. Frontiers fixed according to an incomprehensible logic gave it a fictional unity that has bound it as one ever since. But the name is misleading. The Uzbeks were merely the last in a long line of horse-borne invaders, who appeared in the 15th century out of what is now Kazakhstan and named themselves after Uzbek Khan, a 14th-century leader of the Golden Horde.

For nearly two millenia, wave after wave of nomads had arrived to settle the desert oases in the west of modern Uzbekistan and the fertile valleys of the east. The Aryans were probably the first to arrive, in around 1,500BC. Alexander the Great captured Samarkand en route to India in the fourth century BC, but the empire he created couldn't survive his death. The next great movement across the desert plains was not of warriors but of goods — along a route through the mountains from China, which from around 100BC carried caravans of silk, spices, weapons and precious stones into the hands of an eager western market. The name, the 'Silk Road', was coined in the 19th century but is misleading: it wasn't a single road but a web of inter-weaving paths that meandered across the desert, some going up to southern Russia and others down through Persia. In its wake it threw up the wealth to create towns and bazaars which flourished for over 1,000 years.

After the death of Mohammed in the seventh century, Arabic invaders brought not just a religion, but an alphabet and an aesthetic lexicon governed by the tenets of the Koran. Various Turkic dynasties rose and fell, but they pale in the face of what was to come: Genghis Khan, or 'Khan of all the Mongols'. His army was a disciplined war-machine that swept out of Mongolia, advancing at the rate of 70 miles a day and creating an empire that stretched from the China Sea to Poland. Their legacy was the Pax Mongolica, a period of peace that lasted nearly 200 years until the birth of another legendary emperor: Timur, known to history as Tamerlane or Timur the Lame, after he received a leg-wound in battle. Born 50 miles/80km south of Samarkand, he created the largest land empire there has ever been, stretching from India northwest to Moscow and south to Damascus. And although a Mongol nomad by birth, Tamerlane created cities the like of which had never been seen. He died in 1405 and his empire was torn apart by quarrelling factions.

In the 16th century the Uzbeks finally came on the scene. They divided the land into three introverted khanates: Khiva, Bukhara and Kokand. They determinedly ignored the rest of the world, ruling over their inhabitants with cruel, despotic fervour. They had little resistance to offer the cannons of the Russian army, which moved inexorably south during the 19th century. By 1873, the last of the Khans in Khiva had fled and Russia stood in control of the region.

Initial support for the Russian Revolution in 1917 was transformed into fierce resistance after the implemenation of a reign of terror. It took the Red Army until 1923 to quell the revolt and in 1924 the Uzbek SSR was created. It wasn't until after World War Two that political control was handed over from the Russians to the Uzbeks. They were doggedly loyal during the Brezhnev years and in return were allowed a degree of autonomy which Sharaf Rashidov, the main post-war political figure, exploited to create a regime that was not only ruthless but also spectacularly corrupt.

The break-up of the USSR spelled disaster for the Uzbek government and its hard-line communist leader, Islam Karimov, who had little option but to back independence. However, he allowed no other candidates to stand in the presidential elections and has since pursued a policy of silencing both the press and opposition members, outlawing all religious parties and playing up to Western governments' fears of Islamic fundamentalism. Neighbouring countries are suspicious of his possible territorial ambitions and human rights groups have lambasted his record. Nevertheless, he has kept the country together and enjoys conspicuous levels of popularity among his people.

THE PEOPLE

Uzbekistan's population of 21 million is constantly growing: the country has one of the highest birth rates in the world, with families of ten or more by no means unusual. Uzbeks themselves make up 71% of the population, with significant numbers of Russians, Tajiks and Kazakhs making up the bulk of the remainder. Since the late 80s there has been a significant increase of tension between the groups; Tajik schools have been closed down and Russian television programmes pulled off the air. Tatars have emigrated to Crimea, Jews to Israel and America, while many Russians have decided that their children will have more of a chance within Russia itself.

Traditional dress is still worn by a majority of people, the men looking particularly fetching in silk quilted coats called *khalats* and small round hats known as *doppa*.

Religion. During the communist years, thousands of mosques were closed down, the observation of Ramadan was banned, as was the wearing of veils and the selling of the Koran. As a result, relatively few Uzbeks have an in-depth knowledge of Islam's teachings, but the majority still call themselves Muslims and Islamic traditions run deep. Mosques have been re-opening steadily and you may even see women wearing the veil. Predictions in the West that Uzbekistan would become a new Iran have so far proved wrong. Uzbeks tend to compare themselves make with their fellow Sunni Muslims in Turkey rather than the Shias of Iran.

Women. In Uzbekistan women still occupy a traditional role at the heart of the family and on the fringes of society. They marry young and tend to have lots of children, while polygamy, although still illegal, is on the rise. Foreign women undoubtedly attract a fair amount of curiosity, as only Uzbek women who have lost the respect of their family would travel unchaperoned. However, the multi-national nature of the country means that if you are Caucasian, it will often be assumed that you're from Russia or the Baltics. Hostility from men is rare, but if you are being hassled, the best advice is to seek out an older woman who will soon sort them out. If you're invited into an Uzbek home, you will usually be treated as an honorary man for the duration of your visit, while the women are in the kitchen cooking up huge feasts. Probably the best way to mingle unobtrusively and meet women in a relaxed environment is in the bath-house of any town.

LANGUAGE

The official language is Uzbek, but the diverse ethnic mix means that Russian is still the only viable *lingua franca* between the different groups. Uzbek shares a common grammar with Turkish but with a vocabulary made up of a mixture of Turkish, Persian and Arabic words. A decision to switch from Cyrillic (introduced by Stalin) back to the Latin alphabet is due to be implemented by the year 2000, but this seems to be an optimistic estimate. Some street signs in Tashkent are now in both scripts, but this is about as far as the reforms have got so far.

Useful words and phrases

hello — *salam aleykum*	hotel — *mehmonhona*
goodbye — *khair*	house — *uyi*
thank you — *rahmat*	breakfast — *sovuk*
please — *merhamat*	lunch — *tushlik*
yes — *kha*	supper — *keschki ovkat*
no — *yok*	money — *pul*
good — *yakshi*	cold — *sovuk*
bad — *yamon*	hot — *issyk*
I — *men*	water — *suv*
you — *sen*	morning — *ertaliap*
we — *biz*	evening — *okshom*

RECOMMENDED READING

As Russia's empire extended southwards during the 19th century, England-fearing an unhealthy interest in her own dominions in India — sent intrepid spies over the borders to sound out the situation. The Russians did the same, in a sport which became known as the 'Great Game'. Some adventurers returned and took to writing. The result is a classic genre of adventure story that makes essential reading. There are plenty to choose from, but among the best known are Fitzroy Maclean's *Eastern Approaches*, and F M Bailey's *Mission to Tashkent* (OUP, 1992). Peter Hopkirk provides the authoritative account of the subject in *The Great Game* (Oxford University Press, 1990), while his wife Kathleen Hopkirk supplies a fine introduction to the area in *Central Asia: A Traveller's Companion* (John Murray 1993).

AIR

If you are travelling from the UK, Uzbekistan is the easiest Central Asian capital to reach. Four times a week there is a direct service from London to Tashkent and once a week from Manchester to Tashkent, both with Uzbekistan Airways (tel 0171-935 1899, fax 935-9554). The cheapest ticket costs £575 return, a hefty price given that a return ticket to Thailand or India via Tashkent with the same airline costs about half as much. On the other hand, if you buy a return to the Uzbek capital, you should be able to travel on to Thailand, China or another eastern destination for the same price. Safety standards are probably better on Uzbekistan Airways than on any other former Soviet airline since Lufthansa is responsible for servicing the planes.

The other options include flying to Istanbul and then on to Tashkent with Turkish Airlines, but the second leg alone costs around £600. Flying to Moscow and to Tashkent from there with Aeroflot, Uzbekistan Airways and Transaero does not work out much cheaper than flying direct from London, and involves crossing Moscow en route. KLM is due to introduce a flight from Amsterdam to Uzbekistan in the near future.

TRAIN

If you're in the mood for a journey of epic proportions, you can catch a train from London's Liverpool Street station, change in Moscow and arrive in Tashkent several days later. A better idea if you're trying to cut costs would be to fly to Moscow and then travel onwards by train from there. There are two trains a day from Kazanskii station and these take about three days to reach the Uzbek capital. If you want to be sure of a ticket, Intourist in London (0171-538 8600) can reserve one for you. There are also trains from (amongst others) St Petersburg, Kiev and Novosibirsk.

BUS

There are regular bus services to Uzbekistan from Almaty in Kazakhstan and Bishkek in Kyrgyzstan. Destinations any further away are serviced by train.

Obtaining the right documentation to travel around Uzbekistan may well be one of the most ardous aspects of your trip. It is not that the country is unwelcoming to tourists but they prefer them to be shepherded around in large groups. The rules are in a state of flux, but this does not mean that they are any more lax. It is impossible to over-stress the importance of having your papers sorted out in advance. If all is not as it should be, you will liable to fines, expensive extensions and time-consuming bureaucracy once inside the country. Without a visa you cannot stay in hotels or even buy bus tickets. At any time of the day or night you are likely to have your papers checked by over-zealous police officers with too much time on their hands.

The Rules. All visitors require a visa. This should specify all the towns you intend to visit. When leaving the country, you may need to produce evidence that you stayed in tourist-designated hotels, so keep all receipts. British nationals are no longer officially required to have all the towns and cities listed on their visa, but this is a new rule and it is unlikely that hotel administrators and local militia will be aware of the finer points of diplomatic agreements.

Individual travellers need to obtain a tourist visa from an Uzbek embassy in their own country or, as is more likely, on arrival at the airport. Tourist visas can officially only be obtained if you pre-pay for your accommodation through an approved travel agent in your home country. Unofficially, in Britain at least, Intourist can obtain Russian tourist visas specifying towns in Uzbekistan and will not ask you to pay for accommodation in advance. Although this is a cheap and easy means of getting hold of the necessary documentation, some officials will claim that they are valid only for three days in any city; that they have been illegally issued by the Russian embassy; and, lastly, that they are insult to the Uzbek nation. Nonetheless, for the time being this remains the best option. If you have problems it is always worth emphasising the fact that there is no Uzbek embassy in your own country.

If you have a CIS visa which does not have towns in Uzbekistan specified on it, you should theoretically be allowed three days grace to transit the country, after which time you should be able to buy an extension. Don't bank on it. Recent travellers have reported being denied entry with CIS visas and forced to buy a non-extendable Uzbek transit visa at the airport. *Extending visas:* it is well worth avoiding having to do this, but if you have to extend your visa, head to the Ministry of Affairs in Tashkent (see below). To extend a tourist visa you'll have to pay not only $30 a week but also be forced to buy accommodation vouchers.

Uzbek embassies and consulates

Germany: Deutschchenstrasse 7, 53177 Bonn (tel 228-953 5715, fax 953 5799).
Pakistan: Suite 712, Hotel Mehran, Islamabad (tel 92-1-515061, fax 533886).
Russia: ul Boshaya Polyanka 49, Moscow (095-2301301).
Turkey: Ahmet Rasim 14, Chankiya, Ankara (tel 90-4-439 2740, fax 440 9222).
USA: 1511 K Street NW, Suite 619/623, Washington DC, USA 20005 (202-638-4266/67/68).

Uzbekistan introduced its own currency, the *som*, in July 1994. Theoretically there are 100 tanga to the som, but coins are thin on the ground and of little use: inflation is running high, at about 25% per month.

Bring most of your money as dollar bills. Make sure that they are not ripped or too worn, and preferably dated after 1990. You will be able to change older notes in Tashkent, but if you're travelling elsewhere it can be difficult. Travellers cheques are practically useless, apart from at the National Bank in Tashkent, which will change Visa travellers' cheques.

The Black Market. Uzbekistan is far stricter than any other country in the CIS when it comes to changing foreign currency. To pay for a hotel room and sometimes even for a bus or train ticket, you will need an official receipt bearing your passport number proving that you have changed your money at the government and not the market rate. There is a thriving black market and dollars are worth at least 30% more if changed unofficially. It is, however, illegal and both you and the traders risk a two-year prison sentence.

If you decide to deal on the black market, you'll find the best rates in the bazaars in Tashkent. Floor-ladies in hotels and shop-owners are usually more than willing to change dollars, but at a slightly reduced rate. Outside Tashkent, rates are lower again.

Credit cards. These are accepted only in a few hotels and restaurants in Tashkent. It is now possible to get a cash advance on a Visa card at the National Bank (see *Tashkent: Help and Information*), which charges 4.5% commisssion.

Telephone. To make calls from a public telephone you need to buy jetons from kiosks. All cities have a central telegraph office where you can book a call to another town or country. It is possible to dial international numbers direct from a private telephone but you need a lot of patience; if you want to try, the best time is late at night when the lines should be less busy. Going through the operator ensures the greatest likelihood of success: dial 061 for international calls, 07 for calls within the CIS.

Uzbekistan is five hours ahead of GMT.

Mail. Stamps, postcards and envelopes can be bought from kiosks, hotel receptions and post-offices.

THE MEDIA

The media in Uzbekistan is entirely state-controlled and rigorously censored. President Karimov is accorded demi-god status and the country's problems are routinely blamed upon Russia. Added to this has been the harrassment of the foreign press corps by both official and unofficial means.

The main newspapers are the Russian-language daily, *Narodnoye Slovo* and the Uzbek version, *Khalq Sozi*. There is one state television channel, which broadcasts in a mixture of Russian and Uzbek. It is possible to pick up Moscow channels and in some places you can watch cable television, which shows a mixture of Star TV, BBC World service and MTV.

You can try picking up BBC radio's world service, but the reception is usually very poor.

Air. The easiest and most comfortable way to get around Uzbekistan is to fly. It is also the most expensive. For example, a one-way ticket to Bukhara costs $63, to Samarkand $51 and to Urgench (for Khiva) $82. There are several flights a day from the capital to the major cities, the main drawback being that the air network is heavily centred on Tashkent, so you may find that you need to return to the capital in order to fly on elsewhere. Note also, that some airports will simply refuse to sell foreigners a ticket, and will redirect you to the Intourist *kassa* at the office in town.

The aeroplanes are either miniature Yak 40s or the propeller-driven Antonovs.

Rail. Uzbekistan does not have an extensive rail network and in general trains are less convenient for getting around than the buses. There are some exceptions to this rule, however. There is, for example, a comfortable overnight train between Tashkent and Bukhara, and a regular service between the capital and Samarkand. Buying tickets in advance is not always feasible due to lengthy queues, but you can usually turn up at the station and pay a conductor.

Bus. Buses cover a more extensive network than the trains and services are more regular. You rarely have to buy a ticket in advance. The buses are not particularly uncomfortable, but don't expect air-conditioning in summer or heating in winter. There are a few smart international vehicles, but in general you'll be aboard hand-me-down Hungarian Ikarus buses.

Officious bureaucrats may insist on registering your movements at the bus station in order to keep tabs on you. If you're leaving from the main bus station in Tashkent, for example, you are supposed to go to the Ovir (foreigners' office) on the first floor, before buying a ticket, to tell the local militia where you're going. And once on the road any vehicle is likely to be stopped every half hour or so by the GAI or traffic police, and buses are no exceptions. The drivers usually inform them immediately of the presence of a foreigner aboard and you will need to be able to show a valid visa.

Taxi. If you have a lot of money, then you can take a taxi between towns. A cheaper alternative, however, are the shared taxis which operate along fixed routes. These are faster and more comfortable than the buses and not necessarily much more expensive. Ask around at the bus station to find out where they depart from.

DRIVING

According to some sources, the only foreigners allowed on the roads unaccompanied are diplomats and employees of registered foreign companies. Even if this is not true, driving your own vehicle will probably attract more problems than it is worth.

It is no surprise that the big foreign car-hire companies haven't been tempted to set up shop in Uzbekistan. The tourist board, Uzbektourism, scorns the very idea of letting a foreigner out behind the wheel of a car. The best option is for you to negotiate with an official or unofficial taxi-driver. The cheapest deals are to be had from the latter.

CITY TRANSPORT

Most cities use a combination of trams, trolley-buses and ordinary buses. The usual procedure is to pay on exit. Tashkent has the only metro in Central Asia and is worth a sightseeing trip in itself.

Thare are three basic kinds of taxi: modern yellow Turkish 'Logan' cars, old black and white Volgas, and unofficial private cabs. With official taxis, try to fix a price in advance since meters do not work. With unofficial taxis simply offer money when you get out. Half a dollar in local currency is more than enough for a medium-length trip within a city. At night it's a good idea to stick to licensed taxis. If you suspect any funny business, make a point of openly writing down the driver's registration number.

Hotels. All hotels have a separate tariff for Uzbeks, Central Asians, Russians, and all other foreigners. Some state hotels are better than others, but all are overpriced. The only redeeming feature of most hotels are the floor-ladies, who more than make up for front-desk curtness and will change money and make you cups of tea.

Private Accommodation. If you travel by local transport, you'll be surpised by how many people offer you a roof for the night. This is the most reliable way of finding a room: during the main tourist season you may find people offering accommodation at the bus or train stations, but this is still illegal and many people are fearful of repercussions. In Tashkent, several of the hotels have *kvartira buros*, which can arrange private lodgings. The price quoted will be an arbitrary sum and you'll need to bargain hard. Check what the transportation links are before accepting.

Specialities. The three staples of Uzbek (and Central Asian) cuisine are *shashlik*, *laghman* and above all *plov*. Plov is a dish made of rice, carrots, lamb and onion, to which an inordinate amount of national pride is attached. It is not only a daily staple but also the main dish at any wedding or other festive occasion.

Shashliks or kebabs are also very popular. Chunks of barbecued lamb mixed with mutton fat are barbecued on a skewer over charcoal and served with raw onion. You find shashlik grills in the bazaars and a whole host of other places. In summer it is a good thing to eat because you know that it has been freshly cooked. Laghman is a soupy broth containing noodles and chunks of lamb and fresh parsley. A soup called *chorba* is similar but without the noodles. The flat round bread served everywhere is called *non*, and should be treated with respect. If eating with other people tear it into pieces and offer it around. Never place it on the floor even if it's safely inside a bag.

Fruit. Uzbekistan grows an abundant amount of delicious fruit which surpasses anything you'll find in a restaurant. Every town has at least one bazaar where you'll find peaches the size of melons and melons the size of footballs. Pomegranates, grapes, apples, apricots, dried fruits, walnuts, salted apricot kernels, home-produced honey, and ready-prepared salads are all available and are infinitely more tempting than the whole skinned horses' heads and sheeps' intestines also on offer. The bazaars are also a boon for vegetarians who will find little they can eat in the average restaurant.

Restaurants. A few private ventures have been set up in Tashkent, but generally you'll be confined to the hotel restaurants or a few huge old state affairs. Given such a dearth of restaurants, during the day *chaikhanas* (see below) are much the best option, though these close at sunset.

DRINKING

Chaikhanas, or tea-houses, are an Uzbek insitutition and offer one of the most interesting and relaxing ways of getting to grips with the country. Drinking large amounts of green tea and trading tittle-tattle is a time-honoured way of passing the day, with fellow drinkers usually more than eager to strike up a conversation. Seating is usually on large wooden beds covered with carpets and cushions; you should either keep your feet upon the ground or, if you want to get more comfortable, remove your shoes. Both green and black tea is served, although if you don't specify it will be assumed that you want green. If you take sugar bring your own, and if you plan to drink in a lot of chaikhanas, invest in your own cup (*peola*), since the ones offered are often unsatisfactory plastic affairs. As a foreigner you won't be expected to know the finer rules of tea-drinking etiquette, but the basic rules are: fill your cup and return the tea to the pot several times, until the liquid reaches a satisfactory weak-green colouring; only half-fill a guest's cup since to fill it completely is to suggest that you would like the guest to leave; always use the right hand to drink with; and finally, to refill a tea-cup before it is entirely empty is a bad omen.

Alcohol. The years of Soviet rule have successfully banished any Muslim misgivings about drinking alchohol. As in Russia, the most popular drink is vodka and the attitude towards it is also roughly the same, i.e. keep going until you fall over. Beer, usually Efes Pilsen imported from Turkey, is available in some places. In Tashkent there are a couple of bars devoted exclusively to alchohol, but in most places it is served only in restaurants. Uzbek women do not drink alcohol.

For the canny shopper prepared to spend time looking, there are bargains to be had in Uzbekistan. Hand-painted plates and bowls in colourful traditional designs are among the best buys. To find good quality items, however, can involve some research. The best bet is to locate a factory and buy the pottery direct. Tourist shops in the big cities will carry a selection, but the same quality is available for much lower prices in the state department stores. Carpets are another good buy, though they are better in Turkmenistan. Hand-knotted carpets made of wool do not come cheap, and if your funds are overstretched colourful woven kilims are a good alternative. Spices can make good presents, particularly saffron which is a fraction of its price in the West and widely available in the bazaars.

Tobacco. Western brands of tobacco are made under license in Uzbekistan and are very cheap. You may be offered *nossovoi*, a green powder containing a small amount of hash that is mixed into a ball and placed under the tongue. It gives a short buzz and is widely seen as the healthy alternative to smoking.

If you intend heading off the beaten track, it is a good idea to get immunistation against Hepatitis A and diptheria, in addition to the standard vaccinations. See the general introduction for further information on how to look after your health. If you do need urgent treatment in Uzbekistan the best hospital is Policlinic No. 1 in Tashkent, but contact your embassy for advice and help.

Whilst surrounding republics grapple with rising crime rates, Uzbekistan is comparatively free of crime. It is not difficult to spot the reasons why: there are police and militia everywhere and they act as a strong deterrent. Even so, poor street lighting and the almost total absence of people on the streets after dark can be unnerving — despite the knowledge that you are probably not in danger. In summer this is not such a problem since it is light until about 9pm. In winter, however, you'll find towns utterly deserted after 6pm.

Tourist information in Uzbekistan is almost non-existent. The official successor to Intourist is Uzbektourism, though staff still seem perplexed by the idea of individual travellers. The only Uzbektourism office abroad to speak of is in Moscow (ul Polyanka 41, 5th floor, room 33; tel 2385632).

TASHKENT

Tashkent is twinned with Tripoli and Birmingham and it is not difficult to spot the connection. With sprawling concrete suburbs, triumphalist boulevards and a relentlessly modern centre, there are few clues as to its 2,000-year long history. This is the largest, most populous and, all things considered, the least immediately appealing capital in Central Asia. The most decisive moment in its modern history came at 5.23am on 26 April 1966, when a massive earthquake struck and within a matter of minutes had reduced the city to rubble. About 30,000 volunteers poured in from all over the Soviet Union and the bulk of the re-building had been completed within a year. Today the Uzbeks are proud of their capital with its modern, well-ordered streets.

Beyond the re-naming of a few streets, there have been few changes since independence. The rooftops carry the latest pearls of wisdom to fall from the mouth of President Karimov. The state shops are well-stocked and the free market has yet to make an impact. This was a show-piece Soviet city and, despite the death of the Union, remains so today.

CITY LAYOUT

The hub of the new town is Ploshchad Markazy, where the towering Hotel Uzbekistan provides one of the city's major landmarks as well as a host of useful services. In addition, the metro station (called Markazij Hieboni) at the intersection of two of Tashkent's three subway lines is next to the hotel. The old town is located at some distance to the west of here, at the end of Prospekt Navoi. As well as old winding streets and a handful of interesting mosques and madrassas (religious schools), this is also where the city's largest bazaar is located.

Maps. It is almost impossible to buy a map of Tashkent. Keep you eyes peeled in the underpasses for street vendors who may be selling an old stray copy. Otherwise, Uzbekistan Airways produces an inflight pamphlet which has a basic street plan.

ARRIVAL AND DEPARTURE

Air. The domestic airport (Tashkent 1) and international airport (Tashkent 2) are next door to one another in the south of the city. Tram number 14 runs to the Alaisky Bazaar, which is fairly central, while bus 67 will drop you right in the centre. A taxi should cost no more than $5, but if you arrive on an international flight you'll have to bargain hard.

If you are leaving on an international flight, allow yourself plenty of time as the check-in procedure is time-consuming not to say completely chaotic. You must pay $10 airport tax, have your visa scrutinised, fill out a customs declaration form and have your luggage examined — and you will encounter huge queues and every turn.

If you want to buy a ticket for an internal flight, there are several means of doing this. The easiest way is to pay 10% commission and let the service desk at the Hotel Uzbekistan sort you out. The second is to go the Uzbekistan Airways *kassa* on Shota Rustavelli and join a queue. The third is to simply turn up at Tashkent 1 airport and go to the Intourist *kassa* on the right-hand side of the building. The staff here are inordinately helpful, and if there is no space on the flight you require they may well suggest the amount you should tip the cashier in order to find you the space.

Airline offices:

Aerotours (which operates a charter service to Moscow), ul Proletarskaya 16a, 3rd floor (333559).
Air India, Tashkent II airport (541621).
Lufthansa, Tashkent II airport (548569).
Pakistan International Airlines, ul Zhukovsky 63 (335446) and at Tashkent II ariport (529215).
Turkish Airlines, Tashkent II airport (548281).
Uzbekistan Airways (Havo Yullari), at Shota Rustavelli 9 (311033, 546721) and at the airport (563837)

Rail. The main train station is at the end of ulitsa Taras Shevchenko, an easy journey south of the centre on the metro (the Tashkent metro station serves the railway terminal). It is well worth trying to obtain tickets in advance from the ticket office just around the corner on ulitsa Proletarskaya, though as a foreigner you are officially required to buy tickets from the Intourist office (around the corner to the right of the main hall). Here, the prices are heavily inflated, particularly for international travel, and you'll also need to change money at the official rate and have a receipt. Tickets for same-day travel can be bought from a desk in the Hotel Lokomotiv immediately adjacent to the train station.

The city's second railway station is some distance south of the centre but easily reached on bus 58 or tram 7. Trains to Samarkand leave from here.

Bus. Long-distance buses depart from the 'Tashkent' terminal at the southern end of ulitsa Sapernaya. You can get there by taking the metro to the Sabir Rahimova stop at the end of the Chilanzarskay line. You'll come out at the hippodrome, where a large daily market is held; walk through the market and along the road back towards the centre of town. There are departures to Samarkand roughly every half hour from 6am, and the journey takes about five hours. There are four buses daily to Bukhara (8-10 hours), three to Fergana, five to Almaty and four to Bishkek. For information try calling 768452.

CITY TRANSPORT

The sparkling clean, endlessly efficient and highly ornate metro system functions 5am to midnight. Payment is by jetons, which are for sale at the entrances and deposited in the turnstiles. Buses and trams are crowded but regular. Taxis can be ordered in advance by calling 062 or 345160, but generally sticking your arm out in the street works well.

ACCOMMODATION

Tashkent's hotels are poor value and often fully booked. A couple of new upmarket hotels are due to open soon, but at the moment the top end of the market is cornered by the Uzbekistan Hotel, on ulitsa Khamza 45 (tel 327270, fax 335120). Its central location, selection of restaurants, coffee-bars and travel agencies are all useful, but the small rooms are hopelessly overpriced at $120. There are, however, a couple of ways of getting the same room more cheaply. The first is to offer to pay by credit card, which at present means that the price mysteriously drops to $75. The other is to buy Uzbektourism hotel vouchers from the foreign exchange desk to the right of the reception; these cost $45 and are good for one night's worth of accommodation at the hotel.

Next in price is the Chorsu, on Chorsu Maydoni (428330), where a single costs $45 and a double $60. It is located right next to the main bazaar and convenient for exploring the old town, but is soulless in the extreme. A much better bet is the Hotel Tashkent at Buyuk Turon 56 (332741/335491). It is an attractive building, central, and looks onto the elegant opera and ballet theatre. A casual enquiry will reveal that the rooms cost $40, but a little persistent questioning should reveal that there are cheaper rooms for $20. These are spacious and have clean bathrooms and satellite television. One notch down is the Rossia (Ploshchad Sapernaya 2; 562874), where the floor-ladies more than make up for any deficiencies in the plumbing.

If these places are all full, try the Yoshlik on Pakhtakorskaya (414410), near metro Pakhtakor. At $30 a double, it costs more than the Turon at ul Yusupov 5 (410705, 427600), with doubles at $18, but this last place treats foreigners with ill-disguised contempt, and your visa will be mercilessly scrutinised for any possible irregularities. There is a new private venture, Hotel Zorbi, on Prospekt Maxima Gorkova 1 (674382, 672404). It is a little out of the centre, but can be reached easily enough on tram 13 or bus 1, 21 or 30 to the Shkola 69 stop. It's very clean, very safe and accepts payment by Visa card. A double costs $45. Cheapest of all is Hotel Bakht on ul Katartal in the Chilianzar district, which charges about $5 for a room.

Private accommodation. There are desks offering private accommodation in Hotels Lokomotif (by the railway station), Rossia and Tashkent, although the last two are rarely open. Otherwise, you could try telephoning the Information Business Service on 244349, which claims to be able to arrange rooms in private apartments.

EATING AND DRINKING

Generally, there are not many options if you don't include the ubiquitous street shaslik vendors. All the hotel restaurants serve average food at average prices. For lunch, try one of the bazaars or the Chagatai district of the old town (nearest metro Tinchlik), where people set up shashlik grills in their courtyards. This is also the place to come for a slap-up Uzbek breakfast. Stalls sell tripe, barbecued liver and soup from 7am onwards. As far as restaurants are concerned, choose from the following:

Bakhor, Akhunbabyev 8, just around the corner from the Hotel Uzbekistan. Come here for the definitive Stalinist eating experience. It has a grand dining room with painted ceilings and sweeping murals portraying smiling peasants and happy workers.

Traktir, ul Nukus 5 (548470). The best of the new private restaurants. It sells good food in intimate surroundings for reasonable prices and as a result it is impossible to turn up without having made a booking.

Zerafshan, on the corner of ul Mustafa Kemal Ataturk and Matbuyochi. This restaurant, a local mafia haunt, provides some of the liveliest entertainment in Tashkent. From the outside it looks like a multi-storey car park, but it has restaurants on three floors and tables outside in the summer.

TV Tower, bus no 72 to the Park Pobeda stop, north of the centre. Two revolving restaurants in the TV tower are good for food with a view.

Blue Domes Café, Prospekt Sharaf Rashidov. This Tashkent icon is a concrete pastiche of a caravanserai, but serves good food in the open air. Next door is an intimate chaikhana where green tea, laghman and plov are served.

EXPLORING

The best place to begin an exploration of the heart of new Tashkent is Ploshchad Mustakkilik Majdon (Independence Square). This is not so much a square as a shapeless expanse, but its changing fortunes have mirrored the city's political transformations. It is here that you'll find the icons of the new state, but it started life as Kaufman Square, a tribute to the Russian general who subdued large tracts of Central Asia. Later, as Lenin Square, it boasted the world's biggest bronze monument of Lenin. In the early 1980s, a huge mausoleum was constructed to house the body of Sharaf Rashidov, the ruthless Brezhnevite who ruled Uzbekistan for several decades. He was quietly exhumed during the Gorbachev years, and where Lenin used to stand is the nation's new symbol: a bronze globe marked with the outline of a grotesquely over-size Uzbekistan.

In summer, when the monumental fountains are working, this square is a popular place for an evening promenade. On the western side is the Bakhor hall, where concerts are sometimes held, and behind that the canal which used to delineate the Russian town from the native quarter. Heading east you'll find Uzbekistan's equivalent of Moscow's Arbat, with various shashlik and ice-cream vendors, and end up at Markazy Square. There is a leafy park in the centre and a statue of Tamerlane, but the square's most obvious landmark is the high-rise Hotel Uzbekistan, a magnet for all foreign business people in the city. Across ulitsa Khamza is the Museum of the History of the Peoples of Uzbekistan.

You'll find another cluster of museums on ulitsa Sharaf Rashidov, near the Opera and Ballet Theatre, a neoclassical building designed by the architect also responsible for Lenin's tomb in Moscow. The old Lenin Museum, a short walk north, is closed pending its transformation into a history museum. To the south is the Exhibition Hall of Uzbekistan Artists. The basement has a cosy café with alcoves and good cakes, but if you prefer to be out of doors, try the Blue Domes Café opposite (see *Eating and Drinking*).

The Applied Arts Museum of Uzbekistan at Shpilkova 15 is a short walk from here and takes you into the most exclusive residential district in town. The area consists of low-level houses from the tsarist period, and the museum itself is housed in a particularly fine building laid out in the traditional courtyard with shady verandahs. Inside is a small but fine colleciton of carpets, hats and ceramics, all characteristic of Uzbekistan and labelled in English. (Note the newly tarmacked road and working street lamps outside: the president's private residence is at the end of the road.)

The Old Town. Despite earthquakes and the wishes of Soviet-era planners to 'cleanse' the city of its retrograde living quarters, the old town covers a deceptively large area. It is interrupted at intervals by huge swathes of concrete, but in the district stretching north of the bazaar, in the western part of the city, you find impossibly narrow streets, houses with courtyards and baked mud walls, and a way of life that is resolutely traditional in spite of the modern city surrounding it. If you follow ulitsa Zaikanar from Ploshchad Hadra at the western end of Prospekt Navoi, you eventually come to the Barak-Khan Madrassa. Freshly restored using copious amounts of gilt, this is the head-quarters of the Sunni mufti. Opposite it is the Kaffelshashi Madrassa, dating from the 16th century and housing the Imama Bukhari institute, the highest seat of Islamic learning in the country. The library houses the oldest Koran in the world, which once belonged to Caliph Othman, the third of Mohammed's successors. You may or may not be allowed in to see the enormous tome, whose pages measure a metre across.

You'll find another madrassa about half a mile south of Ploshchad Khadra, at Druzhba Narodiv. This square is an enormous space surrounded on all sides by modern apartment blocks and dominated by the enormous People's Friendship Palace, so it's easy to miss the plain brick façade of the 17th-century Abdul Khazim Madrassa which shelters behind it. Craftsmen now occupy the cells once used by students.

ENTERTAINMENT

The Alisher Navoi Opera and Ballet Theatre, on Sharaf Rashidov, performs the standard repertory of Russian classics but has a high reputation. The Khamza Drama Theatre on Navoi 34 performs works in the Uzbek language.

Sport. If you're in Tashkent at the end of May you'll catch Uzbekistan's answer to the French Open Tennis Championship, the President's Cup. Despite a singular lack of previous interest in tennis, the government invested some $50 million creating new facilities and inaugurated a competition with a first prize of $150,000. It is apparently intended to boost Tashhkent's desperately optimistic bid to host the Olympic games in 2004.

The main football stadium is on Zaikarni ulitsa. If you fancy a swim, there is a pool in the Hotel Uzbekistan.

SHOPPING

The biggest bazaar is in the old town, housed under a massive concrete dome, but the Alaisky bazaar on ulitsa Amir Timur is closer to the centre. Tashkent has probably some of the best stocked state shops left in the CIS. There is a large Tsum near the old bazaar, opposite the Chorsu hotel, and another opposite the Navoi Theatre. You can find surprisingly good buys here, including cheap ceramics and records (with pirated copies of Western groups selling for $0.25 per record). For jewellery and carpets try the souvenir shop at the Exhibition Hall on Prospekt Sharaf Rashidov.

HELP AND INFORMATION

Tourist information: Uzbektourism, Hotel Uzbekistan, Khorezm 47 (220733,

338068). The Information Business Service (244349) offers all sorts of services, including help with private accommodation, visas and ticket reservations.

There are a few agencies which may be able to help anyone interested in going trekking, though all are happier dealing with groups than with individuals. Try Ansar Travel (567078); Tourist Sports Club, Taras Shevchemko 44 (333440, 442603) and Uzbekintour in Hotel Uzbekistan (332773). The last two agencies claim to be able to organise heli-skiing and desert camel tours.

Money: for cashing Visa travellers' cheques and Visa cash advances into som, go to the National Bank at Taras Shevchenko 29 (551201, 543818).

Communications: The Central Telegraph Office is on Prospekt Navoi 28 (open 8am-6pm, closed noon-1pm), near metro Navoi, from where you can also send faxes. For phone calls, the satellite telephones in the business centres at the hotels Uzbekistan and Tashkent are more expensive but also more reliable. Both charge $6 per minute.

The telephone code for Tashkent is 3712.

Embassies and consulates

Afghanistan, Gogolya 73 (339171).
China, Gogolya 79 (331396, 335375).
India, A Tolstogo 5 (tel 338267, fax 333782).
Iran, Tamiryazev 16-18 (350777, 352546).
Mongolia, Gogolya 67 (338313).
Pakistan, Chilanzarskaya 25 (776977, 771003).
Russia, P Poltoratskogo 15 (559157).
UK, Murtazaeva 6 (347658, 345652).
USA, Chilanzarskaya 55 (tel 771407, fax 776953).

Visa Extension: at the Ministry of Foreign Affairs opposite the Navoi Theatre on ul Uzbekiststankaya. If you need passport photographs, there is a photo machine at Amir Timur 73.

FERGANA VALLEY

The Fergana Valley juts into Kyrgyzstan in the far east of the country. It was formed by the Syr Darya river, and was the most fertile staging post along the entire length of the Silk Road. Five hundred years ago the emperor Babur, who was born here, claimed that melons were so plentiful that they were given away free along the sides of the road, and even in the last century travellers reported the delights of its orchards. But that was before the Russians siphoned off the river to make irrigation channels and imposed the monoculture of cotton. Today it is the most populous and industrialised part of Uzbekistan. Hemmed in by mountains on three sides, the area has become the breeding ground of both religious and ethnic discontent. The biggest city is Fergana, an industrial power base whose sprawling suburbs have now absorbed the older town of Margilan. You would do better to head straight to Kokand. If you travel by bus, it is worth noting that all roads to the Fergana valley have to pass through Tajikistan; since you stay on board, you are unlikely to encounter visa problems.

KOKAND

This was once a notorious place. In the 19th century it was the seat of a powerful khanate, whose rulers were famed for their abject cruelty and absurd decadence. In 1876 it was captured by the Russians, who built a sparkling new colonial town alongside the old; large sections of both were destroyed by the Bolsheviks during an uprising here in 1918. Today Kokand is a small and pleasant place, divided into a new town with colonial-era architecture and an old town with some interesting madrassas, an atmospheric cemetery and the only all-night bazaar in Central Asia.

Getting There. There is one flight a day from Tashkent, which arrives at the airport 6 miles/10km south of Kokand. Buy tickets here or at the Uzbekistan Airways office next door to Hotel Kokand.

There are three trains a day from the capital, taking about six hours, with daily departures for Moscow and Bukhara. The station is at the end of ulitsa Istambul ulitsa. Shared taxis to various destinations depart from in front of the terminal; a ride to Tashkent shouldn't cost more than $10.

Bus is probably the most straightforward way of getting to the Fergana valley, with about three buses a day from Tashkent. There are services at least every hour to Fergana and Margilan, Andizhan and Namangan. The bus station is on ulitsa Furkat, southeast of the centre.

Accommodation and Food. The best place to stay is Hotel Kokand on Imam Ismail Bukharii (36403). A room costs about $5, but don't expect clean sheets. If it's full try the Hotel Vostock, a few hundred metres away at ul Istiklol 16.

There are two old state restaurants with little to choose between them. The first is the Dilshod behind Park Mukimi on Oktyabrysky Square; the second is the Yoshlik on ulitsa Istambul, a short walk south from the Hotel Kokand. Directly opposite the hotel itself is the small Bar Nilufa, but it has irregular opening hours.

Much the best bet after dark is the all-night bazaar, about 3 miles/5km northeast of the centre, which provides this sleepy town with some of the most exciting nightlife in Uzbekistan. It is held in its own custom-built compound with arc lights illuminating the merchandise, throngs of people and little boys letting off Chinese fire-crackers. There are several chaikhanas and lots of stalls serving food.

Exploring. The central attraction is the palace of the last khan of Kokand in the middle of Mukimi Park. Built in the 1860s by the cruel Khudayar Khan, its 113 rooms were completed only three years before the Russians arrived, and are now undergoing restoration. Decorated with multi-coloured tiling and standing next to a toy railway, this symbol of absolute authority now has the air of an abandoned fairground attraction. Inside are a couple of dusty museums, the most exciting of which has a collection of moth-eaten stuffed animals.

If you walk down ulitsa Khamza from here and cross the river, you'll reach the Djuma Mosque. Despite the fact that the front façade has been converted into a hardware shop, inside you'll find an enormous courtyard and a forest of wooden columns supporting up the verandah on the right-hand side. Heading up Islama Akbara Islamova, you come to the Narbutabek Madrassa. Built in 1799, it is in a state of delapidation, but this hasn't stopped the return of about 300 young students. Adjoining it is a Muslim cemetery, but you have to wind your way through the back streets to reach it: follow the small lane directly to the left of the madrassa. Shaded by trees and enclosed by walls, the graveyard is a peaceful place crammed full of tombs. There are two 19th-century mausolea: the larger Dachma-i-Zhakon, with colourful tiling and intricately carved doors, and the smaller Modari-chon-Dachmasi, with its tiny blue dome providing a splash of colour against the austere white and grey tombs.

Help and Information. A detailed but old map is sold at the ticket office in the khan's palace.

SAMARKAND

Fabled Samarkand was once the centre of the vast empire of Tamerlane, a savage one-eyed cripple who divided his time between conquering the world and building a city so magnificent that its name is still synonymous with oriental splendour. Today Samarkand is Uzbekistan's second city, with all that this entails in the way of Soviet industrialisation and modernisation. Yet the sheer scale and brilliance of Tamerlane's turquoise domes and soaring minarets enables them to hold their own against the background of a dusty Asian city.

Between Tashkent and Samarkand is a plain that was so arid it was christened the Hungry Steppe by travellers a few centuries ago. It has kept this title to this day, but intense irrigation has transformed the plain into lush fields populated by grazing cows and the occasional camel. Closer to Samarkand the Zerafshan mountains come into view, named after the river that flows through them.

History. The city was first mentioned in 329BC, as Maracanda, at the time of Alexander the Great's conquest. However, there is archaeological evidence to show that Samarkand was founded over 5,000 years ago by King Aphrosiab, ruler of an empire known as Sogdiana, which in the first millenium BC included much of present day Tajikistan and Uzbekistan. Samarkand grew and eventually dominated the Great Silk Route that led to Europe from China and India. After the devastation caused by the Mongol hordes of Genghis Khan in 1221, Samarkand was given a new lease of life by the notorious Timur, or Tamerlane, who chose to make it his capital.

Timur who is now considered something of a national hero was a great conqueror and brutal ruler and also an incomparable builder. During the 35 years of his reign (1370-1405) he brought artists, architects and skilled craftsmen from Damascus, Baghdad, Delhi and other far-flung cities he had conquered to work on his titanic building projects. Timur drove his workers with the whip and the threat of death. The result was a city so splendid that Timur called it the 'eye and the star of the earth'. Thanks to Ulugbek, Timur's grandson and a great scholar and statesman, Samarkand also became one of the centres of medieval science. It was after his death in 1449 that the capital was moved to Bukhara, resulting in the steady decline of Samarkand.

Arrival and Departure. *Air:* there are 2 flights a day from Tashkent. The airport is about 15 minutes' drive north of the city centre, near the long-distance bus station. Foreigners cannot buy tickets at the airport and instead must go to the Uzbekistan Airways office on ul Gagarina (ask for Agentsva Aeroflota) or to the service desk at the Hotel Samarkand. In summer there are also direct flights to and from Moscow.

Rail: Samarkand is not a major railway junction, but there are connections with Tashkent. The journey takes six hours and works out much more expensive than the bus. The station is northwest of the city centre.

Bus: there are at least 10 buses a day covering the 180 miles/290km between Tashkent and Samarkand, taking 5-6 hours. Buses also run to Bukhara (5 hours), Khiva (12 hours) and Termez (12 hours), but these services are less regular.

Accommodation. Private accommodation with a family or in a self-contained flat can be arranged through Orient Star, located on the third floor of the Hotel Samarkand (35-88-19). Bed and breakfast works out around $10-15 per person. There is another agency at number ul Sovietskaya 33, where a French-speaking Georgian woman called Valya may be able to find you a cheaper deal.

The Samarkand and the Zerafshan are the best hotels in terms of location and value for money. Hotel Samarkand, at bulvar Maxima Gorkovo 1 (35-88-19, 35-71-52), has clean, comfortable rooms and reliable supplies of hot water, with double rooms for $60 in high season and $40 in low; and American Express charge cards are accepted. The Zerafshan at ul Sovietskaya 65 (33-33-72) charges about $15 for an ordinary double and $20 for a lux. If these hotels are full, try the less central Turist, a modern highrise at ul Gagarina 85 (24-07-04) or the Leningrad at ul Karla Marxa 36 (33-52-25). An Indian joint-venture hotel is due to open on ulitsa Registanskaya.

Eating and Drinking. A limited choice of restaurants which tend to close early makes eating out in Samarkand something of a challenge. In daytime, it is easy to fill up on shashlik, plov and laghman, which are sold at numerous stalls along the pedestrian stretch of ulitsa Tashkentskaya. Alternatively, you could buy your own picnic at the bazaar and eat it in one of the chaikhanas along this same road. In the evening try the following:

Dilshod, ul Sovietskaya 65, behind the Zerafshan Hotel. Standard dishes served in a pseudo-elegant dining room with a fountain and dance floor inside and a large verandah outside.

Abir-Rakhmat, near the Ulugbek observatory on Tashkentsaya. A monumental pagoda decked out with Chinese lanterns and serving genuine Chinese food. Open only in summer.

Sogd, on ul Registanskaya, less than five minutes' walk from Hotel Samarkand.

The best restaurant in the city, with its Mongolian dishes billed as the house speciality.

Exploring. The centre of Samarkand is compact and most of the major sights are within easy walking distance of one another. The Gur Emir Mausoleum is a few minutes' walk southeast of the Samarkand Hotel along ulitsa Akunbabaeva and is a good place to begin a tour of the city's treasures.

Gur Emir Mausoleum: at the age of 69, the insatiable Timur set out in 1405 to conquer China, but to the great relief of the Chinese he expired en route. His body was brought back to Samarkand and laid to rest in the Gur Emir, the gigantic mausoleum which Timur had commissioned for his favourite nephew, Muhammad Sultan. The basic structure is an octagon topped by a magnificent ribbed cupola. Inside, eight tombs lie in an opulent chamber decorated with alabaster panels, elaborate vaulting made of *papier mâchê* and two and a half kilos of gold leaf. In keeping with his wishes, Timur's tomb is 'only a stone and my name upon it', though it happens to be the largest slab of nephrite in the world. Other notables interred here include his grandson, Ulugbek, but the tombs are only reproductions of the real ones, which are kept in a vault below. A small tip to the curator may convince him to take you down there. Strangely, Timur's original tomb is considered an auspicious place for newly-weds to leave flowers.

The Registan: ulitsa Registanskaya, with its vodka factory and hideous new hotel, is a model of insensitive town-planning. Running east from Gur Emir, it helps mar the approach to Central Asia's most famous square, the Registan. But turn your back on the drab apartment blocks and feast your eyes on the Registan itself. This vast square that was once the central market is sur-rounded on three sides by monumental madrassas.

On the right is the Ulugbek Madrassa, commissioned by Timur's grandson and adorned with kaleidoscopic suns and stars. Built between 1417 and 1420, it is the oldest building in the ensemble and generally considered the finest artistically. The bulging façade and slanting minarets are not an illusion but the result of a succession of earth tremors. Ongoing restoration work means that you cannot go inside.

Opposite stands the Sher Dor Madrassa, built almost two centuries later (1619-35). The lion motif in the spandrels marks a break from the earlier tradition of Islamic art that vetoed the representation of living beings on religious buildings. Inside, forlorn souvenir shops occupy the cells where students once slept, and loitering youths offer to take you up on the roofs.

Tillya-Kari Madrassa was the last addition to the square, built 1648-60. Its main façade is markedly different from the other two in that instead of being smooth it is broken up by the outward-facing balconies of the students' cells. Pieces of original masonry and alabaster panels from Afrasiab (see below) are displayed in a small museum to the left of the central courtyard. Walk through the museum to reach the magnificent prayer room, embellished with gold.

The stairs to the right of the Sher Dor Madrassa emerge opposite the Museum of History, Culture and Art, which is worth a quick browse. From Tsum, Samarkand's central department store, ulitsa Tashkentskaya begins. This tree-lined avenue has recently been pedestrianised and is in the process of being smartened up. Donkey-drawn carts trot up and down, carrying those for whom either the heat or the cold get too much. A picturesque quarter of narrow, shaded streets and one-storey houses extends east from Tashkentskaya, providing a pleasant contrast to Timur's exhuberance.

Bibi Khanum: the Bibi Khanum or Queen Lady Mosque (1399-1404) is named after Timur's Chinese wife. According to legend, she commissioned the building as a surprise for her husband on his return from a campaign in India. But the architect fell in love with Bibi and refused to finish the mosque unless she granted him a kiss. She allowed him to kiss her through a cushion but the ardour of the architect's kiss was so great that it left a mark on her cheek. Timur discovered the mark and the architect, fearing execution, promptly sprouted wings and flew away from the top of the minaret. In fact, Timur built the mosque himself on a scale grander than anything he had seen before in order to commemorate his victorious cam-paign in India.

Close up, Bibi Khanum looks like a deserted building site, with birds' nests in the minarets and large slabs of marble and fragments of turquoise tiling scattered over the ground. Successive earthquakes and centuries of neglect have left it in ruins and restoration work seems to have ground to a halt — although there are plans to finish it by 1996, in time for the 600th anniversary of Samarkand. In its original condition, the mosque was a vast open-air affair; the main structure standing today, surmounted by the largest turquoise dome in Samarkand, was the prayer room. Step through the web of geriatric scaffolding to see the deep cracks and fissures in the inner dome. In the middle of the courtyard is a massive Koran stand that looks like an open book. If you want to do as some locals do, walk around it twice and make a wish, or crawl under it to cure backache or have lots of babies.

The Bazaar: high walls and the even higher ruins of Bibi Khanum seal the bazaar off from the encroaching modernity, making it one of the most photogenic spots in Samarkand. Rocks of crystallised sugar, decorative non-bread, paprika, cinnamon, cumin, saffron and countless other spices are all for sale. You may also be offered *momiyo*, a black paste made from mountain rodent droppings that is supposed to cure everything from burns to broken bones.

Shahi-Zinda: the main entrance to Shahi-Zinda is through an arch on ulitsa Usta Umara Dzhurakulova, the street running east from the bazaar.

Shahi-Zinda is perhaps the most exotic sight in Samarkand. It consists of a narrow sloping street hemmed in on either side by the most exquisitely tiled mausolea. The burial complex was built by Timur at the beginning of the 14th century, around the site of a memorial to Kusam ibn Abbas, a seventh-century holy man. According to legend, Kusam ibn Abbas was beheaded by infidels as he was giving a sermon, but unperturbed he finished his address, picked up his head and disappeared with it down a cave where he still lives today: thus the Shahi-Zinda or the 'Living King' was christened. His mausoleum and shrine are at the far end of the street on the right. Opposite it stands the mausolea of Tuman-Aka (one of Timur's wives), perhaps the finest of all those at Shahi-Zinda. A number of rare colours, including a pinkish stone, have been used in the delicate star and flower mosaics.

Afrasiab: the partially excavated ruins of Afrasiab, the ancient site of Samarkand, cover an elevated parcel of land northeast of the bazaar. You can still make out a few streets and baked brick walls, but this is above all a place to come in the evening and watch the sun set over Samarkand. The best finds at Afrasiab, including fascinating frescoes depicting merchants on the Silk Road, are kept in the archeaology museum which is on the road to Ulugbek's observatory.

Ulugbek Observatory: this is about 15 minutes' walk northeast of the bazaar, up the continuation of ulitsa Tashkentskaya and past ancient graveyards.

Timur's grandson, Ulugbek, was a historian, geographer, mathematician and keen astronomer. He calculated the number of days in the year to within a minute of modern calculations. Sadly, little remains of the remarkable observatory he built in 1428 because some 200 years later Ulugbek was denounced as a heretic and the observatory was razed to the ground. Just the foundations and part of the sextant have survived. The latter, an elaborate device used to measure the movement of the stars, was discovered only in 1908. The small museum in the neighbouring pavilion has several drawings showing what the complete observatory must have looked like.

Help and Information. The service desk at the Hotel Samarkand organises city tours as well as excursions to Shakrisabz and Pendzhikhent. Prices for individuals are high, e.g. $94 for one person to Pendzhikent.

The central telegraph office is on ulitsa Postova and opens 24 hours a day. The code for Samarkand is 3662.

AROUND SAMARKAND

Shakrisabz. This town lies 50 miles/80km south of Samarkand in the foothills of the Zerafshan Ridge. Alexander the Great, Genghis Khan and, more recently, Soviet troops on their way to Afghanistan have all passed through Shakrisabz. Timur was born here and chose this spot to build the Ak Sarai or White Palace. Only a fragment of his most ambitious building project has survived to this day, but it is no ordinary fragment. Measuring 125ft/ 38m and decorated with ornamental Arabic inscriptions, the huge portal dwarfs even Bibi Khanum — though the arch collapsed some 200 years ago. Other sights of interest include the Kok Gumbaz Mosque, built by Ulugbek, and several fine mausolea.

Getting There: two buses a day take the long road to Sharkrisabz from Samarkand (4 hours). However, unless you are short of money or the weather is very cloudy, try to go by car: a shared taxi costs around $4 per person. Smaller vehicles can take a more direct road than the buses, over the 5,494ft/ 1,675m Tashtakaracha Pass, which offers unrivalled views of the surrounding mountains. Cars depart from behind the Museum of History, Culture and Art as well as from the long-distance bus station in Samarkand. In Shakrisabz, the best place to organise a lift is at one of the two bus stations (at opposite ends of ulitsa Sholkoviput, the main street). The main hotel is the Hotel Shakrisabz on Sholkoviput (3-38-61).

Pendzhikent. Though Pendzhikent is actually in Tajikistan, it is usually visited from Samarkand (just 43 miles/70km away as opposed to the 95 miles/158km to Dushanbe). Since 1947, architects have been excavating a fifth-century Sogdian town here. The ruins themselves are of specialist rather than general interest but the setting is superb. Pendzhikent lies on the River Zeravshan and is flanked by mountains on two sides. Whether you go independently or on an organised trip, you must have a Tajik visa. Given the current unrest in Tajikistan (see page 364), it is not worth attempting to go without all the right papers.

BUKHARA

If you don't go anywhere else in Central Asia but Bukhara, it doesn't matter. Despite seven decades of Soviet neglect, Bukhara has retained more of the spirit of a Silk Road city than any other. The old centre is still densely populated, the 16th-century baths are still functioning, and every afternoon elderly gentlemen congregate at the edge of the sacred pool of Lyab-i-Khauz to drink tea and trade gossip.

Surrounded by the flat open expanses of the Kyzyl-Kum Desert, Bukhara is flooded in light. The rich golds, browns and pinks of brick and clay are the dominant colours, but here and there splashes of turquoise and cobalt blue tiling compete with the almost permanently azure skies. In addition to its wealth of monuments, narrow medieval streets and a gentle pace, Bukhara has a couple of fine places to stay. Spend at least four days here to sap up the atmosphere.

Bukhara's climate is extreme due to the city's location in the middle of the Kyzyl-Kum desert. Summers are suffocatingly hot and winters bitingly cold. The best months to visit are September and October, when the evenings are balmy and day-time temperatures hover around 25°C/ °F.

History. Bukhara's heyday was in the ninth and tenth centuries, when the city flourished as capital of a Persian dynasty called the Samanids. Lying at the crossroads between India, Iran and China, it became a major trading post on the Silk Road and attracted a great number of scholars and artists. Most famous among these was Abu ibn Sina, the doctor and philosopher who became known to the West as Avicenna. Only a couple of monuments survive from this golden era as a succession of invaders did their utmost to wipe Bukhara off the map. Following Genghis Khan's campaign of death and destruction in 1220, Bukhara sank into decline until the 16th century, when the Sheibanid Khans gave it a new lease of life.

By the middle of the 18th century the city had fallen into the hands of the Mangit dynasty (of Persian origin), whose rule earned Bukhara an almost global notoriety. The few foreign visitors who dared to visit the city were appalled by the depravity and cruelty they encountered. There was a thriving slave market, unfaithful wives were thrown off the top of minarets and anyone who offended the Emir would be flung into the bug pit, a deep hole filled with fleas, snakes and other vermin.

In 1868 Bukhara was absorbed into the Russian empire, but the last Emir was not deposed until 1920, when the Bukharan People's Republic was formed in the aftermath of the Bolshevik Revolution. Initially this incorporated both present-day Uzbekistan and Tajikistan, but in 1924 the two new Socialist Republics were formed.

Arrival and departure
Air: there is a daily flight from Tashkent, and in summer there are also connections with Samarkand and Urgench (for Khiva). The airport is a few miles east of the city; bus 10 goes there from ulitsa Lenina, west of the old town.

Train: there are daily trains to and from Ashkhabad, Dushanbe, Moscow and Tashkent. The best overnight service to Tashkent is the Zerafshan Express, a freshly outfitted train which is exceptionally clean and comfortable. The station is not in Bukhara itself but in Kagan, 10 miles/16km east of the city. Buying tickets in advance is an ordeal and it is far easier to turn up at the station and to buy a ticket from a *provodnik* (carriage attendant). Buses from Bukhara to Kagan depart from ul Lenina.

Bus: there are five buses a day to Tashkent (12 hours) and Samarkand (6½ hours) and one to Andizhan (16 hours) and Urgench (8 hours). The bus station is north of the city centre on ul Gizhduvanskaya.

Accommodation. Bukhara is blessed with two exceptionally cosy guest houses, which are ten times better than the city hotels. Mubin John's (Ichoni pir 4; 42005) is a 200-year old house run by the enthusiastic owner and his wife and ruled by their young daughter Bibi Khanum. Mubin John is a fixer *par excellence* and claims to be able to organise anything from renting a car to finding an antique rug. The rooms are ideal in spring and autumn, but the lack of heating or air-conditioning makes them cold in winter and hot in summer. Beds come in the form of the colourful mattresses seen in traditional Uzbek homes. The washing facilities are basic, but this is still a charming place to stay. The charge is $10 per person including breakfast. Mubin John's is in the Jewish quarter of the old town; head to Lyab-i-Khauz pool and ask for directions — it is past the synagogue just south of here.

Sasha and Lena's (ul Maladyohznaya 13; 33890) is five minutes' walk east of the centre. Both Sasha and Lena used to work as Intourist guides and speak excellent English. Their bed and breakfast is known to all the resident foreign community in Tashkent and is often fully booked, so it is worth ringing in advance. Comforts include large rooms, a sauna and satellite TV. This place offers superb value at $15 per person including breakfast. An evening meal costs less than $5.

If by some misfortune you cannot stay at either of the above places, try calling Alex (42382), who rents out his spare flat to visitors; it isn't central but is good value at $10 a night for two people. Alternatively, the best of an extremely poor choice of hotels is the Bukhara at ul Sovietskaya 6 (30124, 30289), with rooms for $50. The Varaksha (pr Navoi 5; 38494) is a standard Soviet high-rise hotel, but is at least cheap at $15 per person. Only in extremis should you resort to the appalling Zerafshan at ul 40 Let Uzbekistana 7 (34067/340173), with double rooms for $10.

Eating and Drinking. Possibilities for eating out are even more limited here than in Samarkand — another good reason to stay in bed and breakfast accommodation, where your hosts can provide far better food than you are likely to find in the restaurants. During the daytime, a number of informal semi-outdoor eateries serve the Central Asian staples, plov and shashlik. The best of these is the chaikhana on the edge of Lyab-i-Khauz. It is also possible to eat in the House of the Rich Merchant: see below.

Exploring. The centre of Bukhara, where all the main sights are located, is a fairly compact area surrounded on all sides by the narrow and labyrinthine streets of the old town. The sights described below are placed approximately in the order that you would come across them starting at Lyab-i-Khauz and heading west all the way to the Samanid Park.

Lyab-i-Khauz (At the Pond): come here to idle away an afternoon or a month sipping tea at the edge of a pool shaded by 600-year old mulberry trees and flanked by two brilliantly tiled portals. Old men dressed in turbans loll on wooden beds discussing politics and only occasionally rising to fill their teapots, whilst gulls glide across the opaque waters. Appropriately, this was the site of the tea bazaar in centuries past.

On the eastern edge of the pool is a statue of Khodja Nasreddin, the wise fool of Sufi legend astride a donkey, and looming above him the Nadir Divanbeg Madrassa, built 1630-1631. Although the scale of the building is modest compared to that of the madrassas surrounding the Registan in Samarkand, the decoration above the portal is at least as impressive. Two mythical birds gripping white deer in their talons fly in a riot of colour under the watchful eye of the sun personified as a Mongol face. Across the pool and reflected in its waters is the Khanaka Divanbegi (1619-1620), once a hostel for Muslim dervishes and now a souvenir shop. Up some steps on the northern side of the pool is the Kukeldash Madrassa, the largest in Bukhara (1578-9).

The Jewish Quarter: the narrow winding streets just south of Lyab-i-Khauz lead into the Jewish Quarter, where Jews have lived for as long as anyone can remember. Under the rule of the Emirs, Bukhara's Jews were only one step up the social ladder from slaves. They were made to wear a rope around their waists to remind them that they may be hanged. Ten years ago the Jewish community numbered 120,000, but since then so many have emigrated that today only about 1,000 still live here; and more families are leaving every month. The remaining children attend the Jewish school which is around the corner from the synagogue on ulitsa Centralnaya.

Bazaars and Magoki Attari Mosque: heading west from Lyab-i-Khauz, you reach the Moneychangers' Bazaar, a domed intersection that marks the entrance to the old trading centre. Just south of here builders are restoring the 16th-century Sarrafon baths, due to re-open in 1996. In the meantime, men can use the modern public baths next to the Magoki Attari Mosque, north of the bazaar.

Sunken 13ft/4m below ground level, the 12th-century Magoki Attari

Mosque was discovered only in 1939. For the past eight centuries, its ornate brick and alabaster main façade had been hidden and preserved by layers of sand blown in from the desert.

Beyond the mosque and west of the Kalyan Minaret, three clay igloos stand in a row, the sole survivors of a vanished epoch. Until the late 19th century, this whole area was a maze of narrow streets linked by several domed bazaars, each one devoted to a particular trade and each one built in this particular style to keep heat and bright light at bay. The first was and still is home to the milliners, who sell Astrakhan hats made of the distinctive tightly curled pelts of Karakul lambs. The second is devoted to silk, though the delicate embroidered scarves have been replaced by gaudy rougher fabrics. The third and largest bazaar devoted to jewellery must have been the most magnificent in its heyday, but is now home to a handful of forlorn souvenir shops.

Kalyan Mosque and Minaret and the Mir-i-Arab Madrassa: west of the jewellers' bazaar and dominating both the centre and the skyline of the city are Bukhara's three most impressive monuments. The Kalyan ('Great') Minaret, erected in 1127, is one of only three medieval buildings to have survived Genghis Khan's rampage in the 13th century. The only other structures to escape his wrath were the Samanid mausolem and the Magoki Attari mosque, both of which were buried out of sight. The Kalyan minaret, which once served as a beacon for caravans navigating across the desert, measures 30ft/9m in diameter and is 150ft/45m high. Halfway up the names of the architect, Bako, and of the ruler of Bukhara at the time, Arslan-Khan, can be deciphered. Inside, a spiral staircase leads to a gallery at the top, where the muezzin called the faithful to prayer and from where the unfaithful were thrown to their death. The last recorded death by 'deminorisation' was in 1884.

A small bridge links the minaret to the Kalyan Mosque, the largest in Bukhara. The existing structure was built in the first half of the 15th century, and gives a good idea of the scale and design of Bibi Khanum in Samarkand before it fell into ruins. The inside is simply enormous and semi-derelict, although some of the rooms around the central courtyard serve as extra classrooms for the madrassa opposite. Perched atop the huge turquoise dome that crowns the prayer room is one of the last remaining storks' nests in Bukhara. Until the middle of this century these gigantic nests, rising like chimneys from the tops of Bukhara's domes, were one of the city's best-known and best-loved features. Their diminishing numbers are ascribed to the change in ecological balance brought about by large-scale irrigation programmes in the region.

Opposite the Kalyan Mosque stands the equally huge Mir-i-Arab Madrassa, one of just two madrassas that remained fully functional during the Soviet era. Students come here from all over Central Asia to study the teachings of the Koran and to learn Arabic. It is closed to visitors.

Women's Hammam: down a back street just south of the Kalyan Mosque, the women's hammam or baths (open 7am-5pm except Tuesdays) provide a sultry respite from spiritual Bukhara. Bring a towel, soap and shampoo and enter another world. The first chamber on the ground floor is a cosy wooden panelled changing room, where both inhibitions and garments are shed. From here head down the stairwell into a cavernous twilight zone. Seven domed underground chambers, each heated to a slightly different temperature, have served for ablutions since the 16th century. The basic principle is as follows: sit in the hot chambers, gently perspire, soap thoroughly and then exfoliate by rubbing the entire body vigorously with a cotton mitt, rinse and repeat the whole procedure several times over. Massage, hair treatments and medicinal cures are also available at this informal women's centre. Males under five can accompany their mothers; those over-five have their own baths: see above.

The Ark: heading west from the jewellers' bazaar along ulitsa Kommunarov, which becomes Ploshchad Registan, you eventually reach the Ark, the lofty citadel where the Emir and his entourage lived 65ft/20m above the common rabble. According to a 16th-century legend, the Ark — meaning 'winter palace' in Farsi — was founded in the first century AD by a certain Siavush, son of an Iranian king. Over the centuries the Ark was destroyed and rebuilt at least five times, and every time the hill got higher. By the beginning of the 20th century, it was a small town with its own mosques and 3,000 inhabitants. Very few buildings have survived since most were made of wood and were destroyed during a fire in 1920 after the departure of the last Emir.

You enter the citadel through the Dolon, a covered passage lined with chambers where prisoners once languished and guides now ambush unsuspecting tourists. The first building at the top of the plateau is the Djuma, or Friday Mosque, which houses an exhibition of Korans, including a pocket-size one for travellers from the 15th century. The Emir's palace is a reduced and quite unregal version of its former self, the one surviving wing now given over to an eclectic collection of exhibits relating to Bukharan history. These include the staff, gourd and psychedelic robes of wandering dervishes.

The open space below the Ark was the Registan or Central Square, where public executions were held until the beginning of this century. The infamous bug pit, where thieves and other rotters were punished, was probably located directly below the disused water tower that now dominates the area.

Towards the Samanid Park: opposite the gateway to the Ark but half hidden by the water tower is the Bolo-Khauz Mosque, with a long porch supported by 20 very tall wooden pillars. A five-minute walk west of here takes you to Chaysma Aub, a quirky brick building with a lopsided conical dome that was built — so the story goes — over the Spring of Job. As well as providing a roof for the spring, which trickles out of a rusty tap, the building shelters a small exhibition on the lack of water in the region.

A little further west, ensconced in the greenery of the Samanid Park, stands one of the best preserved monuments of early Islamic architecture. Built above the tomb of Ismail Samani in the 10th century, the Samanid Mausoleum is characterised by the combination of simple design and intricate brickwork. Tiny bricks are angled in every conceivable direction and combination to create a variety of honeycomb surfaces, jagged edges and circular patterns.

The House of the Rich Merchant: this informal house museum used to belong to the family of Khojaev, who became the first president of the Bukharan SSR in 1920 and was later executed by Stalin. The recently restored interiors are not directly concerned with Khojaev but give an impression of the lifestyle of a wealthy 19th-century family. The combination of erratic opening hours and an impossibly difficult location in the southwestern part of the old town means that it is essential to phone in advance to organise a visit. By far the most enjoyable way to view the house is as a backdrop to an evening meal. Given a day's notice the curator is more than willing to cater for visitors: contact Zinat at the Ark to organise a meal (41378, 41404).

Shopping. A daily market is held in the street that runs from the jewellers' bazaar to the Ark, but the largest and best market is held just outside the city walls at the northern end of the Samanid park every Thursday and Sunday.

Help and Information. A number of day trips can be booked from the service bureau of the Hotel Bukhara, though these are expensive for individuals; other local tourist agencies include the Salom Tourist Agency (23398, 37277) and Bukhara Visit (60085).

International calls can be made from the telephone office on ul 40 Let Oktyabrya just east of Hotel Bukhara; connections are almost instantaneous. The most central post office is along a tiny passageway accessible via a narrow staircase just east of the Moneychangers' Bazaar. The phone code for Bukhara is 36522.

AROUND BUKHARA

Chor Bakr Necropolis. Just 15 minutes' drive west of Bukhara, Chor Bakr seems a million miles from anywhere. This vast cemetery was developed in the 16th century around the site of the alleged tomb of Abu Bakr, a descendant of Mohammed. Beyond a cluster of peasant shacks, a monumental mosque rises above the surrounding wilderness, its twin portals and crumbling blue domes visible from afar. The walls of the main prayer hall are riddled with cracks and the dome looks on the point of collpase, but this doesn't seem to deter the faithful who have returned to pray here since the mosque re-opened in 1990. All around, thousands of engraved tombs lie half hidden in the tall pampas grass that has taken root after decades of neglect. Sunset, when the ruins blush a deep shade of gold, is the most atmospheric time to visit.

Sitorai-Mokhi-Khosa. Just over 2 miles/4km north of Bukhara, Sitorai-Mokhi-Khosa was the favourite residence of the last Emir who came here to forget the humiliation of Bukhara's subjugation to Russian rule. The palace itself is an arresting mixture of tastelessness and opulence, every successive room more ornate than the last, with mirrors, niches and frescoes vying for wall space. The Emir's 400-strong harem was housed in the pavillion overlooking the pool and the oriental pagoda nearby was the Emir's personal viewing tower. He would stand there and watch the women frollicking in the water and then toss an apple to the beauty of his choice. The Bolsheviks brought an end to these games when they captured the palace in 1920, though the Emir had already fled to Afghanistan.

Just over 2 miles/4km north of Bukhara, Sitorai-Mokhi-Khosa is easily reached by taxi or by public transport. Take bus 9 or 13 from ul Nizami, east of the historic centre, or bus 12 from the Registan.

KHIVA

Medieval Khiva feels like an abandoned stage set. The inner city, encircled by 26-ft/8m high fortifications, has enjoyed the status of a museum since 1968. Though this means that Khiva has preserved its unity better than any other city in Central Asia, the bustle and colour that characterised the old trading centre have long since gone — as have most of the inhabitants, lured to the new town beyond the walls by modern facilities such as running water. Still, this is no reason not to come. Khiva may have lost its vitality but the ghostly atmosphere that has taken its place has its own charms. You need one long day to see the sights, but try and stay at least one night to see Khiva at its most appealing in late evening or early morning.

Khiva has existed since at least the sixth century. During the Middle Ages became an important stopping place for caravans heading north through the desert, though it rose to prominence only in the 16th century, when the river Oxus changed its course, leaving the more ancient city of Gurganj (now known as Kunya Urgench) stranded in the desert. From that time until 1873, when the town was absorbed into the Russian empire, it was the capital of the Khivan Khanate, whose territory at one time stretched from the Caspian Sea right into India.

Getting There. all routes to Khiva go through Urgench, about 20 miles/ 32km northeast, and unless you have you own car it is impossible to avoid this unexciting modern city.

To Urgench: the journey by land to Urgench is arduous at any time of year since it invloves travelling at least six hours across two of Central Asia's vast deserts, the Kara-Kum and Kyzyl-Kum. Temperatures are extreme and you tend to shiver or sweat all the way. If you opt out and fly, there is a daily flight from Tashkent, with occasional flights from Bukhara in summer. There are regular buses from the airport into the centre of town.

For land travellers there are rail connections from Moscow, Dushanbe and Ashkhabad, and several buses a day from Tashkent (16 hours), and one or two a day from Bukhara (8 hours) and Samarkand (12 hours). The bus and train stations are adjacent at the southern end of ulitsa Kommunisticheskaya, the town's main artery.

To Khiva: there are regular bus and *marshrutnoyes* (minibuses) to Khiva from Urgench bus station. Most buses stop by Khiva's northern gate. Since the taxis stop where you want, you can ask to be dropped at the western gate (Zapadnaya Vorota), which is the main entrance; most *marshrutnoyes* wait here too.

Accommodation. There is only one possibility in Khiva itself — the Hotel Khiva (527275), just inside the west gate. It is actually the Amin Khan Madrassa, which was built in 1854 and has remained virtually unchanged since the last students left after the Bolshevik Revolution. This is probably the most atmospheric hotel in Central Asia, where the rooms are the old student cells with balconies overlooking the courtyard on one side and the old city walls on the other. You'll pay about $15 per person in the high season and $10 at other times. If it's full, ask whether the Hotel Khorezm, in the newer part of Khiva has re-opened, or better still wander the streets with a rucksack and see what offers you get.

In Urgench, the cheapest option is the Hotel Urgench at ulitsa Kommunisticheskaya 27, but it does not officially accept foreigners; getting a room will depend very much on who's working on reception. Otherwise, you will be forced to pay $60 for a double at the Hotel Khorezm on ulitsa Al-Biruni (65408) or $40 for a room at the Hotel Dzheykhoum on ulitsa Kommunisticheskaya.

Eating and Drinking. The underground chaikhana inside the Hotel Khiva is cool in summer and warmish in winter. If you wish to eat, you need to order ahead of time. There are various other chaikhanas dotted around the old town, most notably near the bazaar just outside the eastern gate, although these tend to pack up as soon as the weather starts cooling down.

Exploring. The Ishan-Kala or Inner City of Khiva consists of a maze of narrow medieval streets lined with mosques, madrassas, caravansarais and palaces. Much the best way to appreciate its charms is to wander aimlessly. Virtually every building houses a museum, usually consisting of an improvised assortment of bric a brac and providing an excuse to charge an entrance fee. The best exhibits tend to be black and white photos of Khiva at the turn of the century, with the Khan's Guards in tall fur hats and long flowing robes.

There are few outstanding buildings, and most are no more than one or two hundred years old. The Kalta Minaret and Kunya Ark dominate the western end of the old town. Had Khiva's famous sacred tower been completed it would have been the tallest minaret in Central Asia. Decorated with multi-coloured stripes of tiling, the squat minaret nevertheless remains impressive in its unfininshed state. Just north of here the Kunya Ark, the principal residence of the Khivan Khans, has been partially restored. A chamber by the entrance documents the horrible punishments devised by the Khans. The best thing about the Ark, however, is the view from the top. The roof is high enough to reveal all of Inner Khiva but low enough to hide the modern sprawl beyond the walls.

About halfway down ulitsa Karla Marksa, the Dzhuma or Friday Mosque is a haven of shade and tranquillity. The interior is like a symmetrically planted glade, with 212 carved wooden columns supporting the roof. The minaret can be climbed and provides another excellent vantage point, though there is an even better view from the minaret adjoining the Mausoleum of Pakhlavan Mahmud on ulitsa Bukhara, just south of here. According to legend, Mahmud was a 14th-century tanner turned poet-philosopher, who gave away all his money to the poor. After the death of this folk hero, a mausoleum was built above his grave and it has remained Khiva's holiest shrine to this day. Some of Mahmud's sayings and verses are inscribed in the glazed tiles. One of the inscriptions reads: 'It is better to live a hundred years in prison than to talk for one minute to a fool.'

Finer than the Ark is the Tash Kauli Palace, by the eastern gates, which was commissioned by the 37th Khan, Allakuli, at the beginning of the 19th century. The residence is a city within a city, with covered passages linking various courtyards decorated with dazzling blue and white tiling. The first courtyard is the harem, where the Khan's four principal wives lived in spacious rooms along the shady façade, whilst his 40 spare wives lived in more cramped style along the sunny façade. A tip to the guide will ensure that you see the most impressive part of the palace, the courtyard where dancing boys twirled on a raised stage decorated with paisley-patterned tiling which is unique in Central Asia.

South of Tash Kauli is Khiva's strangest sight, an old caravansarai converted into a Soviet department store or *univermag*. Only the Soviet authorities would have thought of roofing over the liveliest, most colourful part of the old town, and filling it with factory-made nylon carpets and cheap underwear. Commercial transactions are of secondary importance here; an army of cashiers sit by their tills knitting and sipping tea whilst old men play chess under the Leninist slogans painted on the walls. There is an open-air bazaar just east of here.

Help and Information. Maps can be bought from shops just inside the western gate. The Hotel Khorezm in Urgench organises group excursions and sells airline tickets.

AROUND KHIVA

Kunya Urgench or Gurganj, the medieval capital of the kingdom of Khorezm, is actually in Turkmenistan but is easier to reach from Urgench than from

Ashkhabad. The most impressive surviving monument is the 14th-century Kutluk Timur Minaret which, at 203ft/62m is the tallest in Central Asia. Several daily buses go from Urgench to Tashauz (30 miles/48km), the first town beyond the Turkmen border from where there are regular connections to Kunya Urgench, a further 55 miles/90km away. Although you officially need a Turkmen visa to visit Kunya Urgench, it is unlikely that anyone will check local buses plying their way across the desert. If, however, you plan to stay the night in Tashauz, ask at the Hotel Khorezm in Urgench about getting a visa. Visiting Kunya Urgench from Urgench is likely to become easier in the coming years as there is talk of an Uzbek-Turkmen agreement to improve transport links for tourists.

Public Holidays

January 1	New Year's Day
March 8	International Women's Day
March 21	Navroos, the vernal equinox
Late March	Khait, Muslim holiday
May 9	Victory Day
Variable	Khuraban Khait, Muslim celebration
September 1	Independence Day
December 8	Constitution Day

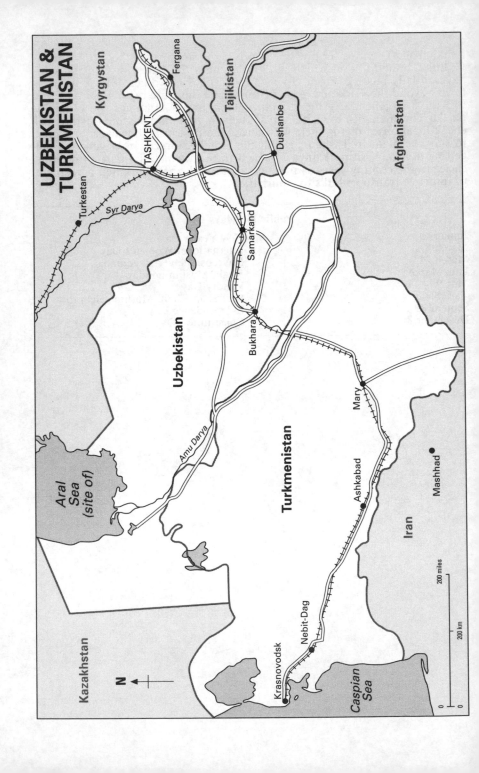

TURKMENISTAN

Population: 3.7 million   **Capital:** Ashkhabad (population 450,000)

Turkmenistan is the last frontier, until recently the very outpost of the old Soviet Empire, bordered by Afghanistan and Iran. The country is covered by the very large, very empty and very hot Kara-Kum desert — for centuries Turkmenistan's most effective defensive weapon, successfully repelling adventurers, armies and most forms of human life. But the people who adapted to its environs, the Turkmen, are probably the most charismatic in Central Asia. It is not just their enormous sheepskin hats that make them so distinctive but also their sense of *chilik*, a uniquely Turkmen concept involving a mixture of pride, hospitality and courage. In the 19th century they developed a reputation for ferocity and mystery which to some extent still holds true today. The country's president sponsors a cult of personality that would make even Stalin blush. Wherever you go, you will never be far from the words and wisdom of Turkmenbashi, or 'Leader of the Turkmen', as he likes to be known.

Despite attempts to woo Western leaders with some celebrated gift-giving (in 1992 President Niyazov presented British prime minister John Major with a thoroughbred race-horse), tourists are not exactly welcomed with open arms. Visas can be problematic, police-checks frequent and the cost of accommodation astronomically high. But this in turn means that Turkmenistan is one of the least visited and altogether wildest corners of the former USSR.

GEOGRAPHY AND CLIMATE

Four-fifths of Turkmenistan is covered by the Kara-Kum, or Black Sands desert, so-called not so much because of its colour but because of the proverbial suffering borne by its inhabitants. According to an old legend, after God created Earth he gave the first arrivals, the Turkmen, a vast territory. When the sun was shared out the Turkmen arrived first again and received more than the others; but when the day to share out the water came, the Turkmen didn't wake up and so got nothing. Water has always been a problem. For centuries the Amu-Darya River provided the only irrigation, and a string of towns grew up along its banks and tributaries. In modern times its water has been siphoned off into the Kara-Kum canal which, at 682 miles/1,100km, is the longest in the world, built by the Soviets to enable them to grow cotton in the south of the country.

Summers are long and hot with temperatures in the shade reaching 40°C/104°F. Winters are bitter with lows reaching −25°C/−13°F, but mercifully short. Average temperatures in Ashkhabad are 4°C/38°F in January and 30°C/86°F in July. Spring is the only time you're likely to see rain.

HISTORY

No one is quite sure where the Turkmen came from, though it is thought they first appeared from the Altai mountains in northern Mongolia during the fifth century. They were first recorded as living in the area that is now Turkmenistan in the 15th century. They were hardy nomads noted for their ability to ride as much as 80 miles/130km a day and survive on nothing more than wheat and sour milk. When the Russians arrived, they found the

Central Asian people with the firmest sense of 'nationhood' and the strongest will not to be subdued. Subdued they were, however, in 1881, but only after 20,000 of them had been massacred at the Battle of Geok-Tepe. The Anglo-Russian Treaty of 1895 established the present borders between Turkmenistan, Iran and Afghanistan; this left one to two million Turkmen in Iran and a further million in Afghanistan.

After the Revolution there was more resistance, and for a time counter-revolutionaries controlled the area propped up by a small British force. In 1934 the Turkmen Soviet Socialist Republic was formed, though political control was handed over to native Turkmen only after World War II.

The 1991 coup in Moscow brought no new faces to power in Turkmenistan. Niyazov, the first secretary of the Turkmen Communist Party, was voted president in an election in which no other candidate was allowed to stand. Attempts at democratisation have been limited to renaming the Communist Party the Democratic Party, while the opposition has been suppressed. For the time being, Niyazov's position seems almost unassailable.

THE PEOPLE

Despite the years of Soviet rule, the Turkmen people still identify themselves by tribe and clan. The new national flag introduced by President Niyazov acknowledged this by including carpet patterns distinctive to each of the major tribes. Turkmen make up 72% of the population, but in the cities the percentage of Russians can be as high as 40%.

LANGUAGE

Turkmen is the official language though Russian is widely spoken. In 1929 the Arabic script was scrapped in favour of the Latin alphabet and then in 1940, in keeping with Soviet policy in all the republics, the Cyrillic alphabet was introduced. Turkmen is a Turkic language with more in common with Anatolian Turkish than any other Central Asian language. If you plan to stray beyond the capital, it is well worth mastering the basics.

Useful words and phrases

1 — *bir*	thank you — *tangyr*
2 — *iki*	yes — *howa*
3 — *uch*	no — *yok*
4 — *durt*	good — *yakhsheh*
5 — *byash*	where is? — *niredeh?*
6 — *altih*	bread — *churuk*
7 — *yeddih*	water — *su*
8 — *sekiz*	
9 — *dokuz*	
10 — *on*	

GETTING THERE

Air. The cheapest and easiest route to Turkmenistan from the UK is with Turkish Airlines via Istanbul. Trailfinders (42/48 Earls Court Road, London, W8 6EJ; 0171-938 3366), for example, offer return tickets for around £500. Another good option is to fly with Azerbaijan Air via Baku. East West Travel and Tours (93 Regent Street, London W1 7OA; 0171-734 0099) can do a return ticket for around £530. Iran Air (73 Piccadilly, London W1X

5AA; 0171-409 0971) has flights to Ashkhabad via Tehran, but this costs around £700 and is made complicated by overnight stops en route and the relevant visas. Aeroflot no longer operates flights from Moscow to Ashkhabad as this route is now covered by Turkmen Air, which currently has no agent in the UK. Both Turkmen Air and Uzbekistan Airways fly from Tashkent. The former charges more, around $60 one way compared with $40, but uses a larger aeroplane so it is generally easier to get a seat and may be safer. There are also flights to and from Almaty in Kazakhstan.

Rail. Plans exist to build a railway line to link Turkmenistan with Iran. Construction of the Iranian section of the track has already begun. For the time being, the country is linked by rail to Moscow, Dushanbe and Tashkent.

Bus. There are no long-distance bus services from neighbouring republics, but local buses travel between Uzbekistan and Tashauz, the Turkmen town closest to the border on the Nukus-Ashkhabad road, and also to Chardzhou, the first Turkmen town on the road linking Bukhara to Mary.

Boat. It is possible to take a boat from Baku in Azerbaijan across the Caspian Sea to Turkmenbashi (formerly Krasnovodsk). The journey, aboard an old Soviet liner, takes about 14 hours. Services are not as frequent as they used to be so be prepared for an overnight stay or longer at either end. Another option is to sail down the Volga from Moscow to Astrakhan, and from there find a passage on a cargo ship sailing to Turkmenbashi. Enquire at the River Port (Rechnoi Vokzal) in Moscow.

Driving. Road checks and random fines from the police are even more frequent in Turkmenistan than in Uzbekistan, and despite the country's abundant oil resources petrol can be surprisingly difficult to obtain. As in all other Central Asian countries, bringing your own vehicle into the country and getting it out again is fraught with difficulty. Those undeterred by the bureaucratic hurdles can check with the Iranian Embassy in London whether it is possible to obtain transit visas through the border crossing at Gaudan for entry into Turkmenistan. At the time of writing it is open to local traffic only, but this could change in the future.

RED TAPE

Russian and Central Asian visas are not valid in Turkmenistan. This should not cause any problems if you fly into the country since Turkmen visas are obtainable on arrival at Ashkhabad airport. In 1995 a one-week visa cost $20. If you arrive by bus or train, you may or may not be troubled by border formalities. Travellers have entered the country from neighbouring Uzbekistan without having their passports checked, but this may change. Given that Turkmenistan is virtually a police state, it may not be wise to flout the law; and note that without a visa it is unlikely that you will be given a room in a hotel.

If you do manage to enter the country by an overland route without a visa, head to the foreigners' registration office (Ovir) at the international airport as soon as you arrive in Ashkhabad; if need be, claim you arrived by plane. If you want to stay ovenight in Mary en route to Ashkhabad, ask at Hotel Mary for Tanya and George, who may be able to help you.

Obtaining a Turkmen visa in advance is virtually impossible as Turkmenistan has few missions abroad. The private tourist office on the third floor of the Hotel Tashkent in Uzbekistan may, however, be able to help.

MONEY

1 manat = 10 tenga   1995: $1 = 90 manat

Bring all your money in small denomination post-1990 dollar bills as travellers' cheques and credit cards are rarely accepted. Unofficial exchange rates are better than bank rates, but trading on the black market is illegal. If you do change your money outside the official channels, it is obviously safer to do so with a floor lady in a hotel than in the street.

GETTING AROUND

There are daily connections by air and rail linking Ashkhabad with Turkmenbashi, Mary, Chardzhou and Tashauz, the four main towns outside the capital. Buses serve these main routes as well as more rural areas. For short journeys, hiring a taxi is by far the easiest option and is not too expensive since petrol is still cheap.

ACCOMMODATION

The Turkmen Minstry of Tourism has done absolutely nothing to encourage foreign visitors, so the hotel situation has if anything deteriorated since the demise of Intourist. The choice is extremely limited and prices are exhorbitantly high. Private accommodation offices are non-existent so the only option is to get to know local people. Luckily, their hospitality is legendary.

EATING AND DRINKING

Traditional Central Asian fare such as shashlik, plov, manti and samsa are Turkmen staples too, but fish is often used instead of meat. Fish plov is delicious, but raw fish manti may be an aquired taste. Bread, which goes by the name of *churuk*, looks and tastes like that found in other Central Asian countries.

CRIME AND SAFETY

A strong police presence throughout the country means that crime rates are relatively low. Still, the streets of Ashkhabad and other cities are eerily dark at night which makes it uncomfortable if not unwise to wander alone after dusk. Take the usual precautions and be particularly careful on overnight trains.

SHOPPING

Turkmen carpets attracted the admiration of Marco Polo in the 13th century, and were first exported to Europe in Renaissance times, when they appeared in Italian art. If you have any desire at all to buy a carpet, then Turkmenistan is undoubtedly the place to come. The skill and effort involved in the making of a single carpet is immense. The craft and tribal motifs are passed on from mother to daughter and even today are signifiers not just of wealth but of clan allegiances. 'Unroll your carpet and I shall see what is written on your heart' goes a Turkmen saying. The basic design element is the *gul* or flower, an octagonal or diamond shape motif filled with a variety of geometric forms.

The most expensive carpets are the old hand-knotted ones, which have as many as 500 knots to the square inch, though you may need to get an export certificate from the Ministry of Culture to take it out of the country. Much cheaper, but equally colourful, are the woven kilims which can be bought for as little as $5. Other good purchases include the huge shaggy hats that Turkmen wear year-round to insulate against both heat and cold.

ASHKHABAD

In Arabic, Ashkhabad means 'lovely settlement', which you could politely call an exaggeration. In 1948 an earthquake, still known locally as 'the catastrophe', levelled the city and killed all but 20,000 of the 130,000 inhabitants. The capital today is a small modern town with a provincial atmosphere, situated on the edges of the Kara-Kum desert. Although its ancient history goes back a good 2,500 years, when the Russians arrived in 1881 they found nothing more than a ramshackle village. For the best part of the 20th century it has been a garrison town, closed to Western visitors and full of soldiers brought in to patrol the sensitive Iranian border, just 30 miles/48km away. Natural gas and oil reserves in the Caspian sea have also brought hordes of businessmen to Ashkhabad, together with a spate of new developments to cater for their expense accounts. Otherwise, life has changed little here. The best reason for coming is to see old-style state communism in action and to visit the fine weekly market. Every Sunday, Turkmen traders take over a vast stretch of desert and will sell you anything from a carpet to a camel, at prices which are far lower than elsewhere in the region.

CITY LAYOUT

The main artery running from east to west is Makhtumkuli prospekt (formerly Prospekt Svobody). The principal shopping area is around the Russian market on ulitsa Engelsa.

ARRIVAL AND DEPARTURE

The ultra-modern airport is about 6 miles/10km north of the city and served by bus number 18, which stops near the Hotel Ashkhabad. The Turkmen Air ticket office is behind this same hotel at ulitsa Pushkina 3. Turkish Airlines has an office at Makhtumkuli prospekt 71 (510666, 511666).

The train station is at the northern end of prospekt Lenina, near the centre of the town. The bus terminal is on ulitsa Engelsa, opposite the Tikinsky bazaar.

ACCOMMODATION

By the time this book goes to press, a cluster of deluxe hotels on the edge of the desert should be completed. But while this is good news for businessmen, it provides scant comfort for poorer visitors, who might balk at paying $250 for a room. Not that the existing options are good value. On the contrary, a double room at the main tourist hotel, the Ashkhabad (Makhtumkuli prospekt 74; 90447), will set you back in the region of $120. The exact price is at the discretion of the administrator, so it is worth trying to bargain. A more comfortable and slightly better value option is the Jubilyenaya on prospekt Tehran (formerly prospekt Temirayesev) at the western end of Makhtumkuli prospekt. A double here costs $100. If all else fails, try turning up at the American Embassy (in the same hotel) with a good excuse and a polite smile. They have the names of a couple of people who are able to provide bed and breakfast, and have been known to help out stranded travellers.

EATING AND DRINKING

The choice of restaurants is limited. Some of the best food is served at the Hotel Ashkhabad, but more fun is Restaurant Ayna, opposite the Hotel Jubileynaya. Although the lighting here is dim verging on gloomy, an energetic band plays Turkish, Russian and Iranian hits to an appreciative audience. During the day you can fill up on shashlik and other fast food at a number of chaikhanas dotted around the Russian bazaar.

EXPLORING

The one unmissable sight in Ashkhabad is in fact not so much a sight as an event: the weekly Sunday market, held beyond the Kara-Kum canal, a few miles south of the city. This is probably the most colourful market in Central Asia, with the biggest woolliest hats on sale as well as acre upon acre of carpets. Here you'll have the chance to sample camel-milk yoghurt or buy a thoroughbred horse: at about $500 they are a snitch at the price, though it would cost about ten times that amount to ship the animal home.

In Ashkhabad itself there are two interesting museums. The Fine Arts Museum at Makhtumkuli prospekt 84 has a collection of rugs and jewellery, and several rooms of Soviet, French and Italian works as well as 20th-century Turkmen paintings. The History Museum, at ulitsa Shevchenko 1 (two blocks south of Hotel Ashkhabad), is housed in a one-storey building that somehow managed to survive the 1948 earthquake. It has an extensive collection of second-century BC Parthian artefacts found in nearby Nisa (see below), but due to the lack of funds only a tiny of portion are on display. The best exhibits include some exquisitely carved ivory drinking horns, and a fine display of Turkmen clothing. Opposite the museum is a small park with the last remaining statue of Lenin in Ashkhabad. Lenin himself is outshone by his enormous three-tiered pedestal draped in a Turkmen carpet made entirely of tiles.

The main shopping hub is one block west of the History Museum. Tsum, entered from ulitsa Shevchenko, is still stuffed full of state-subsidised produce, while just down the road on ulitsa Engelsa is the only Benetton in Central Asia. The main *kolkhoz* or farmers' market, where traders sell a vast array of fruit and vegetables, is called the Tikinsky bazaar and occupies a whole block between Engelsa and Pervovo Mai.

VDNKh, the old exhibition hall of Soviet excellence, is about a mile southeast of the centre on ulitsa Atabaeva. It is chiefly notable for having what is purported to be the largest carpet in the world measuring 1,935 square metres.

ENTERTAINMENT

At the weekends and on national holidays the Turkmen relive their nomadic past with a number of highly popular horse and camel-back games in the Hippodrome, 3 miles/5km east of the centre and accessible on bus 4 from Makhtumkuli prospekt. Betting is strictly forbidden.

HELP AND INFORMATION

Turkmen Tourism has an office in the Hotel Ashkhabad. The main post office is on the corner of Libknekhta and 50 Let Turkmenskoye SSR. The telephone code for Ashkhabad is 3632.

Britain is contemplating opening up an embassy in Ashkhabad but has not got around to it yet. In an emergency, contact the US Embassy in Hotel Jubilenaya (244925, 244994). To extend your visa or sort out immigration problems, go to the Ovir office in the interntaional lounge at the airport.

FURTHER AFIELD

Nisa. Just 10 miles/16km west of Ashkhabad you can visit the remains of Nisa, the royal fortress of the Parthians who between the third century BC and the third century AD ruled over a vast empire that stretched as far as Iraq and Syria. The site is protected by UNESCO and still under excavation. The best finds are now in the Hermitage in St Petersburg and in the History Museum in Ashkhabad, but the ruins still give a good impression of a fortified town and occupy a beautiful elevated site in the mountains. Tanya, an English-speaking guide at the History Museum in the city can organise an excursion.

Bakharden. Travelling about 60 miles/100km northwest of Ashkhabad on the road to Krasnovodsk you reach Bakharden, in the foothills of the Kopet Dag Mountains. There is a cave here with an underground lake where you can bathe in the warm emerald green water and soak up its sulphuric salts. Note that if you go for a dip, you must observe the rule of silence enforced to keep the bats at bay.

Merv. At one time the second city in the Islamic world and an important trading post on the silk route, Merv lies 217 miles/350km west of Ashkhabad on the road to Bukhara. There are many apocryphal stories attached to the city, the most appealing of which is that it was the setting and inspiration for *A Thousand and One Nights*. The partially-excavated site is enormous: it covers an area of 125 square kilometres and encompasses at least four different settlements, the seats of successive dynasties which ruled over the region from the fifth century BC right up until the 18th century. The most important of these was the Seljuk city of Sultan Kala, where today the best-preserved monuments are the Sanjar mausoleum, the most magnificent of all the Seljuk tombs with a huge double dome, and the sixth-and seventh-century Kyz-Kala palaces built with strange fluted walls. Hiring a guide is definitely worthwhile to find you way round and make sense of the maze of brick walls and mausolea.

Mary, a bleak industrial town 20 miles/32km away is the hotel base for visiting Merv. There are daily flights to Mary from Ashkhabad as well as a weekly flight from Tashkent. A daily overnight train (in both directions) and several buses also link Mary to the capital, taking six hours and eight hours respectively. The only hotel that puts up foreigners is the Sandzar at ulitsa Malomitez 58 (57644, 57144). A double room costs $60-80. Insist on tourist class if you object to cockroaches. The chaikhana opposite the hotel serves much better food than the hotel restaurant.

The easiest way to reach Merv from Mary is by taxi. Tanya and George who work at the Hotel Sandzar can help you organise an excursion (39422, 35874).

Kazakhstan

Population: 16 million   **Capital:** Almaty (1.5 million)

Imagine the population of Holland living in a country the size of western Europe. That's Kazakhstan. Very big, and very empty, the country consists of a million square miles of steppeland between China and the Caspian Sea. Kazakhstan was created only in the 1920s, when the Bolsheviks fixed some arbitrary borders and turned it into a dumping ground for political prisoners and entire communities of unwanted nationalities. This was Stalin's brave new world, a previously blank patch of the world from where scientists catapulted rockets into orbit, exploded 15 nuclear bombs a year and hatched crazy agricultural plans that were to wreak havoc on a fragile ecology and pollute the land for future generations.

Nine-tenths of Kazakhstan is steppe, and the 16 million people who live here are concentrated in a handful of cities created by Stalin. The country may not be overflowing with attractions, but it has the most invigorating capital city in Central Asia and, on the southeastern fringe, the high drama of the Tien-Shan and Altai mountains.

CLIMATE

Kazakhstan's climate is characterised by drastic variations. In the desert areas east of the Caspian Sea, temperatures range from 40°C/104°F to −40°C/−40°F. Droughts are common and in summer the area is ravaged by sandstorms. The south is warmer than the north and summers are long with an average temperature of 30°C/86°F in July.

Almaty has very hot summers, with temparatures reaching 40°C/104°F, and extremely cold winters, with lows of −34°C/−28°F in January. The sun shines for most of the year.

HISTORY

For centuries the only people who lived in what is now Kazakhstan were nomads migrating across the huge plains according to season. Nobody can be quite sure when and from where they appeared. It was probably around the fifth century that various Turkic tribes swept down from the northeast, mingling with later Mongol invaders in the 15th century. In the 18th century, the Russians began their inexorable progress southwards and found the people sprinkled across the plains and sub-divided into three confederate hordes. The Russian nationalist view maintains that there followed a 'voluntary unification' between the tsarist settlers and two of the hordes. By the mid-19th century, the Kazakhs had been subdued into servitude, though they were still nomads.

It was only in the 1930s, following incorporation into the Soviet Union, that the nomadic lifestyle which had been practised for centuries was brought to an abrupt end. A ferocious regime oversaw the slaughter of Kazakhs, as the people were eventually starved into submission. Out of a population of four million only one million survived, a holocaust from which the Kazakhs have yet to recover. Their numbers were swamped by the wholesale exporting of *personae non grata* from all parts of the Soviet Union.

During the Brezhnev years the Kazakh government, led by Dinmukhamed Kunaev, was thoroughly corrupt but absolutely loyal to Moscow. Change came in late 1986, when Gorbachev replaced Kunaev with a reformist. He was a Russian, however, and large demonstrations by young Kazakhs succeeded in having him replaced by Nursultan Nazarbaev, a local man who remains president to this day. Kazakhstan was the last republic to leave the USSR in December 1991. Since then the country has been relatively stable, due mostly to the firm grip Nazarbaev has maintained on the government, press and all opposition parties.

THE PEOPLE

The Kazakhs, peaceable nomads forcibly settled into concrete farms and suburbs only a generation ago, are a minority in their own country. Kazakhstan means 'Land of Kazakhs', but they represent only 43% of the population. They are outnumbered mainly by Russians and Ukrainians, but the country has a truly multinational society, with significant groups of Koreans, Tatars, Belarusians and Germans to name just a few. The hundred or so different nationalities live together remarkably well, lending a truly cosmopolitan air to the cities.

Kazakhs, historically repressed and discriminated against, have been enjoying a national renaissance in the last few years, but there has been little inter-ethnic tension and little in the way of a religious resurgence. The people were not convincingly Islamicised, and the women have never worn the veil. The Kazakhs' traditional nomadic lifestyle, which meant moving from pasture to pasture on horseback and living inside the large circular felt tents known as yurts, has disappeared, but there is still an almost mystical affection for the steppe.

LANGUAGE

In 1990 Kazakh became the official language of the republic. In response to

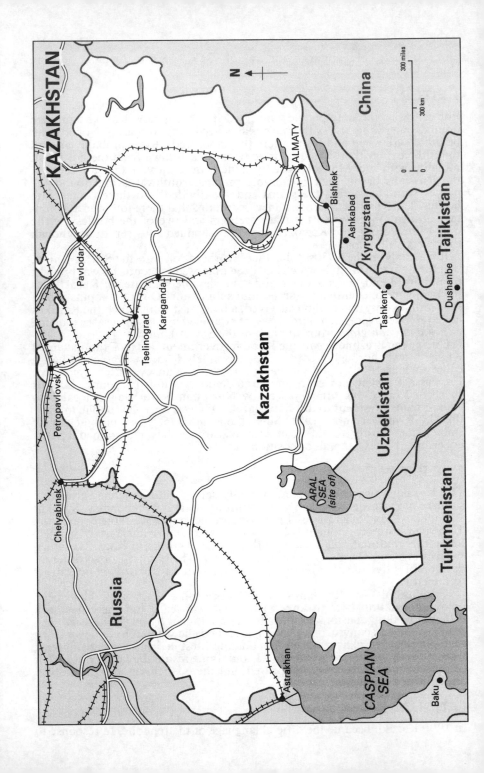

demands by the Russians and other nationalities, however, Russian has now been designated the language of inter-ethnic communication and some amendments introduced. The new banknotes, for example, have Kazakh script on one side and Russian on the other.

The Kazakh language belongs to the Turkic family, like other Central Asian language, and is most similar to Kyrgyz. The language has its own peculiarities, though: eight extra letters were added to the Cyrillic alphabet to accommodate its strange vowels. Eskimoes are (wrongly) said to have countless different words for 'snow', but the Kazakhs certainly have 100 different ways of saying 'horse'.

AIR

With international flights to Kazakhstan expanding rapidly, Almaty rivals Tashkent as a gateway to Central Asia. Austrian Airlines, KLM and Lufthansa fly from Vienna, Amsterdam and Frankfurt respectively, but discounted fares are hard to find. Kazakh Air, the national airline, operates a number of flights to and from western Europe including Frankfurt, Vienna and Hannover. There is no agent in the UK so far, but when a route begins to London it is likely to be handled by United Travel (0171-493 4444/fax 493 2195). Turkish Airlines flies from Istanbul, and this could be the most economical route: specialist agents such as those listed on page 14 should charge around £570 return from London. Pakistan International Airlines operates from Islamabad to Almaty, and could also provide some discount fares.

You can pick up some real bargains once in Kazakhstan, using Kazakh: flights from Almaty to Urumqi in China for $290 return, Istanbul for $600 and Delhi from $350 return. Cheapest of all, however, are the regular charter flights operated between Almaty and leading shopping destinations, notably in the Middle East but also occasionally to western Europe. Prices are about $120 return to the Gulf, and $200 to Islamabad. It is hard to find out about these last flights: if you read Russian, check the local newspapers for advertisements or ask the owner of the restaurant in the Hotel Alau-Tau in Almaty (see page 343).

From within the CIS, Kazakh Air has flights from St Petersburg and Tashkent, as well as dozens of flights a week from Moscow. Aeroflot and Transaero also operate from Moscow, but charge a little more. Even so, you should not have to pay more than about $200 for a one-way ticket from Moscow to Almaty.

TRAIN

The journey by train from Moscow is much cheaper than the flight, and it is a fine way to take in the vastness of Kazakhstan's empty steppe. It also takes about three days, so pack plenty of provisions and a good book. There are services from Irkutsk, Tomsk, Omsk and Novosibirsk too.

Genghis Khan Express. It is now possible to follow the route of the old silk caravans out of China aboard the Genghis Khan Express, a twice-weekly train between the Chinese city of Urumqi and Almaty. It runs along a track 762 miles/1,230km long and took more than half a century to complete. Linking Rotterdam to Shanghai, this is a less well-known but equally tempting alternative to the heavily subscribed Trans-Siberian Express.

If you are planning to take this train out of Kazakhstan, it is possible to get a Chinese visa in Almaty (see below). However, it is even better to sort this out in advance. The best way to get a Chinese visa in London is through the China Travel Service, 7 Upper St Martin's Lane, London WC2H 9DL (0171-836 3688); a fee of £10 is added to the visa fee of £25, but buys you exemption from having to say where you will be going and staying in China.

Tickets out of Kazakhstan are available most cheaply in Almaty, but you can buy a ticket in advance and be assured of a berth if you book through Intourist in London (0171-538 5965). See also *Almaty: Arrival and Departure.*

BUS

Taking a bus to Kazakhstan is only really feasible if you are coming from Kyrgyzstan or Uzbekistan. There are regular services from both Bishkek and Tashkent to the Kazakh capital.

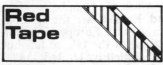

At the time of writing, in early summer 1995, you can enter Kazakhstan if you have a CIS visa issued by a Russian consulate. There is some difference of opinion amongst Kazakh officials as to whether this is strictly legal, but on the whole Kazakhstan has a more relaxed attitude towards visa requirements than some of its neighbours. To be on the safe side, have Almaty and any other towns you intend to visit specified on your visa. If you arrive by bus or train, however, it is highly unlikely that you will encounter any border controls.

Arriving by air with no visa is a potentially expensive risk. Although it is perfectly possible for the authorities to issue you with a Kazakh visa on the spot, the price for a week is likely to be in excess of $100.

Kazakhstan has few representations abroad, although there is an embassy in Washington (tel 244-4305, fax 833-3843).

Forced out of the rouble zone by Russia's tough new membership criteria, Kazakhstan introduced its own currency in 1993. It is called the tenge and is proving relatively stable. There are no dividends to be won by exchanging money on the black market.

Credit Cards. Kazakhstan presents m ore possibilities for spending money by credit card than anywhere else in Central Asia. You can use it to pay for hotel rooms, meals and even to draw out cash. The most popular brand is Visa.

Telephone. The standard mediocre Soviet telecommunications network is in place in Kazakhstan. If you have a lot of cash and need to make an international call in a hurry, Almaty has a burgeoning number of satellite cardphones that (almost) guarantee an instant connection. Bear in mind that Kazakhstan is six hours ahead of GMT

Broadcasting. Kazakhstan's state television station has changed little since independence. In much of the country it is possible to pick up two Moscow stations, and one apiece from Uzbekistan and Kyrgyzstan. In addition, the cities have four commercial channels on cable, which show a mixture of pirated movies, MTV, CNN, Prime Sport and, at 7pm every evening, BBC Worldwide TV news.

In Almaty, the most popular radio station is Radio Max on 102.2FM. It broadcasts in English between 6pm and 7pm every evening.

Getting Around

In a country the size of Kazakhstan, flying is the only practicable way to travel if you are short of time. Kazakh Air has several flights a day to the big cities from Almaty. If you have a little more time, there are trains from the capital to all the large towns and cities. Regional bus networks serve rural villages.

Driving. Generally, the condition of the roads in Kazakhstan is good, but be prepared for adverse weather conditions. A thick layer of snow covers most roads for up to five months of the year. Avoid the roads in western Kazakhstan, where there is little traffic and highwaymen are said to operate. Road signs are in both Kazakh and Russian, and some are also transliterated into the Latin alphabet.

Petrol is not of the highest quality but is widely available. The speed limit is 60km/h (37 mph) in urban areas, 90km/h (55 mph) on main roads outside the cities. Fines range from $5 for not observing traffic lights to $100 for drink driving.

Car hire: the first Western car rental agency to open in Central Asia is Hertz, based in Almaty; this is still the only official place in the region at which to rent a self-drive car. To hire a Ford Escort for one day costs $45 plus $0.40 per kilometre. All credit cards are accepted. Sadly, it is not possible to drive a hired car over the border into China nor to drop it off in another Kazakh city.

Eating and Drinking

Specialities. The standard Central Asian dishes of *shashlik* (kebabs), *non* (flat bread) and *laghman* (noodle broth) are as ubiquitous as elsewhere, but Kazakhstan also has its own specialities. Look out for *besh-barmak*, a type of meat pie that literally translates 'five fingers' because it takes that many to eat it. Other dishes to look out for or avoid are *kazbl* (fried horsemeat), *zhaya* (horse steak) and *tjuzhuk* (tripe). *Manti*, meat-filled ravioli cooked over steam, are very popular here, as are *samsa*, a distant relation of the Indian samosa but less spicy. For dessert, keep your eyes open for *chukchuk*, a honey pastry not unlike baklava.

Restaurants. Almaty has the only thriving restaurant culture in Central Asia. The large numbers of foreign business travellers, plus locals with large amounts of excess cash, have sponsored the development of a wide range of eateries. Outside Almaty, the scope for eating out is less promising — bazaars are usually the best place to find good freshly cooked food.

DRINKING

The Kazakh speciality is *koumiss*, fermented mare's milk, which has been drunk by nomads for centuries. It is slightly sour, slightly fizzy and is definitely an acquired taste. If you're in the country during the spring, don't fail to try some, though tea is more refreshing. Homesick Britons may be happy to know that Kazakhstan is one of the few other countries in the world where tea is taken with milk.

Despite Kazakhstan's nominally Muslim nature, it has the same relaxed attitude towards alcohol as other Central Asian countries. Particularly popular is imported Chinese beer, which is strong and good. Chinese vodka should on all counts be avoided: it is sold in cheap plastic bottles which make it easy for black marketeers to siphon out the vodka and replace it with home-produced moonshine, the cause of a recent spate of deaths.

Hiking. After Bishkek (see page 356), Almaty is the next easiest place in Central Asia from which to organise a trek. Several new private companies are willing to take you up into the Tian Shan mountains, whose snow-covered peaks visible from Almaty are just a fraction of the enormous range. The most important thing to remember when planning a trip is to arrive in the right season. July and August are considered best.

Whilst the Tian Shan are the most dramatic of Kazakhstan's mountains, there is also the Altai range, which is not as high but spreads into Siberia, Mongolia and China. The only way to take an organised expedition into the Altai, however, is to go with an adventure holiday firm based abroad. If you want to head out by yourself, the nearest big city is Ust Kamenogorsk in the northwest of the country.

Kazakhstan has an increasing crime problem, though is mainly in the form of racketeering. Street lighting is poor or non-existent, which makes wandering around at night uncomfortable. Bring a torch, stick to the major thoroughfares and take licensed taxis at night. A number of foreigners have been mugged close to the large hotels in Almaty. This invariably occurs at night, so avoid walking around after dark alone and stick to official taxis.

ALMATY (ALMA-ATA)

Stand in Almaty with your eyes straight ahead and there is nothing to suggest that you are in Asia: it is a modern Soviet city with nothing that is older than the century. Raise your eyes, however, and you see the jagged snow-capped peaks of the Tian Shan Mountains, just 10 minutes from the centre by car. China is a mere 200 miles/320km away.

It is not just the mountains which give Almaty a whiff of excitement. This is Central Asia's boom-town, where there is more happening — and more changing — than anywhere else in the region. People have become millionaires overnight, smart Western cars cruise the tree-lined boulevards and the people dressed in their imported Chinese clothes have an air of easy confidence. At weekends you can skate on the world's highest skating rink, by night you can dance in the old KGB headquarters and by day drink cappuccinos in any number of new restaurants.

CITY LAYOUT

Almaty is laid out on a simple grid pattern, stretching from north to south up an incline into the foothills of the Tien-Shan. The main street is Lenina Prospekt, which stretches up the hill from Panfilov Park, past the high-rise Hotel Kazakhstan (a useful landmark) and the Presidential Palace, and eventually becomes the mountain road leading up to the ice-rink at Medeo.

Maps. The local Hertz office (see *Car Hire* below) produces a small but up-to-date map of the city centre. The best place to pick up a more detailed map is at the Akademikniga bookshop next door to the US Embassy at Formonova 91/97.

The street names have been systematically overhauled although you'll still find rogue communist-era signs and cartographic confusion in the minds of the city's inhabitants. To confuse things further, streets are sometimes referred to by the Russian *ulitsa* and sometimes by the Kazakh *kuchasi*; this book uses the former. Prospekt Lenina is still Prospekt Lenina. The main changes include:

Old Name	New Name
ul Komsomolskaya	ul Tole
ul Mira	ul Zheltoksan
ul Sovietskaya	ul Aiteke Bi
ul Karla Marxa	ul Kunaev
ul Kirova	ul Bogenbai Batyr
ul Dzerzhinskogo	ul Naurysybai Batyr
ul Karla Marxa	ul Kunaev

ARRIVAL AND DEPARTURE

Air. The airport is north of the city, about 20 minutes from the centre on buses 92 and 97 (to ulitsa Zheltoksan) or by taxi.

Airline offices:

Lufthansa: airport, tel 340404/344475.
Pakistan International Airlines: tel 344397.
Kazakh Air: for both domestic and international tickets, go to the office ('Aerovoksal') at the corner of Zhibek Zholu and Zeltoksan. Visa cards accepted.
Aeroflot: tel 390594 (reservations), 541555 (information).
Transaero: Mamteova 47 (tel 632989).
Uzbekistan Airways: Seyfulina 531, ground floor (tel 635085, 634010).

Intourist Southern, which has an office in the Hotel Otrar on ulitsa Gogolya, can sell tickets to Moscow with any of the above airlines and also onward tickets from there. The staff speak excellent English and are efficient.

A couple of UK-based business travel specialists have offices which can help with air tickets and other travel requirements: Time Travel, at Apartment 34, 75 Abai Avenue, Almaty (tel/fax 671774); and Overseas Business Travel, 50-25 Lenin Prospect, 48011 (tel 613618, 616094).

Rail. Almaty has two railway stations. The main one, Almaty II, is close to the centre at the northern end of Prospekt Ablai Khan, served by trolley-buses 4, 5 and 6. From here trains go to Moscow (one daily, taking about 75 hours), Bishkek and all stations in Siberia. Tickets are sold inside the station and should be bought as far in advance as possible. The other station is Almaty I, located a good 6 miles/10km out of town, and linked by trolley-bus 13 to Almaty II.

The most exciting train to pull out of Almaty II is the twice-weekly

Genghis Khan Express: see *Getting There*. Buy your ticket as soon as possible after you arrive in the city. Tickets go on sale the Tuesday before departure. Note that it is impossible to buy one without a valid Chinese visa in your passport. As well as the price of the ticket you may be required to pay a $15 booking fee.

Bus. The bus station is 15 minutes west of the centre at the end of ulitsa Tole. There are regular services to Bishkek, Tashkent, Dzambul and Chimkent.

Car hire. Hertz is on the first floor of the business centre opposite Hotel Kazakhstan on ulitsa Formanova. There is also an office at the airport.

CITY TRANSPORT

Work has still to begin on the city's planned metro system, but in any case it is perfectly possible to walk between most sites in Almaty. There are buses, trolley-buses and trams for when you get tired. Buy a ticket from the driver when you board.

ACCOMMODATION

Cheap hotel rooms hardly exist in Almaty. For the moment, the cheapest option is the Daulet at Kunaev 150 (620409). If you ask for directions, the hotel is still known by its old name, the Kapsosepstroyuza. Double rooms costs $23, but the hotel is due for renovation shortly so the prices will rise. The next most affordable place is Hotel Medeo (688568) near the ice-rink; take bus 6 from the stop opposite the Hotel Kazakhstan. This charges $30 for a double room. Hotel Turkestan (ul Mukagli Makataeva 49; 301832) charges $34 for a double room, but its location opposite the main bazaar gives it a reputation for night-time business negotiations.

If you have more money to spare, you may want to stay at the luxurious Hotel Dostuk at ul Kurmangazi 36 (636555), with double rooms costing over $100. This place is worth a look if only for historical interest: until 1991 it was the Communist Party guest house. Of the more expensive hotels, Hotel Otrar (Gogolya 73; 330046), opposite Panfilov Park, is probably the best located and equipped; a double costs $90. Hotel Issyk (ul Bogenbai batyr 140; 600211) is the best value. A double with a fridge and TV costs $52. There is also a lively restaurant, with good live blues music. The brand-new (as of May 1995) Rachat Palace Hotel is an Austrian-Kazakh joint venture, boasting an atrium, a health club, three tennis courts, three restaurants and room rates of around $200.

In summer, you could try the student dormitories at Formanova 176.

Private Accommodation. People offering private flats for rent tend to hang around the entrance to Hotel Zhetysu on Prospekt Ablai Khan at the corner with Mukagli Mataeva; $15 per person is the usual starting price. A better option is to walk around the corner onto Zhetoksan, where you'll find an apartment agency in a small blue kiosk opposite the Aerovoksal. It opens 9am-9pm.

EATING AND DRINKING

Over the last few years, the restaurant scene in Almaty has flourished. If you plan to try one of the smarter venues, make a reservation first and dress up.

Restaurants

Adriatica, on the corner of Dzhambula and Mechnikova, (672244). This is one of the classiest restaurants in town, with reasonably authentic Italian food and crooning divas.

Hotel Alau-Tau, Prospekt Lenina 105. The hotel is being renovated by a Turkish firm but the dining room is run by a Pakistani. The décor is extraordinary, and there is a huge stage for an erotic floorshow.

Chen-Yan, on the corner of Zheltoksan and Bogenbai batyr, (691971). The busiest, best and most authentically Chinese restaurant in town.

Hotel Otrar, ul Gogola 73. Shaped like a yurt, with painted walls and cosy red velvet alcoves, this is better for lunch than dinner, when an electric band drowns out all chances of conversation. Kazakh dishes, reasonable prices.

Giris, on the corner of Ablai Khan and Kabanbai batyr. Excellent cheap Turkish restaurant. The *pide* or Turkish pizza is especially good.

Il Sorriso shares the basement of the circus building with a furniture warehouse, at the western end of Prospekt Abai, and serves pizzas, ice cream and very good capuccinos for reasonable prices. This is one of the most popular night-time spots with the locals.

Korean Restaurant, on the ground floor of Hotel Kazakhstan (619679). Expensive with probably the most erotic floorshow in town.

One Thousand and One Nights, Naurybaj Batyra 37a (390851), at the corner of Gogolya. Garden furniture and dubious music can't detract from the very good and cheap Lebanese food.

Shaggies, next to the Hotel Kazakhstan, Prospekt Lenina 52. A Korean fast-food outfit which is good if you want food fast.

Tomaris, Prospekt Lenina 48 (616807). Expensive food and cheap beer served in an elegant dining room. In summer the astroturf and fairy lights outside provide one of the few possibilities in Almaty for al-fresco dining.

Cafés.

Café Nezik, Prospekt Lenina 31. Warm cheap and smoky, frequented primarily by the students from the main university building just one block down the road.

Italian Café, 2nd floor of the business centre opposite the Hotel Kazakhstan on Prospekt Lenina. Excellent ice-cream and capuccinos.

Viennese Café, in the new Rachat Palace hotel — the cheapest of the hotel's options, but still extremely expensive.

EXPLORING

The city's best-known landmark is the Zenkov Cathedral. It stands shaded by silver-birch trees in the middle of Panfilov Park, the most central of the city's green areas. It is an elaborate affair with hexagonal domes made of green and blue tiles which are themselves topped with small gold cupolas. Knock the walls and they sound quite hollow: the entire building is made of wood, although it has been deceptively overlaid with stucco. The remarkable structure was built in 1904 and, so the story goes, without the help of a single nail. If you've got a few hours to kill, the central chess club is in a shack opposite and you are welcome to challenge one of the old men who congregate here.

Just east of the church is an enormous bronze memorial to the 28 soldiers of the Panfilov division, raised in Almaty, who routed an armoured assault during the Battle for Moscow in 1941. There are small tablets commemorating the USSR's 13 hero cities, an eternal flame and large amounts of red and black marble. Opposite stands the huge concrete mass of the Dom Officierov (see *Entertainment*), pierced by a strenous arch which on a clear day frames a background of Tian Shan peaks. In front of it, creating an awkward juxtaposition, is an old wooden house topped by a belfry which contains the Museum of Musical Instruments (open 9.30am-5.30pm daily except Monday). This is a fascinating place. There are horse-hoof castanets, a goat-skin bagpipe and a large collection of *domras*, the national instrument that looks rather like a lute. And on request the staff will press a button on the side of each cabinet, giving you a demonstration of how each instrument sounds. Don't miss the beautiful sixth-century harps, one in the shape of a bow and arrow and another with the strings between the gaping jaws of a crocodile.

Around Ploshchad Republiky. Republic Square, a huge space in the south of the town off Prospekt Abai, is where the main government buildings are located. On the north side of the square is the old presidential palace, not to be confused with the new one being built next door. The enormous structure, involving large amounts of glass, was originally conceived as a Lenin museum, a purpose that was quickly reconsidered upon independence.

On the other side of Prospekt Lenina is the National Museum, an example of Soviet monumentalism at its most extravagant. It roughly covers the history of the republic from earliest times to February 1917. The museum opened only in 1991 and the top-floor covering the period from 1917-1945 has been closed for revision. However, there is a small hall covering the years from perestroika to the present. It is an uncertain display covering the horrors of Semi-Palatinsk (the nuclear-testing zone in the northeast), gifts given to the President and a teepee covered in messages of love and peace from the people of North America to the people of Kazakhstan.

A cable-car runs from behind the museum up to a viewpoint and kebab restaurant called Kok-Tyube or Green Hill.

Medeo. At 5,545ft/1,691m above sea level, Medeo is the highest ice-rink in the world and also one of the fastest. It is open to the air, sited at the foot of an Alpine valley with mountain peaks towering above you and the city laid out below. Bus no. 6 climbs to Medeo from opposite the Hotel Kazakhstan, past the old party dachas which line the road to the top of the hill. If you take a cab you have to pay an extra $2 to get into the park, which is a clean-air zone. Not that it puts off the lines of Mercedes and Korean cars, which cruise up here on Sundays between November and May. This is when the ice rink opens for a public free-for-all, from 10am to 2pm. If you decide to hire skates and join the throng, it's worth remembering that everyone else has probably been able to skate since they could walk. For even greater embarrassment, you can join the Russian and Kazakh national speed-skating teams, who train here for six months of the year. The rink is officially closed to the public, but the trainer Alec Turgeyev is happy to let stray tourists join the Olympic athletes.

ENTERTAINMENT

Almaty has two of the strangest nightclubs in the former Soviet Union, or indeed anywhere. The first is known as the Italian disco and is located inside the old KGB building on the corner of Shevchenko and Dzherzinskovo. It is best at weekends, the cover price is steep and a fairly arbitrary smart dress code is enforced. The other club is in an equally unlikely building, the top floor of Dom Officierov, where the Red Army's officers used to relax over a stiff drink.

If you're in the city in the last week of July or the first week of August, don't miss the Voice of Asia. This is the eastern answer to the Eurovision Song Contest and is held over several days at Medeo. It is not strictly Asian, as past competitors have come from countries as diverse as Mali and Ireland.

For cut-price opera and ballet try the Abai Theatre on Kabanbay Batyr, near the intersection with Panfilova. This is an elegant neo-Classical structure inlaid with Islamic arches and adorned by quotes from Lenin about art and the edification of the masses. The ticket office is open 10am-7pm. The Museum of Musical Instruments sometimes hosts concerts of traditional Kazakh music. The circus is at the eastern end of Prospekt Abai.

SPORT

The Kayrat football stadium on Prospekt Abai is the home of the first division side, Kayrat. The Palace of Sports next door has an ice-rink and swimming pool. In Gorky Park you'll find rowing boats, camels, miniature ponies and a selection of fairground rides. The city baths are on ulitsa Kunaev, opposite Panfilov Park. You can choose between Finnish, Turkish and Russian steam.

Skiing. The Chimbulak Ski Base is in use from November to May. Although the lifts are old and the equipment for hire is not the best, the snow could not be better, being dry and powdery. To get there, walk up the enormous dam behind the Medeo ice-rink, turn to the right and follow the road up the valley for about an hour; or take a cab. Hotel Chimbulak rents out skis and boots.

SHOPPING

The city's main shopping street, Zhibek Zholu, is a pleasant pedestrian boulevard replete with fountains. This is where you'll find Tsum — supposedly the Central Universal Store, in reality a handful of boutiques, lots of kiosks and an express Kodak developing franchise. The main shopping section is between Formanova and Panfilova. Further east along the same street, between Pushkina and Vosmoye Marta, you'll find the main bazaar, where Chinese clothes and pirated tapes are among the many things on offer.

HELP AND INFORMATION

Tourist information: Intourist has a desk in Hotel Otrar (tel 330045, 330075; fax 332056). Bekkojina Umikaiam speaks fluent English and can organise anything you care to name, for a price. A car with driver costs $10 per hour.

Money: Amex and Visa travellers' cheques can be exchanged for tenge at both the Otrar and Dostuk hotels; the latter will also do Visa card cash advances for tenge. For dollar cash advances, go to the Alem Bank either at Prospekt Lenina 39 or M. Toreza 152 (open mornings only).

Communications: the main post office is at Prospekt Lenina 36. The telegraph office is on Zhibek Zholu, not far from Tsum, but the queues are long. A more expensive but much more efficient way to call abroad is to use one of several new satellite phonebooths. The most conveniently located ones are inside the Kazakh Business Centre opposite the Hotel Kazakhstan; inside the joint British/French/German Embassy building at Formanova 173; or at the business centre in the Hotel Dostuk. Phonecards can be bought from the nearest shop or from the doorman.

Embassies and consulates

Canada: Abai 155, 6th floor (tel 509381, fax 509380).
China: Formanova 137 (639291/632482). The consular section opens 9am-noon, Monday, Wednesday and Friday.
Kyrgyzstan: Ploshshad Republiky 15 (631390).
Mongolia: Ablai Khan 24-47 (326288).
Pakistan: Tulebayev 25, ul Makatayev (331502)
Russia: Dzhandsova 4 (448332)
Tajikistan: Hotel Kazakhstan (619148).
UK: Formanova 173 (tel 506191/2, fax 506260).
Uzbekistan: Baribaeva 36 (618316).
USA: Formanova 97, (632426).

Medical Treatment. There is a big pharmacy at Formanova 91. For anything more serious, call the private 24-hour ambulance service (621288/621289). There is a VIP hospital at Panfilova 139 (632792/622828).

TREKKING

One of the most enjoyable treks you can take from Almaty is over the mountains to Lake Issyk-Kul in Kyrgyzstan. There are various routes and levels of difficulty, but a person of reasonable fitness can probably do it in a comfortable three days. Large-scale maps are sometimes available from the hotel in Chimbulak (see *Sport* above) or from a company called Parcek on the sixth floor of the business centre opposite the Hotel Kazkhstan. In any case, plenty of professional outfits can kit you out and provide a guide. These include:

Asia Tours, Korolenko 8, apt 25 (478164)
Kramds Mountain Company, ul Zheltoksan 115 (696242).
Pilgrim, Prospekt Abai 68/74 (tel/fax 426209).
Yuggeo Ltd, Formanova 338 (tel 692241, after 7pm 247030; fax 621284).

Alma-Arasan. This is a lovely mountain valley about 12 miles/20km nor-thwest of Almaty and a good starting point for a trek. Buses 61 and 63 from the Aerovokzal in the city centre go as far as Al Farabi bus station, and from there bus 68 will take you into the mountains.

PANFILOV

Even if you don't make it to China, a trip to the border crossing of Panfilov is an interesing excursion from Almaty. The drive is impressive, with the peaks of the Tien-Shan mountains on one side and vast empty steppe on the other. At Panfilov itself, is an enormous market and the largest concentration of 'biznizmen' in Central Asia. Buses serve Panfilov from Almaty's central station.

KAPCHIGAI LAKE

This enormous lake, measuring 50 miles/80km by 25 miles/40km, was formed 27 years ago when a valley was flooded to make a reservoir. The incredibly blue, and apparently clean, water has helped turn Kapchigai into a poor man's Issyk-Kul and on summer weekends is busy with people trying to escape the heat of Almaty, almost 100 miles/160km north. To get there, take a bus from the central bus station to Chingildi and ask for the *zona otdikha* or 'rest area'. There are lots of campsites and rest houses along the shores; most are still tied to local trade unions, but your novelty value and willingness to pay in dollars will probably get you a bed for the night.

BAIKONUR COSMODROME

Responsible for catapaulting the first dog (Laika) into space in 1957 and then in 1961 the first man (Yuri Gagarin), Baikonur Cosmodrome is the stuff dreams are made of. It is located in its own territory, which is about the size of Britain, and has its own attached city, built specifically to supply it with manpower. The city of Leninsk and its 100,000 inhabitants has been systematically left off all Soviet maps and it remains a closed city today. If you're thinking of just turning up in the city, you'll be swiftly turned out again.

Although the space programme is run and funded by Moscow, the base is now jointly operated by the Kazakh and Russian governments and you need to secure permission from both parties before you can pay it a visit. It is, however, theoretically possible to do so, and if you manage to find a way through the bureaucracy you'll have the satisfaction that you'll be among the first Westerners to ever do so (not counting Norman Thagard, the American astronaut who spent a year here before taking off for the space station Mir.). The place to head is the National Aerospace Agency in Almaty, on the 5th floor of Formanova 50 (336257). Jaksi Bek, in charge of international relations, speaks fluent English and can tell you when the next launch will be.

Bekkojina Umikaiam at Intourist in Almaty can organise trips, but expect the price to be well in excess of $1,000.

AKMOLA

Look for the city of Akmola on a map, and you'll eventually find it surrounded by steppe 620 miles/1,000km north of Almaty. In 1994, the Kazakh parliament took the decision to move the capital of the country here, with the President saying that it would be a more effective seat of government because of its central location. It is widely seen as a populist move, appealing to Kazakh nationalists who find Almaty too Russian in appearance and population. However, the business community is trying its best to forestall the plan, which is supposed to be completed by the year 2000.

Until the capital moves to Akmola, which currently has a population of 300,000, there is little reason to go there — and it's worth noting that the climate is particularly inclement, with temperatures reaching −50°C in January.

TURKESTAN

Although Turkestan is firmly within Kazakhstan's borders, it has closer ties with neighbouring Uzbekistan. This was once part of Tamerlane's vast empire and, for reasons which no one has satisfactorily deduced, in 1394 he chose it as the site for a massive mausoleum to house the remains of Khodja

Ahmed Yasavi, the founder of a powerful Sufi order. It is now the holiest site in Kazakhstan, a place of pilgrimage second in importance only to Mecca. The massive dome and exquisite tilework make this small, sleepy town Kazakhstan's second-most interesting attraction after the capital itself.

Getting There. Two trains a day run from Tashkent, and one from Almaty, Bishkek and Andizhan. Buses run hourly from Chimkent (100 miles/160km south of the mausoleum), the last one leaving at 6.30pm.

If you negotiate a car and driver, it is possible to regard Turkestan as a long day trip from Tashkent.

Accommodation and Food. Hotel Turkestan, behind the mausoleum at Prospekt Lenina 88 (51172), is the only place to stay. For food, try the chaikhanas opposite the mausoleum, which serve shashlik and plov. Otherwise, try Restaurant Nauryz on Ploshchad Lenina.

Exploring. The Khodja Ahmed Yasavi Mausoleum (open daily 10am-7pm) is in the centre of the town, the entrance guarded by massive 100ft/30m towers. From here, you can see the turquoise cupola and enormous ribbed dome, the largest in Central Asia. The battlements which used to circle the complex have fallen into ruin, no doubt helped by the barbed wire fence erected during the Khrushchev years, when the mausoleum was shut down completely.

The central prayer hall is now a museum, with old photos, prayer rugs and a stack of rams' skulls. The main exhibit, however, standing proudly beneath the dome is an enormous water urn. It is made out of bronze and gold and weighs over two tons. It bears the inscription, written in Arabic, 'This is a gift from Timur for having built this mausoleum.' In 1935 it was carted off to the Hermitage, but in 1989 made a triumphant return.

Kyrgyzstan and Tajikistan

KYRGYZSTAN

Population: 4.5 million   **Capital:** Bishkek (population 500,000)

Kyrgyzstan is a remote land of extraordinary beauty that was mostly off-limits to foreign visitors until the late 1980s. The Kyrgyz people call their land *altyn beshik*, the 'golden cradle', and it is not hard to see why. Their country has some of the lushest alpine scenery anywhere in the world, where several peaks surpass 22,000ft/7,000m, where bears and snow leopards roam wild, and where mountain people still hunt with trained falcons. Nestling between the gigantic peaks are over 2,000 lakes; the largest is Issyk-Kul, where you can swim in crystalline waters heated from below by volcanic activity.

As if all this weren't enough to lure you here, hospitality in these parts is overwhelming; it is not unusual for a herdsman to sacrifice the last of his sheep in honour of a casual guest. Furthermore, the country is more open and relaxed than neighbouring states. Perhaps because Kyrgyzstan has fewer natural resources than Kazakhstan or Uzbekistan, it has actively welcomed foreign development and promoted tourism. Visa regulations for once are straightforward and independent firms have been allowed to mushroom, offering a greater choice of accommodation and endless possibilities for trekking.

CLIMATE

Sunshine characterises the Kyrgyz climate; on average there are 247 sunny days a year. Summers are hot and dry with temperatures reaching 40°C/

104°F in the valleys; winters are cold and snowy, with lows of –40°C/–40°F high up in the mountains. Temperatures vary greatly between night and day as well as according to altitude. The little rain the region sees falls mainly in April and November. The best time of year to visit is from May to October; from November many of the mountain passes are closed due to snow.

HISTORY

The Kyrgyz, a nomadic people who have inhabited the region of the Tian Shan mountains since the tenth century, trace their ancestry to Turkic tribes who once populated southern Siberia. Until 1924, when the Kara-Kyrgyz Autonomous Region (later to become the Kyrgyz Soviet Socialist Republic) was created, Kyrgyzstan had never existed as a country. It had always been incorporated into the dominion of the most powerful force in the region, latterly the Russian Empire. The Kyrgyz people did not establish any towns since they moved every season in search of new pastures for their livestock. The strongest force uniting the various nomadic tribes, then as now, was the *Manas* — an epic poem which tells of the Kyrgyz people's past and has been handed down orally from generation to generation. *Manastchi*, rather like troubadours, still recite the *Manas* from memory.

During the early years of Soviet rule, Moscow allowed a flowering of indigenous culture in Kyrgyzstan, but this halted with the Stalinist purges of the 1930s. Like the other nomadic people of Central Asia, the Kyrgyz suffered badly during the era of collectivisation and thousands fled across the border into China. The Kyrgyz language was marginalised and a massive influx of Slavic workers in the middle of the 20th century temporarily rendered the Kyrgyz a minority in their own republic. Such a situation encouraged the formation of nationalist movements in the 1980s.

Since independence in 1991, Kyrgyzstan has established a reputation as one of the most progressive states to emerge from the former Soviet Union. President Akayev has embraced economic reform and cultivated good relationships with neighbouring states. Even so, the majority of the population are experiencing considerable economic hardhsip as the country struggles to establish a market economy.

THE PEOPLE

According to a 1989 survey, the Kyrgyz make up 52% of the population, the Russians 21% and the Uzbeks 13%. Though Stalin's policies of collectivisation brought an end to traditional nomadic life, many Kyrgyz are still engaged in livestock herding in the mountains. In summer shepherds leave the settlements in the foothills for the higher pastures and move into yurts, the circular tents that have become the symbol of the country, as represented on the Kyrgyz national flag. The greatest affection is reserved for their horses, and the highest honour for guests is to be presented with a glass of *koumiss* or fermented mare's milk.

The main religion is Islam but shamanist beliefs are still widespread and the wave of religious fervour that has spread in neighbouring Uzbekistan finds no followers among the Kyrgyz.

LANGUAGE

The state language is Kyrgyz, a Turkic language closely related to other

Central Asian languages. Though Russian is more widely spoken, especially in Bishkek and other urban centres, a basic knowledge of Kyrgyz is useful in rural areas and to read signs. The Cyrillic alphabet, imposed in 1941, is still used but the possibility of returning to Latin script is being debated.

Useful words and phrases

1 — *bir*	hello — *salamatsyszby*
2 — *iki*	thank you — *yrakhmat*
3 — *ooch*	yes — *ova*
4 — *turt*	no — *yawk*
5 — *besh*	good — *jakshe*
6 — *alte*	where is? — *khayede?*
7 — *yete*	bread — *nan*
8 — *seygis*	water — *su*
9 — *togus*	hotel — *meimankanagha*
10 — *on*	

Getting There

Air. There are no direct scheduled flights from anywhere in western Europe to Kyrgyzstan. The most direct route from Britain is probably via Uzbekistan (see page 300); there are daily connections from Tashkent to Bishkek, providing fuel is available (otherwise it is a 12-hour bus journey). Bishkek's airport code is FRU, short for Frunze and a reminder of the capital's old name in honour of a Stalin crony.

Another relatively direct but more expensive route is to Almaty in Kazakhstan (see page 337), from where it is only a four-hour drive, six-hour bus ride or short flight to Bishkek.

A cheaper option is provided by the charter flights between Bishkek and Hanover in Germany, organised by Neufeld Reisen, 199/82 ul Bonkonbaeva, Bishkek (248304/268734); the partner in Germany is based in Lemgo (tel 052-612-271, fax 052-108-66). From Turkey, a return flight from Istanbul with Kyrgyz Airways costs $480 and is bookable through Track Travel in Istanbul (255-56-56). Asia Star, a new independent airline based in Bishkek offers an even cheaper deal to Istanbul: $380 for a round ticket with fixed dates; contact Raisa Janilbaeva (263-455/130, 265-927, 226-901 or 223-122).

In theory, there are several flights a week linking Bishkek to Baku, Moscow, Almaty, Tashkent and other cities in the CIS. In practice, these are often cancelled due to fuel shortages.

Train. There is a daily train from Moscow, taking three days, with services from Tashkent and Almaty on alternate days.

Bus. Several services a day link Bishkek with Tashkent (12 hours) and with Almaty (six hours). For the time being, passengers are still rattled about in the old Hungarian-made Ikarus buses, but there are plans to introduce a new fleet of Mitsubishi coaches, which will provide a faster and more comfortable service.

Driving. The main road from Almaty to Tashkent passes through Bishkek. Between the Kazakh and Kyrgyz capitals, you have to cross a 4,050ft/ 1,233m mountain pass at Kurdai, but from Bishkek onwards the road widens considerably and it is an easy drive to Tashkent. The approximate journey time from Almaty to Bishkek is four hours, and from Tashkent eight hours.

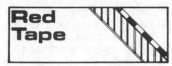

Red Tape

Visas. All foreign visitors require a visa. In countries with no Kyrgyz embassy, travellers should obtain a Russian visa that specifies Bishkek. Note, however, that Kyrgyzstan has a reciprocal arrangement with Kazakhstan and Russia that allows a traveller who has a valid visa for any of the three countries to transit in the other two for up to three days.

All visitors, irrespective of visa status, staying longer than three days are required to register at the Ovir (visa registration) office in Bishkek. In practice, this is not always necessary since hotels are not particularly fussed about seeing visas, and most travellers arrive in the country via overland routes without border controls so the date of their arrival is not registered. If, however, you are found to be infringing this regulation, you will probably be fined.

Anyone planning to go trekking without the support of an agency, particularly anywhere near the border with China, should definitely register with Ovir and enquire about having particular towns or regions specified on their visas. This is not required by law but militia outside the capital are not always kept informed on latest rules and regulations. In any case Ovir in Bishkek is an uncharacteristically friendly and helpful place; unlike its counterparts in neighbouring countries, staff there may even be able to help with visas to other CIS countries.

Kyrgyz law also requires that individuals staying more than one month demonstrate that they have tested negatively for Aids, but this law is rarely enforced.

Kyrgyz embassies and consulates abroad include:

Kazakhstan: Ploshchad Respubliki 15, Almaty (tel 3272 61-92-73).
Russia: ul Bolshaya Ordynka 64, Moscow (tel 095 237-4601, fax 237-4452).
Turkmenistan: prospekt Turkmenbashi 13, Ashkhabad (tel 3632 46-88-04).
USA: 1511 K Street NW, Washington, DC 20005 (tel 202-347-3732, fax 347-3718).
Uzbekistan: ul Alleya Pravdy 5, Tashkent 700078 (tel 3712 39-45-43, fax 39-16-78).

Customs. Customs regulations are in a state of flux, but if arriving by air you will have to fill in the usual old Soviet customs declaration form. It is worth obtaining a clearance certificate for any object that could be construed as having considerable scientific, historical or artistic value as it is illegal to export any such item. This can be obtained from from the Kyrgyz Ministry of Culture located at 205 Abdymomunova in Bishkek (22-59-54). It is forbidden to export or import nuclear materials and appliances for opium smoking, but you can obtain special permission to export silkworm cocoons, racehorses and hen's dung.

Money

In 1993, Kyrgyzstan introduced its own currency, the som. In early 1995 $1 was worth 10 som. At the time of writing, only one or two hotels in Bishkek accepted credit cards, none accepted or exchanged travellers' cheques and cash advances from credit cards were also impossible. So take all your money in cash; bills that are torn, defaced, or printed before 1990 will not be accepted.

All hotels have exchange offices, otherwise look out for kiosks and shops sporting dollar signs. As inflation is relatively low in Kyrgyzstan, there is little advantage in changing money on the black market.

Telephone. There are public phones for both local and long-distance calls; local calls are free. For international calls, go to the local telegraph office, which is usually adjacent to the local post office. Satellite links between Kyrgyzstan and western Europe are a thing of the future so it is still necessary to book a call if phoning from a private phone. Kyrgyzstan is five hours ahead of GMT.

The telephone code for Bishkek is 3312.

Mail. Given Kyrgyzstan's location and lack of fuel, it is not surprising that the postal service is extremely slow and cannot be relied upon. Faxes, telexes and electronic mail can however all be dispatched from the capital (see *Bishkek: Help and Information*).

Newspapers. There are several national newspapers in both Russian and Kyrgyz and two English-language weeklies: the *Kyrgyzstan Chronicle* and *Kyrgyzstan Today*.

Internal air links have virtually ground to a halt due to shortages of fuel and spare parts. The railway network is also extremely limited. More often than not buses provide the only public transportation links within the country; services are cheap and frequent if over-crowded.

Shared taxis for day excursions can be a good idea to reach otherwise inaccessible mountain regions. By western standards, taxi fares are still reasonable, although fuel shortages have led to price increases in the last few years. Negotiate a price before departure with either an official taxi or a private car. To give an indication of prices, in early 1995, $20 a day was the going rate for driving within Bishkek and up to twice that beyond the city limits.

Driving. At present there is nowhere to hire a self-drive car in Kyrgysztan. An accompanying driver is both complimentary and compulsory with any vehicle you try to hire in Bishkek, so driving amounts to taking taxis. If you wish to drive yourself, the only options are to bring your own or buy one — for example at the secondhand car bazaar held on weekend mornings in the village of Vayenno-Antonovka, nine miles/14km west of Bishkek.

Petrol is widely available in the capital, from small tanker trucks parked along the edge of the road (though some sell milk rather than fuel). Outside Bishkek you would be well advised to bring as many jerry cans as you need.

Road signs are written in both Kyrgyz and Russian.

Cycling. If you haven't brought your own bicycle, you can pick up a used one in the bazaars. For mountain bike enthusiasts, Kyrgyzstan has a huge amount of undiscovered territory.

Apart from a few over-priced 'business' hotels in Bishkek, hotels in Kyrgyzstan have changed little since Soviet days. The good news is that prices are on the whole much lower than in neighbouring countries. If the old Intourist hotel is a fleapit at least it's a cheap fleapit. Bishkek may therefore be a better base than Almaty for budget travellers who wish to go trekking in the Tian Shan mountains. The cheapest accommodation outside the capital is usually to be found in climbers' hostels called *alpbaza*; facilities are usually basic — don't count on a bathroom. In the mountains themselves, you need to bring all your own equipment unless you are going on an organised trek.

Eating and Drinking

Like the Kazakhs, the Kyrgyz people's tradition of breeding animals has determined their eating habits. Fatty meat and rich meat broths are common, as are dishes made from fresh and sour milk such as *kurit* (dried curds). Cow, camel and mare's milk are all used. Typical Kyrgyz dishes include: *besh barmak* ('five fingers'), which is a medium spicy stew combined with noodles and bouillon; *shorpa*, mutton soup with vegetables; and *manty*, giant meat-filled ravioli which are steam cooked. Plov, laghman and shashlik, the Central Asian staples, are also ubiquitous.

Exploring

Trekking. The lush valleys, unexplored paths and dizzying heights of the Pamir and Tian Shan mountains are undoubtedly Kyrgyzstan's greatest attraction. There are three main areas for mountain adventure:

The Central Tian Shan: also known as the Muztag or 'ice fortress', on Kyrgyzstan's eastern border with China, the Central Tian Shan is the harshest range of mountains in all of Central Asia. Experienced mountaineers can reach Pik Pobeda, the highest peak in the country at 24,600ft/7,499m, by trekking up the Inilchek glacier — at 38 miles/62km in length, this is the largest of some 7,800 glaciers in the Tian Shan mountains.

On its northern side, Lake Marzbacher is the setting every summer for an impressive geological drama. Some time between the end of July and mid-August, the brilliant blue waters of the lake emit a mighty roar as the lower frozen part of the lake cracks from the prolonged summer heat and explodes violently, sending huge icebergs up to the surface. These mountains are usually reached from Bishkek via Kara-Kol on Lake Issyk-Kul.

The Northern Tian Shan: these are the mountains closest to the capital and include the Kyrgyz Alatau and the Zailiisky Alatau, which separate Bishkek and Almaty. Numerous trails run from Bishkek via Lake Issyk-Kul to Chimbulak, just north of Almaty. Several one or two-day treks along gorges and canyons also begin within an hour's drive of the Kyrgyz capital. The less experienced and completely inexperienced can go trekking on horseback in alpine pastures, where semi-nomadic Kyrgyz bring their animals to graze in the summer months.

The Pamirs: these extend from Samarkand in Uzbekistan across Tajikistan and western Kyrgyzstan until they merge with the Tian Shan. As well as including the two highest peaks in the former Soviet Union, Pik Lenina and Pik Communisma (both in Tajikistan), the Pamirs are home to countless wild uninhabited valleys and racing rivers. Professional support is essential for trekking in these mountains as the political situation in Tajikistan remains unstable after several years of brutal civil war.

The best months for mountaineering are July and August. Trekking is possible from May to November, but by mid-November the cold has set in and snow blizzards are a distinct possibility even in the foothills. Spring, when the Greig tulip blooms, and summer, when the meadows in the sub-alpine pastures are strewn with poppies, buttercups and gentian, are the most beautiful seasons in which to explore these stunning mountain regions.

For a list of trekking agencies in the Kyrgyz capital, see page 360. There are also several agencies in the UK which specialise in trekking and mountaineering. These include Explore Worldwide (1 Frederick Street, Aldershot GU11 1LQ; tel 01252-344161) and Exodus (9 Weir Road, London SW12 OLT; tel 0181-675 5550, fax 673 0779). The latter has been running two to three-week treks in the Pamir and Tian Shan mountains since 1990 and has established an extensive network of local contacts. If time is an important consideration, or if your patience is easily stretched, booking a tour with the experts is undoubtedly the easiest option.

Maps. Within Kyrgyzstan, crude maps of the country can be bought from hotel kiosks in Bishkek and Russian; 1:200,000 topographical maps arc available from the State Geodetic and Cartographic Agency at ul Kievskaya 107 (21-22-15). The US Defense Mapping Agency's satellite maps (the most useful being the Operational Navigation Charts on a scale of 1:1,000,000) are available from Stanford's in London or direct from the National Oceanic and Atmospheric Administration in the USA (301-436-6990).

Trekking in Russia and Central Asia by Frith Maier, published by Cordee is an excellent general reference book.

The local health service is extremely poor by western standards. See the general introduction for the necessary precautions you should take before visiting Kyrgyzstan. In particular, travellers going trekking in the summer months should consult their doctor about the usefulness of immunisation against tick encephalitis.

Kyrgyzstan has a low rate of crime committed against foreigners. However there has been an increase in street crime recently particularly in Bishkek. Avoid unmarked taxis at night and avoid walking around on your own after dark. As elsewhere in the CIS, the streets are extremely poorly lit, if at all.

The state-run tourist board, Kirghiztour, is moderately helpful but is still geared to group rather than individual travel. A number of private tourist firms that specialise in trekking have sprung up in recent years, however, and these are listed on page 360. Two useful publications to look out for in Bishkek are *Discovery of Kyrgyzstan* and the *Bishkek Handbook* by Daniel Prior.

BISHKEK

Bishkek is the closest thing to a metropolis in Kyrgyzstan, but it is still just a small town with a small town feel. And that is precisely its appeal. Scant traffic, an abundance of trees and a backdrop of snow-capped peaks make it an ideal place to rest after a dusty train ride or an exhausting bureaucratic wrangle.

Bishkek is not old. The most ancient site is an amorphous mound where the Khan of Kokand built a fortress in 1825 — one of a series that lay along the caravan trail from Tashkent to Kashgar. Pishpek, as the fort was known, was razed to the ground by the Russians in 1862, as the tsar stretched the boundaries of his empire southwards. Following the Revolution, Pishpek was renamed Frunze (after a Bolshevik general who was born here) and became the capital of the new Kyrgyz SSR. Bishkek's present appearance was largely determined during the ensuing Soviet period. Thoughtful urban planning turned it into the leafiest capital in the former USSR, with over 100 square metres of greenery per inhabitant. In 1991, following the declaration of independence, the capital was renamed Bishkek — an adaptation of the original Pishkek, which apparently sounded Kazakh rather than Kyrgyz.

CITY LAYOUT

Orientation is easy in Bishkek as the city is laid out on a neat grid plan. All streets run north to south or east to west, and the mountains to the south provide a permanently visible compass point. The two main axes are prospekt Erkindik (formerly Dzerzhinskovo), a broad tree-lined boulevard, and prospekt Chui (formerly Leninsky). The intersection of these two streets is the heart of the city and most sights of interest are within easy walking distance of this point. Note that if you are catching taxis, it is more useful to say which intersection you need than to give street numbers.

Various city maps are available from hotel kiosks and street vendors, though most of these were published some time ago and many street names have changed.

ARRIVAL AND DEPARTURE

Air. Manas International Airport lies 22 miles/35km north of the city centre. Regular buses run between the airport and the West Bus Station, from where you can take either a city bus or a taxi to your hotel.

The ticket office for Kyrgyz Airlines, still usually referred to as Aeroflot, is located in the old airport building on prospekt Mira, south of the centre (42-29-22,42-24-72). For general flight information call 25-77-47.

Rail. The main train station is at the southern end of prospekt Erkindik and can be reached from the centre on Trolleybus 7. The ticket office is just east of the station at ulitsa Lineynaya 49, open 7am to 5pm (22-09-07).

Bus. There are two bus stations. The East Bus Station (Vostochny Avtovokzal), on the corner of Jibek Jolu by the Alamedin River, serves destinations nearby. The West Bus Station (Zapadny Avtovokzal), on the corner of Jibek Jolu and Chimkentskaya, serves destinations further afield, including Almaty, Tashkent and Issyk-Kul.

Driving. If you want to hire a car, which automatically comes with a driver, the staff at the Business Centre of the Hotel Dostuk can advise you on the going rates.

ACCOMMODATION

Bishkek has a surprisingly good choice of affordable hotels so finding a cheap, comfortable room should not be a problem. Choose from the following:

Ak-Sai, ul Ivanitsyna 117 (26-14-65), directly behind the circus but with no sign on the door. The rooms in this truckers' hostel are basic but at $4 probably the best value you'll find in Bishkek.

Ak-Kuu, ul 50 Let Komsomola Kyrgysi 3-g (47-22-62, 24-73-68), near the intersection with Sovietskaya. Run by the travel agency of the same name, the Ak-Kuu has just three rooms: $10 per person in a double room with shared bathrooms, $15 for full board.

Ala-Too, at the bottom of prospekt Erkindik, opposite the train station (22-60-41). The former Intourist hotel is neither good value nor central, but the rooms are comfortable. Double $40, deluxe $60.

Dostuk, ul Frunze 426b, at the corner of Pravdy (28-42-51). Extras at the most luxurious hotel in town include a business centre, a sauna and the best breakfast in town. A double costs about $140. Credit cards are accepted.

International School of Business and Management Studies, ul Panfilova 237 (22-04-14), near the intersection with Frunze. This is a student hostel that leases its free rooms to visiting foreigners. The rooms are comfortable, excellent value and there is a cosy café on the ground floor. Doubles cost $10, payable in som.

Interservice, apt 17, ul Politekhnicheskaya 4 (tel 44-00-88, fax 21-97-96), near the corner of 50-Let Oktyabrya. This agency can help with short and long-term flat rental.

Jurta Ak-Tilek, ul Sovietskaya 101/108 (tel/fax 28-45-65). Jurta ak-Tilek organises homestays in Bishkek, Samarkand, Bukhara and various other cities in the CIS. One week half-board costs $90.

EATING AND DRINKING

For a city its size Bishkek has a surprisingly large number of restaurants, though most close early so you'll find it hard finding a meal after 9pm. In terms of drinking, the only bar as such is on the ground floor of the Hotel Dostuk; otherwise, most of the restaurants listed serve alcohol.

Ak-Orgö, ul Frunze 368, in Panfilov Park. Noodle dishes are served on the second floor and in summer you can sample *koumiss* on the first. Open 10am-10pm.

Belly Ollen, 8th floor, Hotel Issyk-Kul (44-89-75). Good Korean cuisine and an outdoor terrace with views of the mountains.

Dostuk, ul Frunze 426b, on the corner of Pravdy. There are three restaurants in Hotel Dostuk, but the one you shouldn't miss is on the ground floor of the round structure that looks like a spaceship. Come here for breakfast, which includes blinis, eggs, cheese, pastries and endless coffee, all for $3. The glitzy Arizona Restaurant next door serves pricey Western-style dishes.

Flash Pizza and Burger, prospekt Chui 36. A fast food joint with glaring

neon lights that serves Turkish-style pizzas and lamb burgers. Open
11am-11pm.

Primavera, ul Toktogula 175 (21-17-26), across the street from the Chinese
Embassy. The entrance is through an unmarked basement door so you
will need help finding it; if you take a taxi from Hotel Dostuk, the driver
should be able to help. The Moldovan food is expensive but excellent.

Tête a Tête, on the ground floor of the International School of Business and
Management (ul Panfilova 237). This is a cosy café with a young crowd
and friendly waiters. Open 7am-10pm.

Tian Shan, at the corner of Turusbekova and Moskovskaya (24-71-90).
Chinese cuisine.

EXPLORING

Prospekt Chui is a natural starting point for a tour of Bishkek. Begin at Ala-
Tau Square (between Pervomaiskaya and Orozbekova), where an enormous
statue of Lenin stands facing the mountains; he seems set to stay as the
government is reluctant to foot the bill for his removal. The white marble
cube behind him used to be the Lenin Museum and is now the History
Museum (open 9am-6pm except Mondays). The exhibits are in the process
of being reshuffled; recent additions on the third floor include documentation
of Stalin's purges. The much larger white marble building some 100m west
of the Lenin statue houses the presidential and government offices and also
the Parliament. It is popularly known as the White House.

Two blocks North of Ala-Tau, on the corner of Frunze and Pervomaiskaya,
is the Frunze Museum — dedicated to Mikhail Frunze, the Bolshevik general
who gave his name to the capital of Kirghizia from 1926 to 1991 (open
9am-5pm except Mondays). The ground floor contains a thatched cottage
that was supposedly his childhood home, though contemporary photographic
evidence suggests the wrong house was preserved. Guides of the old school
will reverently explain how 'Misha' (as Mikhail Frunze was affectionately
known) was sent to Tashkent in 1919 to prevent a counter-revolution and
how he subsequently became a Red Army hero.

Heading east across prospekt Erkindik, you reach the Fine Art Museum
on the corner of Kirova and Sovietskaya (open 9am-5pm except Mondays).
It covers traditional Kyrgyz decorative and applied arts as well as Soviet
art, and is worth at least a browse. A block further east, ulitsa Kirova opens
onto a vast square — the site of the central bazaar until 1983, when the
whole area was bulldozed to make way for the Victory memorial that can
be seen today. The three joined arches of the lone monument represent the
frame of a yurt. The absence of the fourth supporting arch symbolises loss,
since the death of a relative is marked in Kyrgyz tradition by the removal
of one of the poles supporting the yurt frame.

Rabochy Gorodok. Architects and others with an interest in urban planning
may like to visit Rabochy Gorodok or 'Workers' Town'. It is located
southwest of the city centre between ulitsa Tolstovo and prospekt Mira: the
spoke and wheel plan is instantly recognisable on a map. This housing estate
was built in 1928-32 by a Czech co-operative called Interhelpa — just one
of many groups that flooded into the Soviet Union to help build a communist
Utopia following Lenin's appeal to the workers of the world in 1921.
Rabochy Gorodok was Bishkek's first purpose-built suburb.

ENTERTAINMENT

The Philharmonia, located in the white marble building on the corner of prospekt Chui and ulitsa Belinskovo, puts on excellent concerts ranging from classical European to traditional Kyrgyz. Other venues for the performing arts include the Kyrgyz Drama Theatre at ulitsa Panfilova 273 and the circus on ulitsa Frunze, close to the Dostuk Hotel.

Sport. The hippodrome at ulitsa Termechikova 1, stages a variety of equestrian events. Most of these take place at weekends in July and August.

There is an Olympic-size outdoor pool at the Sports Palace on ulitsa Togolok Moldo, which opens June to August. Russian steam baths, saunas and massage can be enjoyed at the Jyrgal Baths on the corner of Toktogula and Pravdy.

SHOPPING

Most trading is done in the city's bazaars, the most colourful of which is the daily Osh Bazaar, held in the western part of the city between Toktogula, Kievskaya and the Ala-Archa river. Felt hats, Taiwanese shell suits and cheap cigarettes are all sold at the stalls surrounding the food market. Take a peek inside the meat hall to see a most artistic (not to say tasteful) display of carcasses and horse, sheep and goat heads, carefully arranged against a backdrop of socialist realist friezes.

Tsum, the central department store, is on prospekt Chui between Shopokaya and Sovietskaya. It has an unpredictable stock of goods but you can usually find felt carpets and *al-kalpaks*, the traditional black and white felt hats.

HELP AND INFORMATION

Tourist information: Khirgiztour Travel, based at Hotel Ala-Tau, organises day trips and treks, but individual travellers will do better at one of the independent trekking companies (see *Trekking* below). The excellent *Bishkek Handbook* is published locally and should be on sale in the Hotel Dostuk; otherwise, you can get hold of a copy by calling Jane on 44-52-83 or 43-47-11.

Communications: the main post office is at prospekt Chui 114, with the international telphone office in the same building. All offices open 7am-7pm weekdays and 7am-5pm at weekends. There is a 24-hour international phone office at prospekt Chui 227, on the corner of ulitsa 40 let Oktyabrya. The telephone code for Bishkek is 3312.

*Medical treatment:*there is a fairly well stocked chemist on the first floor of the Hotel Dostuk. In an emergency, ask your hotel or host for advice or call one of the foreign embassies. Medical evacuation can be arranged through SOS Switzerland (022 47-61-61).

Embassies and Consulates

China, ul Toktogula 196 (22-24-23).
Kazakhstan, Bishkek Hotel, pr Erkindik 21 (22-45-57).
Russia, ul Piervomayskaya 17(22-16-91).
USA, pr Erkindik 66 (22-26-31).

Visa extension: the Bishkek branch of Ovir (for visa registration and any visa enquiries/problems) is at ul Kievskaya 58 (26-90-627).

Trekking. See page 354 for information about the main areas for trekking in Kyrgyzstan. There are several agencies in Bishkek which can organise trips for you. They include:

Ak-Kuu Excursion Group, ul 50 Let Komsomola Kirgizii 3-g. If you speak Russian, call 47-22-62; otherwise try the American partner, John Sevcik, on 24-73-68. The Ak-Kuu offers trekking on foot or on horseback from its base camp at the Issyk-Ata canyon. They can also help with visas, rent you a car with a driver, and arrange transport to Kashgar in China.

Dostuk Trekking, ul Vosemnadtsataya Liniya 42-1 (tel 42-74-71, fax 22-39-42). If you have trouble locating the office, go to the Hotel Ala-Too and ask for directions from there. This is probably the most professional trekking company operating in Kyrgyzstan. It offers a wide choice of itineraries of varying difficulty in the Central and Western Tian Shan and in the Pamirs, as well as heliskiing and overland trips to China and silk road cities.

International Mountaineering Centre 'Tian Shan', ul Togoloka Molko 17 (tel 27-28-90, fax 27-05-76). Offers a wide range of expeditions and has its own base camp on the south side of the Inilchek glacier.

Kirghiz Sayakat, ul Sovietskaya 49 (44-54-50, 44-44-49). Offers similar services to the Ak-Kuu Excursion Group and also runs a small guest house.

ALA-ARCHA AND ALAMEDIN

The Ala-Archa and Alamedin valleys are ideal places to go on one, two or three-day excursions if you don't have the time or desire to go on a long trek. The entrance to the Ala-Archa National Park is just 15 miles/24km south of Bishkek, and yet within two days' walking you can be as far removed from civilisation as you could ever dream of being. Even on a day-trip you can hike up slopes covered in juniper and fir forest where wild boar, lynx and eagles may be sighted. Experienced trekkers can reach the summit of Korona peak, which at a height of 15,390ft/4,692m lords it over the surrounding mountains — but this requires crampons and ideally a guide. The Tyoplie Klyuchi or Hot Springs, located a couple of miles up the Alamedin Canyon, are the starting point for a number of treks in the area, including an exerting three to four-day hike east over to Ala-Archa. The springs themselves are a dubious attraction as the curative waters are walled in an unattractive concrete bathouse; there is, however, the possibility of spending the night in the adjoining guest houses.

In summer, bus 177 from the Osh bazaar should run to the entrance of the Ala-Archa National Park, but recently services have been affected by fuel shortages. The easiest way to get there is by taxi and to arrange a pick-up time for the return journey. To reach the Alamedin Canyon, about 12 miles/20km from Bishkek, head south along ulitsa Alma-Atinska and continue until you reach the canyon wall.

LAKE ISSYK-KUL

Measuring 113 miles/182km long and 36 miles/58km wide, Lake Issyk-Kul is the second-largest mountain lake in the world after Lake Titicaca in South America. Volcanic activity heats the waters so that despite the 5,000ft/1,600m elevation the saline waters of the lake never freeze, and the whole surrounding area enjoys a mild microclimate. In the summer months, you can swim in the clear blue waters enclosed on all sides by the snowy peaks of the Tian Shan mountains. These natural advantages were not overlooked by the communists, who built their usual concrete sanatoria. But providing you avoid Cholpon-Ata on the northern shore of the lake, where the biggest and ugliest sanatoria lurk, you can still enjoy the glorious natural surroundings. Kara-Kol, a small 19th-century town at the eastern end of the lake and formerly known as Przhevalsk, is a much better base. The nearest beach is 6 miles/10km northwest and can be reached by bus.

At least 10 buses a day run from Bishkek to Kara-Kol, the journey taking about nine hours. The scheduled daily flight is subject to the availability of fuel. There are two decent hotels in the town: the Kara-Kol at ul Kalinina 118 (31922 2-41-55) and the Intourist on ul Fuchika (31922 2-07-11, 2-17-21).

TRAVELLING TO CHINA

The only border point officially open between China and Kyrgyzstan is the Torugart pass, which lies about 250 miles/400km south of Bishkek and 100 miles/160km north of Kashgar, at an altitude of 12,300ft/3,752m. Getting to the Kyrgyz side of the border is relatively straightforward. Buses run from Bishkek to Naryn, about halfway to the border, and from there you can try hitching a lift or enquire about private buses. Alternatively, it is possible to hire a car and driver from one of the trekking agencies in Bishkek to take you all the way. The difficulty, however, lies in crossing the border itself. Chinese visas are not available at the frontier, and the Chinese embassy in Bishkek will only issue a visa if you can prove — in the form of an official letter or faxed invitation — that someone is meeting you on the Chinese side to escort you as far as Kashgar.

At the border itself, the CIS border guards will not let you cross the 3-mile/5km stretch of no man's land until the Chinese border guards have radioed through that your Chinese escort has arrived. To arrange transport on the Chinese side, you will probably have to go through one of the trekking agencies in Bishkek, but the cost of this is extremely high. Expect to pay in the region of $250 for the border to Kashgar section of the journey alone.

If you do have your own transport, two interesting side trips can be made along the road from Bishkek to Torugart Pass. The first is to Son-Kul, a beautiful mountain lake west of the main road between Balychky and Naryn. The second is to the Tash Rabat caravanserai, a 15th-century stone fort that served as a shelter for silk road caravans. The caretakers can show you around and give advice on one-day treks in the area. The turning to Tash Rabat is about halfway between At-Bashi and Torugart. Should you get stuck in Naryn, you can always stay overnight at the Hotel Beshbek.

Another road pass linking China and Kyrgyzstan is theoretically due to open at a place called Irkyeshtam, south of Torugart. The road to Irkyeshtam begins at Sary Tash, which can be reached only from Osh, 125 miles/200km north, or from Tajikistan. Enquire at the Chinese embassy or at Dostuk Trekking for the latest news. Both the Irkyeshtam and Torugart passes are only open in the summer months.

Public Holidays

January 1	New Year's Day
January 7	Russian Orhodox Christmas
March 8	International Women's Day
March 21	Nooruz, Muslim New Year, a feast of renewal
May 1	International Workers' Solidarity Day
May 5	Constitution Day
May 9	Victory Day
mid-May	Orozo Ait (Muslim holiday)
May 29	Armed Forces Day
June 13	Kurban Ait (Muslim holiday)
August 31	Independence Day

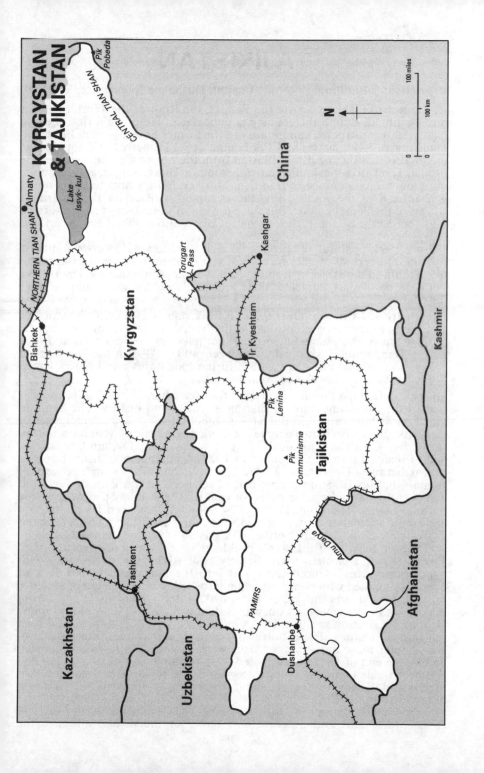

TAJIKISTAN

Population: 5.4 million   **Capital:** Dushanbe (population: 600,000)

At the heart of Tajikistan are the Pamirs, the Roof of the World, and for high mountain drama the country is unbeatable. Here you'll find the two biggest unreconstructed communists in the former Soviet Union: Pik Communisma at 7,495 metres and Pik Lenina at 7,134 metres. It's not just the mountains that distinguish Tajikistan from the rest of Central Asia but the people. The Tajiks speak a Persian rather than a Turkic tongue, and culturally have more in common with Iran than Moscow. With China to the east and Afghanistan to the south Tajikistan occupied a place on the outermost fringes of the Soviet empire, but since the union's break-up it's been thrown into the centre of the torturous nationalist politics that have resurfaced everywhere.

Since 1991 a painful and protracted civil war has veered between intense fighting and periods of uneasy peace. If you're planning a trip it's important to get as up-to-date information as you can and even though foreigners have not been particularly targeted, there are simply far too many guns at large for comfort.

Geography and Climate. Over 93% of Tajikistan is mountain. The people and the industry are concentrated at the bottom of the valleys in the west of the country and the nodule of land that pokes up into Uzbekistan in the north. Temperatures veer wildly between 40°C/104°F in the sub-tropical valleys in summer and −50°C/−58°F in the mountains in winter. There is little rainfall and what there is falls in spring.

History. Before the Bolsheviks arrived the area which is now Tajikistan was part of the Bukharan emirate, sharing its rulers and history. The Saminid kingdom with its capital in Bukhara is sometimes seen as the emergence of the Tajiks as a consolidated people but it ruled very little of what is Tajikistan today. In 1924 an autonomous Tajik region was created within Uzbekistan, and formalised into a full republic in 1929. A bureaucratic distinction was drawn between Uzbeks, or Turkic speakers, and Tajiks, or speakers of Iranian dialects. But the people had never been territorially divided and had been living in the same cities for centuries with many people speaking both languages. The result of the 1924 boundary has been lasting tension and ethnic anomalies: most people in Samarkand and Bukhara were declared Tajik, while Khodzhent in northern Tajikistan is predominantly Uzbek.

However most of Tajikistan's problems date from more recent times. *Perestroika* and *glasnost* were fiercely resisted by the party elite, with opposition voices silenced until well into the late eighties. The lack of openness coupled with poor living standards led to an explosion of violence in 1990, but it was only after the failed Moscow coup in 1991 that an opposition finally emerged. A new president was elected, Rakhmon Nabiev. He took his election as a mandate to impose old-style communism and soon ran into difficulties. The country split along regional lines into those pro-Nabiev and those anti-Nabiev. Arms were smuggled in from Afghanistan and by the end of 1992 an estimated 20,000 people had died, and 500,000 had been made homeless. Nabiev stepped down, replaced by Imamli Rakhmanov and the government set about reasserting its authority with the help of forces from the CIS.

Since then there has been little way forward. Despite a ceasefire in 1994 cross-border raids and assassinations have continued, and although the capital is peaceful much of the rest of the country is still highly unstable. The opposition has based itself in Afghanistan, the unrest is still based on regional loyalties, and the hardline government is unwilling to enter into negotiations.

The People. The Tajiks not only speak a different language from the rest of Central Asia, they look different with European faces and Persian genes. Uzbeks make up a quarter of the population and Russians about 8%, although the numbers have been steadily declining. The Pamiris in the remote Gorno-Badakhshan region speak a different dialect from the rest of Tajikistan and regard themselves as a distinct nationality. They have been demanding autonomy and have been systematically targeted by government forces.

Despite hard times, or maybe because of them, the Tajiks display an incredible degree of good humouredness, and that anything works at all in the country is testimony to their resilience and resourcefulness.

Language. The Tajiks are alone in Central Asia in speaking a language which is not Turkic. Tajik is a dialect of Farsi, as spoken in Iran, but is written in the Cyrillic script. In Khodzhent in the north there is a large Uzbek speaking minority, and Russian is understood more or less everywhere.

Religion. Thousands of mosques have been built in Tajikistan since Gorbachev's time, many of them funded by religious foundations in Saudi Arabia and Iran. Religious worship has burgeoned since the collapse of the USSR and Tajikistan was the only country in Central Asia which did not immediately outlaw the Islamic Renaissance Party (IRP). They swiftly ousted the existing government and it was at that point that Taikistan descended into civil war. Now that the old guard is back in place the IRP has been banned and thousands of its supporters fled to Afghanistan where soldiers have been receiving instruction at the hands of the *mujahadin*. The hardline governments of neighbouring countries fear that religious fundamentalism could spread throughout Central Asia, although others claim that the opposition was forced to seek assistance in Afghanistan and Iran because they lost the civil war.

GETTING THERE

In 1994, Tajik Air enjoyed a brief flowering when it rented a 747 from United Airlines and began a London-Dushanbe-Delhi flight. The airline sadly failed soon afterwards, leaving plenty of angry people behind.

At present there is no way to fly into the country. The alternatives are to fly from Tashkent to Termez and take a bus from there, or to take the bus to Khodzent (formerly Leninabad) and catch an internal flight from there to Dushanbe.

It takes about 30 hours to reach Dushanbe from Tashkent going via Samarkand, and about 11 hours from Termez. Trains run every other day from Ashkabad to Dushanbe and pass through Bukhara on the way.

There are buses roughly every half an hour from Tashkent to Khodzent, as Uzbekistan's absurd border arrangements mean that every bus to the Fergana valley has to go this way.

RED TAPE

It's not possible to obtain a Tajik visa anywhere in Central Asia so it should theoretically be possible to enter the country with just a CIS visa and then to go and register at the OVIR office in Dushanbe. However it should be remembered that foreigners are an unknown quantity in Tajikistan and it's difficult to explain this little bureaucratic procedure from the wrong end of an AK47. To be on the safe side, try to have Dushanbe explicitedly stated on your visa.

MONEY

Tajikistan is the only former Soviet republic that never left the rouble zone. However there is an extreme lack of bank-notes with reports that some rural areas are operating without cash. What notes there are tend to be pre-1993 roubles no longer valid in Russia itself. There were plans to introduce a Tajik currency, the somon, but this is unlikely to get off the drawing board any time soon.

GETTING AROUND

Travelling by air should be the easiest way to get around the country, but erratic fuel-shortages and periods of intensified fighting tend to disrupt the services. Tajikistan does not have an extensive rail system but there are services between Dushanbe, Kurgan-Tyube and Kulyab. Most roads are extremely bad, but this is the only feasible way of getting around much of the country. In summer it's easy enough but in winter many of the passes are blocked by snow.

EATING AND DRINKING

In recent times there has been an extreme shortage of food in Tajikistan, with army troops reportedly being brought in to guard Dushanbe's bread factories. Don't expect to find too much in the way of restaurants. Your best bet will be to seek out bazaars and shashlik stands.

EXPLORING

The most compelling reason to come to Tajikistan is for the mountains. The Pamirs form a quadrangle of high ridges and peaks that reaches its greatest heights in the east of the country where you'll find three out of four of the former Soviet Union's highest peaks. Several of the ranges can be accessed from neighbouring countries, the Pamir Alai mountain system can be reached from Samarkand in Uzbekistan or Osh in Kyrgyzstan, and this is worth bearing in mind. Trekking alone in Tajikistan should only be undertaken with extreme caution and a good grasp of the language. Weapons from Afghanistan have reached even the most remote villages and while most people will be perfectly hospitable to random Western tourists, some may not.

HELP AND INFORMATION

You could consult the Foreign Office's travel information line (0171-270 4129) before you go but a better idea would be to approach the British Embassy in Tashkent when you get to Central Asia. If you run into problems when in Tajikistan head to the American Embassy (see the end of this chapter).

DUSHANBE

Probably the most preposterous of all the unlikely capitals in the former Soviet Union, Dushanbe consisted of 40 tents and 250 people in 1924 when it was made administrative centre of the new autonomous republic. By definition a modern city, dating mostly from after World War II, the Tajik capital lies on the banks of the Dushanbinka river. The Hissar foothills form the northern edge of the city, and provide the life-saving cool breezes in the evening. Temperatures can hit 40°C in the city during the summer. Plentiful vegetation as well as the usual aryks (irrigation channels) not only give relief but, with the orchards that surround the city, adds to the atmosphere of Dushanbe.

CITY LAYOUT

The main street is prospekt Rudaki (formerly prospekt Lenina) running north to south more or less parallel to the river and where most shops, hotels and cafes are located. In the south it starts at the railway station and passes through the three squares: Aini, Moscow Anniversary and Lenin.

GETTING THERE

Air. From the airport, which lies a few miles south of the centre, take bus 3,9 or trolleybus 2 to reach prospekt Rudaki. Aternatively a taxi shouldn't set you back a fortune as the drive to the centre takes no more than 15 minutes. Airline tickets can be bought at the airport itself or from the Intourist service bureau at the Hotel Tajikistan.

Rail. The station is at at the southern end of prospekt Rudaki.

Bus. The bus station is on the western bank of the Dushanbinka river and linked to prospekt Rudaki by bus 15 and marshrutnoye 16.

ACCOMMODATION

At the very top end of the scale the Oktyabrskaya, at 105a prospekt Rudaki (24-63-03), offers double rooms for $100 upwards. The Tajikistan at 22 ulitsa Shotemur (formerly ulitsa Kommunisticheskaya) with air-conditioning, hip baths and balconies is the standard hotel used by foreigners. Double rooms start at $80, (tel 27-43-93). Better value and slightly older but still comfortable, is the Dushanbe at 7 prospekt Rudaki (23-36-60), a double room will set you back about $30.

EATING AND DRINKING

All the hotels have restaurants but more lively and interesting than any of these is the Rokhat Chaikhana in Putovsky Square, a modern building incorporating traditional Tajik woodcarving and frescoes inside. Tajiks gather here to drink kok chai (green tea) but you can also eat manti, plov and other Central Asian fast foods. The open-air Farokhat restaurant, among the trees opposite the Tajikistan hotel, serves good shashliks and beer.

EXPLORING

There is frankly not all that much to see in Dushanbe but the two local museums are worth visiting. The Museum of Ethnography at 14 ulitsa Ismail Somoni (formerly ulitsa Putovskaya), two blocks north of the hotel Tajikistan, has an excellent collection of 20th century Tajik art including pottery, costumes, carpets, embroidery and musical instruments. The Tajikistan Unified Museum in Aini Square at the southern end of porspekt Rudaki spans a fair section of Tajik history with exhibits ranging from prehistoric flints to 20th century cartoons.

Dushanbe's main mosque is the Haji Yacoub at ulitsa Shomolni 58. Work began on it almost 5 years ago, and although the roof has yet to be finished, Tajik holy men show a blithe disregard for the cement mixers and scaffolding.

ENTERTAINMENT

The Opera and Ballet Theatre is on Moscow Square. The Philharmonic Concert Hall, plus the Russian and Tajik drama theatres are all on prospekt Rudaki.

SHOPPING

The main market is one block northeast of Aini Square at the southern end of prospekt Rudaki. Another market is behind the Hotel Tajikistan, down a typical old street where they still make the traditional flat bread in old ovens and you can see the craftsmen at work.

HELP AND INFORMATION

The Tajik state tourism organisation has an office on the second floor of the Hotel Tajikistan (273903).

Communications. The central post office is on ploshchad Lenina. The code for Dushanbe is 3772.

Embassies and consulates. The American Embassy is in the Hotel Oktabrskaya (210356), while Pakistan and Iran's representations can be found in the Hotel Tajikistan.